CATIA V5-6R2017: Advanced Part Design

Learning Guide

1st Edition

ASCENT - Center for Technical Knowledge®
CATIA V5-6R2017: Advanced Part Design
1st Edition

Prepared and produced by:

ASCENT Center for Technical Knowledge
630 Peter Jefferson Parkway, Suite 175
Charlottesville, VA 22911

866-527-2368
www.ASCENTed.com

Lead Contributor: Scott Hendren

ASCENT - Center for Technical Knowledge is a division of Rand Worldwide, Inc., providing custom developed knowledge products and services for leading engineering software applications. ASCENT is focused on specializing in the creation of education programs that incorporate the best of classroom learning and technology-based training offerings.

We welcome any comments you may have regarding this learning guide, or any of our products. To contact us please email: feedback@ASCENTed.com.

AS-56CAT17-APD1-E // RS-56CAT17-APD1-E

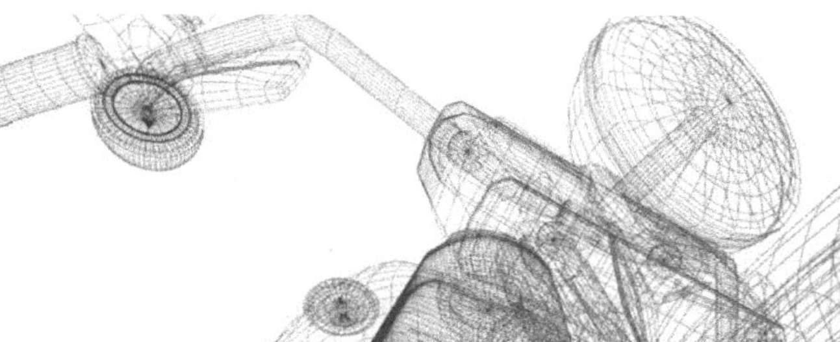

Contents

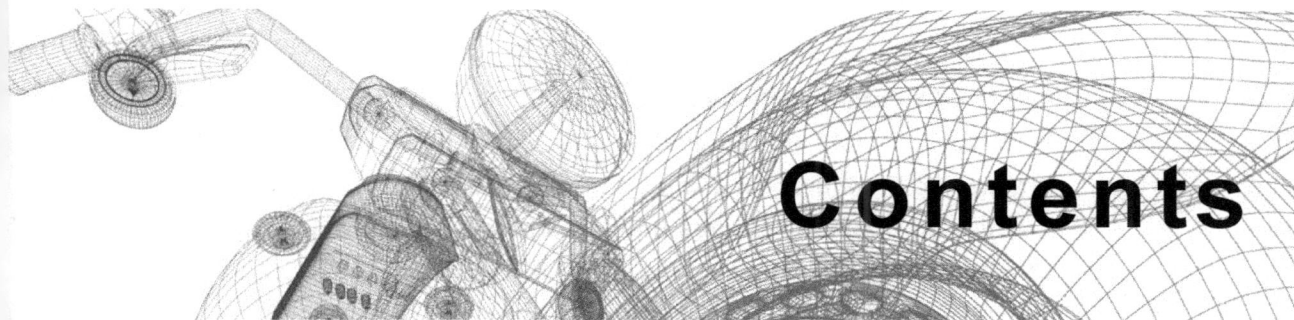

Preface

The *CATIA V5-6R2017: Advanced Part Design* learning guide is ideal for experienced CATIA users who want to extend their modeling abilities with advanced functionality and techniques. This extensive hands-on guide contains numerous projects focused on process-based exercises to give students practical experience while improving design productivity. Students will learn techniques for reusing data, tackling complex geometry, using wireframe, working through feature failure, and investigating the model with analysis tools.

Topics Covered:

- Effective modeling practices and design methodology review
- Advanced multi-section solid and rib/slot operations
- Advanced draft and fillet creation and troubleshooting techniques
- Advanced patterning techniques and user patterns
- PowerCopy creation and instantiation
- Design tables
- Catalog creation
- Creating and managing multi-model links
- Multi-body modeling techniques
- Performing Boolean operations
- Knowledge Templates
- Wireframe Lines and Curves
- Analysis Tools
- Feature Failure Resolution

- Thickness, Remove Face and Replace Face features
- Introduction to Automation
- Project Exercises

Note on Software Setup

This learning guide assumes a standard installation of the software using the default preferences during installation. Lectures and practices use the standard software templates and default options for the Content Libraries.

This guide was developed against CATIA V5-6R2017, Service Pack 1.

Lead Contributor: Scott Hendren

Scott Hendren has been a trainer and curriculum developer in the PLM industry for almost 20 years, with experience on multiple CAD systems, including Pro/ENGINEER, Creo Parametric, and CATIA. Trained in Instructional Design, Scott uses his skills to develop instructor-led and web-based training products.

Scott has held training and development positions with several high profile PLM companies, and has been with the Ascent team since 2013.

Scott holds a Bachelor of Mechanical Engineering Degree as well as a Bachelor of Science in Mathematics from Dalhousie University, Nova Scotia, Canada.

Scott Hendren has been the Lead Contributor for *CATIA: Advanced Part Design* since 2013.

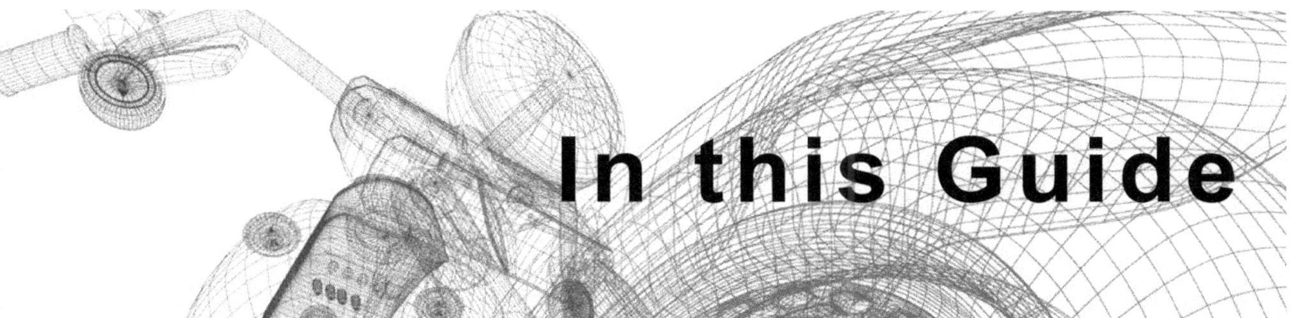

The following images highlight some of the features that can be found in this Learning Guide.

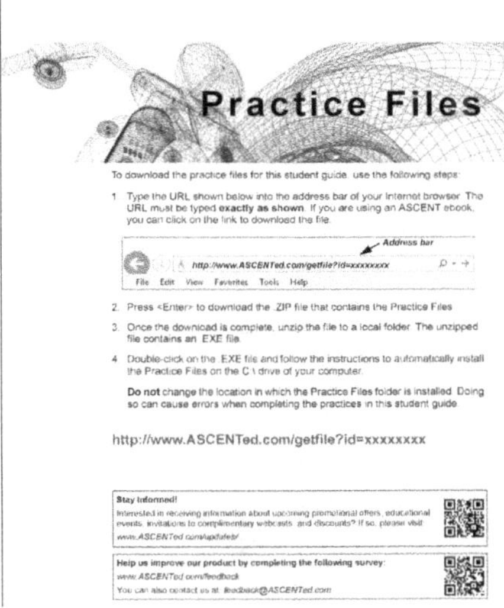

Practice Files

To download the practice files for this student guide, use the following steps:

1. Type the URL shown below into the address bar of your Internet browser. The URL must be typed **exactly as shown**. If you are using an ASCENT ebook, you can click on the link to download the file.

http://www.ASCENTed.com/getfile?id=xxxxxxxx

Address bar

File Edit View Favorites Tools Help

2. Press <Enter> to download the .ZIP file that contains the Practice Files.
3. Once the download is complete, unzip the file to a local folder. The unzipped file contains an .EXE file.
4. Double-click on the .EXE file and follow the instructions to automatically install the Practice Files on the C:\ drive of your computer.

   Do not change the location in which the Practice Files folder is installed. Doing so can cause errors when completing the practices in this student guide.

http://www.ASCENTed.com/getfile?id=xxxxxxxx

Stay Informed!
Interested in receiving information about upcoming promotional offers, educational events, invitations to complimentary webcasts, and discounts? If so, please visit:
www.ASCENTed.com/updates/

Help us improve our product by completing the following survey:
www.ASCENTed.com/feedback
You can also contact us at: *feedback@ASCENTed.com*

FTP link for practice files

Practice Files

The Practice Files page tells you how to download and install the practice files that are provided with this learning guide.

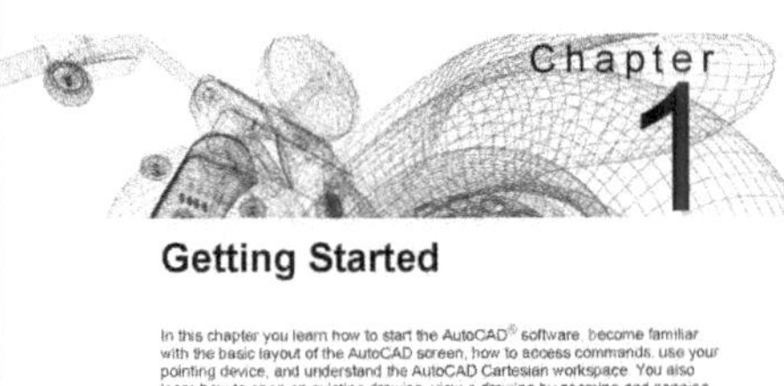

Getting Started

In this chapter you learn how to start the AutoCAD® software, become familiar with the basic layout of the AutoCAD screen, how to access commands, use your pointing device, and understand the AutoCAD Cartesian workspace. You also learn how to open an existing drawing, view a drawing by zooming and panning, and save your work in the AutoCAD software.

Learning Objectives in this Chapter

- Launch the AutoCAD software and complete a basic initial setup of the drawing environment.
- Identify the basic layout and features of AutoCAD interface including the Ribbon, Drawing Window, and Application Menu.
- Locate commands and launch them using the Ribbon, shortcut menus, Application Menu, and Quick Access Toolbar.
- Locate points in the AutoCAD Cartesian workspace.
- Open and close existing drawings and navigate to file locations.
- Move around a drawing using the mouse, the **Zoom** and **Pan** commands, and the Navigation Bar.
- Save drawings in various formats and set the automatic save options using the **Save** commands.

Learning Objectives for the chapter

Chapters

Each chapter begins with a brief introduction and a list of the chapter's Learning Objectives.

Side notes

Side notes are hints or additional information for the current topic.

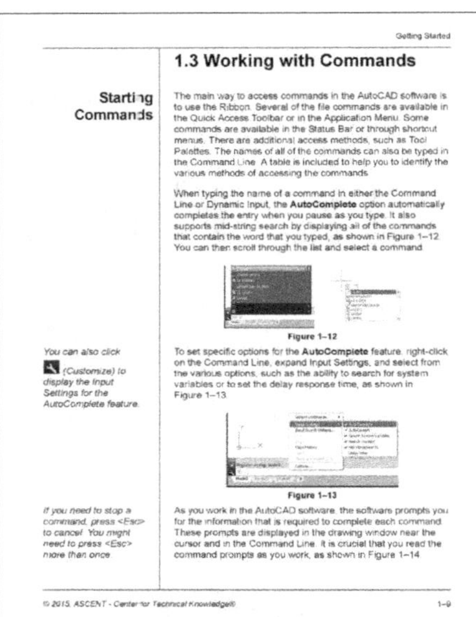

Getting Started

1.3 Working with Commands

Starting Commands

The main way to access commands in the AutoCAD software is to use the Ribbon. Several of the file commands are available in the Quick Access Toolbar or in the Application Menu. Some commands are available in the Status Bar or through shortcut menus. There are additional access methods, such as Tool Palettes. The names of all of the commands can also be typed in the Command Line. A table is included to help you to identify the various methods of accessing the commands.

When typing the name of a command in either the Command Line or Dynamic Input, the **AutoComplete** option automatically completes the entry when you pause as you type. It also supports mid-string search by displaying all of the commands that contain the word that you typed, as shown in Figure 1–12. You can then scroll through the list and select a command.

Figure 1–12

You can also click (Customize) to display the Input Settings for the AutoComplete feature.

To set specific options for the **AutoComplete** feature, right-click on the Command Line, expand Input Settings, and select from the various options, such as the ability to search for system variables or to set the delay response time, as shown in Figure 1–13.

Figure 1–13

If you need to stop a command, press <Esc> to cancel. You might need to press <Esc> more than once.

As you work in the AutoCAD software, the software prompts you for the information that is required to complete each command. These prompts are displayed in the drawing window near the cursor and in the Command Line. It is crucial that you read the command prompts as you work, as shown in Figure 1–14.

© 2015, ASCENT - Center for Technical Knowledge® 1–9

Instructional Content

Each chapter is split into a series of sections of instructional content on specific topics. These lectures include the descriptions, step-by-step procedures, figures, hints, and information you need to achieve the chapter's Learning Objectives.

Practice Objectives

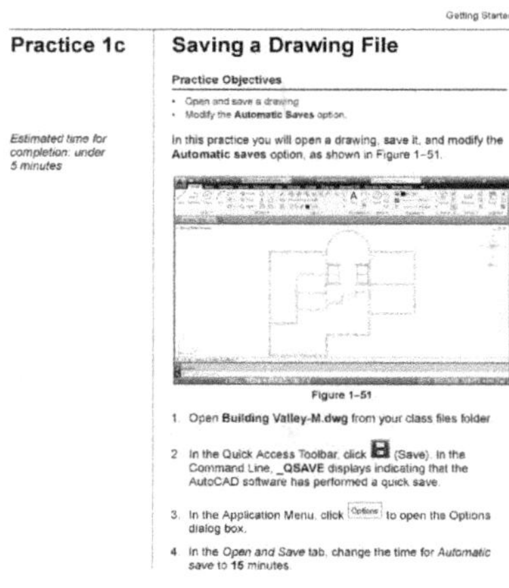

Getting Started

Practice 1c **Saving a Drawing File**

Practice Objectives

- Open and save a drawing.
- Modify the **Automatic Saves** option.

Estimated time for completion: under 5 minutes

In this practice you will open a drawing, save it, and modify the **Automatic saves** option, as shown in Figure 1–51.

Figure 1–51

1. Open **Building Valley-M.dwg** from your class files folder.
2. In the Quick Access Toolbar, click (Save). In the Command Line, **_QSAVE** displays indicating that the AutoCAD software has performed a quick save.
3. In the Application Menu, click Options to open the Options dialog box.
4. In the *Open and Save* tab, change the time for *Automatic save* to **15** minutes.

Practices

Practices enable you to use the software to perform a hands-on review of a topic.

Some practices require you to use prepared practice files, which can be downloaded from the link found on the Practice Files page.

Getting Started

Chapter Review Questions

1. How do you switch from the drawing window to the text window?
   a. Use the icons in the Status Bar.
   b. Press <Tab>.
   c. Press <F2>.
   d. Press the <Spacebar>.
2. How can you cancel a command using the keyboard?
   a. Press <F2>.
   b. Press <Esc>.
   c. Press <Ctrl>.
   d. Press <Delete>.
3. What is the quickest way to repeat a command?
   a. Press <Esc>.
   b. Press <F2>.
   c. Press <Enter>.
   d. Press <Ctrl>.
4. To display a specific Ribbon panel, you can right-click on the Ribbon and select the required panel in the shortcut menu.
   a. True
   b. False
5. How are points specified in the AutoCAD Cartesian workspace?
   a. X value x Y value

Chapter Review Questions

Chapter review questions, located at the end of each chapter, enable you to review the key concepts and learning objectives of the chapter.

Practice Files

To download the practice files for this learning guide, use the following steps:

1. Type the URL shown below into the address bar of your Internet browser. The URL must be typed **exactly as shown**. If you are using an ASCENT ebook, you can click on the link to download the file.

2. Press <Enter> to download the .ZIP file that contains the Practice Files.
3. Once the download is complete, unzip the file to a local folder. The unzipped file contains an .EXE file.
4. Double-click on the .EXE file and follow the instructions to automatically install the Practice Files on the C:\ drive of your computer.

   Do not change the location in which the Practice Files folder is installed. Doing so can cause errors when completing the practices in this learning guide.

http://www.ASCENTed.com/getfile?id=relucesco

Stay Informed!

Interested in receiving information about upcoming promotional offers, educational events, invitations to complimentary webcasts, and discounts? If so, please visit:

www.ASCENTed.com/updates/

Help us improve our product by completing the following survey:

www.ASCENTed.com/feedback

You can also contact us at: *feedback@ASCENTed.com*

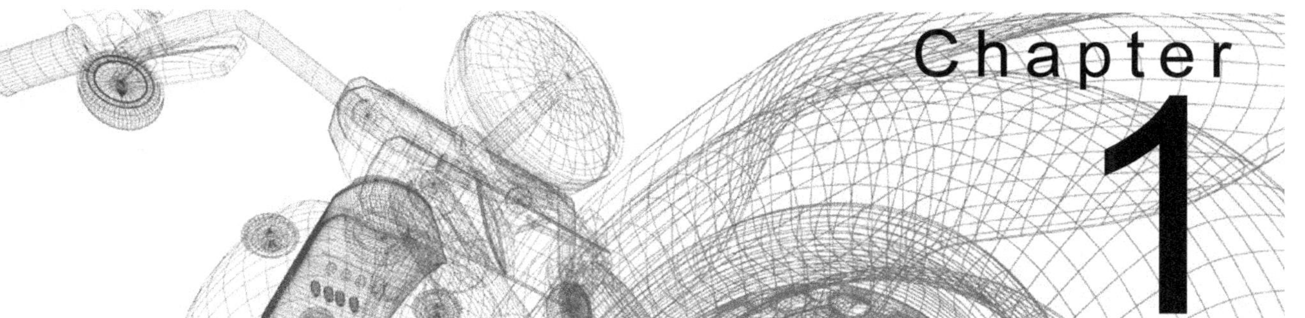

Part Design Overview

Starting with this chapter, you build on the fundamentals of modeling in CATIA. You learn new techniques to help create and manage your part designs. These techniques help to ensure that a part design remains flexible and leads to the creation of robust models.

Learning Objectives in this Chapter

- Review the design intent items to consider when creating a new model.
- Review the tools available for manipulating a design.

1.1 Part Design Philosophies

Before creating any part in CATIA, consider the design intent of the part. By doing so, you can maximize the flexibility of the design. Considering *what if* scenarios that might be introduced into the part helps you to create a robust model that requires minimal effort when incorporating modifications. Remember that CATIA is a design tool. Consider the following questions when starting a new model:

Default Reference Planes

Why use default reference planes? Every part contains three default reference planes, as shown in Figure 1–1. They form a foundation for your model and cannot be deleted. Reference planes make an excellent selection as parents for subsequent features, thereby reducing the number of unwanted parent-child relationships.

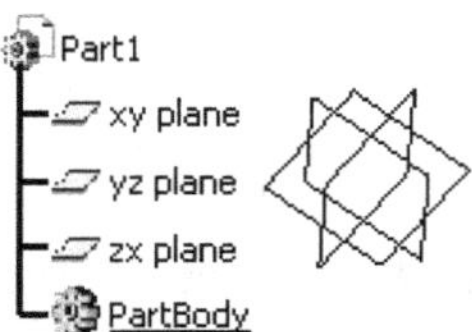

Figure 1–1

Base Feature

What is the best choice for the Base feature? The Base feature of the part is the first geometry feature added to the part (e.g., Pad, Spline, or Surface). Select a form that captures the fundamental shape of the model.

Active Body

Which body should be set to the active body in the model? As new features are created, they are added to the active body. These bodies can be used to perform boolean operations, group features, and separate model geometry. Features added to one body might not be accessible to other bodies in the same model. The active body is set by right-clicking it in the specification tree and selecting **Define in Work Object**.

Sketch Support

What is the best sketch support plane? It is important to carefully consider this reference, because it establishes parent-child relationships. Do not randomly select a sketch support simply because you think you must. This might create an unwanted parent-child relationship. Whenever possible, use a default reference plane to minimize the number of unwanted parent-child relationships. The selection of this reference also affects the default view of the model.

Sketcher References

Which entities should be selected as sketcher references? As you dimension and constrain your sketch, you select references that determine how the sketch reacts to modification. References can be removed and added as required in each sketch. Select references that incorporate your design intent.

Positioned Sketch

The use of a positioned sketch is highly recommended. It enables you to locate the origin of the sketch so that it updates correctly.

- Standard sketches are also called *Sliding* sketches. When the model is modified, it can reposition itself unexpectedly because its origin is not constrained.
- Positioned sketches enable you to develop the required parent-child relationships between features. For example, if the vertical axis of the sketch is constrained to a specific line or edge, the relationship is maintained throughout the design changes.
- If you need to translate, copy, or paste the sketch to another location, it can be done more easily with a positioned sketch.

Dimensions

Which dimensions are required to drive the design? CATIA is associative. You can take advantage of this with an intelligent dimensioning scheme. Place dimensions so that they enable modifications. The dimensions that are automatically added to the sketch by **Auto Constraint** are based on the references and sketched geometry that were originally selected. Additional dimensions can be added as required to capture the required design intent.

Which dimensions on the part would change? Always check that the dimensioning scheme works correctly by flexing the model. Test as many *what if* scenarios as possible.

Parent-Child Relationships

Which parent-child relationships work the best? Which parent-child relationships should be avoided? As mentioned earlier, parent-child relationships are established when selecting the sketch support, as well as all other references throughout the creation of a feature (e.g., dimensioning, using or offsetting edges, or the depth option).

Depth Options

Which limit type should be used to create features? The selection of the limit type affects the feature. Always consider the consequences if additional features are added or if other dimensions in the model are modified. Remember that some depth options result in parent-child relationships (e.g., **Up to next**, **Up to plane**, or **Up to surface**).

Formulas

Should any formulas be added? Formulas are user-defined mathematical equations used to capture and control design intent in a model. In CATIA, you can use formulas in features, parts, and assemblies.

Feature Order

Which feature order best captures the design intent? The feature order of a model is important. For example, should a hole be placed before or after a Shell feature? Consider this type of question from the beginning to the end of the modeling process. Use the specification tree to easily review the feature order at any time during model creation.

Multi-body

Typically, all of the features that you create are added to the PartBody in the specification tree. This linear tree structure is acceptable for models with a low feature count or simple geometry. CATIA enables you to create multiple bodies in a single CATPart model. This enables you to structure your model based on your design intent. An important reason for creating multiple bodies is to be able to use the Boolean commands.

Using a multi-body approach to create a model provides the following advantages:

- Update times are reduced.
- Features are grouped by function or area, making the model easy to interpret.
- Bodies can be shown or hidden independent of each other.
- The creation of the part model becomes easier when the model is divided into smaller, functional areas.
- Features (such as a Shell or Fillet) can be restricted to a finite area of the model.

Boolean Operations

Boolean operations in CATIA V5 are a powerful design tool. The ability to combine feature-based modeling with boolean operations permits the creation of robust geometry. Working with various bodies in a single part file provides flexibility in design scenarios, promotes concurrent engineering, and enables the display and manipulation of multiple model states.

1.2 Maintaining Design Intent

*The **Feature Definition**, **Edit Parameters**, **Reorder**, and **Define in Work Object** options can also be accessed by selecting the geometry in the main window and right-clicking.*

Not all possibilities can be foreseen. CATIA offers tools for manipulating the design when a change is required. They are as follows.

Option	Description
Feature Definition	Attributes used to create a feature can be modified by double-clicking on the feature in the specification tree. The Feature Definition dialog box opens, enabling you to modify any aspect of the feature, including the sketch.
Sketch Definition	A section can be edited directly in the model. The Feature Definition dialog box does not need to be opened. Expand the feature in the specification tree and double-click on the sketch.
Edit Parameters	Dimensions that are associated with a specific feature can be modified.
Reorder	The feature order can be reordered for any number of features in the model.
Define in Work Object	Features can be inserted into the specification tree after the feature is selected.

Practice 1a

Capturing Design Intent in Sketcher

Practice Objective

- Use the sketcher tools to capture design intent.

The intent of this practice is to demonstrate how design intent can be captured using sketcher tools and techniques. As with every modeling process, you should use the simplest and most effective methods of capturing design intent. A proficient CATIA V5 user can create robust models that enable design changes to be made quickly and easily, resulting in predicable changes throughout the model.

Create the part using the following information:

- Figure 1–2 shows an isometric view of the completed pipe model.
- Figure 1–3 shows the design requirements that must be captured.
- Figure 1–4 shows the dimensioned drawing views.

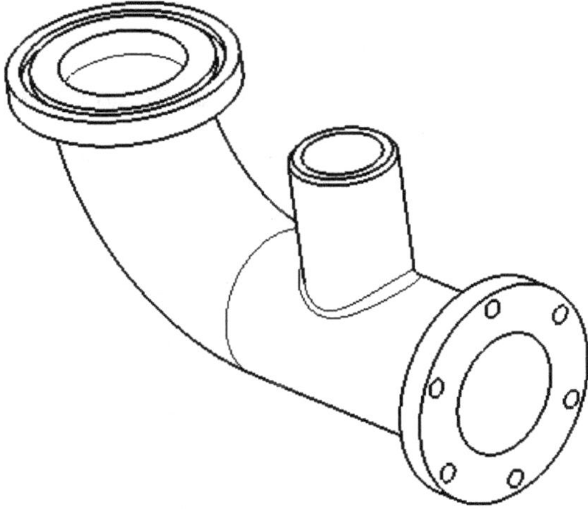

Isometric view
Scale: 1:1

Figure 1–2

Design Considerations

Consider the following design requirements, as shown in Figure 1–3. Note that relations (formulas) cannot be used.

The surface of the flange and the end of this pipe segment must remain co-planar.

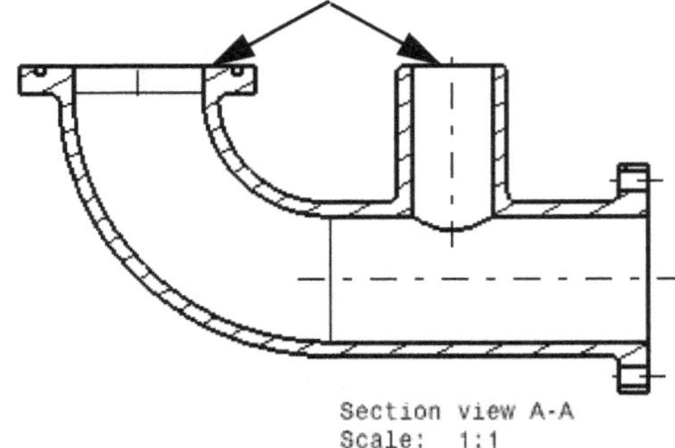

The outside diameter of both flanges is the same. The pipe segment and flange outside diameters must automatically update if the inside diameter of the pipe is changed.

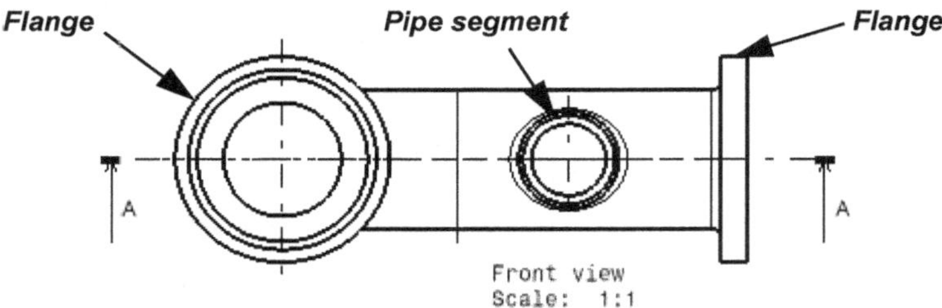

Figure 1–3

Before you begin modeling, ask the following questions:

- What is the best selection for a Base feature?
- What is the second feature going to be?
- What is the complete feature order going to be?
- Which references are going to be used in Sketcher?
- How are you going to incorporate the design requirements shown in Figure 1–4?
- Which depth options should be used?

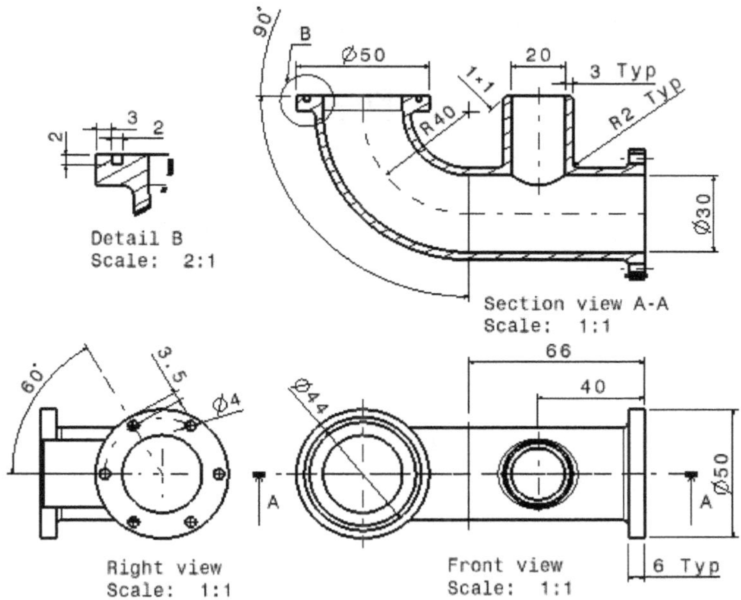

Figure 1–4

When you have completed the Pipe model, flex it by modifying the inside diameter of the pipe from *30* to **40**. The model updates, as shown in Figure 1–5.

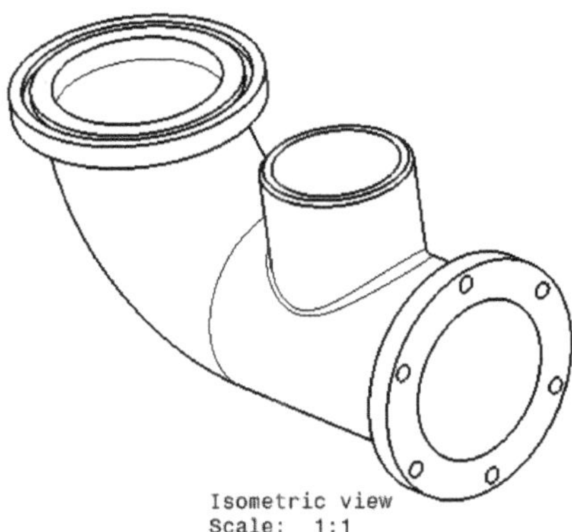

Figure 1–5

A step-by-step solution for this practice can be found in *Appendix C*.

Practice 1b Locking Insert

Practice Objective

- Create a model without any instructions.

In this practice you will evaluate the level of your knowledge of CATIA. A proficient CATIA V5 user should be able to create robust models that enable design changes to be made quickly and easily, resulting in predictable changes throughout the model. You will create Pads, Holes, Pockets, and Drafts. The completed model is shown in Figure 1–6.

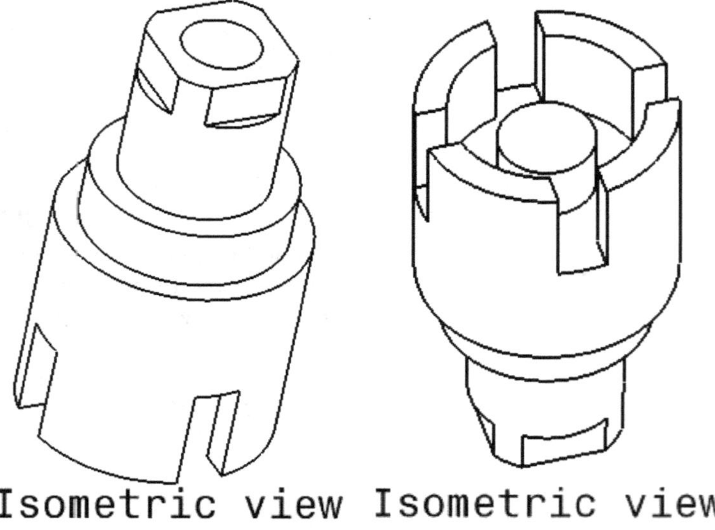

Figure 1–6

Use the drawing shown in Figure 1–7 to create the model.

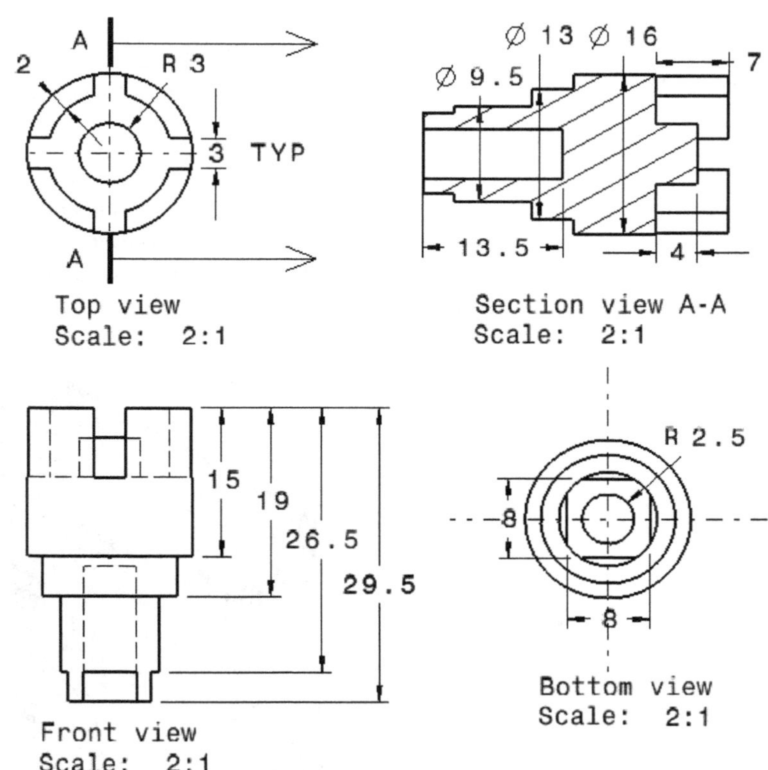

Figure 1–7

The part will be molded. To ease the process of removing the part from the mold, apply a **0.2deg** draft to the correct faces.

Practice 1c (Optional) Sketcher Analysis

Practice Objective

- Create a model with limited instructions.

In this practice, you will create the cooling fins for an aluminum heat sink extrusion. The base geometry has been created for you, as well as the sketch that defines the cooling fin geometry. Use the **Sketch Analysis** tool to solve the problem(s) with the sketch. The completed model displays as shown in Figure 1–8.

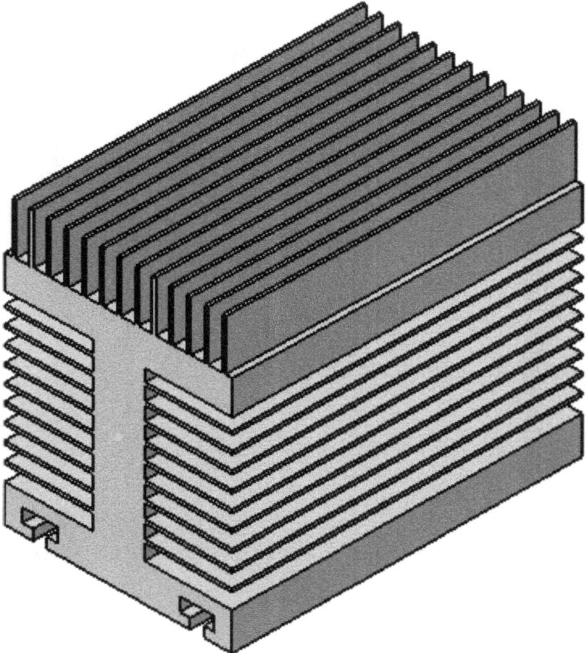

Figure 1–8

Task 1 - Open the part.

1. Open **HeatSinkExtrusion.CATPart**. The model displays as shown in Figure 1–9.

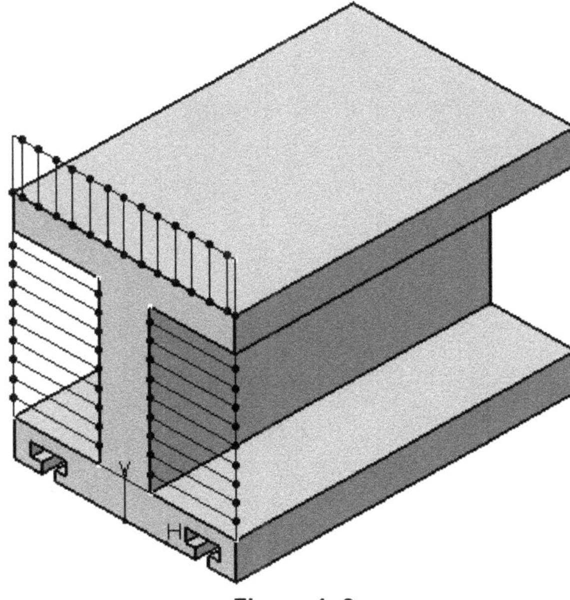

Figure 1–9

Task 2 - Create a pad.

1. Attempt to create a Pad feature using **Sketch.2**.

   The sketch cannot be used to create a Pad feature, as shown in the warning in Figure 1–10.

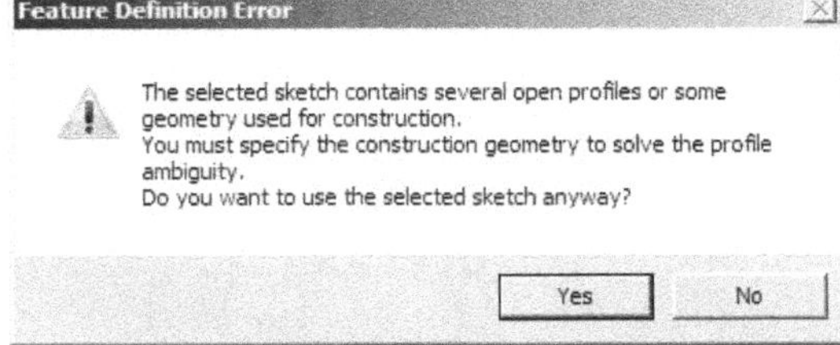

Figure 1–10

2. Click **No**.
3. Click **Cancel** to cancel the creation of the Pad feature.

Task 3 - Analyze the sketch.

1. Edit **Sketch.2** and click (Sketch Solving Status). The sketch status indicates that the sketch is fully constrained, as shown in Figure 1–11.

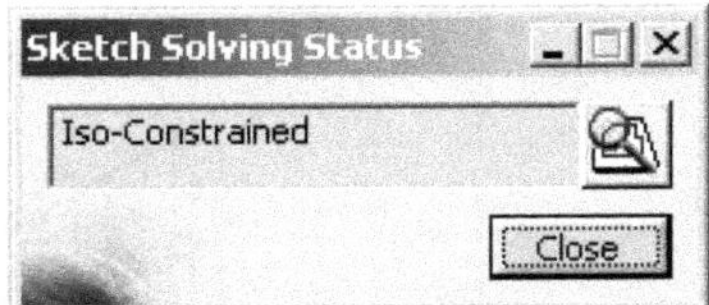

Figure 1–11

2. Click (Sketch Analysis).
3. In the Sketch Analysis dialog box, select the *Geometry* tab.
4. Press and hold <Ctrl> and select the following:
   - **Projection.9/Mark.1** and **Projection.13/Mark.1**.
   - The three Implicit Profiles at the end of the list.
5. In the *Corrective Actions* area, click (Set in Construction Mode) to set the appropriate sketch geometry in Construction mode, as shown in Figure 1–12.

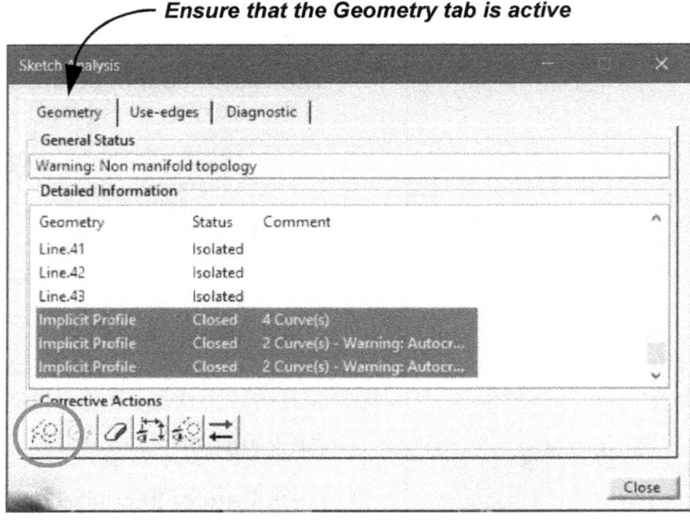

Figure 1–12

6. Verify that all of the geometry has a status of **Isolated**, as shown in Figure 1–13.

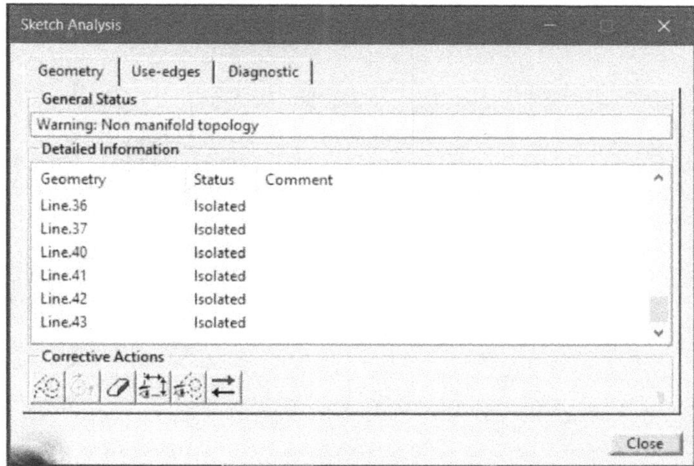

Figure 1–13

Once complete, the sketch displays as shown in Figure 1–14.

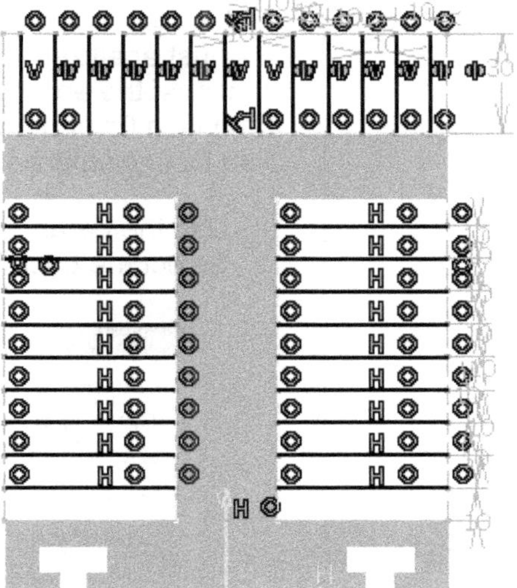

Figure 1–14

7. Click **Close**.

8. Exit the Sketcher workbench. The model displays as shown in Figure 1–15.

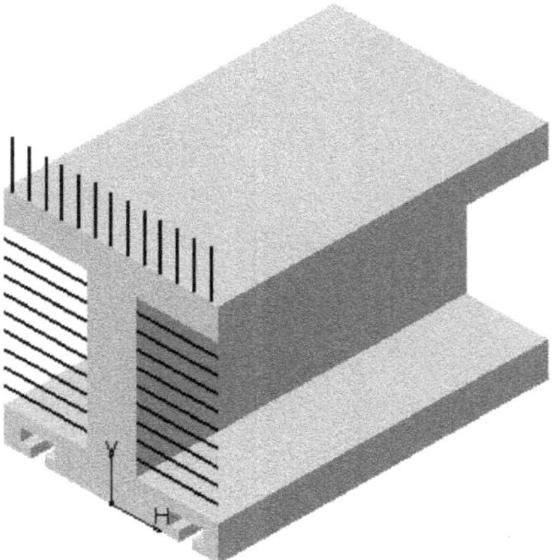

Figure 1–15

Task 4 - Create a Pad.

In this task, you will create a Pad feature using the sketch that you just analyzed. Because the sketch still contains open sections, the application continues to display the Feature Definition Error message until the **Thick** option is selected in the Pad Definition dialog box.

1. Use the parameters shown in Figure 1–16 to define **Pad.2**. Select the back face of the part for the up to plane reference.

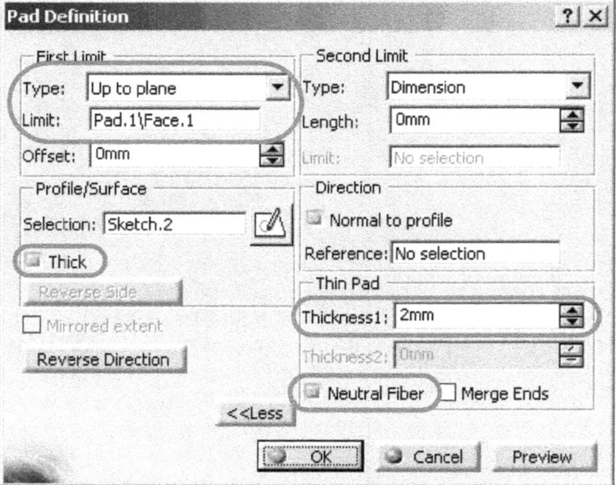

Figure 1–16

The completed model displays as shown in Figure 1–17.

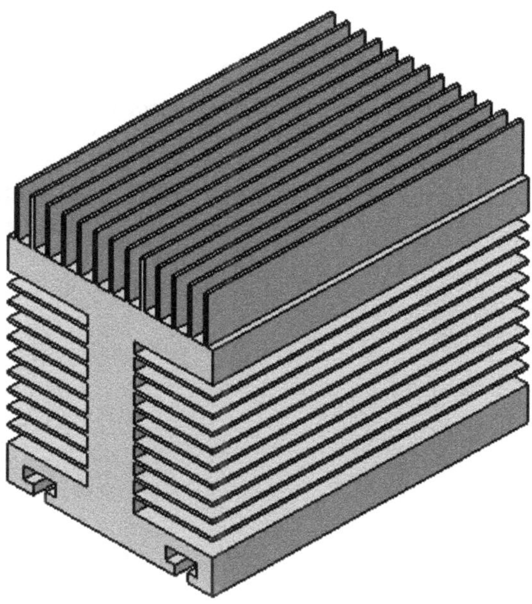

Figure 1–17

2. Save the model and close the file.

Practice 1d (Optional) Sketcher

Practice Objective

- Create various sketches.

In this practice, you will create several closed sketches without instructions. Try to complete at least three of the profiles shown in Figure 1–18, Figure 1–19, Figure 1–20, Figure 1–21, Figure 1–22, and Figure 1–23. Make sure all the sketches are fully constrained, and that no open profiles are in the sketches.

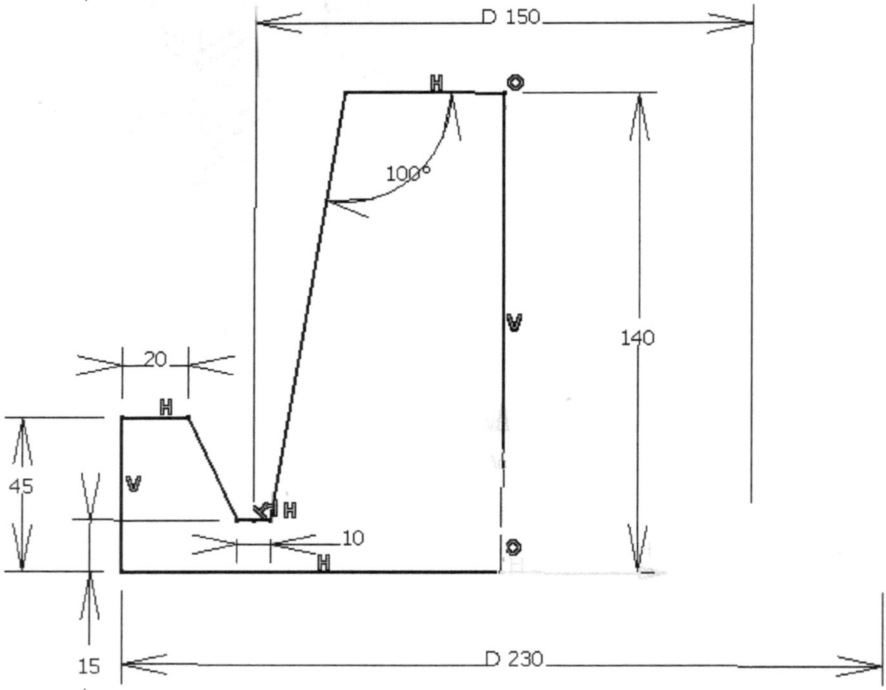

Figure 1–18

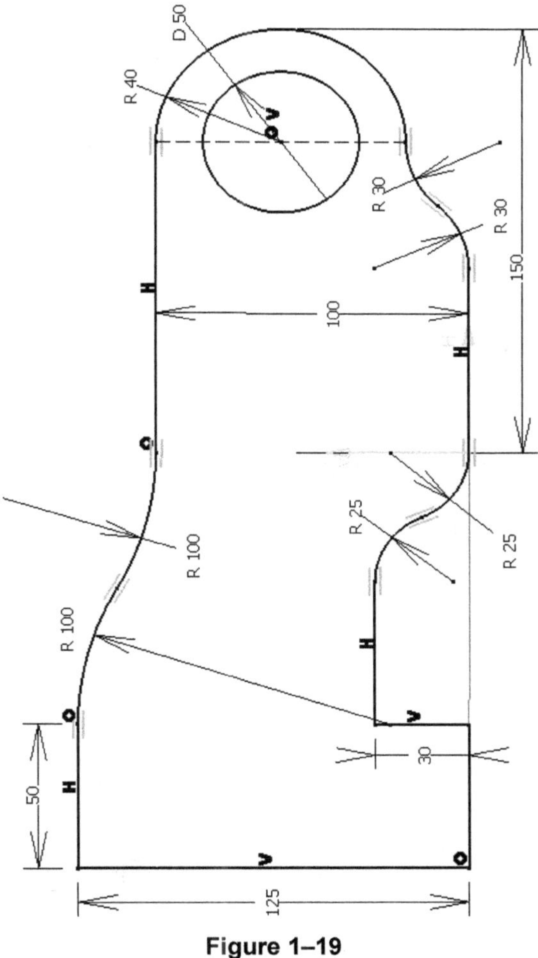

Figure 1–19

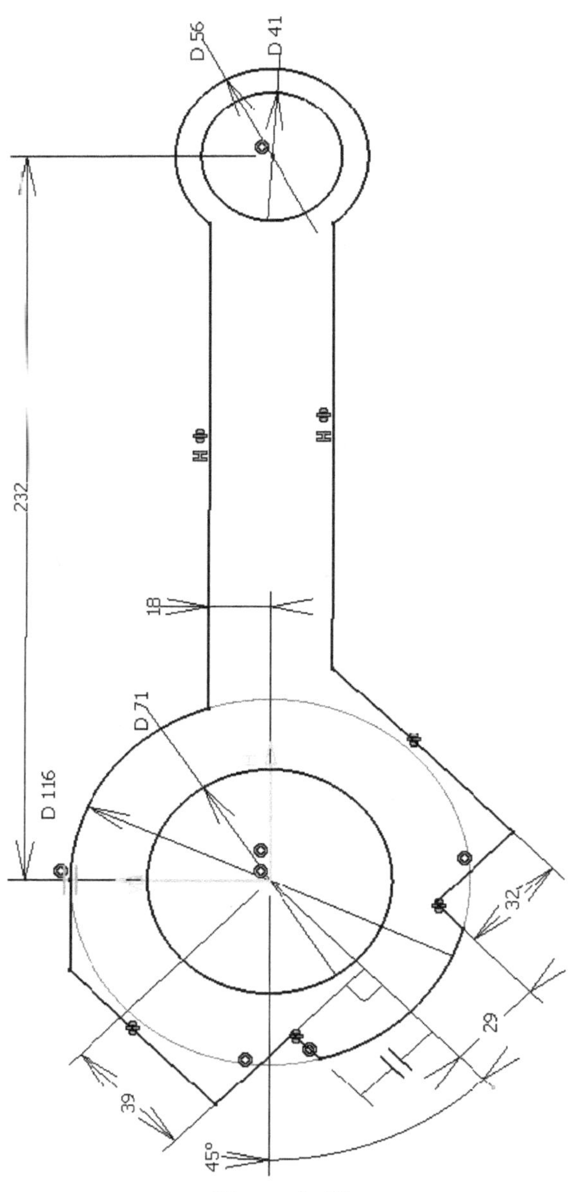

Figure 1–20

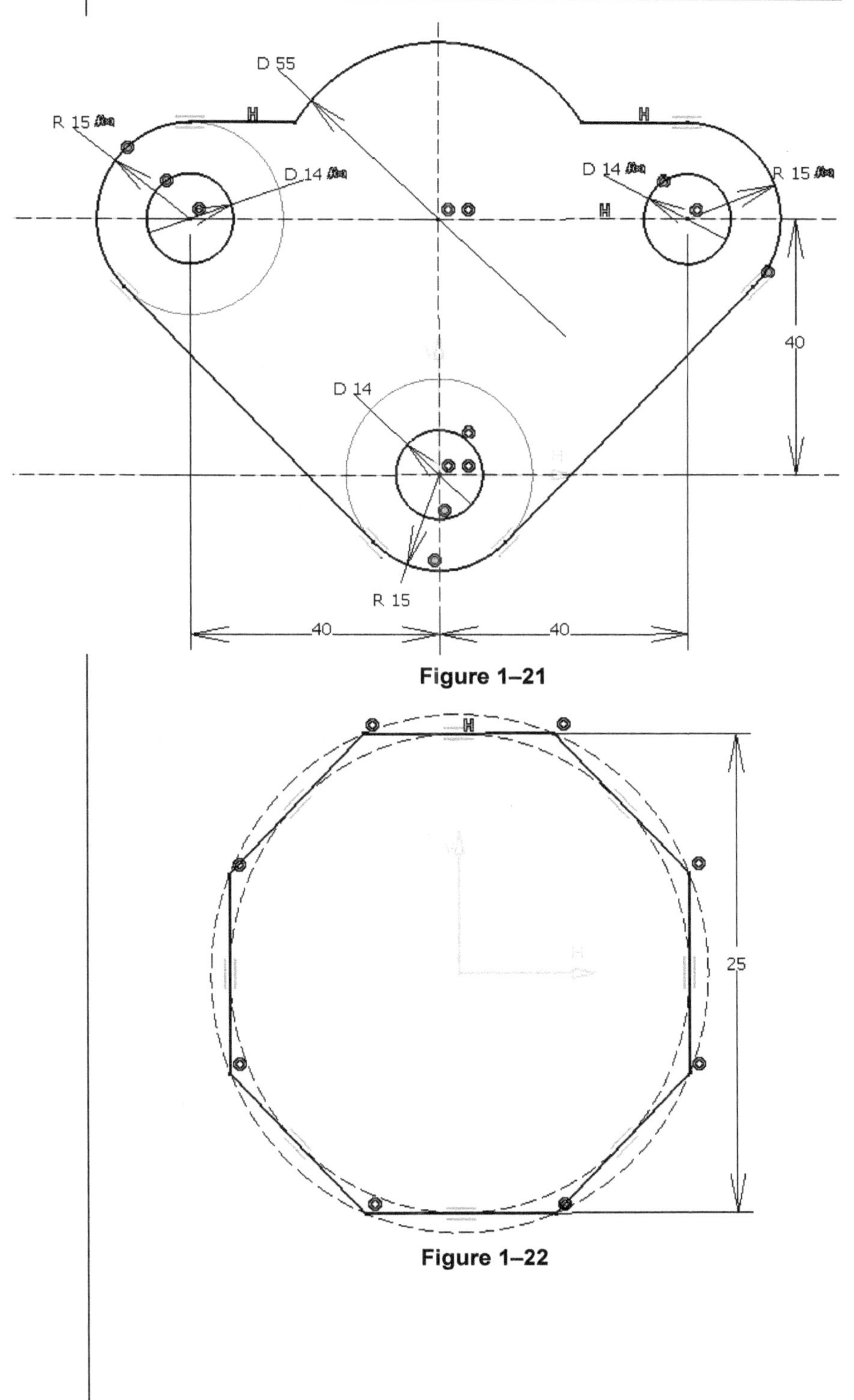

Figure 1–21

Figure 1–22

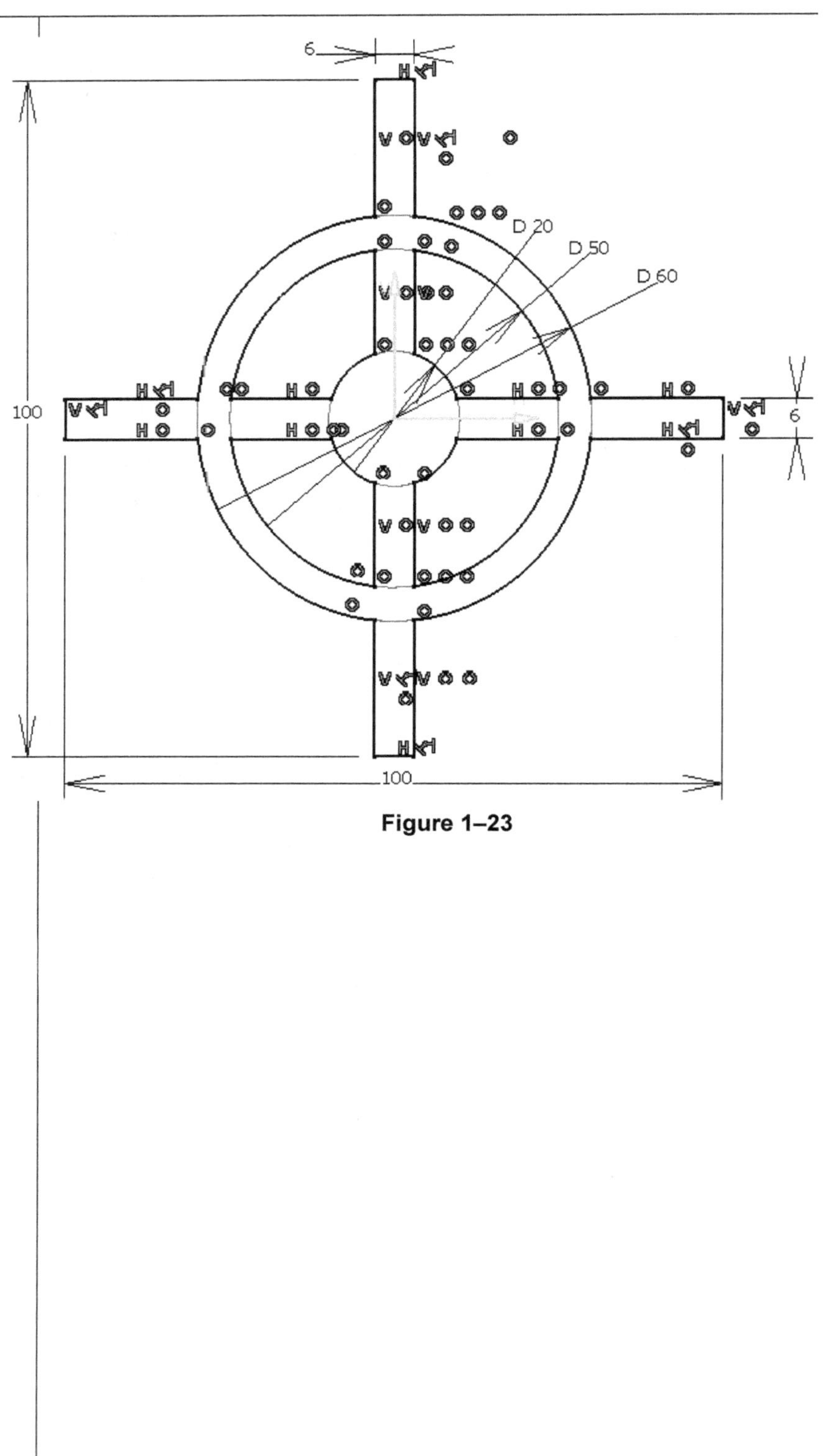

Figure 1–23

Chapter Review Questions

1. Why should you use the default reference planes?
    a. Every part contains three default reference planes, providing consistency from model to model.
    b. They form a foundation for your model and cannot be deleted.
    c. Referencing the default planes helps to reduce the number of parent/child relationships.
    d. All of the above.
2. One of the main problems with using a standard sketch is that when the model is modified, it can reposition itself unexpectedly because its origin is not constrained.
    a. True
    b. False
3. Why is it important to carefully select a sketch support?
    a. The selection of a sketch support dictates the type of feature being created.
    b. The selection of a sketch support creates a parent-child relationship.
    c. The selection of a sketch support dictates the dimensions and constraints that are available for sketching.
    d. All of the above.
4. What are the advantages of using a multi-body approach when modeling?
    a. Features are grouped by function or area, making the model easy to interpret.
    b. The creation of the part model becomes easier when the model is divided into smaller, functional areas.
    c. Features (such as a Shell or Fillet) can be restricted to a finite area of the model.
    d. All of the above.

5. To change the sequence in which features display in the specification tree, use _______.
    a. **Resequence**
    b. **Regenerate**
    c. **Reorder**
    d. None of the above.

Advanced Pattern Options

Patterning provides options for creating efficiency and consistency in your part designs. The Advanced Pattern options introduced in this chapter aid in capturing design intent. Formulas and exploding patterns provide useful controls for meeting specific design requirements. User patterns enable you to create customized patterns by specifying pattern locations through the use of sketched points.

Learning Objectives in this Chapter

- Explore various pattern options.
- Use pattern formulas to automate changes to the model.
- Learn how to manage individual instances of a pattern using Explode Pattern.

2.1 Advanced Pattern Options

Patterns can be a great time-saver when you are creating multiple identical features. The additional options available in the Pattern Definition dialog box can help you create more complex models.

Click **More** to expand the Pattern Definition dialog box to display the additional options for patterning. These options help you to position the pattern.

Rectangular Patterns

Use the options in the *Position of Object in Pattern* area in the Rectangular Pattern Definition dialog box to change the position of the original feature in the pattern. For example, in Figure 2–1, the position of the original feature has been changed so that it is in the second column (first direction) and in the third row (second direction) of the pattern.

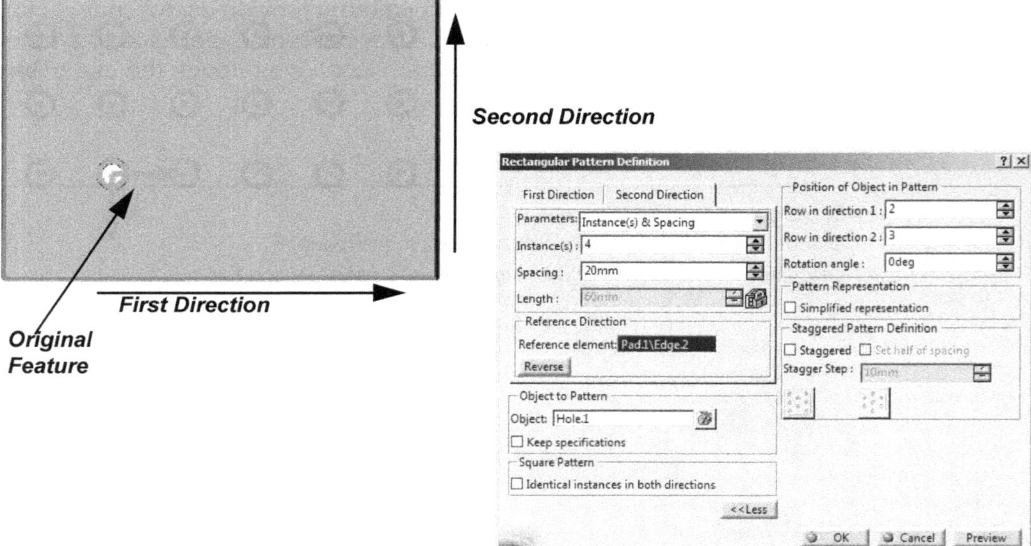

Figure 2–1

The position of the original feature has been changed so that it is in the first column (first direction) and in the third row (second direction) of the pattern.

In Figure 2–2, a rotational angle of 35° has been added to the feature.

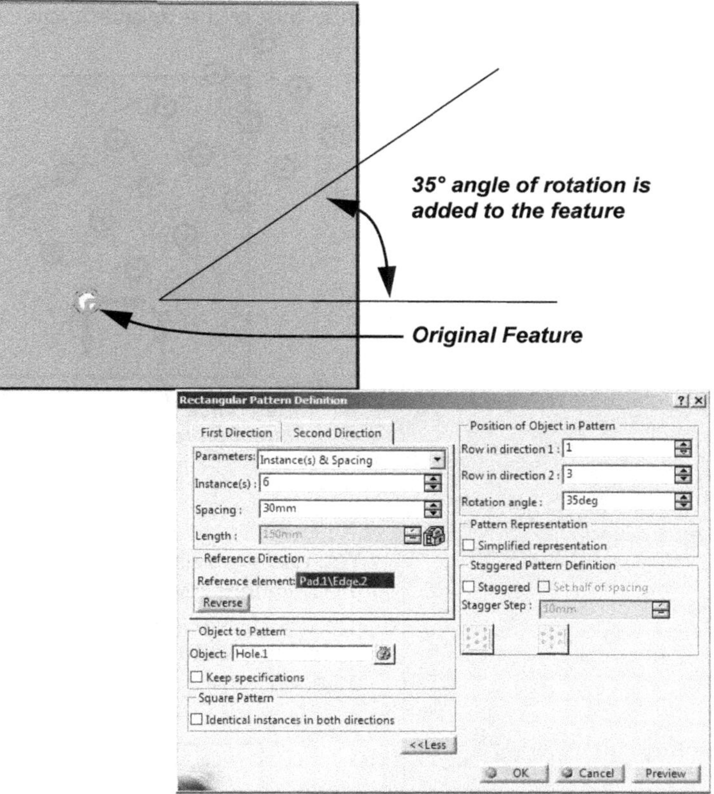

Figure 2–2

In a rectangular pattern, you can create a staggered pattern configuration in which alternate rows are offset by a specified value. To enable a staggered pattern, select **Staggered** in *Staggered Pattern Definition* area, as shown in Figure 2–3.

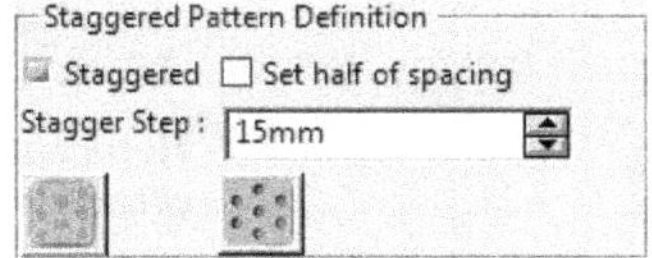

Figure 2–3

The **Stagger Step** is the offset value, and there are two options for the resulting pattern, The default option ( ) ensures that the number of instances in the reference direction row is more than that of the adjacent row, as shown in Figure 2–4.

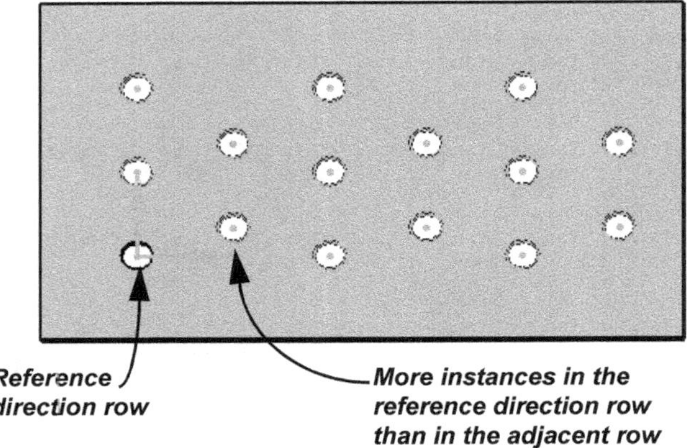

Figure 2–4

You can then use to ensure that the number of instances in the adjacent row is greater than that of the reference direction row, as shown in Figure 2–5. The **Set half of spacing** option will keep them auto-aligned in the middle of the instances of the adjacent row.

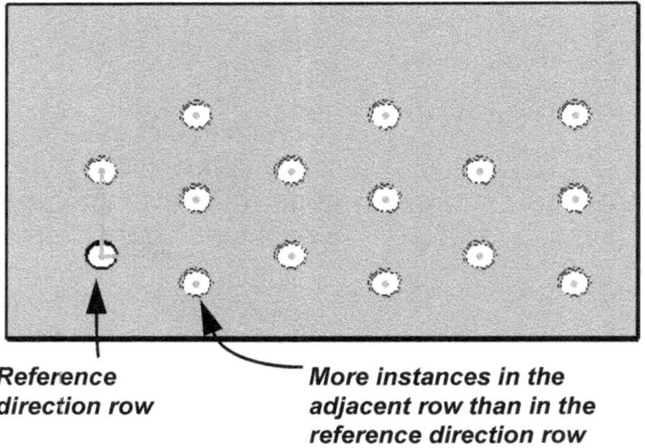

Figure 2–5

Circular Patterns

The Circular Pattern Definition dialog box has similar advanced options, except that the first direction is known as the *Angular direction*, and second direction is known as the *Radial direction*.

A simple circular pattern rotated by 45° is shown in Figure 2–6.

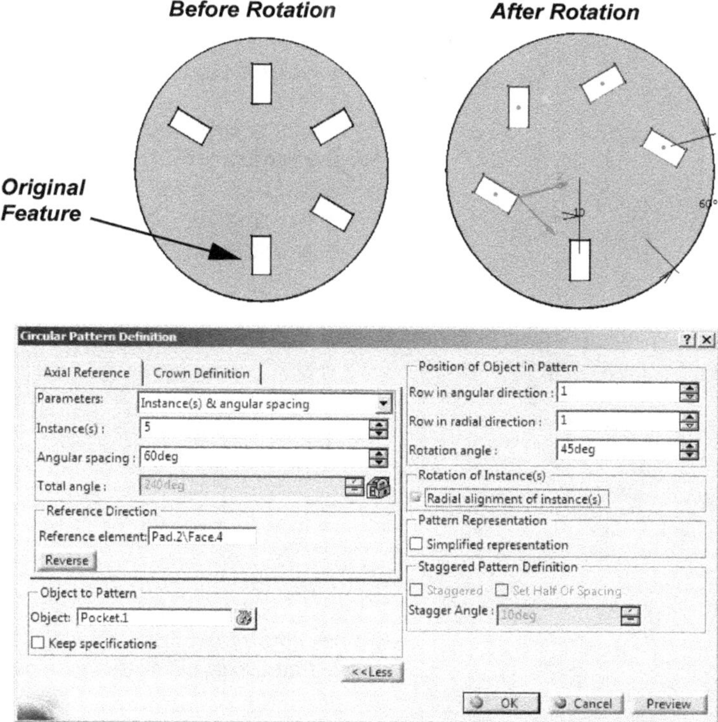

Figure 2–6

Additionally, you have the option of defining how to align the instances of a circular pattern. If the **Radial alignment of instance(s)** option is selected (default option), all instances remain tangent to the circle, as shown on the left in Figure 2–7. If this option is not selected, all of the instances remain in the same orientation as the original object, as shown on the right in Figure 2–7.

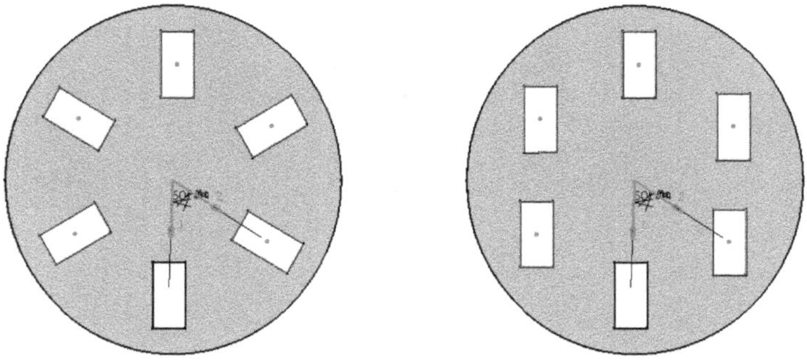

Figure 2–7

Simplified Representation

The **Simplified Representation** option for both rectangular and circular patterns enables you to display some of the pattern instances to represent the entire pattern. This option saves display and regeneration times if your pattern has a large number of instances and reduces the file size of the model.

To create a simplified representation, select **Simplified Representation**. For a circular pattern, all instances are removed except for the two innermost and two outermost rings. For a rectangular pattern, all instances are hidden except for several at each corner, as shown in Figure 2–8.

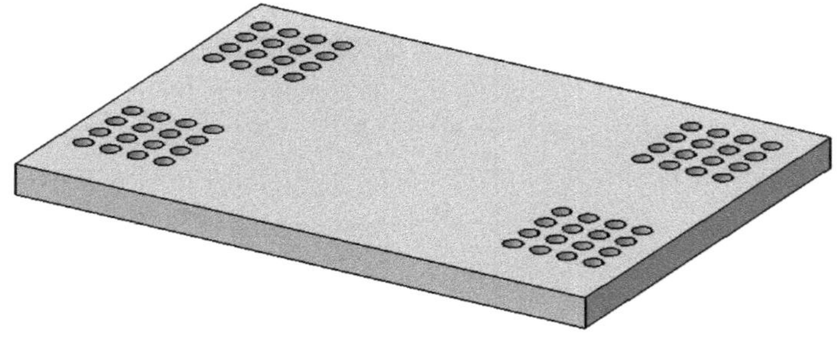

Figure 2–8

To re-display the full pattern, open the Use Pattern Definition dialog box and clear the **Simplified Representation** option.

Keep Specifications

You can also keep the specifications of the original feature by selecting **Keep specifications**. For example, in Figure 2–9, the Pad feature is created using the **Up to surface** option. If the Pad feature is patterned without selecting **Keep specifications**, the patterned feature is identical to the original Pad feature.

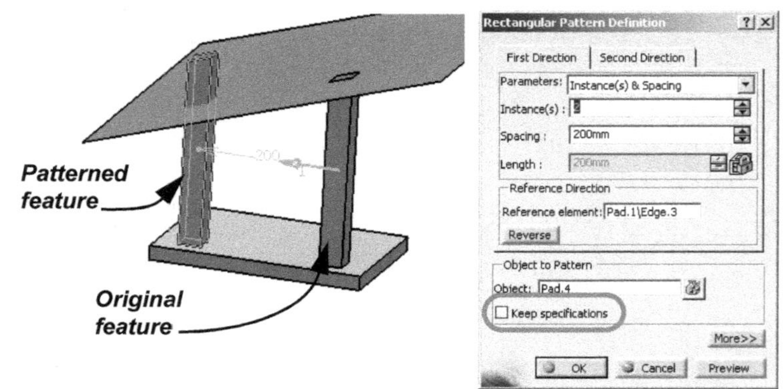

Figure 2–9

In Figure 2–10, the Pad feature is patterned with the **Keep specifications** option selected. The patterned feature is also created using the **Up to surface** option. The disadvantage of using this option is that it increases the update time.

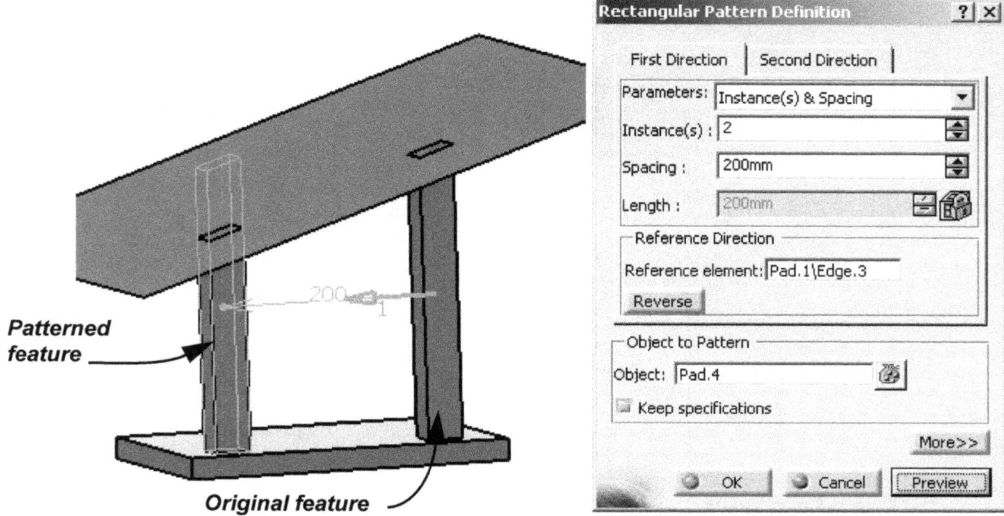

Figure 2–10

If the surface is modified, the patterned features update according to the changes. However, if the surface is modified so that the patterned features lose their references, the pattern fails. To avoid this, the original feature must be created using the Dimension type.

Pattern Formulas

Patterns can be controlled by formulas to automate changes in the model. For example, you might want to generate a relationship between the length of your geometry and the number of instances in a pattern. If the length of the geometry changes, the formula ensures that the number of pattern instances updates accordingly.

The need to generate a formula is often realized during the process of creating a pattern. A formula can be generated while creating a pattern by right-clicking in a field and selecting **Edit Formula**, as shown in Figure 2–11.

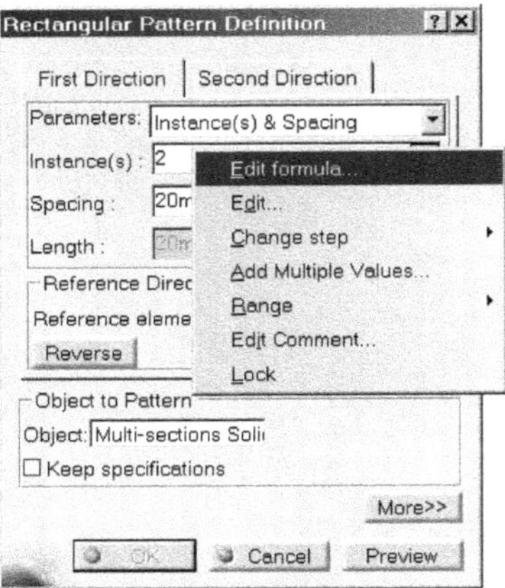

Figure 2–11

Exploding Patterns

After a pattern has been created, you might need to edit individual instances of a pattern. To do this, you need to explode the pattern. Once exploded, each instance of the pattern displays as a separate feature in the specification tree.

To explode a pattern, right-click on the pattern in the specification tree and select **<pattern name> object>Explode**. Once you explode the pattern, the specification tree displays as shown on the right in Figure 2–12.

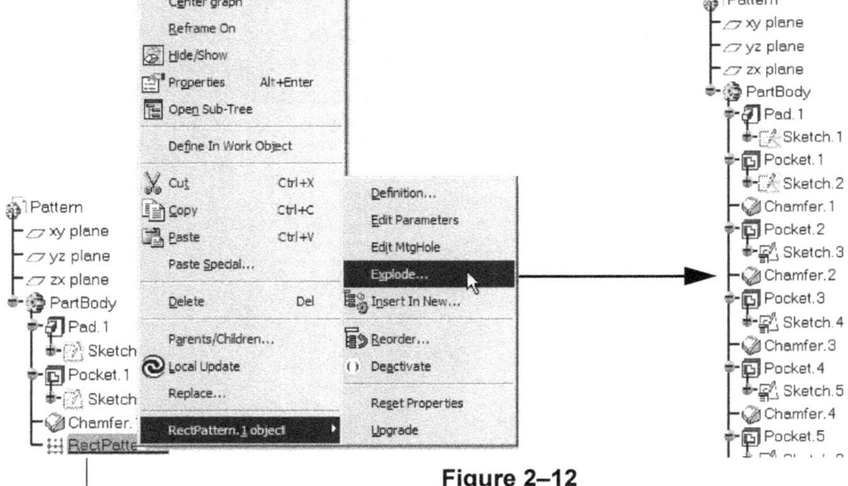

Figure 2–12

Practice 2a

Pattern Options

Practice Objectives

- Use Advanced Pattern options.
- Drive a pattern with a formula.

In this practice, you will create circular patterns of ventilation slots and drill holes in a brake Pad. You will use **Advanced Pattern** options to ensure that the drill holes penetrate the entire model and to ensure that the number of slots equal the number of drill hole groups. The model displays as shown in Figure 2–13.

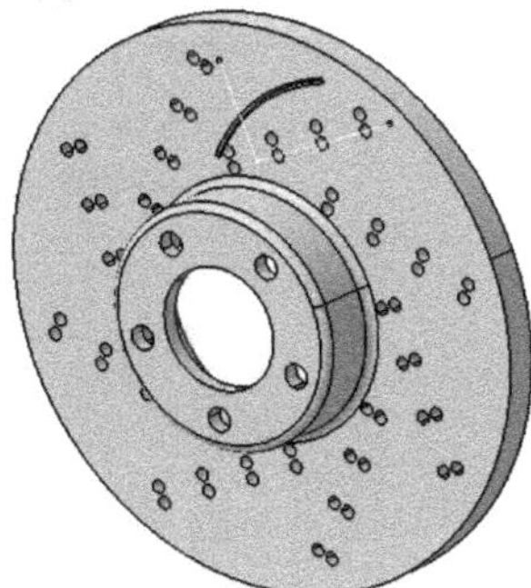

Figure 2–13

Task 1 - Open the part.

1. Open **BrakeRotor.CATPart**. The model displays as shown in Figure 2–14.

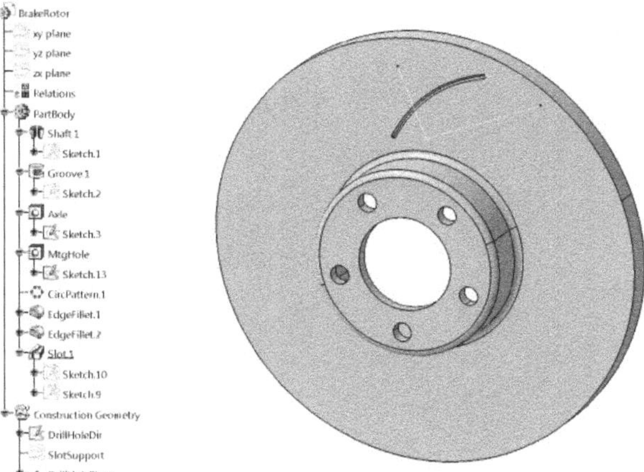

Figure 2–14

2. Investigate the features that have been created in the part model:

   - A Slot has been added to the face of the rotor that aids cooling.
   - In addition, a point (**DrillHolePlace**) and a sketch (**DrillHoleDir**) have been added to the **Construction Geometry** geometrical set. These features are used to create a drill hole pattern.

3. Measure the length of the longer line in the **DrillHoleDir** sketch. The line is approximately 100mm in length.

Task 1 - Create the drill hole.

1. Preselect the face of the rotor and the **DrillHolePlace** point element, as shown in Figure 2–15.

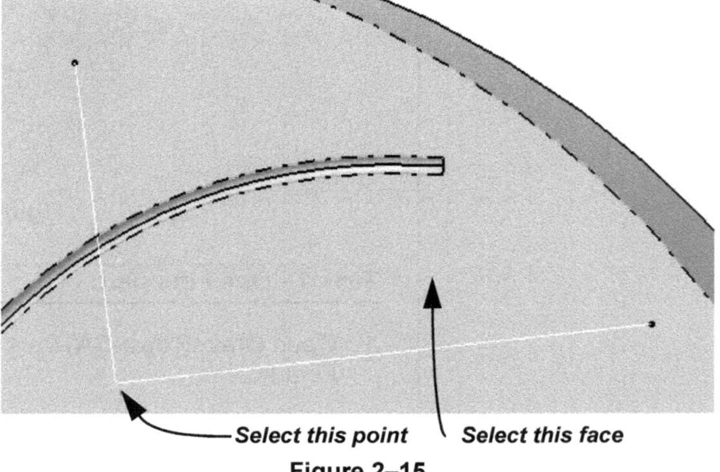

Figure 2–15

2. Create a Hole feature with the following parameters:

   - *Depth*: **Up To Last**
   - *Diameter*: **8mm**

3. Rename the feature as **DrillHole**.

Task 2 - Create a rectangular pattern.

1. Select **DrillHole** and click (Rectangular Pattern) to create a rectangular pattern. Make the following selections:

   * *Parameters:* **Instance(s) & Length**
   * *Instance(s):* **4**
   * *Length:* **100mm**
   * *Reference Direction:* **DrillHoleDir** (Select the long line of the sketch.)
   * If required, clear the **Keep specifications** option.

   The completed pattern displays as shown in Figure 2–16.

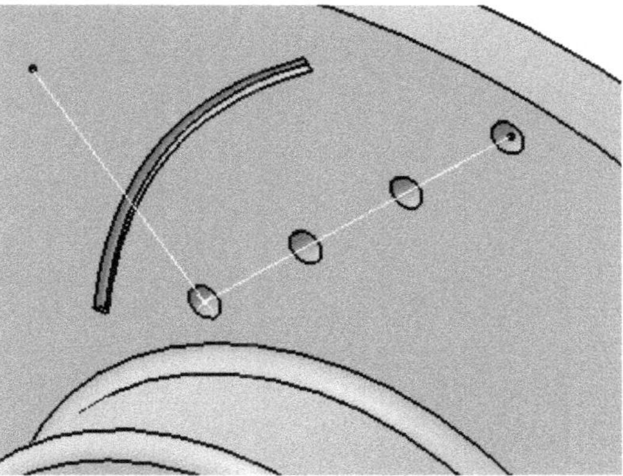

Figure 2–16

2. Rotate the model to display the back of the rotor. Note that the patterned holes do not go through the entire model, as shown in Figure 2–17.

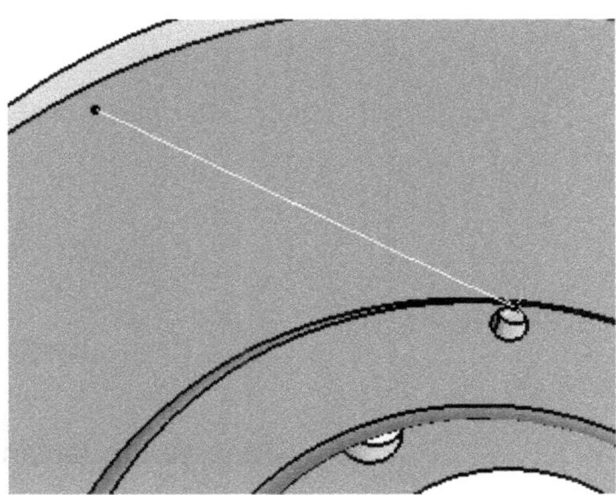

Figure 2–17

Design Considerations

By default, a patterned instance is an exact replica of the Lead Pattern feature. When the **Keep specifications** option is cleared, the patterned instances maintain the same depth as the original feature. In this case, the patterned features no longer cut through the entire model. To resolve this issue, the pattern must be forced to use the specifications of the original Hole feature.

3. Modify **RectPattern.1** and select **Keep specifications**, as shown in Figure 2–18.

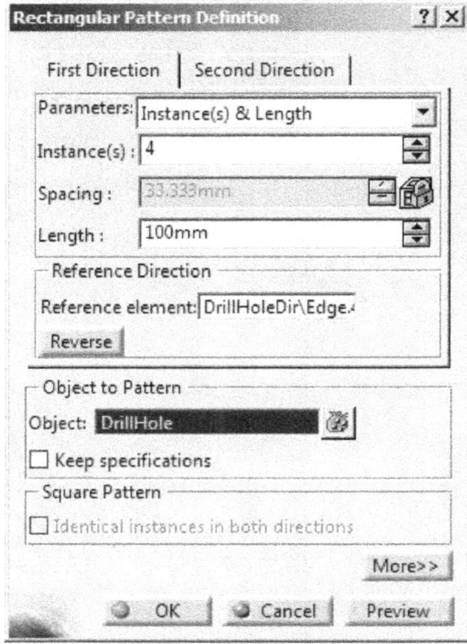

Figure 2–18

The completed pattern displays as shown in Figure 2–19.

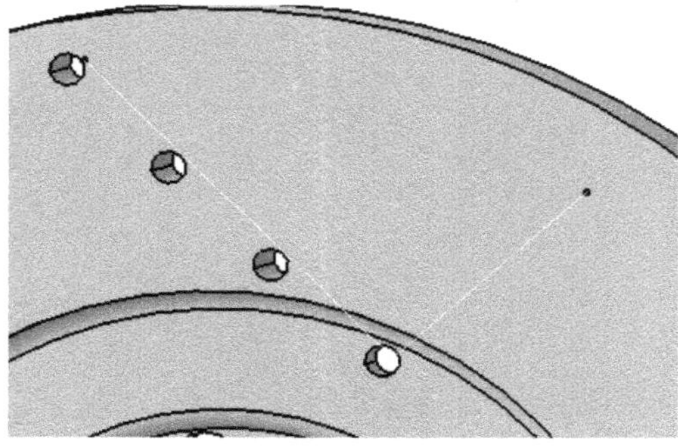

Figure 2–19

4. Rename the rectangular pattern as **DrillHoleRect**.

5. Apply the isometric saved view.

Task 3 - Investigate the Staggered pattern options.

1. Edit the definition of **DrillHoleRect**.
2. In the Rectangular Pattern Definition dialog box, select the *Second Direction* tab.
3. Expand the Parameters drop-down list and select **Instance(s) & Spacing**.
4. Enter **2** for the number of instances.
5. Enter **10** for the spacing.
6. Select the *Reference element* field and then select the short arm of **DrillHoleDir** sketch.

   The pattern updates as shown in Figure 2–20.

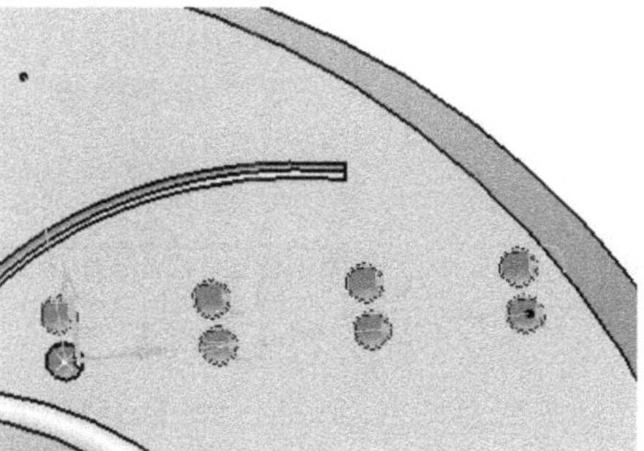

Figure 2–20

7. Click **More** to expand the Rectangular Pattern Definition dialog box.
8. Select **Staggered**.
9. Select **Set half of spacing**.
10. Reorient the model slightly and click **Preview** to display the result, as shown in Figure 2–21.

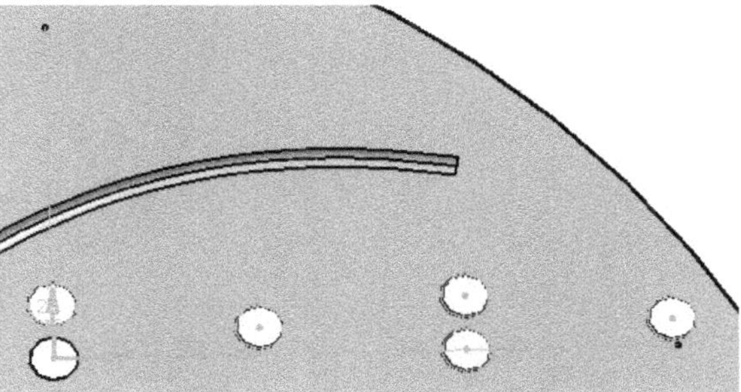

Figure 2–21

11. Click and click **Preview** to change the stagger pattern, as shown in Figure 2–22.

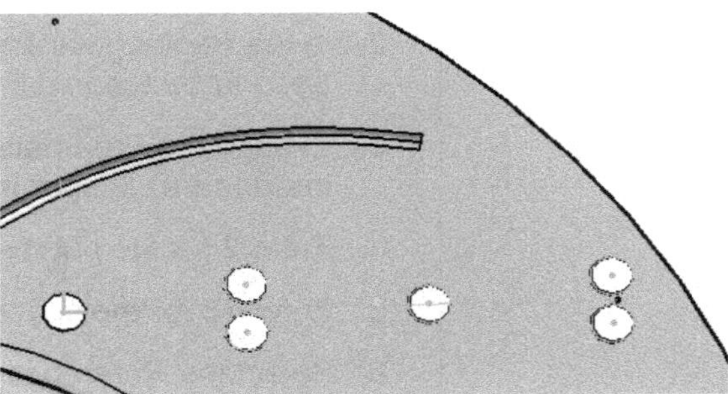

Figure 2–22

12. Click **Staggered** to disable it.

13. In the Rectangular Pattern Definition dialog box, click **Less** and complete the pattern.

14. Apply the isometric saved view.

Task 4 - Create a circular pattern.

1. Select **DrillHoleRect** and click (Circular pattern) to create a circular pattern. Make the following selections:
   - *Parameters:* **Complete crown**
   - *Instance(s):* **8**
   - *Reference element:* (Select the cylindrical face shown in Figure 2–23.)

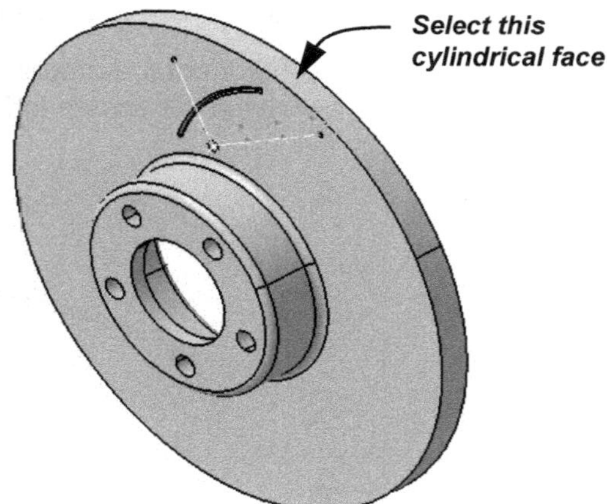

Figure 2–23

2. Rename the circular pattern as **DrillHoleCirc**. The resulting pattern is shown in Figure 2–24.

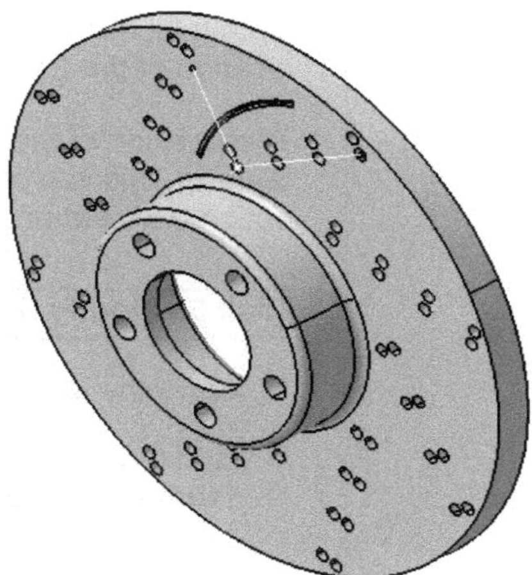

Figure 2–24

3. Rotate the model to display the back face of the rotor. The model displays as shown in Figure 2–25. Although the Lead Pattern feature cuts through the entire part, none of the circular pattern instances do so.

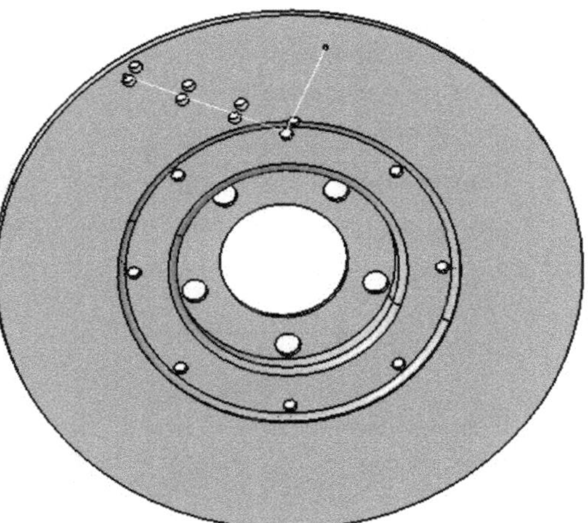

Figure 2–25

Design Considerations

When patterning a pattern, the **Keep Specification** option is not available. To resolve this issue, you must move the Lead Hole feature to an area on the rotor that has the maximum thickness, so that all other instances cut through the entire part. The location of the Lead feature in the pattern can then be adjusted.

The position of the Hole is located using the **DrillHolePlace** feature. This is a point element created using the **On curve** option and referencing the **DrillHoleDir** linear sketch.

Task 5 - Modify the Lead Pattern feature.

1. Apply the isometric saved view.
2. Modify **DrillHolePlace** and change the *Length* value to **110mm**, as shown in Figure 2–26. This moves the hole 110mm (or approximately halfway) up the longer line. It also pushes the patterned instances further up the line so that the last instance leaves the part model.

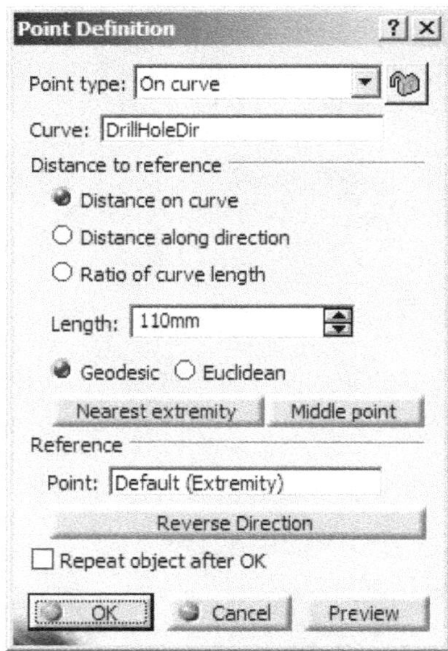

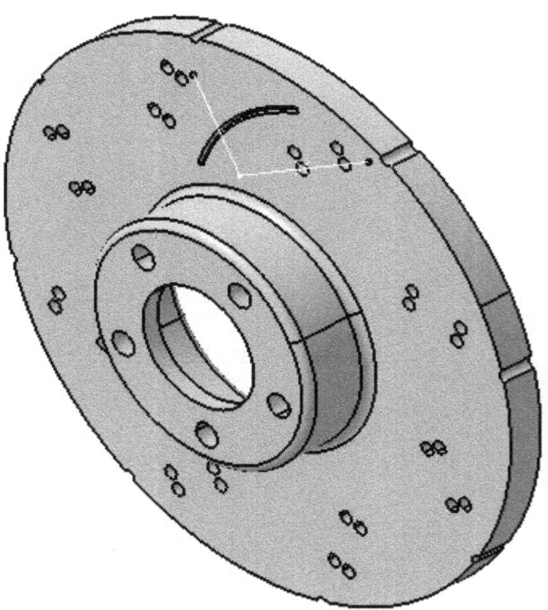

Figure 2–26

3. Click **OK**.

Task 6 - Modify the pattern.

To reposition the pattern instances, you will modify the rectangular pattern and make the Lead Pattern feature the third instance in the pattern.

1. Modify **DrillHoleRect**.
2. Click **More** to display the **Advanced Pattern** options, as shown in Figure 2–27.

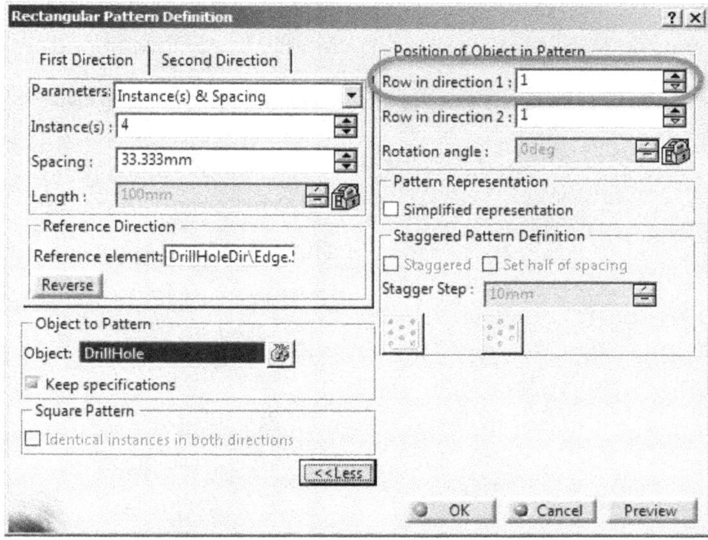

Figure 2–27

3. In the *Row in direction 1* field, enter **3**. This places two instances before the Lead feature and one after the Lead feature. The model displays as shown in Figure 2–28.

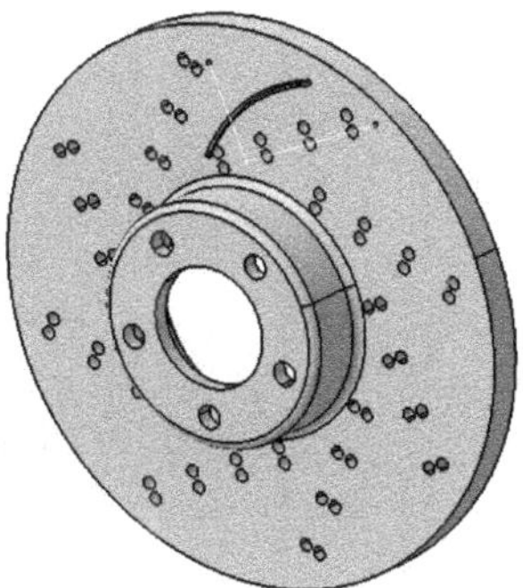

Figure 2–28

Task 7 - Modify the pattern by removing instances.

You have received a design change that requires you to change the spacing of the pattern to provide a greater cooling effect in the contact area between the brake pad and the rotor. This change requires an uneven spacing of the patterned instances. This uneven spacing is accomplished by modifying the rectangular pattern to correctly position the holes, and then disabling the extra instances.

1. Edit the **DrillHoleRect** feature and click **More**.
2. Modify the following pattern parameters:
   - *Parameters:* **Instance(s) & Spacing**
   - *Instance(s):* **6**
   - *Spacing:* **18mm**
   - *Row in direction 1:* **4**

   The dialog box opens as shown in Figure 2–29.

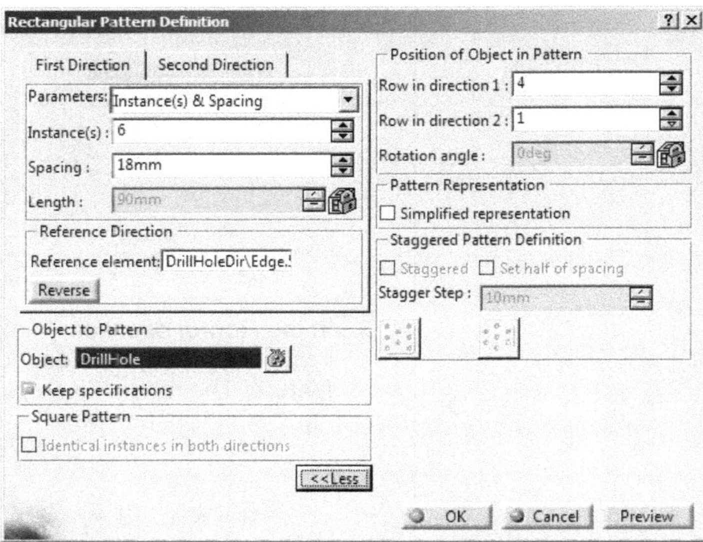

Figure 2–29

3. Zoom in on the pattern and disable the four pattern instances shown in Figure 2–30. This is done by selecting the dot at the center of the instances to be removed.

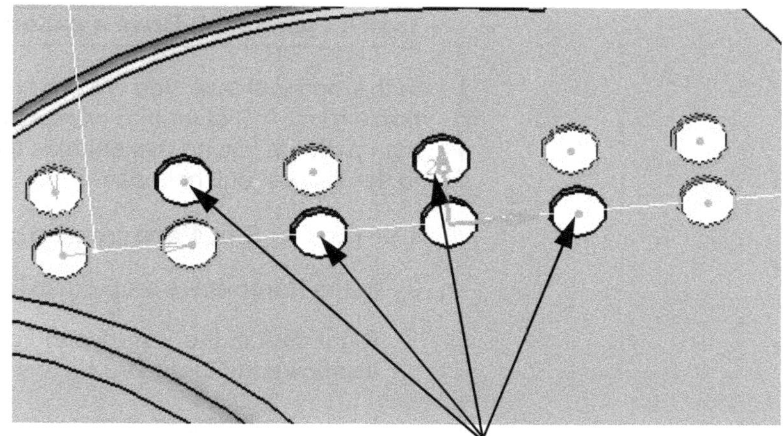

Figure 2–30

4. Complete the Pattern feature. The updated model displays as shown in Figure 2–31.

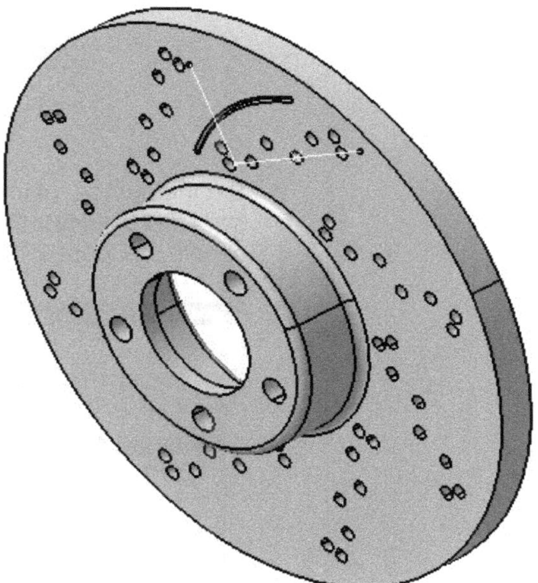

Figure 2–31

5. Hide **DrillHoleDir** and **DrillHolePlace**.

6. Save the model.

Task 8 - (Optional) Drive a pattern with a formula.

In this optional task, you will pattern the Slot feature around the brake rotor. A Slot feature will display between each of the drill hole patterns. Doing this enables the pattern values to be linked to the circular drill hole pattern.

1. Preselect **Slot.1** and create a circular pattern.
2. In the Parameters drop-down list, select **Complete crown**.
3. Right-click in the *Instance(s)* field and select **Edit Formula**, as shown in Figure 2–32.

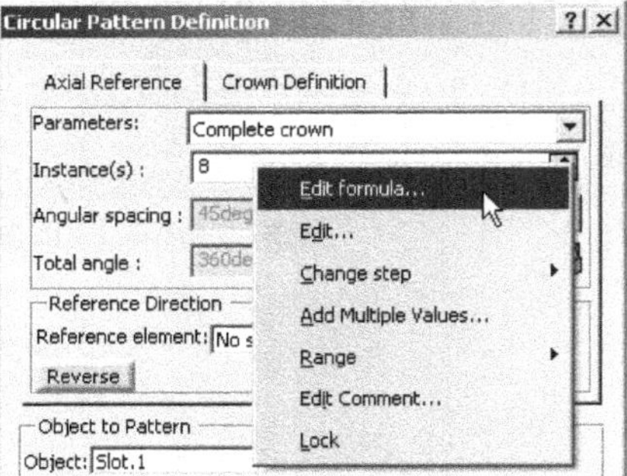

Figure 2–32

4. Set the number of instances equal to the number of instances from the **DrillHoleCirc** pattern. The formula will display as shown in Figure 2–33.

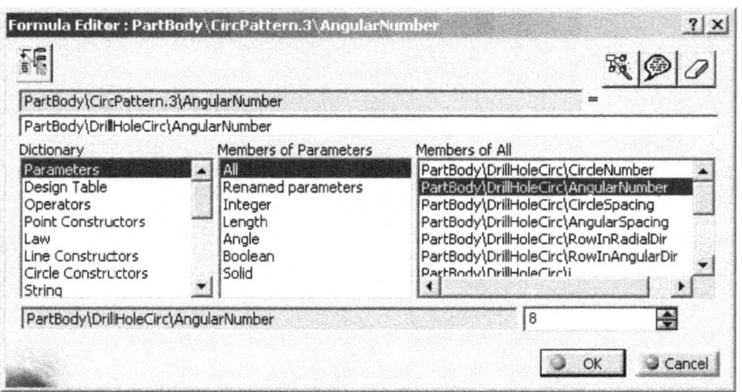

Figure 2–33

5. Select an appropriate reference element to drive the pattern. The completed pattern displays as shown in Figure 2–34.

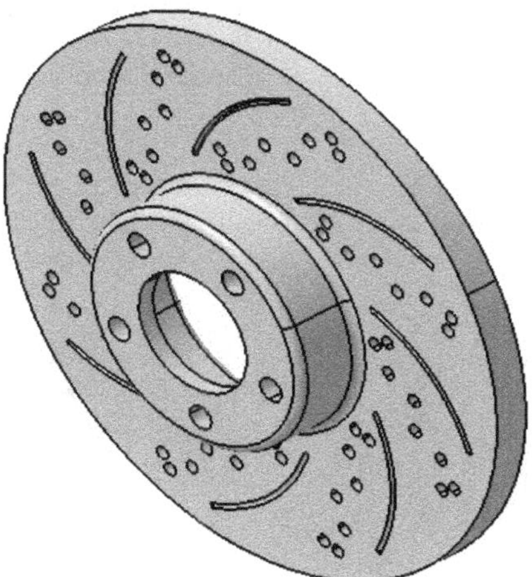

Figure 2–34

6. Rename the pattern as **SlotCirc**.

7. Modify the number of instances in the **DrillHoleCirc** pattern to **10** and update the model. The model displays as shown in Figure 2–35.

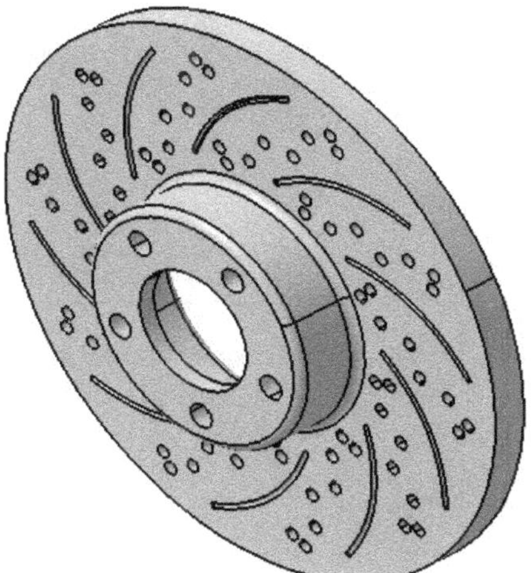

Figure 2–35

8. Save the model and close the window.

Practice 2b Simplified Representations

Practice Objective

- Create a simplified representation of a pattern.

In this practice, you will create a simplified representation of a large rectangular pattern and examine the resulting geometry. When using simplified representations, the model display, file size, and moment of inertia of the part will change.

Task 1 - Open the part.

1. Open **SimpRep.CATPart**. The model displays as shown in Figure 2–36.

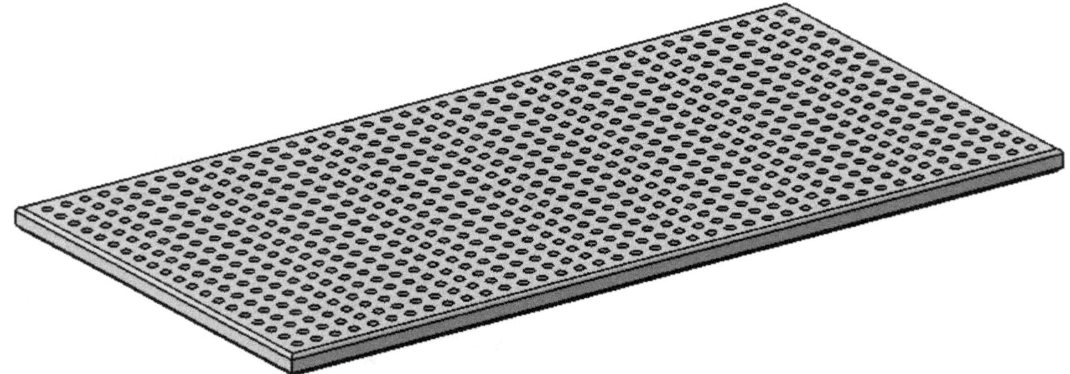

Figure 2–36

Task 2 - Check the file size of the model.

Check the file size so that you can compare it to the size after using a simplified representation.

1. Select **File>Document Properties**. Note in the *Document* tab that the file size is over 4000 KB, as shown in Figure 2–37.

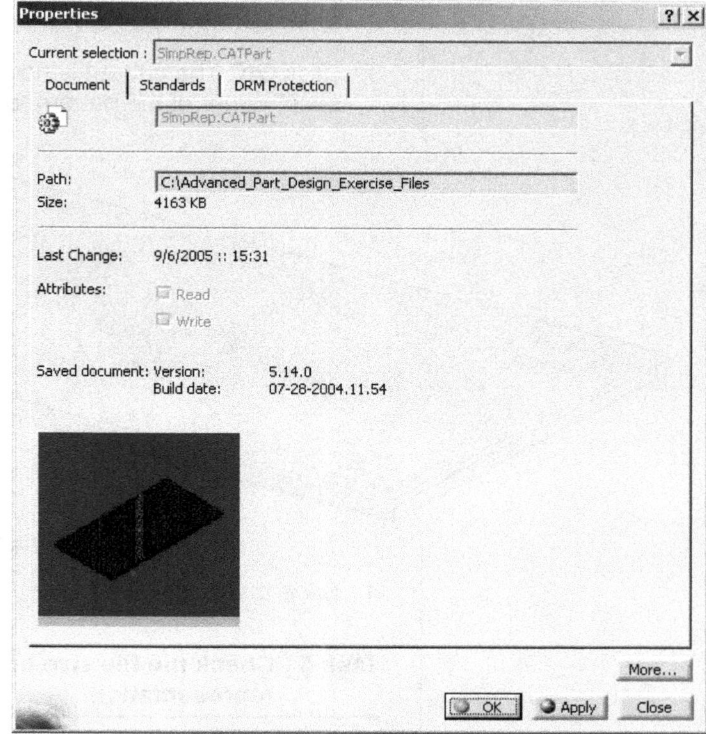

Figure 2–37

2. Close the Properties dialog box.

Task 3 - Measure the mass of the part.

1. Obtain the inertia properties of the PartBody by clicking  (Measure Inertia).

   Note that the mass of the part is 5.505 kg.

2. Close the Measure Inertia dialog box.

Task 4 - Create a simplified representation of the pattern.

1. Edit the rectangular pattern and click **More**.
2. Select **Simplified representation**.
3. Click **OK**. The pattern is now represented by instances at each corner of the pattern, as shown in Figure 2–38.

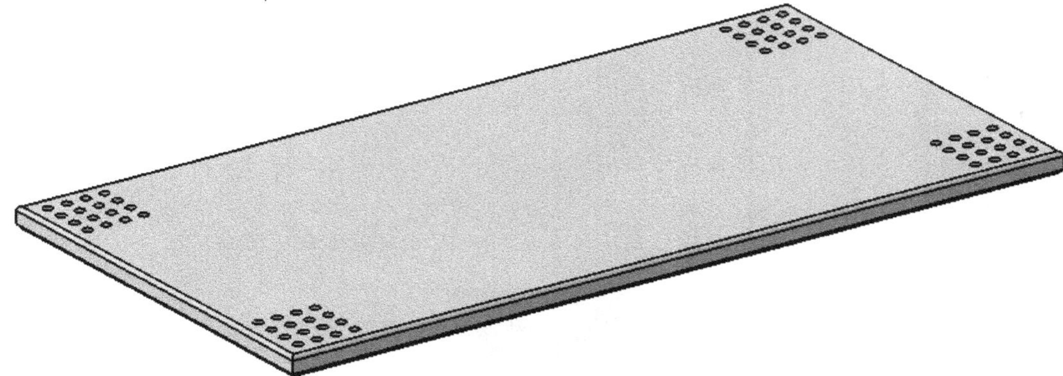

Figure 2–38

4. Save the model.

Task 5 - Check the file size of the model with the simplified representation.

1. Select **File>Document Properties**. Note that the file size has been significantly reduced. Although the pattern is intact, less data is required to describe the model since all hole instances are not currently visible on the part.
2. Close the Properties dialog box.

Task 6 - Measure the mass of the part with the simplified representation.

1. Obtain the inertia properties of the PartBody. Note that the mass of the part has increased to 6.641 kg. When using a simplified representation, the mass and inertia properties are not correct.
2. Close the Measure Inertia dialog box.
3. Close the file without saving.

Practice 2c

Engine Cover

Practice Objective

- Use the Keep specifications option.

In this practice, you will clear the **Keep specifications** option for a rectangular pattern and examine the resulting geometry. You will then replace a reference surface for a Pad feature that is patterned.

Task 1 - Open the part.

1. Open **Engine_Cover_JY.CATPart**. The model displays as shown in Figure 2–39.

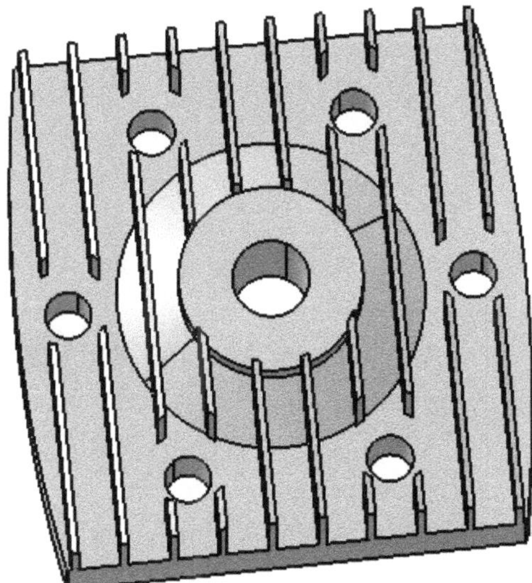

Figure 2–39

Task 2 - Modify the Rectangular pattern.

In this task, you will deactivate the **Keep specifications** option for the rectangular pattern.

Design Considerations

The rectangular pattern is created using a Pad feature. The **Up to surface** option is used to create the Pad feature, which uses an isolated surface as the limit.

1. In the **Surfaces** geometrical set, show **Surface.1**.

2. Orient the model, as shown in Figure 2–40.

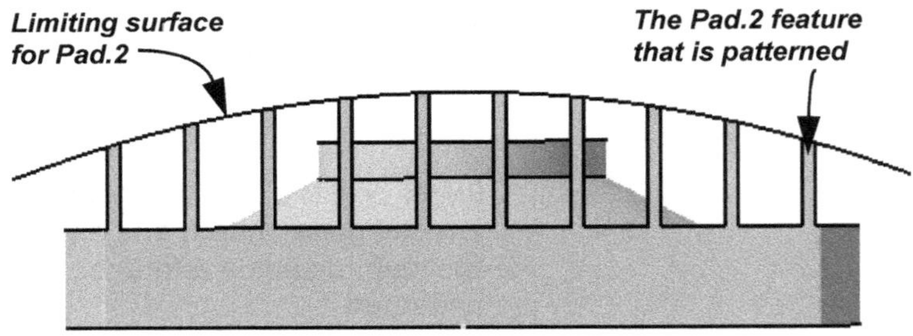

Figure 2–40

3. Double-click on **RectPattern.1**. The Rectangular Pattern Definition dialog box opens as shown in Figure 2–41.

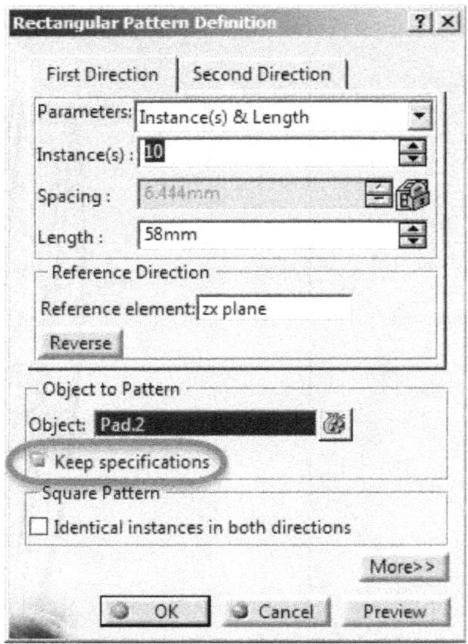

Figure 2–41

4. Clear the **Keep specifications** option.

5. Click **OK**. The model displays as shown in Figure 2–42. Note that the pattern is identical to the original Pad feature.

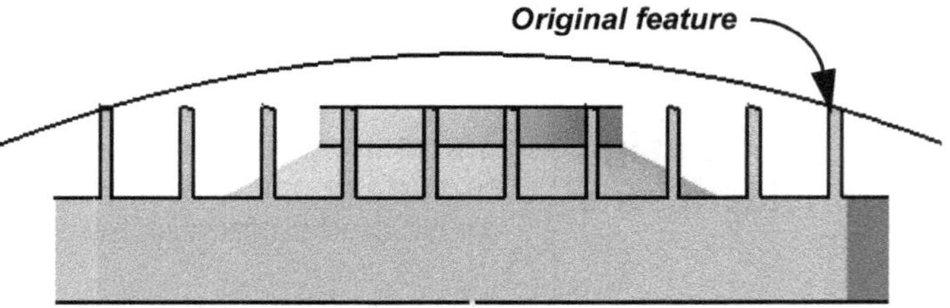

Figure 2–42

Task 3 - Replace the reference surface.

1. In the specification tree, double-click **RectPattern.1** to open the Rectangular Pattern Definition dialog box.
2. Select **Keep specifications** for the rectangular pattern.
3. Click **OK**.
4. Hide **Surface.1** and show **Surface.2**. The model displays as shown in Figure 2–43.

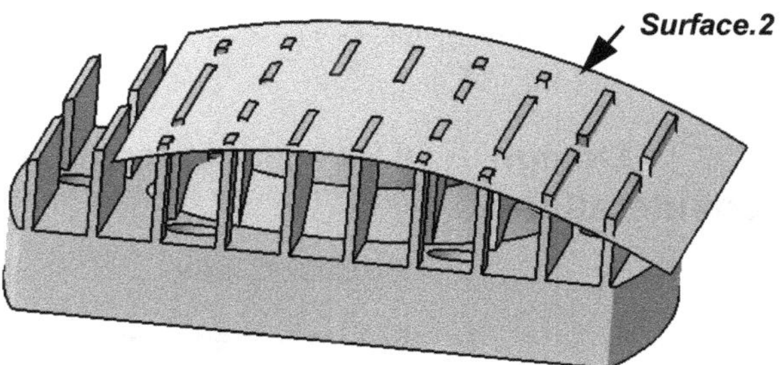

Figure 2–43

5. Double-click on **Pad.2** and select **Surface.2** as the limit, as shown in Figure 2–44.

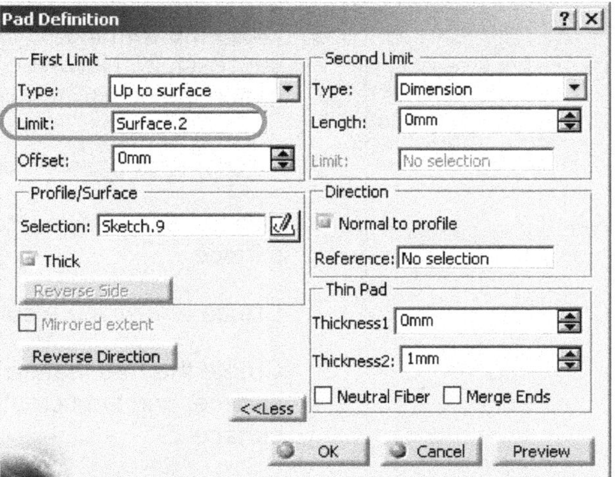

Figure 2–44

6. Click **OK**. The Update Diagnosis:Pad.2 dialog box opens as shown in Figure 2–45, indicating that some of the patterns are not intersecting the limiting element.

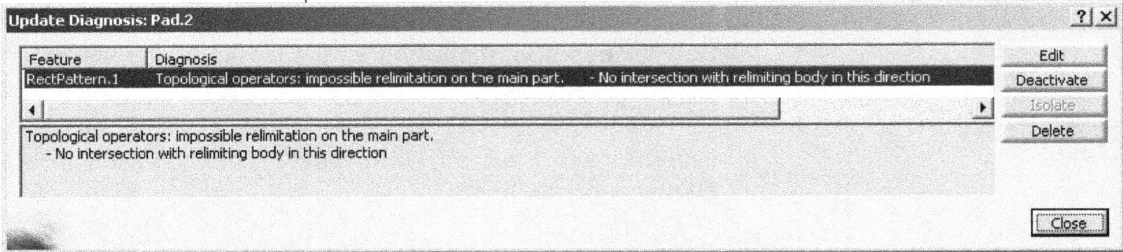

Figure 2–45

Design Considerations

If the surface does not intersect the patterned feature, the pattern loses its reference. This causes the pattern to fail.

7. Click **Close**.

8. Clear the **Keep specifications** option for the rectangular pattern. A warning message opens prompting you that the **Pocket.1** feature is unnecessary. Clearing the **Keep specifications** option results in the model not having any material for the **Pocket.1** feature to cut. This is why it no longer required.

9. Close the warning. This time, the rectangular pattern updates successfully. However, the shape of the pattern does not match the design requirements.

There are a few possible solutions for this situation:

- Use the Generative Shape Design workbench to fix the surface.
- Create a new, more suitable surface.
- Create the Pad feature with a dimension that intersects the surface, and then create a Pocket feature using the suitable surface.

10. Save and close the model.

Practice 2d

Copying Features Between Models

Practice Objectives

- Copy and paste between models.
- Create a User Pattern.
- Explode a pattern.

In the practice, you will copy the HolePositions sketch from the **MeasureTapeBack** part to the **MeasureTapeFront** part. You will also copy a Pad and Hole feature, and then create a User Pattern using the copied sketch and features. You will also explode the pattern. The completed model displays as shown in Figure 2–46.

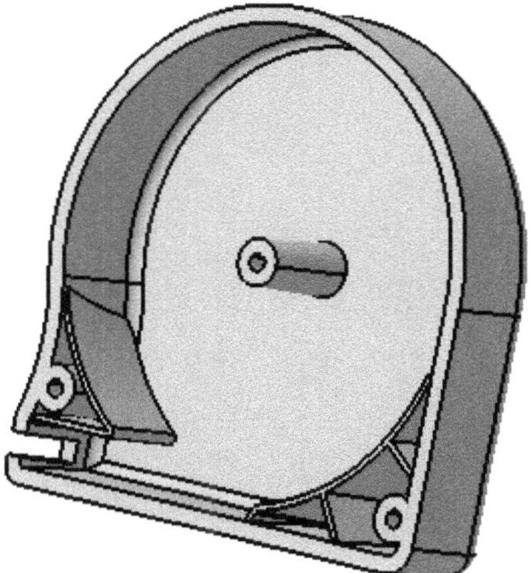

Figure 2–46

Task 1 - Open the part.

1. Open **TapeMeasureBack.CATPart** and **TapeMeasureFront.CATPart**. The TapeMeasureFront.CATPart model displays as shown in Figure 2–47.

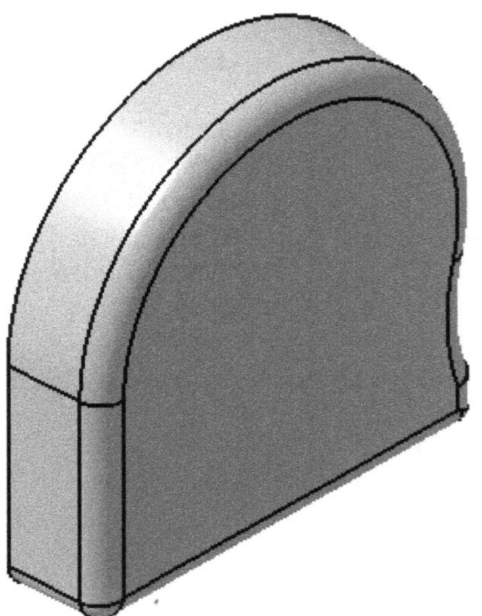

Figure 2–47

2. Activate the **TapeMeasureBack.CATPart** window.

3. Right-click on the **HoleLocations** sketch and select **Copy**, as shown in Figure 2–48.

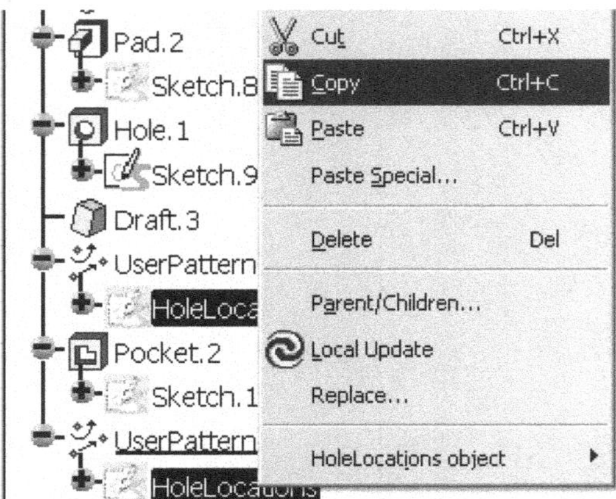

Figure 2–48

4. Activate the **TapeMeasureFront.CATPart** window.
5. Right-click on the PartBody and select **Paste**, as shown in Figure 2–49.

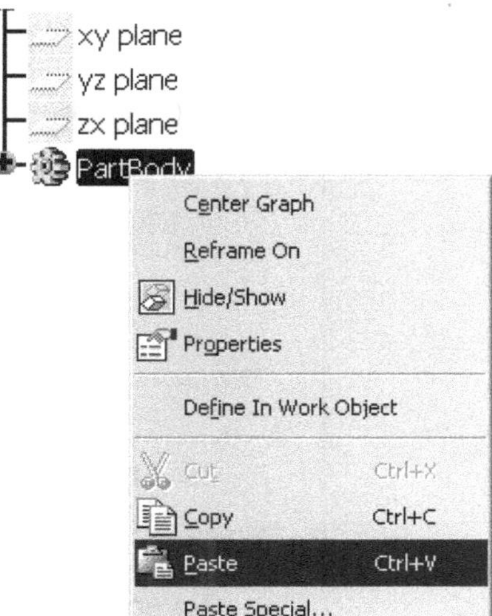

Figure 2–49

The **HoleLocations** sketch displays as shown in Figure 2–50.

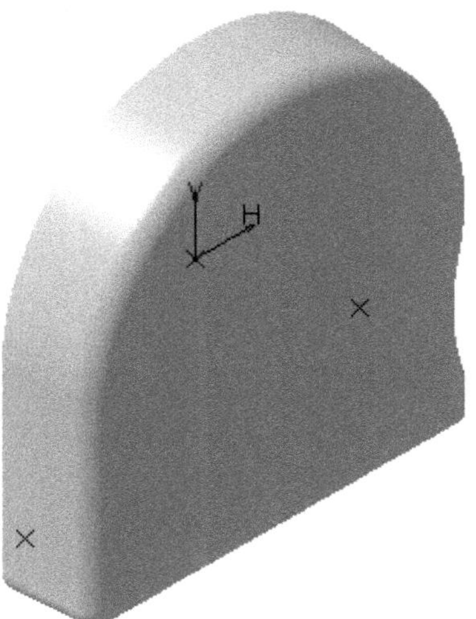

Figure 2–50

6. Copy and paste **Pad.2** from the **TapeMeasureBack** to the **TapeMeasureFront** model. The feature fails due to an incorrect direction of feature creation, as shown in Figure 2–51.

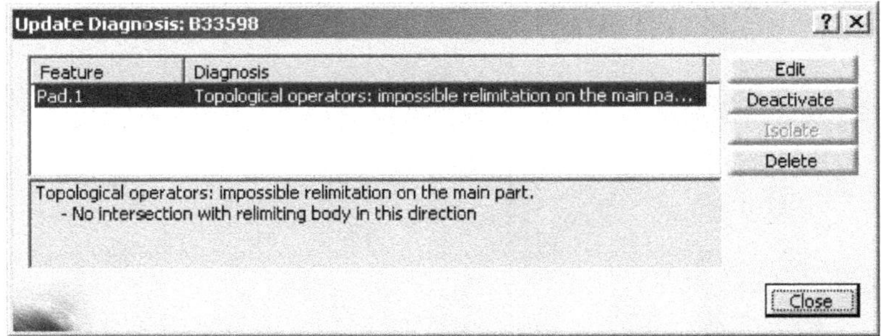

Figure 2–51

7. Click **Edit**. The Feature Definition Error dialog box opens.
8. Click **OK** in the Feature Definition Error dialog box.
9. Reverse the direction of feature creation. The correct direction for the Pad feature is shown in Figure 2–52.

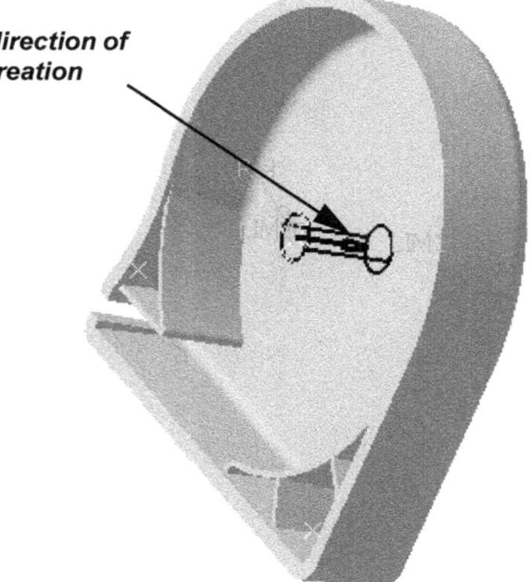

Figure 2–52

The pasted Pad feature displays as shown in Figure 2–53.

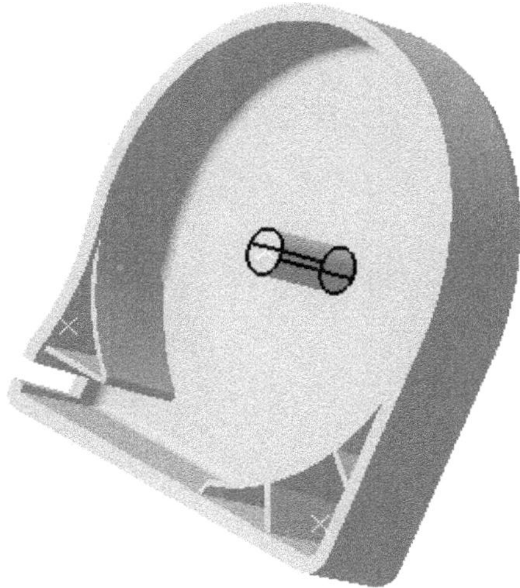

Figure 2–53

10. Copy **Hole.1** from **TapeMeasureBack.CATPart**.

11. Activate **TapeMeasureFront.CATPart**.

12. Select the face of **Pad.1**, right-click, and select **Paste**, as shown in Figure 2–54.

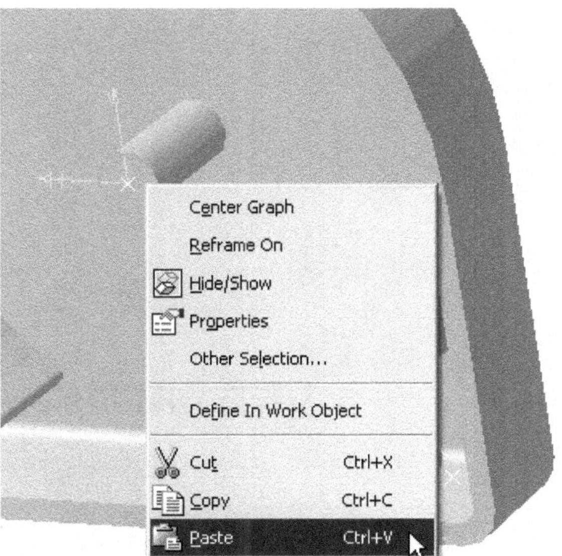

Figure 2–54

The result displays as shown in Figure 2–55.

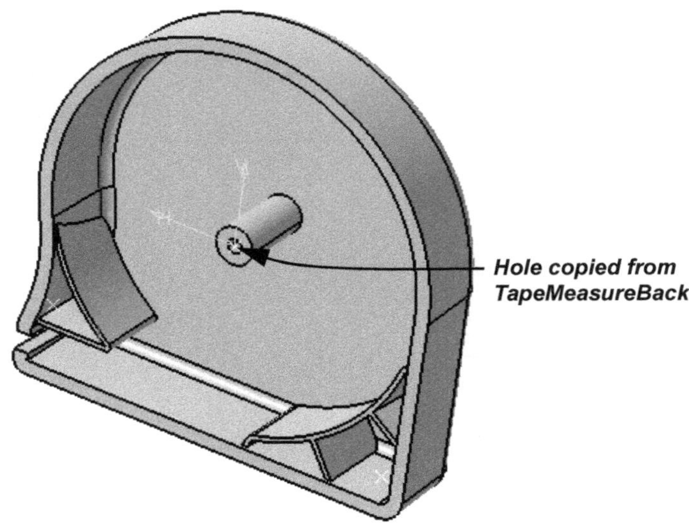

Figure 2–55

13. Make the following changes to the Hole feature, as shown in Figure 2–56:
    - Verify that the Hole direction is pointing to the model.
    - *Extension:* **Blind**
    - *Depth:* **15**

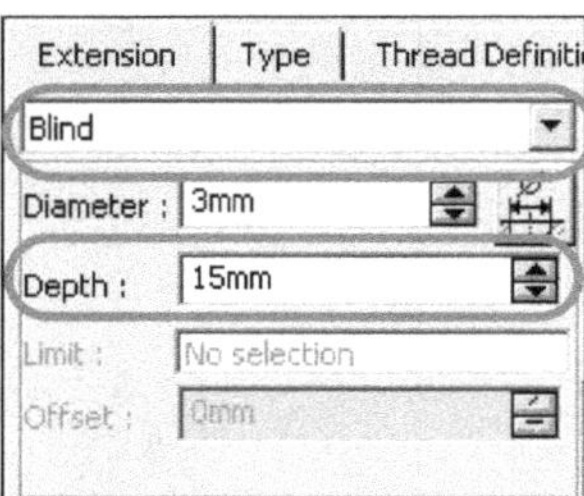

Figure 2–56

Task 2 - Create a Draft feature.

1. Add the following Draft to the cylindrical surface of the Pad:
    - *Angle:* **2**
    - *Surface(s) to draft:* (cylindrical surface, as shown in Figure 2–57)
    - *Neutral element:* (planar surface, as shown in Figure 2–57)

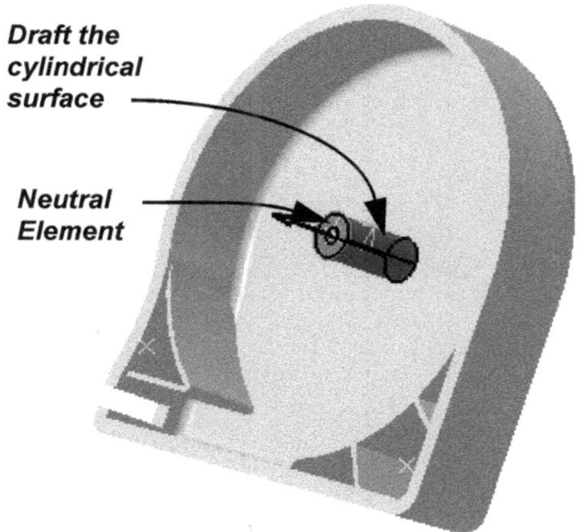

Figure 2–57

Task 3 - Create a User Pattern.

1. Create a user pattern of the Pad, Hole, and Draft features using the pasted **HoleLocations** sketch, as shown in Figure 2–58. Select the features in the specified order. Selecting the draft first will cause the User Pattern to be created incorrectly.

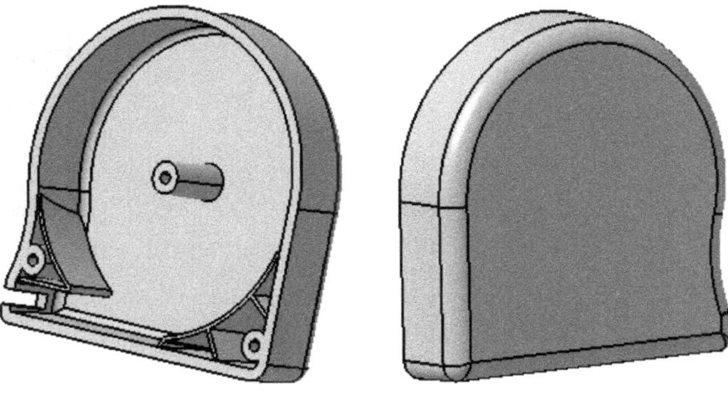

Figure 2–58

Design Considerations

Copying and pasting features is an effective method of duplicating features between part files. Remember that the pasted features are located in the same position as the source model. The pasted features are not associative using the **Paste** functionality.

2. Save the model, but keep **TapeMeasureFront.CATPart** open for the next task.

Task 4 - Explode the pattern.

1. Right-click on **UserPattern.1** and select **UserPattern.1 object>Explode**, as shown in Figure 2–59.

Figure 2–59

After the pattern has been exploded, the specification tree displays as shown in Figure 2–60.

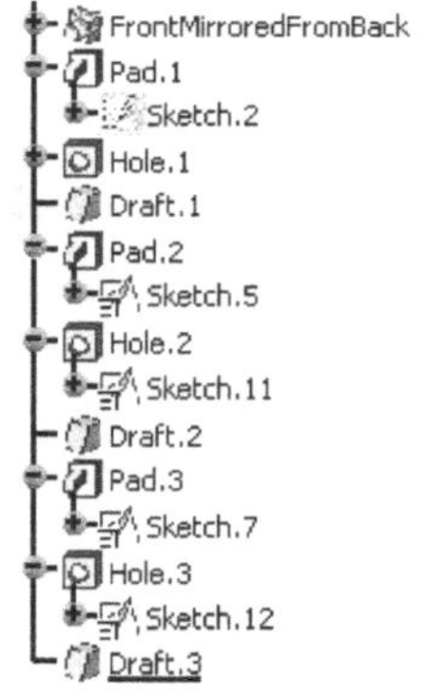

Figure 2–60

2. Undo the explode with the **Undo** option.
3. Close **TapeMeasureFront.CATPart** without saving.

Design Considerations

Be cautious when using the **Explode** command. It cannot be undone once it no longer exists in the Undo history list. It is recommended that you save a backup of the model immediately before performing an explode.

Chapter Review Questions

1. When creating a rectangular pattern that extends in two directions, the original feature always displays in the first row and first column of the pattern.
   a. True
   b. False
2. To create a rectangular pattern in which alternate rows are offset by specified values, use the _____ option.
   a. **Offset**
   b. **Alternating**
   c. **Pivot**
   d. **Staggered**
3. To create a circular pattern, you need to define the _______ directions.
   a. **First** and **Second**.
   b. **Angular** and **Radial**.
   c. **Rotation** and **Offset**.
   d. None of the above.
4. You can use the **Simplified Representation** option to display some pattern instances instead of the full pattern.
   a. True
   b. False
5. Once a pattern has been created, you cannot break the pattern into separate features.
   a. True
   b. False
6. To create pattern instances that are identical to the original, disable the _______ option.
   a. **Keep specifications**
   b. **Maintain status**
   c. **Hold definition**
   d. None of the above.

Working With Multi-Profile Sketches

A Multi-Profile sketch enables you to sketch multiple profiles in one sketch. In this chapter, you learn how to integrate Multi-Profile sketches with a variety of other features.

Learning Objectives in this Chapter

- Understand how sketches with multiple profiles can be used in a single pad feature.
- Select one or more sketch sub-elements to create a pad feature.
- Use Output features to make sketched elements independent of the sketch.
- Understand how to define a set of sketched elements as a single profile, using the Profile Feature.
- Learn the available propagation modes.
- Understand the domains in a multi-profile sketch.
- Understand multi-pad features that can have unique lengths for each domain.
- Learn about the available length options.

3.1 Multi-Profile Sketches

In some design situations, you might want to sketch multiple profiles in one sketch. If you use a multi-profile sketch to create a Pad feature, you end up with a solid feature that adds material in the areas between the profiles, and leaves a void in other areas that resemble a hole or a pocket. An example is shown in Figure 3–1.

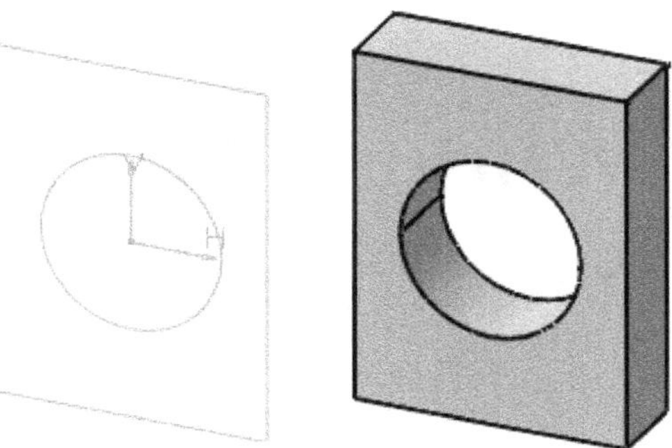

Figure 3–1

For a multi-profile sketch to work for a Pad feature, the profiles cannot intersect one another. This results in the error message shown in Figure 3–2.

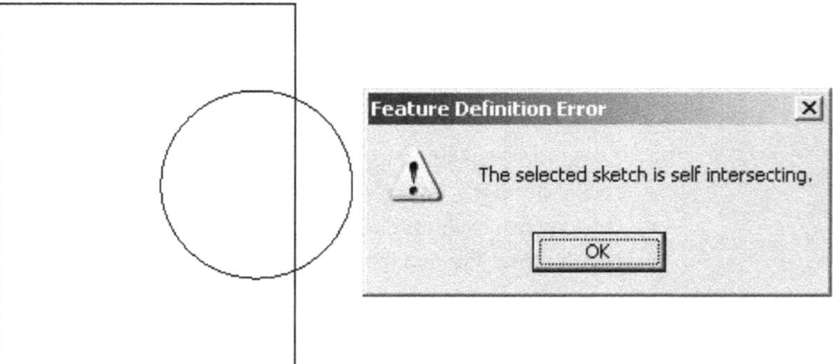

Figure 3–2

3.2 Creation of Sketch Sub-Elements

You can use multi-profile sketches to construct solid features by using a sub-element of the sketch for feature creation, instead of the entire sketch. The result of creating a Pad feature using each sub-element is shown in Figure 3–3.

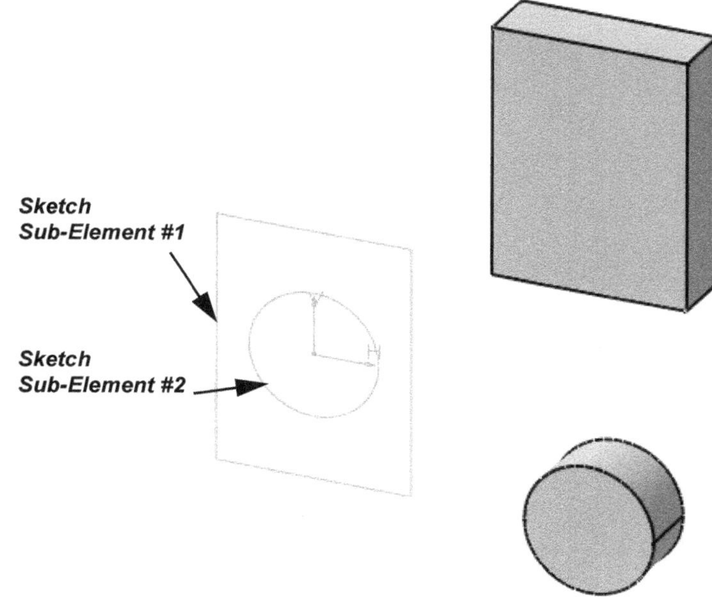

Figure 3–3

How To: Construct Solid Features Using a Sub-element of a Sketch

1. Create a Pad feature without preselecting a sketch.
2. In the Pad Definition dialog box, place the cursor in the *Profile Selection* field and right-click.

3. Select **Go to profile definition** as shown in Figure 3–4. The Pad Definition dialog box temporarily hides and the Profile Definition dialog box opens.

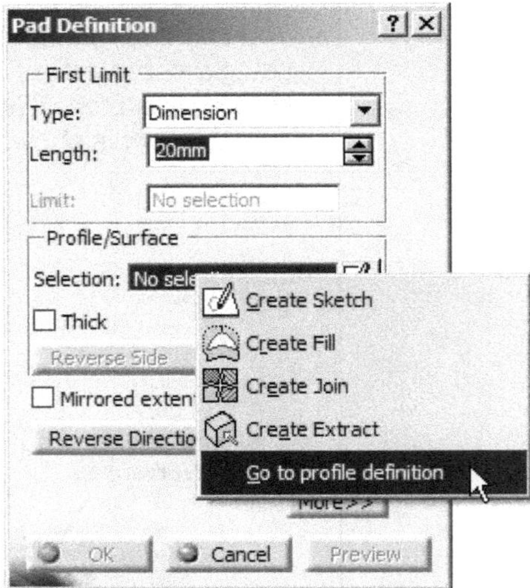

Figure 3–4

4. Select the required edge of the profile. In the Profile Definition dialog box, click **OK** as shown in Figure 3–5.

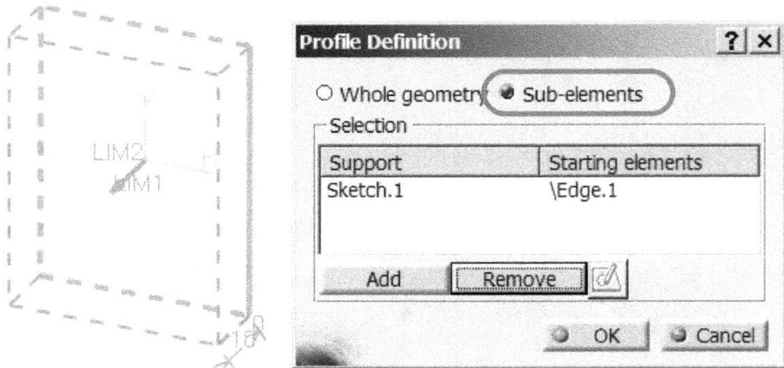

Figure 3–5

5. Continue to define the Pad feature as usual. Note that the *Profile Selection* area lists **Complex**, instead of the name of the sketch, as shown in Figure 3–6.

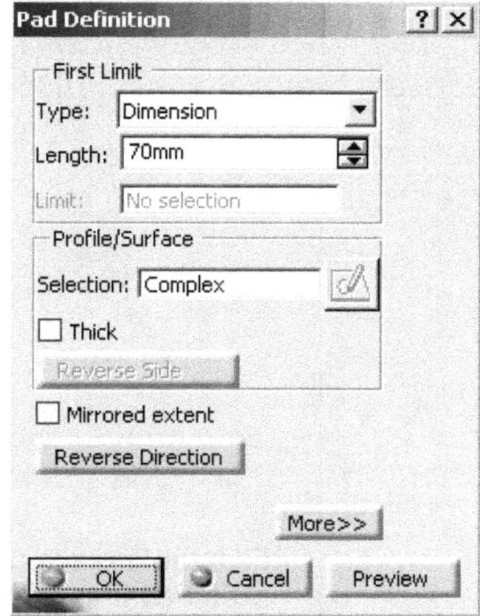

Figure 3–6

The sketch is not automatically hidden, as is the case when you use the entire sketch for a feature. The system assumes that you need to refer to the sketch again at a later time, and therefore leaves it displayed, as shown in Figure 3–7. You must manually hide the sketch if you want to clean up the display.

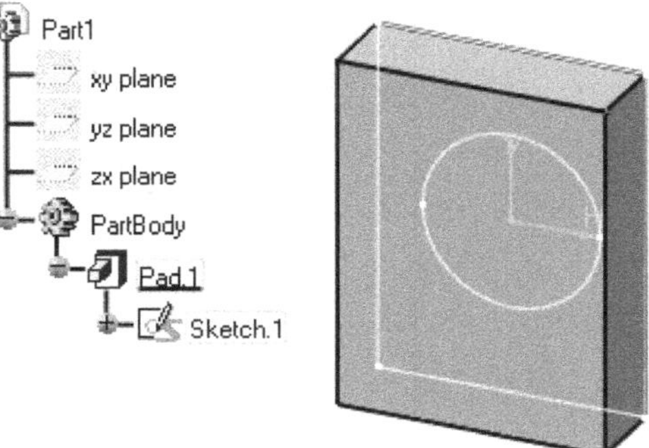

Figure 3–7

In some cases, creating a multi-profile sketch is more efficient than developing a series of separate sketches. Consider the sketch shown in Figure 3–8.

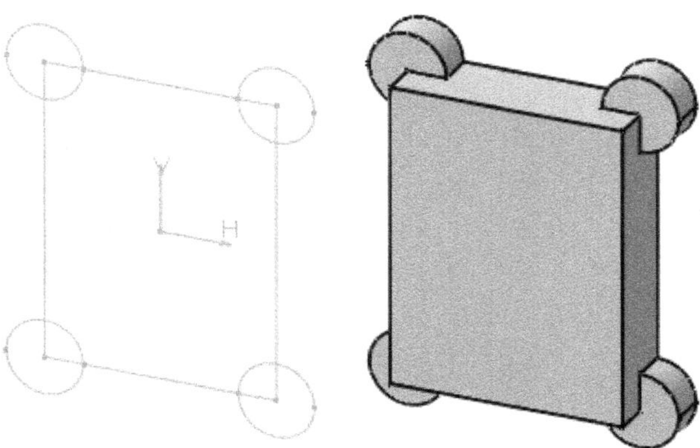

Figure 3–8

Five profiles are created in one sketch. With the rectangle sketched first, the centers of the four circles can be quickly constrained to the four corners of the rectangle. Construction geometry can also be added quickly to ensure that all four circles are the same size and controlled by a single diameter dimension.

3.3 Output Features

Output features enable you to make selected sketched elements independent of the sketch in which they were created. The independent elements can then be used independent to the rest of the sketch.

How To: Create an Output Feature

1. With the sketch active, click (Output feature) in the Tools toolbar, as shown in Figure 3–9.

Figure 3–9

2. Select the sketched geometry that you want to make independent. In Figure 3–10, the spline entity is made independent from the rest of the sketched geometry.

Figure 3–10

3. A completed output feature is listed under the Outputs node in the specification tree. It displays under the sketch in which it was created, as shown in Figure 3–11. The line thickness of the output feature is different from the rest of the sketched geometry to help visually distinguish it from the rest of the sketch.

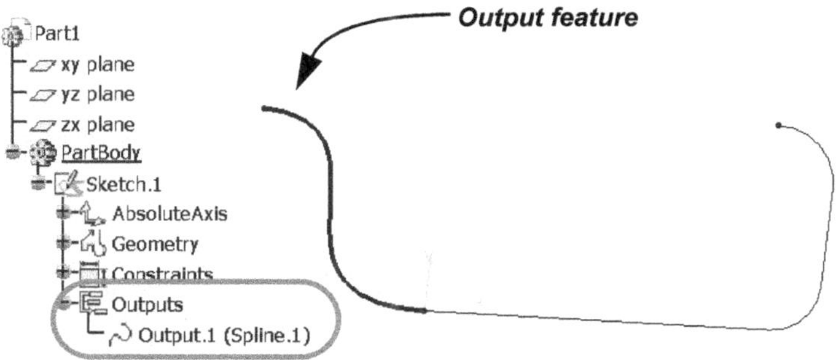

Figure 3–11

3.4 3D Outputs

3D axes and planes can be created by referencing sketcher entities, using (3D Axis) and (3D Plane) from the Tools toolbar, as shown in Figure 3–12.

Figure 3–12

3D Axis

You can use sketch points to output 3D axes. In the Tools toolbar, click (3D Axis) and select a point. The system generates an axis running through the point and perpendicular to the sketch support. The created output axis displays under the **Outputs** node in the specification tree, as shown in Figure 3–13.

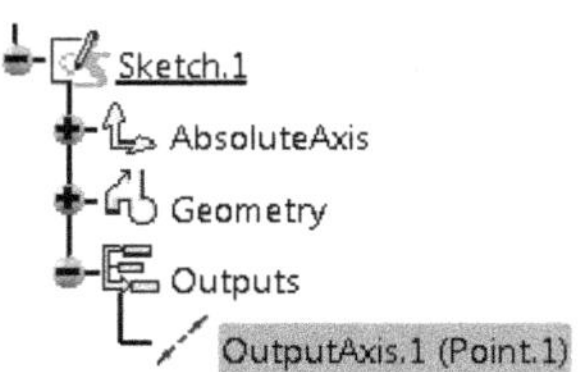

Figure 3–13

3D Plane

You can use a sketched line to output a 3D plane. In the Tools toolbar, click (3D Plane) and select a line. The system generates a plane running through the line and perpendicular to the sketch support. The created output plane displays under the **Outputs** node in the specification tree, as shown in Figure 3–14.

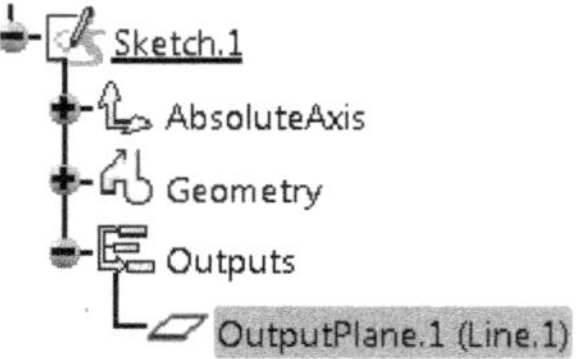

Figure 3–14

3.5 Profile Feature

The **Profile Feature** tool enables you to define a set of sketched elements as a single profile. As with output features, profile features become independent of the sketch in which they are created.

How To: Create a Profile of Sketched Elements

1. In the Tools toolbar, click (Profile feature) as shown in Figure 3–15.

Figure 3–15

2. The Profile Definition dialog box opens as shown in Figure 3–16. You can enter a user-defined name for the profile and define a color.

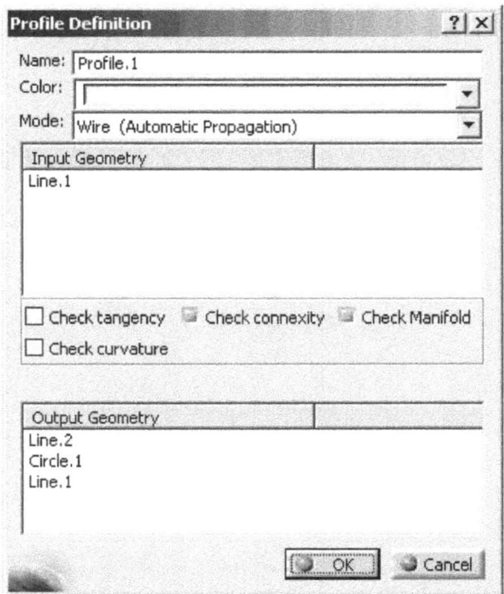

Figure 3–16

3. The *Input Geometry* field lists the items that have been selected to add to the profile. The *Output Geometry* field lists the items that are included in the profile. The type of geometry that you can select is dependent on the Mode being used.

Three different modes can be used for geometry selection. They are described as follows:

Mode	Description
Wire (Automatic Propagation)	The default mode. The system selects all of the point continuous entities, until a loop is selected or the system encounters a point that connects more than two entities.
Point (Explicit Definition)	Only points and vertices can be added to the profile. All entities must be explicitly selected. The *Input* and *Output Geometry* fields are the same.
Wire (Explicit Definition)	All sketched entities can be added to the profile. All entities must be explicitly selected. The *Input* and *Output Geometry* fields are the same.

4. Click **OK** to complete the profile. A completed profile is listed under the Outputs node in the specification tree, under the sketch in which it was created, as shown in Figure 3–17.

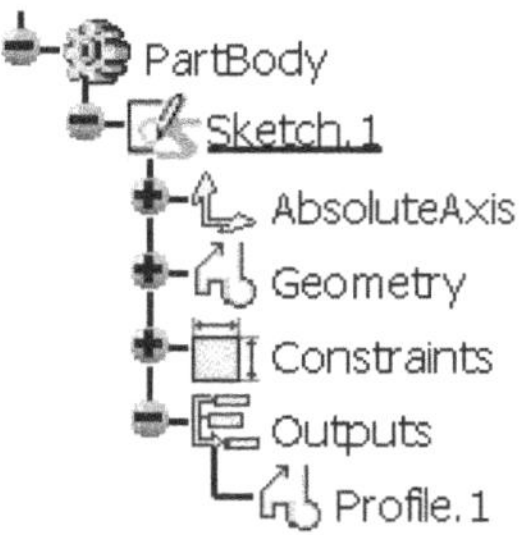

Figure 3–17

3.6 Creation of Multi-Pad Features

Multi-pad features enable you to specify a different length for each domain of the sketch, in which the domain is the space enclosed by each sub-element of the sketch. The domains cannot overlap. An example is shown in Figure 3–18.

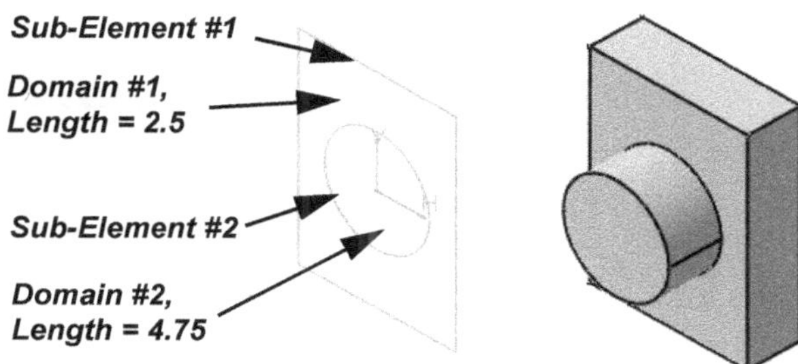

Figure 3–18

The system does not extrude the full area inside each profile to the length that you specify. It extrudes the domain, or the area **between** the profiles to the specified length. Note the results of different length values for each domain, as shown in Figure 3–19.

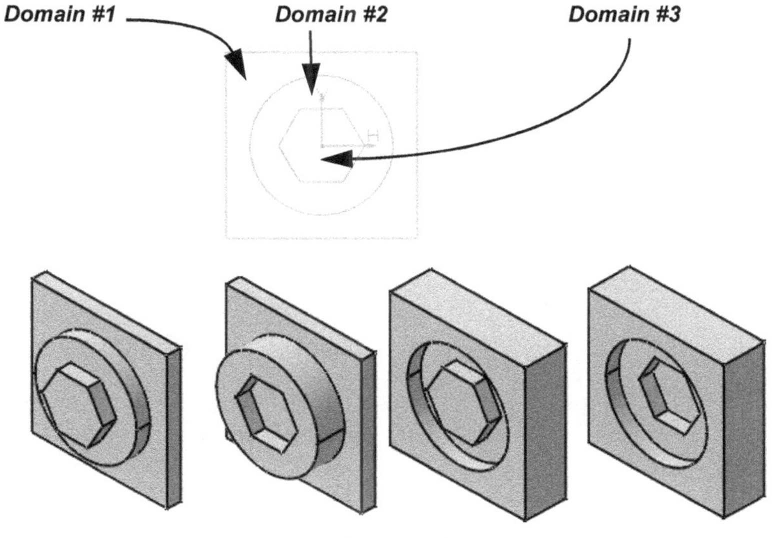

Figure 3–19

How To: Create a Multi-pad Feature

1. Select a sketch with multiple profiles and click (Multi-Pad). The Multi-Pad Definition dialog box opens.
2. Select a domain from those listed in the dialog box.
3. In the *Length* field, enter a value for the distance at which to extrude the selected domain.
4. Repeat this process for all domains, as shown in Figure 3–20.

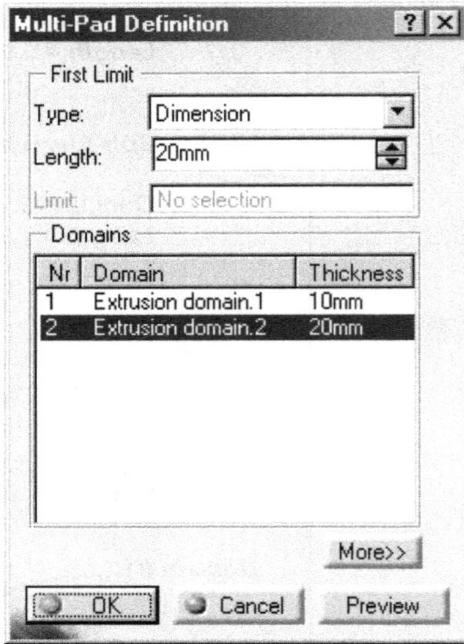

Figure 3–20

Length Options

When specifying the length of the domains, you can use one of the following options:

- Enter a positive or negative value to extrude the domain to opposite directions from the sketch.
- Use the second limit to specify the length of the domain in two directions.
- Enter a zero depth to create voids in the feature to resemble Holes or Pockets.

Practice 3a

Creating a Multi-Pad Feature

Practice Objectives

- Use a sketch with multiple profiles to create a multi-pad feature.
- Add dress-up features to finish the part model.

In this practice, you will create the part shown in Figure 3–21. After creating a multi-profile sketch, you will use the multi-pad feature to create the Pad geometry. Later, you will modify the depths of the various profiles of the multi-pad feature using the Multi-Pad Definition dialog box.

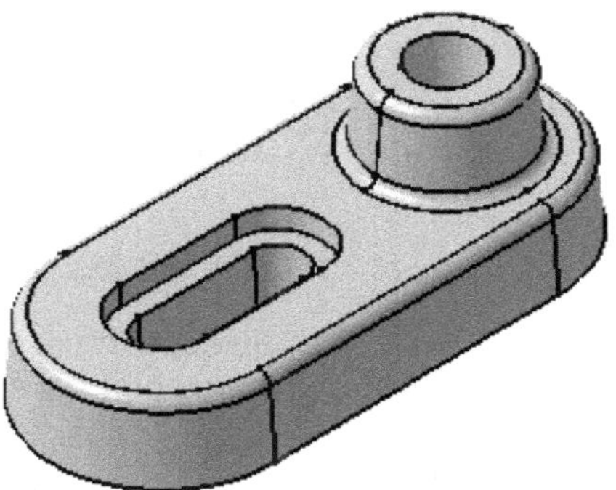

Figure 3–21

Task 1 - Create a new part.

1. Create a new part called **Sliding_Cam.CATPart**. Ensure that the **Enable hybrid design** option is cleared.
2. Set model units to millimeters (mm).

Task 2 - Create a sketch with multiple profiles.

Design Considerations

A sketch with multiple profiles cannot be extruded to different heights using a single Pad feature. This multi-profile sketch will be used with a multi-pad feature to create a part that has surfaces of different heights.

1. Select the **xy Plane** and click (Sketch).

2. Create the sketch shown in Figure 3–22. The geometric constraints are hidden to clarify the display.

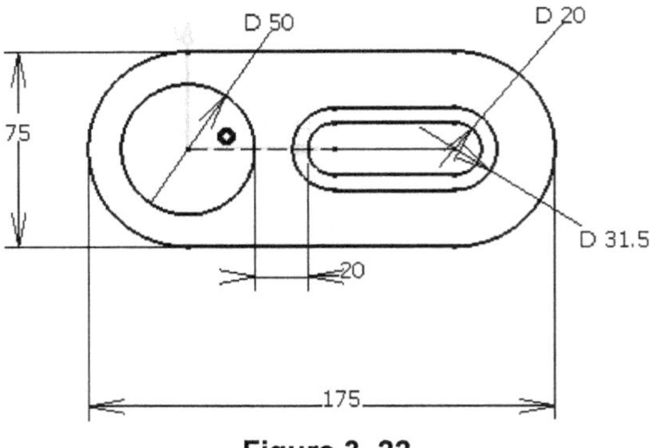

Figure 3–22

Task 3 - Create a multi-pad feature.

1. With the sketch still highlighted, click (Multi-Pad).
2. Select each of the domains listed in the Multi-Pad Definition dialog box, as shown in Figure 3–23.

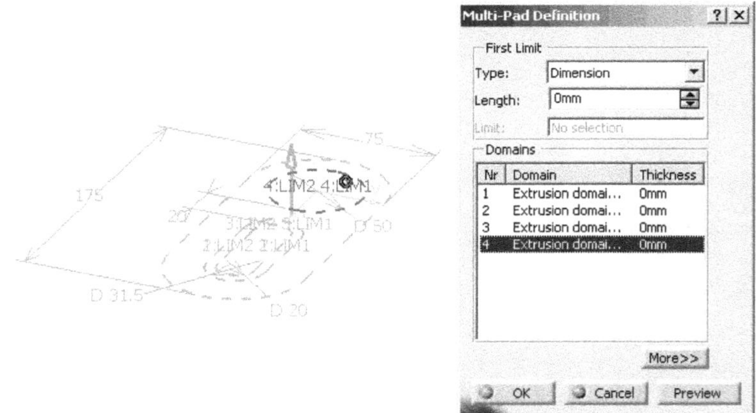

Figure 3–23

3. When the circle highlights, enter **50.0** for the *Length* and click **Preview**. The part displays as shown in Figure 3–24.

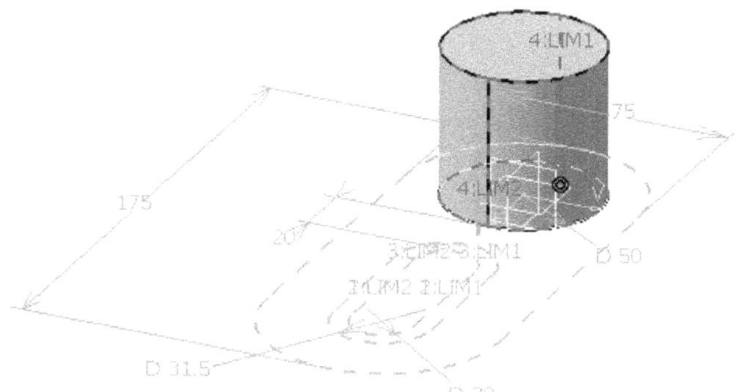

Figure 3–24

4. Highlight the domain for the two inner elongated holes. Enter **19.00** for the *Length* and click **Preview**. The part displays as shown in Figure 3–25.

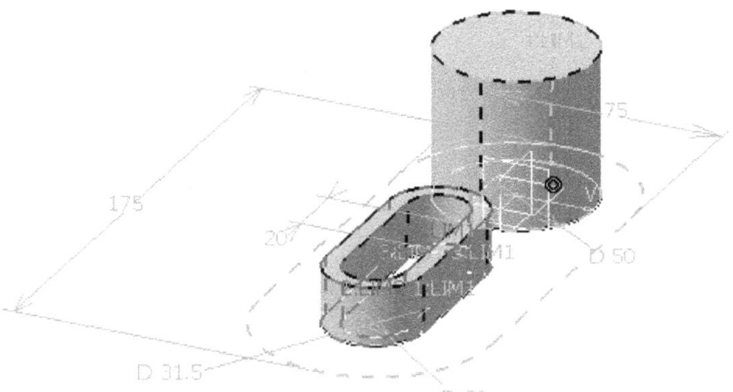

Figure 3–25

5. Highlight the domain for the large, outer elongated hole. Enter **25.0** for the *Length* and click **Preview**.

6. Leave the *Length* of the remaining domain at **0**.

7. Click **OK** to complete the feature.

8. Hide the three default planes.

Task 4 - Add a hole that is coaxial to the cylindrical boss.

1. Select the top circular face of the boss, hold <Ctrl> and select the circular edge, as shown in Figure 3–26.

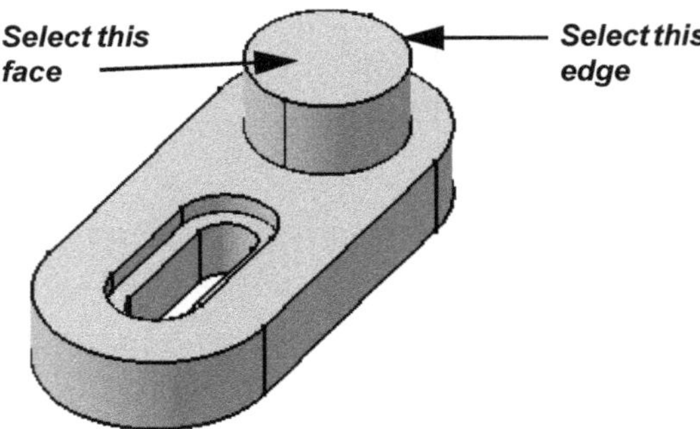

Figure 3–26

2. Click (Hole) to create a hole.
3. Enter **19.00** for the *Diameter* and select **Up to last** for the depth.
4. Click **OK** to complete the feature.

Task 5 - Add a draft to the part.

1. Click (Draft Angle).
2. Select the five surfaces shown in Figure 3–27 as the faces to draft, and enter **5** for the draft *Angle*.
3. Select **Neutral Element** to activate it and select the top face of the part for the reference, as shown in Figure 3–27.

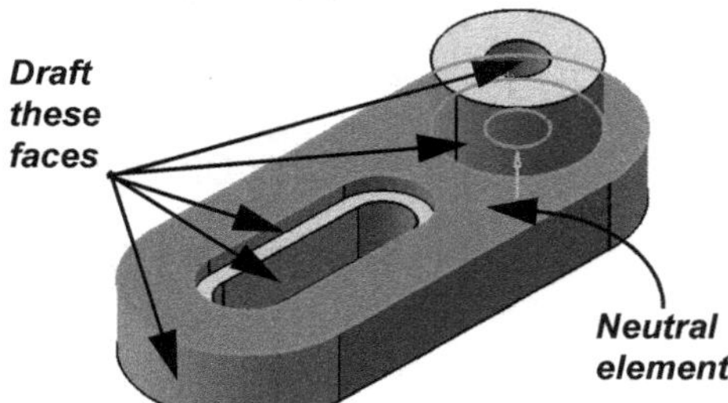

Figure 3–27

4. Click **OK** to complete the feature.

5. Go to the Back quick view and set the display to

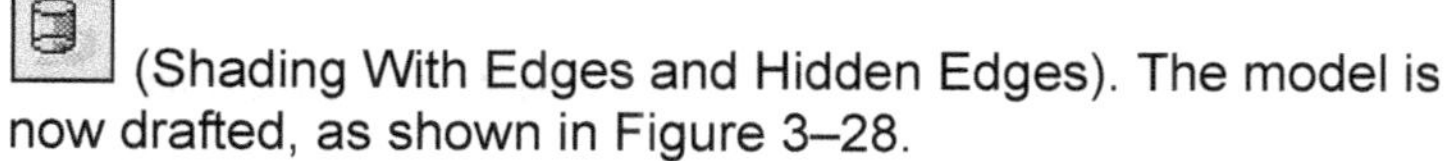

(Shading With Edges and Hidden Edges). The model is now drafted, as shown in Figure 3–28.

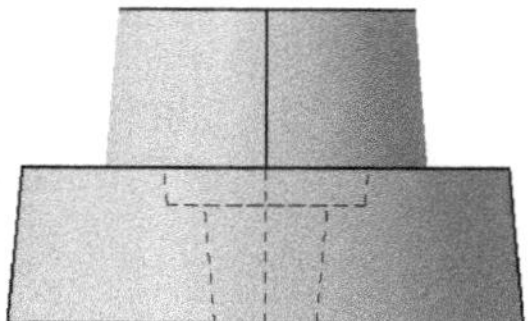

Figure 3–28

6. Set the display back to (Shading with Edges).

Task 6 - Add fillet features to the part.

1. Click (Edge Fillet).
2. Enter **3.80** for the *Radius*.
3. Select the three edges shown in Figure 3–29 as the objects to fillet.

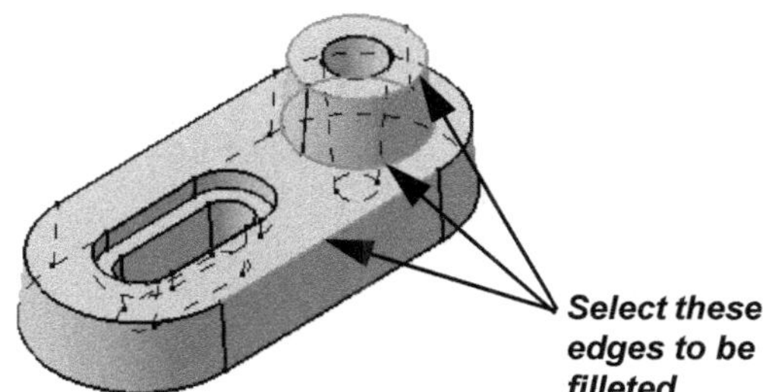
Select these
edges to be
filleted

Figure 3–29

4. Click **OK** to complete the feature. The part displays as shown in Figure 3–30.

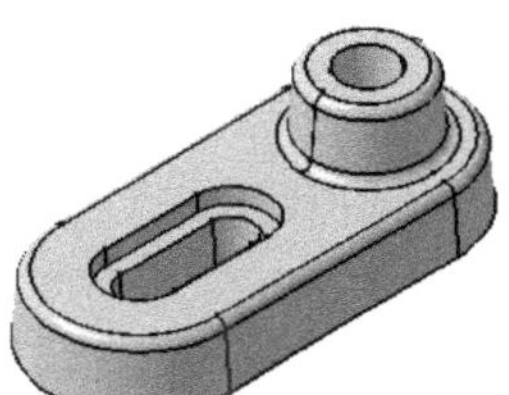

Figure 3–30

Task 7 - Change the depth of the multi-pad feature.

1. In the specification tree, double-click on **Multipad.1**.
2. Change the *Depth* of the large outer domain from *25.00* to **12.5**.
3. Click **OK** to complete the feature. The part displays as shown in Figure 3–31.

When working with multi-pad features, ensure that you make changes to all of the domains to maintain your design intent.

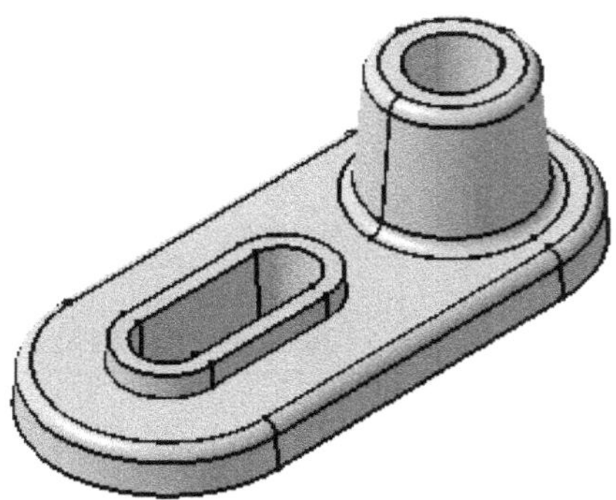

Figure 3–31

4. Select **Edit>Undo** to remove the last change.

Task 8 - Save the part and close the window.

1. Save the file.
2. Select **File>Close**.

Practice 3b

Using Sketch Sub-Elements

Practice Objective

- Use portions of a multi-profile sketch to create several Pad features.

In this practice, you will create the part shown in Figure 3–32. You will begin by creating a self-intersecting multi-profile sketch. From this sketch, you will create Pad features using individual profiles from the sketch. You will also create Hole features on the cylindrical surface of one of the Pad features.

Figure 3–32

Task 1 - Create a new part.

1. Create a new part called **Conn_Rod**. Ensure that the **Enable hybrid design** option is cleared.

Task 2 - Create a sketch with several intersecting profiles.

Design Considerations

When a sketch is created with intersecting profiles, it cannot be directly used as a profile for a Pad feature. However, you can select individual profiles to create Pad features (performed in the following task).

1. Select the **xy Plane** and click (Sketch).

2. Create the sketch shown in Figure 3–33.

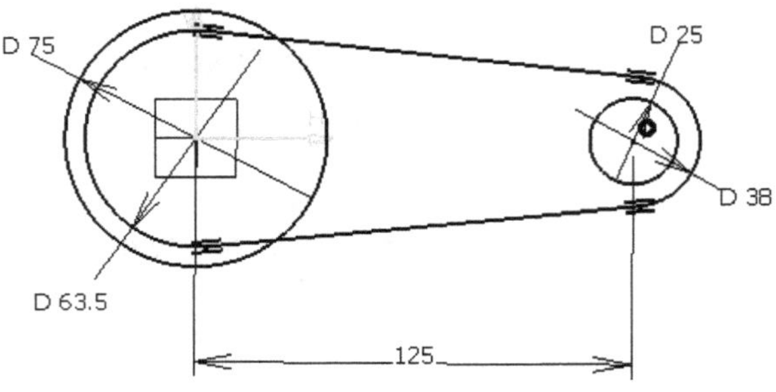

Figure 3–33

Task 3 - Create a Pad feature from a portion of the profile.

In this task, you will create a Pad feature using the sub-elements of a sketch.

1. With the sketch still highlighted, click (Pad). An error message opens prompting you that the sketch is not valid. The sketch is invalid because the profiles intersect each other.
2. Click **OK** to continue using the selected profile.
3. Right-click in the *Selection* field and select **Go to profile definition**, as shown in Figure 3–34.

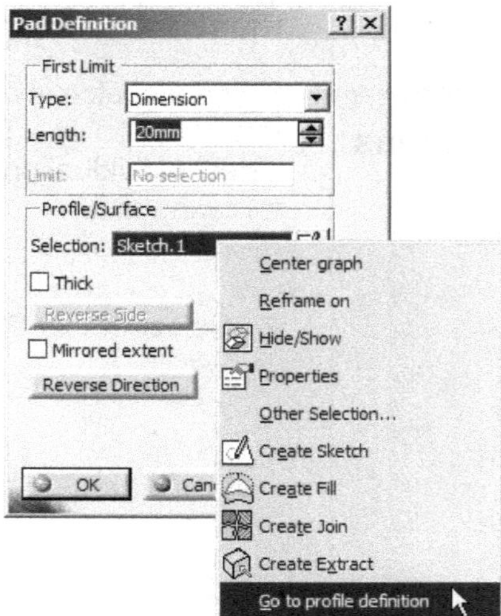

Figure 3–34

4. If required, select **Sketch.1** in the *Support* column and click **Remove**.
5. In the Profile Definition dialog box, select **Sub-elements**.
6. Select one of the bi-tangent lines of the sketch to add the profile to the feature, as shown in Figure 3–35.

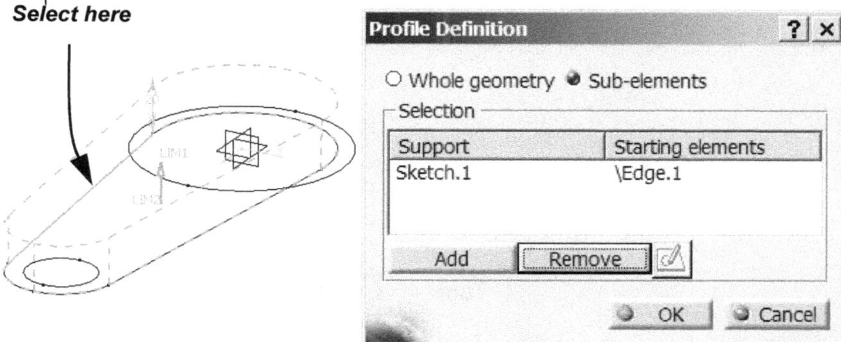

Figure 3–35

7. In the Profile Definition dialog box, click **OK** to complete identification of the sub-element of the sketch.
8. In the Pad Definition dialog box, for the *Length*, enter **6.25**. Select **Mirrored extent**.
9. Click **OK** to complete the feature. The part displays as shown in Figure 3–36.

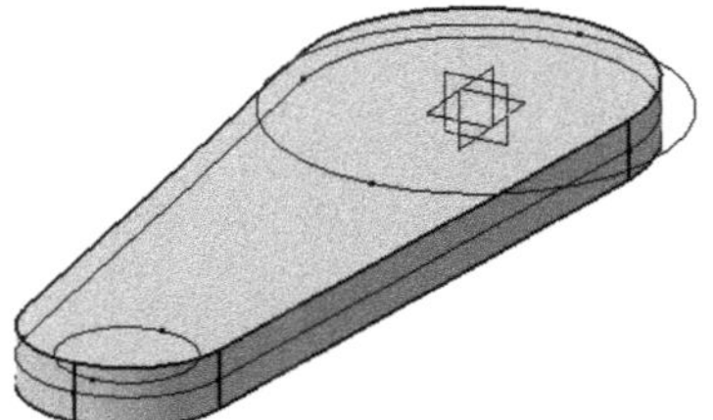

Figure 3–36

10. In the specification tree, select **Sketch.1** and repeat the process to create a second Pad feature, using the small circle sub-element. Set the *Length* to **12.50** and select **Mirrored extent**.
11. Repeat the process and create a third Pad feature, using the large circle sub-element. Set the *Length* to **16.00** and select **Mirrored extent**.

12. Hide the sketch and three datum planes. Two views of the model are shown in Figure 3–37.

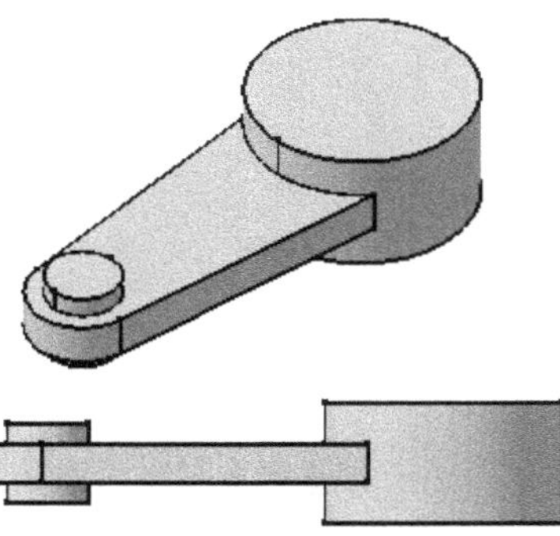

Figure 3–37

Task 4 - Create two holes that are coaxial to the bosses on the part.

1. Create a hole that is concentric to the large cylindrical boss, as shown in Figure 3–38, using the following values:
   - *Depth:* **Up To Last**
   - *Diameter:* **38.00**
2. Create a **12.50** diameter hole that is concentric to the smaller cylindrical boss.

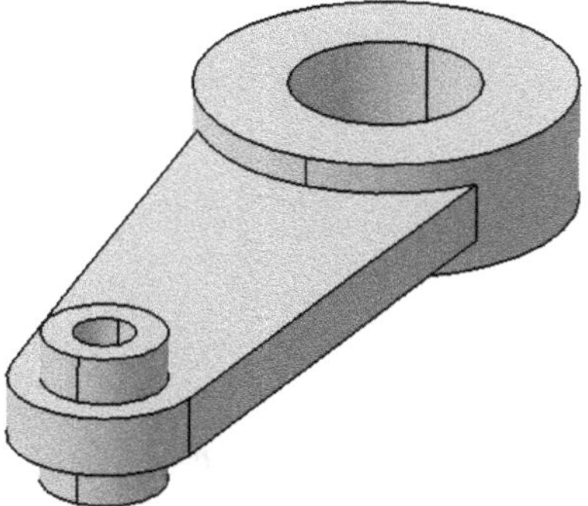

Figure 3–38

Task 5 - Create several holes on the large cylindrical boss.

1. Select the cylindrical surface of the large boss for the first hole, as shown in Figure 3–39, and click (Hole).

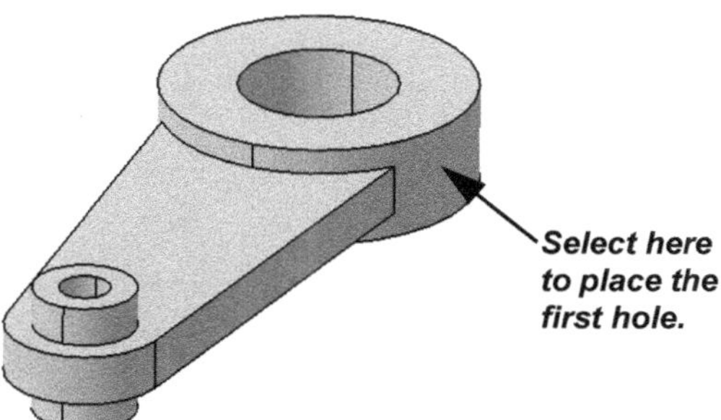
Select here
to place the
first hole.

Figure 3–39

2. For the *Diameter*, enter **6.25**. The **Up to last** option remains selected from the previous feature.
3. To locate the hole around the cylinder, click .
4. Show the three datum planes.
5. Constrain the asterisk to be coincident with the xy plane and the yz plane, as shown in Figure 3–40.

*Go to the **Isometric** quick view and generate the geometric constraints.*

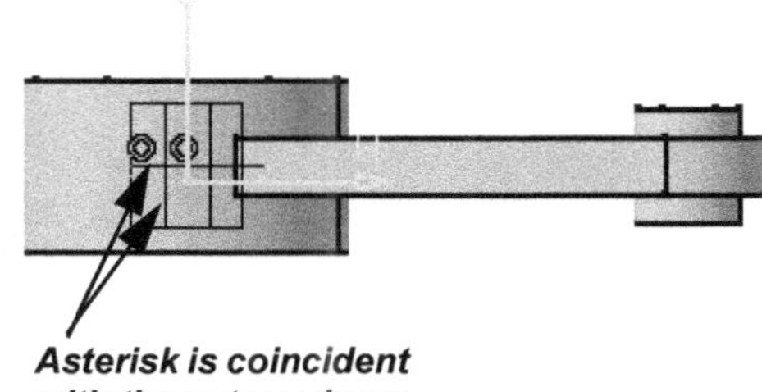
Asterisk is coincident
with these two planes

Figure 3–40

6. Click (Exit workbench) to exit the sketch.
7. Click **OK** to complete the Hole feature.

8. Repeat the process to create a second **6.25** diameter hole. Select **Up To Next** for the extension and make the asterisk coincident with the xy plane and zx plane. The part displays as shown in Figure 3–41.

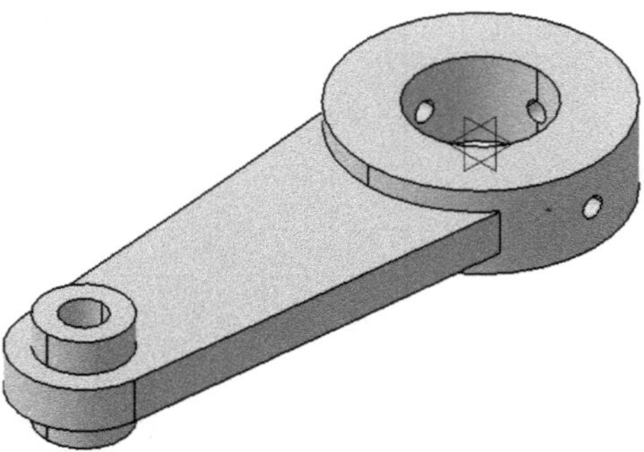

Figure 3–41

9. Hide the three datum planes.

Task 6 - Create several Fillet features to complete the part.

1. Complete the model by adding **2.50** radius edge fillets to the four faces shown in Figure 3–42.

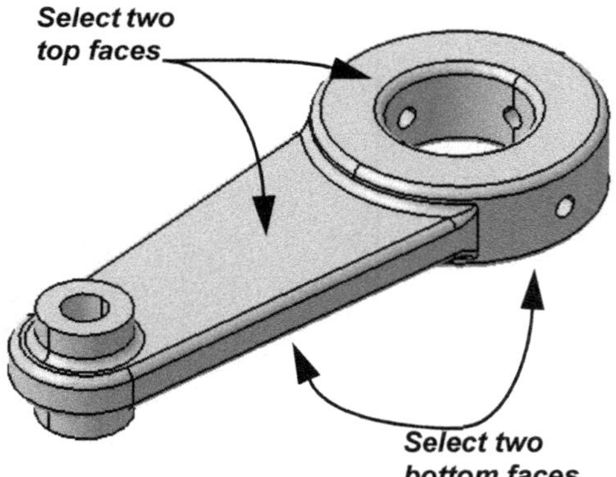
Select two top faces
Select two bottom faces

Figure 3–42

Task 7 - Save the part and close the window.

1. Save the part.
2. Select **File>Close**.

Practice 3c

Engine Block

Practice Objectives

- Create profiles.
- Replace profiles.

In this practice, you will create an engine block, as shown in Figure 3–43. You will create the engine block using a .DXF file. The .DXF file contains all of the required 2D sections for the engine block. After creating the engine block, you will modify the model according to a set of design changes.

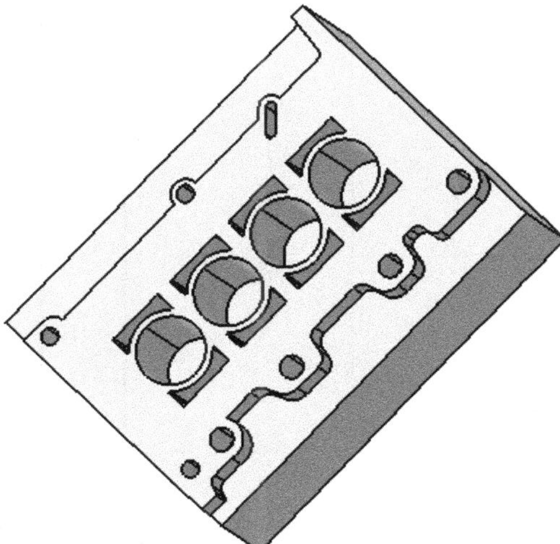

Figure 3–43

Task 1 - Create a new part.

1. Create a new part called **Engine_block**. Ensure that the **Enable hybrid design** option is cleared.

Task 2 - Open a part.

1. Open **Engine_block.dxf**. The file displays as shown in Figure 3–44.

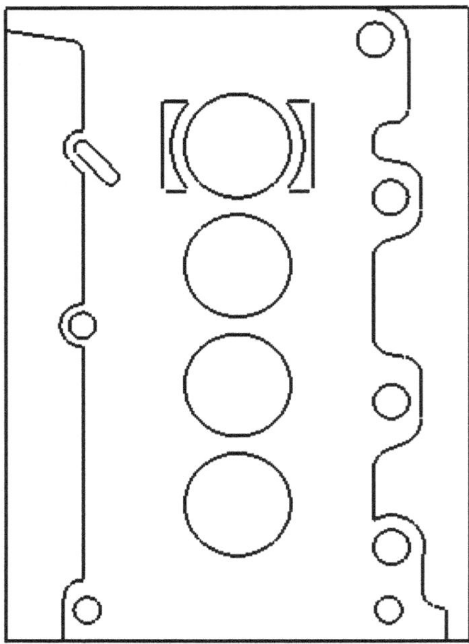

Figure 3–44

Task 3 - Copy the data to a CATPart.

1. Switch to the new part file.
2. In the menu bar, select **Insert>Geometrical Set** to insert a new geometrical set.
3. Leave the *Name* field empty and click **OK** to create a geometrical set with the default name.
4. Switch to the **Engine_block.dxf** window.

5. In the specification tree, copy the Main View. Paste it into **Geometrical Set.1**. The Main View sketch displays in the specification tree, as shown on the left in Figure 3–45, and in the drawing shown on the right.

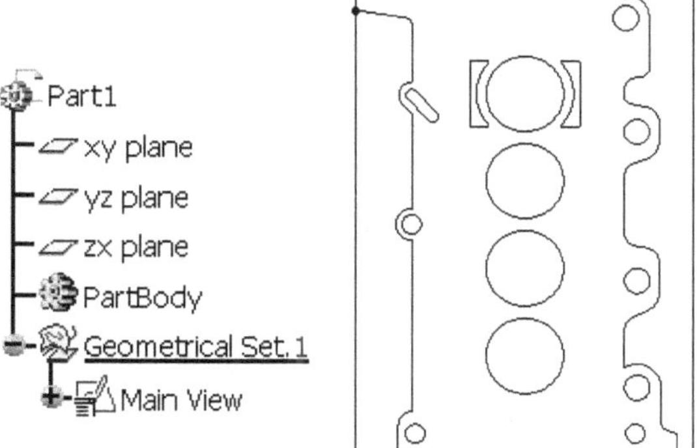

Figure 3–45

Task 4 - Create profiles.

In this task, you will create profiles from the Main View sketch. You will also create three lines, which are used to create one of the profiles.

1. Double-click on the Main View sketch to enter the Sketcher workbench.

2. Create the three lines shown in Figure 3–46.

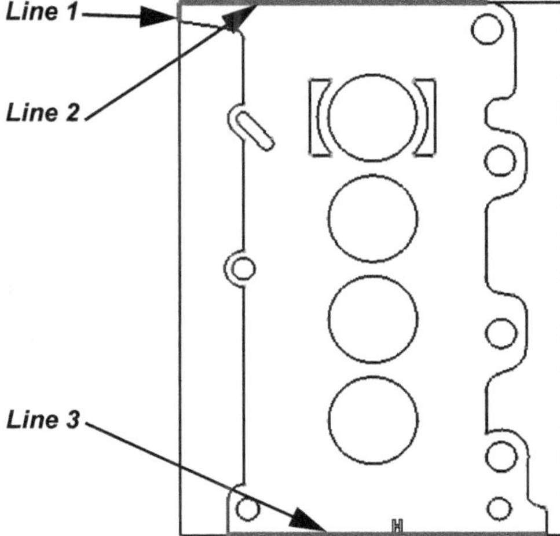

Figure 3–46

3. In the Tools toolbar, click (Profile feature). Select the line as shown in Figure 3–47. Change the *Color* to **Red**.

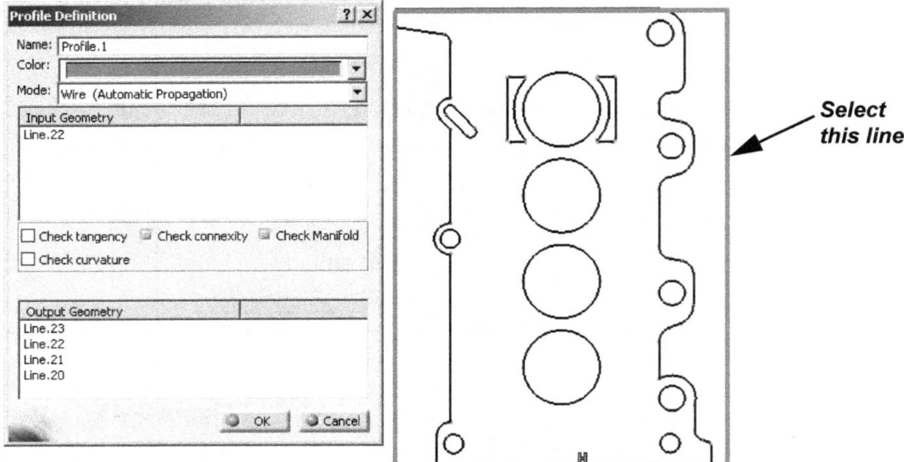

Figure 3–47

4. Click **OK** to complete the feature.

5. In the Tools toolbar, click (Profile feature). Select the line, as shown in Figure 3–48. Change the *Color* to **Blue**.

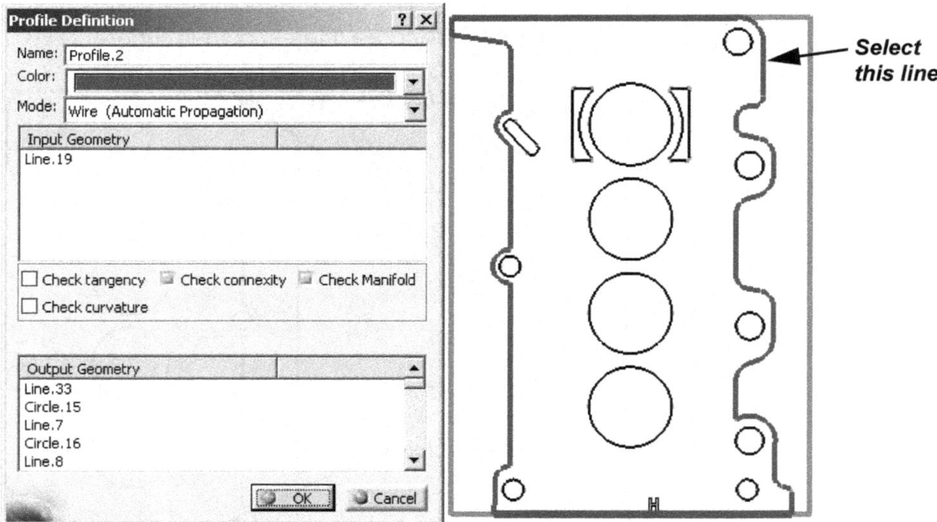

Figure 3–48

6. Click **OK** to complete the feature.

*The **Check connexity** option analyzes the profile for any gaps between the elements.*

7. In the Tools toolbar, click (Profile feature). Select the four large circles and change the *Color* to **Pink**. Ensure that the **Check connexity** option is cleared.

8. Create the other profiles, as shown in Figure 3–49. Color the profiles as follows:

   - *Elongated hole:* **Orange**
   - *Seven small circles:* **Green** (one profile)
   - *Cooling channels:* **Brown** (one profile)

   Ensure that the **Check connexity** option is cleared for complex profiles (for the Green, Brown, and Pink profiles).

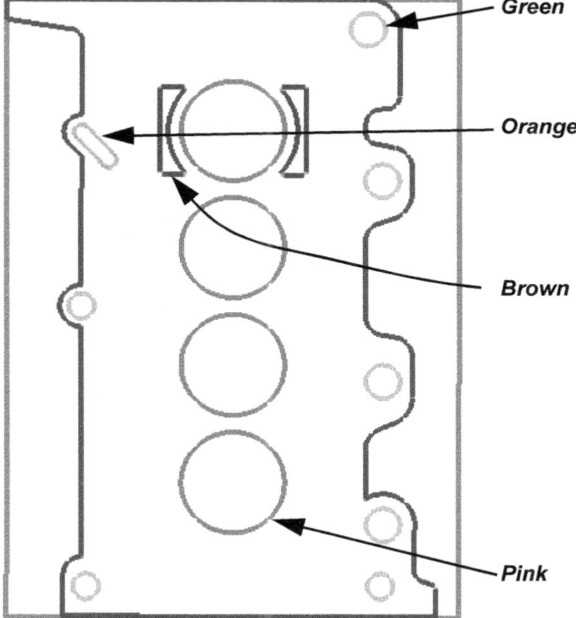

Figure 3–49

9. Create seven points that are concentric to the centers of the small green circles, as shown in Figure 3–50.

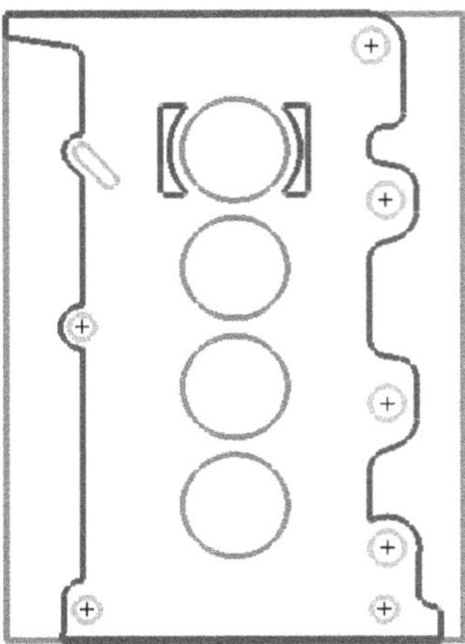

Figure 3–50

10. Exit the Sketcher workbench.

Task 5 - Create sketch-based features using the profiles.

In this task, you will create Pads, Pockets, and Holes using the profiles you have created.

1. Define the PartBody as the In Work Object.
2. Create a Pad with the red profile shown in Figure 3–51, as follows:
    - *Type:* **Dimension**
    - *Length:* **130mm**

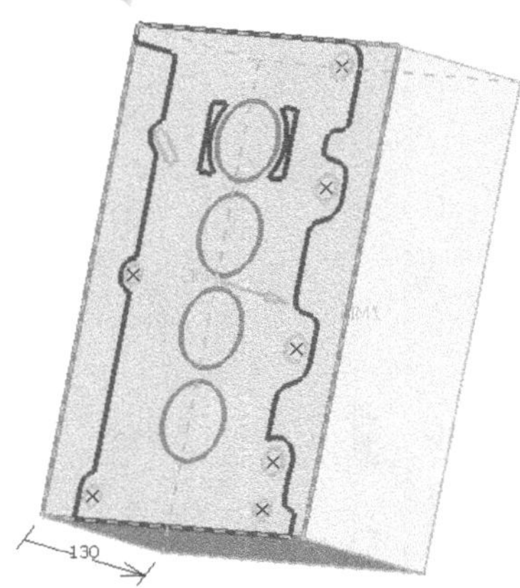

Figure 3–51

3. Create a Pad with the blue profile shown in Figure 3–52, as follows:

   - *Type:* **Dimension**
   - *Length:* **30mm**

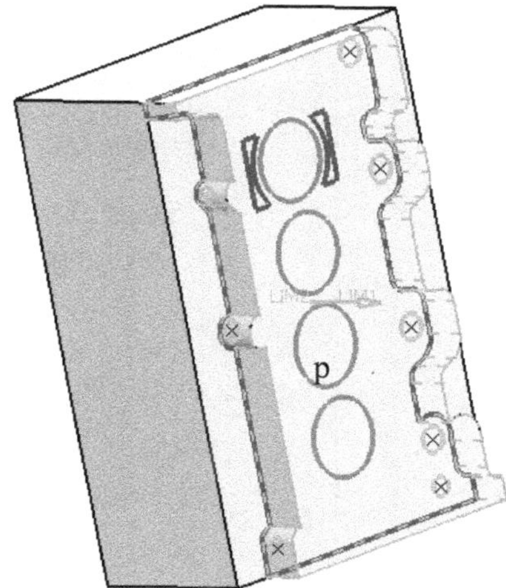

Figure 3–52

4. Create a Pocket with the pink profile. The total length of the Pocket from the top surface is **110mm**.

5. Create two more Pockets with the brown and orange profiles. The total length of the Pockets from the top surface is 110mm. Hide **Profile.5** for the green circles. The model displays as shown in Figure 3–53.

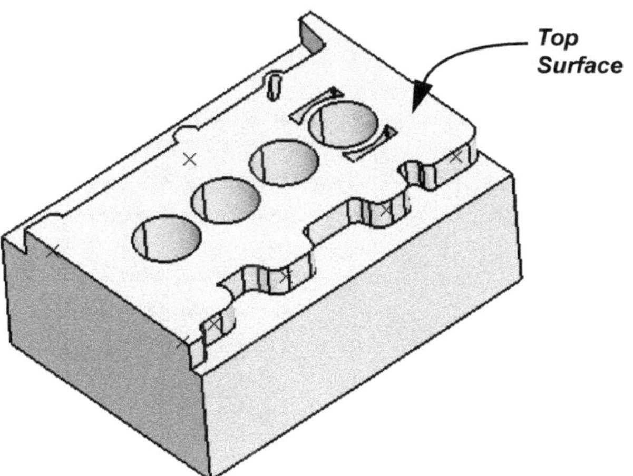

Figure 3–53

6. Create a threaded Hole as shown in Figure 3–54. Select the *Extension* tab and enter the following parameters:

    - *Diameter:* **20mm**
    - *Depth:* **60mm**
    - *Bottom:* **V-Bottom**
    - *Angle:* **100deg**

7. Select the *Thread Definition* tab and enter the following parameters:

    - Select **Threaded**.
    - *Thread diameter:* **22mm**
    - *Hole diameter:* **20mm**
    - *Thread Depth:* **60mm**
    - *Hole Depth:* **60mm**
    - *Pitch:* **1mm**

    The model displays as shown in Figure 3–54.

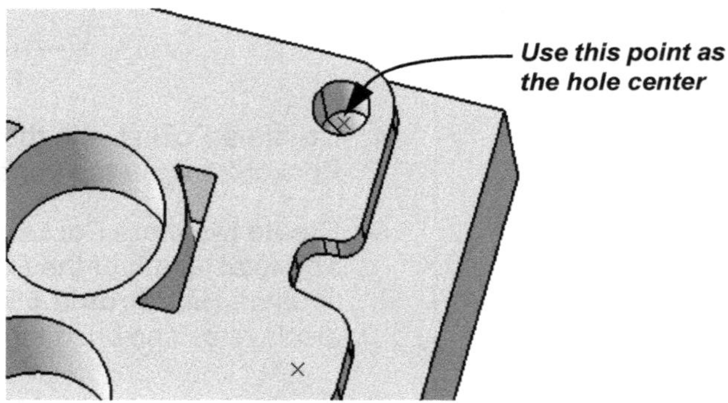

Figure 3–54

Task 6 - Create the patterns.

1. Create a rectangular pattern, as shown in Figure 3–55 with the following parameters:

    - *Parameters:* **Instance(s) & Spacing**
    - *Instances:* **4**
    - *Spacing:* **70mm**

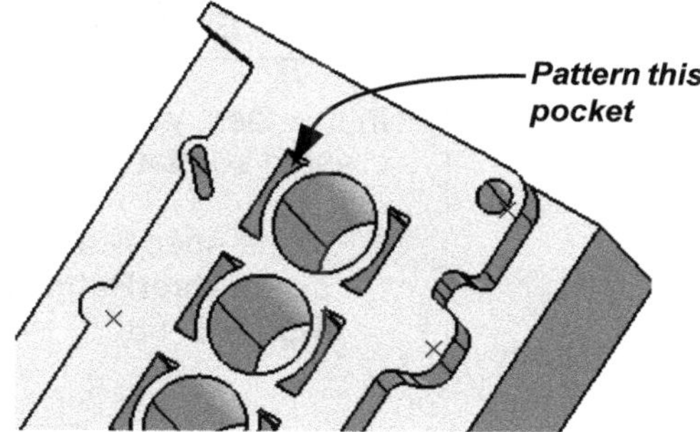

Figure 3–55

2. In the specification tree or the model, highlight the hole that you created in the previous task. In the Transformation Features toolbar, expand the Patterns flyout, and click  (User Pattern).

3. In the specification tree, select the **Main View** sketch. The User Pattern Definition dialog box opens as shown in Figure 3–56.

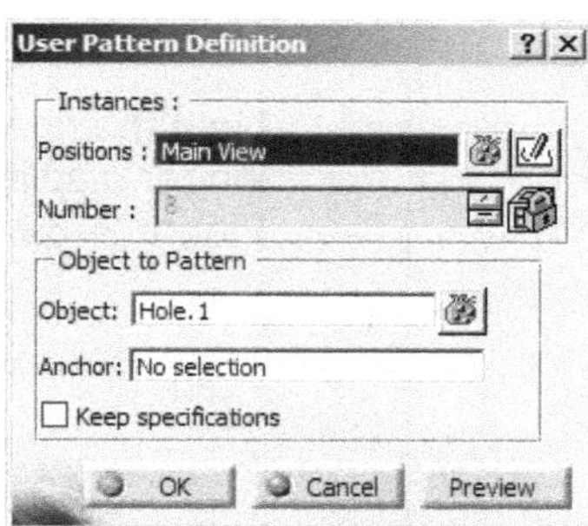

Figure 3–56

4. Click **OK** to complete the feature. The model displays as shown in Figure 3–57.

Figure 3–57

Task 7 - Explode a user pattern.

In this task, you will explode the user pattern that you have just created so that you can modify each hole separately.

1. In the specification tree, right-click on **UserPattern.1** and select **UserPattern.1 object>Explode**, as shown in Figure 3–58.

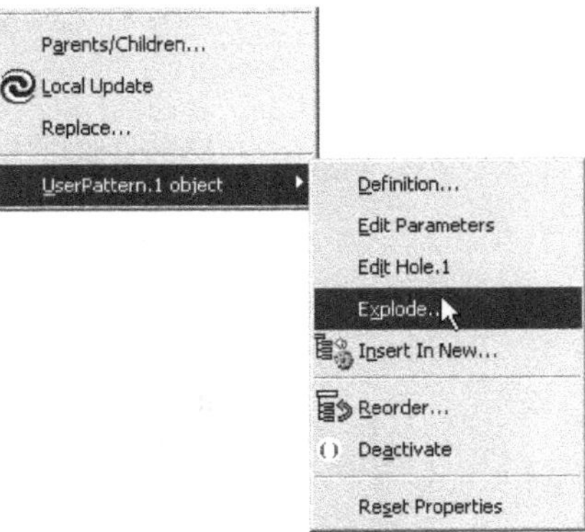

Figure 3–58

Note the change in the specification tree. **UserPattern.1** no longer displays and six new holes are added, as shown in Figure 3–59.

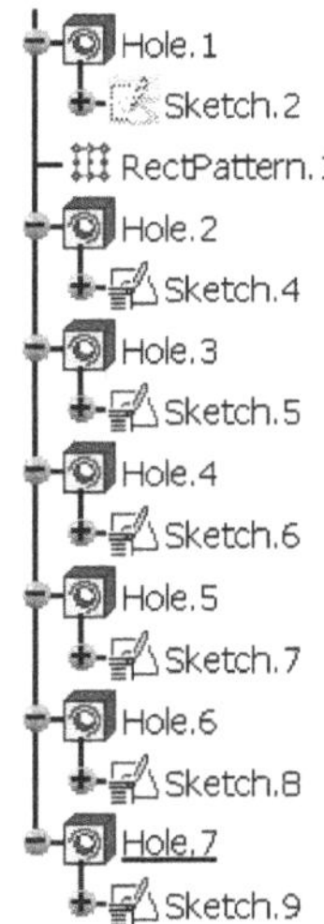

Figure 3–59

2. Show **Profile.5** for the green circles and then zoom in and inspect the diameter of the holes. Three holes need to be modified, as shown in Figure 3–60.

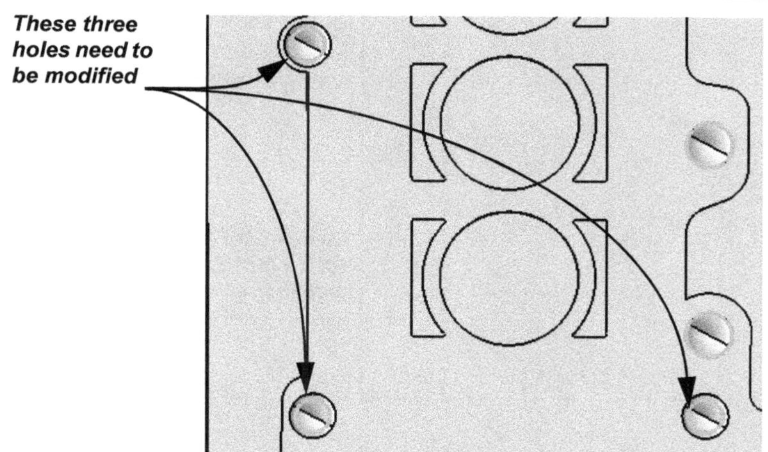
These three holes need to be modified

Figure 3–60

3. Change the hole diameters of the three holes to **15mm**, and the thread diameters to **17mm**. The model displays as shown in Figure 3–61.

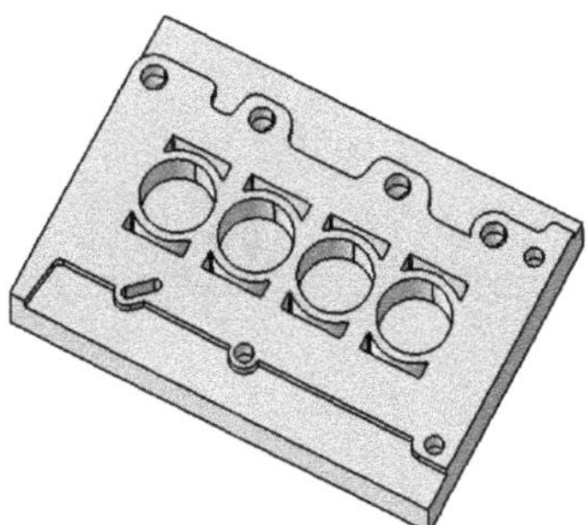

Figure 3–61

Task 8 - Replace a profile.

In this task, you will work with a revised 2D section .DXF file. According to the updated version, the cooling channels have changed and these changes need to be applied to the model.

1. Open **Engine_block_updated.dxf**.
2. In the specification tree, copy the **Main View**.
3. Switch to the new part file.
4. Paste the Main View into **Geometrical Set.1**. The **Main View** sketch displays in the specification tree and model.
5. Rename the sketch as **Updated_version**.

6. Double-click on the **Updated_version** sketch to enter the Sketcher workbench. The 2D section updates to the modified cooling channels, as shown in Figure 3–62.

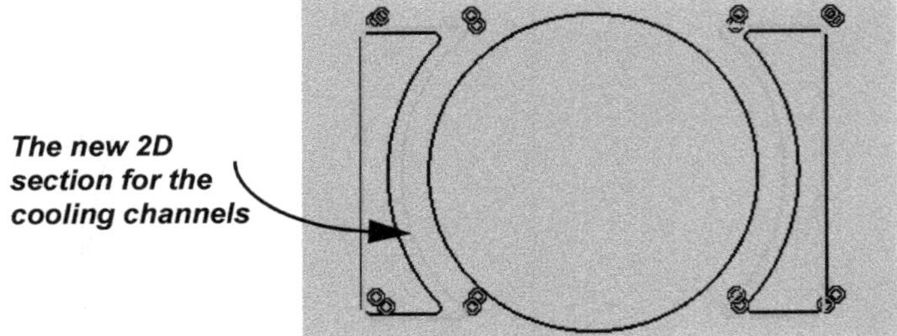

Figure 3–62

7. In the Tools toolbar, click (Profile feature). Select the cooling channels and change the *Color* to **Purple**. Ensure that the **Check connexity** option is cleared.

8. Click **OK** to complete the feature.

9. Exit the Sketcher workbench.

10. In the specification tree, locate the Pocket feature for the cooling channels and locate the brown profile. Right-click on the brown profile and select **Replace,** as shown in Figure 3–63.

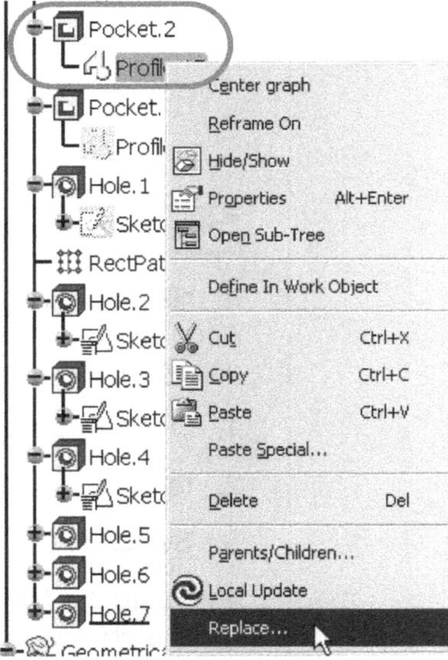

Figure 3–63

The Replace dialog box opens as shown in Figure 3–64.

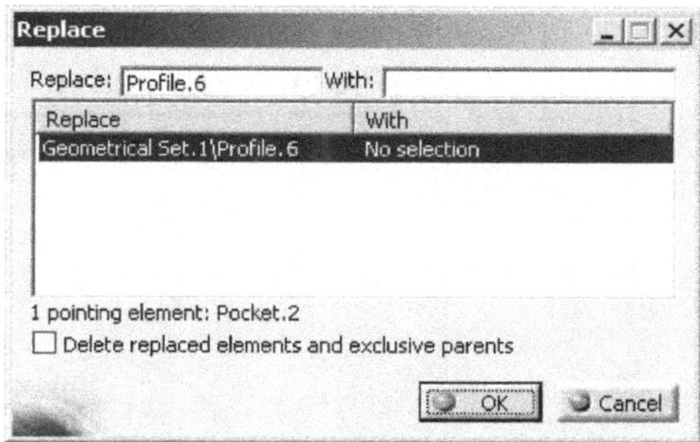

Figure 3–64

11. To replace the brown profile with the purple profile, select the purple profile in the specification tree or model.

12. Click **OK** to complete the feature. The model displays as shown in Figure 3–65.

Figure 3–65

13. Save and close the file. Close the two DXF files as well.

Practice 3d Adjustable Bracket

Practice Objective

- Create a part without any instructions.

Create **AdjustableBracket.CATPart** from a single sketch as shown in Figure 3–66.

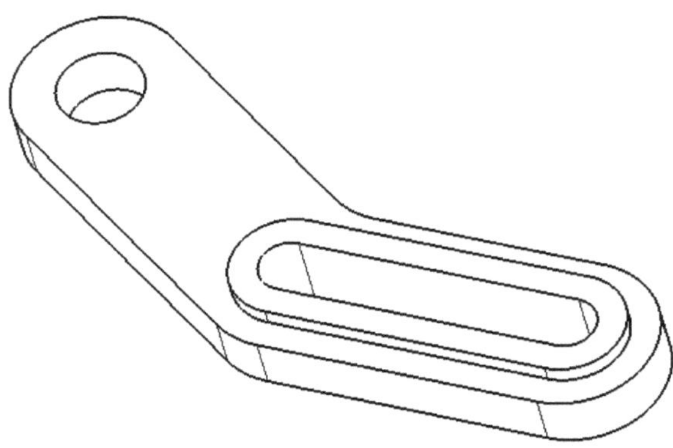

Figure 3–66

The drawing views are shown in Figure 3–67.

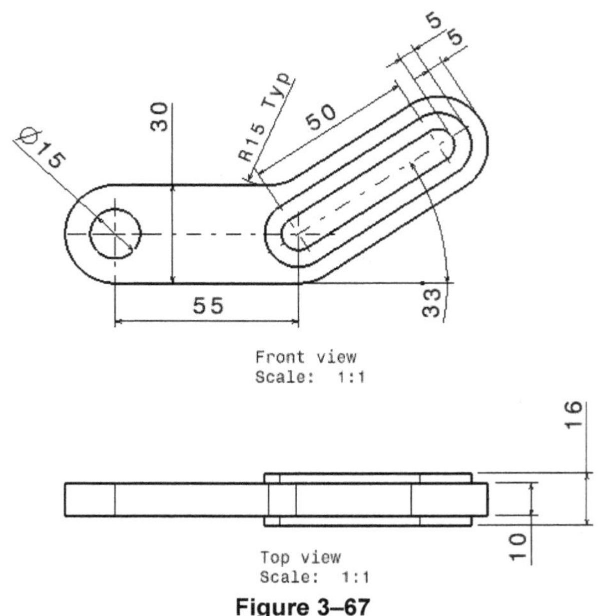

Figure 3–67

Chapter Review Questions

1. In a multi-profile sketch, if the two profiles intersect one another, CATIA eliminates the intersecting parts of the profile, and creates the geometry.
    a. True
    b. False
2. With multi-profile sketches, you can create geometry from any closed portion of the profile by using the ________ option in the Profile Definition dialog box.
    a. **Whole geometry**
    b. **Domain**
    c. **Sub-elements**
    d. None of the above.
3. The purpose of an Output Feature is to make selected sketched elements independent of the sketch in which they were created.
    a. True
    b. False
4. When selecting the entities to include in a Profile Feature, which mode includes all of the point continuous entities?.
    a. Wire (Automatic Propagation)
    b. Point (Explicit Definition)
    c. Wire (Explicit Definition)
    d. None of the above.
5. When creating Multi-Pad features, you can use the different sketch sections to define unique depths for each resulting pad.
    a. True
    b. False

6. The areas between each sketch section are called _____.
    a. Sub-sections
    b. Pad Areas
    c. Faces
    d. Domains

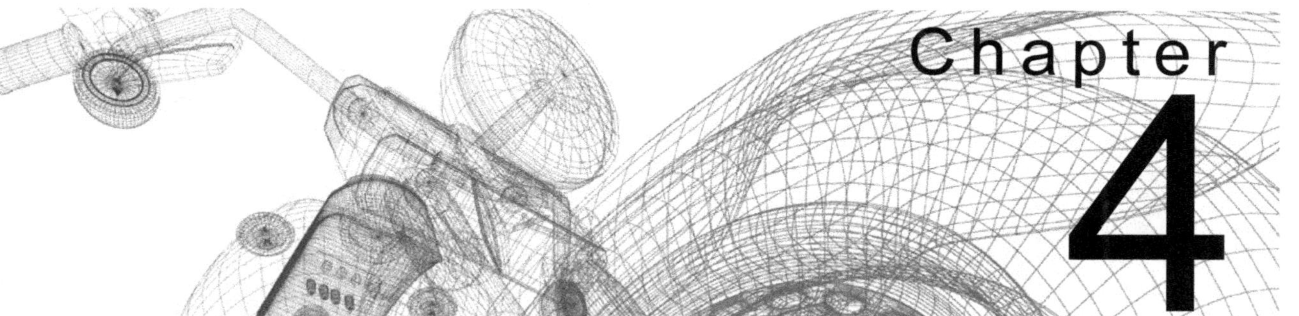

Advanced Part Design

Complex models often require more advanced creation options to create the required geometry. You might need to consider using advanced sketch-based features, such as Multi-sections Solids, Ribs, or Slots throughout the design cycle of complex parts. Multi-sections Solids have advanced options that control the transition surfaces using guides and spines. Ribs and Slots can be created using advanced options, which enable you to control the relationship between the profile and the center curve.

Learning Objectives in this Chapter

- Create a solid from the intersection of two profiles using a Solid Combine feature.
- Learn how to use Multi-sections solids to create a solid between two or more sections.
- Understand the impact of closing points on resulting geometry.
- Understand the Rib feature and the Slot feature.
- Learn how to use the advanced options in the Shell Definition dialog box.

4.1 Solid Combine Feature

The Solid Combine feature enables you to create a solid from the intersection of two profiles that are projected perpendicular to their profile planes or along a specified direction. Think of it as creating a Pad feature from the profiles and then trimming everything except for the common volume between the solids. The sketch for each profile must consist of a single, closed chain of elements.

General Steps

Use the following general steps to create a solid combine:

1. Open the Solid Combine dialog box.
2. Select the two profiles.
3. Specify the direction (if required) and complete the feature.

Step 1 - Open the Solid Combine dialog box.

Click (Solid Combine) in the Sketch-Based Features toolbar, as shown in Figure 4–1.

Figure 4–1

The Solid Combine dialog box opens as shown in Figure 4–2.

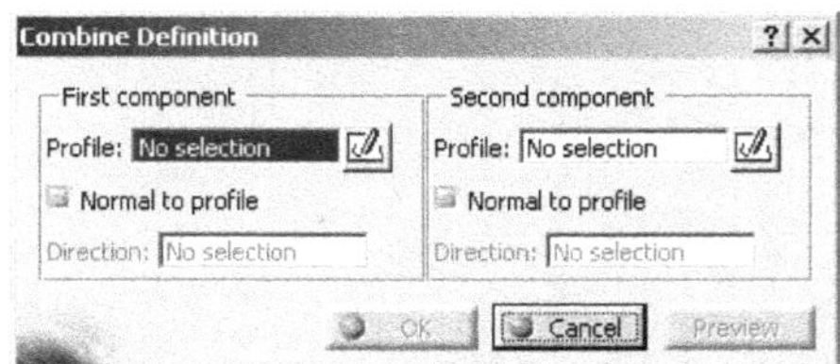

Figure 4–2

Step 2 - Select the two profiles.

Select the two sketches that define the profiles for the Solid Combine feature. In the example shown in Figure 4–3, two profiles have been developed to create the Base feature for an offset box end wrench.

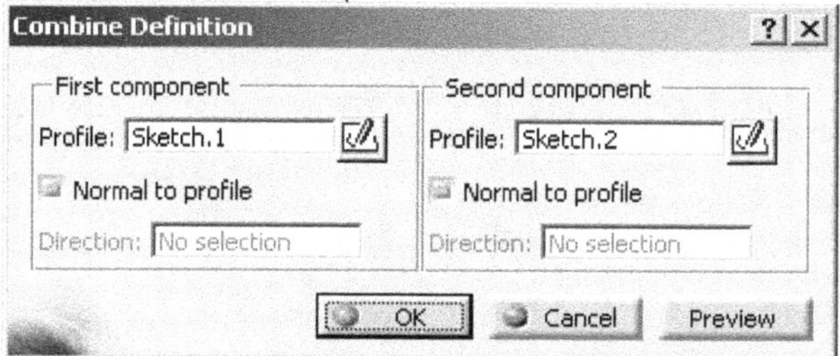

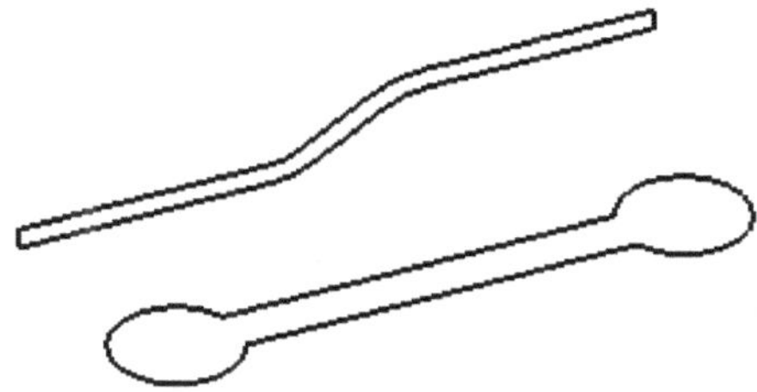

Figure 4–3

Step 3 - Specify the direction (if required) and complete the feature.

By default, the **Normal to profile** option is enabled. You can define a custom direction by clearing this option and specifying another direction. The direction can be defined by a sketch, line, or plane or by right-clicking and selecting the X-, Y-, or Z-axis.

Click **OK** to complete the feature. The offset Wrench Base feature displays as shown in Figure 4–4.

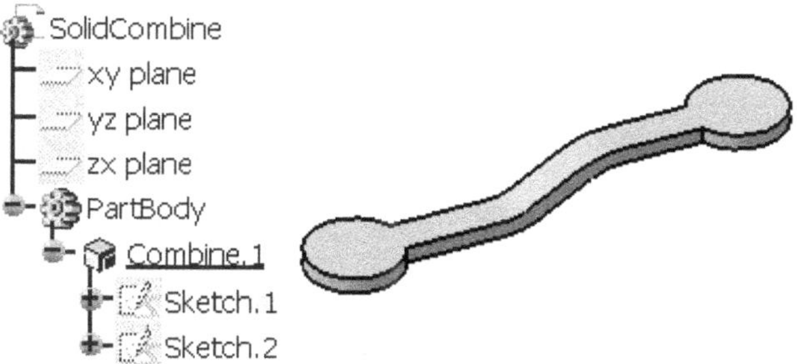

Figure 4–4

4.2 Creation of Multi-sections Solids

A Multi-sections Solid feature involves transitional surfaces being created between multiple selected sketches. The creation of a Multi-sections Solid between two sketched sections is shown in Figure 4–5.

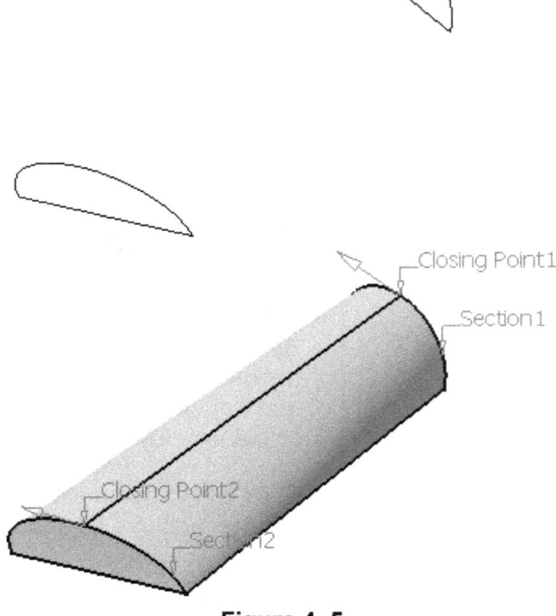

Figure 4–5

The transitional surfaces are created by connecting the vertices of the selected sketches with splinar surfaces. The closing points indicate the first two vertices to connect. The system follows the sections in the direction indicated by the arrow.

The shape of a Multi-sections Solid feature is controlled using one or more of the parameters described in . These parameters are defined using the Multi-sections Solid Definition dialog box.

Parameter	Description
Sections	Any number of sections can be added to the feature to control its shape. A closed profile must be used to create the section.
Closing Points	Each section has a closing point that determines the starting point and direction of the Solid creation. The closing points must be located at the correct positions. The orientation arrows of the closing points must be pointing in the same direction.
Guides	A guide is a curve that defines the path that the Multi-sections Solid must follow as it transitions between sections. The guide must intersect each section. More than one guide can be specified.
Spine	A spine is a curve to which the cross-section of the Multi-sections Solid must remain perpendicular. There can only be one spline curve per Multi-sections Solid.
Coupling	Determines the transition type between sections. Coupling curves can be specified to explicitly define the Solid creation. A coupling curve must intersect each section.
Relimitation	Enables a Multi-sections Solid to be extended beyond the first or last section, up to the shortest guide curve.
Area Law	You can define and control the shape of a multi-sections solid between its sections

General Steps

Use the following general steps to create and control a Multi-sections Solid feature:

1. Start the creation of the Multi-sections Solid feature.
2. Control the profile geometry with guides and spines.
3. Set the **Coupling** and **Relimitation** options.

Step 1 - Start the creation of the Multi-sections Solid feature.

The techniques used to create sections for an advanced Multi-sections Solid are the same as those used to create sections for basic Multi-sections Solids.

To begin the creation of a Multi-sections Solid feature, click (Multi-sections Solid) in the Sketched-Based Features toolbar. The Multi-sections Solid Definition dialog box opens as shown in Figure 4–6.

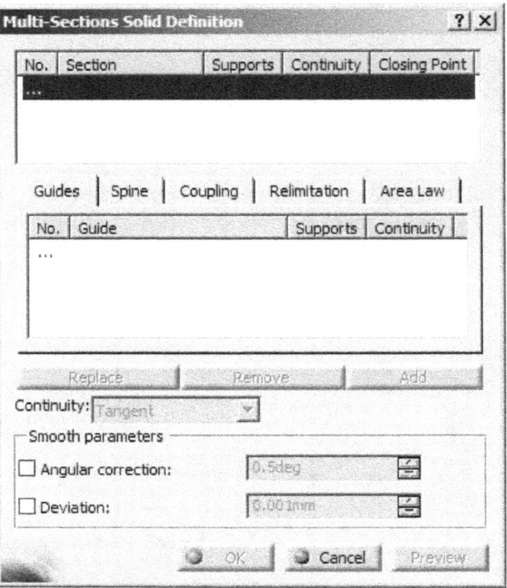

Figure 4–6

Sections for the feature are added by selecting curve geometry or sketches in the model or specification tree. The sections are added to the top of the dialog box, as shown in Figure 4–7.

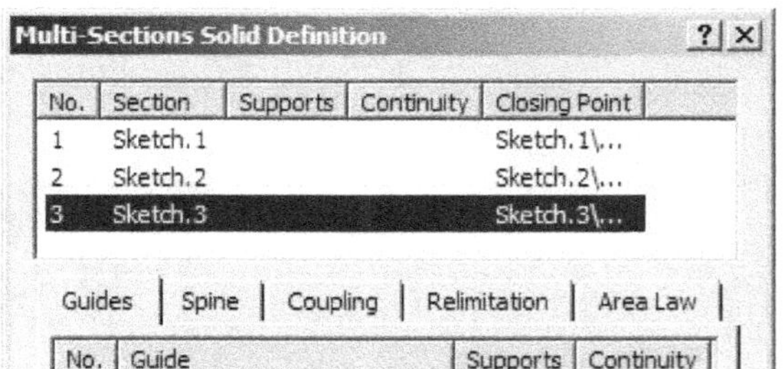

Figure 4–7

A section for a Multi-sections Solid can also be specified by selecting a face on the model that consists of a closed boundary. A Multi-sections Solid section requires the selection of curves. Therefore, CATIA automatically adds an Extract and Boundary feature under the Multi-sections feature. The Extract feature creates an associative copy of the selected face. The boundary of the extract surface is then used as the Multi-sections Solid section. An example is shown in Figure 4–8.

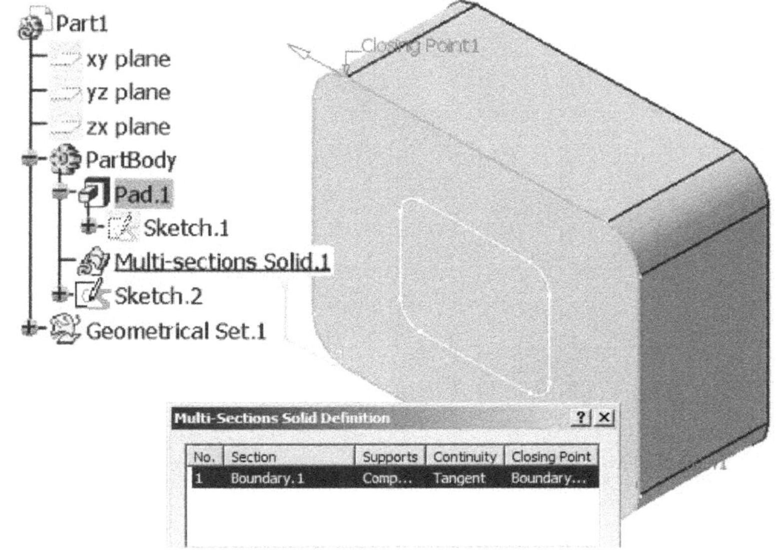

Figure 4–8

Step 2 - Control the profile geometry with guides and spines.

Once the sections have been selected, advanced options (such as guides and spines) can be added.

Guides

Guides provide an absolute path to blend the sections of the Multi-sections Solid together. The guide curve must intersect each section of the Solid feature. More than one guide can be used to control the Multi-sections Solid. The Multi-sections Solid only progresses as far as the last section, regardless of the length of the guide.

Although a guide can be created using a sketch, the curve is typically three-dimensional and created using wireframe features (e.g., Spline) in the Generative Shape Design workbench. In Figure 4–9, a splinar guide is created that connects the two sketches and extends past the end section.

The intersection of the guide and the Multi-sections Solid creates a vertex.

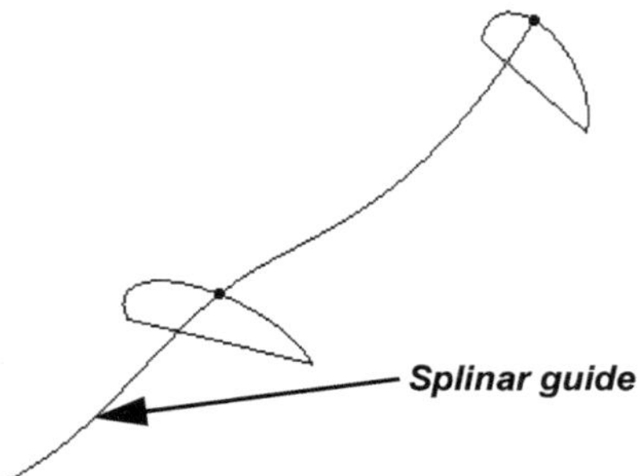

Figure 4–9

To use the guide in the Multi-sections Solid feature, select it in the *Guides* tab in the Multi-sections Solid Definition dialog box, as shown in Figure 4–10, and select the guide from the screen.

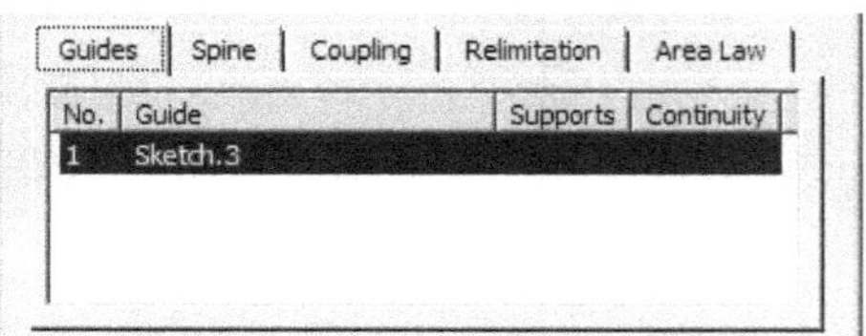

Figure 4–10

The Multi-sections Solid shown in Figure 4–11 is created with a guide to control the internal surface. Note the difference between this Multi-sections Solid and the Multi-sections Solid in Figure 4–5.

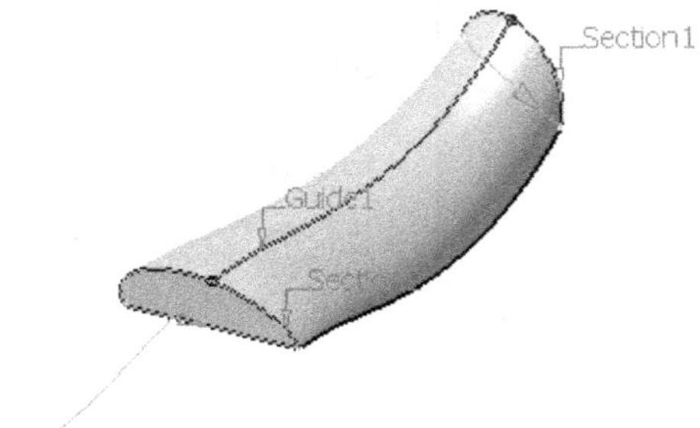

Figure 4–11

Spine

A spine controls the shape of the Multi-sections Solid as it progresses from one section to the next. The cross-section of the Multi-sections Solid must always be perpendicular to the spine. Therefore, only one spine can be selected for a Multi-sections Solid. The spine can be defined by a sketch, edge, or curve.

To specify a spine, select the *Spine* tab in the Multi-sections Solid Definition dialog box, as shown in Figure 4–12, and select the spine geometry to use.

If the Multi-section feature cannot remain perpendicular to the spine while traveling through each section, because the feature might fail.

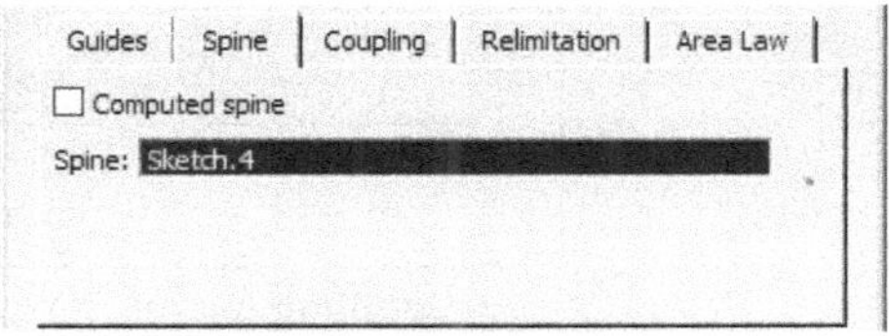

Figure 4–12

If a spine is not specified, CATIA computes a default spine to control the shape of the Multi-sections Solid throughout its progression. To clear a spine and specify a system-default spine, select **Computed spine**.

Step 3 - Set the Coupling and Relimitation options.

Coupling

The **Coupling** option is used to define the transitions between the sections. These options are shown in Figure 4–13 and are as follows.

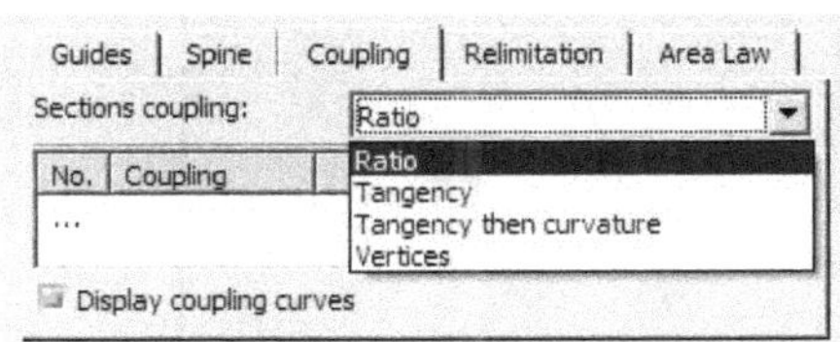

Figure 4–13

Coupling Option	Description
Ratio	If the sections are connected at positions, the ratio is computed by the percentage of the section profile. This option is recommended when non-equal numbers of vertices are present in the sketch sections.
Tangency	If the sections have the same number of tangency discontinuity points, these points are coupled together between sections.
Tangency then curvature	If the sections have the same number of tangency and curvature discontinuity points, tangency discontinuity points are coupled together between sections, and then curvature discontinuity points are coupled together between sections.
Vertices	If the sections have the same number of vertices, these points are coupled together between sections.
Coupling curves	You can create a coupling curve by selecting points on each section. After all of the coupling points have been selected, the coupling curve displays on the model.

An example of a model with coupling curves is shown in Figure 4–14.

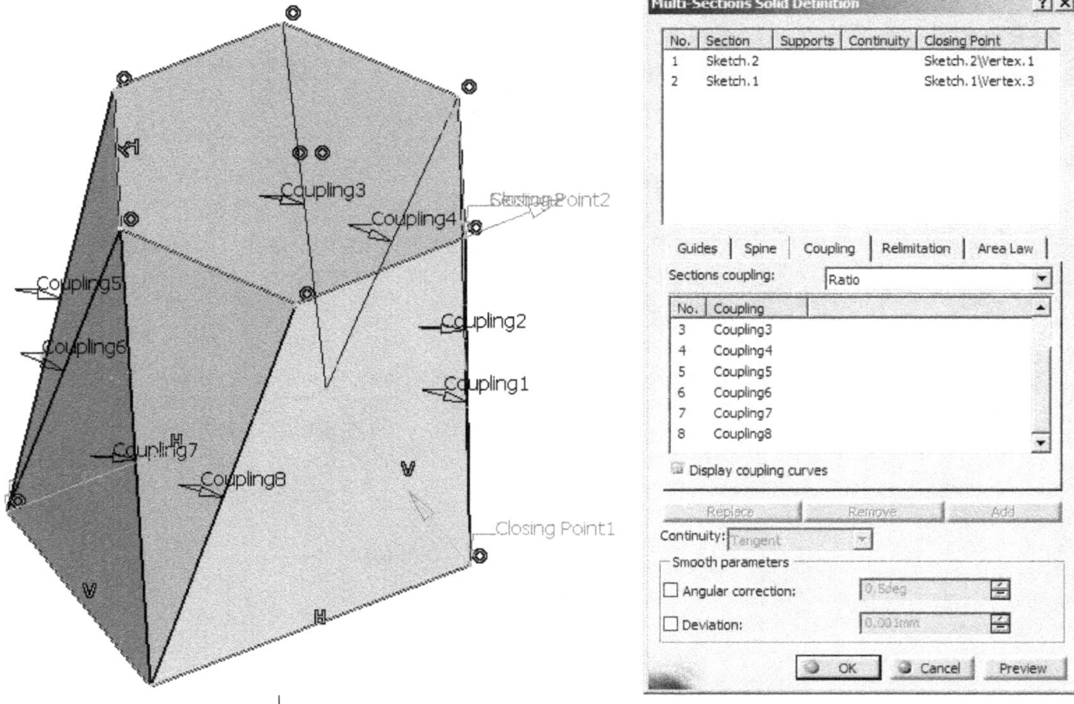

Figure 4–14

If the **Coupling** option is used and the criteria described are not met, an error message opens when you try to generate the Multi-sections Solid feature. For example, setting the **Coupling** option to **Vertices** results in an error message if you are trying to create transitions between a square and a circular section. This error occurs because the circular section does not have any vertices to couple with the square section.

Relimitation

Relimitation controls the progression of the Multi-sections Solid feature beyond the sections. By default, a Multi-sections Solid is relimited at both the start and end sections. CATIA only creates the transitional surfaces of the Multi-sections Solid between the first and last selected sections.

Disabling the Multi-sections Solid relimitation and using a guide, enables the geometry to extend as far as the shortest guide. Figure 4–15 shows the Multi-sections Solid shown in Step 2, except that the **Relimited on the end section** option is not selected. Note that the Multi-sections Solid now extends past the last section. The shape of the Multi-sections Solid's cross-section in this area is controlled by the last section. The trajectory of the Multi-sections Solid is controlled by the guide.

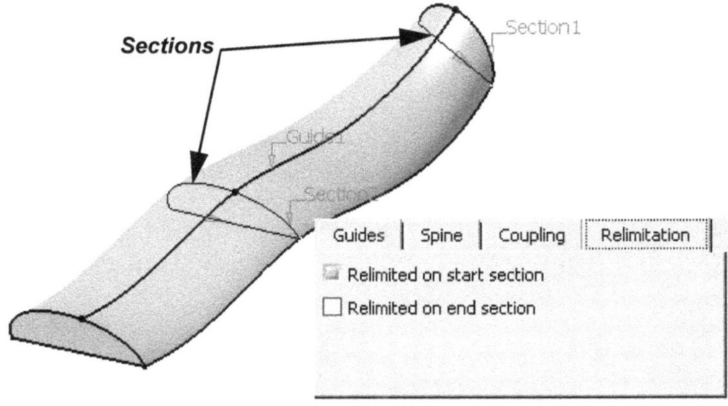

Figure 4–15

To specify Relimitation, select the *Relimitation* tab in the Multi-sections Solid Definition dialog box and clear the **Relimited on the end section** option.

A spine can also control the relimitation of a Multi-sections Solid. The two models shown in Figure 4–16 are created with the **Relimited on the end section** option not selected.

- The Multi-sections Solid on the left in Figure 4–16 uses the system-defined spine and a guide. The cross-section at the end of the Multi-sections Solid is parallel to the last selected section.
- The Multi-sections Solid shown on the right in Figure 4–16 uses a selected spine. The cross-section at the end of the Multi-sections Solid feature is normal to the spine.

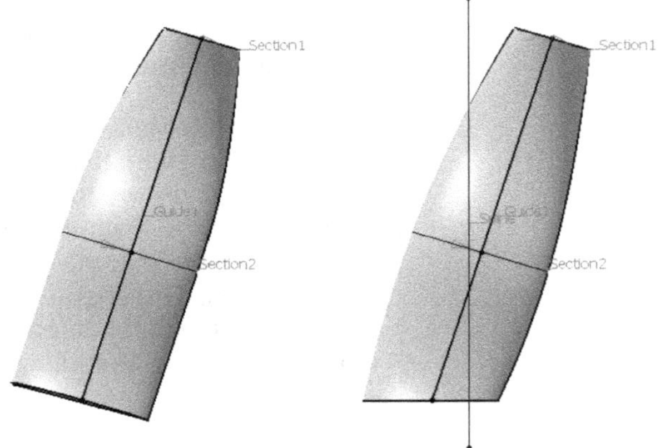

Figure 4–16

Smooth Parameters

Smooth parameters provide additional control over the shape of the Multi-sections Solid feature by attempting to smooth the shape between sections. The **Smooth Parameters** options are located at the bottom of the Multi-sections Solid Definition dialog box, as shown in Figure 4–17. These options are described in .

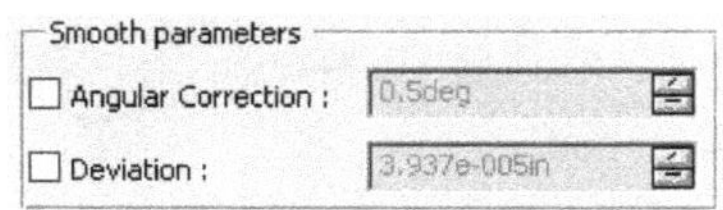

Figure 4–17

Option	Description
Angular Correction	Smooths any portion of the Multi-sections Solid feature with an angular deviation less than the value specified in degrees.
Deviation	Permits deviation from the guide curves by a specified distance to smooth the Multi-sections Solid feature.

4.3 Creation of Rib and Slot Features

The profile of a Rib feature is swept along a center curve that acts as the trajectory for the profile. It creates a feature that adds material. A Slot uses the same technique as a Rib, except that it removes material. Both Slots and Ribs are useful for creating features with non-linear trajectories, unlike Pads and Pockets. A part with Rib and Slot features displays as shown in Figure 4–18.

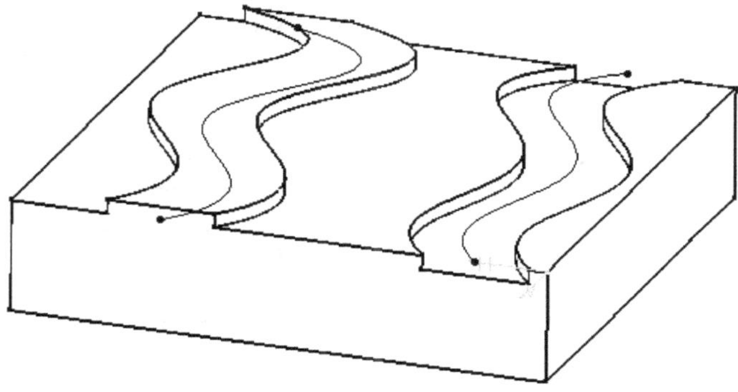

Figure 4–18

The profile of a Rib or Slot is the 2D geometry that is swept along a given center curve. The profile and the center curve can be created before clicking (Rib) or (Slot), or they can be created from the Rib or Slot definition dialog box.

- Click to create a Rib feature.
- Click to create a Slot feature.

General Steps

Use the following general steps to create a Rib or Slot feature:

1. Select or create a profile
2. Select or create a center curve.
3. Define the profile control.
4. Preview and complete the feature.

Step 1 - Select or create a profile

Select an existing profile or sketch a new one. Click next to the *Profile* field, as shown in Figure 4–19, to create a sketch to be used for the profile.

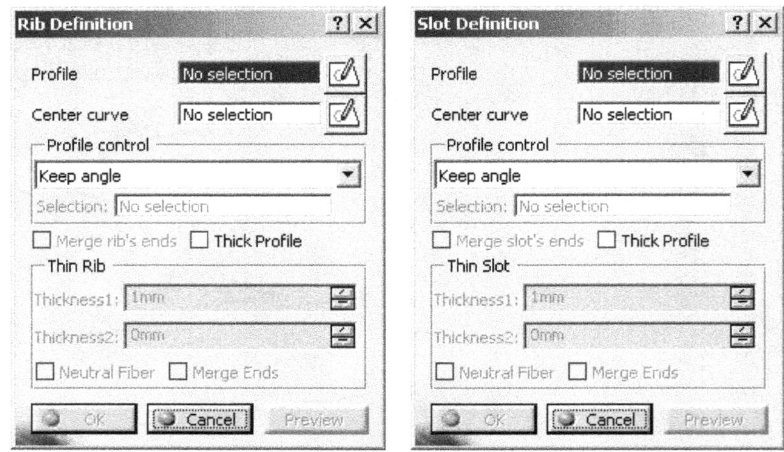

Figure 4–19

Step 2 - Select or create a center curve.

Select an existing center curve or click to sketch a center curve. You can select a sketch, spline, or edge for the center curve.

Step 3 - Define the profile control.

Define the Profile control options, as shown in Figure 4–20.

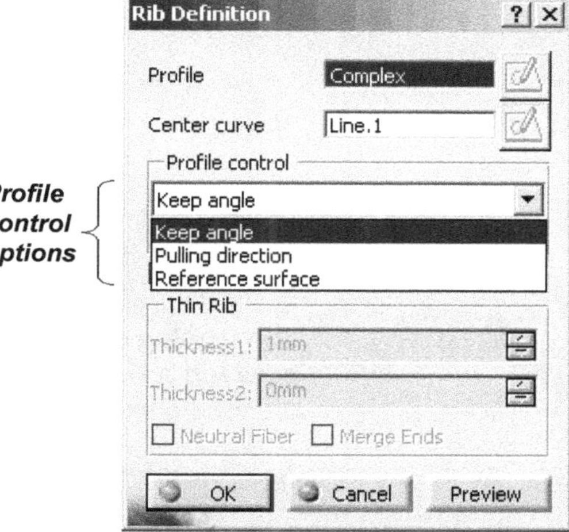

Figure 4–20

Keep Angle

The **Keep Angle** option is the default. This option keeps the angle constant between the support plane of the profile and the center curve along the length of the center curve. For example, if the support plane of the profile is normal to the center curve at the start point, the profile remains normal to the center curve as it is swept, as shown in Figure 4–21.

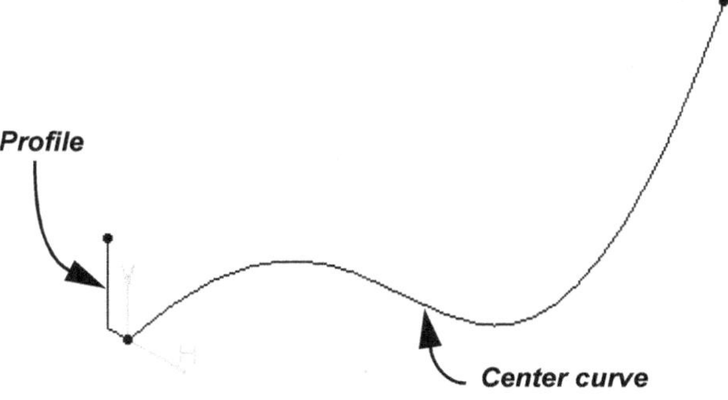

Figure 4–21

The relative angle between the profile and the center curve remains constant, as shown in Figure 4–22.

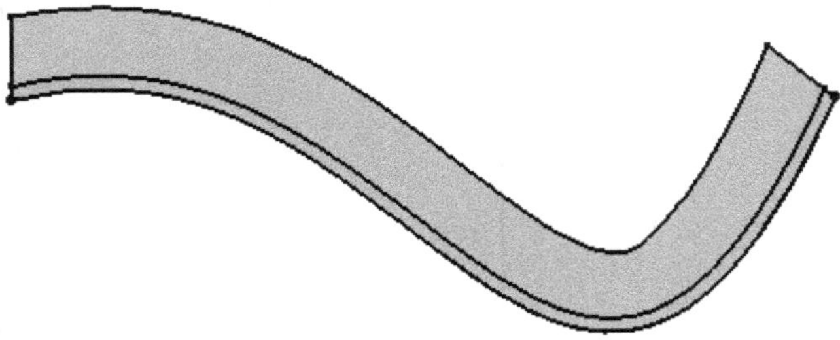

Figure 4–22

Pulling Direction

The **Pulling Direction** option maintains a constant angle between a selected reference plane or planar surface and the profile, as shown in Figure 4–23.

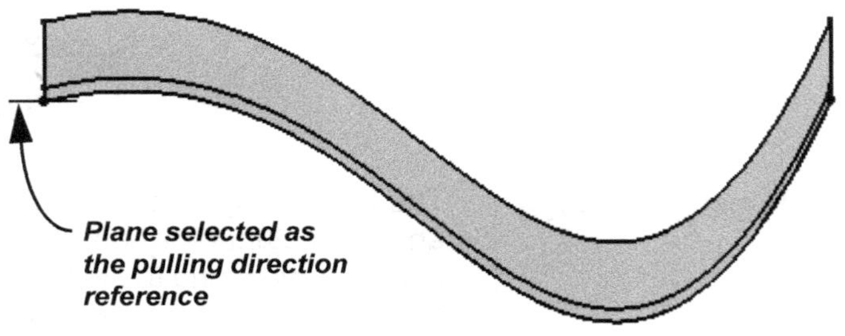

Figure 4–23

Reference Surface

The **Reference Surface** option ensures that the profile follows the shape of a selected Surface feature. A Surface feature that has been selected as the reference surface is shown in Figure 4–24.

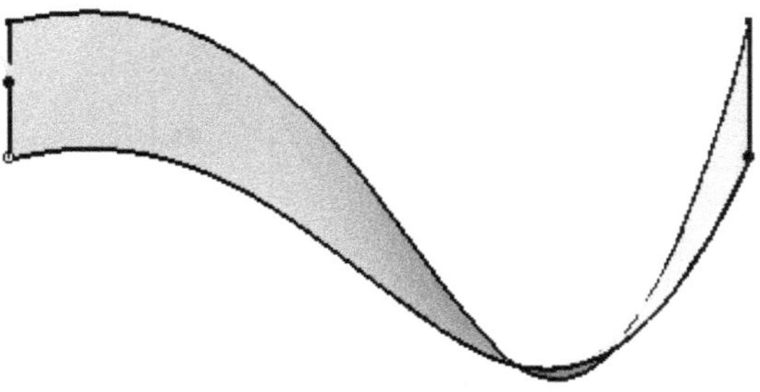

Figure 4–24

*When using the **Reference Surface** option, the edge of the surface feature must lie on the center curve.*

The Rib feature shown in Figure 4–25 follows the shape of the reference surface as it is swept along the center curve.

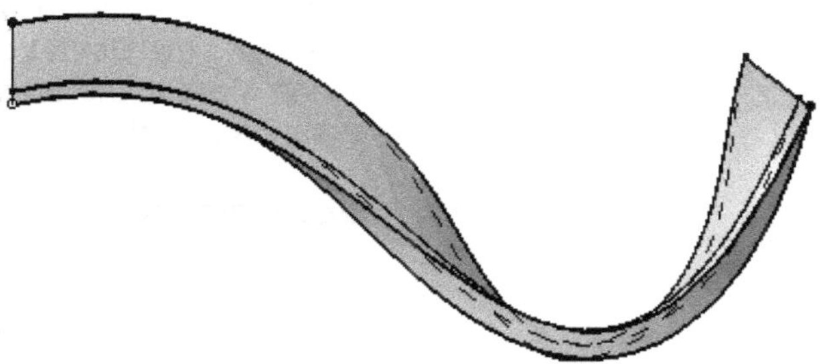

Figure 4–25

Step 4 - Preview and complete the feature.

Preview the feature before exiting the feature creation dialog box. This ensures that the geometry can be created. Click **OK** to complete the feature.

4.4 Advanced Shell Options

If you have a CFO license, you can control the resulting shell surfaces using the **Deviation** parameters. These are accessed by clicking **More** in the Shell Definition dialog box. The dialog box expands as shown in Figure 4–26.

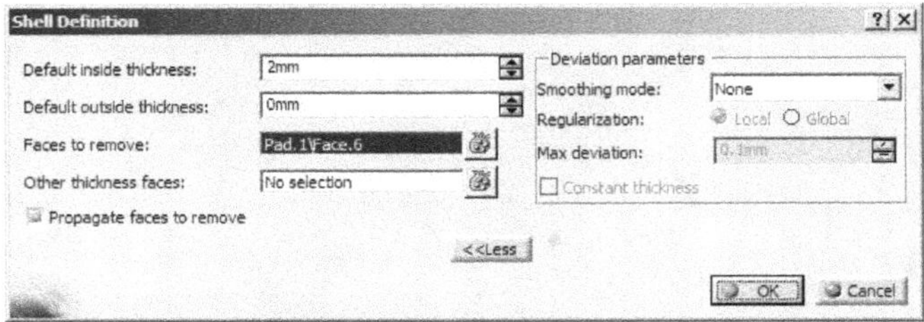

Figure 4–26

Three options are available for the Smoothing mode:

- **None:** This is the default option in which no smoothing is applied. When selected, the **Max deviation** and **Constant thickness** options are disabled.
- **Manual:** When selected you can apply a maximum deviation (the default is 0.1 mm) and can also apply a constant thickness.
- **Automatic:** When selected, smoothing is automatically determined and applied. In this case, the **Max deviation** option is disabled, but the **Constant thickness** option is enabled.

Note that the **Regularization** option is only available with **Automatic** and Manual **Smoothing** modes. It permits for the offset surfaces to be calculated either locally or globally and effects the accuracy wall thickness for each wall.

The Shell Definition dialog box includes the **Propagate faces to remove** option, as shown in Figure 4–27.

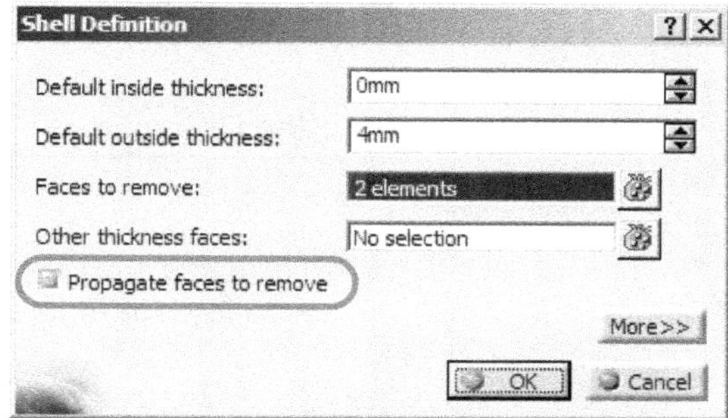

Figure 4–27

With this option selected (this is the default setting), the software removes any additional faces that result from tangent continuous edges. For example, in the model shown in Figure 4–28, the highlighted surface has been selected for removal.

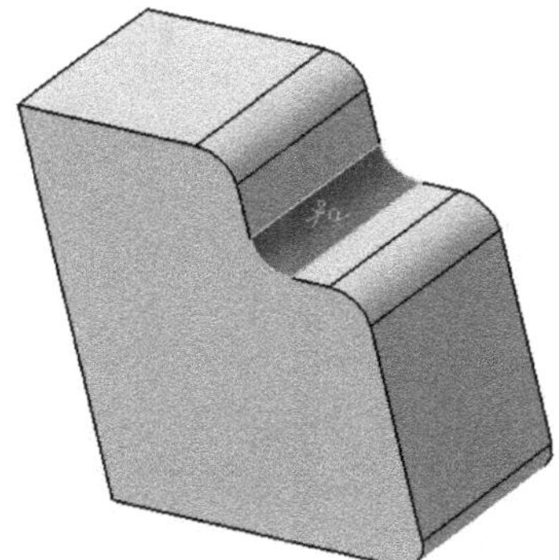

Figure 4–28

The resulting shell feature with **Propagate faces to remove** selected is shown on the left in Figure 4–29. All of the surfaces that have tangent continuous edges are removed. The resulting shell with the option toggled off is shown on the right. Only the selected surface is removed.

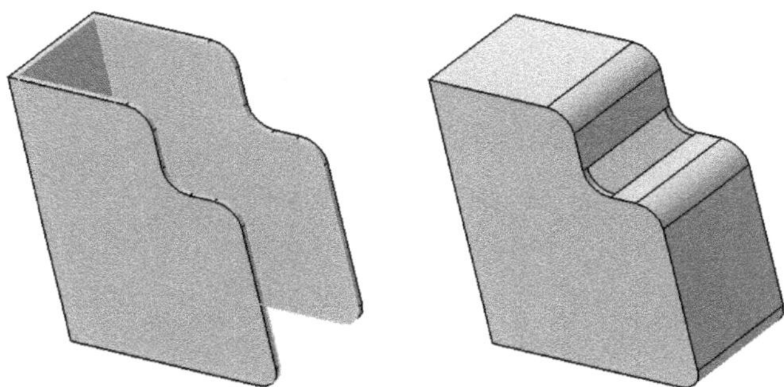

Figure 4–29

Practice 4a Solid Combine

Practice Objective

- Create a Solid Combine feature.

In this practice, you will use the Solid Combine feature to create the part shown in Figure 4–30.

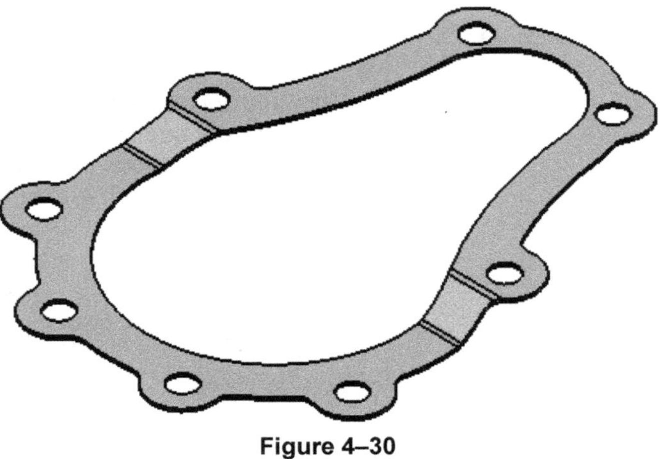

Figure 4–30

Task 1 - Open the part.

1. Open **Combine.CATPart**, as shown in Figure 4–31. The part file contains two sketches as the base of the Solid Combine feature.

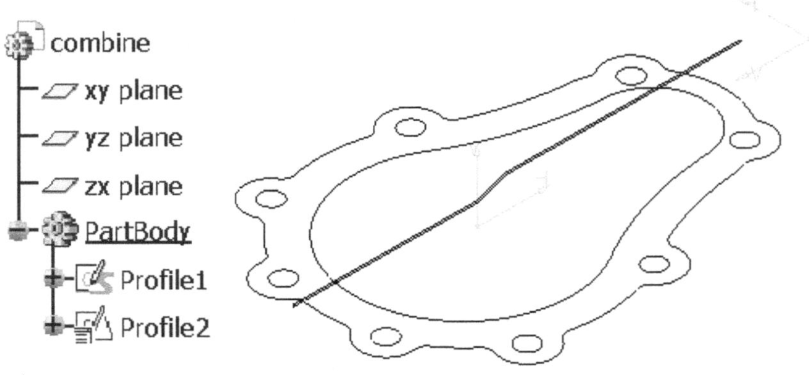

Figure 4–31

Task 2 - Create a Solid Combine feature.

1. Click (Solid Combine). The dialog box opens as shown in Figure 4–32.

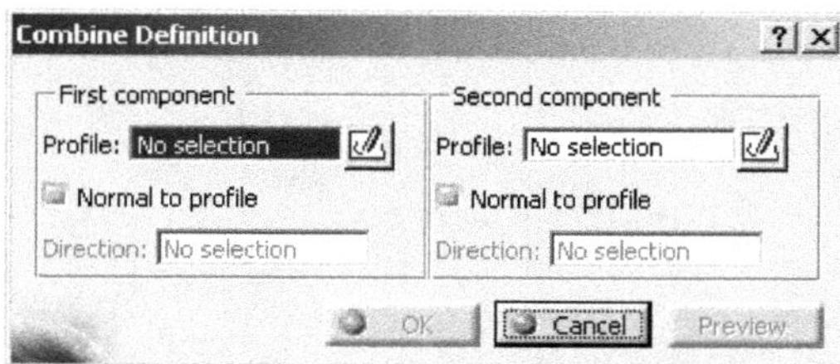

Figure 4–32

2. Select **Profile1** as the first component. An error message opens as shown in Figure 4–33. The sketch has too many domains and cannot be used as a component. Click **OK** and then cancel the Combine Definition.

Figure 4–33

3. Edit **Profile1**.

4. Select any outer element of the sketch and use **Auto Search**, as shown in Figure 4–34.

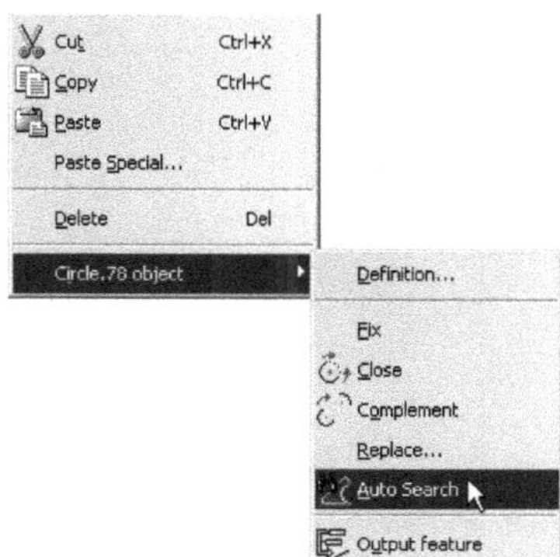

Figure 4–34

The display of Profile1 has been modified to simplify the visualization.

The sketch now displays as shown in Figure 4–35. Note how the entire outer edge is selected by the **Auto Search**.

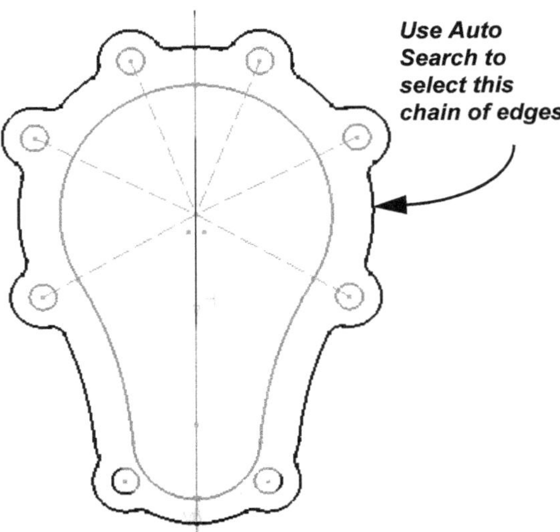

Figure 4–35

5. With the outer edge active, click (Profile feature) in the Tools toolbar. The Profile Definition dialog box opens as shown in Figure 4–36. The selected elements are added.

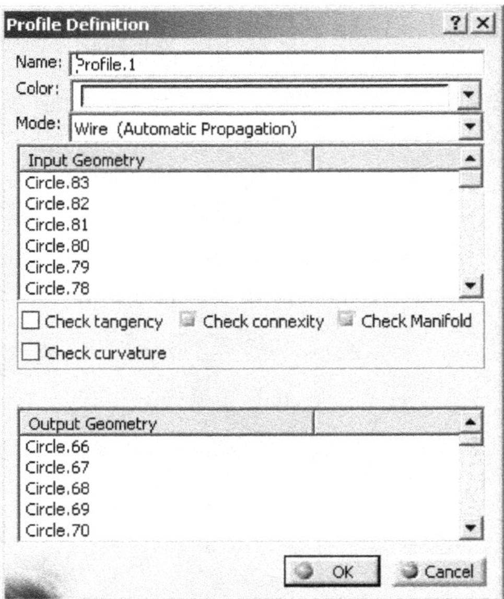

Figure 4–36

6. Click **OK** and exit Sketcher. The profile now displays as shown in Figure 4–37.

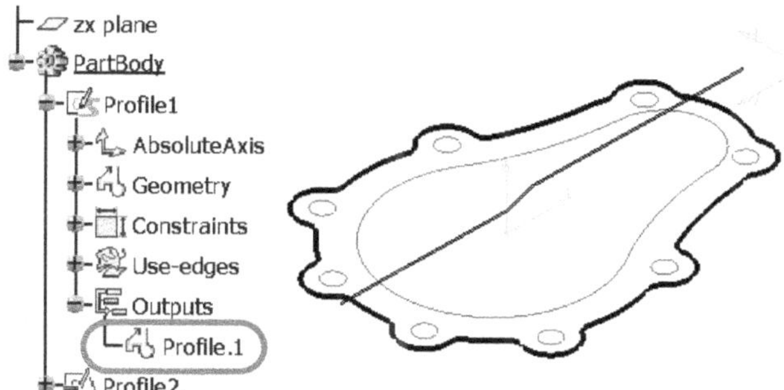

Figure 4–37

7. In the specification tree, locate the profile under Profile1 and rename it as **OuterProfile**, as shown in Figure 4–38.

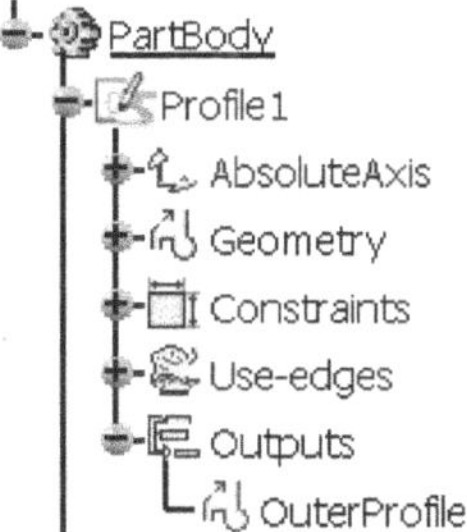

Figure 4–38

8. Click (Solid Combine).

9. For the first component, select **OuterProfile** and for the second component, select **Profile2**.

10. Click **OK**. The result of the Solid Combine displays as shown in Figure 4–39.

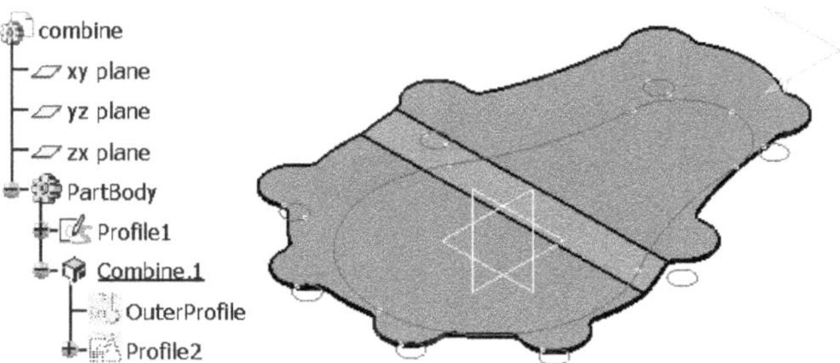

Figure 4–39

Task 3 - Create a Pocket.

1. Create a Pocket feature using Profile1. Note that all of the elements outside the Profile feature created in Sketcher are used. Define the pocket using the **Up to last** depth option. The model displays as shown in Figure 4–40.

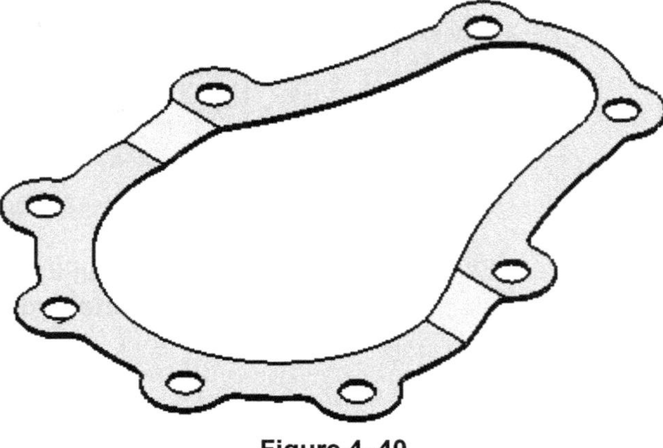

Figure 4–40

2. Save the model.

Task 4 - (Optional) Add edge Fillets.

1. Click (Edge fillet) and select the four edges shown in Figure 4–41.

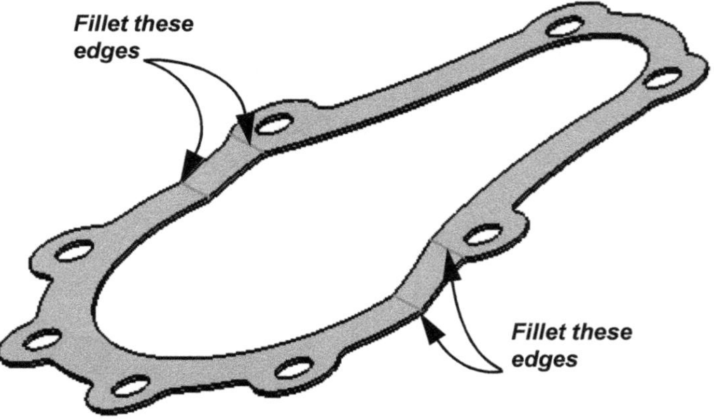

Figure 4–41

2. Enter **6** for the *Fillet radius* and click **OK**.

3. Fillet the 4 edges shown in Figure 4–42 with **6** radius.

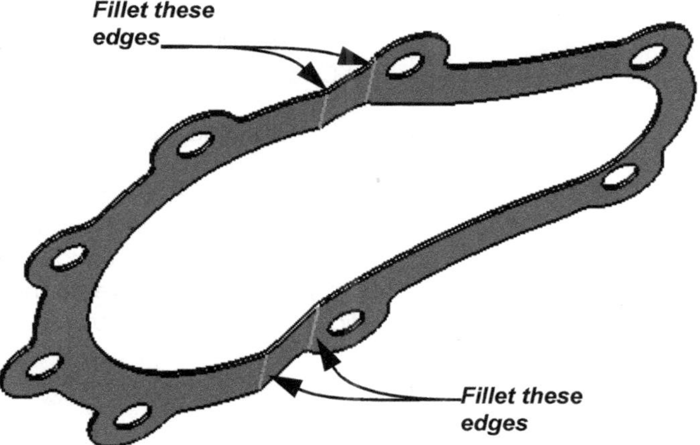

Figure 4–42

The completed model displays as shown in Figure 4–43.

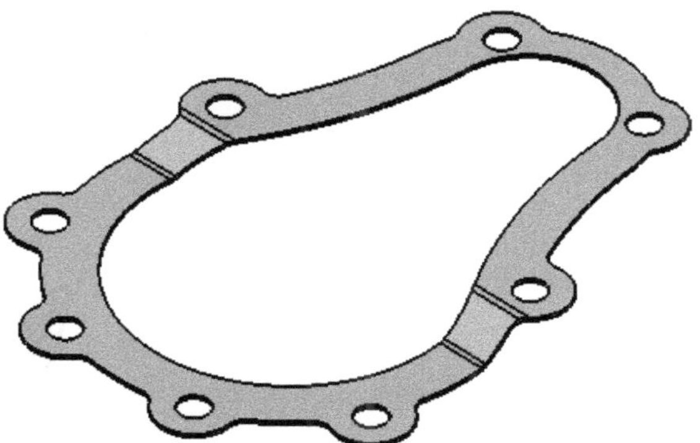

Figure 4–43

4. Save the model and close the window.

Practice 4b Crane Hook

Practice Objectives

- Create a Multi-sections Solid using guide curves and a spine.
- Create a Rib feature.

In this practice, you will create a hook used by a crane or hoist. The hook geometry will be created using a Multi-sections Solid feature between three sections. A spine will be used to control the sections (the sections will stay normal to the spine) and guide curves will be used to control the size of the sections. A Rib will be used to create the eye of the hook. The completed model displays as shown in Figure 4–44.

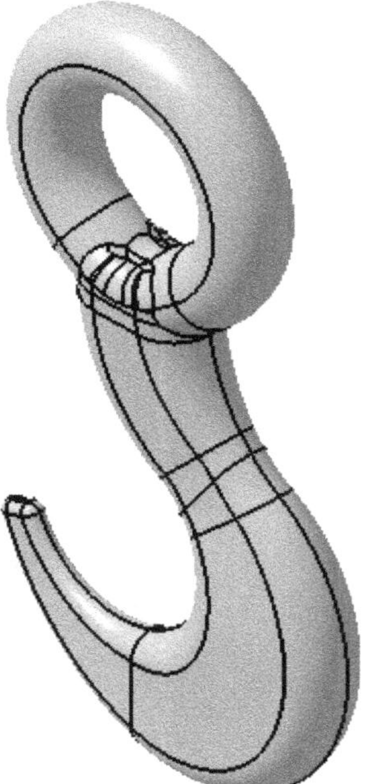

Figure 4–44

Task 1 - Open the part.

1. Open **CraneHook.CATPart**. The model displays as shown in Figure 4–45.

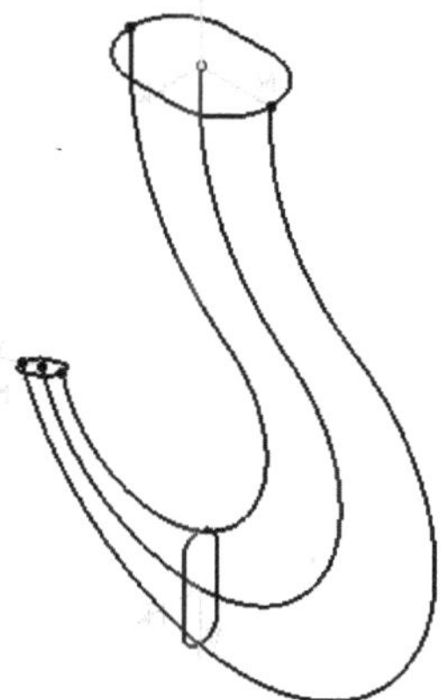

Figure 4–45

2. Click (Multi-sections Solid). Define the Multi-sections Solid feature by selecting the following sketches, as shown in Figure 4–46:

   - **Sketch.1**
   - **Sketch.2**
   - **Sketch.3**

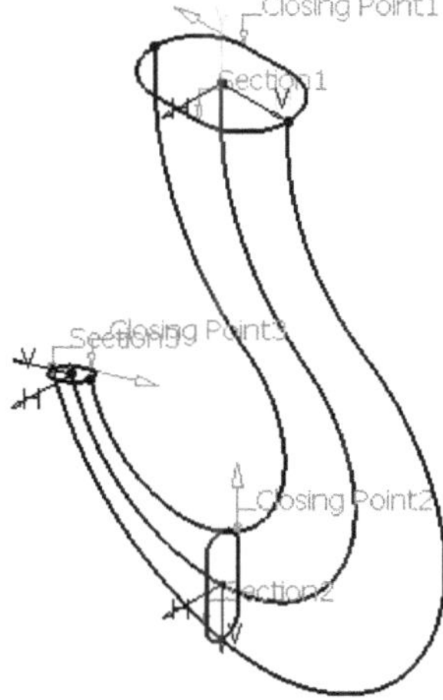

Figure 4–46

3. Select the *Spine* tab and select **Sketch.4**.
4. Click **Preview**. The preview displays as shown in Figure 4–47.

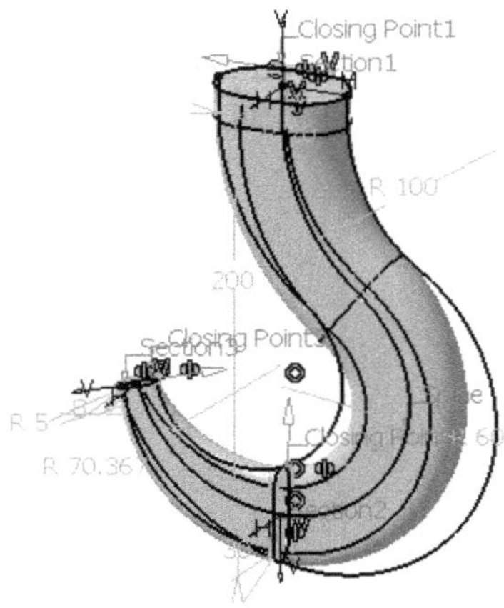

Figure 4–47

Note how the section stays normal to the spine. Without the use of a spine, you could not have used these three sections to create a Multi-sections Solid.

5. Select the *Guides* tab and select the following:
    - **Sketch.5**
    - **Sketch.6**
6. Click **OK**. The completed Multi-sections Solid feature displays as shown in Figure 4–48.

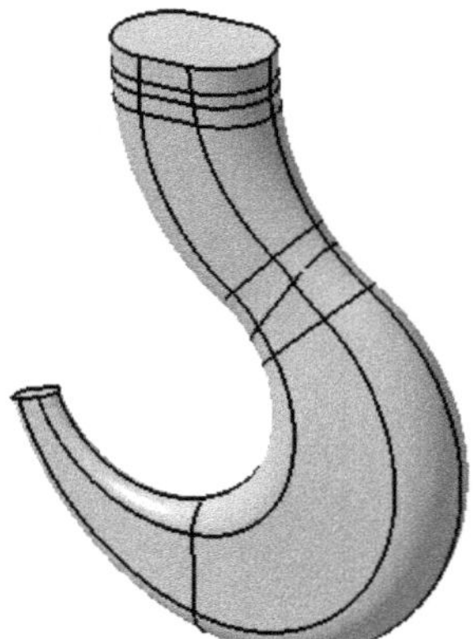

Figure 4–48

Task 2 - Create sketches for the eye of the hook.

1. Create the sketch shown in Figure 4–49 using the **yz** plane as the sketching plane.

Design Considerations

Click (Intersect 3D Elements) and select the top planar surface of the hook to use as a reference for the sketched arc.

Use (Construction/Standard Element) to convert the projection to a construction element. By referencing the projection, the sketch will be associative to the hook geometry.

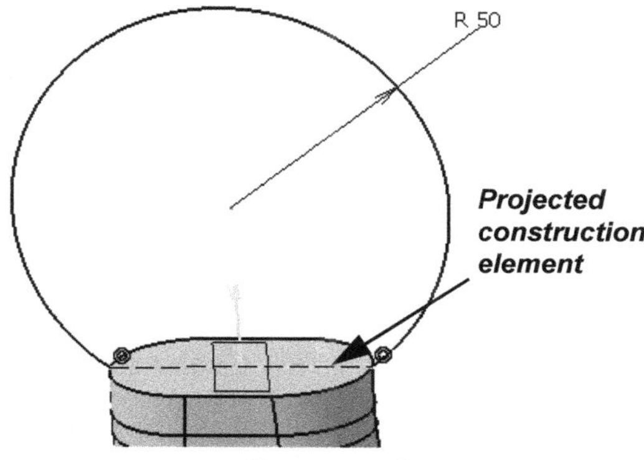

Figure 4–49

2. Create the reference plane shown in Figure 4–50.
   - *Plane type:* **Normal to curve**

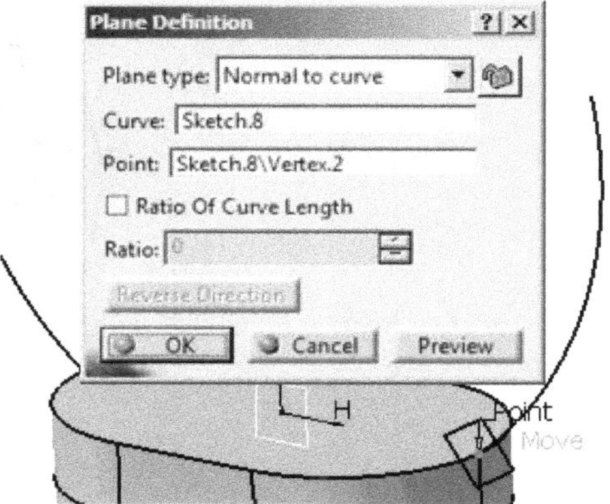

Figure 4–50

3. Create the sketch shown in Figure 4–51, using the plane you just created as the sketching plane.

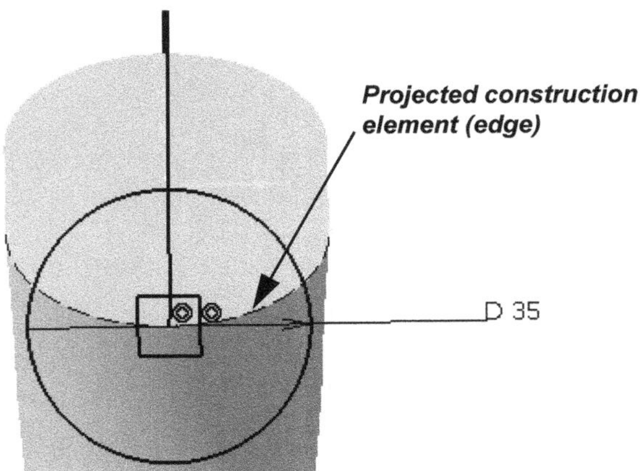

Figure 4–51

4. Click (Rib). Define the Rib feature by selecting the following sketches:
   - *Profile:* **Sketch.9**
   - *Center curve:* **Sketch.8**
5. Preview the Rib. The feature displays as shown in Figure 4–52. Note that the Rib does not merge with the Multi-section Solid feature.

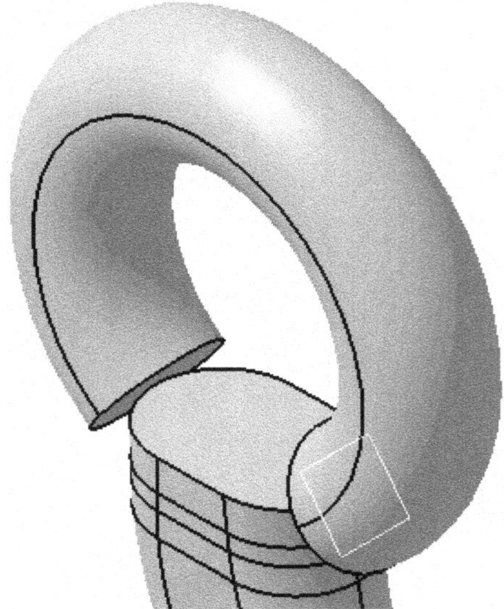

Figure 4–52

Design Considerations

Use the **Merge rib's ends** option to achieve the correct geometry. This option extrapolates the profile to meet the next solid surface.

6. Select **Merge rib's ends** and complete the feature. The model displays as shown in Figure 4–53.

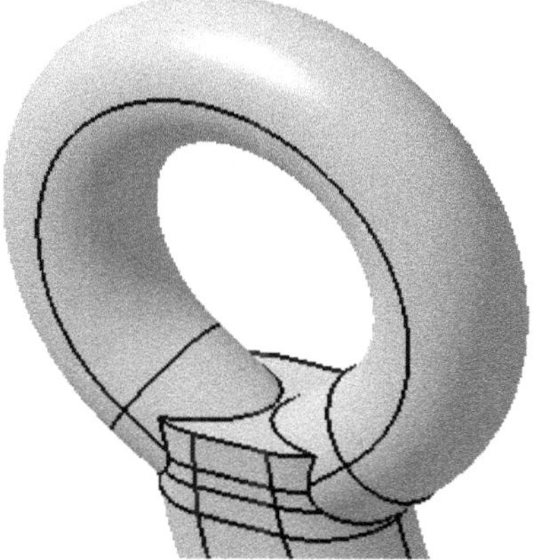

Figure 4–53

Task 3 - Create an edge Fillet.

1. Create an edge Fillet with the following parameters:

   - *Radius:* **12**
   - *Object(s) to fillet:* **1 Face** (the top planar surface of the hook)

   The completed Fillet displays as shown in Figure 4–54.

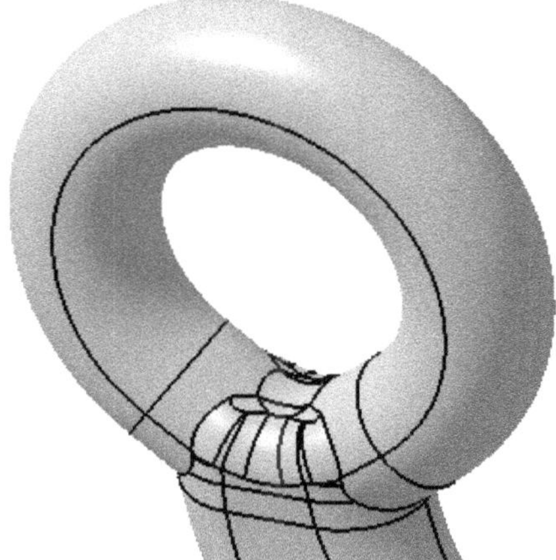

Figure 4–54

2. Create an edge Fillet with the following parameters:

   - *Radius:* **4**
   - *Object(s) to fillet:* **1 Face** (the planar surface at the tip)

   The completed Fillet displays as shown in Figure 4–55.

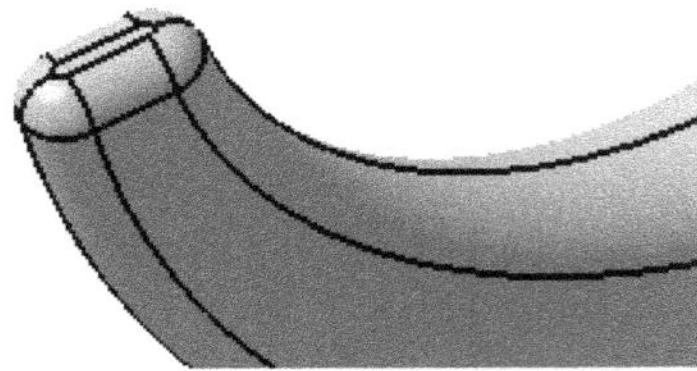

Figure 4–55

3. Save the model and close the file.

Practice 4c

Truck Bumper

Practice Objectives

- Create a Multi-sections Solid feature.
- Use a spine to control a Multi-sections Solid feature.
- Create an unrelimited Multi-sections Solid feature.
- Create a negative Multi-sections Solid feature.

In this practice, you will model the rear bumper for a truck. The bumper must fit the contours of the rear of the truck. Multi-sections Solid features are used to control the shape of the bumper, which will transition from a small section at the ends to a large section near the license plate cut out. The Multi-sections Solid feature will also enable the bumper to wrap around the rear corner of the truck. Only half of this model is created using Multi-sections Solid features. The geometry is then mirrored to create the completed model shown in Figure 4–56.

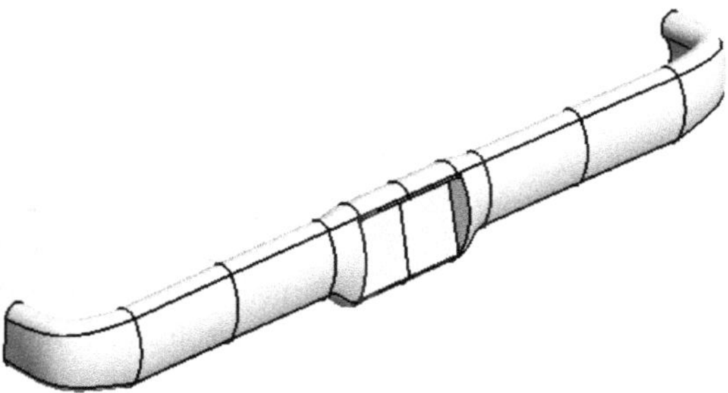

Figure 4–56

You will start with a model that contains the construction geometry required to create the bumper model. The model displays as shown in Figure 4–57.

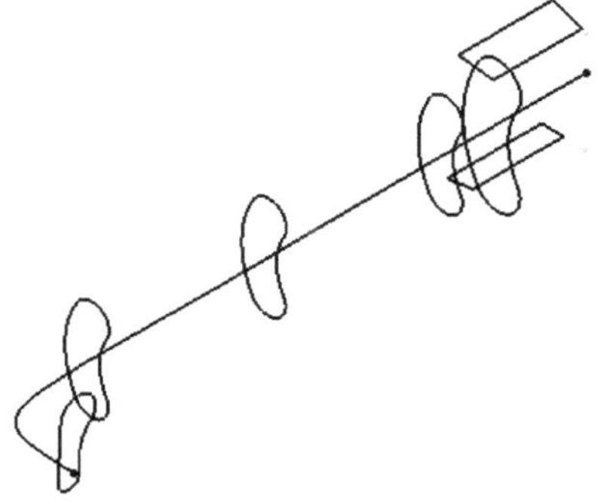

Figure 4–57

Task 1 - Open the part.

1. Open **Truck Bumper.CATPart**. The model displays as shown in Figure 4–58.

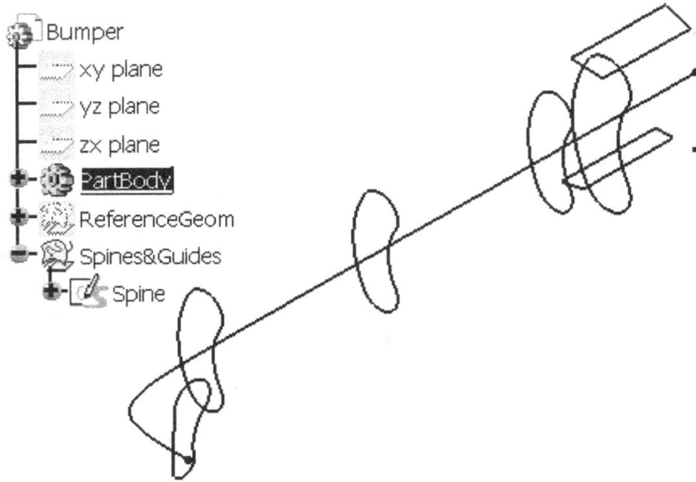

Figure 4–58

2. Expand the specification tree to display the different planes and sketches in the model. Sketches 1 to 5 are used to develop the shape of the bumper. The PlateTop and PlateBottom sketches are used to define a negative Multi-sections Solid, creating a cutout for the license plate.

Task 2 - Create the first Multi-sections Solid.

1. Click (Multi-sections Solid). The Multi-sections Solid Definition dialog box opens as shown in Figure 4–59.

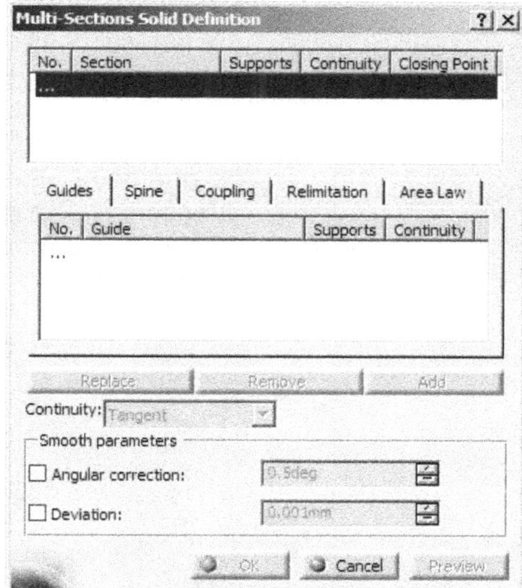

Figure 4–59

2. In the model or specification tree, select the **1stSec** sketch. The section is added to the top field in the Multi-sections Solid Definition dialog box. Note the location of **ClosingPoint1**, as shown in Figure 4–60.

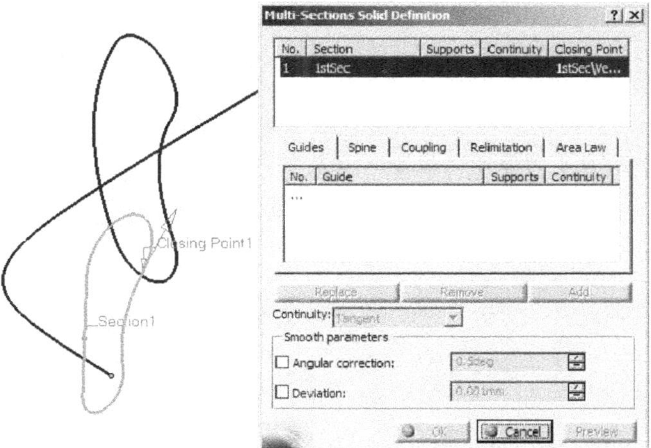

Figure 4–60

3. Select the **2ndSec** sketch. Ensure that the closing points of the two sections are in the same positions, as shown on the right in Figure 4–61. To change the position of the closing point, right-click on the **Closing Point 2** text and select **Replace**. Select the point or vertex for the new location of the closing point. Verify that the arrows point in the same direction. Select the arrow to flip it, if required.

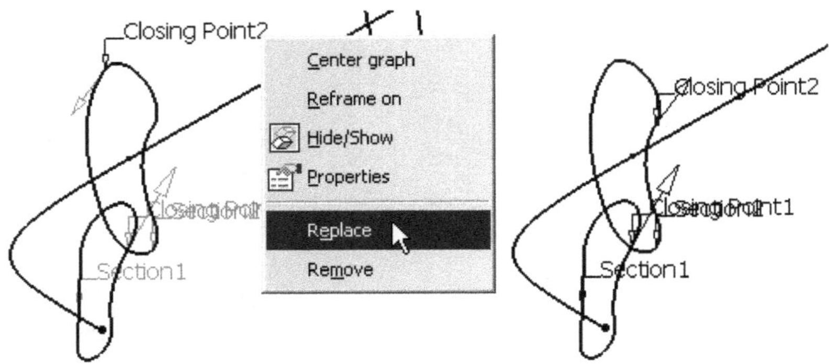

Figure 4–61

4. Click **Preview** to display the Multi-sections Solid feature. The model displays as shown in Figure 4–62. Note the relative position of the Solid feature and Spine sketch feature.

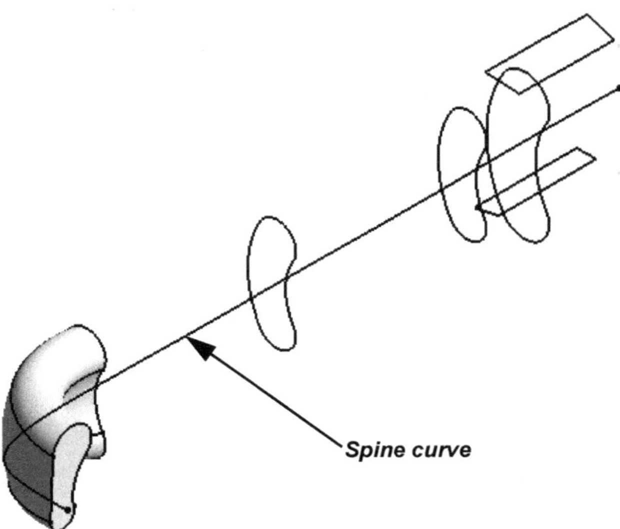

Figure 4–62

The Spine sketch is developed to determine the orientation of the cross-section as the bumper rounds the rear corner of the truck.

5. Select the *Spine* tab. In the **Spines&Guides** geometrical set, select the **Spine** sketch.

6. Click **OK**. The model displays as shown in Figure 4–63. Note that the Spine curve and two sections have been added under the Multi-sections Solid.1 feature in the specification tree. All of the sketches are hidden automatically to simplify the display of the Solid feature.

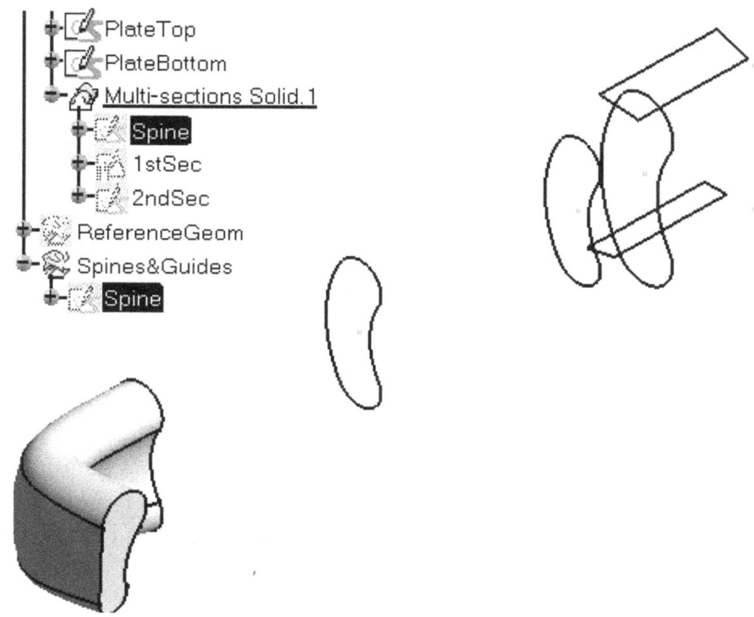

Figure 4–63

7. Show the **2ndSec** and **Spine** sketches. They are used in the next Multi-sections Solid feature.

Task 3 - Create an unrelimited Multi-sections Solid feature.

1. Click (Multi-sections Solid).

2. Select these sections in the following order: **2ndSec**, **3rdSec**, **4thSec**, and **5thSec**.

3. Ensure that the closing points for all of the sections are in the same place and point in the same direction, as shown in Figure 4–64.

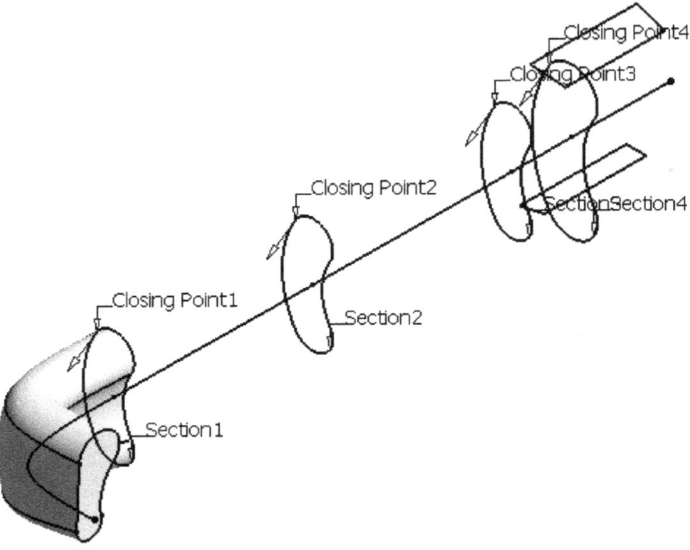

Figure 4–64

4. Add the Spine sketch as the Spine curve for the Multi-sections Solid feature and click **Preview**. The model displays as shown in Figure 4–65.

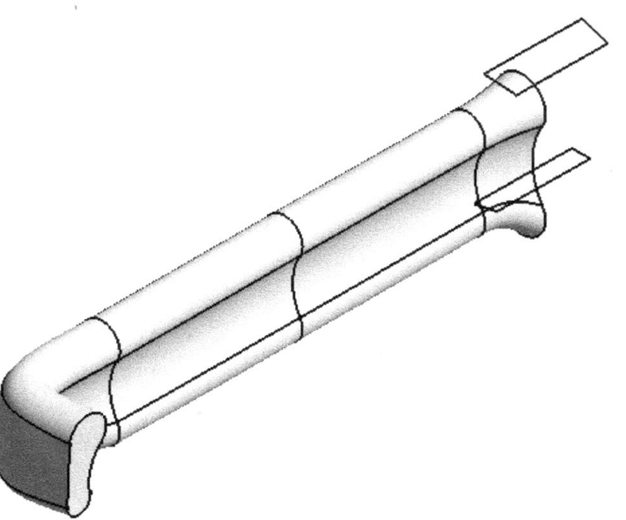

Figure 4–65

5. Select the *Relimitation* tab and clear the **Relimited on end section** option, as shown in Figure 4–66. The Multi-sections Solid turns red, indicating that it needs updating.

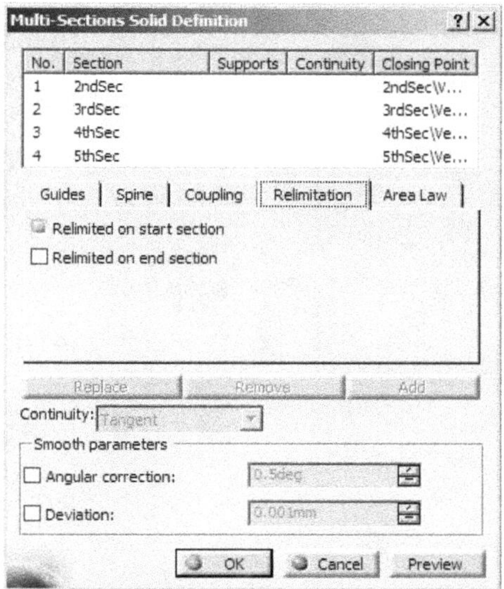

Figure 4–66

6. Click **OK**. The model displays as shown in Figure 4–67. Note that the Multi-sections Solid only extends as far as the longest Spine or Guide curve.

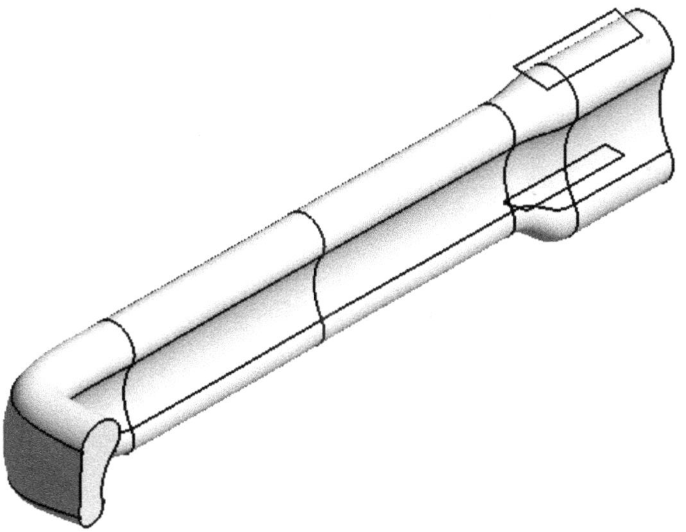

Figure 4–67

7. Save the model.

Task 4 - Create a negative Multi-sections Solid for the license plate space.

1. Click (Removed Multi-sections Solid). The Removed Multi-sections Solid Definition dialog box opens. Note that it is identical to the Multi-sections Solid Definition dialog box.
2. Select the **PlateTop** and **PlateBottom** sections from the PartBody.
3. Ensure that the closing points match between the two sections.
4. Complete the feature. The model displays as shown in Figure 4–68.

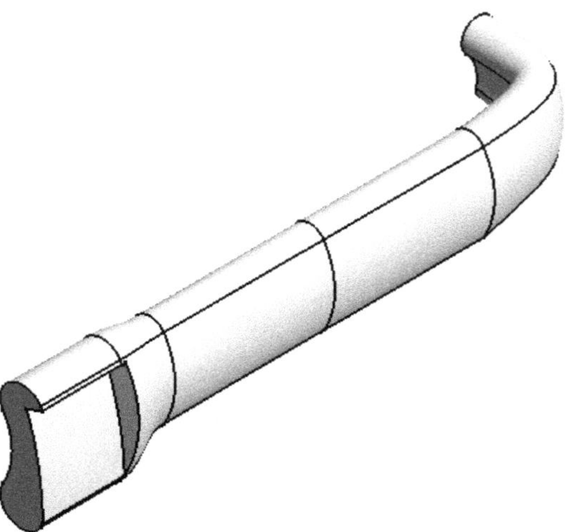

Figure 4–68

5. Show the **PlateTop** and **PlateBottom** sketches.
6. Right-click on the **Spines&Guides** geometrical set and select **Define In Work Object**.

7. Create a line using the Point - Point definition. Select the vertices of the **PlateTop** and **PlateBottom** sketches, as shown in Figure 4–69.

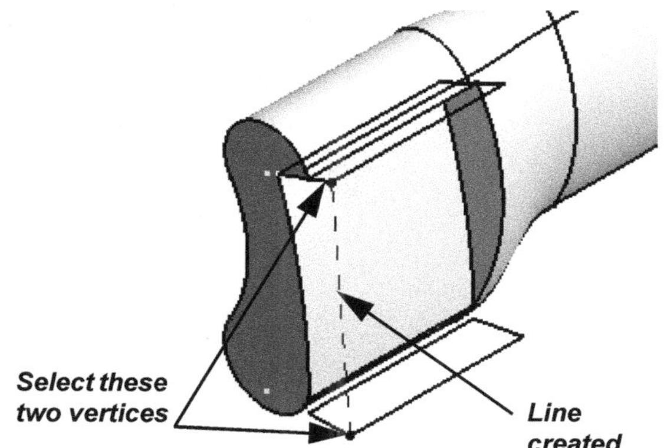

Figure 4–69

8. Rename the line as **PlateGuide**.

9. Edit **Multi-sections Solid.3** and select the *Guides* tab.

10. Select the three dots in the *Guides* field. Add **PlateGuide** as a guide curve and complete the feature.

11. Hide all of the sketches and lines used to develop the Multi-sections Solids for this model. The model displays as shown in Figure 4–70.

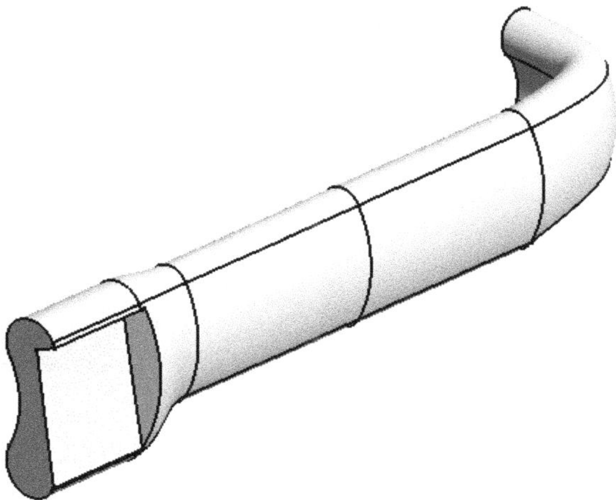

Figure 4–70

12. Right-click on the PartBody and select **Define In Work Object**.

Task 5 - Mirror the bumper.

1. Click (Mirror) to perform a mirror operation.
2. Select the **yz plane** or an appropriate model surface so that the complete model displays as shown in Figure 4–71.

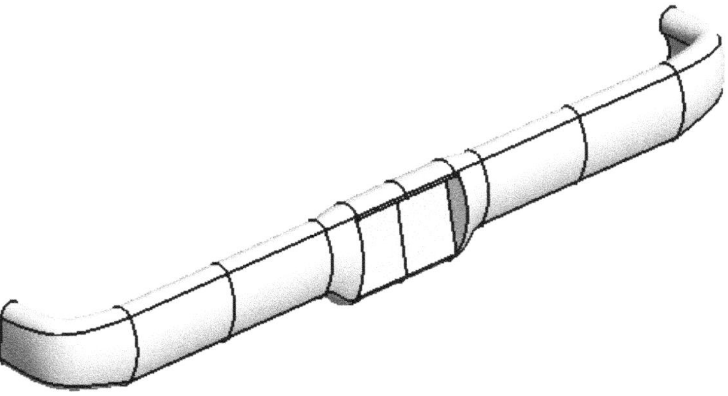

Figure 4–71

3. Save the model.

Task 6 - (Optional) Modify the spine curve.

1. Double-click on the Spine sketch in the **Spines&Guides** geometrical set and zoom in on the spline on the right side of the sketch, as shown in Figure 4–72.

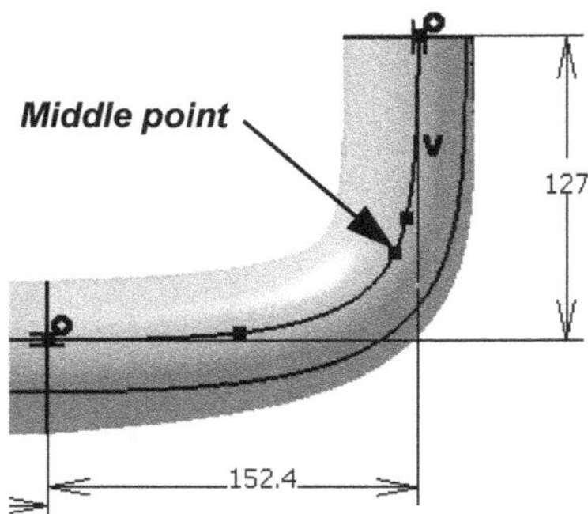

Figure 4–72

The spline has five control points. You will move the middle point to see how it affects the shape of the Multi-sections Solid. Experiment with a variety of locations.

2. Drag the middle control point to a new location and exit the Sketcher. Note how the Multi-sections Solid feature updates. Some examples are shown in Figure 4–73.

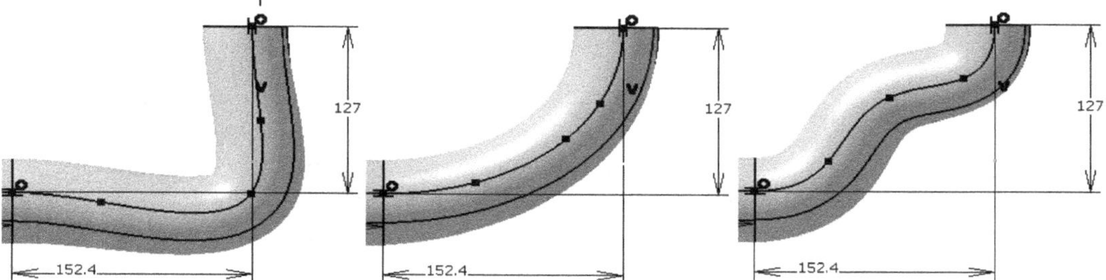

Figure 4–73

3. Close the model without saving.

Practice 4d

Speaker Cover

Practice Objective

- Create a Slot feature using the **Keep Angle** option.

In this practice, you will create the vents on a speaker cover for a car stereo. The vent features will be created using a Slot with the **Keep Angle** and **Merge Ends** options. The **Keep Angle** option ensures that the vent geometry follows the center curve. The **Merge Ends** option brings the vents to the edge of the cover. You will pattern the Slot to complete the speaker cover. The completed model displays as shown in Figure 4–74.

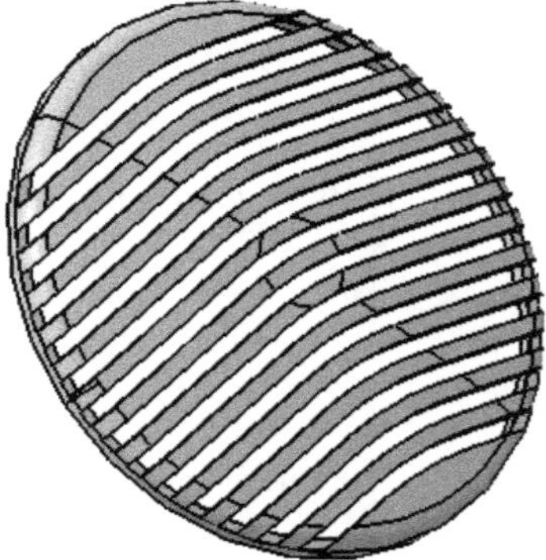

Figure 4–74

Task 1 - Open the part.

1. Open **Speaker.CATPart**. The model displays as shown in Figure 4–75.

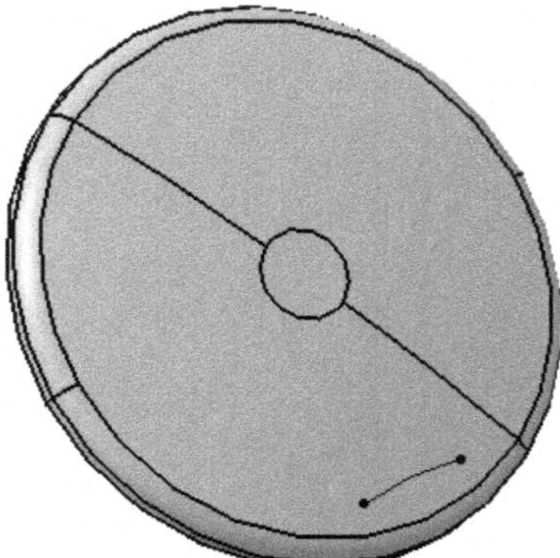

Figure 4–75

Task 2 - Complete reference geometry.

1. Define **ConstrGeom** to be the In Work Object.
2. Create a reference plane for the slot's profile sketch using the following options:
   - *Plane type:* **Normal to curve**
   - *Curve:* **Center Curve**
   - *Point:* **end point of Center Curve**, as shown in Figure 4–76

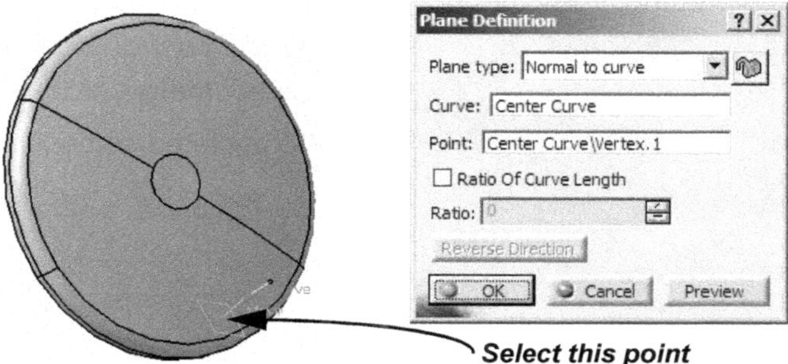

Figure 4–76

3. Rename the plane as **Profile Plane**.
4. Create a sketch on the Profile Plane. Sketch and constrain the section, as shown in Figure 4–77. Note the equidistant constraint between the vertical edges and the end point of the Center Curve.

Create an Equidistant constraint between the end point of the center curve and the vertical edges.

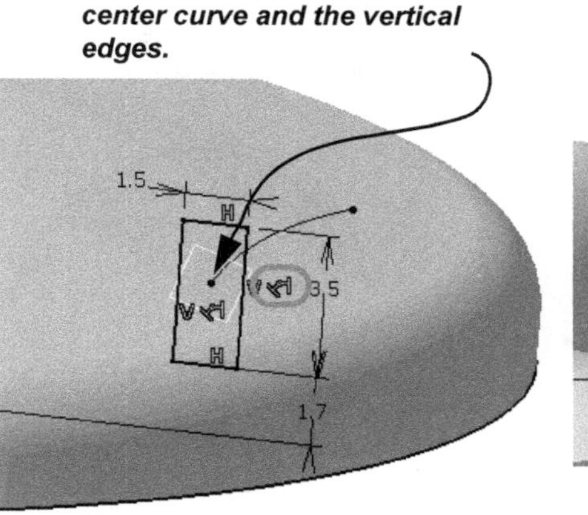

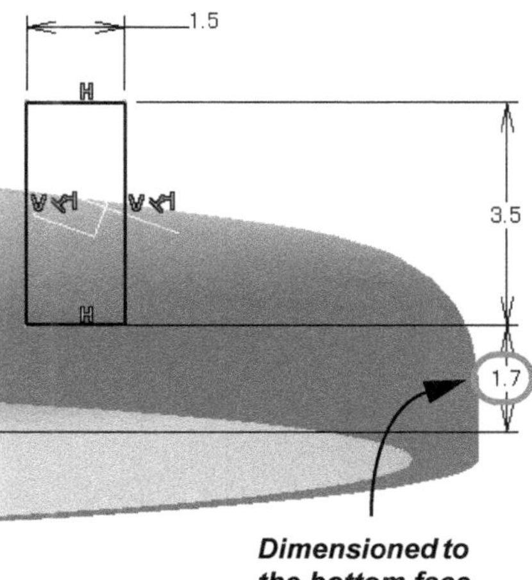

Dimensioned to the bottom face

Figure 4–77

5. Exit the Sketcher workbench.
6. Rename the sketch as **Vent Profile**.

Task 3 - Create the Slot feature.

1. Define the PartBody as in the Work Object.
2. Click (Slot) to create a Slot. Select the **Vent Profile** feature as the slot profile, and the **Center Curve** feature as the slot center curve, and then make the following selections in the Slot Definition dialog box:
   - *Profile control:* Keep angle
   - Select **Merge slot's ends**.

   The completed settings are shown in Figure 4–78.

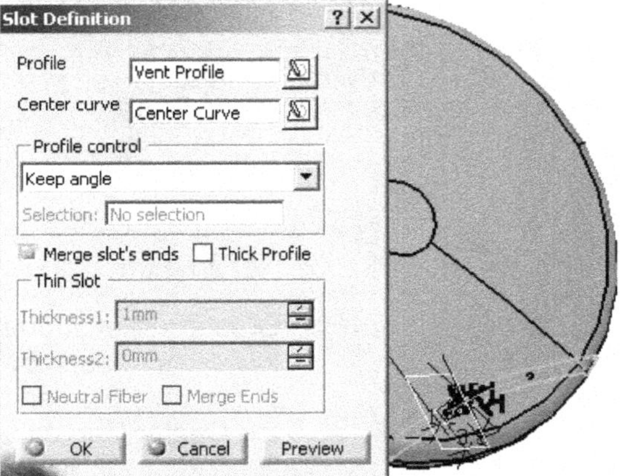

Figure 4–78

3. Click **OK** to complete the Slot feature. The speaker cover displays as shown in Figure 4–79.

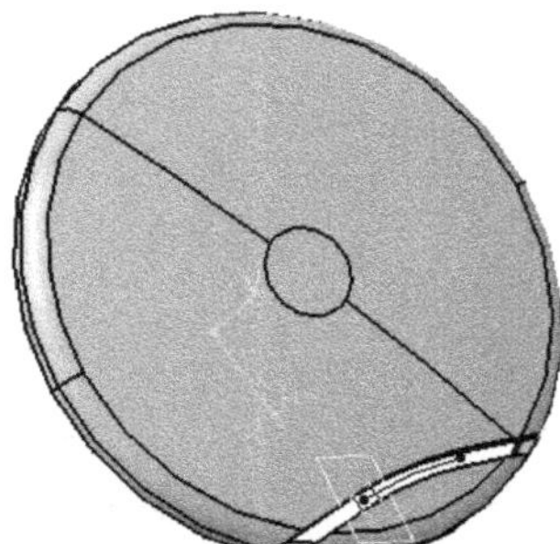

Figure 4–79

Task 4 - Pattern the Rib feature.

1. Preselect the Slot feature and click (Rectangular Pattern). Make the following selections in the Rectangular Pattern Definition dialog box, as shown in Figure 4–80:

    - *Parameters:* **Instance(s) & Spacing**
    - *Instances:* **14**
    - *Spacing:* **3mm**
    - *Reference element:* **yz plane**
    - Select **Keep specifications**.

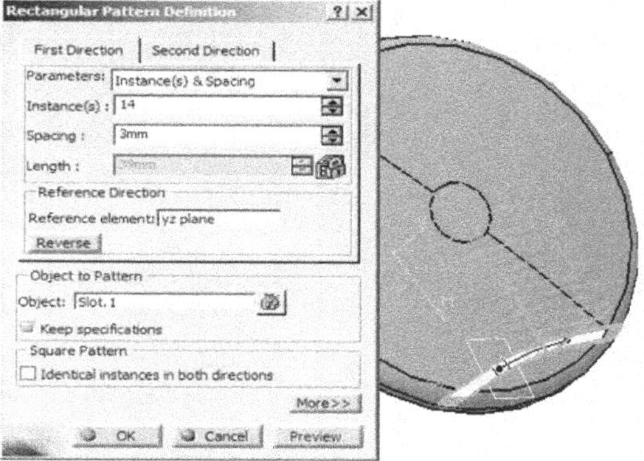

Figure 4–80

2. Click **OK** to complete the Pattern feature.

3. Close the warning dialog box.

4. Hide the Profile Plane, Vent Profile, and Center Curve. The completed model displays as shown in Figure 4–81.

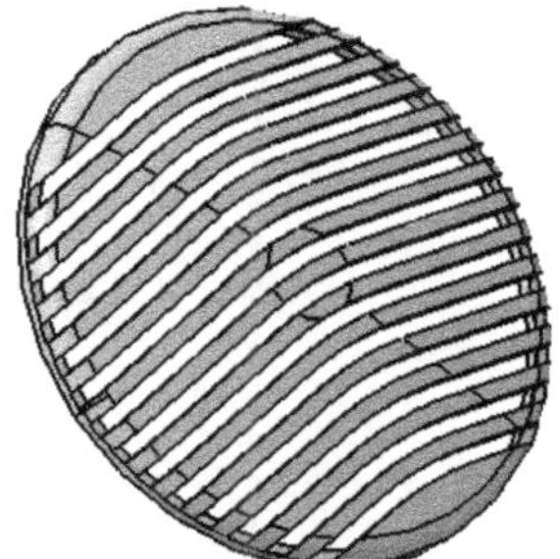

Figure 4–81

5. Save and close the model.

Practice 4e Turbine Wheel

Practice Objective

- Create a Rib feature using a Reference Surface

In this practice, you will create a Rib feature using a reference surface. The reference surface is used to achieve the complex airfoil geometry of the turbine compressor blades. You will then pattern the Rib. The completed model display as shown in Figure 4–82.

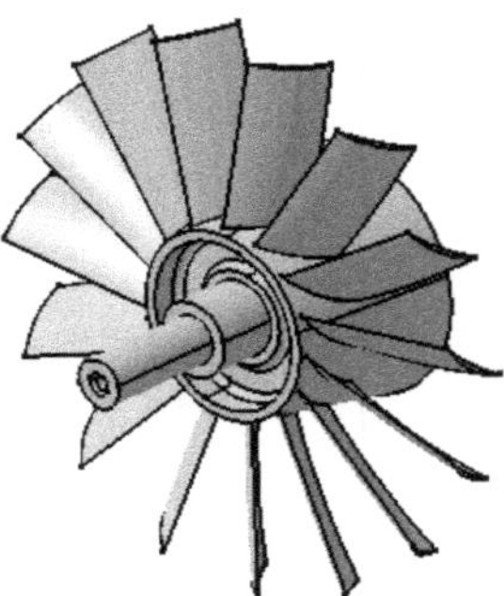

Figure 4–82

Task 1 - Open the part.

1. Open **1stStage.CATPart** in the *Turbine* directory. The model displays as shown in Figure 4–83.

Figure 4–83

2. Note the following features in the specification tree, as shown in Figure 4–84:

- **Blade Profile** sketch in the PartBody
- **Lead Edge** spline curve in the Geometrical Set
- **Trail Edge** spline curve in the Geometrical Set

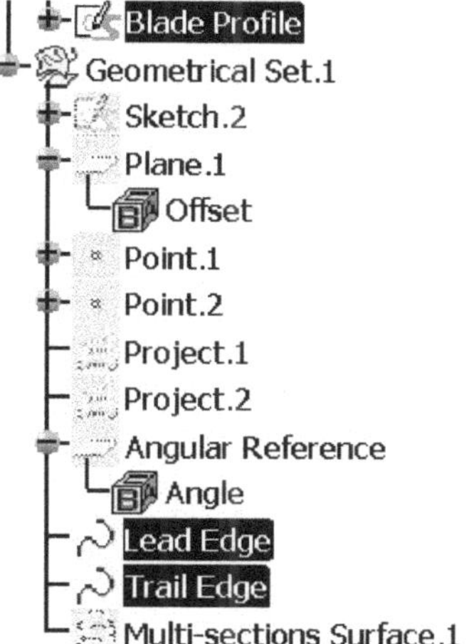

Figure 4–84

Task 2 - Create a Rib feature.

1. Create a Rib by selecting the **Blade Profile** feature as the *Rib Profile* and the **Lead Edge** feature as the *Rib Center curve*, as shown in Figure 4–85.

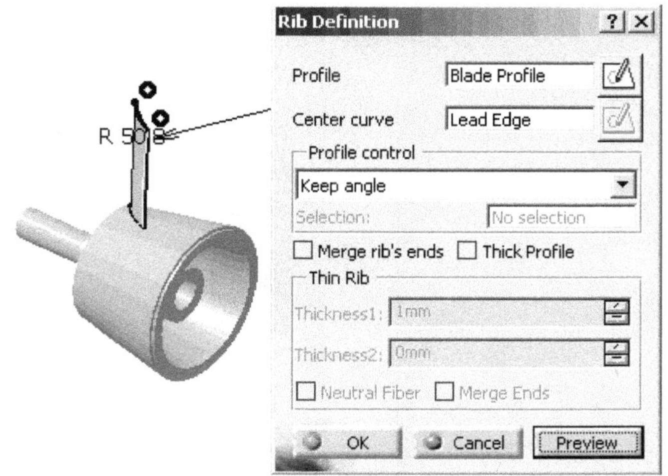

Figure 4–85

2. Keep the default **Keep angle** option selected as the **Profile control** option. This setting will be temporary. You will later modify the Profile control to **Ref Surf** to compare the resultant geometry.

3. Click **OK** to complete the Rib feature.

4. Zoom in on the area shown in Figure 4–86.

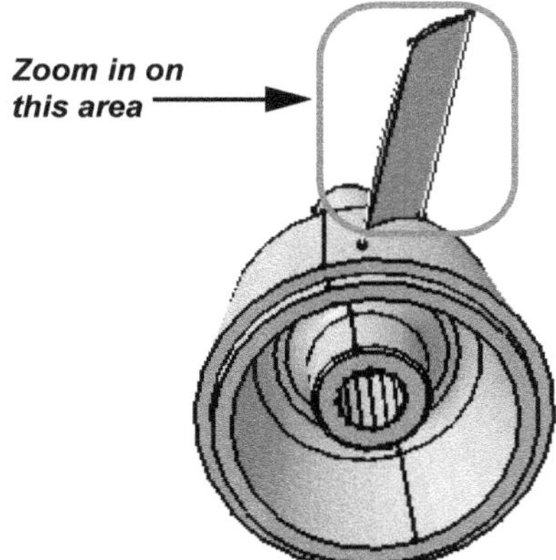
Zoom in on
this area

Figure 4–86

5. Show **Multi-sections Surface.1** under Geometrical Set in the specification tree. The Surface feature displays as shown in Figure 4–87.

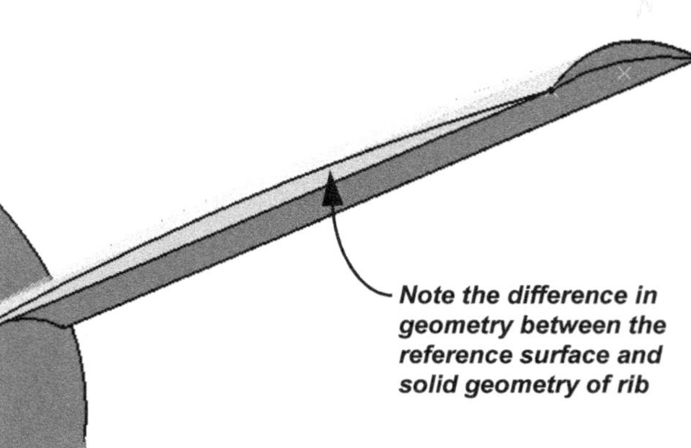
Note the difference in
geometry between the
reference surface and
solid geometry of rib

Figure 4–87

Task 3 - Redefine the Rib feature.

1. In the specification tree, double-click on **Rib.1** to redefine the **Profile control** option.
2. In the Profile control drop-down list, select **Reference surface**.
3. In the Geometrical Set, select the **Multi-sections Surface.1** feature, as shown in Figure 4–88.

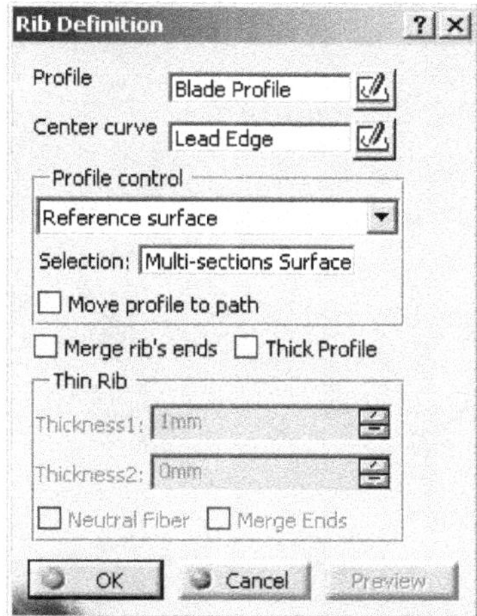

Figure 4–88

4. Click **OK** to complete the Rib feature. The resulting geometry is modified to follow the reference surface shape, as shown in Figure 4–89.

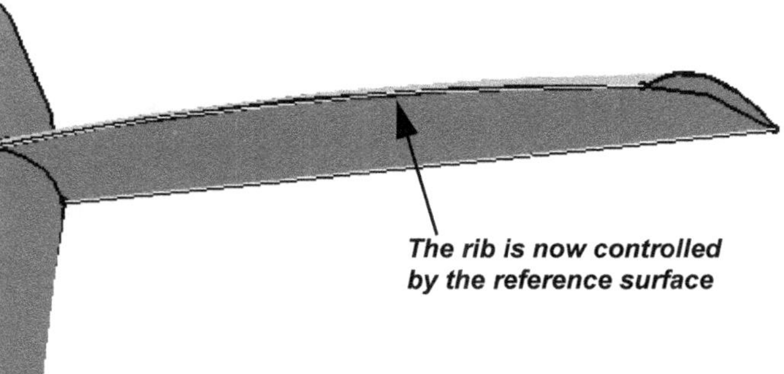

Figure 4–89

Task 4 - Pattern the Rib feature.

1. In the specification tree, select the **Rib.1** feature.

2. In the Transformation Features toolbar, click (Circular Pattern) to create a circular pattern of the blade.

3. Define the circular pattern as shown in Figure 4–90.

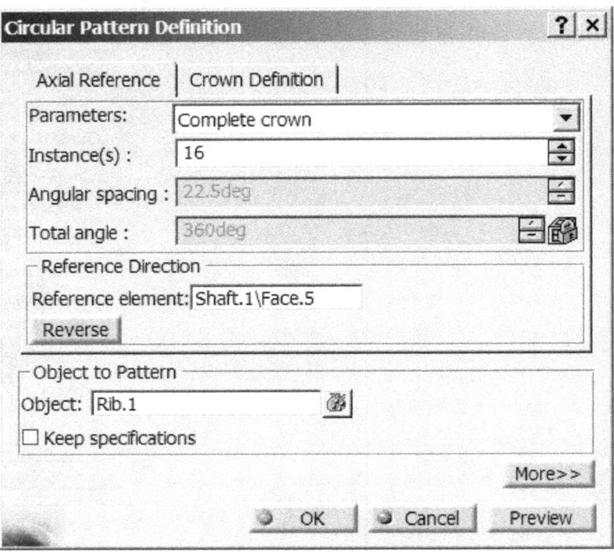

Figure 4–90

4. For the Reference Direction, select the surface shown in Figure 4–91.

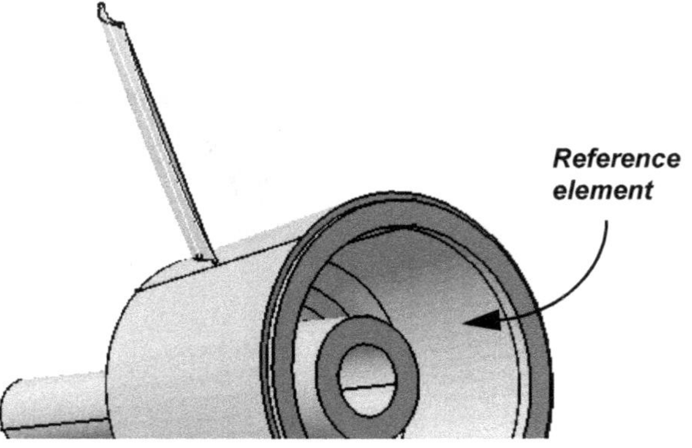

Figure 4–91

5. Click **OK** to complete the Rib feature.
6. Hide the Reference Surface feature (Multi-sections **Surface.1**) in the Geometrical set. The completed model displays as shown Figure 4–92.

Figure 4–92

7. Save and close the model.

Practice 4f Hammer Head

Practice Objectives

- Create Multi-sections Solid
- Create a Rib using pulling direction

In this practice, you will create the head of a hammer. The Base feature will be a Multi-sections Solid. The **claw** geometry is created using a Rib with pulling direction profile control and the hammer geometry is created using a Multi-sections Solid. The completed model displays as shown in Figure 4–93.

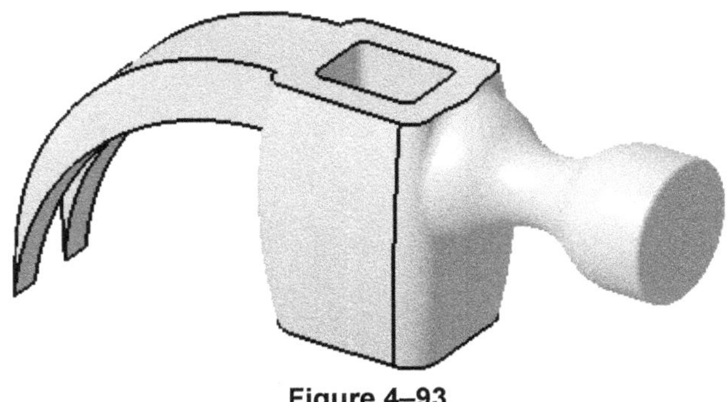

Figure 4–93

Task 1 - Open the part.

1. Open **HammerHead.CATPart**, as shown in Figure 4–94.

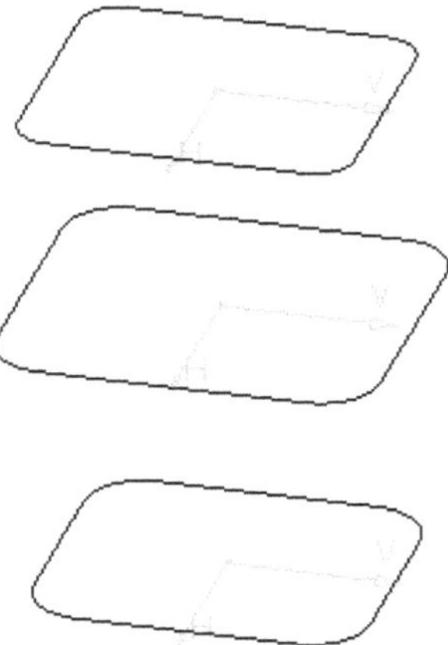

Figure 4–94

2. Click (Multi-sections Solid). Define the Multi-sections Solid feature by selecting the following sketches, as shown in Figure 4–95:

- **Sketch.1**
- **Sketch.2**
- **Sketch.3**

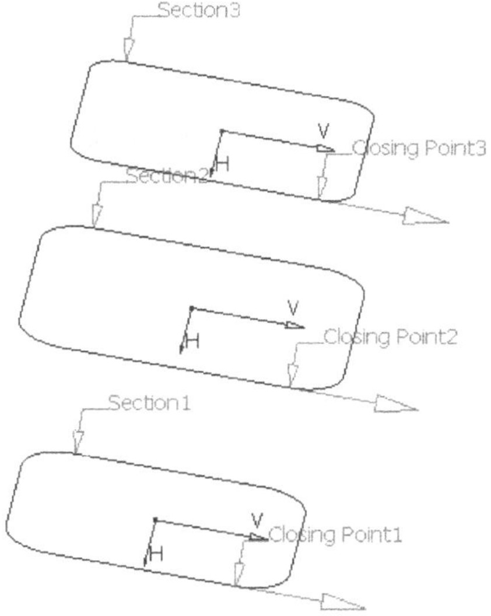

Figure 4–95

The completed Multi-sections Solid displays as shown in Figure 4–96.

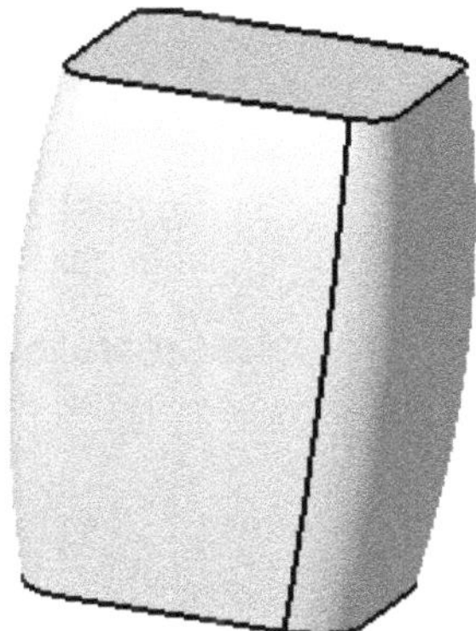

Figure 4–96

Task 2 - Create sketches for a Rib feature.

1. Click (Isometric View), if required.
2. Create a reference plane with the following parameters:
   - *Plane type:* **Through two lines**
   - *Line 1:* (as shown in Figure 4–97)
   - *Line 2:* (as shown in Figure 4–97)

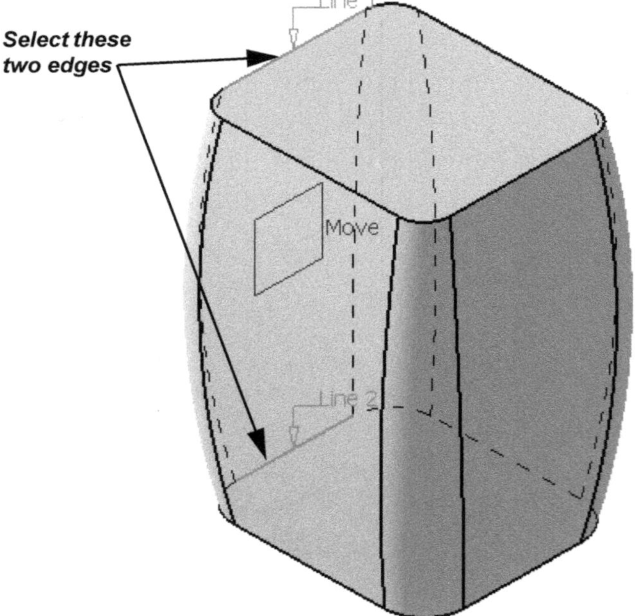

Figure 4–97

3. Select the reference plane that you have just created and activate the Sketcher workbench.
4. Create the sketch shown in Figure 4–98. Trim the projections with the sketched line.

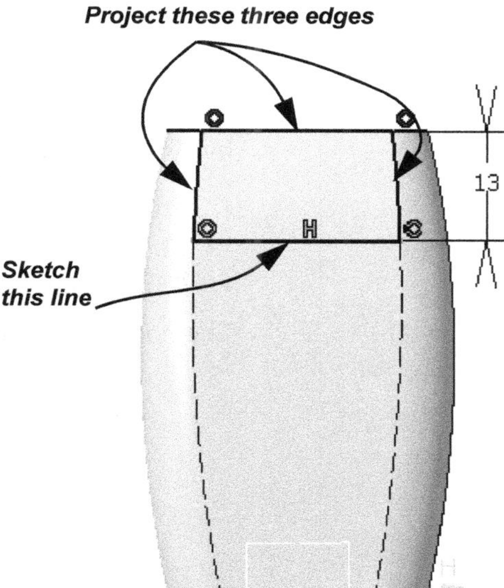

Figure 4–98

Design Considerations

The projected edges help capture the design intent of this feature. Your intent is to ensure that the claw uses the same outline as the Base feature. This also builds in associativity. If the Base feature changes in size, the claw profile will update with the changes.

5. Create a sketch shown in Figure 4–99, using the yz plane for the sketching plane.

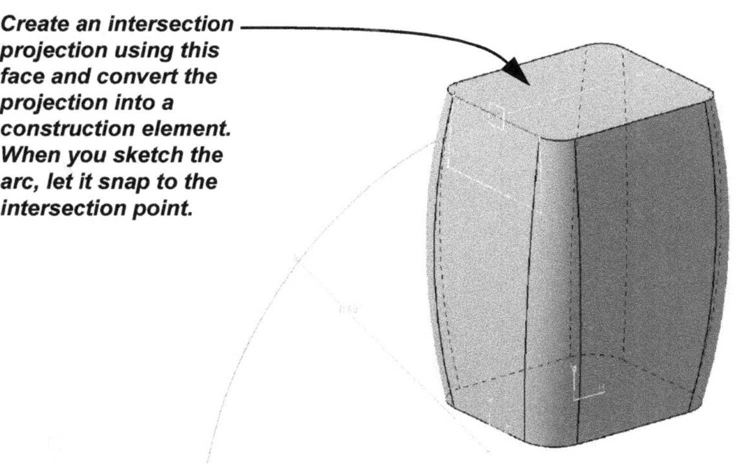

Create an intersection projection using this face and convert the projection into a construction element. When you sketch the arc, let it snap to the intersection point.

Figure 4–99

Task 3 - Create a Rib feature.

1. Click (Rib). Define the Rib feature by selecting the following sketches:
   - *Profile:* **Sketch.4**
   - *Center curve:* **Sketch.5**
   - *Profile control:* Keep angle

   The completed Rib displays as shown in Figure 4–100.

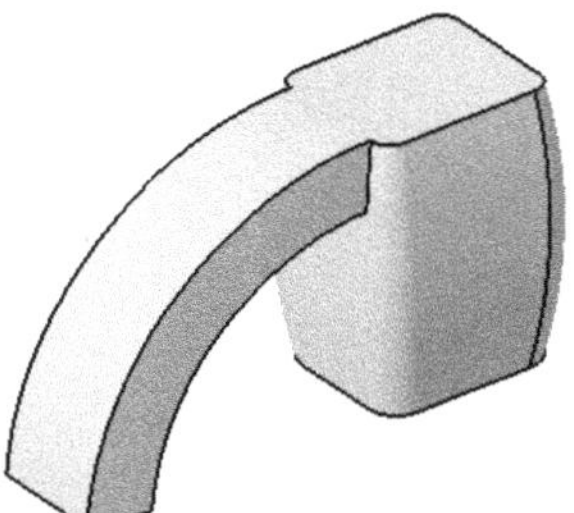

Figure 4–100

1. Edit the Rib feature and make the following change:
   - *Profile control:* **Pulling direction**
   - *Selection:* Select the surface shown in Figure 4–101.

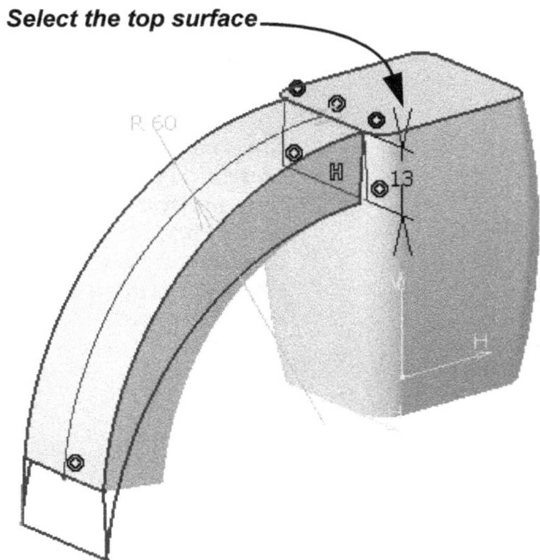
Select the top surface
13

Figure 4–101

2. Complete the Rib feature.

You might need to show ***Geometrical Set.1*** *to display the reference plane.*

Task 4 - Create a Pocket.

1. Create a reference plane with the following parameters:
   - *Plane type:* Through two lines
   - *Line 1:* (as shown in Figure 4–102)
   - *Line 2:* (as shown in Figure 4–102)

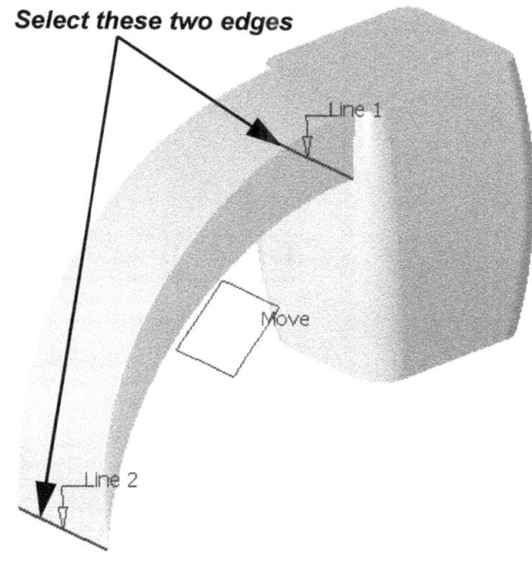

Figure 4–102

2. Use the reference plane from Step 1 as the sketching plane and create a Positioned Sketch.
3. Orient the Positioned Sketch and create the sketch, as shown in Figure 4–103.

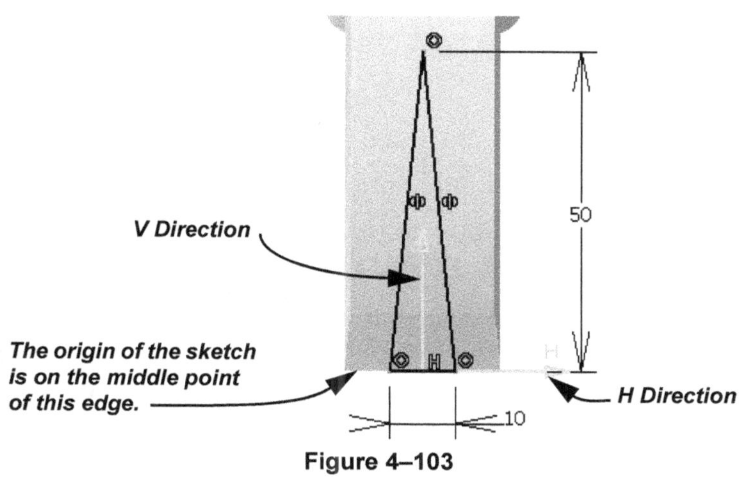

Figure 4–103

4. Create the Pocket shown in Figure 4–104. Select a depth option that best captures your intent.

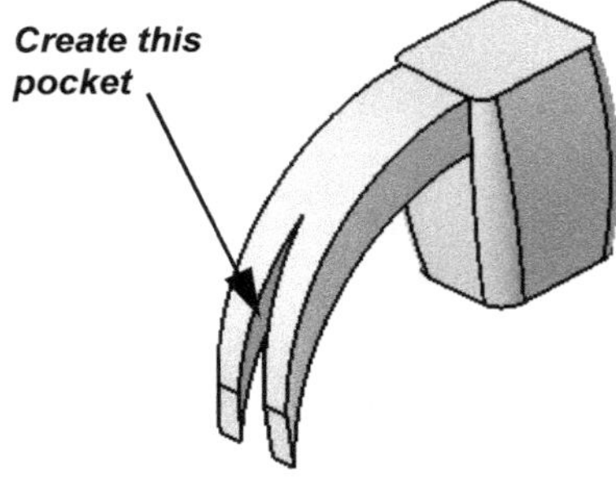

Figure 4–104

Task 5 - Create a Shaft feature.

1. Create the profile shown in Figure 4–105, using a positioned sketch on the yz plane.

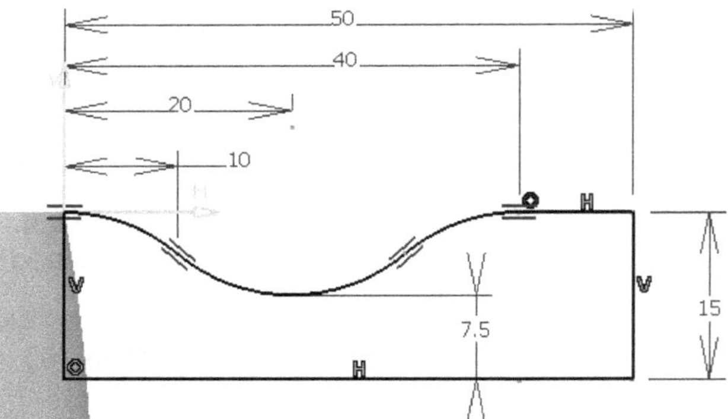

Figure 4–105

2. Create the Shaft shown in Figure 4–106.

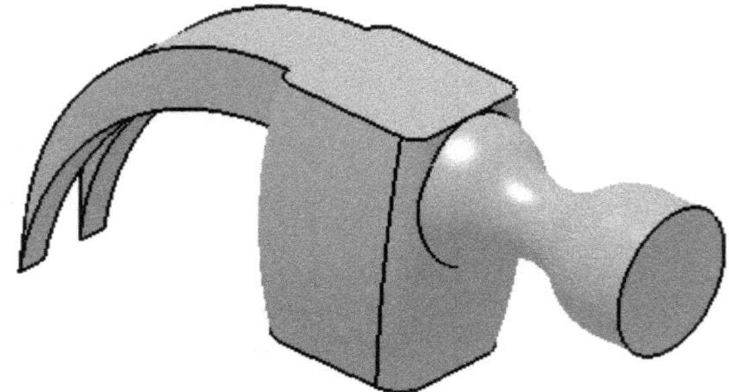

Figure 4–106

Task 6 - Create a Pocket feature.

1. Create the sketch shown in Figure 4–107.

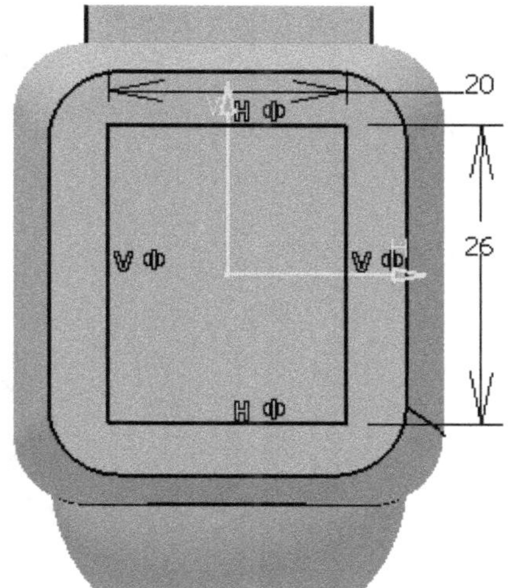

Figure 4–107

2. Create the pocket shown in Figure 4–108.

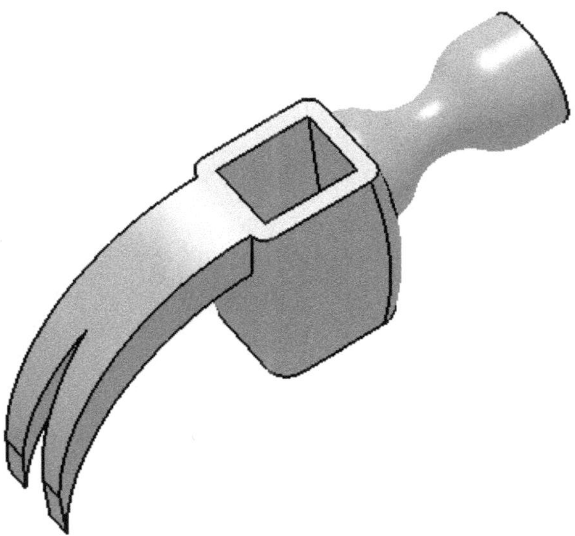

Figure 4–108

Task 7 - Create Dress-up features.

1. Add draft to the Pocket surfaces.
   - *Angle:* **2**
   - *Face(s) to draft:* (the four surfaces of the Pocket)
   - *Neutral Element:* (surface shown in Figure 4–109)

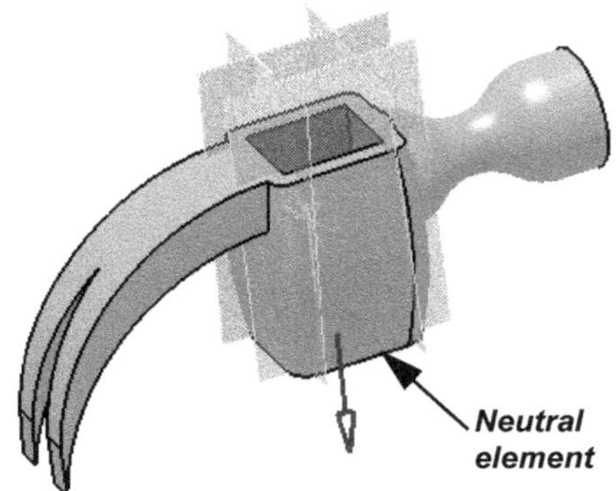

Figure 4–109

2. Create the Fillets shown in Figure 4–110.

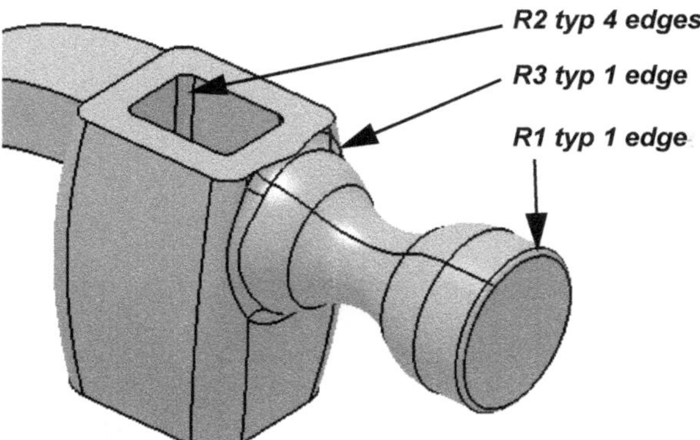

Figure 4–110

3. Save the model and close the file.

Practice 4g

Transition Pipe

Practice Objectives

- Create a Multi-sections Solid.
- Creating output elements.

In this practice, you will create a transition pipe. This transition pipe will be used to connect two different types of pipes. The completed model displays as shown in Figure 4–111.

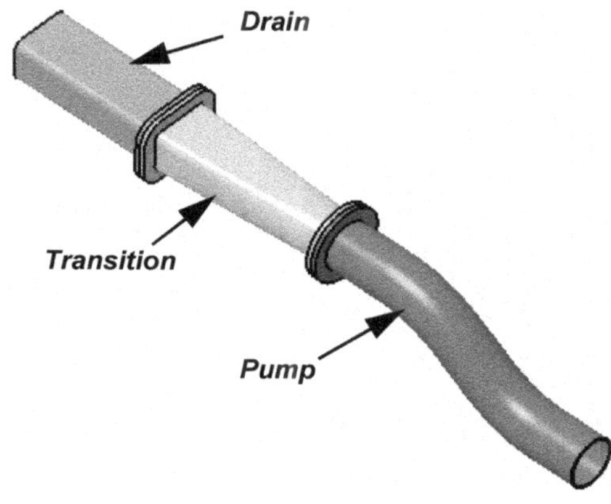

Figure 4–111

Task 1 - Open the assembly and part.

1. Open **The_Pipes.CATProduct** and **Transition_Pipe.CATPart** from the *Pipe* folder. The models display as shown in Figure 4–112 and Figure 4–113. The sections for the connector pipe have already been created.

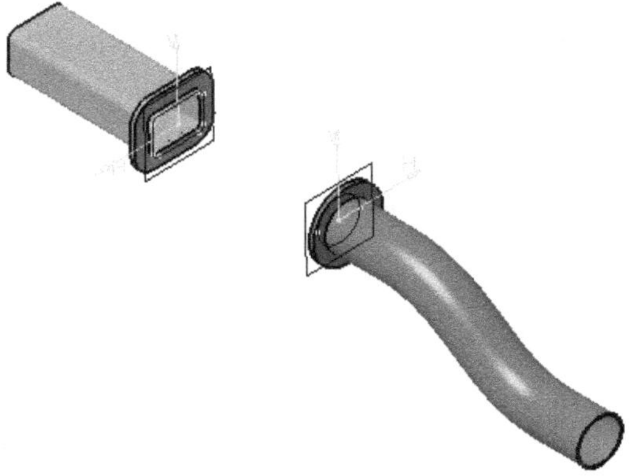

Figure 4–112

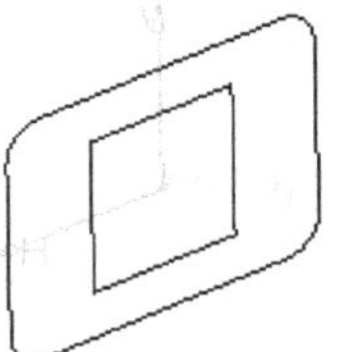

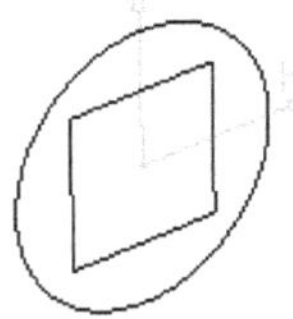

Figure 4–113

Task 2 - Create outputs.

In this task, you will create output points to use as coupling points for the Multi-sections Solid creation. Each section will have eight coupling points to create eight coupling curves.

1. In the menu bar, select **Window>Transition_Pipe.CATPart**.
2. In the specification tree, double-click on Sketch.1 to enter the sketch.
3. In the Tools toolbar, double-click on (Output feature) and select the vertices shown in Figure 4–114.

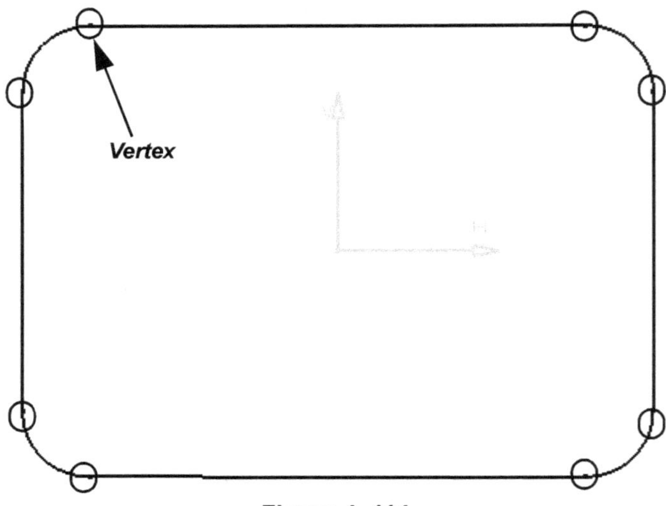

Figure 4–114

4. Exit the Sketcher workbench.
5. In the specification tree, double-click on **Sketch.2** to enter the sketch.
6. Create four construction lines, as shown in Figure 4–115.
7. Toggle off the Construction mode.
8. Highlight the four construction lines and click (Intersection Point), then select the circle to create the points shown in Figure 4–115.

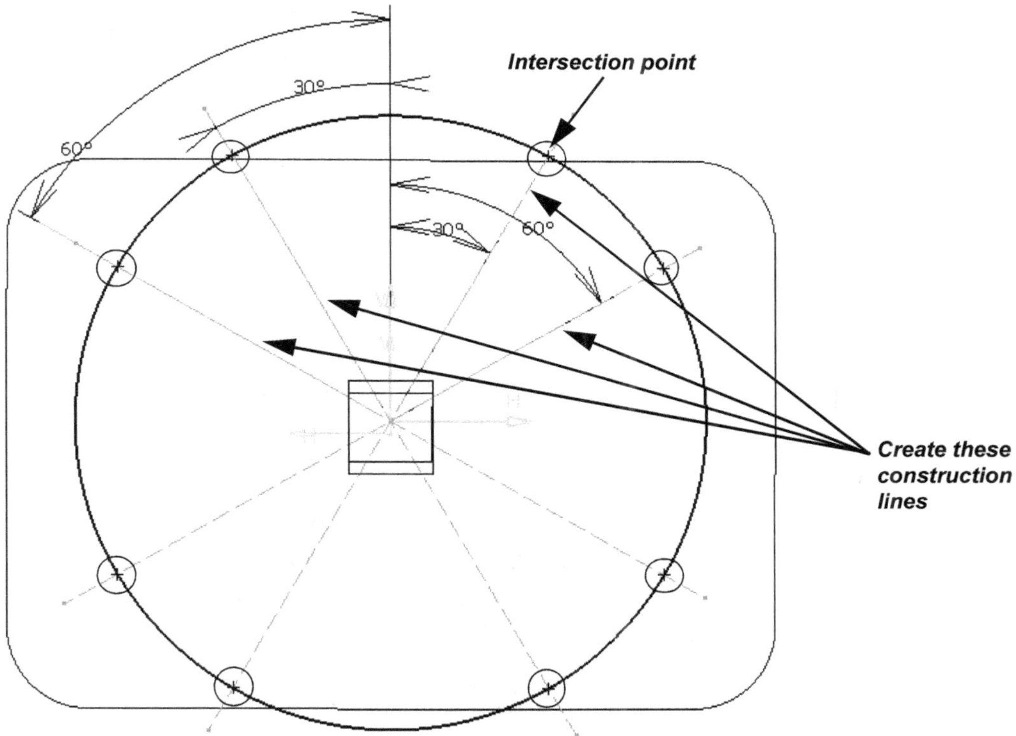

Figure 4–115

9. In the Tools toolbar, double-click on (Output feature) and select the eight intersection points that you just created.
10. Exit the Sketcher workbench.

Task 3 - Create a Multi-sections Solid.

In this task, you will create a Multi-sections Solid using coupling curves. The outputs that you created in the previous task will be used as the coupling points to define the transition between the two sections. This enables you to control the shape of the Multi-sections Solid. If you are not satisfied with the results, you can modify the shape of the Multi-sections Solid by editing the position of the output points.

1. Click (Multi-sections Solid). Select the rectangular shaped profile, and then select the circular profile from the display. The model displays as shown in Figure 4–116.

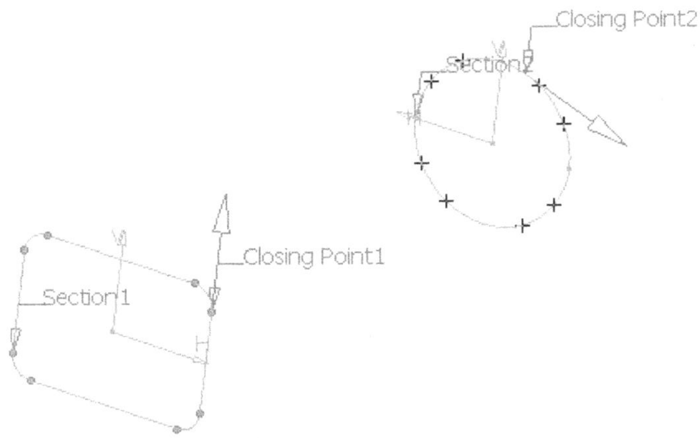

Figure 4–116

2. If required, invert the direction for **Closing Point2** by selecting the direction arrow. The model displays as shown in Figure 4–117.

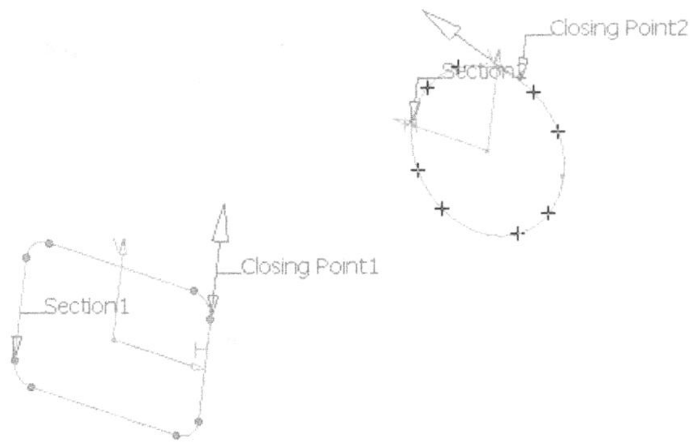

Figure 4–117

3. Select the *Coupling* tab.

4. In the Sections coupling drop-down list, select the **Ratio coupling** option.

5. Preview the Multi-sections Solid. The model displays as shown in Figure 4–118. Note that the Multi-sections Solid has a twisted shape. This is not the correct result.

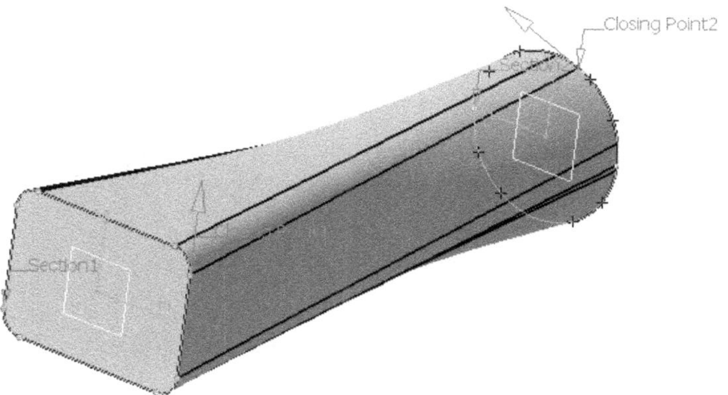

Figure 4–118

6. In the Multi-sections Solid Definitions dialog box, click **Cancel**.

7. Click (Multi-sections Solid). Select the rectangular shaped profile and then select the circular profile.

8. Right-click on the **Closing Point2** and select **Replace**, as shown in Figure 4–119.

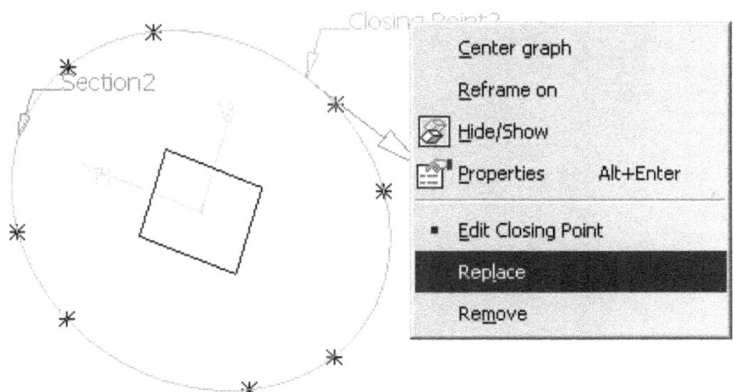

Figure 4–119

9. Select the coupling point and ensure that the closing point directions are pointing in the same direction. The model displays as shown in Figure 4–120.

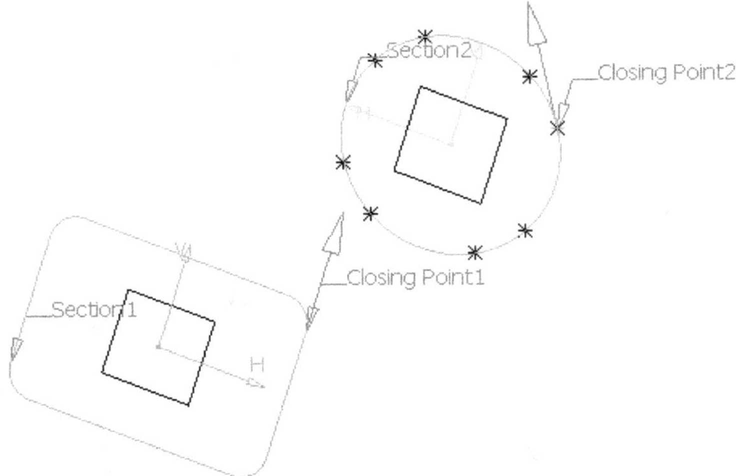

Figure 4–120

10. Select the *Coupling* tab and select in the *Coupling* area as shown in Figure 4–121.

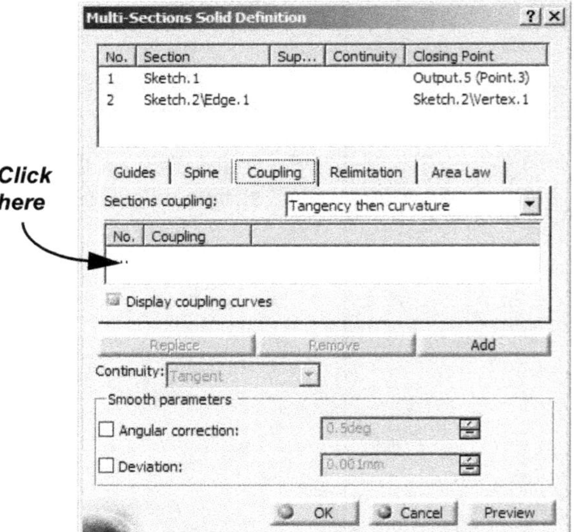

Figure 4–121

11. Select the point shown in Figure 4–122.

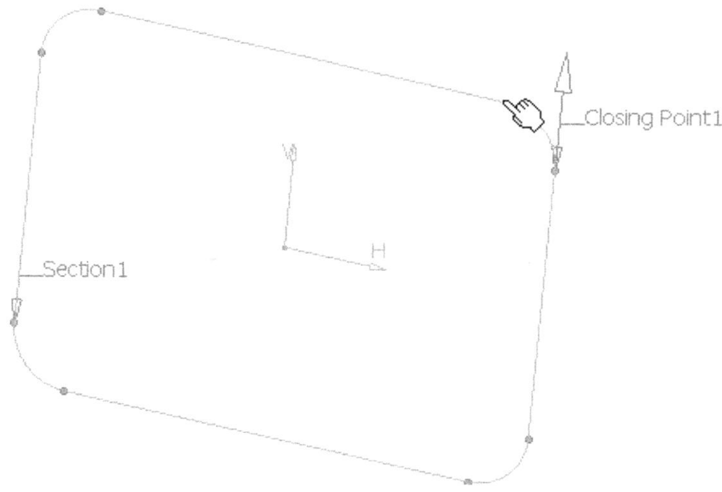

Figure 4–122

The Coupling : Coupling1 dialog box opens as Figure 4–123.

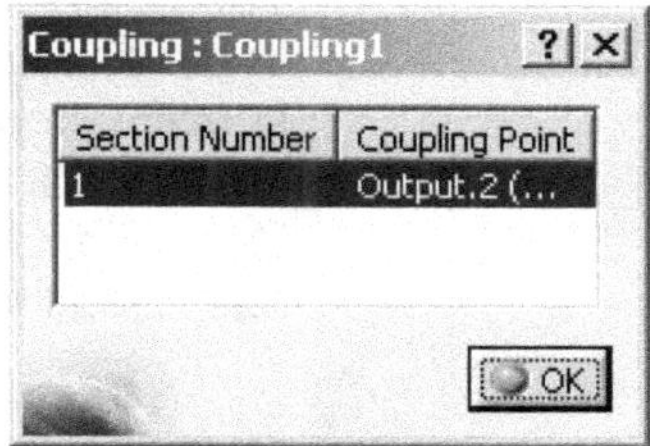

Figure 4–123

12. Select the point shown in Figure 4–124.

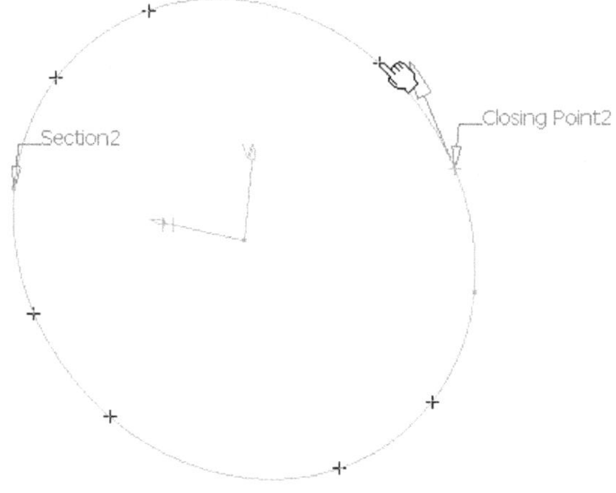

Figure 4–124

The model displays as shown in Figure 4–125.

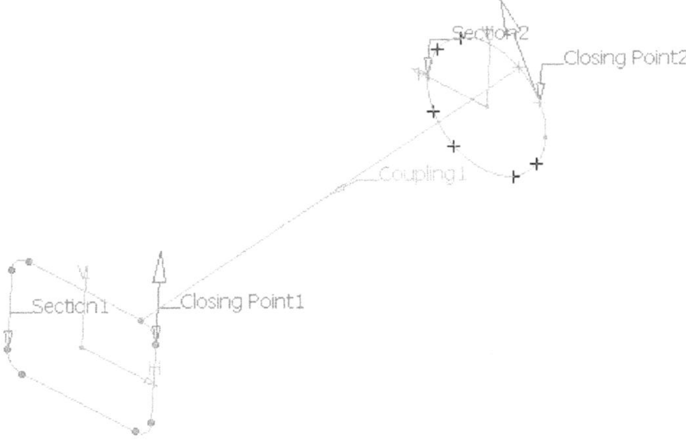

Figure 4–125

13. Create seven more coupling curves using the output points. The model displays as shown in Figure 4–126.

    The points located under the closing points must be selected in the specification tree. To locate the correct point in the specification tree, expand the **Sketch>>Outputs** branches for **Sketch.1** and **Sketch.2**. Move the cursor over the outputs to highlight the points on the model. Once the correct point has been located, select it to add it to the coupling.

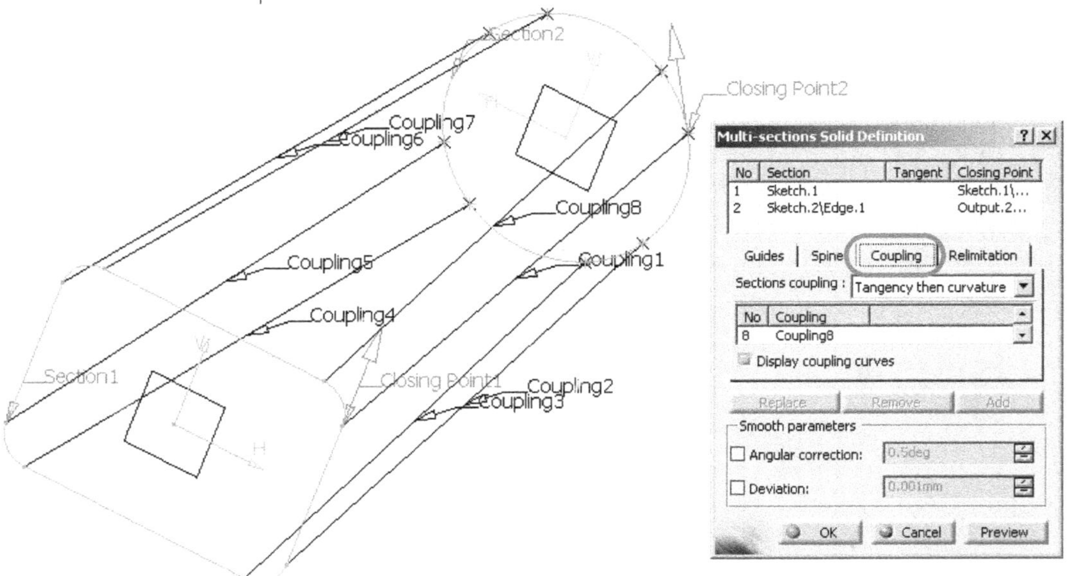

Figure 4–126

14. Click **OK** to complete the feature. The model displays as shown in Figure 4–127.

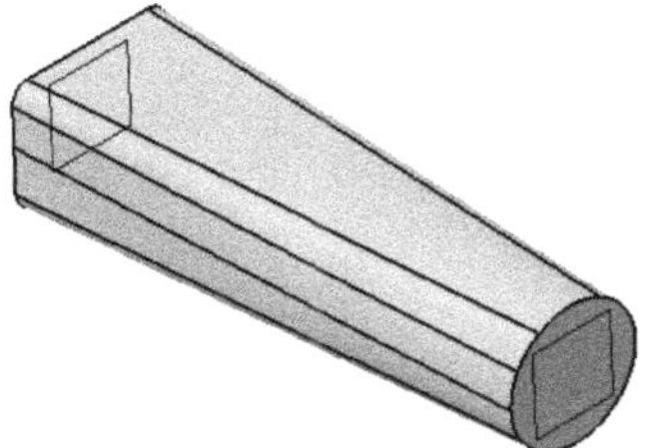

Figure 4–127

15. Hide the eight output points from both **Sketch.1** and **Sketch.2**.

Task 4 - Create a Shell feature.

1. In the Dress-Up Features toolbar, click (Shell).
2. Make the selections shown in Figure 4–128.

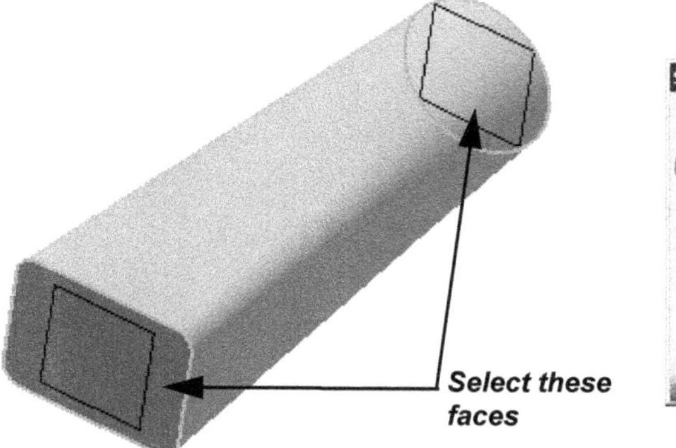

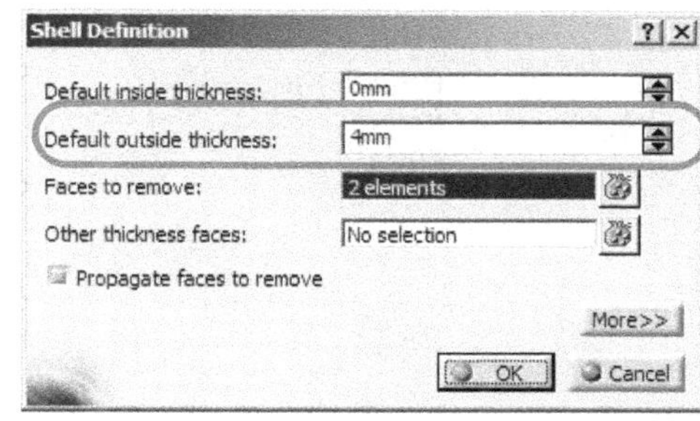

Figure 4–128

3. Click **OK** to complete the feature. The model displays as shown in Figure 4–129.

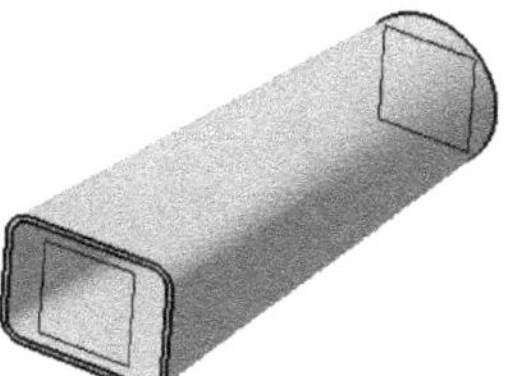

Figure 4–129

Task 5 - Create flange features.

In this task, you will create the flanges to connect the pipes.

1. In the specification tree or model, select **Plane.1** and enter the Sketcher workbench, as shown in Figure 4–130.

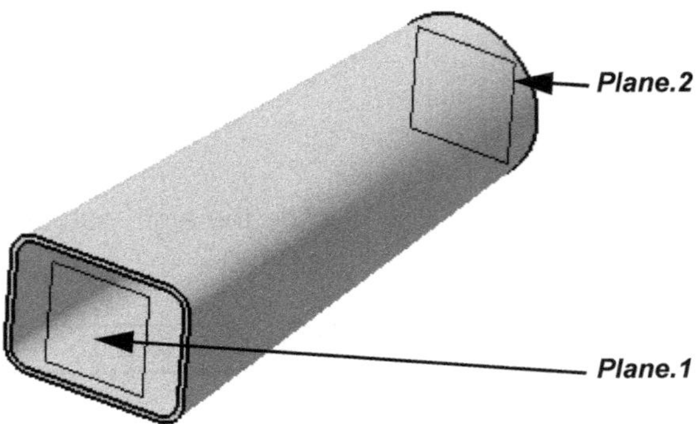

Figure 4–130

2. Sketch the profile shown in Figure 4–131.

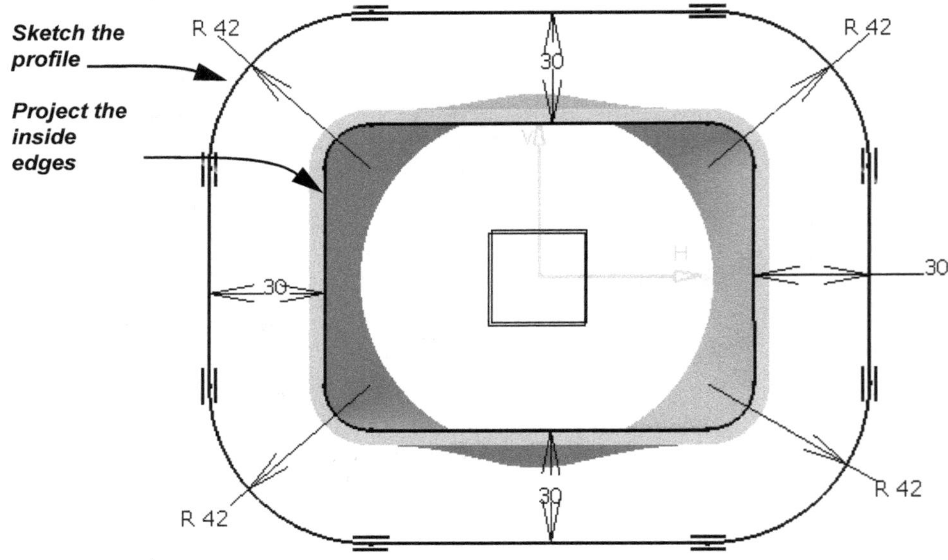

Figure 4–131

3. Highlight the sketch that you just created and click  (Pad).

4. Make the following selections, as shown in Figure 4–132:
    - *Type:* **Dimension**
    - *Length:* **10mm**

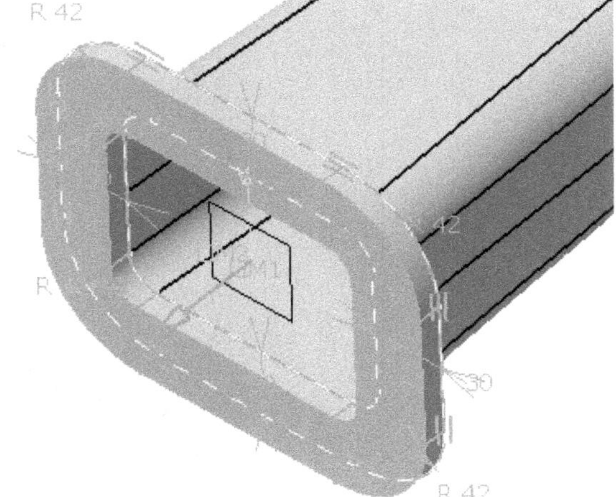

Figure 4–132

5. Click **OK** to complete the feature. The model displays as shown in Figure 4–133.

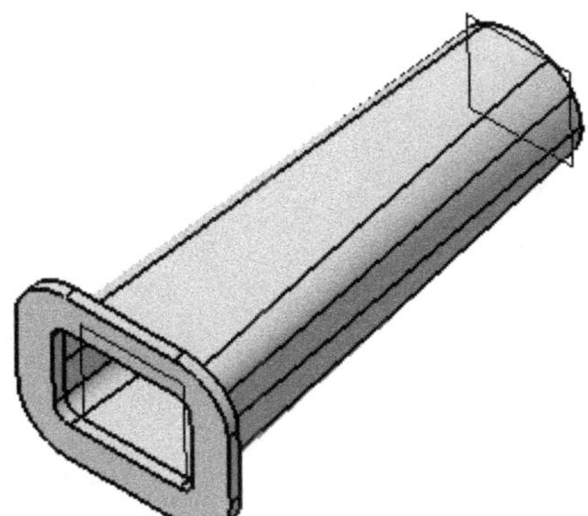

Figure 4–133

6. In the specification tree or model, select **Plane.2** and enter the Sketcher workbench.

7. Sketch the profile shown in Figure 4–134.

Figure 4–134

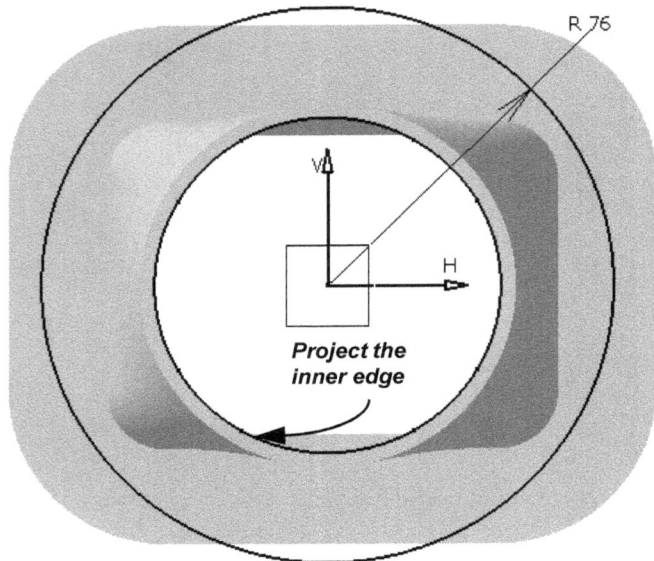

8. Highlight the sketch that you just created and click (Pad).

9. Make the following selections, as shown in Figure 4–135:

   - *Type:* **Dimension**
   - *Length:* **10mm**

Figure 4–135

10. Click **OK** to complete the feature. The model displays as shown in Figure 4–136.

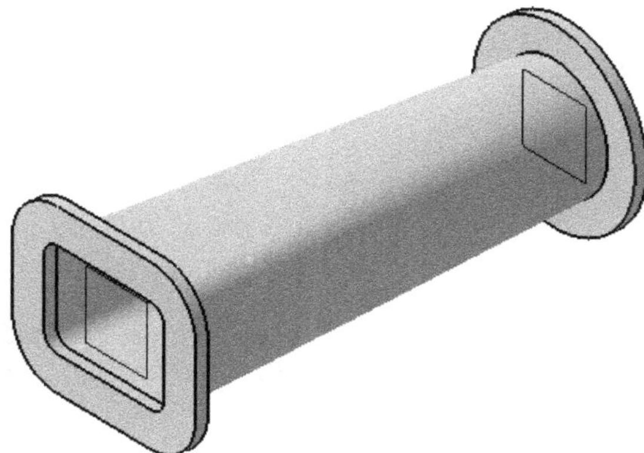

Figure 4–136

11. In the menu bar, select **Window>The_Pipes.CATProduct**. The model displays as shown in Figure 4–137.

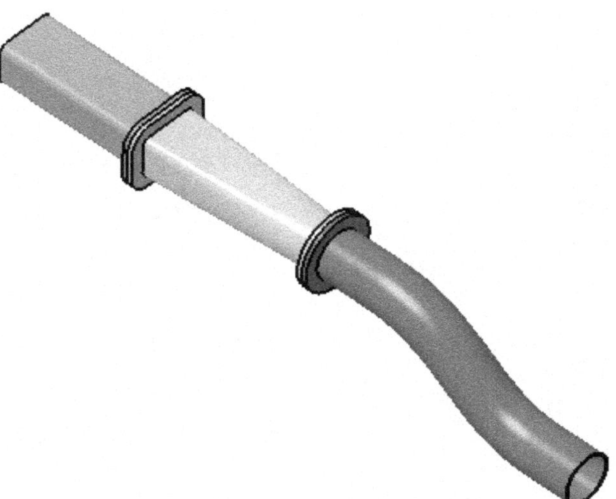

Figure 4–137

12. Save and close the files.

Chapter Review Questions

1. A solid created from the intersection of two projected profiles is referred to as a _______ feature.
   a. Solid Intersect
   b. Solid Join
   c. Solid Combine
   d. Solid Merge
2. When creating a solid feature from the intersection of two projected profiles, the profiles can only be projected perpendicular to the their respective profile planes.
   a. True
   b. False
3. A Multi-sections solid can contain a maximum of two sections.
   a. True
   b. False
4. To avoid twisting the geometry in a Multi-sections solid feature, you must ensure that the _____ line up.
   a. Closing Points
   b. Starting Points
   c. End Points
   d. Coupling Points
5. In a Multi-sections solid feature, a Spine curve defines the path that the feature must follow as it transitions between sections.
   a. True
   b. False

6. In a Multi-sections solid feature, you use _______ to extend the feature beyond the first or last section, up to the shortest guide curve.

   a. **Trim**
   b. **Extend**
   c. **Relimitation**
   d. **Crop**

7. For Shell features, what does the **Propagate faces to remove** option do?

   a. Creates the shell by removing all of the selected faces.
   b. Creates the shell by removing only the internal faces.
   c. Creates the shell by removing all of the curved surfaces.
   d. Creates the shell by removing all of the surfaces with edges that are tangent continuous to the selected surface.

Wireframe Lines and Curves

In this chapter, only wireframe elements that are commonly used during complex, solid-feature creation are discussed.

Learning Objectives in this Chapter

- Understand where to access the Wireframe tools.
- Create points, lines, and planes for Wireframe geometry.
- Create splines for use in creating complex wireframe shapes.
- Learn how a Polyline differs from a Spline.
- Create a Polyline and a Helix Curve.
- Learn how to use a Combine element to create a curve that lies at the intersection of the projection of two curves.
- Understand how to project a curve onto a non-planar support.
- Create a curve at the intersection of two entities.
- Learn how to join two or more curves or surfaces so they can be treated as single entities.
- Extract new surface elements by copying surface or solid faces.
- Lean how to manage situations in which more than one possible solution exists for feature creation.

5.1 Wireframe Elements

Wireframe elements are accessed in the Wireframe toolbar in the Generative Shape Design workbench. Figure 5–1 shows the Wireframe toolbar icons. The Generative Shape Design workbench has more tools for creating wireframes, as compared to the Part Design workbench. You can refer to the example shown in Figure 5–1 at any time if you need to locate a specific tool.

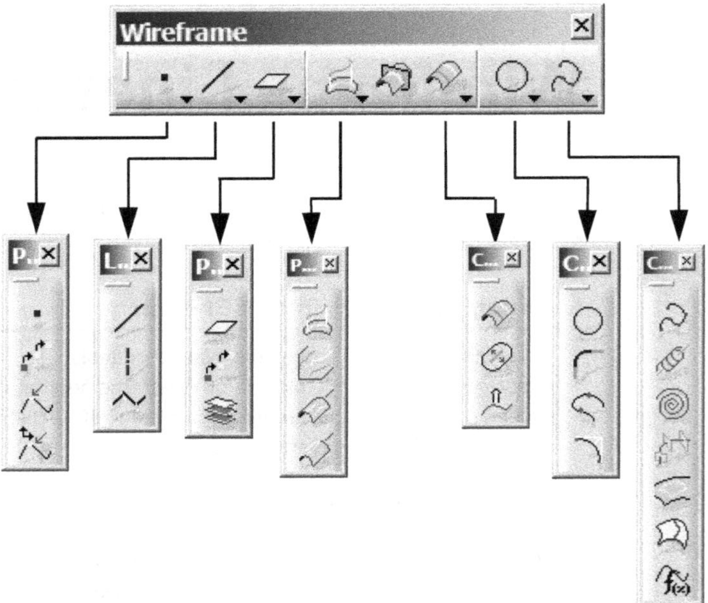

Figure 5–1

5.2 Points, Lines, and Planes

Point, Line, and Plane features are normally used as references that facilitate the creation of other elements.

Points

Points are geometry markers located in 3D space. They can be the building blocks of solid geometry or surface geometry, but are often used to create other wireframe elements.

Click (Point) in the Wireframe toolbar. The Point Definition dialog box opens as shown in Figure 5–2. To create a single Point, select an option in the Point type drop-down list, and click **OK**.

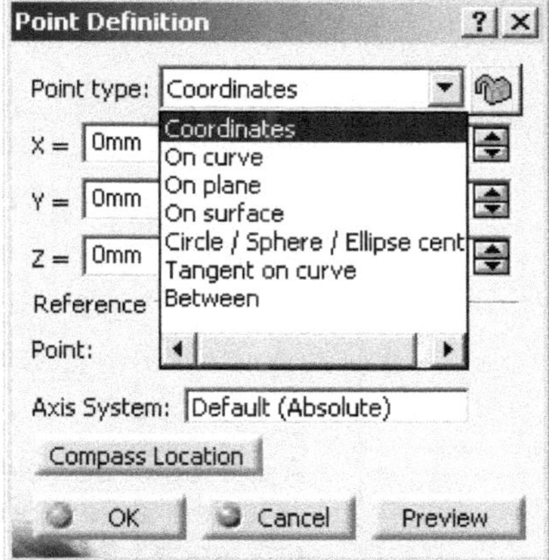

Figure 5–2

To create multiple Points along a Curve, Line, or Edge, click (Points and Planes Repetition). The Points & Planes Repetition dialog box opens as shown in Figure 5–3.

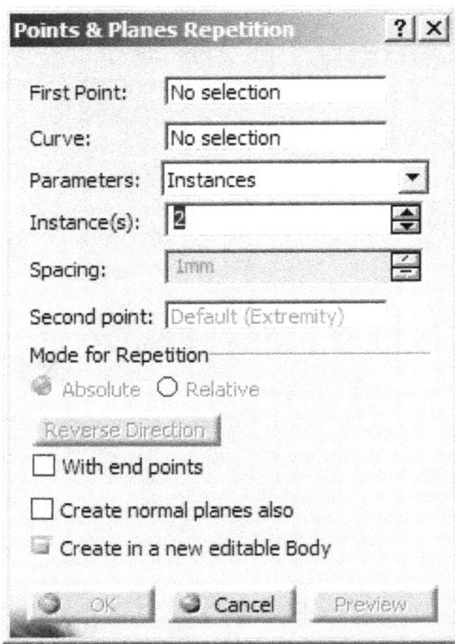

Figure 5–3

A point can be selected for the First Point, but If one is not selected, an endpoint of the Curve is used instead. The reference for the Curve can be an edge, line, or curve.

To obtain evenly-spaced points, select **Instances** in the Parameters drop-down list. Figure 5–4 shows five Points created using the **Instances** option.

Figure 5–4

To obtain Points spaced at a specific distance relative to each other, select **Instances and Spacing** in the Parameters drop-down list. The **Instances and Spacing** option is only available if you have selected a Point to define the start of the repetition. Figure 5–5 shows four Points spaced apart by **0.5 in** using the **Instances and Spacing** option.

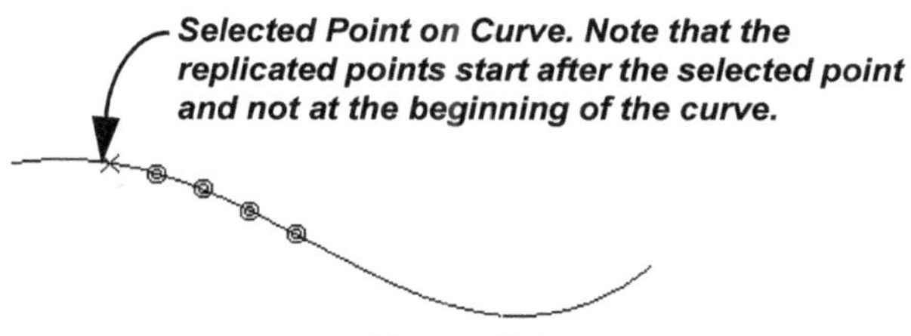

Selected Point on Curve. Note that the replicated points start after the selected point and not at the beginning of the curve.

Figure 5–5

Lines

You can use Lines as a reference to align two components in an assembly or as a reference to define a rotational plane in a part model. Click (Line) in the Wireframe toolbar. The Line Definition dialog box opens as shown in Figure 5–6. To create a Line feature, select an option in the Line type drop-down list.

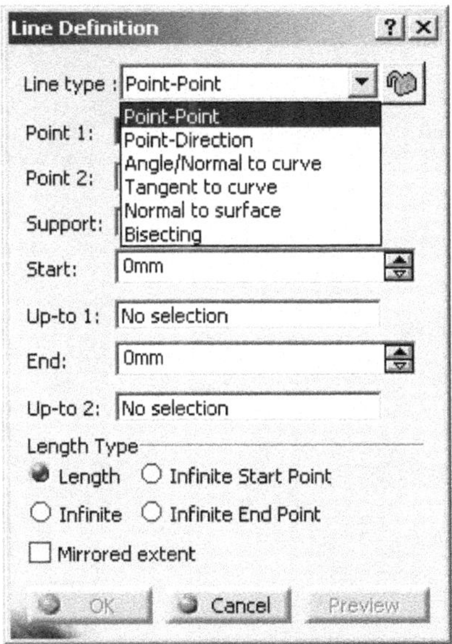

Figure 5–6

Planes

You can use Plane features as a placement and dimensional reference for all types of features. Click (Plane). The Plane Definition dialog box opens as shown in Figure 5–7. To create a Plane, select an option in the Plane type drop-down list.

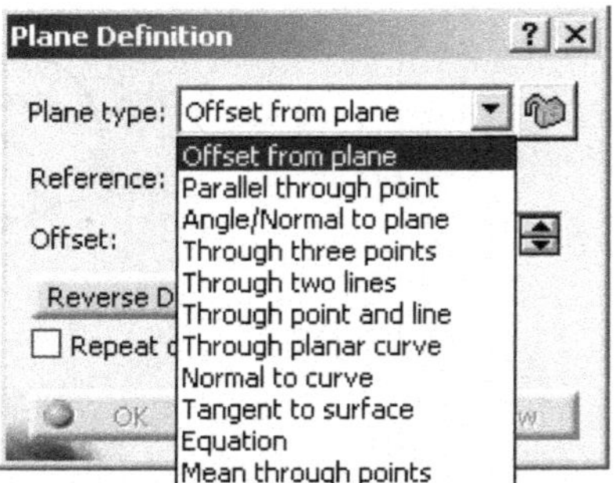

Figure 5–7

5.3 Creating Splines

Splines are curves that pass smoothly through two or more points. The selected points can be point elements or vertices of previous features, including sketched points. These points can be present before you initiate the creation of the Spline, or you can create them on the fly using the shortcut menu. Once the points have been selected, you can insert or replace additional points. You can create a spline as either 2D or 3D. Splines are great tools for creating complex wireframe shapes.

General Steps

Use the following general steps to create a Spline feature:

1. Start the creation of a Spline.
2. Select reference points.
3. Define Spline parameters.
4. Complete the feature.

Step 1 - Start the creation of a Spline.

Click (Spline). The Spline Definition dialog box opens as shown in Figure 5–8.

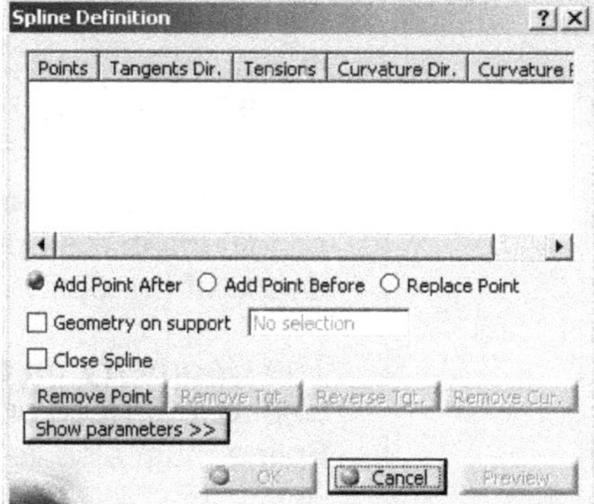

Figure 5–8

Step 2 - Select reference points.

Once you start the creation of the Spline, you can select reference points, end points, and vertices. Add Points to the Spline by selecting them in the specification tree or main window. You can use the options in the Spline Definition dialog box to perform operations on the current, highlighted Point. For example, you can rearrange the order of the Points, close the Spline, or remove a Point.

You can use the **Add Point After**, **Add Point Before**, and **Replace Point** options to control the position of the next selected Point. You can add Points before or after the current Point. You can also replace the current Point.

The **Close Spline** option automatically selects the last Point of the Spline using the first selected Point to close the Spline.

In the Spline Definition dialog box, you can click **Remove Point** to remove the current Point from the Spline. Figure 5–9 shows a Spline passing through five Points.

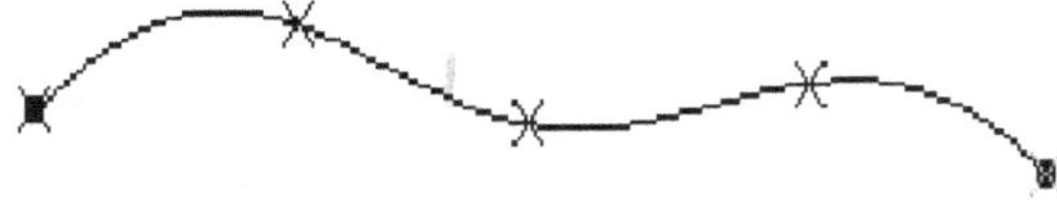

Figure 5–9

Step 3 - Define Spline parameters.

You can use the **Geometry on support** option and tangency conditions in the Spline Definition dialog box to further define the shape of the Spline.

The **Geometry on support** option forces the Spline to lie on the selected Surface or Plane. All of the Points selected for the Spline must also lie on the selected support.

Tangency can be defined for any Point specified in the Spline. To specify tangency or curvature conditions, click **Show parameters** in the Spline Definition dialog box and then select a Line, Plane, or Curve to which the Spline is going to be tangent at the selected point.

Tangency specification is not limited to end points.

The graphic at the top in Figure 5–10 shows a Spline created between two surfaces with no tangency constraints added. The lower graphic shows a Spline created between the same two surfaces with tangency constraints added at both ends of the Spline. The direction of tangency can be set as required.

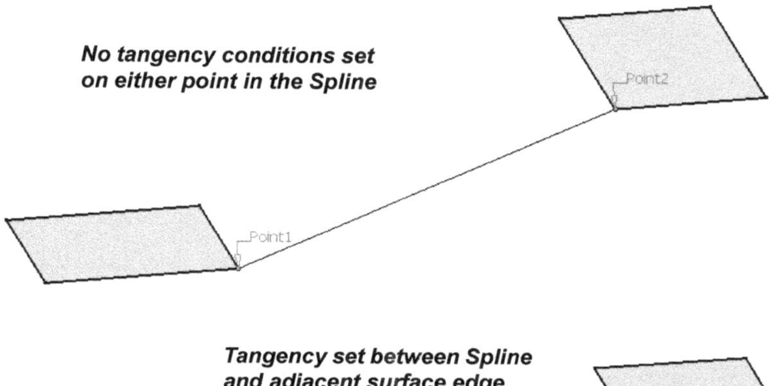

No tangency conditions set on either point in the Spline
Point2
Point1

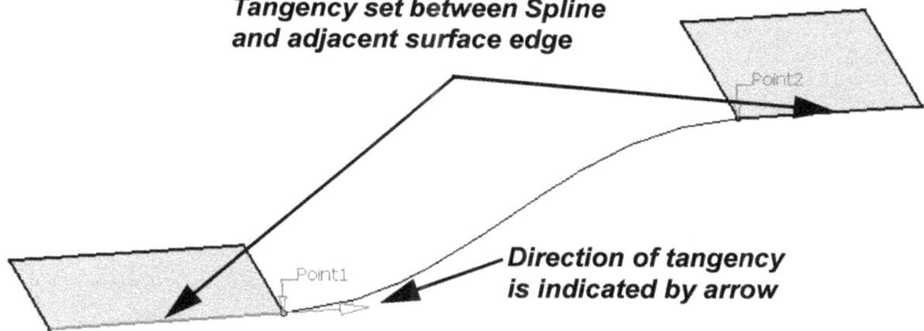

Tangency set between Spline and adjacent surface edge
Point2
Point1
Direction of tangency is indicated by arrow

Figure 5–10

Step 4 - Complete the feature.

In the Spline Definition dialog box, click **OK** to complete the feature.

5.4 Polyline

A Polyline is similar to a Spline, but connects the selected points using straight lines. The Polyline feature is defined by selecting points through which the curve passes. To control the shape of the curve, you can define a radius value at each point. To start creating a Polyline feature, click (Polyline). The Polyline Definition dialog box opens as shown in Figure 5–11.

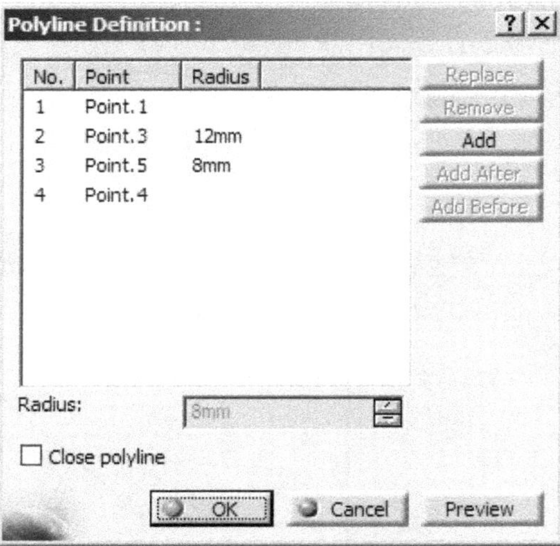

Figure 5–11

The Polyline shown on the left in Figure 5–12 is created using the default straight edges. When a radius is applied at Point 2 and 3 of the Polyline, it displays as shown on the right in Figure 5–12.

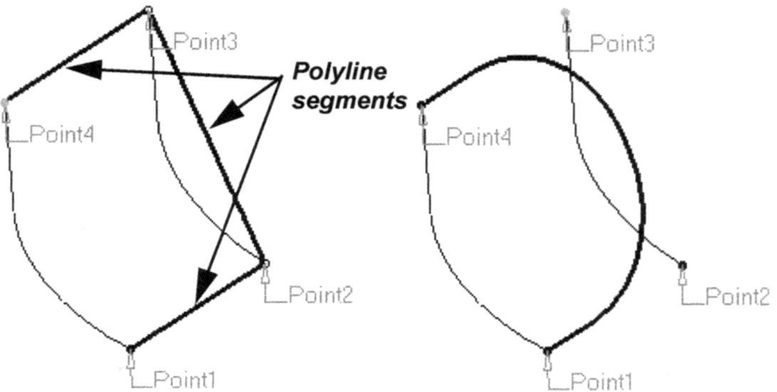

Figure 5–12

5.5 Helix Curve

To start creating a Helix Curve, click (Helix). The Helix Curve Definition dialog box opens as shown in Figure 5–13.

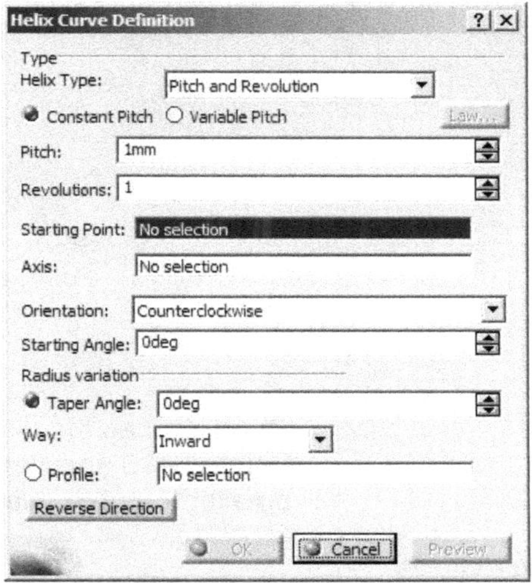

Figure 5–13

A helix is defined by three parameters: **Pitch**, **Revolution** and **Height**. You can create a helix by any two parameters. In the Helix Type drop-down list, select one of the following helix creation methods:

- **Pitch and Revolution**
- **Height and Pitch**
- **Height and Revolution**

Additionally, you must select either **Constant Pitch** or **Variable Pitch**. The **Variable Pitch** option is only available for the **Pitch** and **Revolution** type of helix. When the **Variable Pitch** option is selected, you can define the *Start* pitch value and the *End* pitch value.

A helix can be defined by selecting a starting point and an axis. The starting point defines the radius of the helix and the axis defines the center of the helix, as shown in Figure 5–14. Once specified, you can adjust the remaining parameters to achieve the required results.

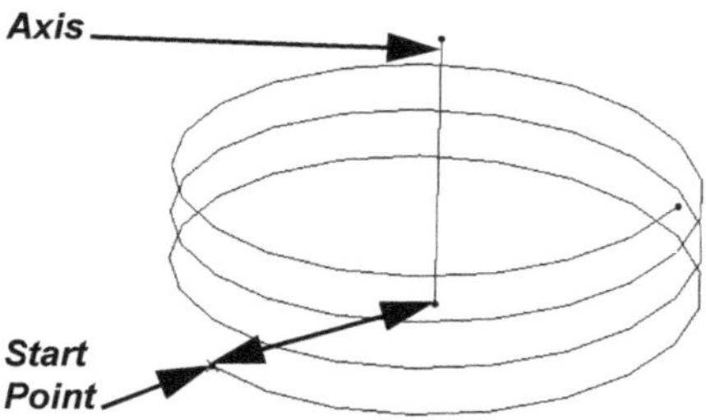

Distance defines radius

Figure 5–14

Pitch defines the distance between the Helix revolutions. In Figure 5–15, the Helix on the left was created with a pitch smaller than the one on the right.

*You can define the pitch using a graph by clicking **Law**.*

Figure 5–15

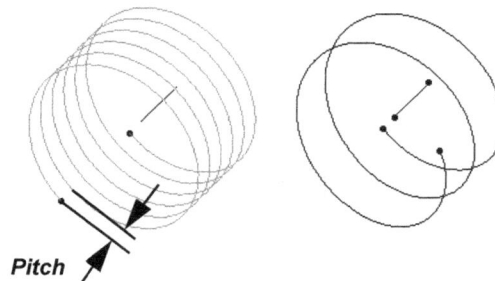

Height defines the length of the axis from the start point of the Helix. In Figure 5–16, a smaller height has been defined for the Helix on the right.

Height is not controlled by the selected axis.

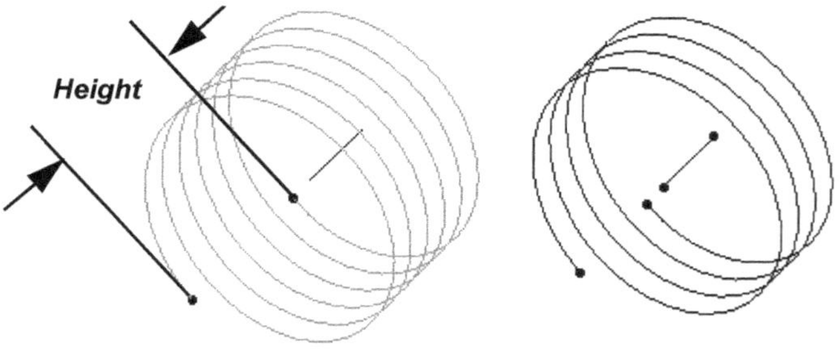

Figure 5–16

Taper defines whether the Helix has a linearly increasing or decreasing diameter. The taper can be defined **Inward** or **Outward** at a specified angle. In Figure 5–17, the Helix on the right tapers inward by 15°.

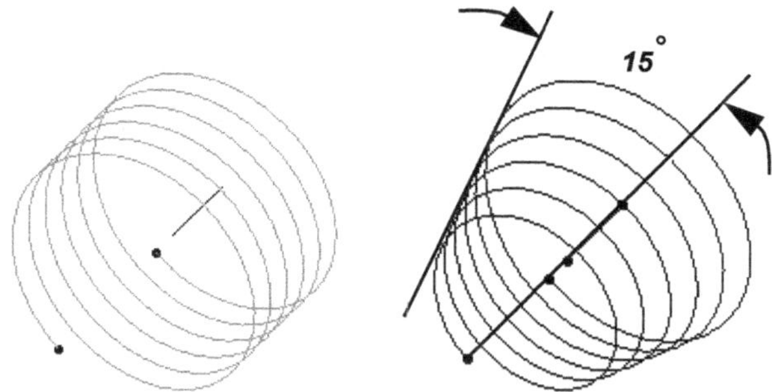

Figure 5–17

Starting Angle starts the Helix offset from the start point, as shown in Figure 5–18.

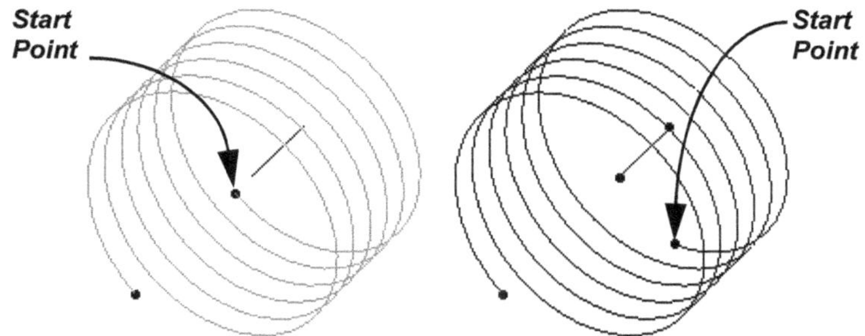

Figure 5–18

In the Helix Curve Definition dialog box, use the options in the *Radius variation* area to further define the Helix Curve. You can use the **Profile** option to define a profile curve that the Helix should follow. An example is shown in Figure 5–19.

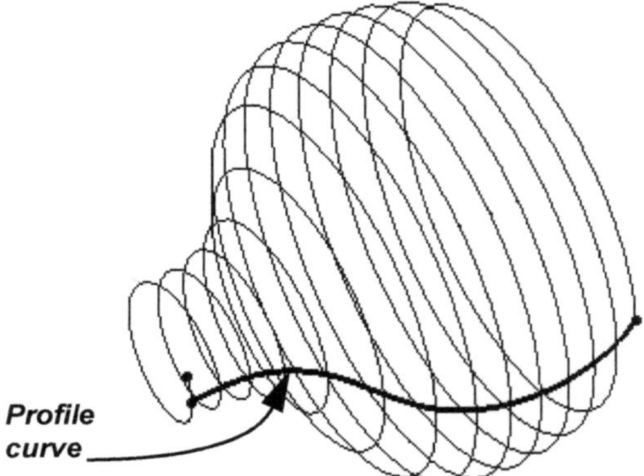

Figure 5–19

5.6 Combine Curve

Combine

A Combine element enables the creation of a curve that lies on the intersection of the projection of two curves or sketches. Each curve or sketch is created independent of the other and can either be projected along the normal or along a specified direction. This method is analogous to creating two extruded surfaces and creating a curve using the intersection element.

A Combine element can be used to define a 3D curve with only 2D information about the curve.

How To: Create a Combine Element

1. Click (Combine). The Combine Definition dialog box opens as shown in Figure 5–20.

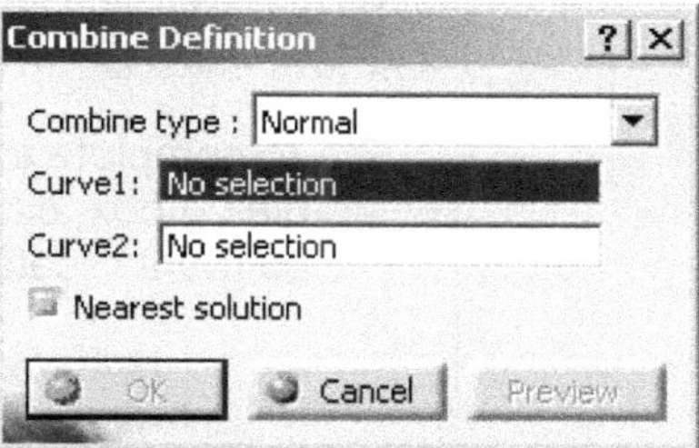

Figure 5–20

2. Specify the Combine type as **Normal** or **Along Direction** and select two curves to define the combine element. Figure 5–21 shows two curves selected to define a Combine element.

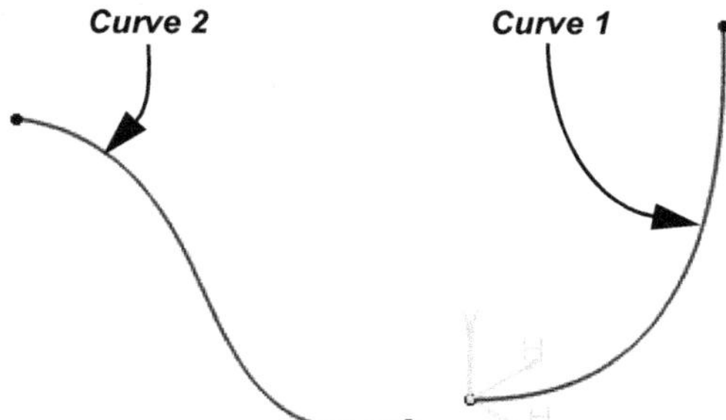

Figure 5–21

Figure 5–22 shows the imaginary extruded surfaces. The resulting intersection defines the location of the combine element.

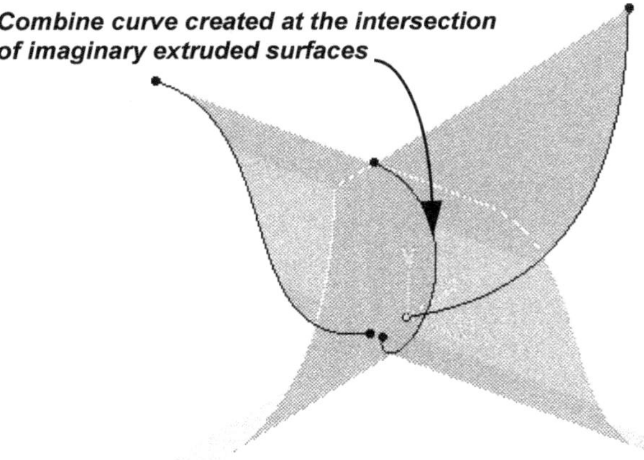
Combine curve created at the intersection of imaginary extruded surfaces

Figure 5–22

3. To complete the Combine element, in the Combine Definition dialog box, click **OK**. Figure 5–23 shows a **Normal** Combine element created from the two curves shown in Figure 5–21.

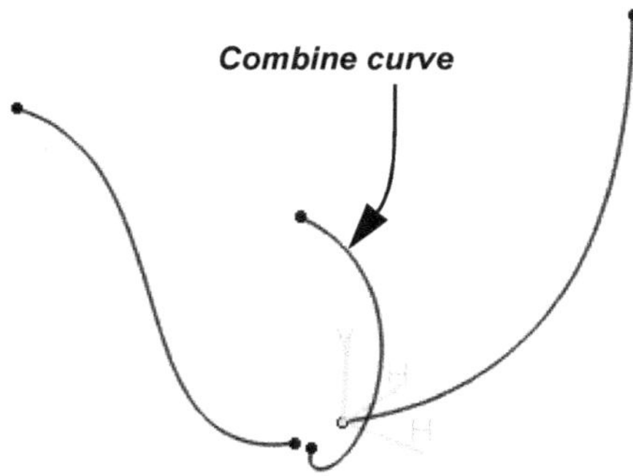
Combine curve

Figure 5–23

If you specify the Combine type as **Along direction**, you must select references for each curve. Planar references denote normal projection, as shown in Figure 5–24.

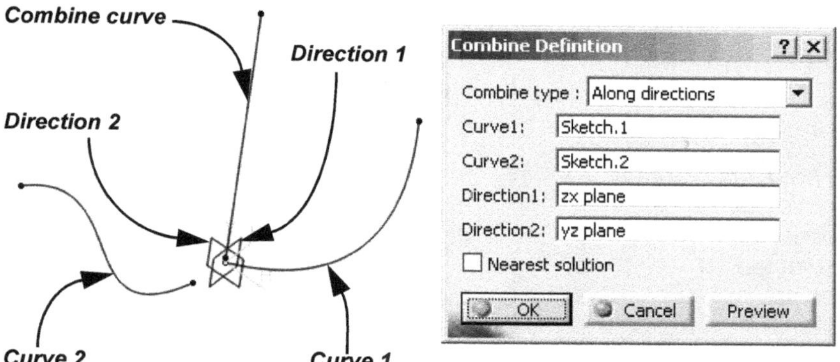

Figure 5–24

5.7 Projection Curve

The Projection feature enables you to project 3D geometry onto a non-planar support. A sketch cannot be created on the non-planar surface shown in Figure 5–25, but a sketch can be projected onto it. The curve can be projected at points normal to the surface or along a direction defined by a surface plane or line.

The direction of the projection is perpendicular to the selected Direction plane.

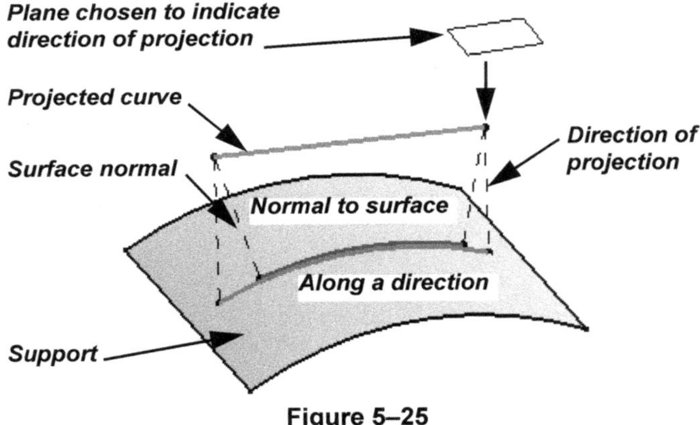

Figure 5–25

To create a projection, click (Projection) in the Project-Combine fly-out, in the Wireframe toolbar. The Projection Definition dialog box opens. You must specify a curve to be projected and a support on which to project the curve, as shown in Figure 5–26.

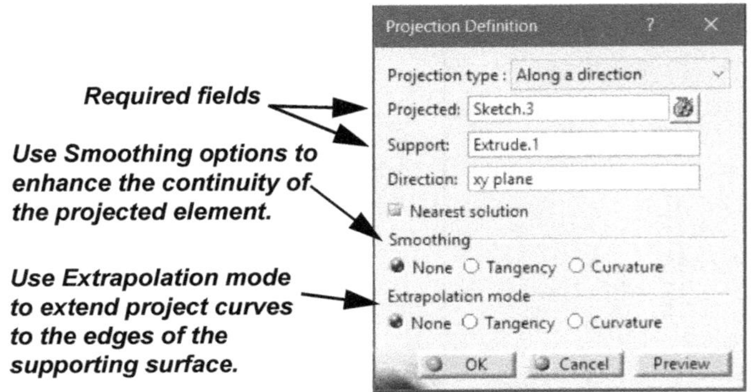

Figure 5–26

Depending on the orientation of the selected curve and support, the resulting feature could be a curve or a point.

5.8 Intersection Curve

The Intersection feature enables you to create geometry at the intersection of two elements. Using this feature, a curve can be created at the intersection of two surface features, as shown in Figure 5–26.

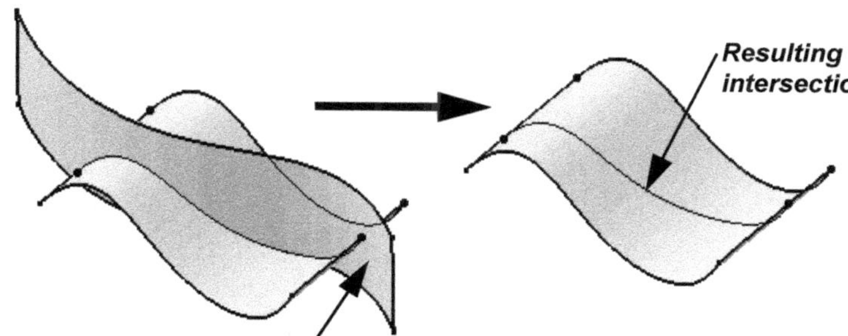

Figure 5–27

How To: Create an Intersection

1. Click (Intersection) in the Wireframe toolbar. The Intersection Definition dialog box opens as shown in Figure 5–27.

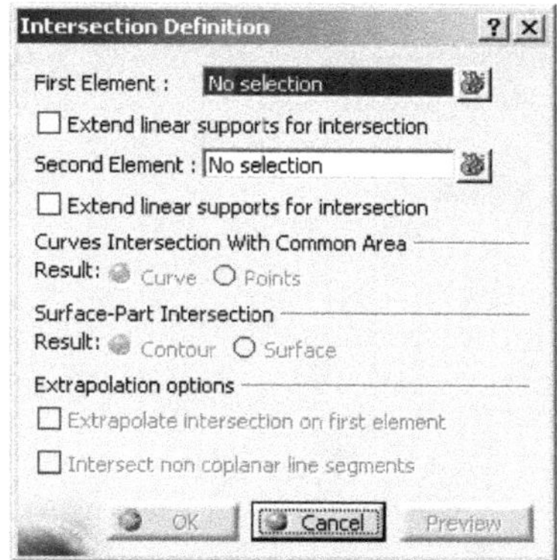

Figure 5–28

2. Select the two elements to intersect. Curves, surfaces, and planes are acceptable elements.
3. Click **OK** to complete the Intersect Definition. The resulting geometry can be curves, points, or a surface area, depending on the options used and the selected geometry.

5.9 Operations

Join

The **Join** operation joins two or more adjacent Curves or Surfaces so that they can be selected as one Curve or Surface. The two Surfaces shown in Figure 5–29 represent two separate features in the specification tree.

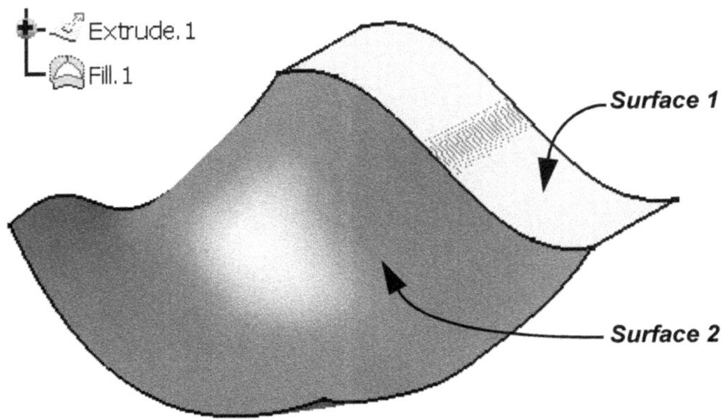

Figure 5–29

To join two surfaces, select both surfaces using <Ctrl> and click 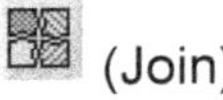 (Join).

You can specify additional parameters using optional elements in the Join Definition dialog box, as shown in Figure 5–30.

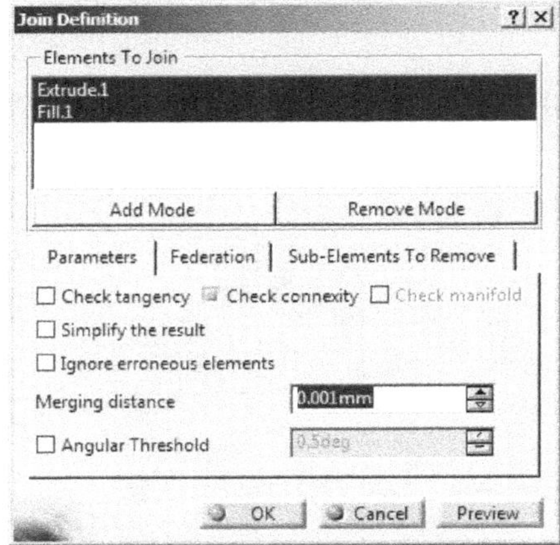

Figure 5–30

Some of the options are described as follows:

Option/Tabs	Description
Check Connexity	Enables you to enter a value in the *Merging Distance* field. If this option is not selected, any two surfaces or curves can be joined into a single element, regardless of the Merging distance value.
Simplify the result	Reduces the number of elements in the Join, if possible.
Ignore erroneous elements	Ignores any elements that prevent the creation of the Join feature.
Merging Distance	Determines the maximum separation permitted between elements, if the **Check connexity** option is selected. The merging distance has a maximum value of 0.1mm.
Federation	Defines groups of elements in the Join. By default, the **No Federation** option is selected. In this situation, each surface in the Join can be selected individually. If the **All** option is selected, all of the elements in the join are selected together.
Sub-Elements to Remove	You can use this tab to exclude sub-elements of elements that have been included in the Join. For example, an individual face of a Surface to be joined can be removed from the Join feature.

If you accept all of the defaults in the Join Definition dialog box, a new Join Surface feature is created, as shown in Figure 5–31. Note that the initial two surfaces now display as grayed out in the specification tree. The new Join Surface represents these two surfaces.

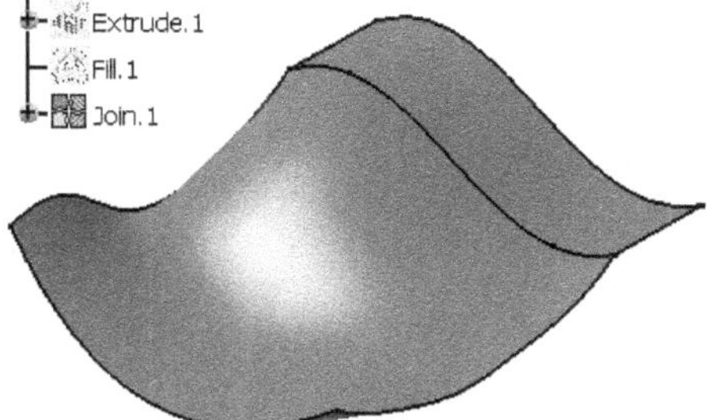

Figure 5–31

Curves selected for a **Join** operation must share a common end point. Surfaces must share an edge, but the edges do not need to have the same length. You can still join features that do not meet these requirements by clearing the **Check connexity** option.

Extract

The **Extract** operation creates new surface elements by copying surface or solid faces. Curves and edges can also be extracted. The resulting surface is a duplicate of the original element that was selected. An example of the **Extract** tool is shown in Figure 5–32, Figure 5–33, and Figure 5–34.

Figure 5–32 shows the solid model of a wing.

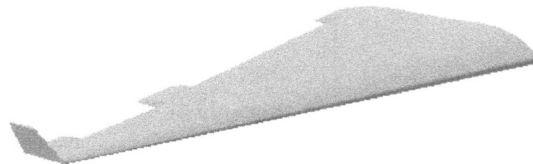

Figure 5–32

Figure 5–33 shows a preview of the surface selected to be extracted.

Figure 5–33

Figure 5–34 shows the resulting extracted surface. The solid geometry is hidden.

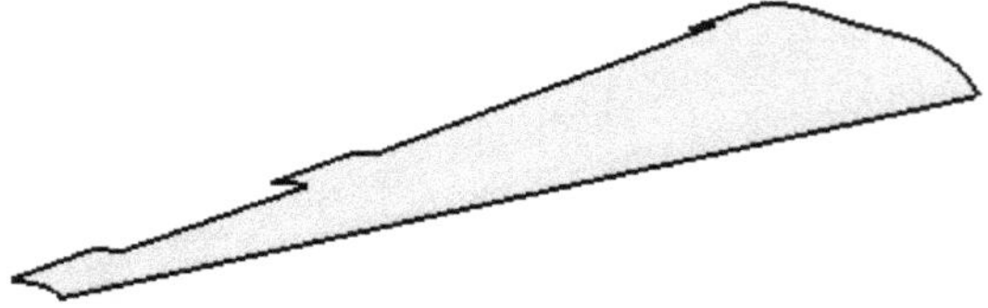

Figure 5–34

General Steps

Use the following general steps to perform an **Extract** operation:

1. Activate the **Extract** tool.
2. Select the entities to extract.
3. Specify the propagation type.
4. (Optional) Define the additional options.

Step 1 - Activate the Extract tool.

Click (Extract). The Extract Definition dialog box opens as shown in Figure 5–35.

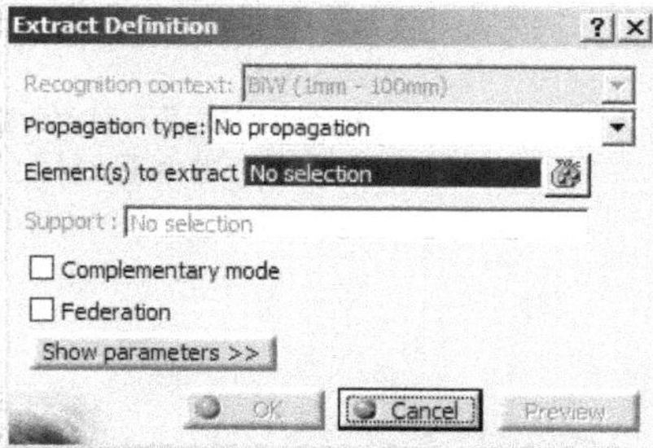

Figure 5–35

Step 2 - Select the entities to extract.

Select a face in the model. You can select multiple faces using , as shown in Figure 5–36. Once the Element(s) to extract dialog box is open, you can select multiple entities.

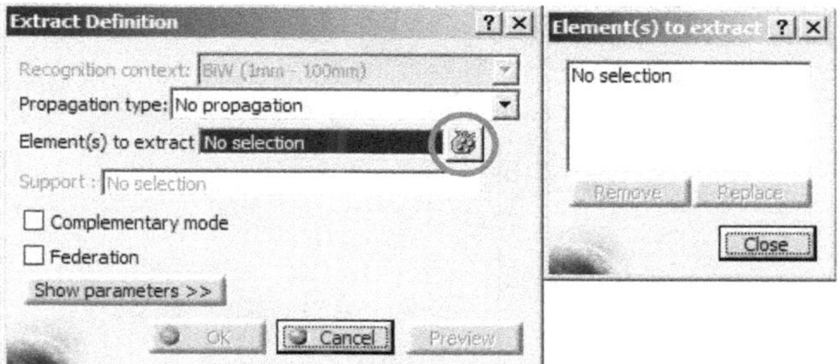

Figure 5–36

Step 3 - Specify the propagation type.

In the Propagation type drop-down list, select one of the following options:

- No propagation
- Point continuity
- Tangent continuity
- Curvature continuity
- Depression propagation
- Protrusion propagation

Figure 5–37 shows some of the different propagation settings used in the **Extract** operation. Only one face was selected in each propagation setting.

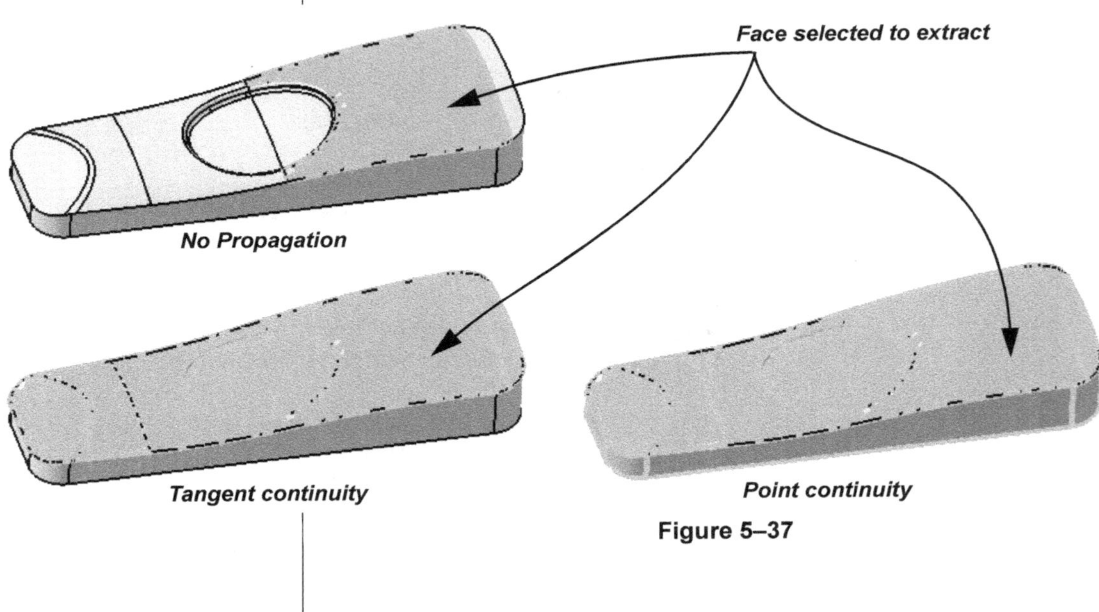

Figure 5–37

Step 4 - (Optional) Define the additional options.

You can apply optional settings, as shown in Figure 5–38.

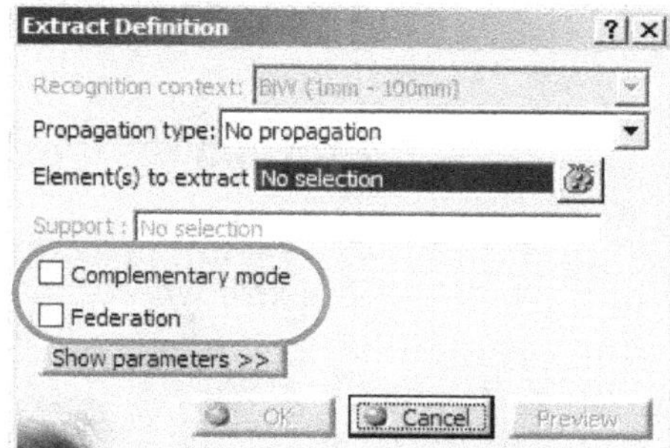

Figure 5–38

Select the **Complementary mode** option to extract the opposite surfaces selected by the **Propagation** tool. An example of this is shown in Figure 5–39.

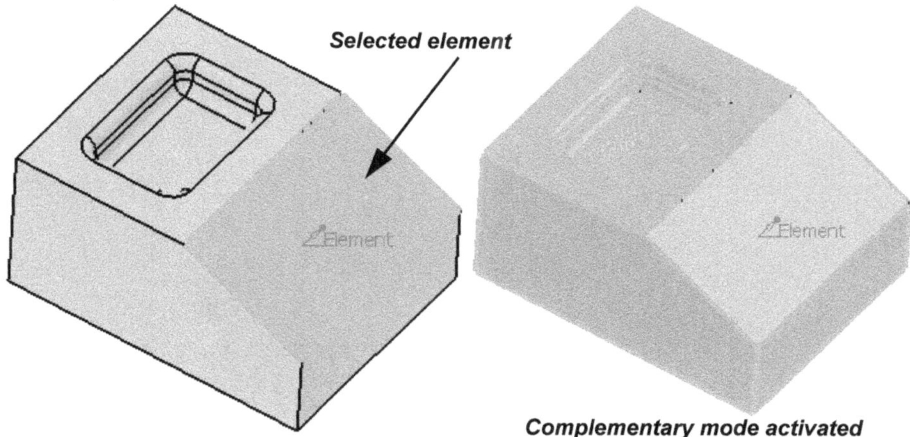

Figure 5–39

Select the **Federation** option if the resultant Surface is considered a representation of all of the Surfaces added to the extract. Do not select the **Federation** option if the resultant Surface is used as a collection of patches representing each individual Surface added to the Extract.

The **Federation** option determines whether the resultant Surface can mathematically represent all of the Surfaces added to the Extract. For example, if a Pad is extruded up to an Extract surface, the **Federation** option should be selected. This enables the stop Surface of the Pad to be calculated at any location on the Extract. If the **Federation** option is not selected and the Pad moves to a new location on the Extract, the Pad feature might fail.

Protrusion/Depression Propagation

Protrusion propagation and **Depression propagation** are available when surfaces are selected to extract. Protrusions and/or depressions of a surface can be selected quickly. When you select a surface, the system will select adjacent convex surfaces for Protrusion propagation, and adjacent convex surfaces for Depression propagation.

When Protrusion or Depression propagation are selected, the **Recognition context** option is available, as shown in Figure 5–40.

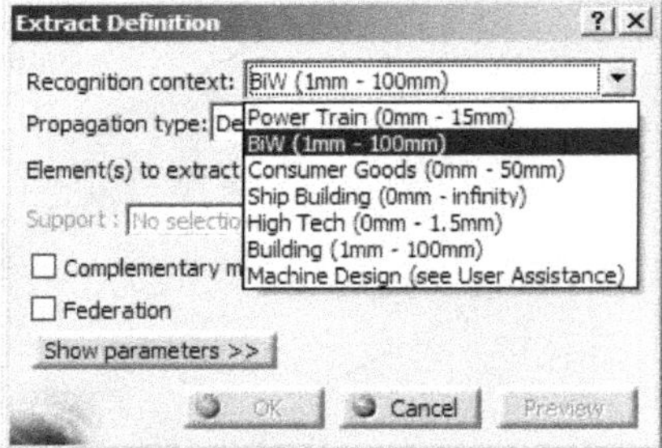

Figure 5–40

The Recognition context options take the industry into consideration by setting the size range of chamfers and fillets that will be recognized.

When the appropriate entities have been selected, click **OK** to complete the Extract.

5.10 Multi-Result Management

Whenever more than one possible solution is available to create a feature, CATIA prompts you to select the sub-element(s) to keep. The Multi-Result Management dialog box contains new options for selecting which sub-element(s) to keep.

For example, two possible lines can be created when a Plane intersects a cylindrical Surface. Once you have clicked **OK** in the Intersection dialog box, the Multi-Result Management dialog box opens as shown in Figure 5–41.

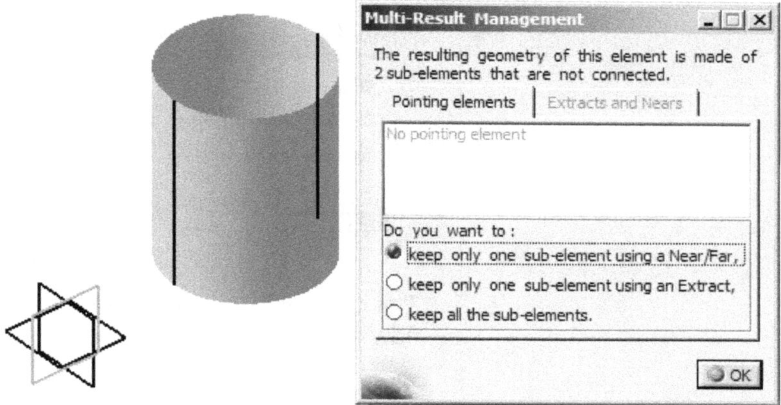

Figure 5–41

The following options are available:

- Keep only one sub-element using a Near/Far
- Keep only one sub-element using an Extract
- Keep all the sub-elements

Keep only one sub-element using a Near/Far

This option opens the Near/Far Definition dialog box in which you select one element that is closest to or farthest from the required output. For example, the zx plane is selected to keep the sub-element shown in Figure 5–42.

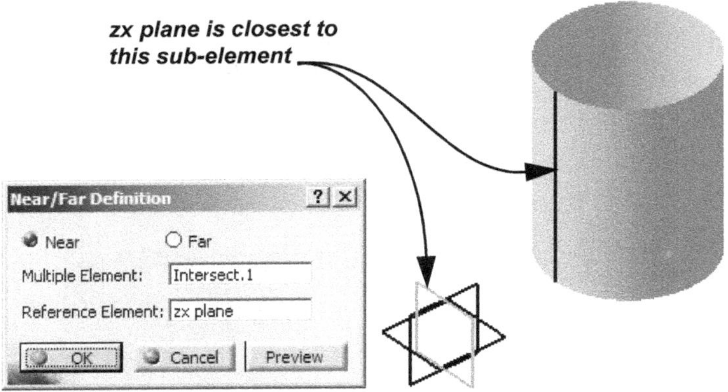

Figure 5–42

The original feature is no longer displayed and the geometry is now stored under the Near feature, as shown in Figure 5–43.

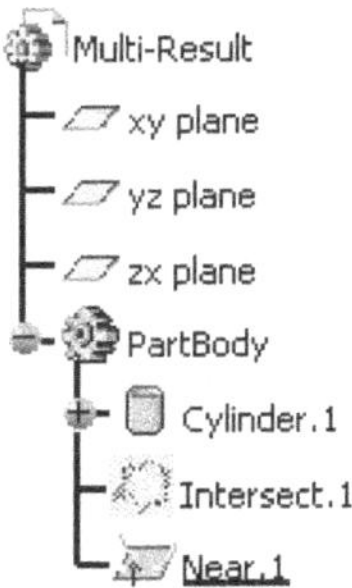

Figure 5–43

Keep only one sub-element using an Extract

You can directly select the element to keep, using an **Extract** operation. This option opens the Extract Definition dialog box, enabling you to select one of multiple results. For example, the opposite line is selected in Figure 5–44.

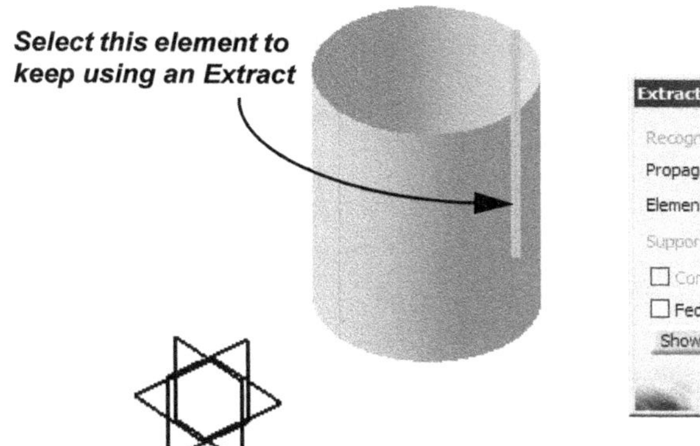

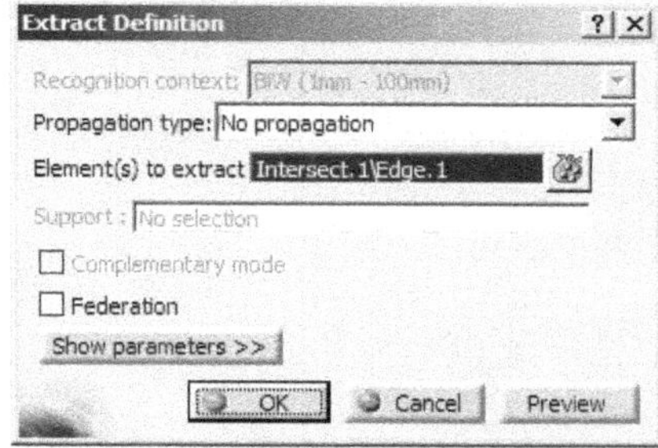

Figure 5–44

The original feature is no longer displayed and the geometry is now stored under the Extract feature, as shown in Figure 5–45.

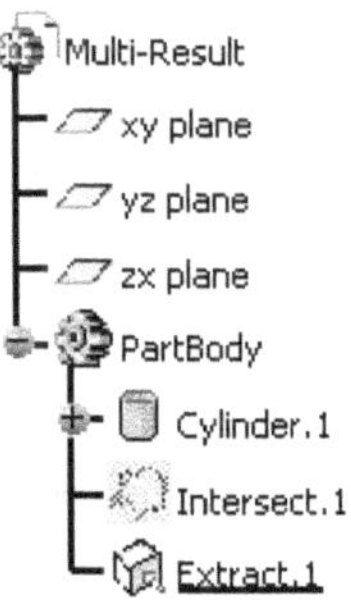

Figure 5–45

Keep all the sub-elements

This option keeps all of the sub-elements. In the case of the intersection of a cylinder and a plane, the Intersection feature consists of two disconnected lines.

Practice 5a

Spline-Polyline

Practice Objective

- Create a Polyline and a Spline.

In this practice, you will create a Polyline and a Spline. You will use these curves to create two Rib features. The completed model displays as shown in Figure 5–46.

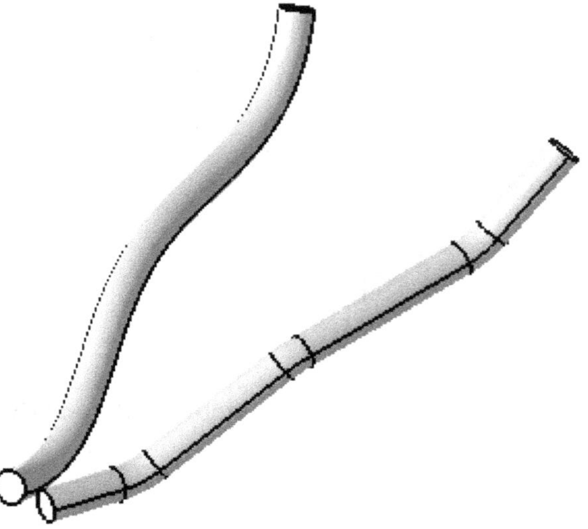

Figure 5–46

Task 1 - Open the part.

1. Open **Spline-polyline.CATPart**. The points for the formation of the curves have already been created, as shown in Figure 5–47.

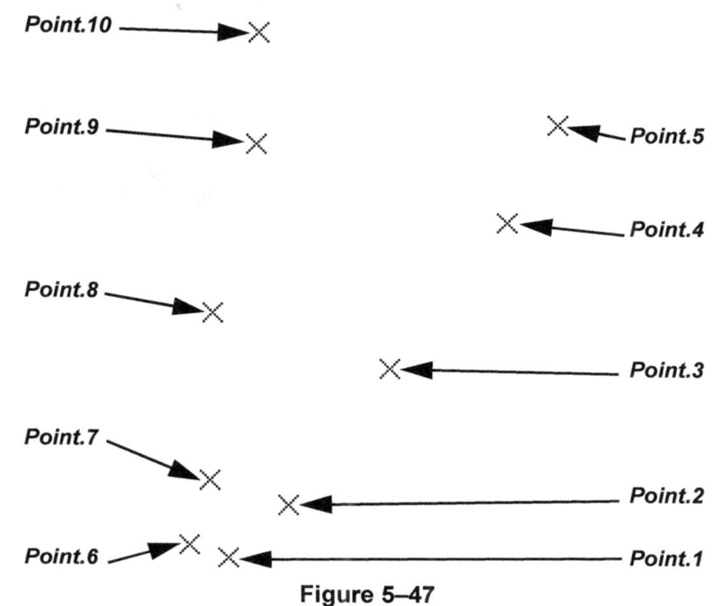

Figure 5–47

Task 2 - Create a polyline.

1. Select **Start>Shape>Generative Shape Design**.
2. In the Wireframe toolbar, expand the Line-Axis flyout and click (Polyline). The Polyline Definition dialog box opens.
3. Select the following points in the same order:
   - **Point.1**
   - **Point.2**
   - **Point.3**
   - **Point.4**
   - **Point.5**

4. In the Polyline Definition dialog box, select **Point.2**. In the *Radius* field, enter **300** as shown in Figure 5–48.

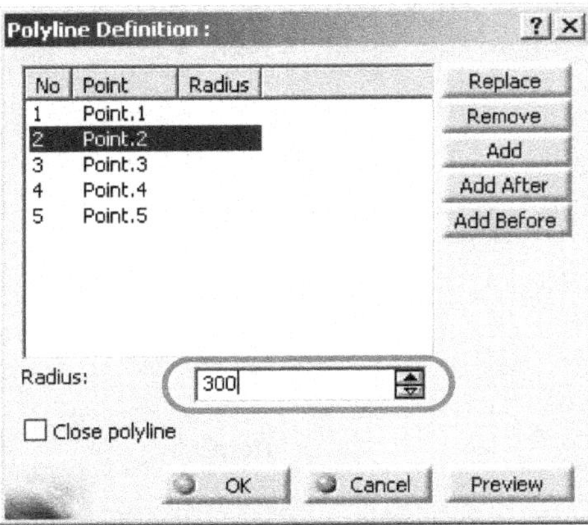

Figure 5–48

5. Select **Point.3** and **Point.4**. In the *Radius* field, enter **300**.

6. Click **Preview**. The model and Polyline Definition dialog box open as shown in Figure 5–49.

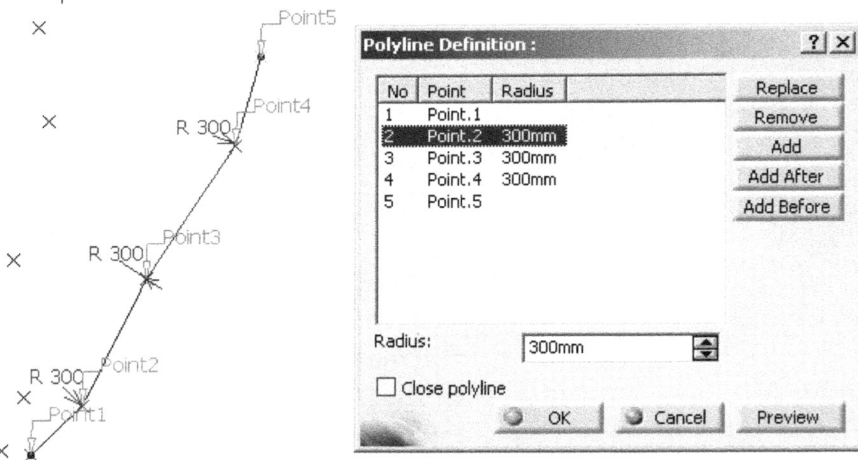

Figure 5–49

7. Click **OK** to complete the feature, which displays as shown in Figure 5–50.

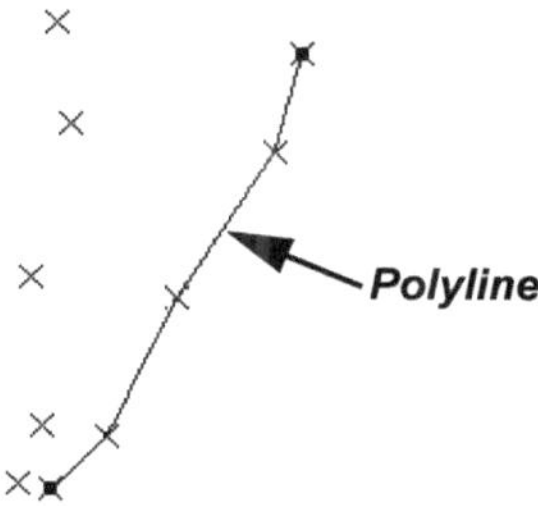

Figure 5–50

Task 3 - Create a spline.

1. In the Wireframe toolbar, expand the Curves flyout and click (Spline). The Spline Definition dialog box opens.
2. Select the following points in the same order:
   - **Point.6**
   - **Point.7**
   - **Point.8**
   - **Point.9**
   - **Point.10**
3. Click **Preview**. The model and the dialog box open as shown in Figure 5–51.

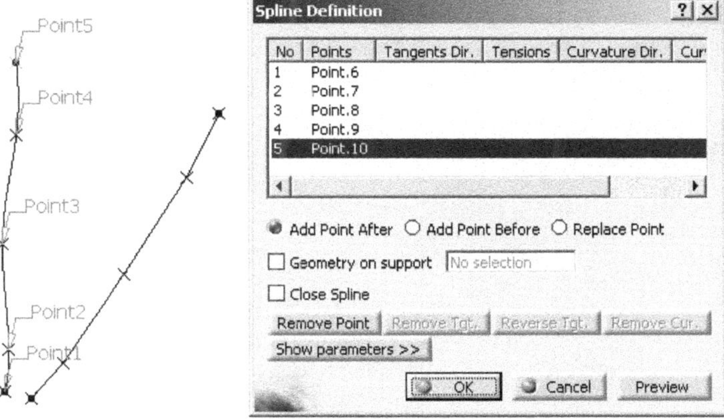

Figure 5–51

4. Click **OK** to complete the feature, which displays as shown in Figure 5–52.

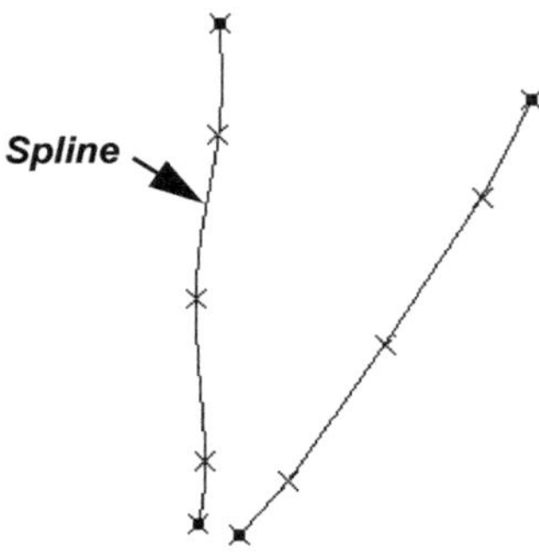

Figure 5–52

Task 4 - Create two Rib features.

In this task, you will create two Rib features with the Polyline and Spline that you created in the previous tasks.

1. Create a Plane using the plane type **Normal to curve**. Use the options shown in Figure 5–53 to define the Plane.

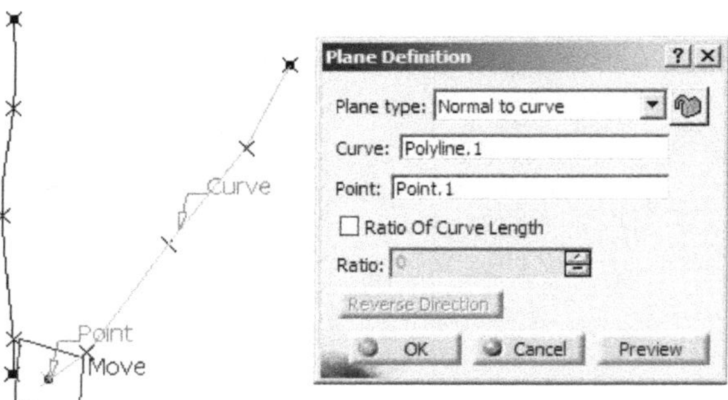

Figure 5–53

2. Create a circle profile, as shown in Figure 5–54 using a positioned sketch. Ensure that the origin of the sketch is positioned at **Point.1**.

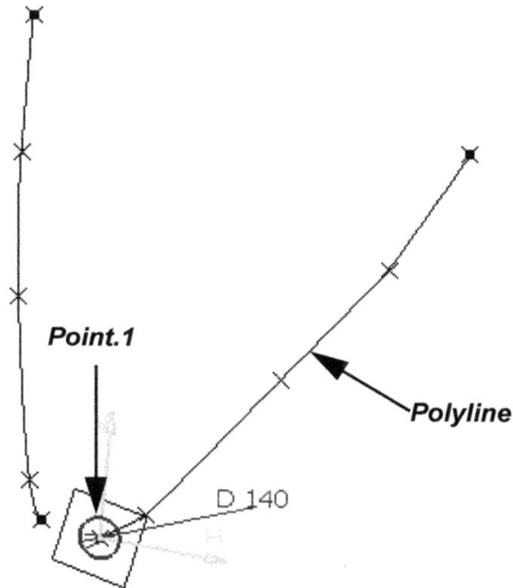

Figure 5–54

3. Create another **Normal to curve** type plane using the Spline and **Point.6**, as shown in Figure 5–55.

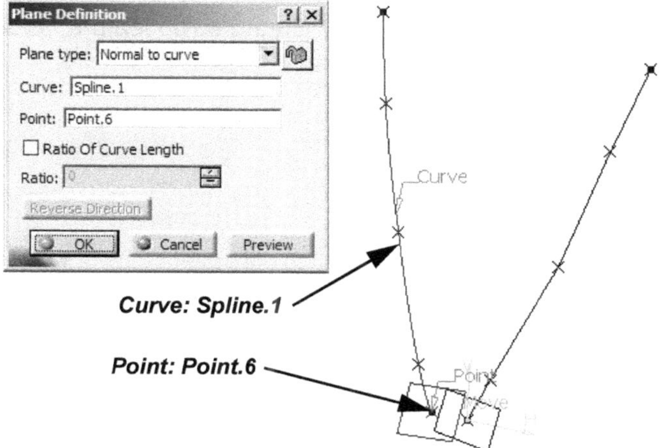

Figure 5–55

4. Using the newly created Plane, create a positioned sketch. Use **Point.6** as the origin of the sketch.

5. Sketch a circular profile as shown in Figure 5–56.

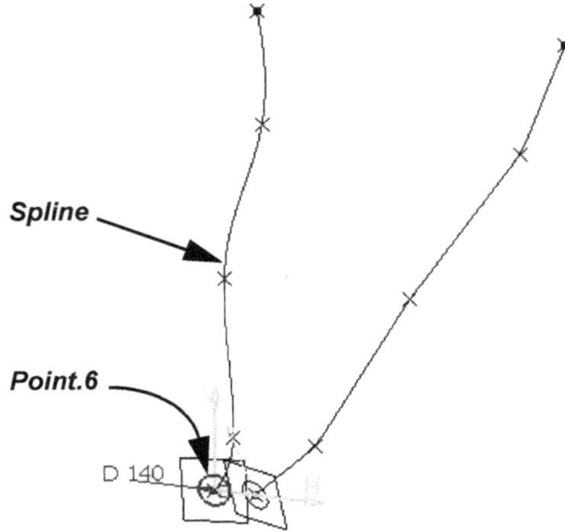

Figure 5–56

6. In the menu bar, select **Start>Mechanical Design>Part Design**.

7. Define the PartBody to be the work object.

8. Create a Rib feature, as shown in Figure 5–57.

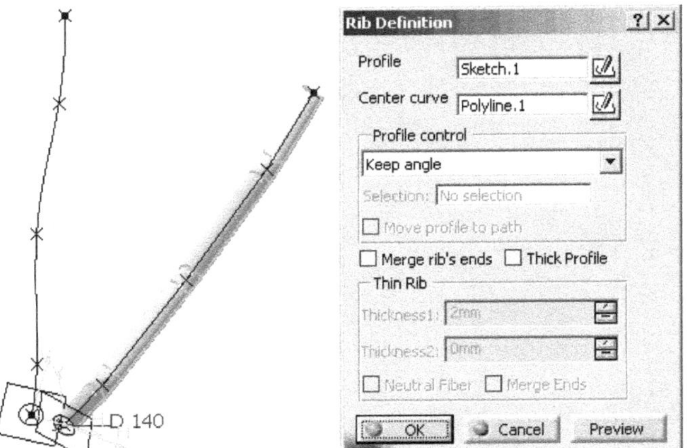

Figure 5–57

9. Create a Rib feature, as shown in Figure 5–58.

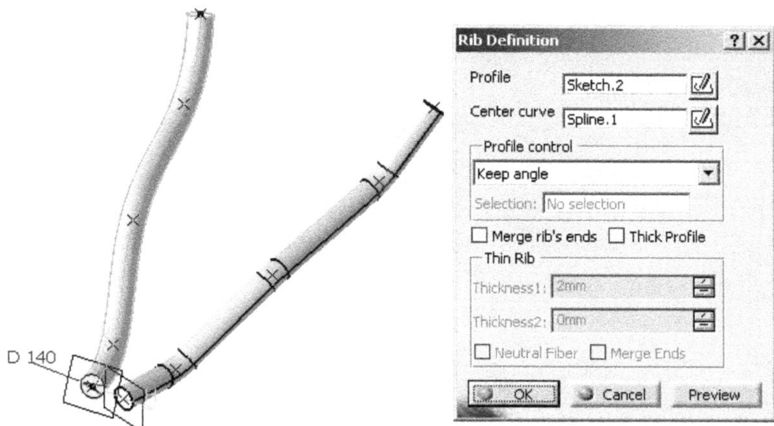

Figure 5–58

10. Hide **Geometrical Set.1**.

11. Save and close the file.

Practice 5b

Spline-Polyline

Practice Objectives

- Create a Projection curve.
- Create a Join Surface.

In this practice, you will create a wavy washer using isolated surfaces. The center curve for the Rib feature is created by projecting the profile onto the surface. The completed model displays as shown in Figure 5–59.

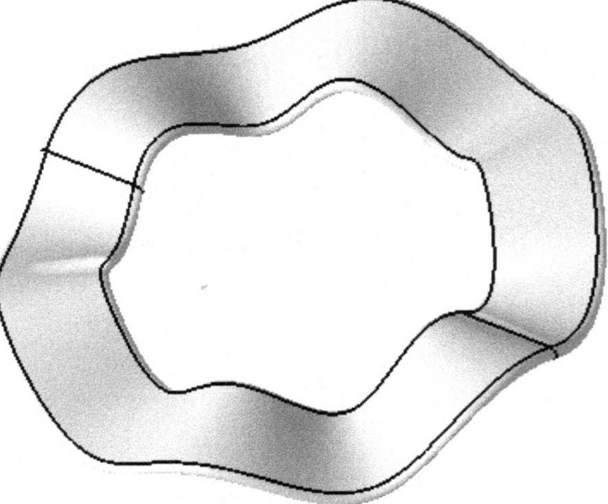

Figure 5–59

Task 1 - Open the part.

1. Open **Wavy_washer.igs**. The model displays as shown in Figure 5–60.

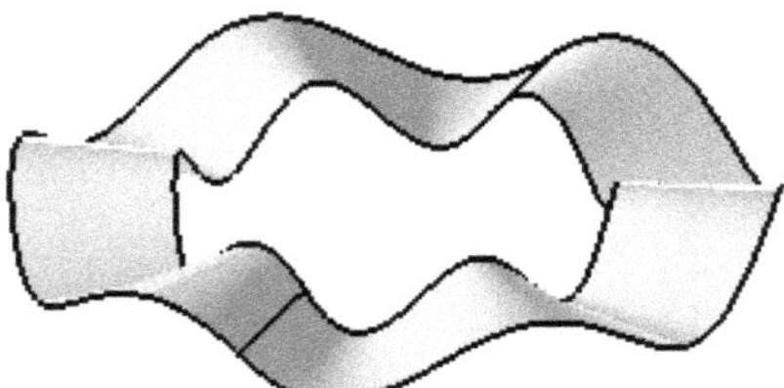

Figure 5–60

Task 2 - Create a Join.

In this task, you will create a Join with the isolated surfaces.

1. Select **Start>Shape>Generative Shape Design**.

2. In the Operations toolbar, click (Join). In the specification tree or model, select the two isolated surfaces. The Join Definition dialog box displays as shown in Figure 5–61.

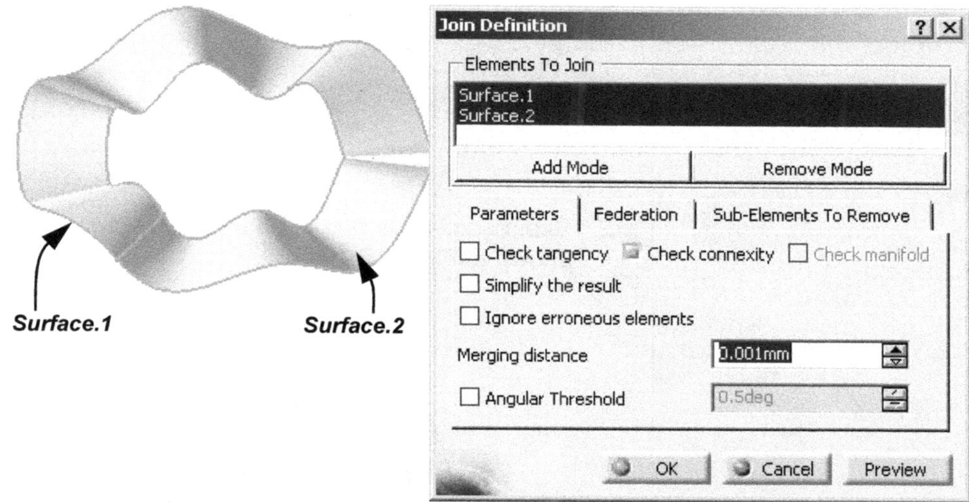

Figure 5–61

3. Click **OK** to complete the feature, which displays in the specification tree as shown in Figure 5–62.

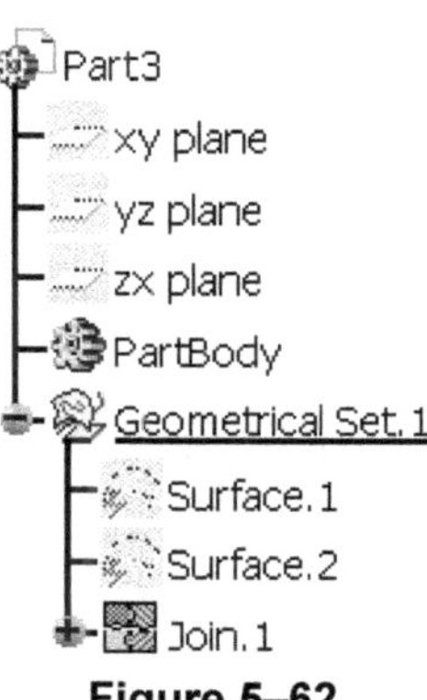

Figure 5–62

Task 3 - Create a Profile.

In this task, you will create a profile that will be projected onto the surface.

1. Create an offset Plane as shown in Figure 5–63.

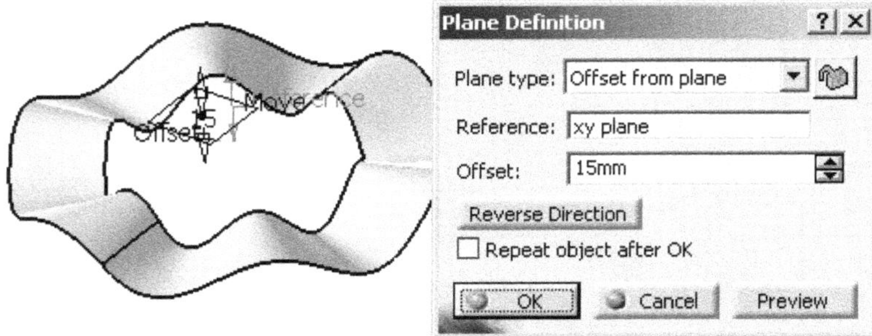

Figure 5–63

2. Sketch a circular profile on the newly created Plane, as shown in Figure 5–64.

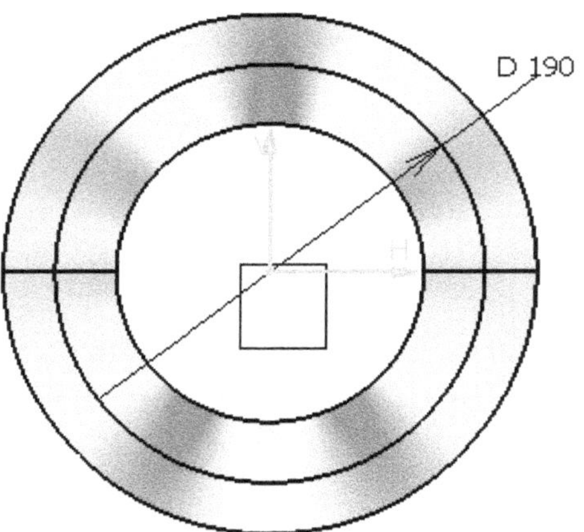

Figure 5–64

Task 4 - Create a Projection curve.

In this task, you will create a projection curve with the profile that you just created.

1. In the Wireframe toolbar, expand the Project-Combine flyout and click (Projection). The Projection Definition dialog box opens.

2. Make the following selections, as shown in Figure 5–65:

- *Projection type:* **Along a direction**
- *Projected:* **Sketch.1**
- *Support:* **Join.1**
- *Direction:* **Plane.1**

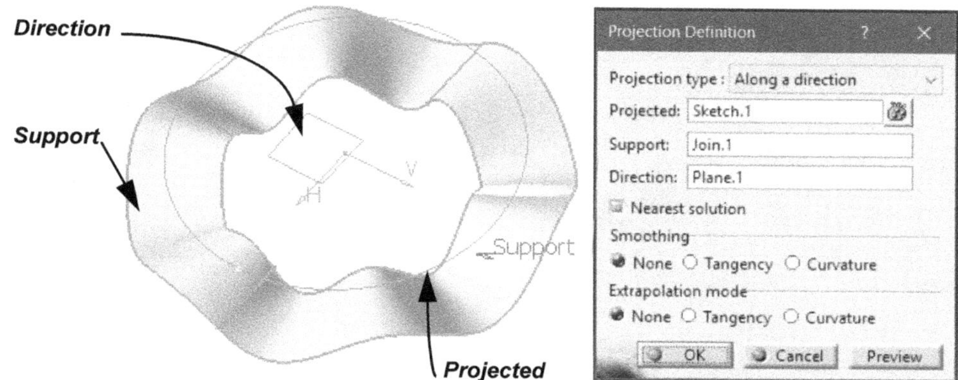

Figure 5–65

3. Click **OK** to complete the feature, which displays as shown in Figure 5–66.

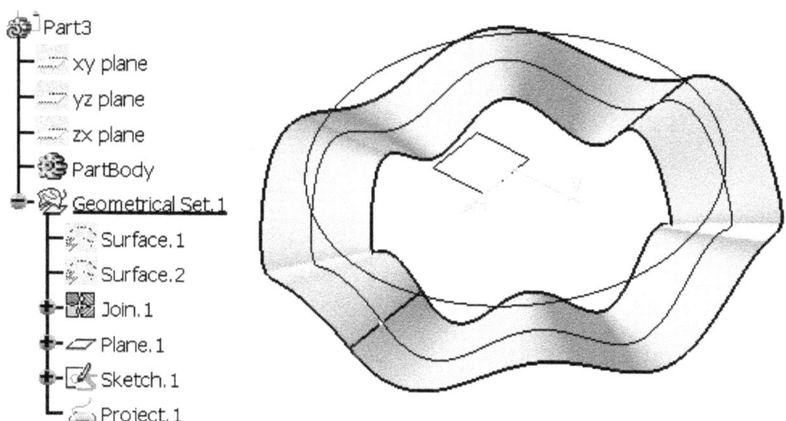

Figure 5–66

Task 5 - Create a Rib feature.

In this task, you will create a profile for Rib creation.

1. Hide **Sketch.1**.
2. Create a reference point on the projection curve, as shown in Figure 5–67.

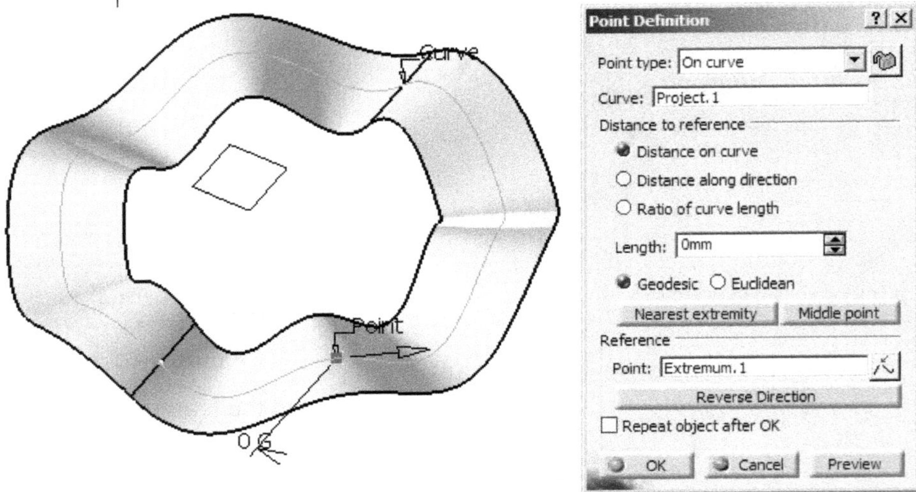

Figure 5–67

3. Create a reference plane, as shown in Figure 5–68.

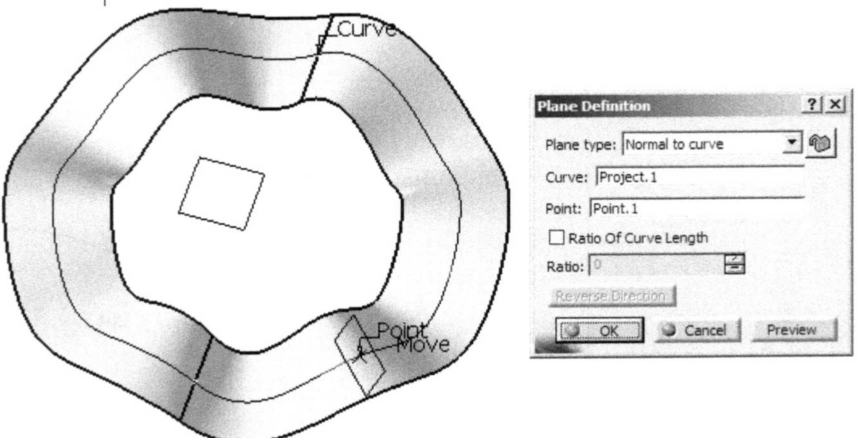

Figure 5–68

4. Create a positioned sketch on the plane that you just created. Ensure that the origin of the sketch is located at **Point.1**, as shown in Figure 5–69.

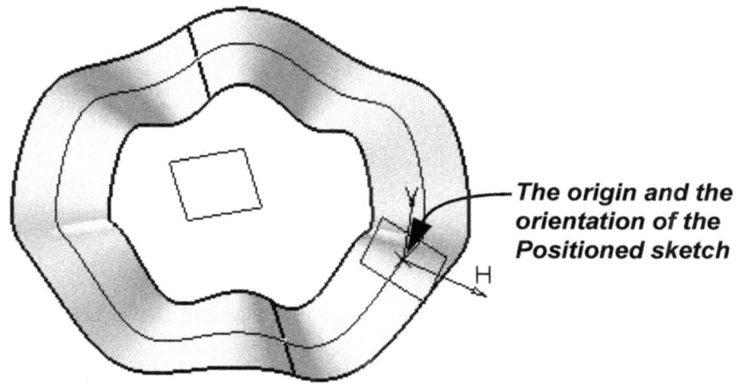

Figure 5–69

5. Create the profile, as shown in Figure 5–70.

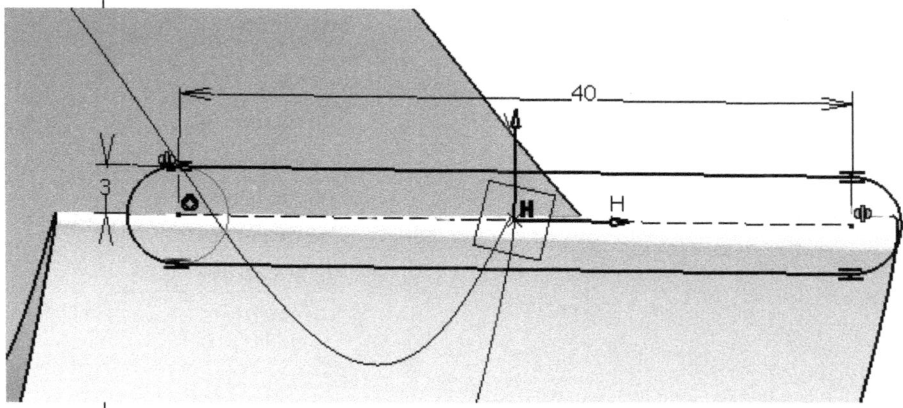

Figure 5–70

6. In the menu bar, select **Start>Mechanical Design>Part Design**.

7. Define the **PartBody** to be the In Work Object.

8. Create a Rib feature using the following specifications:

   - *Profile:* **Sketch.2**
   - *Center curve:* **Project.1**

9. An error message opens as shown in Figure 5–71. It indicates that the center curve is not continuous in tangency.

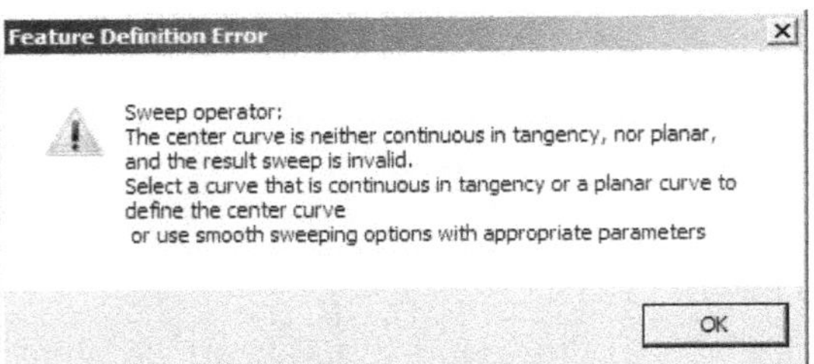

Figure 5–71

10. Close the Feature Definition Error dialog box.

11. In the Profile control drop-down list, select the **Pulling direction** option. In the specification tree or model, select **Plane.1**. The Rib definition dialog box opens as shown in Figure 5–72.

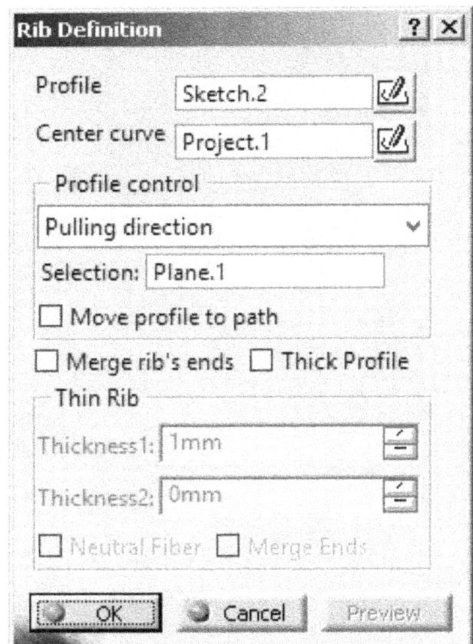

Figure 5–72

12. Click **OK** to complete the feature.

13. Click **Close** in the Warnings dialog box.

14. Hide **Geometrical Set.1**.

15. Save and close the file.

Practice 5c

Handle

Practice Objectives

- Create intersection elements.
- Create a near.
- Create a Join curve.
- Create a Spline curve.
- Create a Combine curve.
- Create a Helix.

In this practice, you will create a handle for a barbeque. First you will create the required 3D profile to create the Rib, and then the profiles to create the threads. The completed model displays as shown in Figure 5–73.

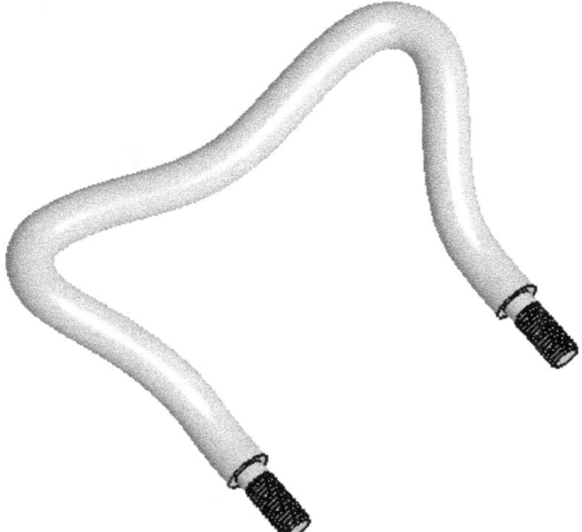

Figure 5–73

Task 1 - Open the part.

1. Open **Handle.CATPart**. There are two sketches in the model that you will use to create a Combine feature. The model displays as shown in Figure 5–74.

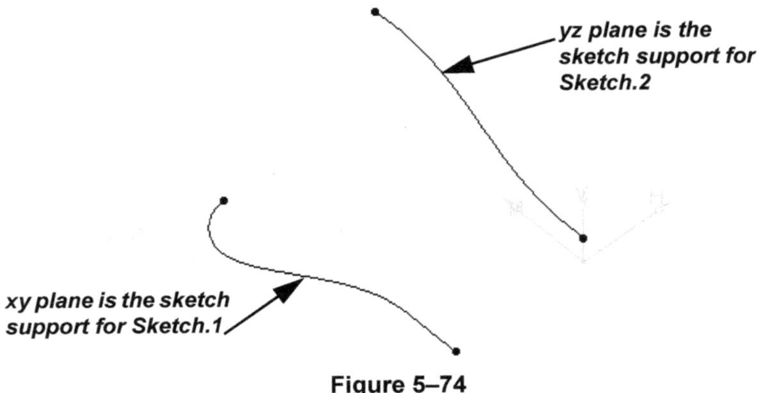

Figure 5–74

Task 2 - Create a combine curve

In this task, you will create a combine curve with the provided sketches.

1. Select **Start>Shape>Generative Shape Design**.
2. In the Wireframe toolbar, expand the Project-Combine flyout, and click (Combine). The Combine Definition dialog box opens as shown in Figure 5–75.

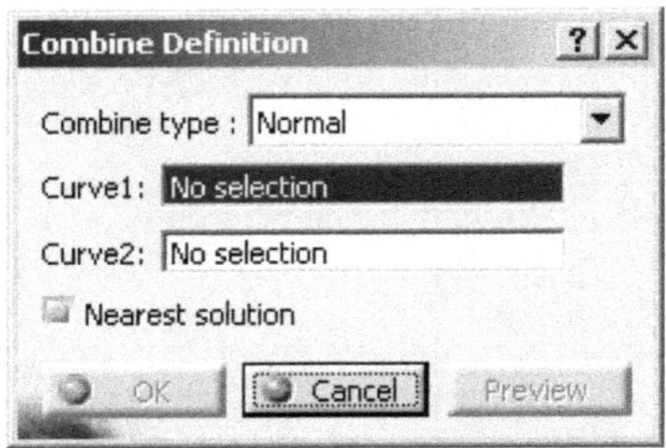

Figure 5–75

3. In the specification tree or model, for *Curve1*, select **Sketch.1** and for *Curve2*, select **Sketch.2**, as shown in Figure 5–76.

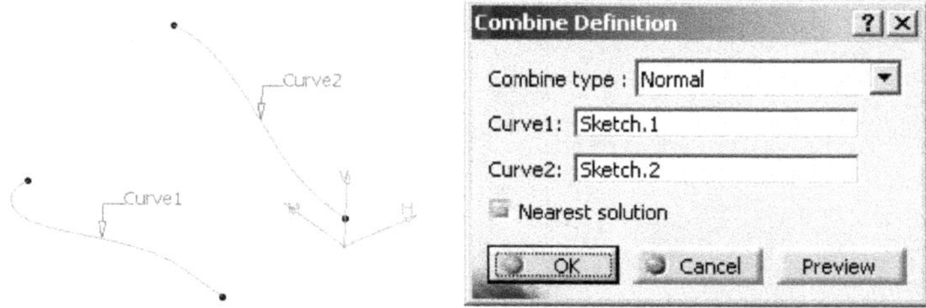

Figure 5–76

4. Click **OK** to complete the feature. The combine curve displays as shown in Figure 5–77.

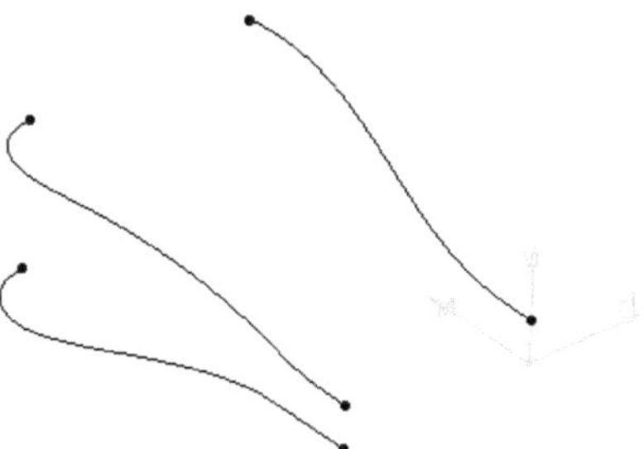

Figure 5–77

Task 3 - Create a spline curve

In this task, you will create two Points that will be used to create a Spline.

1. In the Wireframe toolbar, click (Point) and make the following selections, as shown in Figure 5–78:

   - *Point type:* **On Plane**
   - *Plane:* **yz plane**
   - *H:* **34mm**
   - *V:* **13mm**

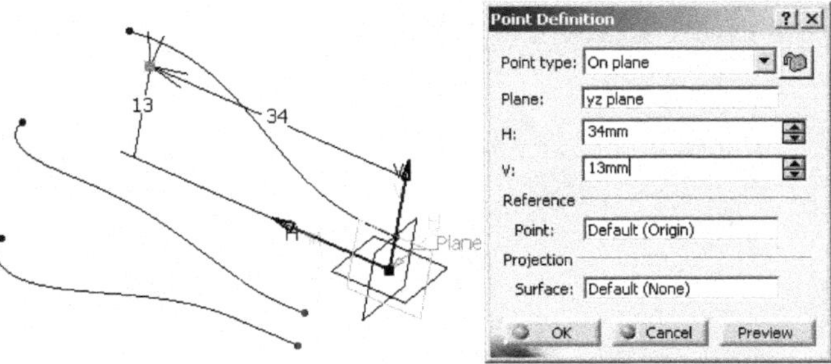

Figure 5–78

2. Click **OK** to complete the feature. The point displays as shown in Figure 5–79.

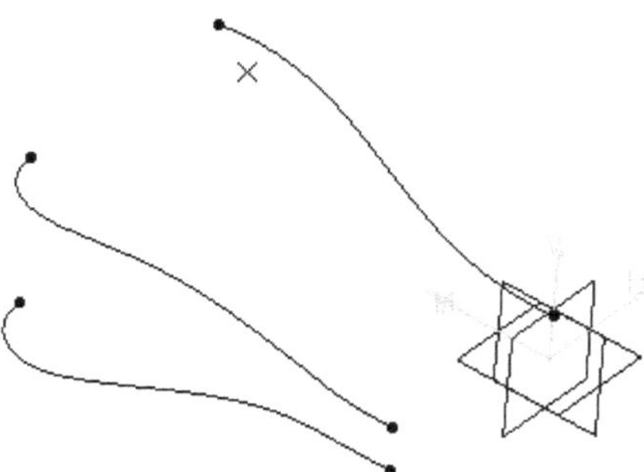

Figure 5–79

3. Create a Point, as specified in Figure 5–80.

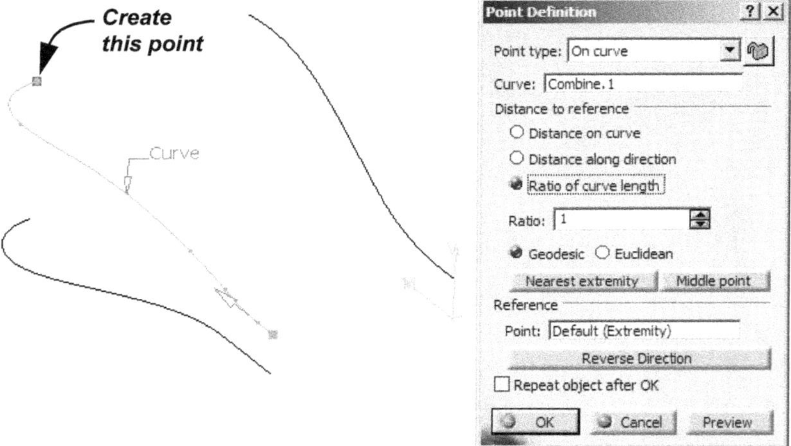

Figure 5–80

4. Create another Point, as specified in Figure 5–81.

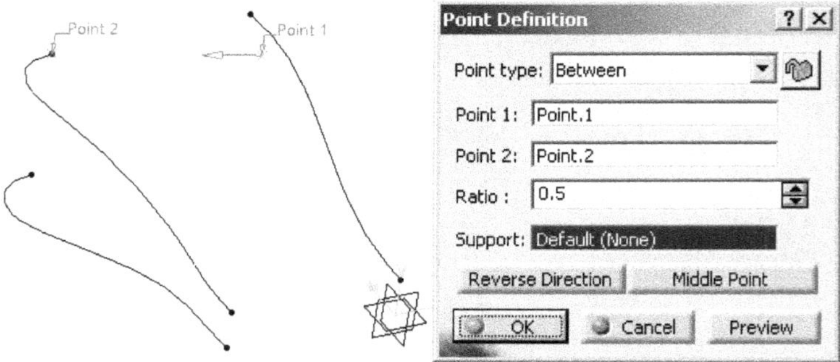

Figure 5–81

The result displays as shown in Figure 5–82.

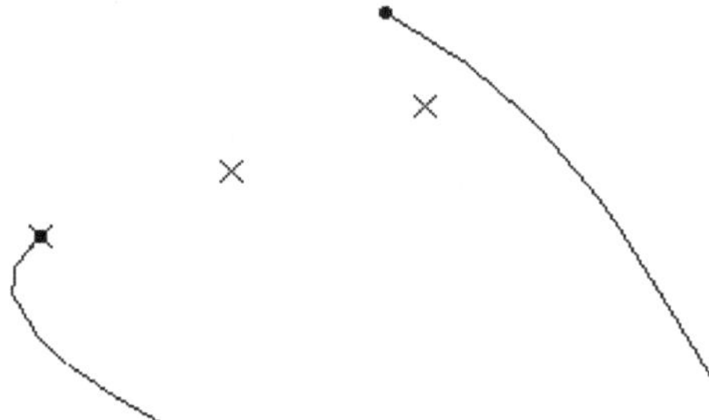

Figure 5–82

5. In the Wireframe toolbar, expand the Curves flyout, and click (Spline). The Spline Definition dialog box opens.

6. Select **Point.2** to specify the start point of the Spline, and then select **Combine.1** to create tangency. Ensure that the tangency arrow is pointing in the same direction, as shown in Figure 5–83. To reverse the tangency direction, select the arrow.

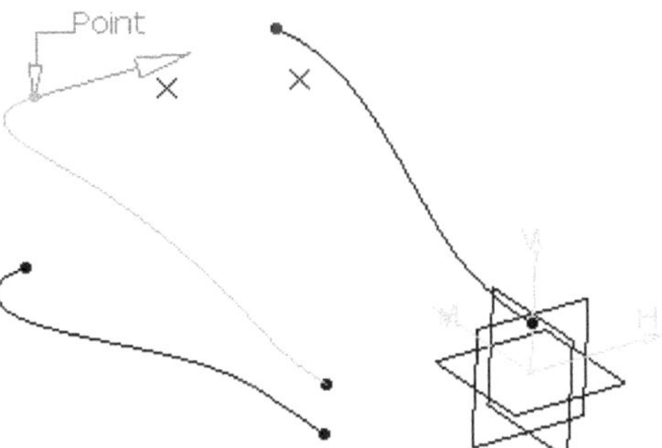

Figure 5–83

7. Select **Point.3**.

8. Select **Point.1**. To make the spline perpendicular to the yz plane, select the yz plane in the specification tree, as shown in Figure 5–84. It is important to have the spline perpendicular to the yz plane, because the spline will be used later to build solid geometry. This is to ensure a smooth result after creating a Symmetry feature.

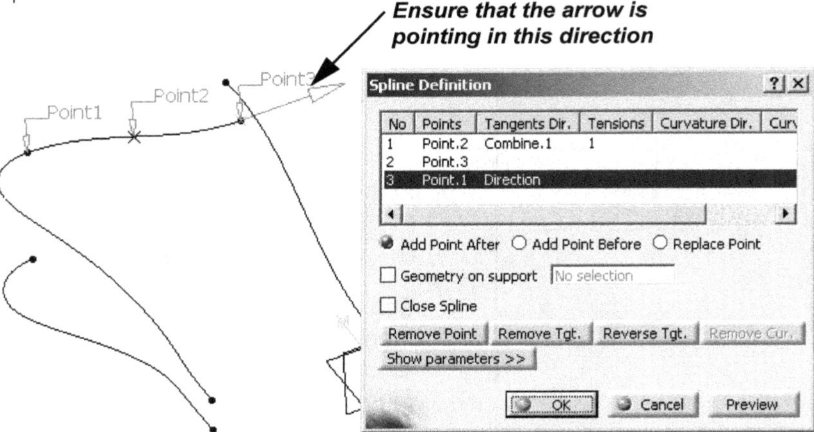

Figure 5–84

9. Click **OK** to complete the feature. The Spline displays as shown in Figure 5–85.

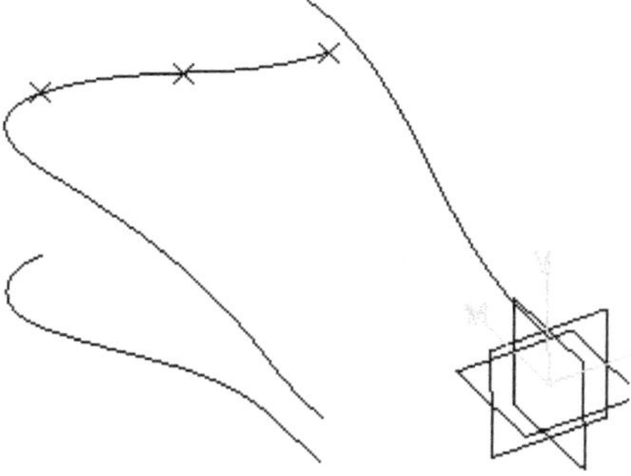

Figure 5–85

Task 4 - Create a Joined curve

In this task, you will join the Combine curve with the Spline curve. You will use this Joined curve as the center curve during the Rib creation.

1. Hide the sketches.

2. In the Operations toolbar, click (Join).

3. In the specification tree or model, select the **Combine.1** and the **Spline.1** curves. The Join Definition dialog box opens as shown in Figure 5–86.

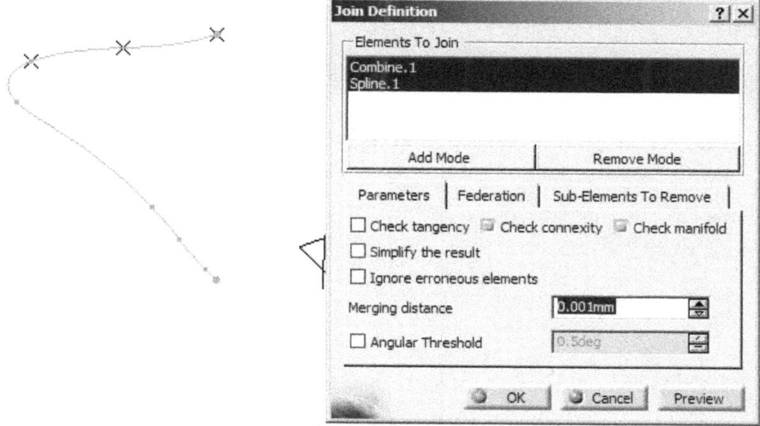

Figure 5–86

4. Click **OK** to complete the feature. The Join feature displays in the specification tree. Note that the Combine curve and the Spline curve are hidden automatically.

Task 5 - Create a Rib feature

In this task, you will first create the Rib profile and then create a Rib feature.

1. Create a plane using the **Parallel through point** type as specified in Figure 5–87.

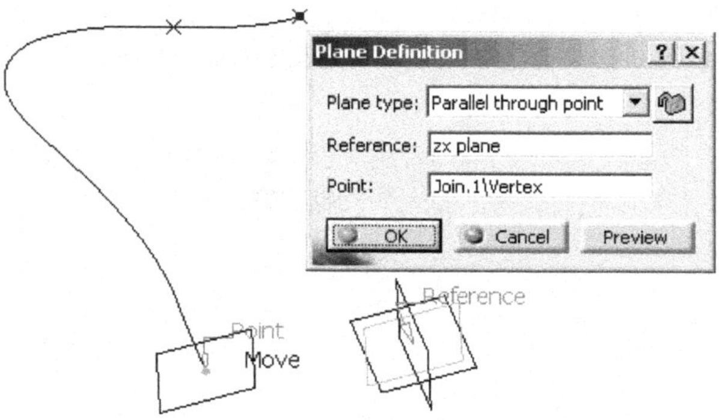

Figure 5–87

2. Rename the reference plane as **Refplane1**.

3. Create a positioned sketch on **Refplane1** as shown in Figure 5–88.

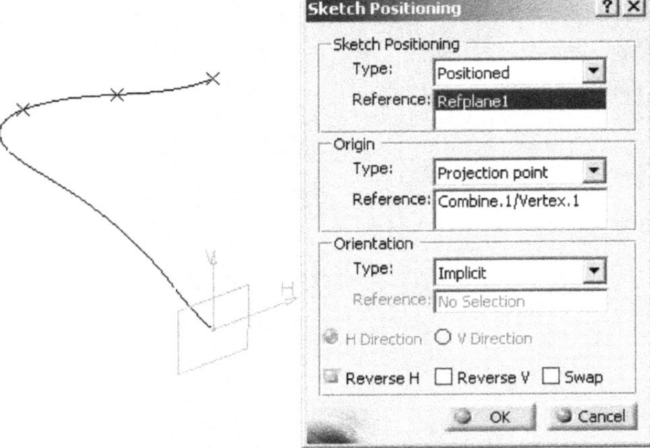

Figure 5–88

4. Create a circle profile, as shown in Figure 5–89.

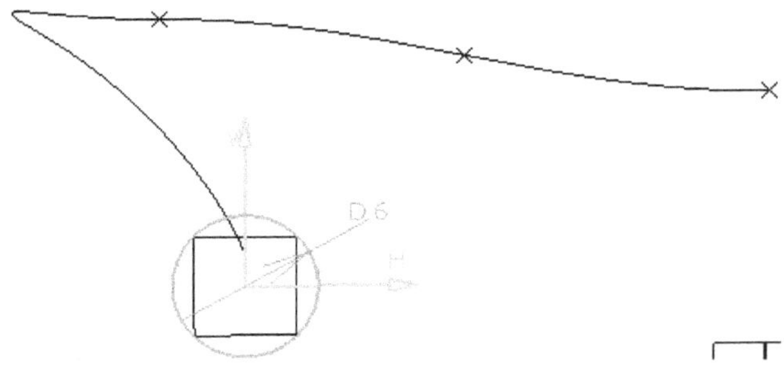

Figure 5–89

5. Switch from Generative Shape Design workbench to the Part Design workbench. Define the **PartBody** to be the In Work Object.

6. Create a Rib using the circle profile and joined curve, as shown in Figure 5–90.

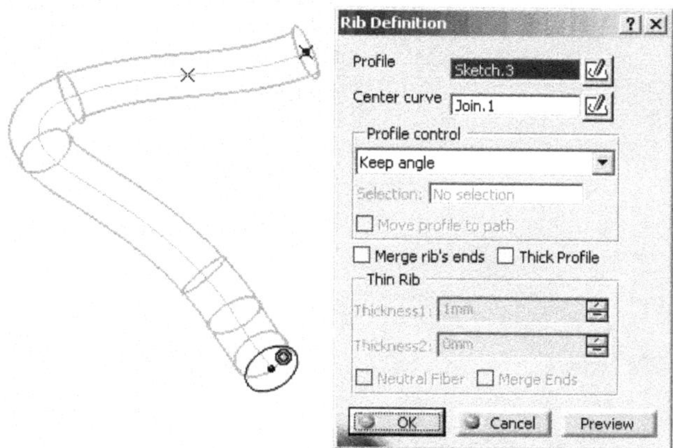

Figure 5–90

7. Complete the Rib feature.

8. Create a positioned sketch on **Refplane1** and then sketch a circular profile, as shown in Figure 5–91.

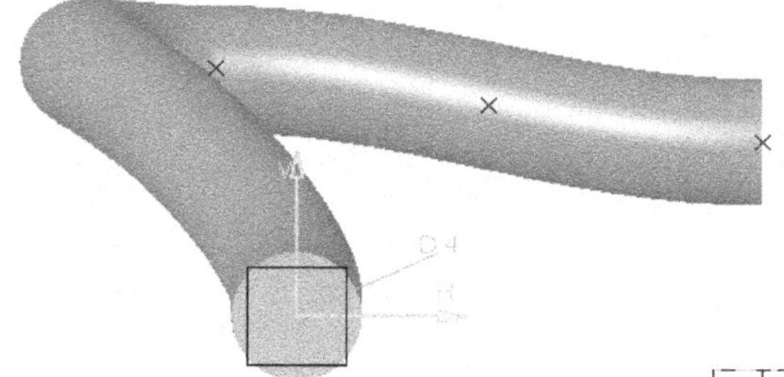

Figure 5–91

9. Create a Pad feature using the profile that you have just created. Use the following specifications (as shown in Figure 5–92).

- *Type:* **Dimension**
- *Length:* **10mm**

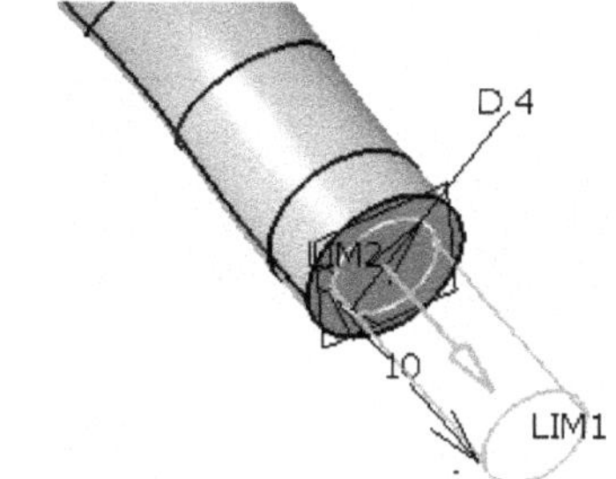

Figure 5–92

10. Hide **Point.1**, **Point.2**, and **Point.3**.

11. Create a Chamfer at the edge of the Pad with following selection (as shown in Figure 5–93).

    - *Mode:* **Length1/Angle**
    - *Length 1:* **0.3mm**
    - *Angle:* **45deg**

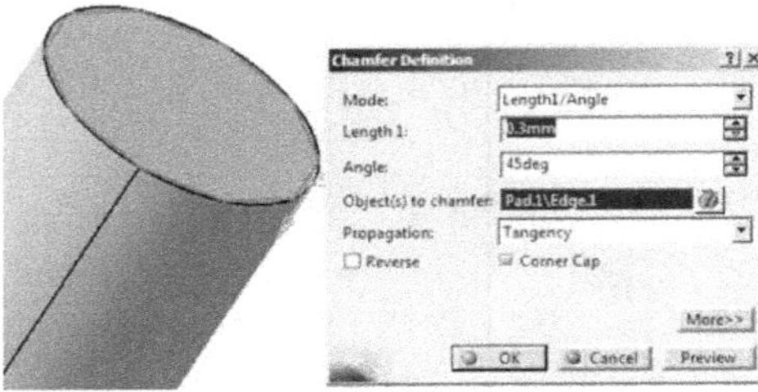

Figure 5–93

12. Mirror the PartBody about the yz plane. The model displays as shown in Figure 5–94.

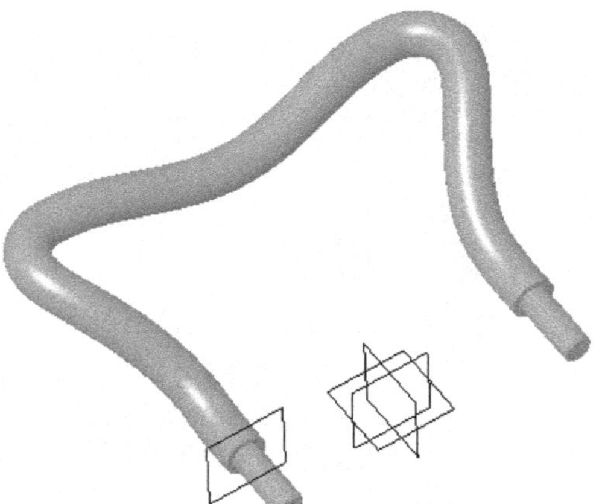

Figure 5–94

Task 6 - Create Wireframe features.

In this task, you will create a Line that will be used as the Helix axis, an intersection point that will be used as the starting point of the Helix, and a profile that defines the shape of the Helix.

1. Select **Start>Shape>Generative Shape Design.**
2. Show the Join feature.

3. Create an **On curve** type point, as shown in Figure 5–95.

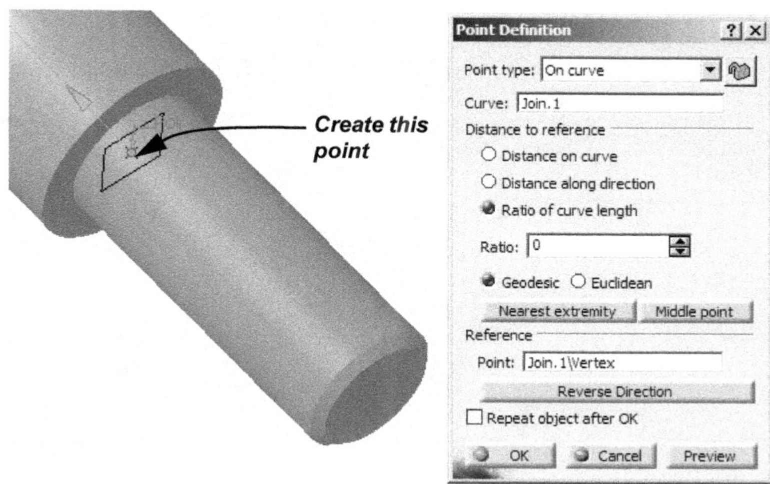

Figure 5–95

4. Create a Line with the following selections, as shown in Figure 5–96:

   - *Line type:* **Point-Direction**
   - *Point:* **Point.4**
   - *Direction:* **Y Component** (in the shortcut menu)
   - *Start:* **0mm**
   - *End:* **10mm**

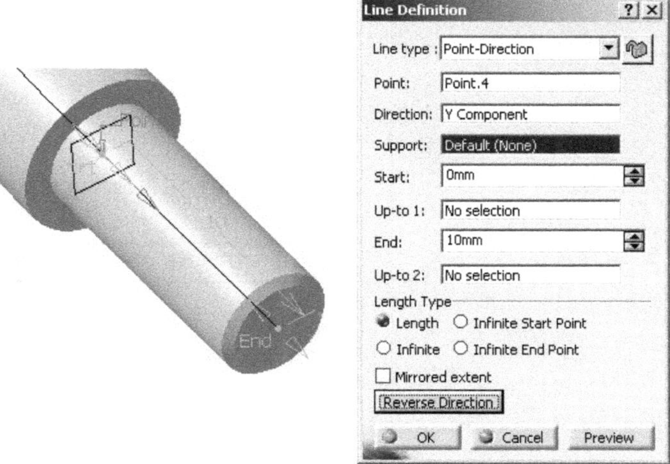

Figure 5–96

5. Rename the line as **Axis**.

6. Hide the joined curve.

7. Create an **On curve** point type, as shown in Figure 5–97.

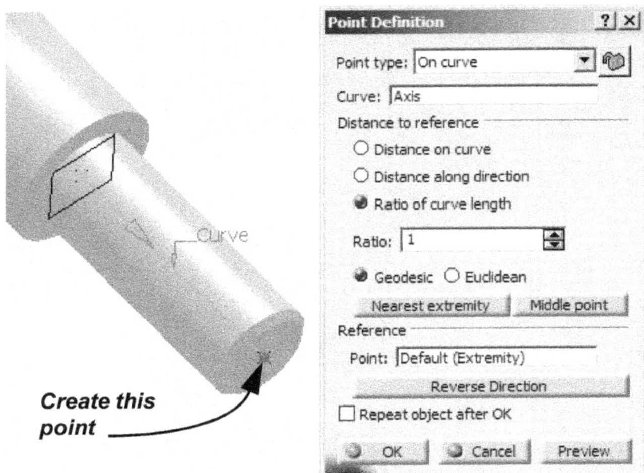

Figure 5–97

8. Create a **Parallel through point** plane type as specified in Figure 5–98.

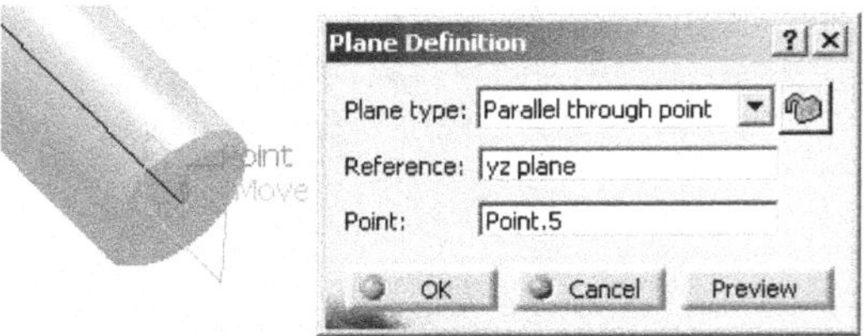

Figure 5–98

9. Rename the reference plane as **Refplane2**.

Task 7 - Create an Intersection feature.

1. In the Wireframe toolbar, click (Intersection).

2. Select the edge of the chamfer as the first element and the reference plane that you just created as the second element, as shown in Figure 5–99.

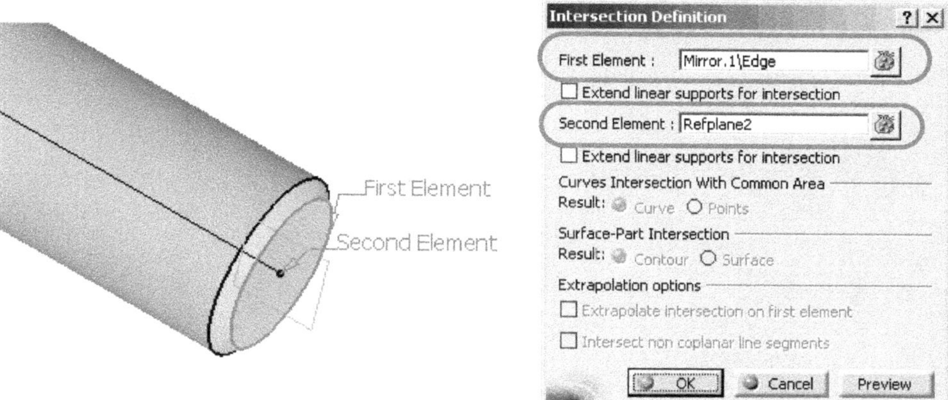

Figure 5–99

3. Click **OK** to continue. Because there are two results for this action, the Multi-Result Management dialog box opens as shown in Figure 5–100. In this dialog box, you can select an option to keep one (by specifying a reference element) or both of the results.

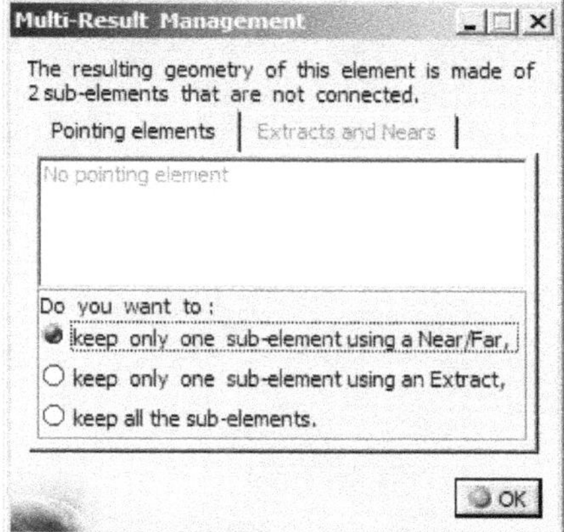

Figure 5–100

4. Ensure that the **keep only one sub-element using a Near/Far** option is selected, and click **OK**.

5. Show **Point.1** and **Point.3**.

6. Select the point shown in Figure 5–101. The result that is closest to this reference point will be kept.

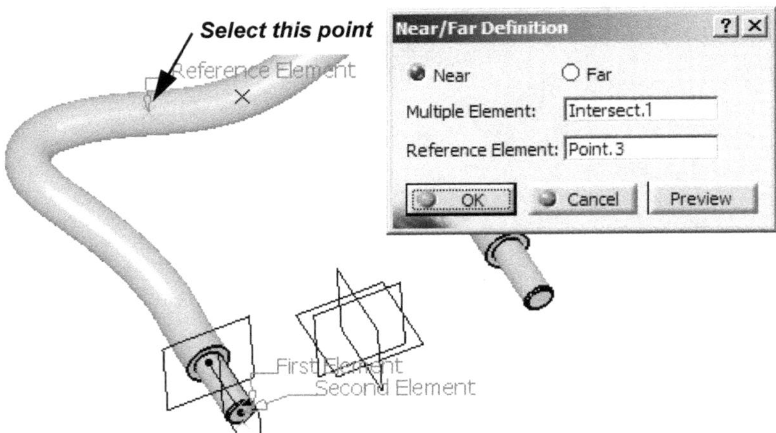

Figure 5–101

7. Click **OK** to complete the feature. The point displays as shown in Figure 5–102.

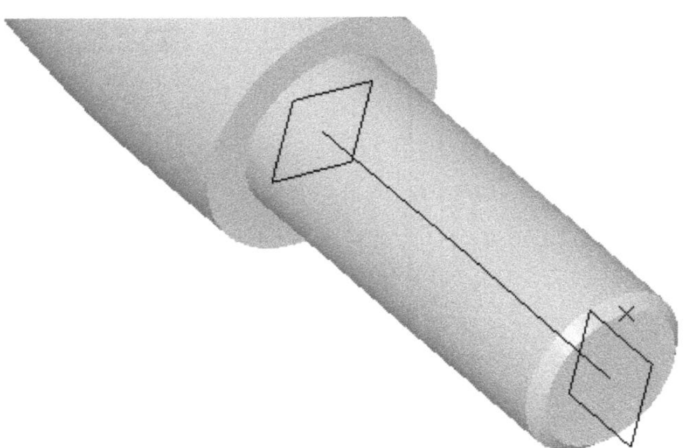

Figure 5–102

Note that the Intersection feature and Near feature display in the specification tree.

8. Rename the Near feature as **Startpoint**.
9. Select **Refplane2** and enter the Sketcher workbench.
10. Sketch the profile on **RefPlane2**, as shown in Figure 5–103.

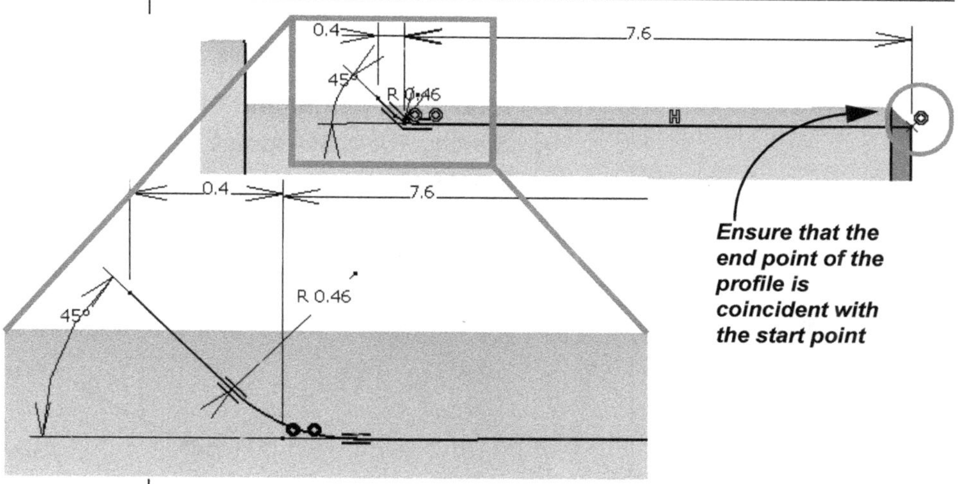

Figure 5–103

11. Complete the sketch.
12. Rename the sketch as **HelixProfile**.

Task 8 - Create a Helix.

In this task, you will create a Helix using the wireframe elements that you created in the previous tasks.

1. In the Wireframe toolbar, expand the Curves flyout, and click (Helix). The Helix Curve Definition dialog box opens as shown in Figure 5–104.

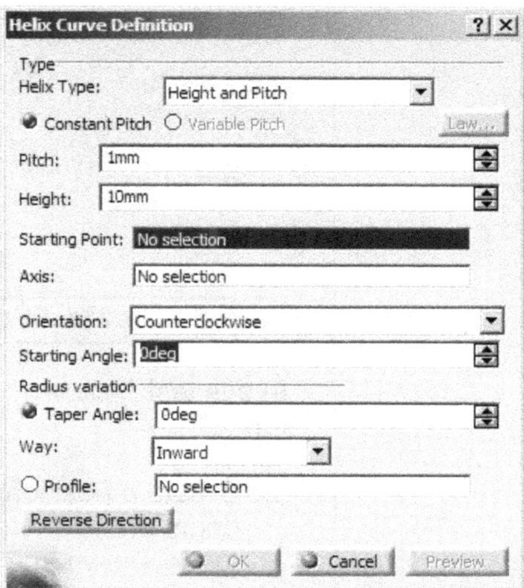

Figure 5–104

2. In the Helix Curve Definition dialog box, enter the following specifications. The result displays as shown in Figure 5–105:

    - *Helix Type:* **Height and Pitch**
    - *Starting Point:* **Startpoint**
    - *Axis:* **Axis**
    - *Pitch:* **0.6mm**
    - Select **Profile** and then select **HelixProfile** in the specification tree.

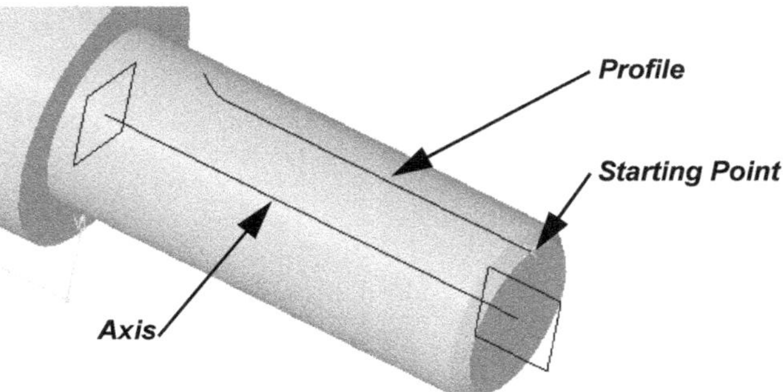

Figure 5–105

3. Click **OK** to complete the feature. The Helix displays as shown in Figure 5–106.

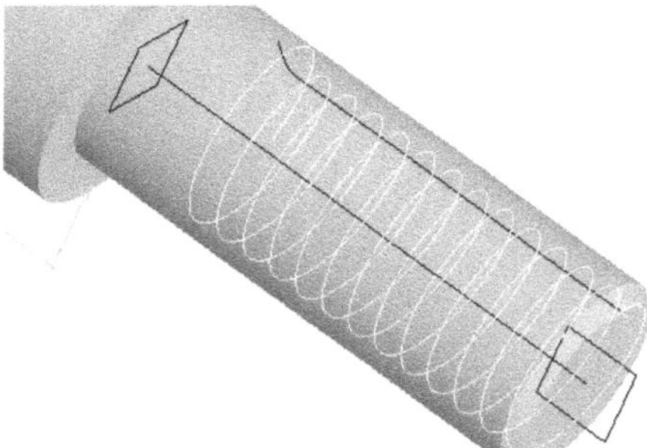

Figure 5–106

Task 9 - Create a Profile.

In this task, you will create a Profile that defines the shape of the thread.

1. Create a positioned sketch on **Refplane2**. Ensure that the origin of the sketch and the orientation of the sketch match those shown in Figure 5–107.

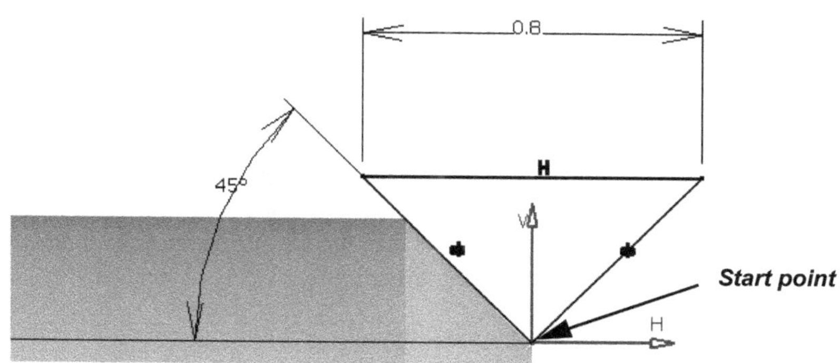

Figure 5–107

2. Rename the sketch as **ThreadProfile**.

Task 10 - Create the thread.

In this task, you will create the thread using the Helix and the profile that you have created in the previous tasks.

1. Switch to the Part Design workbench and define the **PartBody** as the work object.
2. Create a Slot feature with the following selections:
   - *Profile:* **ThreadProfile**
   - *Center curve:* **Helix.1**
   - *Profile control:* **Pulling direction**
   - *Selection:* **Refplane1**

   The model displays as shown in Figure 5–108.

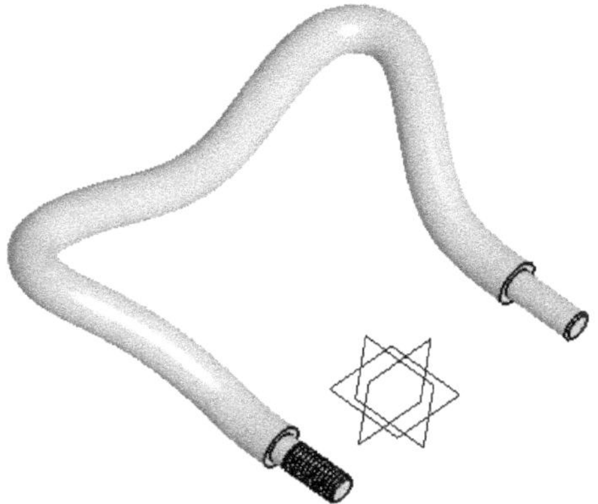

Figure 5–108

3. Save the file.

Task 11 - (Optional) Create another thread.

In this task, you will create another thread for the mirrored side of the model.

1. Create the required wireframe elements.
2. Create the Helix.
3. Create the thread profile.
4. Create the thread.
5. Save and close the file.

   The completed model displays as shown in Figure 5–109.

Figure 5–109

Practice 5d

Sailboat Keel

Practice Objectives

- Create intersection elements.
- Extract elements.
- Create splines.
- Create a Multi-sections Solid feature using a Spline.

In this practice, you will create the keel of a racing sailboat. The keel consists of a hydrodynamic foil and a bulb that holds ballast. You will model the foil using a Multi-sections Solid feature. You will then construct the required wireframe elements to create the bulb creation, using a Multi-sections Solid feature. The completed model displays as shown in Figure 5–110.

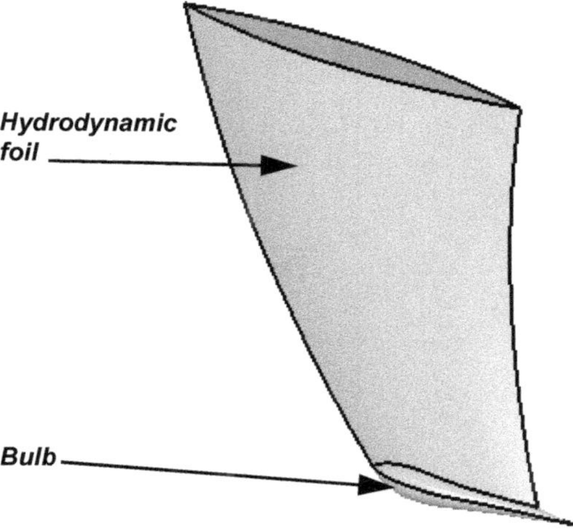

Figure 5–110

Task 1 - Open the part.

1. Open **SailboatKeel.CATPart**. The foil sections have already been created, as shown in Figure 5–111.

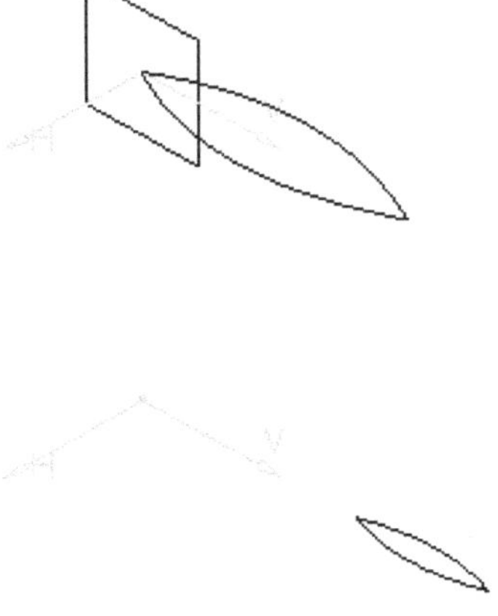

Figure 5–111

Task 2 - Create a profile.

In this task, you will create a profile that will be used to create the Multi-sections Solid.

1. Sketch an arc on the yz plane, similar to the one shown in Figure 5–112.

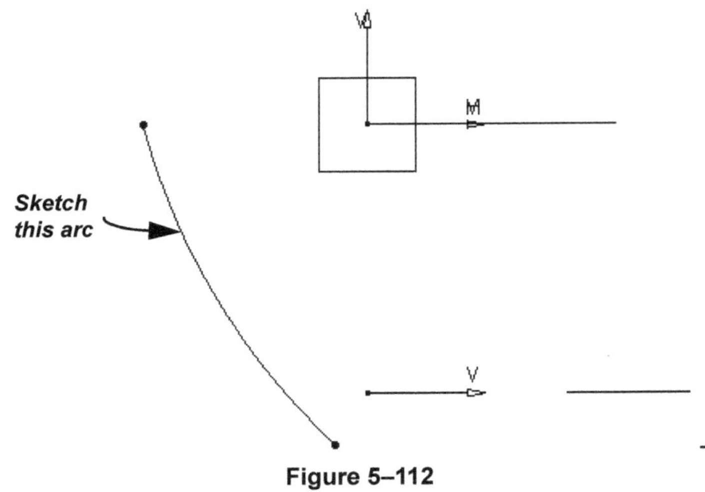

Figure 5–112

Task 3 - Create a multi-sections solid.

1. Click (Multi-sections Solid). Define the Multi-sections Solid feature by selecting the following sketches in the specification tree or model:
   - **RootChord**
   - **TipChord**
2. Click **Preview**. The preview displays as shown in Figure 5–113. The transition between sections is system-defined. Note how different it is compared to the profile.

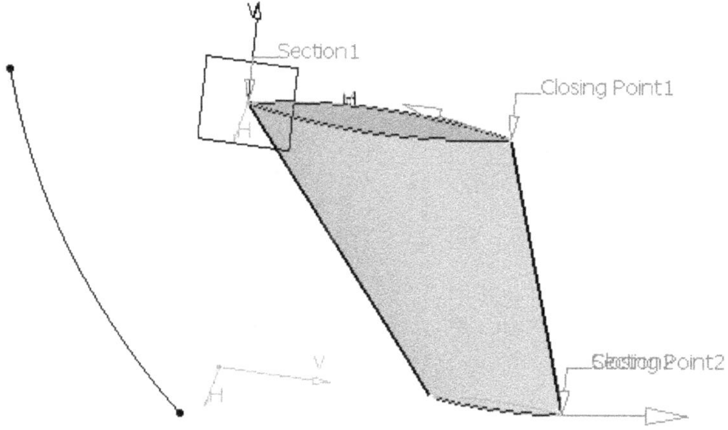

Figure 5–113

3. Select the *Spine* tab and select the profile that you just created.

4. Click **Preview**. The preview displays as shown in Figure 5–114.The geometry is forced to follow the Spine.

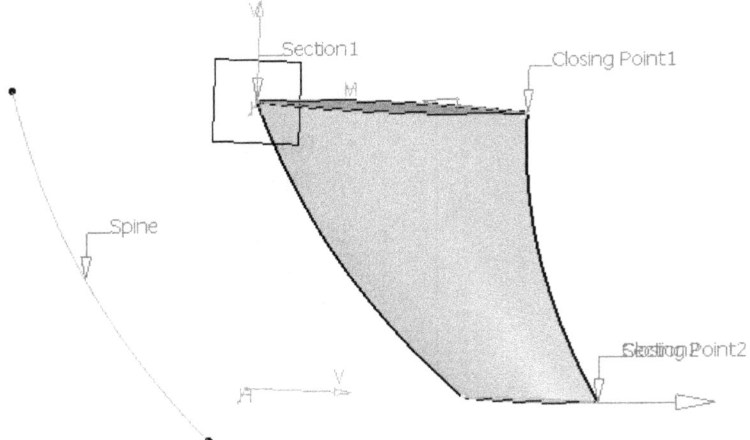

Figure 5–114

5. Complete the feature and hide the yz plane. The Multi-sections Solid feature displays as shown in Figure 5–115.

Figure 5–115

6. Save the model.

Task 4 - Create reference elements for the bulb.

In this task, you will create reference points. You will use these points to create guide curves and as closing points for the Multi-sections Solid creation.

1. Hide the **PartBody**.
2. Show the following geometrical sets:
   - **BulbProfiles**
   - **BulbPointsPlanes**

   The model displays as shown in Figure 5–116.

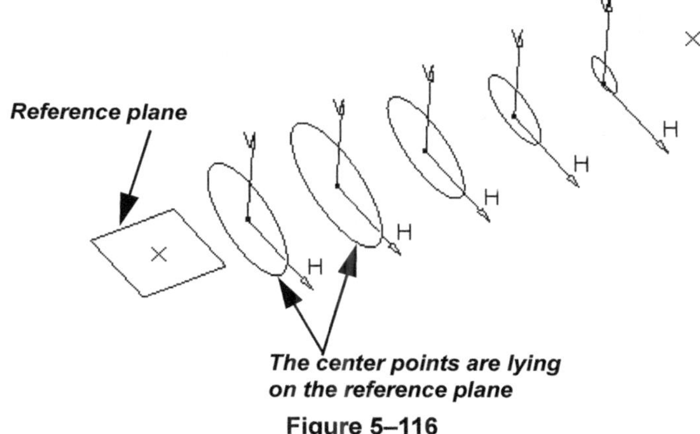

Figure 5–116

Design Considerations

The guide curves will be created using the extremum points of the ellipses. The center points for the first two ellipses are lying on the reference plane. You can make the creation of the extremum points for these two ellipses easier and faster using the Intersection and Extract features. The extremum points of the other three ellipses will be created using the Point feature.

3. Select **Start>Shape>Generative Shape Design**.
4. Define the **BulbGuideCurves** geometrical set to be the work object.
5. In the Wireframe toolbar, click (Intersection).

6. Click [icon] and select the first two profiles as the First element. Select the reference plane as the Second element to create the intersection points, as shown in Figure 5–117.

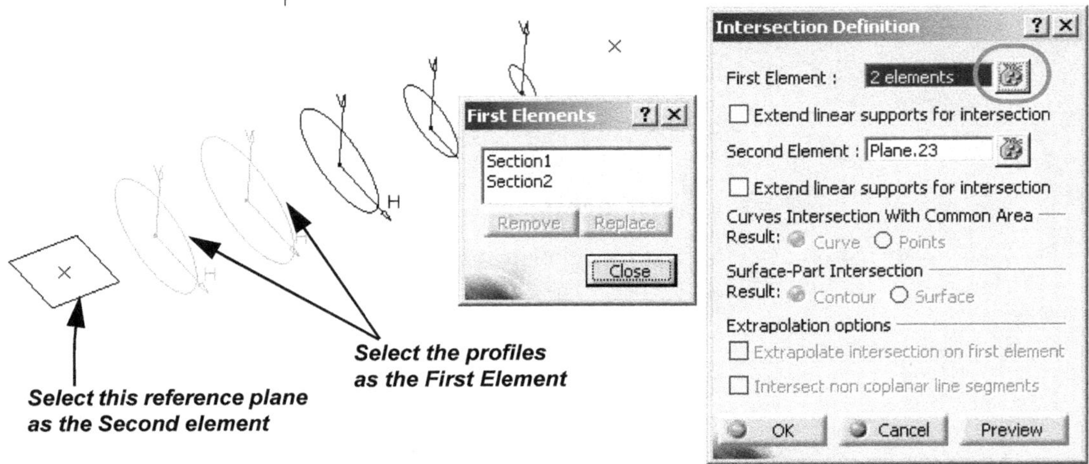

Figure 5–117

7. Click **OK**. The Multi Result Management dialog box opens as shown in Figure 5–118. Click **No**.

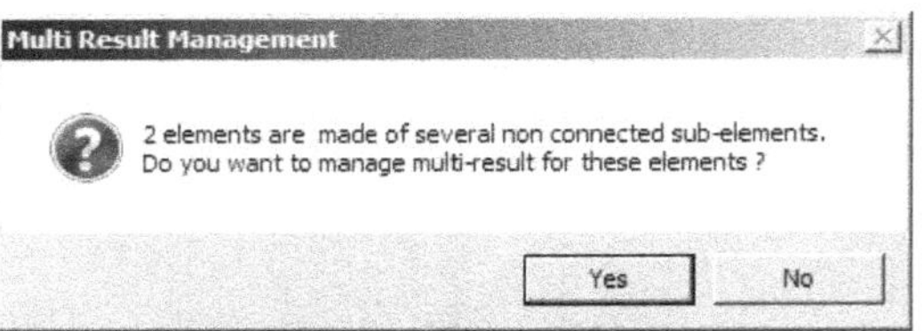

Figure 5–118

The model displays as shown in Figure 5–119.

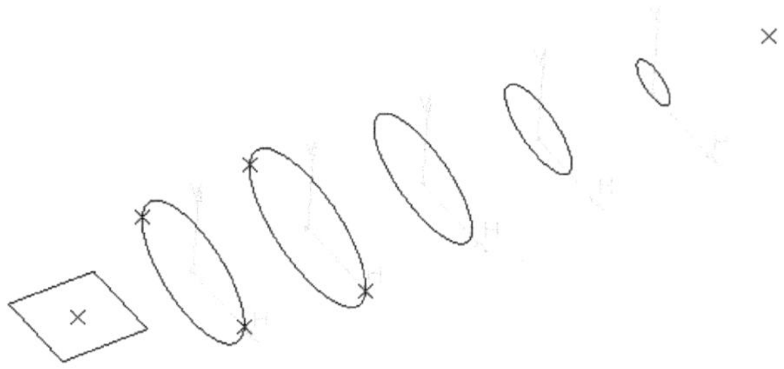

Figure 5–119

Task 5 - Extract the intersection points.

In this task, you will extract the intersection points that you created in the previous task. By doing so, you can use each intersection point as a single element.

You might need to zoom the model to be able to select the points.

1. In the Operations toolbar, expand the Extracts flyout, and click (Extract). The Extract Definition dialog box opens.
2. In the Extract Definition dialog box, click as shown in Figure 5–120. The Element(s) to extract dialog box opens.
3. Select the intersection points one by one from the model. Four elements display in the Element(s) to extract dialog box, as shown in Figure 5–120.

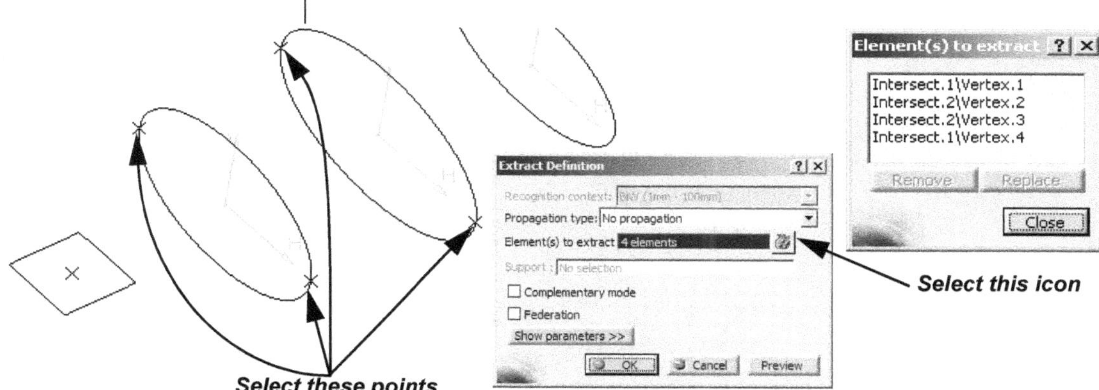

Figure 5–120

4. In the Element(s) to extract dialog box, click **Close**.
5. In the Extract Definition dialog box, click **OK**. The points display in the specification tree, as shown in Figure 5–121.

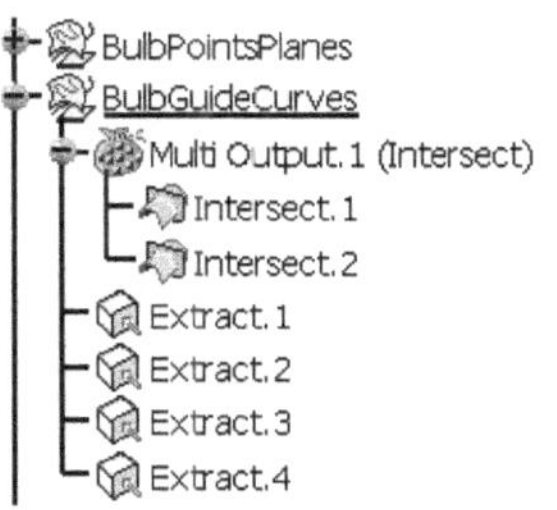

Figure 5–121

6. In the specification tree, hide the **Intersect.1** and **Intersect.2** intersection points.

Task 6 - Create the extremum points

1. In the Wireframe toolbar, expand the Points flyout, and click (Point), Make the following selections in the Point Definition dialog box (as shown in Figure 5–122).

   - *Point type:* **On Curve**
   - *Curve:* **Section.3**
   - *Distance to reference:* **Ratio of curve length**
   - *Ratio:* **0.25**
   - *Reference Point:* **Point.1**

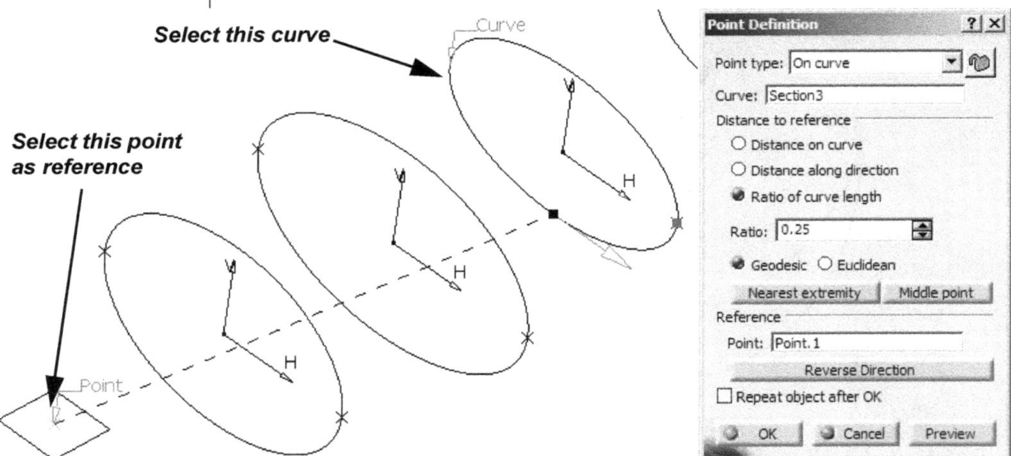

Figure 5–122

2. In the Wireframe toolbar, expand the Points flyout, and click (Point). Make the following selections in the Point Definition dialog box, as shown in Figure 5–123:

   - *Point type:* **On Curve**
   - *Curve:* **Section.3**
   - *Distance to reference:* **Ratio of curve length**
   - *Ratio:* **0.5**
   - *Reference Point:* **Point.11**

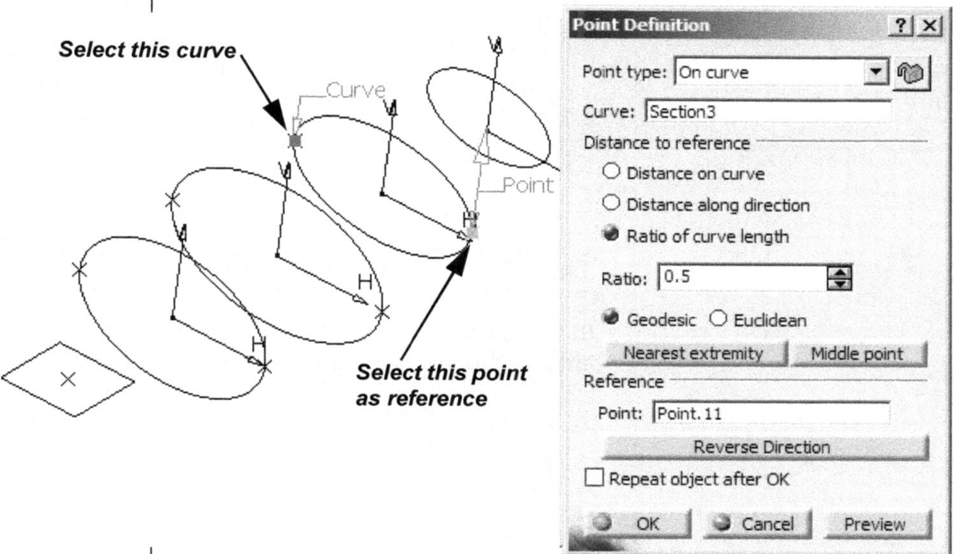

Figure 5–123

The model displays as shown in Figure 5–124.

Figure 5–124

3. Create four more extremum points using **Point.1** as the reference point, as shown in Figure 5–125.

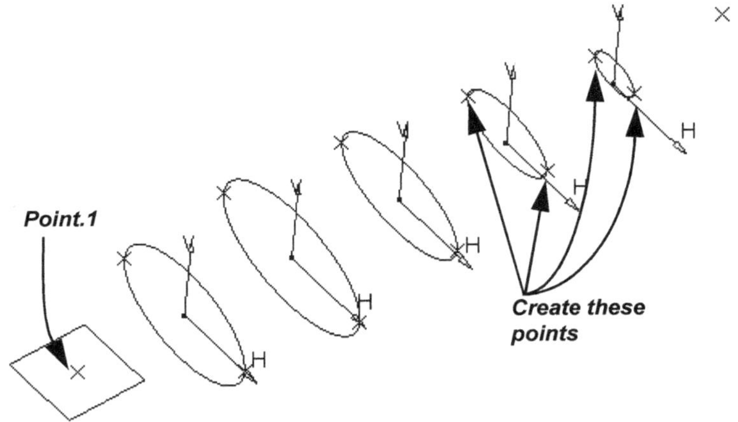

Figure 5–125

Task 7 - Create the guide lines

In this practice, you will create the guide lines. You will use these lines in the next task, during the Multi-sections Solid creation.

1. In the Wireframe toolbar, expand the Curves flyout, and click  (Spline).
2. In the specification tree or display, select the points as shown in Figure 5–126.

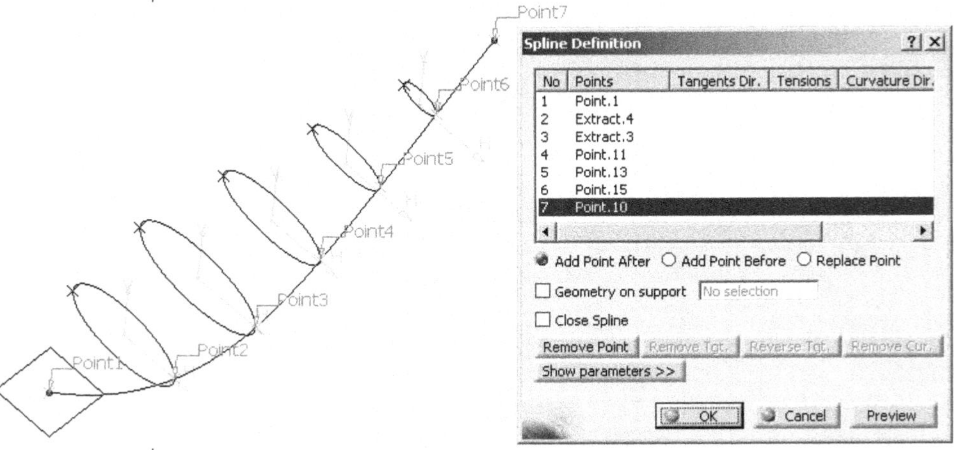

Figure 5–126

3. Click **OK** to complete the feature. The curve displays as shown in Figure 5–127.

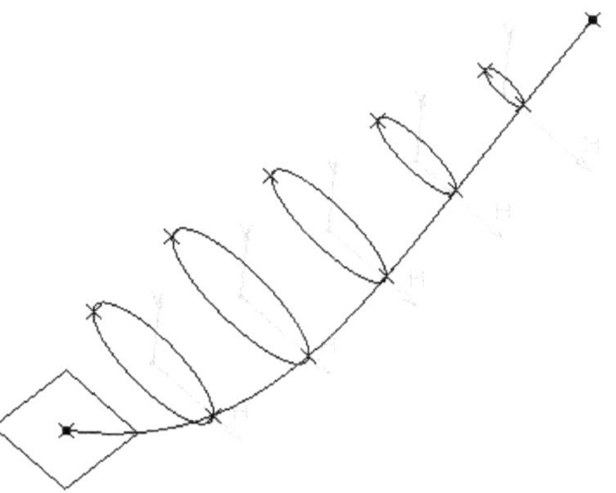

Figure 5–127

4. Rename the spline as **guide1**.

5. Create another Spline as shown in Figure 5–128. Rename the Spline as **guide2**.

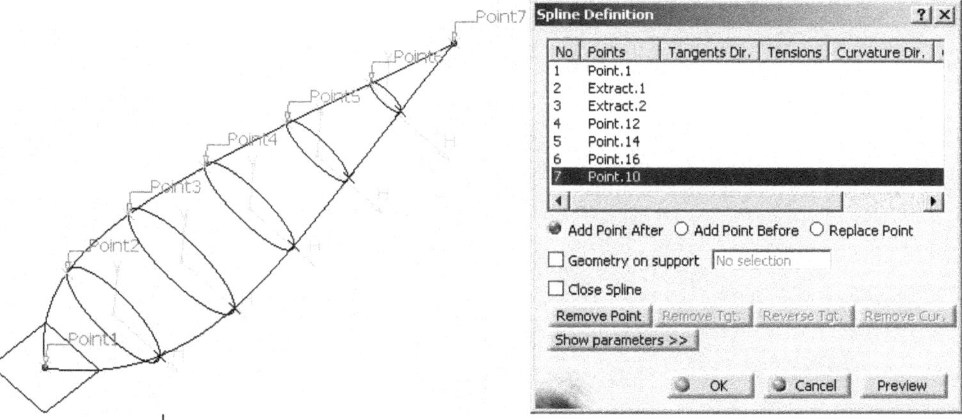

Figure 5–128

Task 8 - Create a Multi-sections Solid.

In this task, you will create a Multi-sections Solid using the profiles, guide curves, and extremum points.

1. Define the **PartBody** to be the work object.
2. Select **Start>Mechanical Design>Part Design**.
3. Click (Multi-sections Solid). The Multi-sections Solid Definition dialog box opens. In the specification tree or model, select the following sketches:
   - **Section1**
   - **Section2**
   - **Section3**
   - **Section4**
   - **Section5**
4. In the *Guides* field, select the three dots. Select the following splines as the guide curves, as shown in Figure 5–129:
   - **guide1**
   - **guide2**

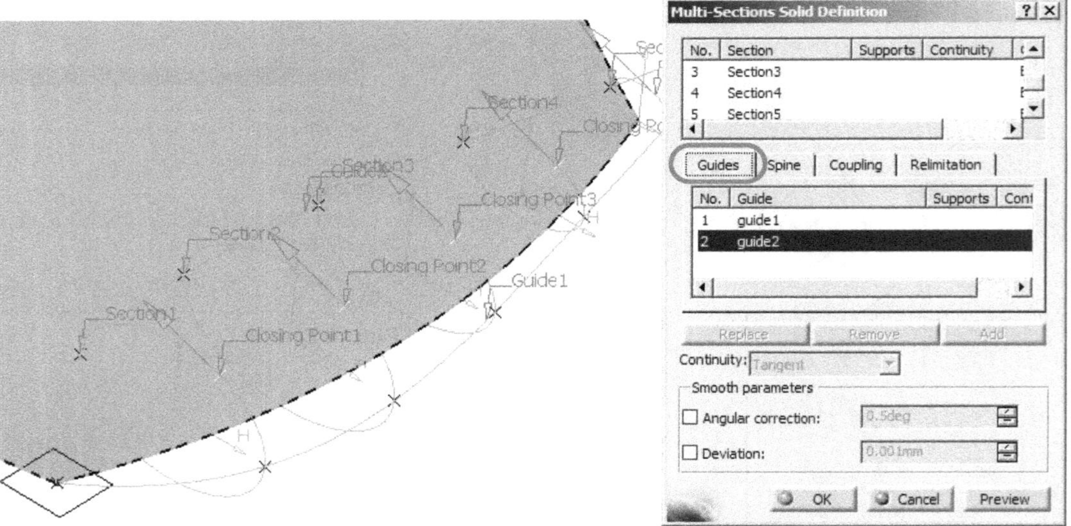

Figure 5–129

5. Right-click one of the closing points and select **Replace**.
6. Select the extremum point. The closing point is now located at the extremum point, as shown in Figure 5–130.

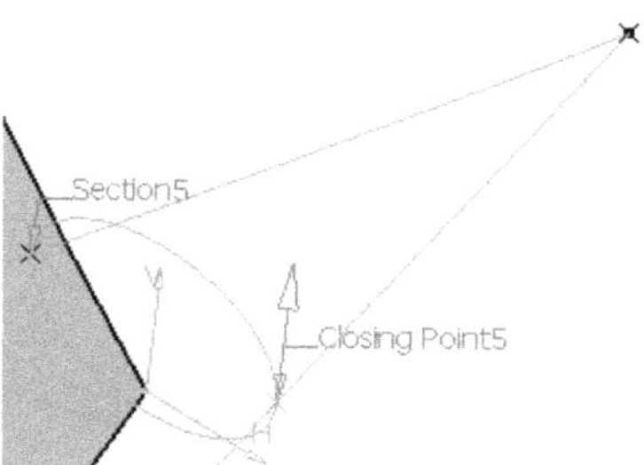

Figure 5–130

7. Replace the rest of the closing points and ensure that they are all pointing in the same direction, as shown in Figure 5–131.

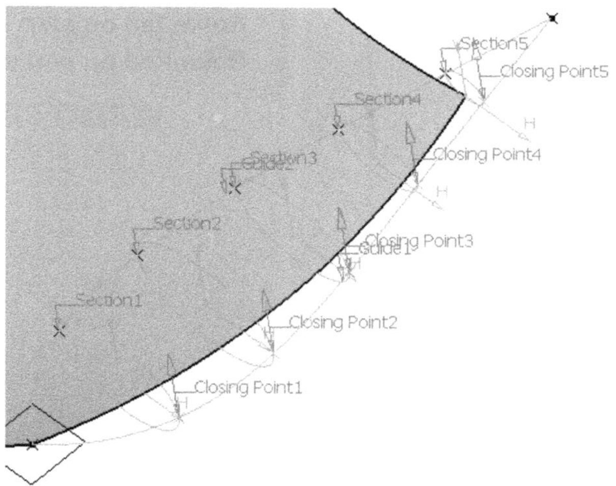

Figure 5–131

8. In the Multi-sections Solid Definition dialog box, click **Preview**. The preview displays, as shown in Figure 5–132.

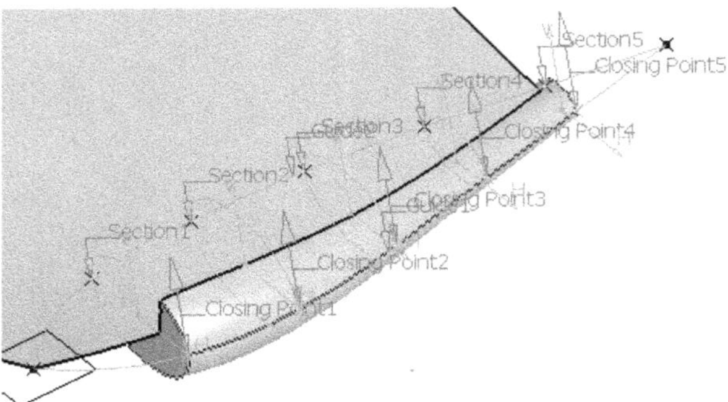

Figure 5–132

9. The solid is only created between the sections. To create the whole bulb, select the *Relimitation* tab and clear the following options, as shown in Figure 5–133:

   - **Relimited on start section**
   - **Relimited on end section**

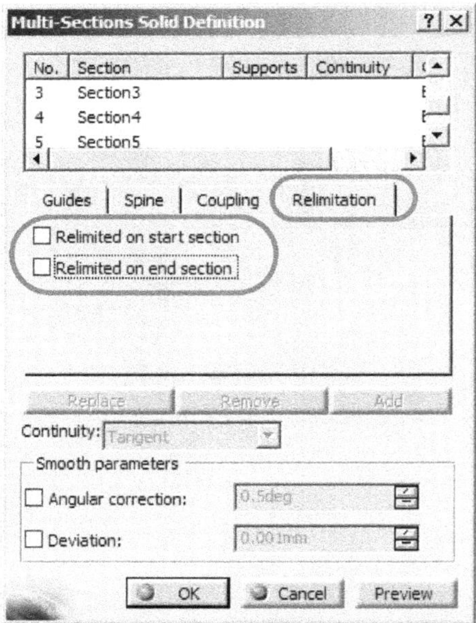

Figure 5–133

Task 9 - Complete the feature.

1. Click **OK** to complete the feature.

2. Hide the **BulbPointsPlanes** and **BulbGuideCurves** geometrical sets. The model displays as shown in Figure 5–134.

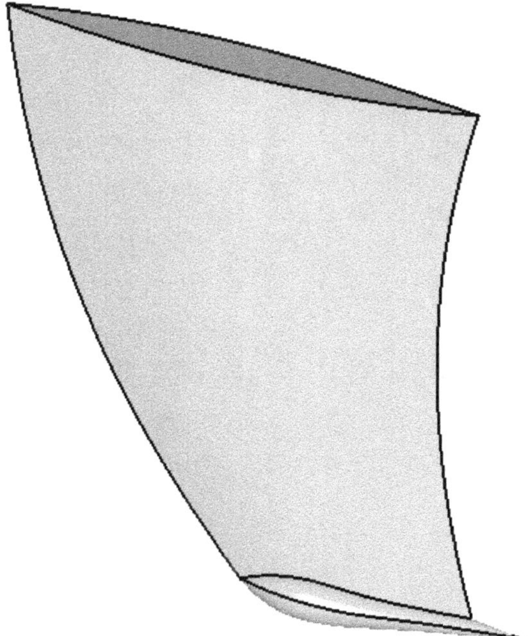

Figure 5–134

3. Save the model and close the file.

Chapter Review Questions

1. To create multiple points along a curve, line, or edge, click

    a. 

    b. 

    c.

    d. None of the above.

2. Which of the following options is valid when creating a line?

    a. Point-Point

    b. Point-Direction

    c. Tangent to curve

    d. All of the above.

3. A spline requires a minimum of three points.

    a. True

    b. False

4. Which of the following options is valid for use as points in a spline?

    a. Reference points

    b. End points

    c. Vertices

    d. All of the above.

5. What can be inferred about the spline curve shown in Figure 5–135?

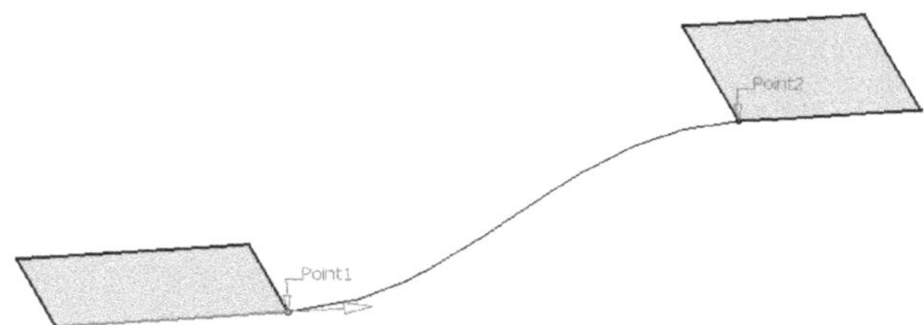

Figure 5–135

   a. There is tangency set between the spline and the adjacent surface edges, at Point1 and Point2.
   b. The arrow indicates the direction of tangency between the spline and the edge of the surface on the left.
   c. Both a and b.
   d. None of the above.

6. The main difference between a Spline and a Polyline, is that a Polyline connects the points with straight lines rather than curves, but can also have a radius defined at each point to control the shape.
   a. True
   b. False

7. The axis of a Helix can be straight or curved.
   a. True
   b. False

8. Once the Axis and Start Point of a Helix have been defined, you can then define _____.
   a. The Pitch
   b. The Height
   c. The Taper
   d. The Starting Angle
   e. All of the above.

9. The curves used to create a Combine are always projected perpendicular to each other.
   a. True
   b. False

Advanced Fillets and Drafts

Dress-up features do not require the creation of a sketch to determine their shape. By default, the underlying geometry of the dress-up feature determines the shape of the resulting geometry. Advanced options for the Fillet and Draft features provide additional control over their shape and propagation. These options also enable you to create the features over more complex geometry.

Learning Objectives in this Chapter

- Understand the advance fillet options for controlling the shape of a fillet.
- Learn about additional types of fillets, including **Variable Radius**, **Chordal**, and **Face-Face**.
- Understand the reflect line draft.
- Learn how advanced draft can provide additional capabilities over regular draft.
- Understand how to manage any failures that occur when creating or editing draft and fillets.

6.1 Advanced Fillets

You can use the Fillet feature to round sharp corners of a part. You can define fillets in the Edge Fillet Definition dialog box by selecting the appropriate reference geometry and specifying a radius value, as shown in Figure 6–1.

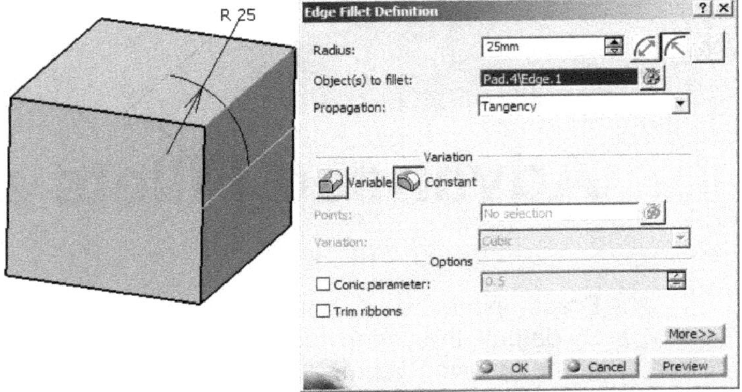

Figure 6–1

You can create fillets using the icons in the Dress-Up Features toolbar shown in Figure 6–2.

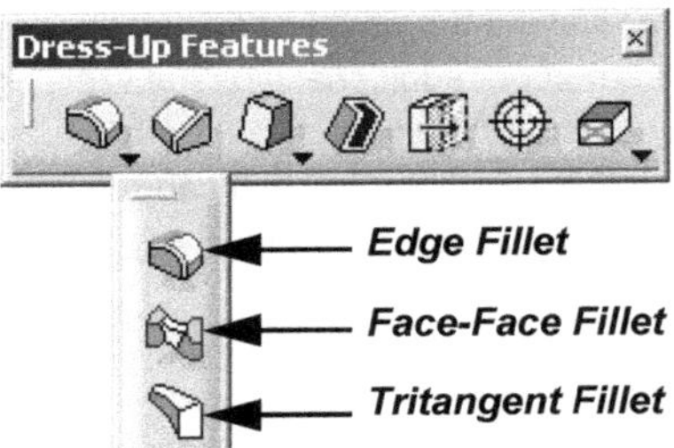

Figure 6–2

In the Edge Fillet Definition dialog box, click **More** to display the advanced Fillet options. You can use the advanced options to further define the shape and propagation of the Fillet feature. The options vary for each type of Fillet feature:

- Edge Fillet
- Variable Radius Fillet
- Chordal Fillet
- Face to Face Fillet
- Tritangent Fillet

Edge Fillet

Note that next time you create an edge fillet, the system will remember whether the dialog box was expanded or not.

The expanded Edge Fillet Definition dialog box is shown in Figure 6–3.

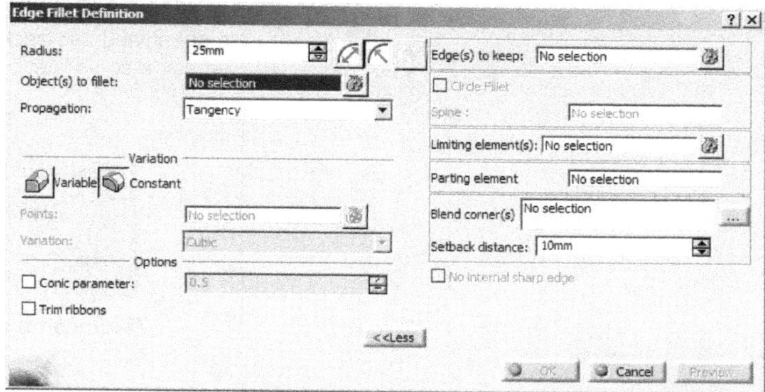

Figure 6–3

The options in the expanded Edge Fillet dialog box are as follows.

Option	Description
Trim Ribbons	Trims overlapping fillets at their intersections. This option is only available when you use the **Tangency** option in the *Propagation* field.

Conic Parameter	Enables you to create conic shaped fillets. By default, a fillet is created with a radial cross-section. To create conic-shaped fillets, the **Conic parameter** option must be activated. The examples show fillet geometry and their respective cross-sections to demonstrate a radial fillet versus a conic fillet. 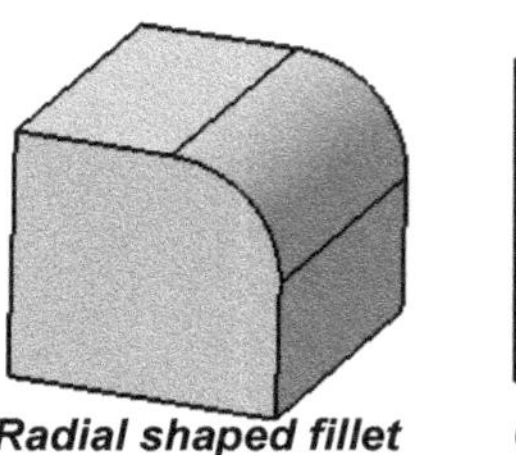  ***Radial shaped fillet*** ***Cross-section*** 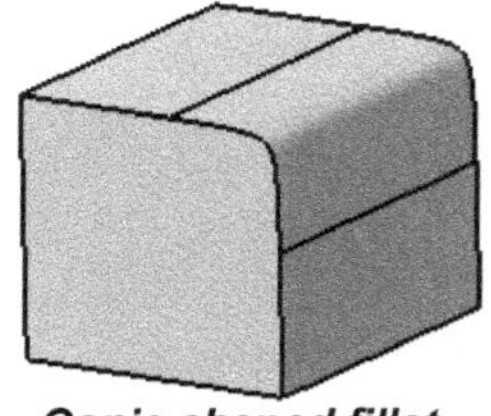  ***Conic shaped fillet*** ***Cross-section***
Edge(s) to Keep	Stops the fillet at the selected part edge. You can add more than one reference. This option is useful when the fillet extends past the boundary of the part geometry.

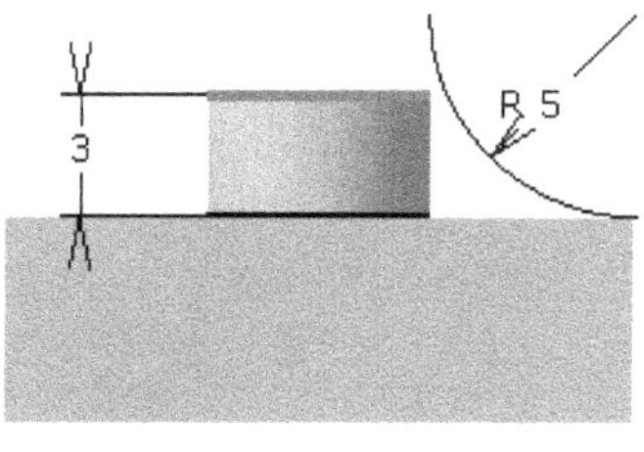

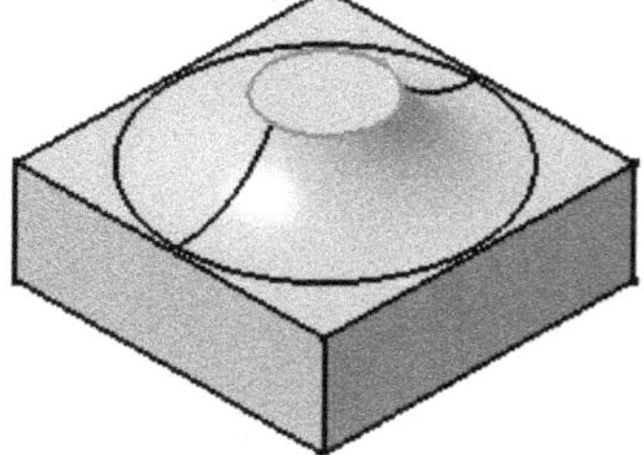

Limiting Elements	Stops the propagation of the fillet at the selected geometry. This geometry can be a reference plane or model surface. The direction of material to be kept is indicated by an arrow. 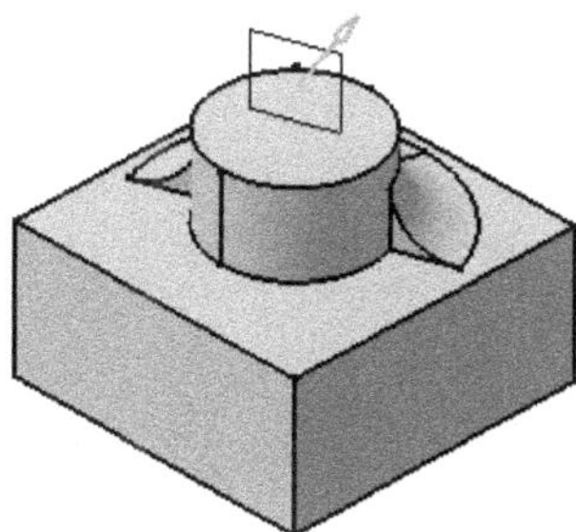
Blend Corners	When more than two edges transition into a corner of a Fillet feature, the **Blend Corner** option is available. It reshapes the way the fillet edges transition together. **How To: Use Blend Corner** 1. In the dialog box, click **More**. 2. Right-click in the *Blend corner(s)* area and select one of the options, as shown below. 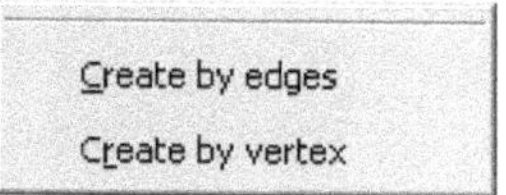 Note that there may only be a single option, **Create by edges or vertex**, depending on your installed service pack. 3. When **Create by edges** is selected, all of the corners are selected automatically. 4. If you want to specify the corners manually, select **Create by vertex** and select a vertex from the model to create or add a corner. 5. Enter a value for the setback distance. The setback distance defines where the fillet shape begins blending into the other fillet shapes. 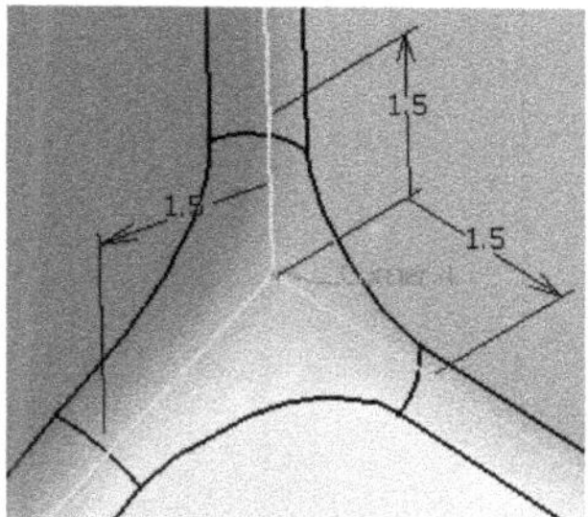

Variable Radius Fillet

To create a variable radius fillet, click (Variable) in the Edge Fillet Definition dialog box. The expanded Edge Fillet Definition dialog box is shown in Figure 6–4.

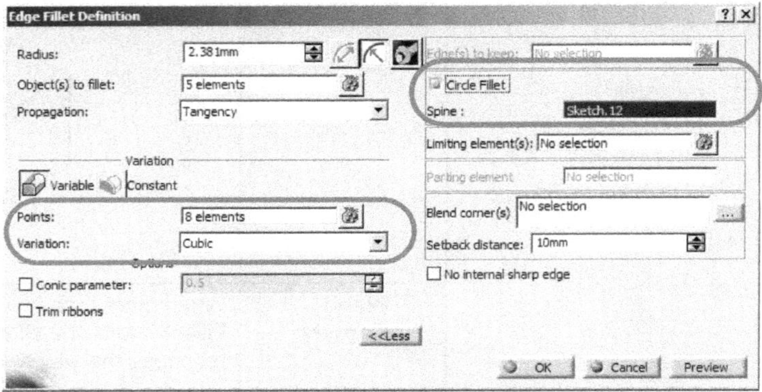

Figure 6–4

The Edge Fillet Definition dialog box updates to enable some additional parameters that were grayed out when the

(Constant) option was selected.

Option	Description
Variation	Determines the shape of the fillet as it blends between two different radii. ***Cubic*** ***Linear*** You can select from the following two options:
Cubic	A third order polynomial curve is fitted between the two radii.
Linear	A first order polynomial curve is fitted between the two radii.

<table>
<tr>
<td>Spine</td>
<td>Provides control over the shape of a Variable Radius Fillet. The radius of the fillet is always perpendicular to the spine.
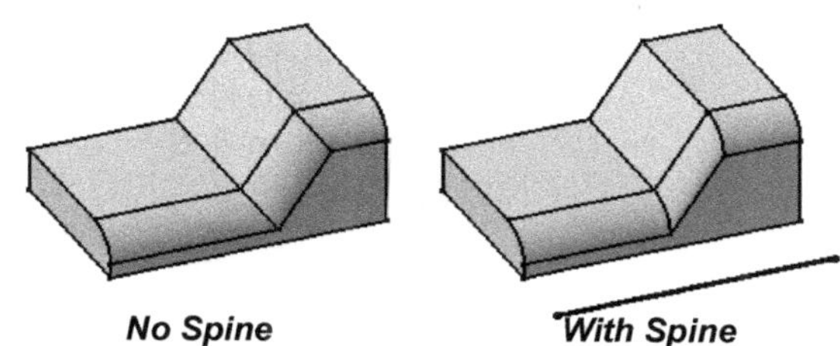

The selection of the spine is disabled by default. To enable selection of a spine, you must first select Circle Fillet.</td>
</tr>
</table>

The variable radius fillet can have unique radii at each point or vertex along the edges being filleted. You can click (Edit Fillet Values) to the right of the *Radius value* field, which opens the Fillet values dialog box, as shown in Figure 6–5.

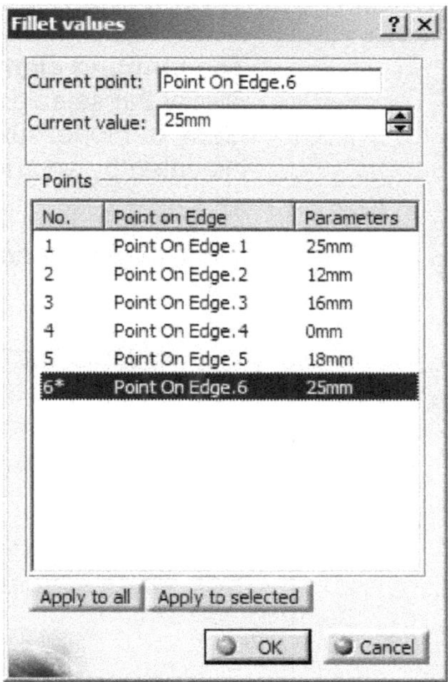

Figure 6–5

Here you can set individual radius values for each point. You can also select several radii and set them to the **Current value** using **Add to selected**, or you can set them all to the **Current value** using **Apply to all**.

Chordal Fillet

To create a chordal fillet, click (Edge Fillet) to open the Edge Fillet Definition dialog box, then click (Chordal). The expanded Edge Fillet Definition dialog box is shown in Figure 6–6.

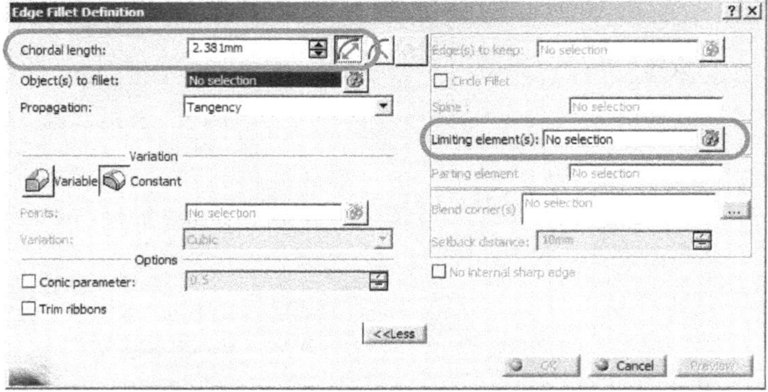

Figure 6–6

The **Limiting element(s)** option stops the propagation of the fillet at the selected geometry. This geometry can be a reference plane or model surface. The direction of material to be kept is indicated by an arrow.

Face-Face Fillet

The expanded Face-Face Fillet Definition dialog box is shown in Figure 6–7.

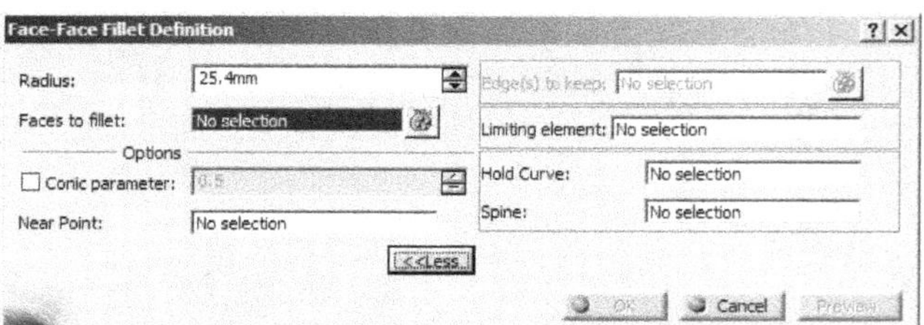

Figure 6–7

In addition to the **Limiting element** option, the Face-Face Fillet Definition dialog box enables you to specify a Hold Curve and Spine. You can use the **Hold Curve** option to specify the radius of the fillet by selecting a sketch or curve created in the Wireframe and Surface workbench. To define the hold curve, you must select a spine. An example is shown in Figure 6–8.

The Generative Shape Design product license is required to create a Face-Face Fillet with a hold curve and spine.

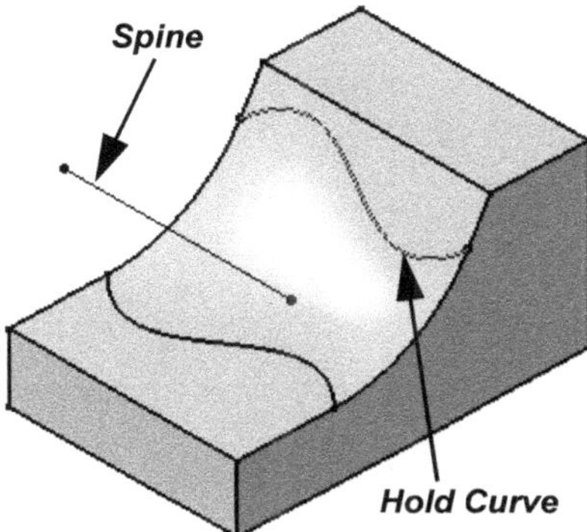

Figure 6–8

6.2 Creating Reflect Line Draft

A reflect line is the external edge of a non-planar face when viewed from a specific direction. Reflect Line Draft uses the reflect lines as neutral lines when drafting the selected faces. The system determines the reflect lines based on the specified pulling direction and Draft angle, as shown in Figure 6–9.

CATIA highlights the reflect line in magenta.

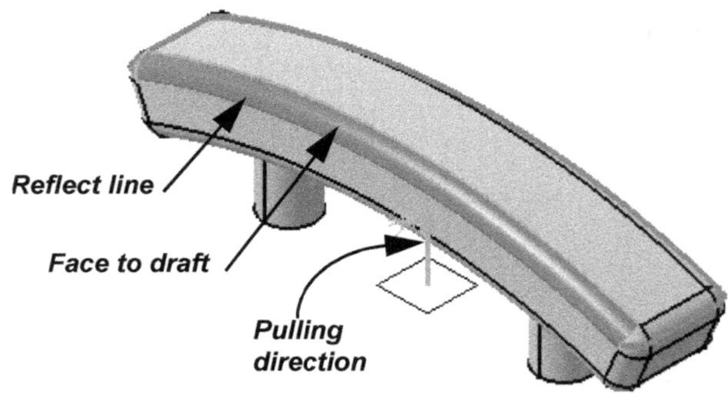

Figure 6–9

Reflect Line Draft is useful when drafting complex models, because their geometry is typically non-planar. This type of Draft enables you to place draft on faces that are already filleted.

General Steps

Use the following general steps to create a Reflect Line Draft:

1. Start Draft creation.
2. Specify Reflect Line Draft elements.

Step 1 - Start Draft creation.

To create a Reflect Line Draft feature, click (Draft Reflect Line) in the Dress-Up Features toolbar. The expanded Draft Reflect Line Definition dialog box opens as shown in Figure 6–10.

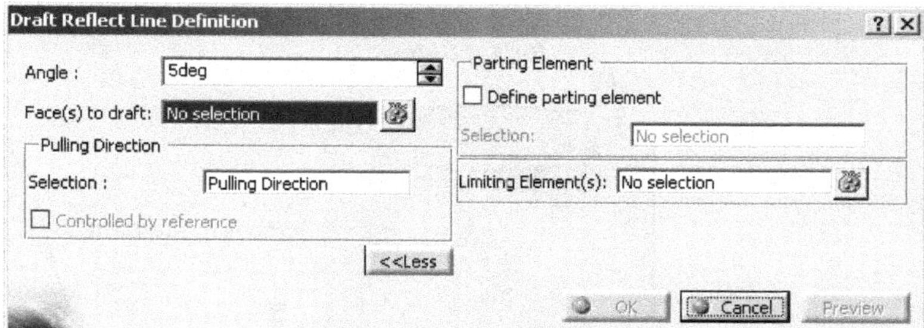

Figure 6–10

Step 2 - Specify Reflect Line Draft elements.

The Draft requires you to enter the following information:

- Draft angle
- Faces to draft
- Pulling direction
- Parting element, if applicable.
- Limiting element(s), if applicable.

Click **OK** to complete the feature.

6.3 Creating Advanced Draft

The Advanced Draft feature provides additional control and functionality over the Constant Draft feature. Advanced Draft incorporates all of the functionality of the constant and variable Drafts. Additionally, different Draft angles can be specified for either side of the parting element, as shown in Figure 6–11.

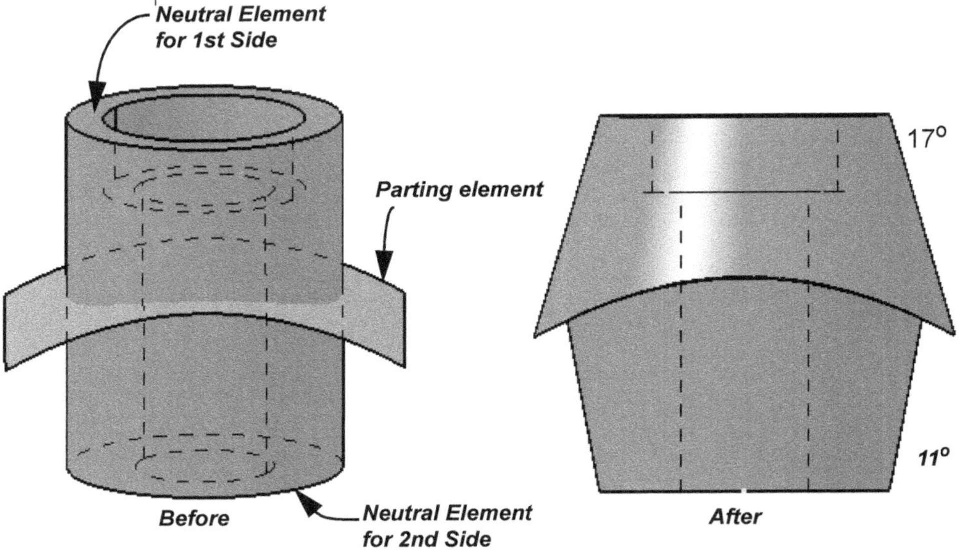

Figure 6–11

General Steps

Use the following general steps to create an Advanced Reflect Line Draft:

1. Start the creation of an Advanced Draft feature.
2. Define the Draft angle conditions.
3. Select the faces to draft in the first direction.
4. Select a pulling direction.
5. Select a parting element.
6. Select the faces to draft in the second direction.

Step 1 - Start the creation of an Advanced Draft feature.

Click (Advanced Draft) in the Advanced DressUp toolbar. The Draft Definition (Advanced) dialog box opens as shown in Figure 6–12.

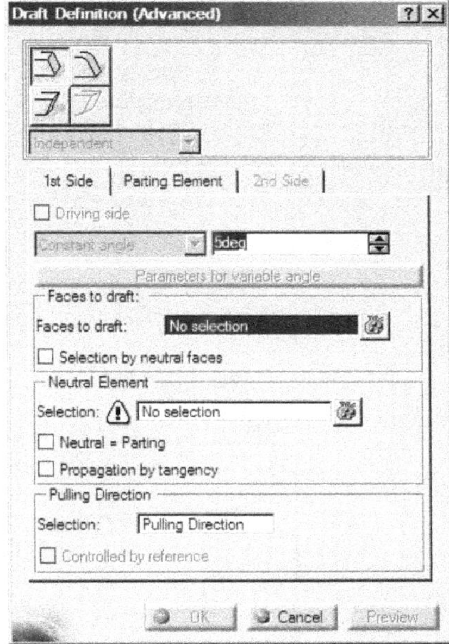

Figure 6–12

Click the required icon in the top of the dialog box. The icons are described as follows:

Icon	Description
	Create a one-sided Draft feature.
	Create a two-sided Draft feature.
	Create a one-sided Draft Reflect Line feature.
	Create a two-sided Draft Reflect Line feature.

Step 2 - Define the Draft angle conditions.

Define the Draft angle conditions, as shown in Figure 6–13.

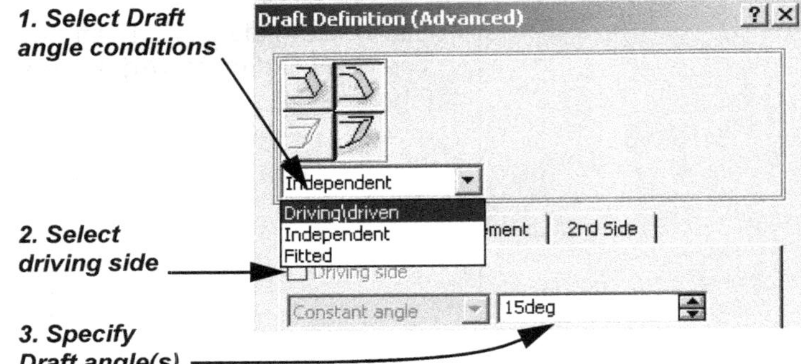

Figure 6–13

When drafting in two directions, two Draft angle conditions can be specified, as follows:

Option	Description
Independent	Specifies the Draft angle independently for each direction.
Driving/driven	Selects a direction as the driving side. The Draft angle that you specify controls draft in both directions.
Fitted	Applies draft symmetrically on two opposite sides of the part line. Using this option, you can apply a parting line adjustment. This option requires a Cast & Forged Part Optimizer license.

Step 3 - Select the faces to draft in the first direction.

In the Neutral Element drop-down list, select the faces to draft and select the faces in the model. If you select the **Tangency** option in the *Propagation* field, tangent faces to the selected face are automatically included in the Draft.

Step 4 - Select a pulling direction.

Select a pulling direction. This option determines the direction in which the mold is pulled away from the part. You can select a reference plane, planar face, or surface. An arrow displays, indicating the pulling direction. You can flip the direction using the arrow.

Step 5 - Select a parting element.

Select the *Parting Element* tab in the Draft Definition (Advanced) dialog box. The parting element determines the surface at which the top and bottom of the mold meet. You can select a reference plane or model face. A parting element is required for a Draft in two directions.

Step 6 - Select the faces to draft in the second direction.

Select the *2nd Side* tab in the Draft Definition (Advanced) dialog box. In the Neutral Element drop-down list, select the faces to draft and select the faces in the model.

6.4 Draft and Fillet Failure Resolution

Fillet Failure Resolution

When a fillet fails, you can use a variety of methods to investigate and resolve the failure. Check the error message reported by the system to determine the cause of the problem. Based on the error message, try one of the following techniques to resolve the error:

- Ensure that the model is of good quality by inspecting it for short edges and very small surfaces that might cause unnecessary complications.
- Reduce the radius of the fillet feature. A large radius often causes the fillet to intersect itself or other complex geometry, which causes it to fail. Create the fillet with a smaller radius and then visualize what the fillet would look like with a larger radius.
- Carefully check your references. When creating large and complex fillets, an incorrect reference is often selected or an important reference is missing. Try breaking a complex fillet into smaller features that are easier to manage.
- Select edges to fillet iteratively by selecting one or two edges and clicking **Preview**, and then selecting more edges as required.
- Fillet the part in a different order. For example, if you have a vertical and horizontal edge that meet, and the vertical edge was filleted first, try filleting the horizontal edge first.
- Try using one of the other types of fillets.
- Extract surface features of a failed fillet or draft and use surface features and surface operations to create the geometry (use this method as a last resort).

Common Filleting Errors and Possible Fixes:

- **Twisted Fillet Error:** Indicates that the radius of the fillet you are attempting is too large for the radius of curvature of the edge you are trying to fillet. A possible solution is to reduce the fillet radius.
- **More than (3) Edges on a Vertex Error:** Indicates that the fillet cannot be re-limited to the point at which the edges come to a point. The solution is to move one of the fillets further up in the specification tree.

- **Interrupted Fillet Error:** Think of the filleting process as a marble rolling between two surfaces. An interrupted fillet is a fillet where the marble cannot stay in contact with the two surfaces through the entire length of the edge. The solution here is to try a smaller radius fillet or a different style of fillet.
- **Coupling:** Indicates that the underlying surfaces and faces cannot be trimmed to complete a closure of the volume. A situation where a fillet is not limited is shown in Figure 6–14.

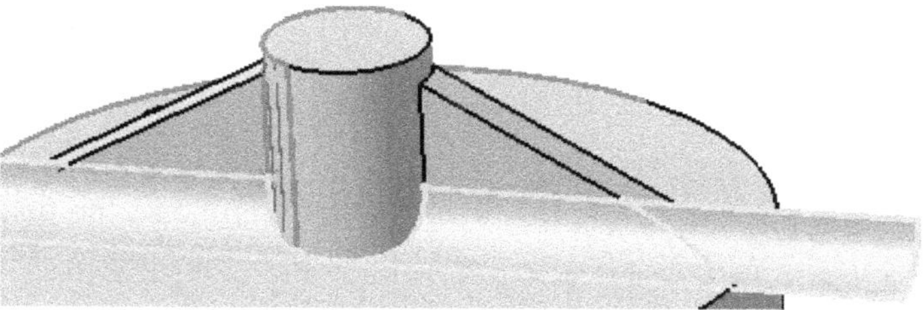

Figure 6–14

The Update Diagnosis dialog box opens as shown in Figure 6–15.

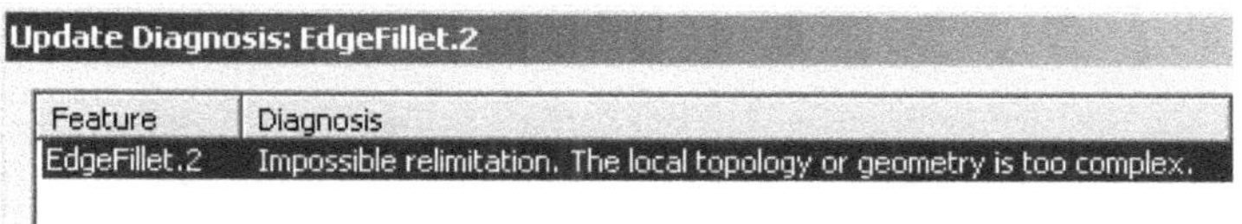

Update Diagnosis: EdgeFillet.2

Feature	Diagnosis
EdgeFillet.2	Impossible relimitation. The local topology or geometry is too complex.

Figure 6–15

Possible solutions:

- Fillet the part in a different order as shown in Figure 6–16.

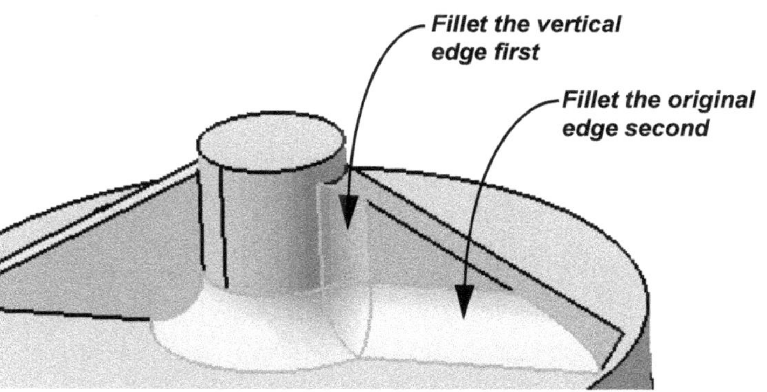
Fillet the vertical edge first
Fillet the original edge second

Figure 6–16

- Reduce the fillet radius as shown in Figure 6–17.

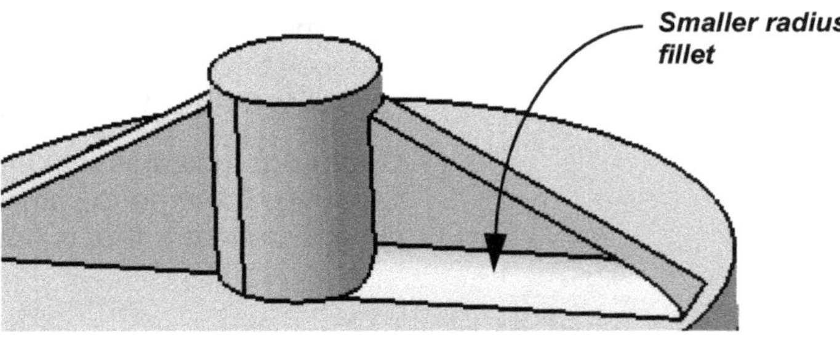

Figure 6–17

Draft Failure Resolution

When a draft fails, you can use a variety of available methods to investigate and resolve the failure. Check the error message to determine the cause of the problem.

Based on the error message, try one of the following techniques to resolve the error:

- Ensure that the model is of good quality by inspecting it for short edges and very small surfaces that might cause unnecessary complications.
- Reduce the angle of the Draft feature. If the Draft feature fails with a large angular value, try to create the draft with a smaller angular value.
- When adding a draft to a model, the system automatically selects tangent faces. Ensure that you have only selected the faces to which you want to add a draft.
- Extract Surface features of a failed draft and use Surface features and Surface operations to create the geometry (use this method as a last resort).

Practice 6a

Advanced Fillet Creation

Practice Objectives

- Use Limiting Elements.
- Use Circle Fillet with Spine.
- Specify the edge(s) to keep.

In this practice, you will create a series of fillets on an existing part. Throughout this practice, be aware of the order in which the fillets are created, and also the type of fillet and fillet options that are used. The completed model displays as shown in Figure 6–18.

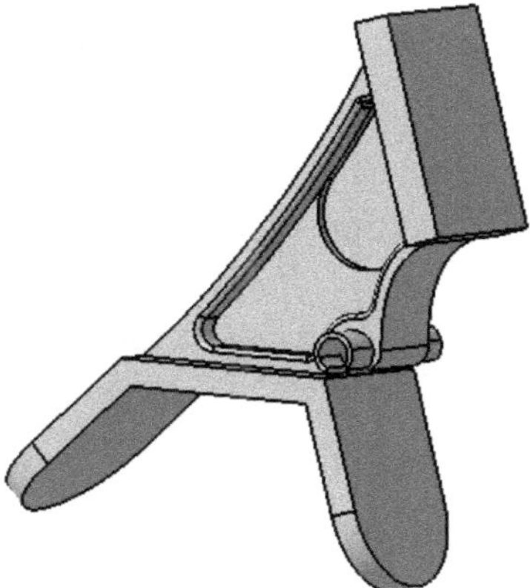

Figure 6–18

Task 1 - Open the part.

1. Open **Support_Fillet.CATPart**. The model displays as shown in Figure 6–19.

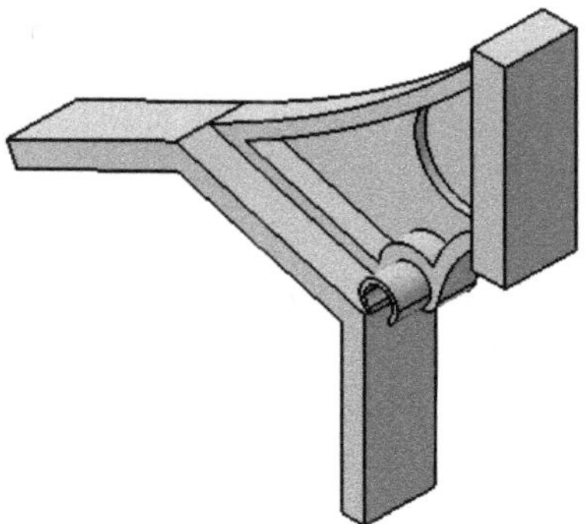

Figure 6–19

2. Create the following Edge Fillet:

   - *Radius:* **3**
   - *Object(s) to fillet:* **5 Edges** (as shown in Figure 6–20)

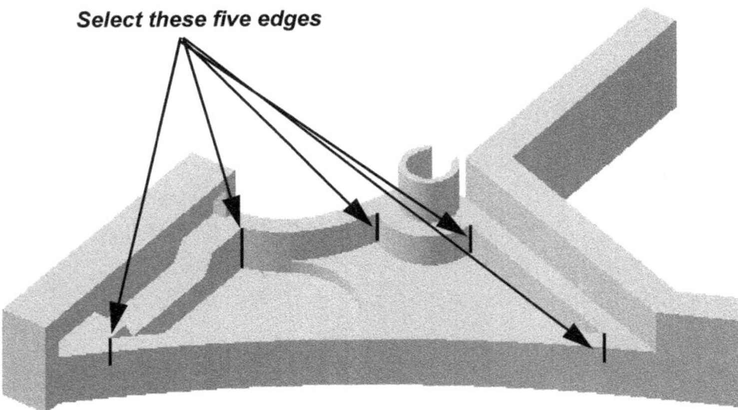

Figure 6–20

3. Create the following Edge Fillet:

   - *Radius:* 3
   - *Object(s) to fillet:* **1 Edge** (as shown in Figure 6–21)

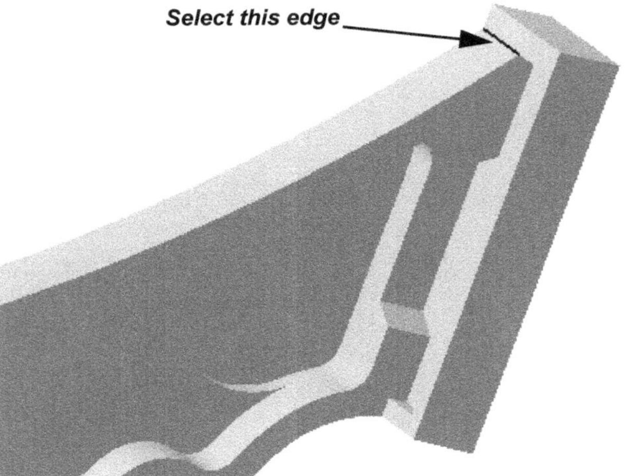

Figure 6–21

4. Click **OK**. The fillet fails due to **Impossible relimitation** as shown in the Update Error dialog box in Figure 6–22.

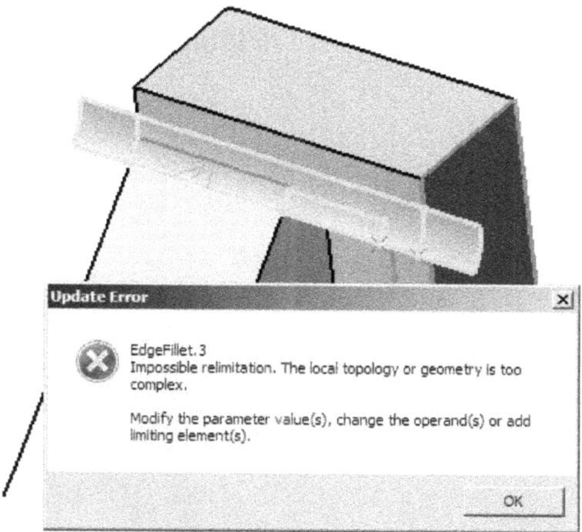

Figure 6–22

5. Click **OK**.

6. In the Edge Fillet Definition dialog box, click **More**, if required, to expand it, and make the following change:

   - *Limiting element(s):* Select the planar face shown in Figure 6–23.

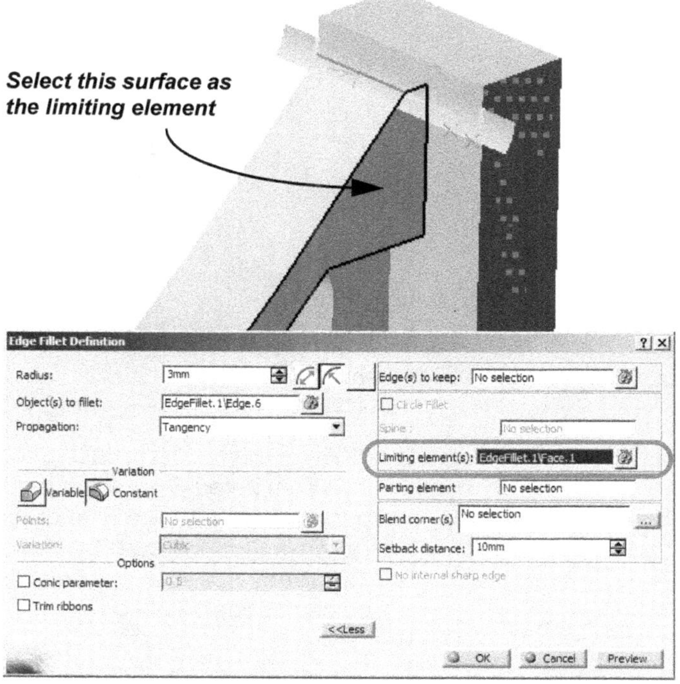

Figure 6–23

7. Click **OK**. The limited Edge Fillet displays as shown in Figure 6–24.

Figure 6–24

8. Create the following Edge Fillet:
   - *Radius:* **1**
   - *Object(s) to fillet:* **7 Edges** (as shown in Figure 6–25)

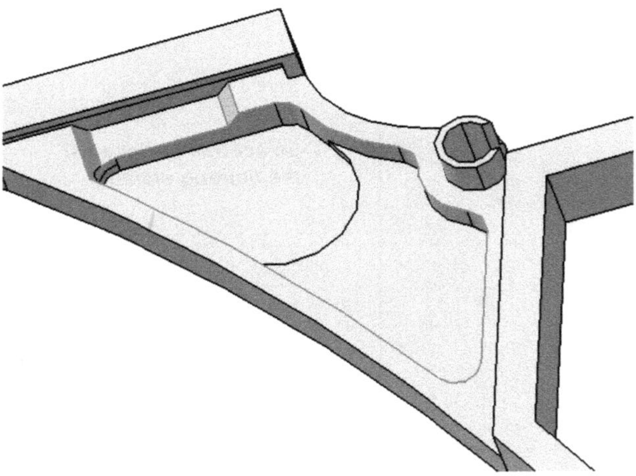

Figure 6–25

Design Considerations

The completed Edge Fillet displays as shown in Figure 6–26. A good design practice is to create as many large radius fillets as possible first, followed by the next largest, etc. If you select the **Tangency** option in the *Selection mode* field, the system permits efficient edge selection.

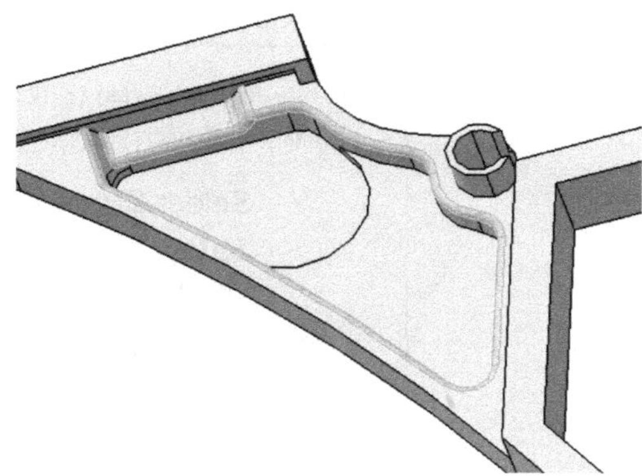

Figure 6–26

Task 2 - Create a Variable Radius Edge Fillet.

1. Click (Edge Fillet) and click (Variable). In the Edge Fillet Definition dialog box, apply the following parameters:
   - *Radius:* **1**
   - *Object(s) to fillet:* **1 Edge** (as shown in Figure 6–27)

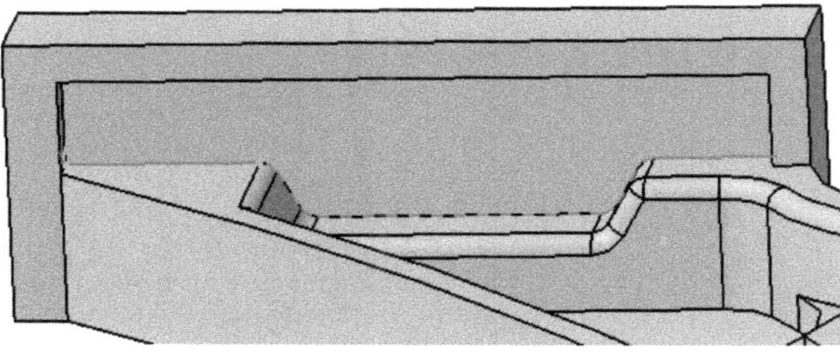

Figure 6–27

The completed Variable Radius Fillet displays as shown in Figure 6–28.

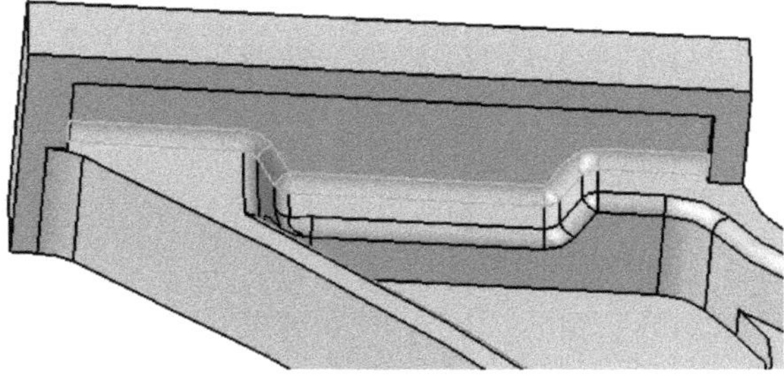

Figure 6–28

Task 3 - Use a spine to control an Edge Fillet.

1. Edit the Variable Radius Fillet that you just created and make the following changes, as shown in Figure 6–29:
    - Select **Circle Fillet**.
    - *Spine:* Select the Line feature named **Spine** under **Geometrical Set.1**

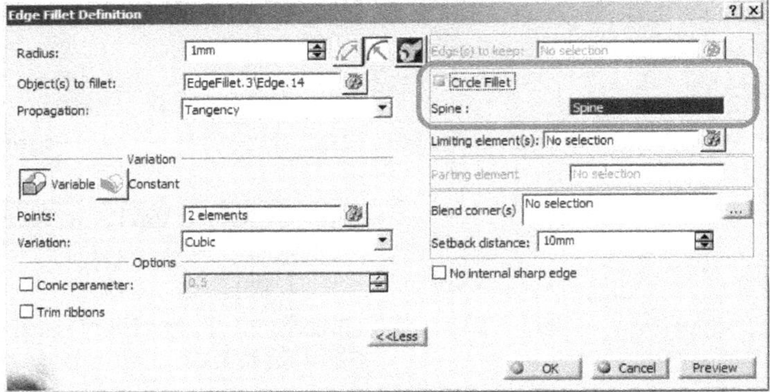

Figure 6–29

The completed fillet displays as shown in Figure 6–30.

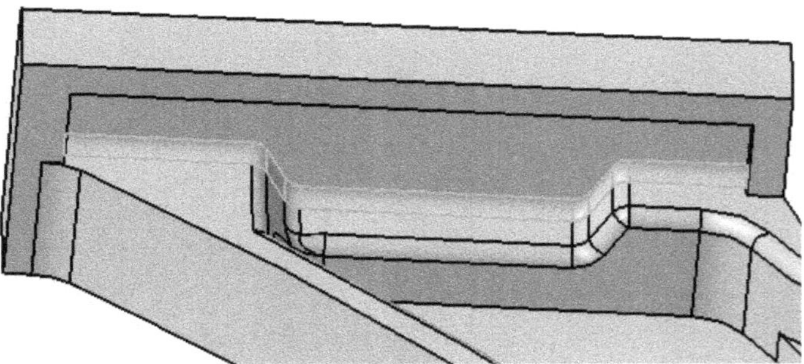

Figure 6–30

2. Show the Spine feature.

Design Considerations

When you use a spine to control the fillet, the fillet remains normal to the selected spine, as shown in Figure 6–31. You cannot use a spine to control an Edge Fillet feature. Note that this fillet was created as a Variable Radius Fillet.

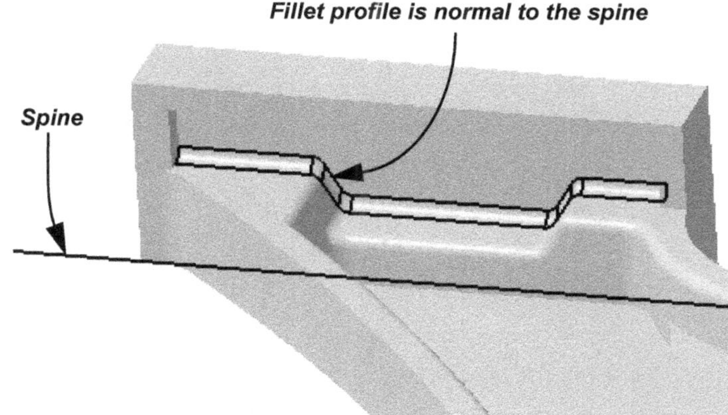
Fillet profile is normal to the spine
Spine

Figure 6–31

3. Hide the Spine.

Task 4 - Use the edge(s) to keep option.

1. Zoom in to the area shown in Figure 6–32.

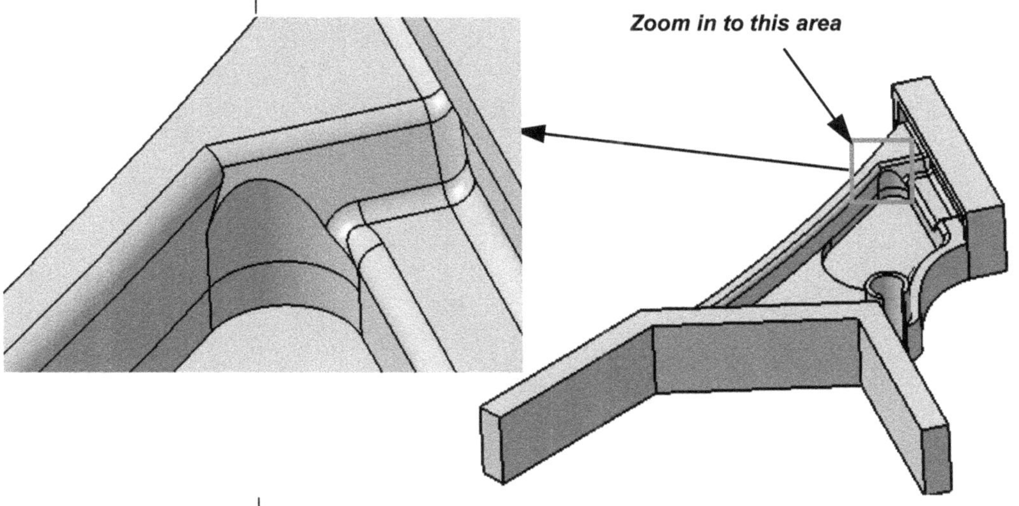
Zoom in to this area

Figure 6–32

2. Edit the fillet shown in Figure 6–33.

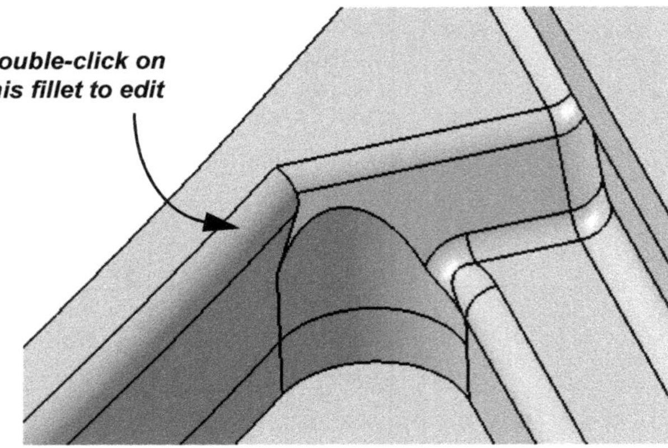

Figure 6–33

3. In the Edge Fillet Definition dialog box, click **More** if required, to expand it. Click in the *Edge(s) to keep* field, then select the edge shown in Figure 6–34.

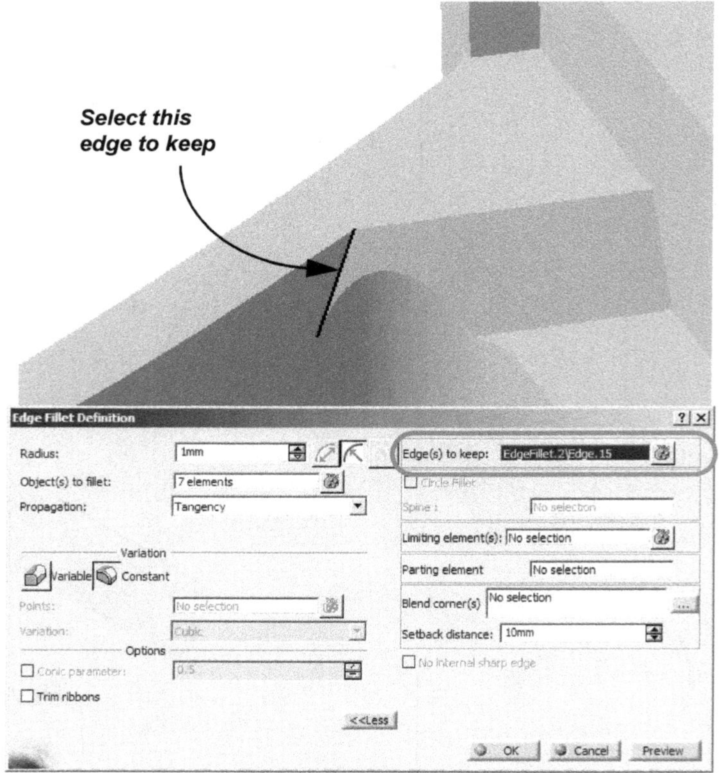

Figure 6–34

4. Click **OK**. Note the difference in the fillet transition, as shown in Figure 6–35.

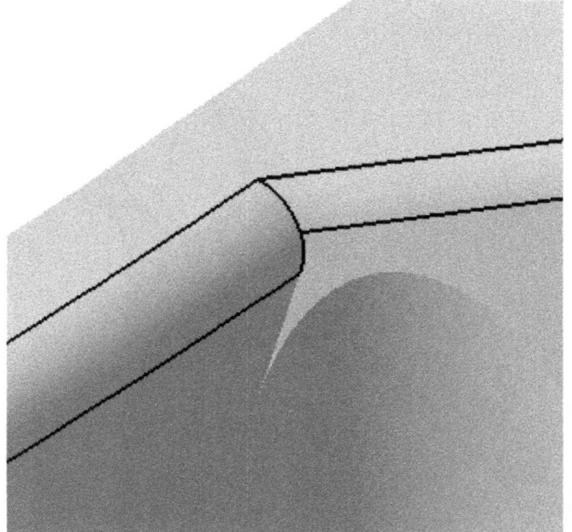

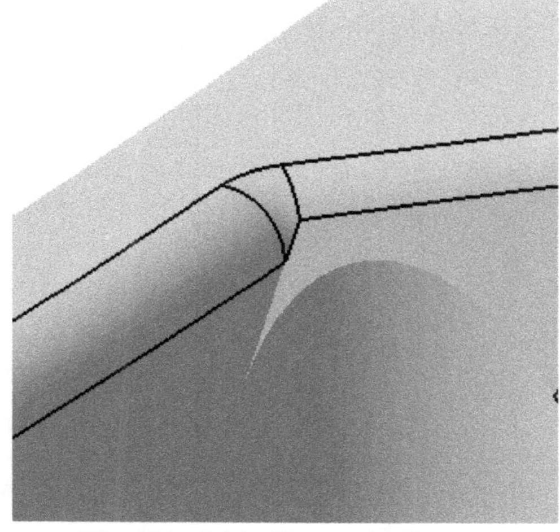

Before Edge(s) to Keep selection ***After Edge(s) to Keep selection***

Figure 6–35

Task 5 - Mirror the geometry.

1. Click (Mirror) to mirror the part geometry about the yz plane. The model displays as shown in Figure 6–36.

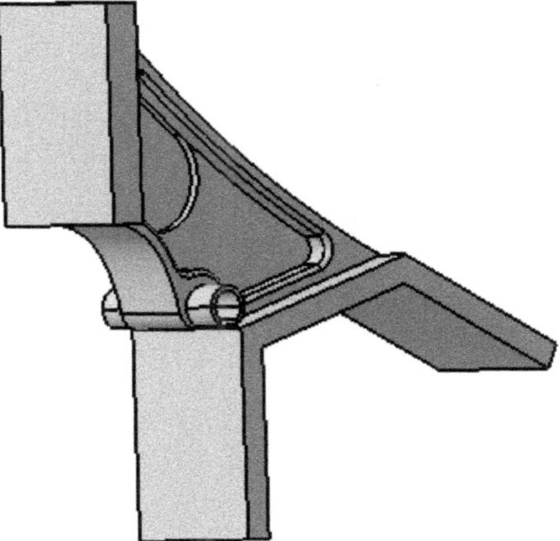

Figure 6–36

2. Create the two Tritangent Fillets shown in Figure 6–37.

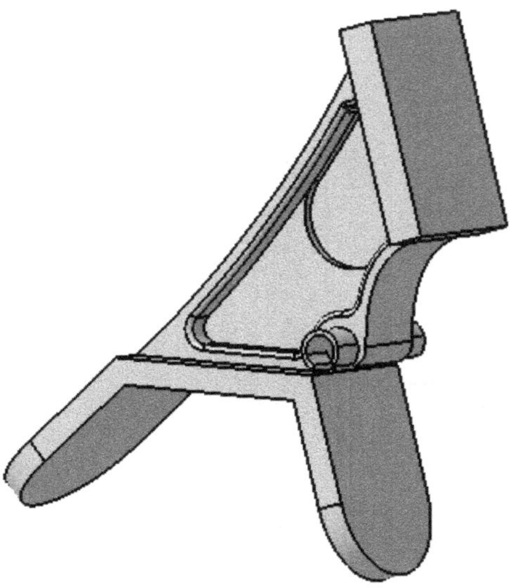

Figure 6–37

3. Save the model and close the file.

Practice 6b

Blended Fillets

Practice Objectives

- Use Blend Corner.
- Use Setback distance.
- Trim Ribbons.

In this practice, you will practice creating blended corners. The completed model displays as shown in Figure 6–38.

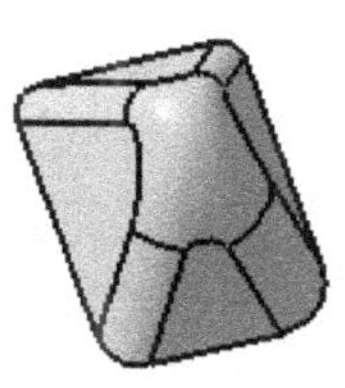
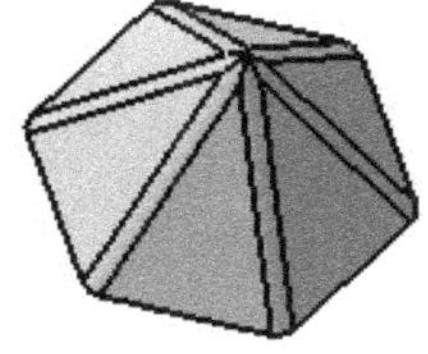

Figure 6–38

Task 1 - Open the part.

1. Open **BlendedCorner.CATPart**. The model displays as shown in Figure 6–39.

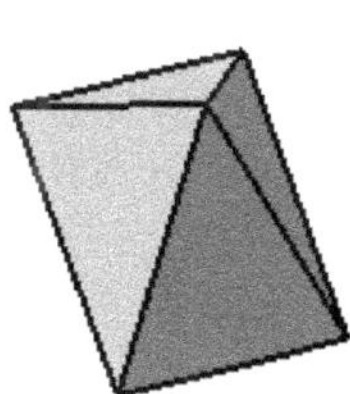
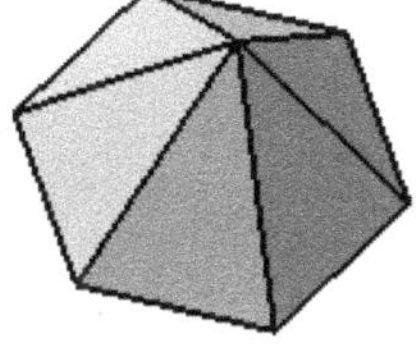

Figure 6–39

Task 2 - Create an Edge Fillet.

1. Click (Edge Fillet) to open the Edge Fillet Definition dialog box, then click (Variable). Create a **2mm** edge fillet along the three edges shown in Figure 6–40.

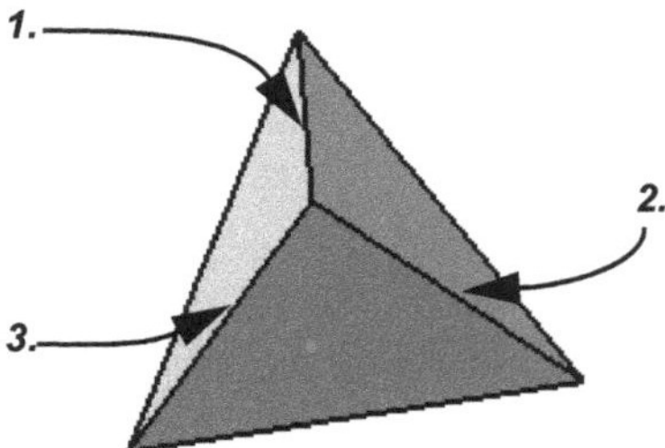

Figure 6–40

The completed Edge Fillet displays as shown in Figure 6–41.

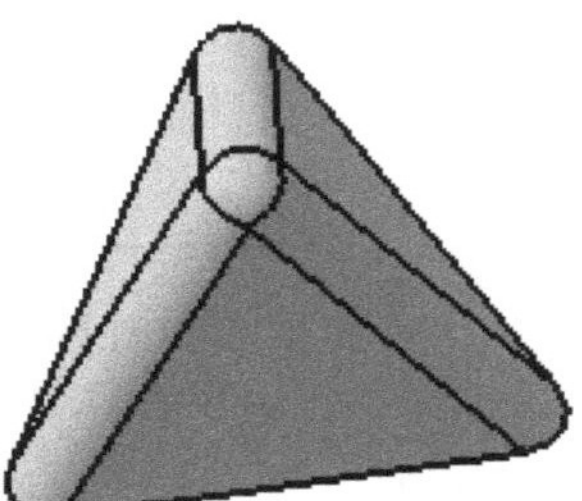

Figure 6–41

Note how the three fillets converge at the top. In the next steps you will modify the edge fillet and use the **Blend Corners** tool to apply a setback distance. A setback distance is a dimension that determines the size of the transition zone where the fillet edges blend together.

2. Edit the edge fillet.
3. Click **More**.
4. Right-click on the *Blend corner(s)* field and select **Create by edges**.
5. Click **Preview**.

*Note that the option may read **Create by edges or vertex**, depending on your installed service pack.*

The setback distance defines where the fillet shape begins blending into the other fillet shapes

6. Note the shape of the fillet with a setback distance of **10mm**.
7. Modify the Setback distance to **6mm** and click **OK**. The model displays as shown in Figure 6–42.

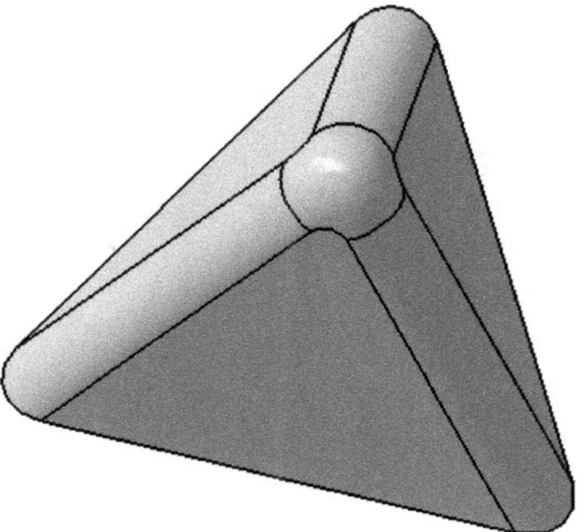

Figure 6–42

Task 3 - Create a Variable Radius Edge Fillet.

1. Click (Edge Fillet) to open the Edge Fillet Definition dialog box, then click (Variable).
2. Select the edge labeled **1** in Figure 6–43. In the Variable Radius Fillet Definition dialog box, enter a *Radius* of **2mm** and press <Tab> to update the radius values of both vertices for the first edge segment.
3. Select the edge labeled **2** in Figure 6–43. In the Variable Radius Fillet Definition dialog box, enter a *Radius* of **3mm** and press <Tab> to update the radius values of both vertices for the second edge segment.
4. Select the edge labeled **3** in Figure 6–43. In the Variable Radius Fillet Definition dialog box, enter a *Radius* of **3.5mm** and press <Tab> to update the radius values of both vertices for the third edge segment.

5. Select the edge labeled 4 in Figure 6–43. In the Variable Radius Fillet Definition dialog box, enter a radius of **5.5mm** and press <Tab> to update the radius values of both vertices for the fourth edge segment.

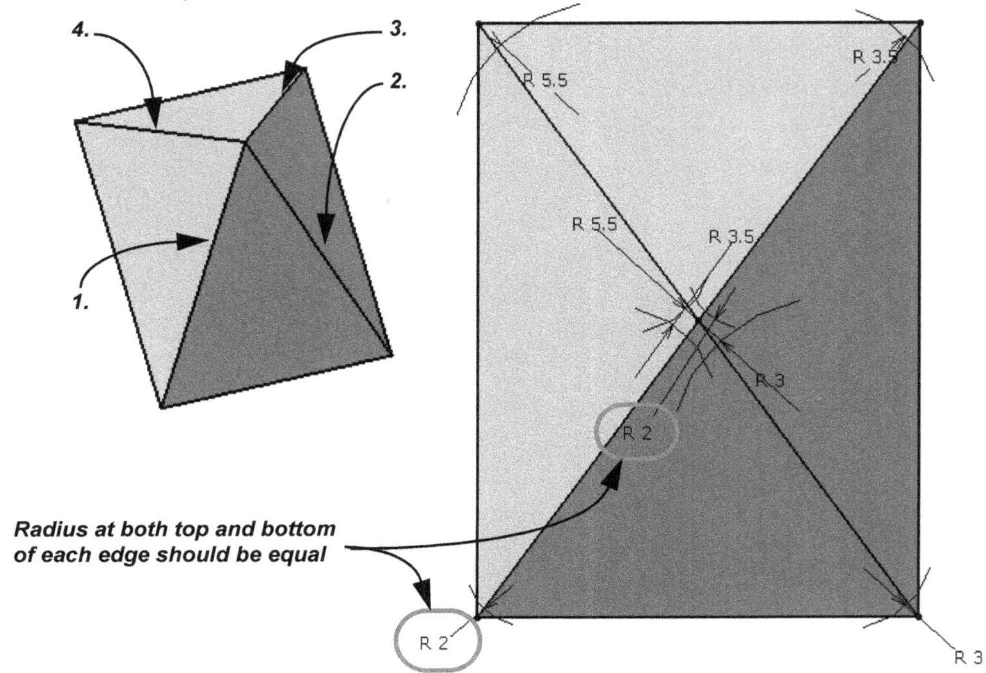

Figure 6–43

6. Click **OK**. The model displays as shown in Figure 6–44.

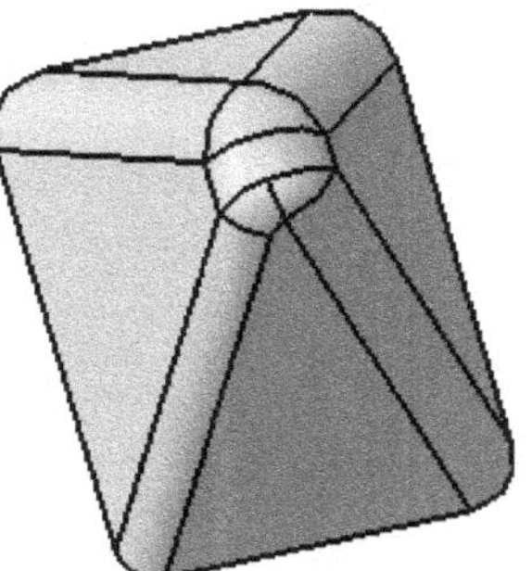

Figure 6–44

7. Edit the Variable Radius Fillet.

8. Click **More** if required, to expand the dialog box.

9. Right-click on the *Blend corner(s)* field and select **Create by edges**. In the *Setback distance* field, enter **10**.

10. Click **OK**. The model displays as shown in Figure 6–45.

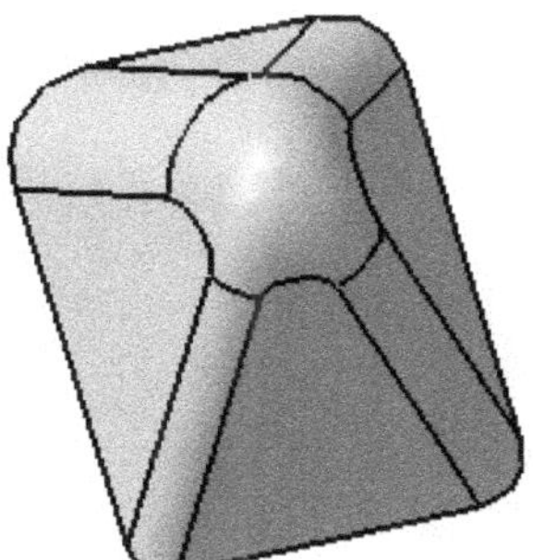

Figure 6–45

11. Rotate the model as shown in Figure 6–46. Note the way the fillets blend into each other at the back of the model. This is not correct and in the next task you will change the setback distance to fix this.

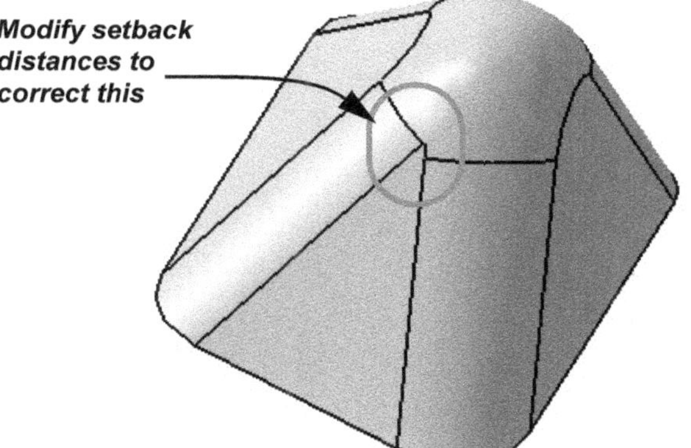
Modify setback
distances to
correct this

Figure 6–46

Task 4 - Modify the Setback distance.

1. Edit the Variable Radius Fillet.

2. Click **More** if required, to expand the dialog box.

3. Double-click on the setback distance for the two values surrounding the area that needs to be corrected, as shown in Figure 6–47, and change both values to **14**.

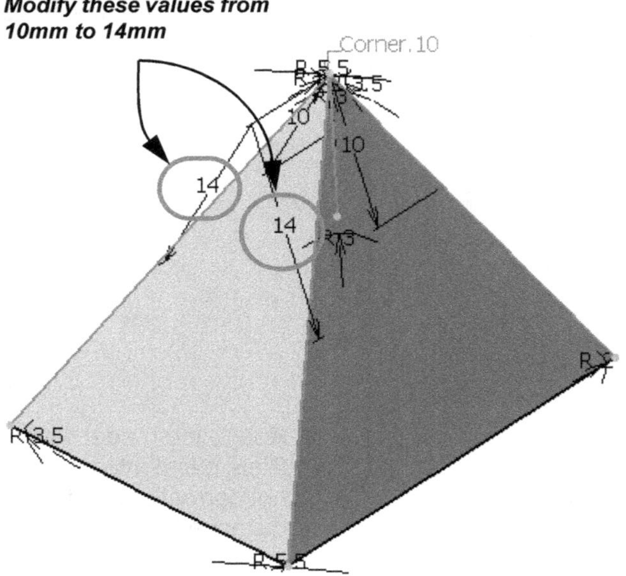

Figure 6–47

4. Click **OK**. The model displays as shown in Figure 6–48.

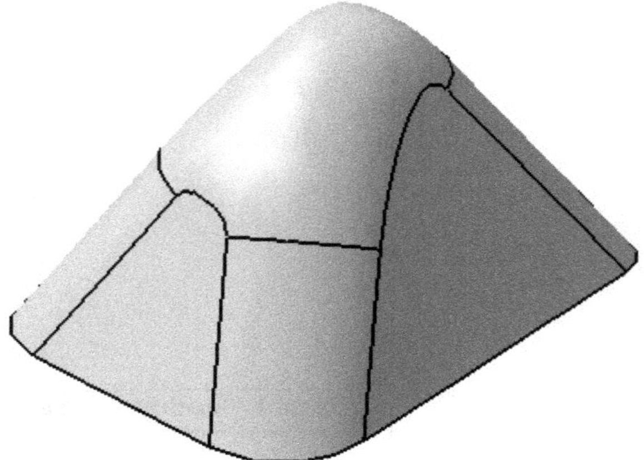

Figure 6–48

Task 5 - Create an Edge Fillet.

1. Click (Edge Fillet). Create a **2mm** fillet on all 6 edges as shown in Figure 6–49.
2. Click **OK**. The model displays as shown in Figure 6–49.

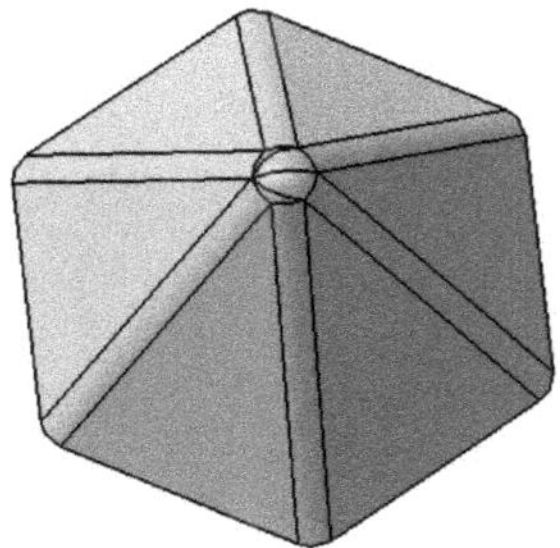

Figure 6–49

Task 6 - Apply the Trim Ribbons option.

In this task, you will modify the fillet created in the last task and apply the **Trim ribbons** option to demonstrate how it will affect the fillet. The **Trim ribbons** option trims overlapping fillets at their intersections.

1. Edit the Edge Fillet created in the last Task.
2. Select the **Trim ribbons** option as shown in Figure 6–50.

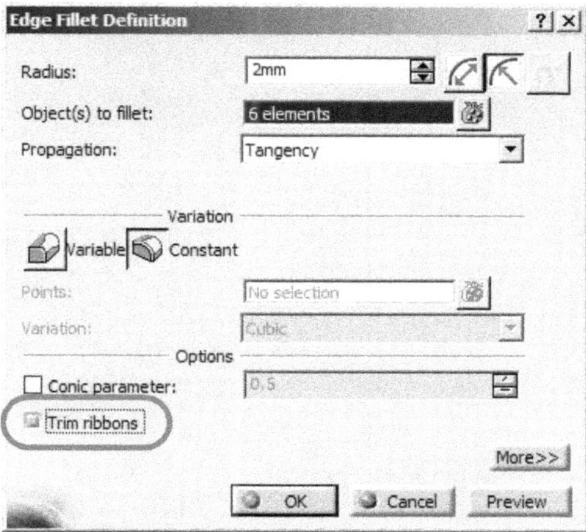

Figure 6–50

3. Click **OK**. The model displays as shown in Figure 6–51.

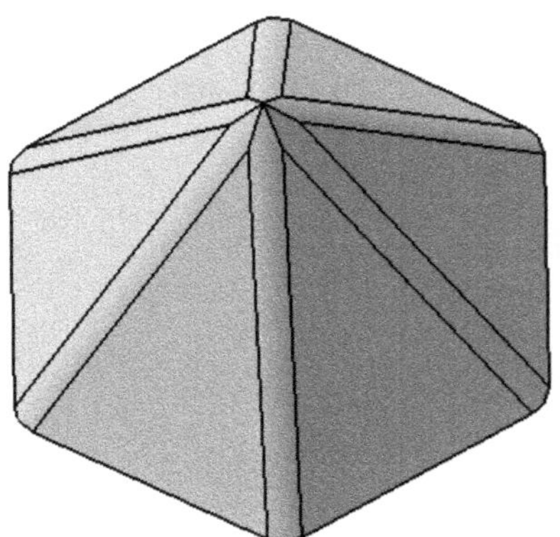

Figure 6–51

4. Save and close the file.

Practice 6c

Advanced Fillet and Draft

Practice Objectives

- Create a Fillet with a hold curve and spine.
- Create a Reflect Line Draft with a parting element.

In this practice, you will add Draft and Fillet to the plastic injection modeled front cover for a small speaker. You will use advanced Fillet and Draft options to create the final geometry of the part, as shown in Figure 6–52.

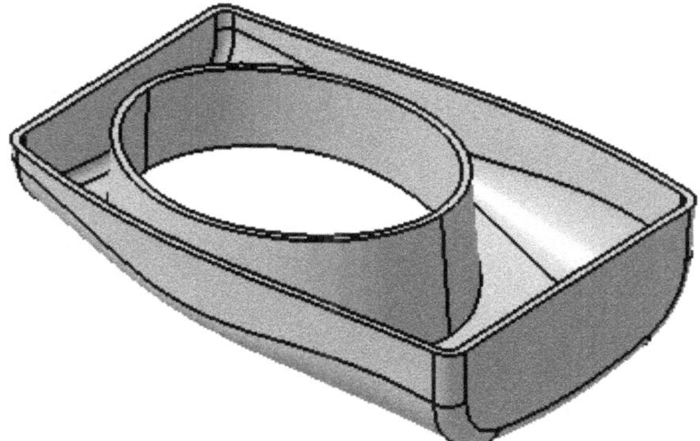

Figure 6–52

Task 1 - Open the part.

1. Open **SpeakerCover.CATPart**. The model displays as shown in Figure 6–53.

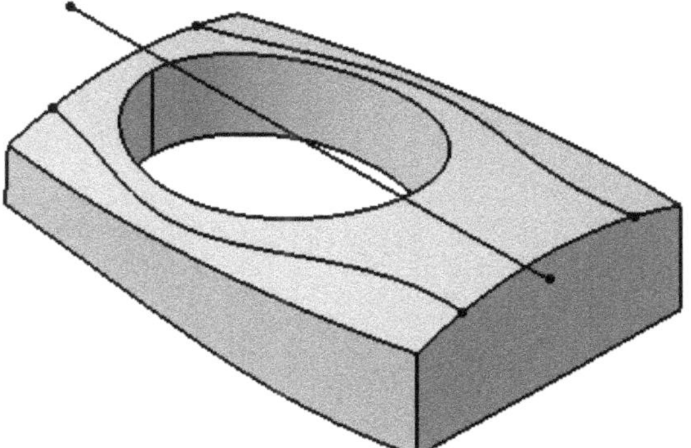

Figure 6–53

Task 2 - Investigate the fillet control curves.

1. In the specification tree, locate the **FilletControlCurves** geometrical set.
2. Hover the cursor over **Line.1**, **HoldCurve1**, and **HoldCurve2** to highlighted them on the model, as shown in Figure 6–54.

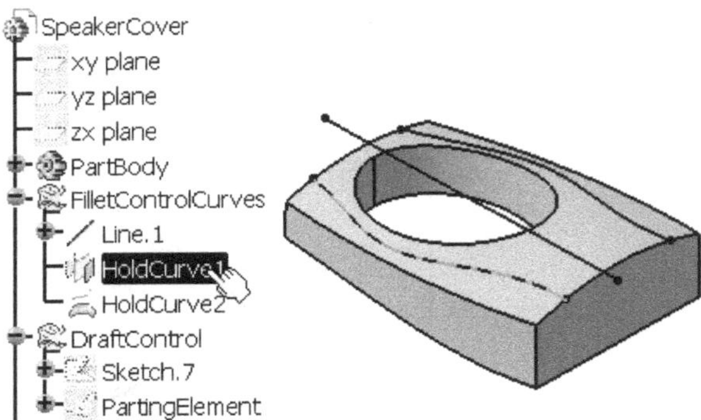

Figure 6–54

Design Considerations

In the next task, you will create a Face-Face Fillet using a spine and a hold curve. A hold curve controls the tangent line of the Fillet. In this case, the hold curve is created to control the formation of the Fillet around the Pocket. The Line will be used as a spine for the Fillet. Note that the profile of the Fillet will stay normal to the spine.

Task 3 - Create a fillet with spine and hold curve.

1. Click (Face-Face Fillet). In the Face-Face Fillet Definition dialog box, define the Face-Face Fillet as follows:
   - *Faces to fillet:* Select the two faces shown in Figure 6–55

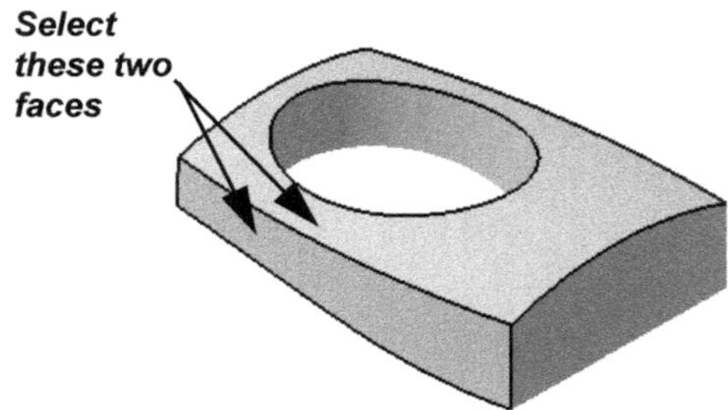

Figure 6–55

2. Click **More** and define the following (as shown in Figure 6–56).

   • *Hold Curve:* **HoldCurve1**
   • *Spine:* **Line.1**

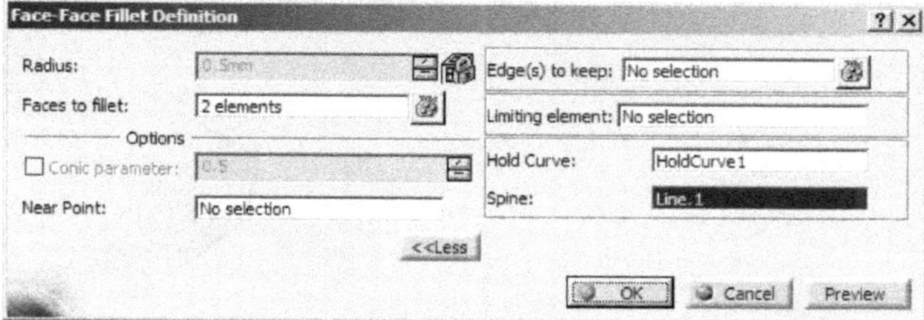

Figure 6–56

3. Click **OK**. The Face-Face Fillet using hold curve and spine displays as shown in Figure 6–57.

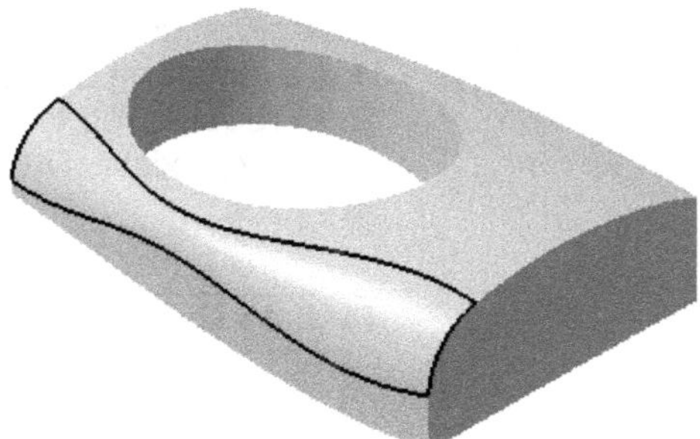

Figure 6–57

4. Create a second Face-Face Fillet by selecting the two faces shown in Figure 6–58.

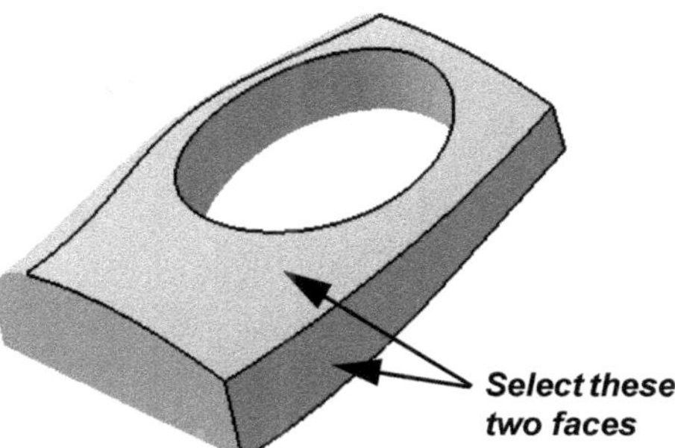

Figure 6–58

5. Select the appropriate hold curve and spine. The completed Fillet displays as shown in Figure 6–59.

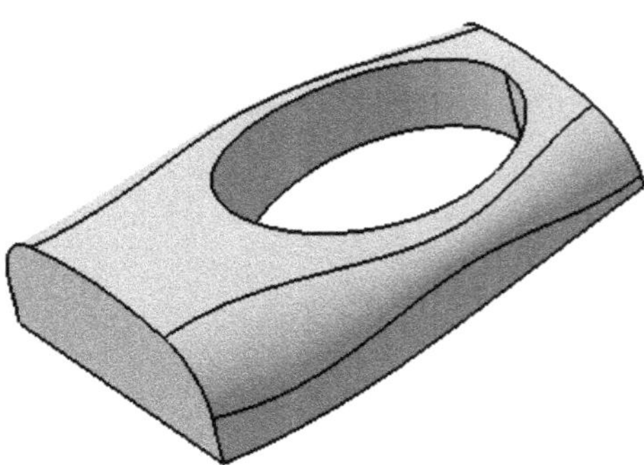

Figure 6–59

Design Considerations

If you are designing a part that requires draft, it is considered good practice to add draft to the model before creating fillets. However, some design scenarios (such as working with imported data) require you to add draft to a model in which some fillet geometry exists. The **Reflect Line Draft** option can be used in this case.

Task 4 - Create reflect line draft

You might need to show the Advanced DressUp toolbar to access the ***Advanced Draft*** *icon.*

1. Click (Advanced Draft). In the Draft Definition (Advanced) dialog box, click (Draft Reflect Line (1st Side)), as shown in Figure 6–60.

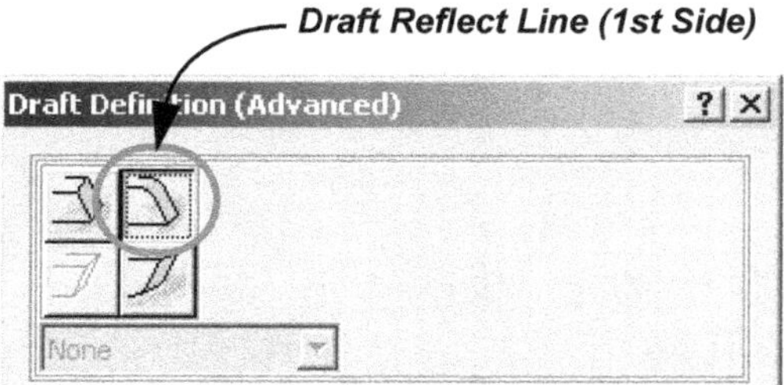

Figure 6–60

2. Make the following selections:

   - *Angle:* **3deg**
   - *Neutral Element Selection:* Select the Face-Face Fillets shown in Figure 6–61

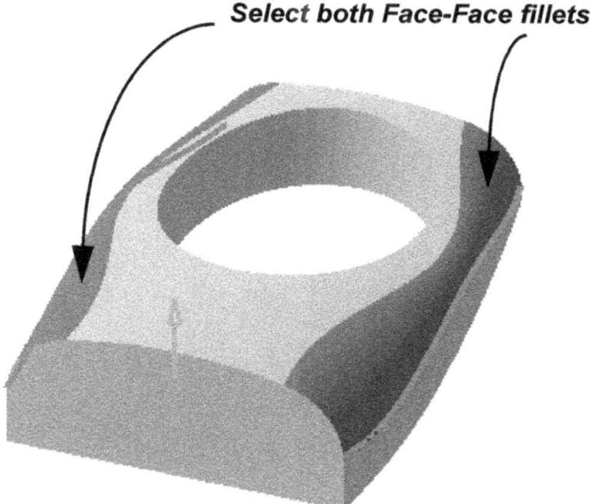
Select both Face-Face fillets

Figure 6–61

3. Click **Preview**. The Reflect Line Draft preview displays as shown in Figure 6–62.

Figure 6–62

4. Click **OK** to complete the feature.

Task 5 - Create Draft that uses a parting element.

1. In the **DraftControl** geometrical set, show **PartingElement**.
2. Use (Draft Angle) to create a standard Draft.
3. Define the Draft with the following parameters:
   - *Angle:* **3deg**
   - *Face(s) to draft:* Select the three faces shown in Figure 6–63
   - *Pulling Direction:* **xy plane**
   - *Neutral Element Selection:* **PartingElement**

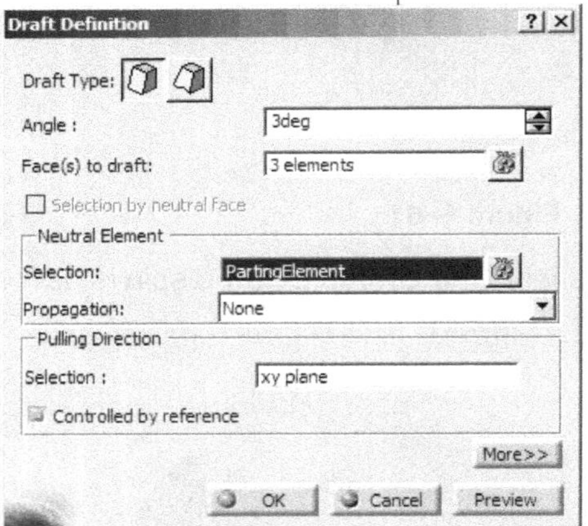

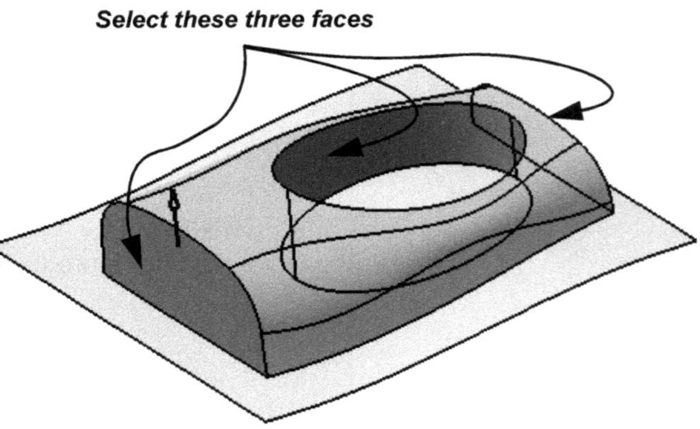

Figure 6–63

4. Click **OK**.
5. In the specification tree, hide the **PartingElement**.
6. Display the model and note the effect of adding draft to the geometry, as shown in Figure 6–64.

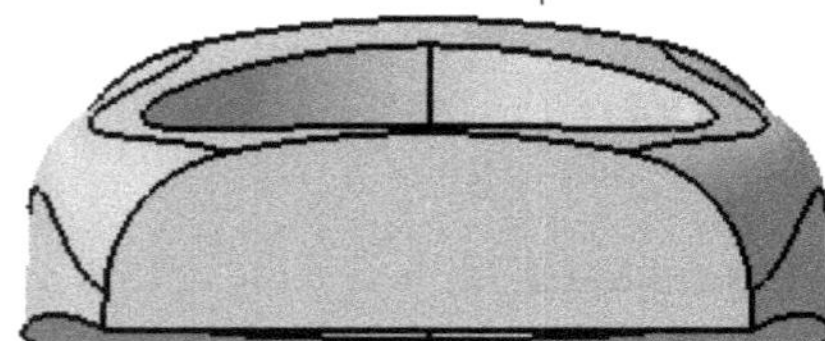

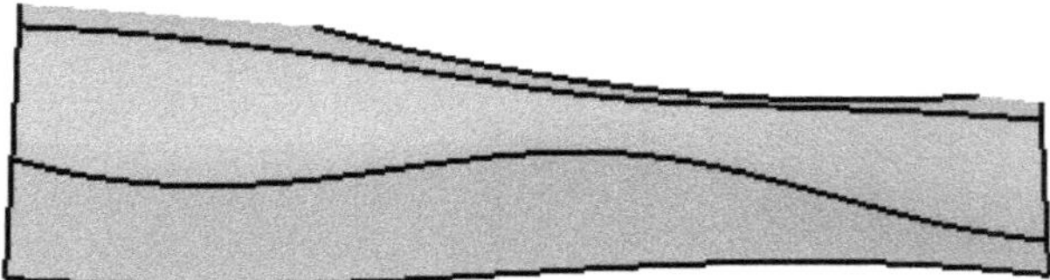

Figure 6–64

Task 6 - Create an Edge Fillet.

1. Create an Edge Fillet by specifying the following parameters in the Edge Fillet Definition dialog box:

    - *Radius:* **5**
    - *Object(s) to fillet:* **2 Edges** (as shown in Figure 6–65)

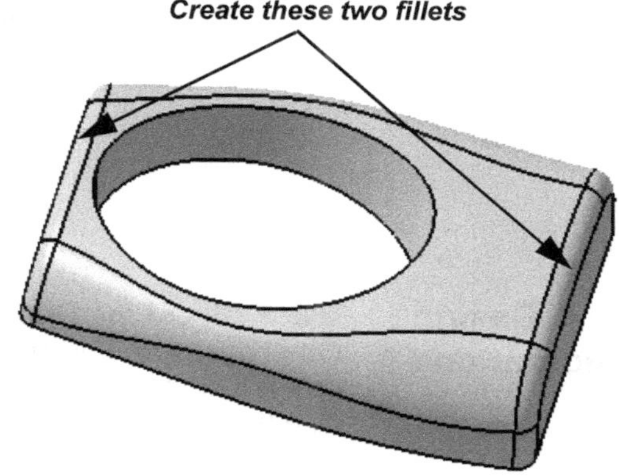
Create these two fillets

Figure 6–65

Task 7 - Shell the part.

1. Create the following Shell:

    - *Default inside thickness:* **2**
    - *Faces to remove:* **1 Face** (select the face shown in Figure 6–66)

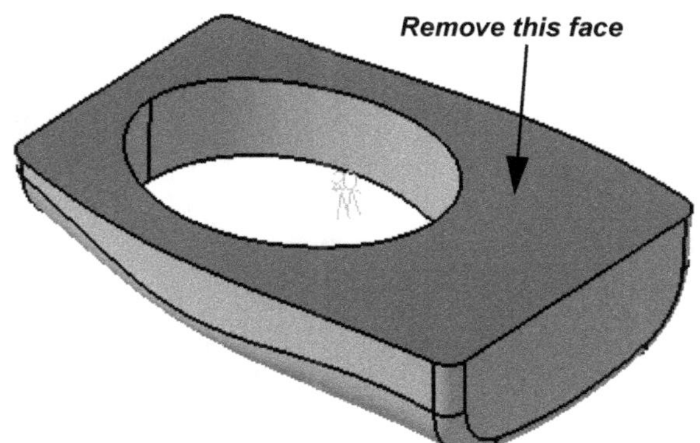
Remove this face

Figure 6–66

The shelled part displays as shown in Figure 6–67.

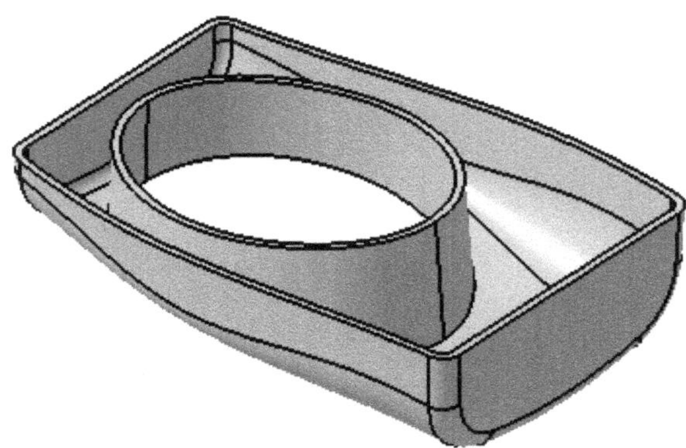

Figure 6–67

Design Considerations

Use **Reflect Line Draft** when the Fillet geometry is created first. Otherwise, you should add draft to the model as required and create Fillets as late in the design cycle as possible, beginning with the largest radius Fillets first. Typically, a model is shelled after Fillet creation.

2. Hide the **FilletControlCurves** geometrical set.

3. Click (Isometric View) to return to the isometric view, as shown in Figure 6–68.

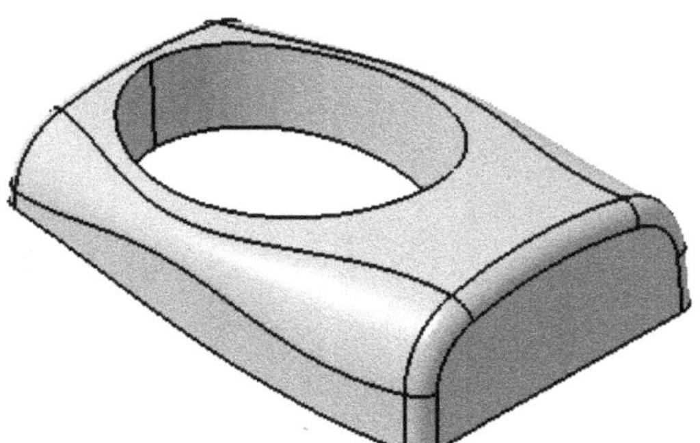

Figure 6–68

4. Save the model and close the file.

Practice 6d

Advanced Draft Creation

Practice Objective

- Use the Standard Draft 1st and 2nd side options.

In this practice, you will create an advanced Draft on a telephone handset and resolve a failure during the creation of another Draft. The completed model displays as shown in Figure 6–69.

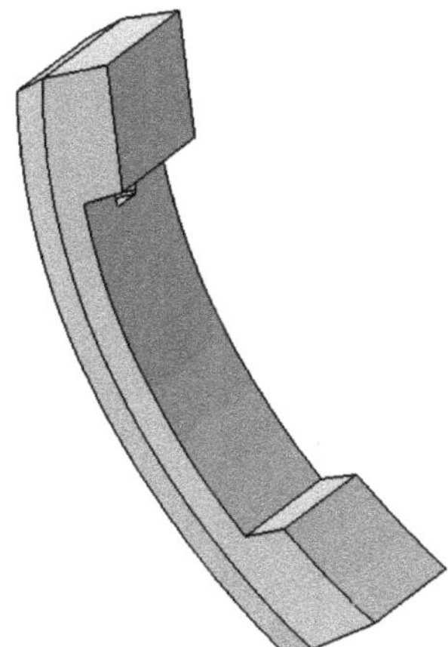

Figure 6–69

Task 1 - Open the part.

1. Open **Phone.CATPart**. The model displays as shown in Figure 6–70.

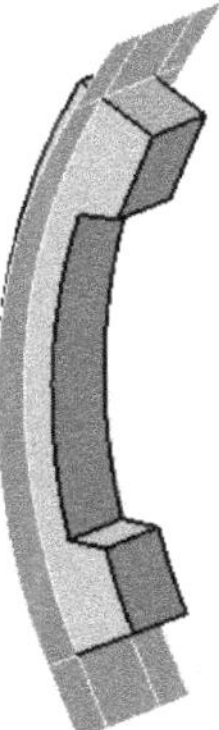

Figure 6–70

Task 2 - Create a Standard Draft on both sides.

You might need to show the Advanced DressUp toolbar to access the Advanced Draft icon.

1. In the Advanced Draft toolbar, click (Advanced Draft). The Draft Definition (Advanced) dialog box opens as shown in Figure 6–71.

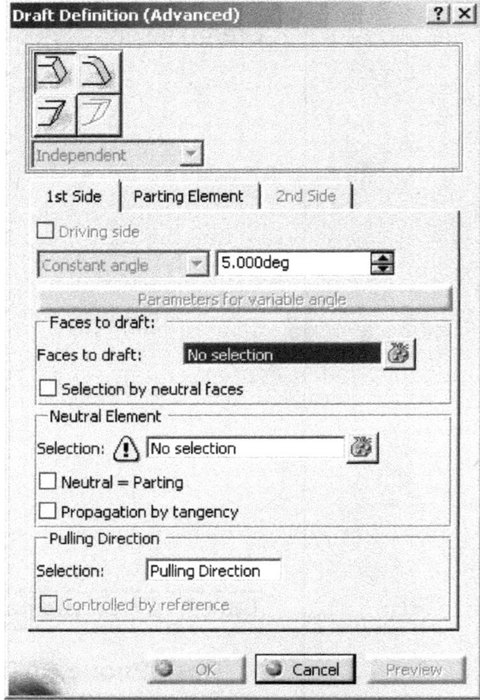

Figure 6–71

2. Create a two-sided Draft feature by clicking (Standard Draft (1st Side)) and (Standard Draft (2nd Side)).
3. Enter a *draft angle* of **5**.

4. Select the *Face(s) to draft* field and select the four surfaces shown in Figure 6–72 (including the hidden one).

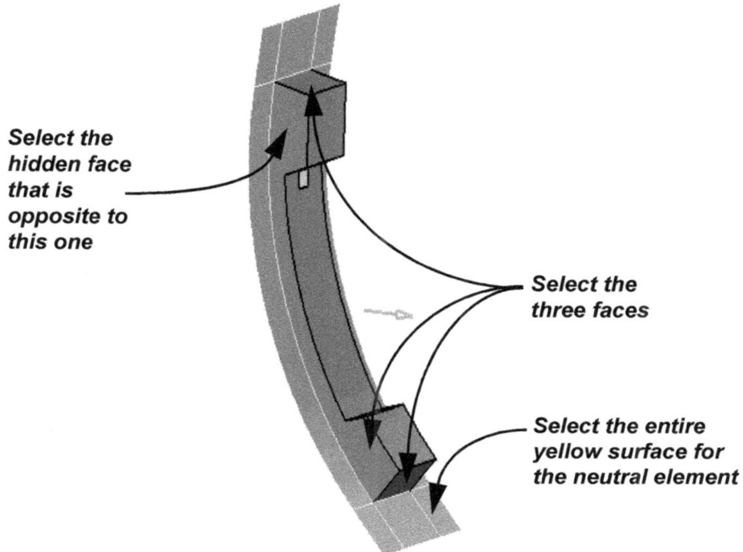
Select the hidden face that is opposite to this one
Select the three faces
Select the entire yellow surface for the neutral element

Figure 6–72

5. Select the *Neutral Element Selection* field and select the entire yellow surface for the neutral element.
6. Right-click on the *Pulling Direction Selection* field and select **Z Axis**.
7. Select the *Parting Element* tab and select the *Use parting element* field.
8. Select the surface that was used for the neutral plane.
9. Select the *2nd Side* tab.
10. For the *draft angle*, enter **10**.
11. Select the *Neutral Element Selection* field and select the entire yellow surface for the neutral element.

12. Click **OK** to complete the feature. The part displays as shown in Figure 6–73.

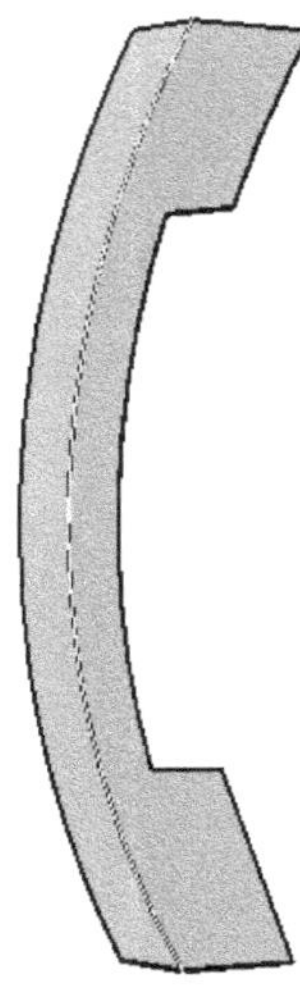

Figure 6–73

13. Hide the yellow surface used as the neutral plane in draft.

Task 3 - Add fillets.

1. Click (Edge Fillet). The Edge Fillet Definition dialog box opens.
2. Select the four edges shown in Figure 6–74.

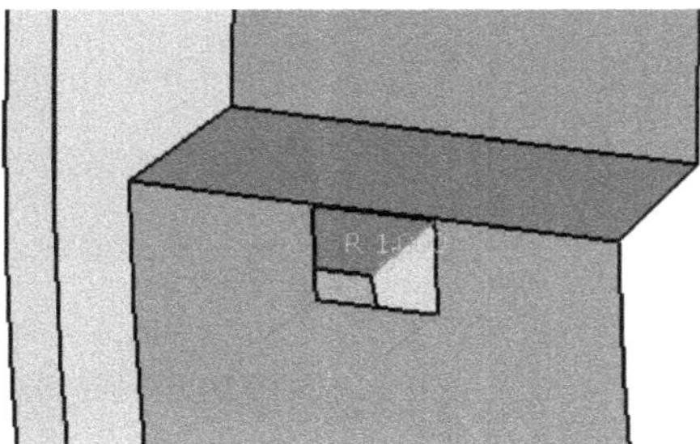

Figure 6–74

3. Enter a *Radius* of **1 mm**.
4. Complete the feature.

Task 4 - Draft additional surfaces and extract geometry to resolve the Draft failure.

1. Click (Draft Angle). The Draft Definition dialog box opens.

2. Select one of the inside faces of the Pocket as the *Face(s) to draft*. Because the vertical surfaces are tangent to each other, all of the inside vertical surfaces of the Pocket are automatically selected, as shown in Figure 6–75.

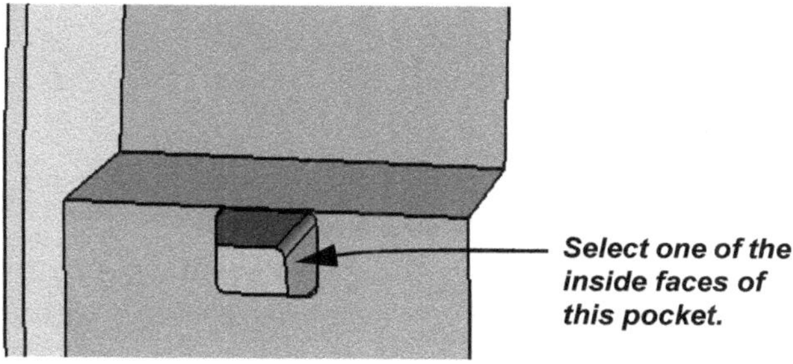
Select one of the inside faces of this pocket.

Figure 6–75

3. For the *Draft angle*, enter **7**.

4. For the *Neutral Plane*, select **Plane.5**.

5. Ensure that the Draft direction displays as shown in Figure 6–76.

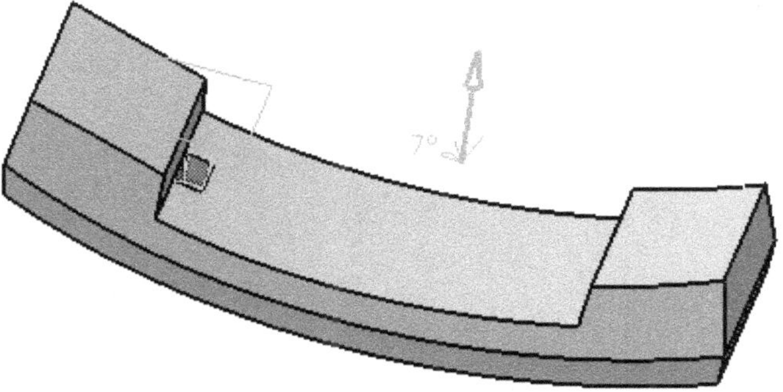
7°

Figure 6–76

6. Preview the Draft feature. The model displays as shown in Figure 6–77. Note that the Draft edges overlap.

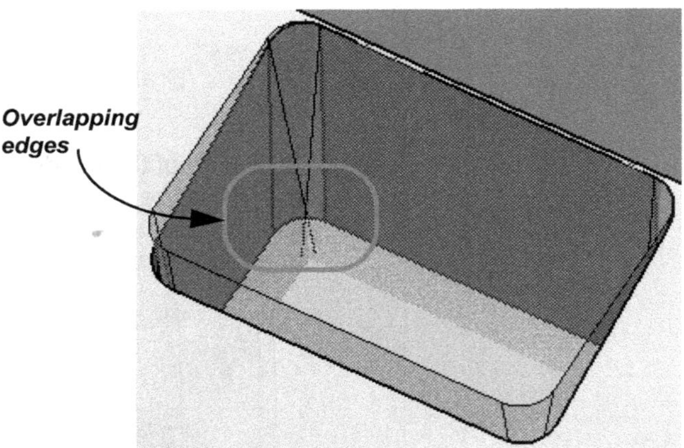

Figure 6–77

7. Click **OK**. An Update Error message opens, indicating that there are twisted faces during the feature creation.

8. Close the Update Error dialog box. The Feature Definition Error dialog box opens, prompting you to deactivate the Draft and extract the geometry, as shown in Figure 6–78.

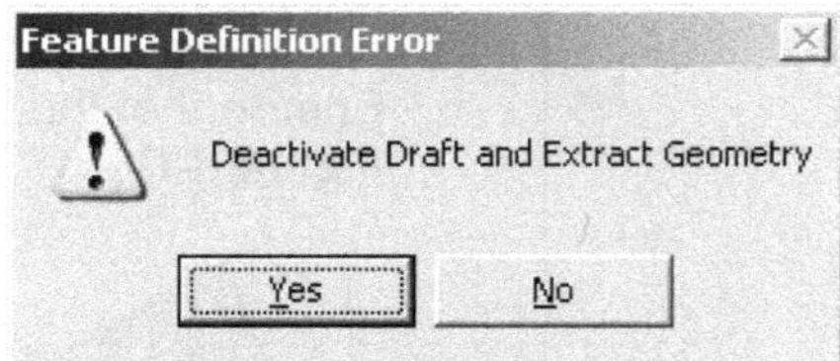

Figure 6–78

9. Click **No**.

10. Modify the *Draft angle* to **5** and complete the feature.

11. Save the model and close the file.

Chapter Review Questions

1. A Variable Radius Fillet requires the start and end radii to be the same.
   a. True
   b. False
2. In the Variable Radius Fillet Definition dialog box, what does do?
   a. Opens a dialog box with a list of points and you can edit the radii at those points.
   b. Opens a dialog box with a list of points, and you can add or delete points as required.
   c. Enables you to edit the edge on which the fillet has been created.
   d. None of the above.
3. When you select a Spine curve with a Variable Radius Fillet, the radius of the fillet is always perpendicular to the spine.
   a. True
   b. False
4. **Reflect Line Draft** uses the reflect lines as neutral lines when drafting the selected faces.
   a. True
   b. False
5. **Advanced Draft** allows for different draft angles on either side of the parting line.
   a. True
   b. False
6. Possible draft angle conditions are:
   a. Independent
   b. Driving/driven
   c. Fitted
   d. All of the above.

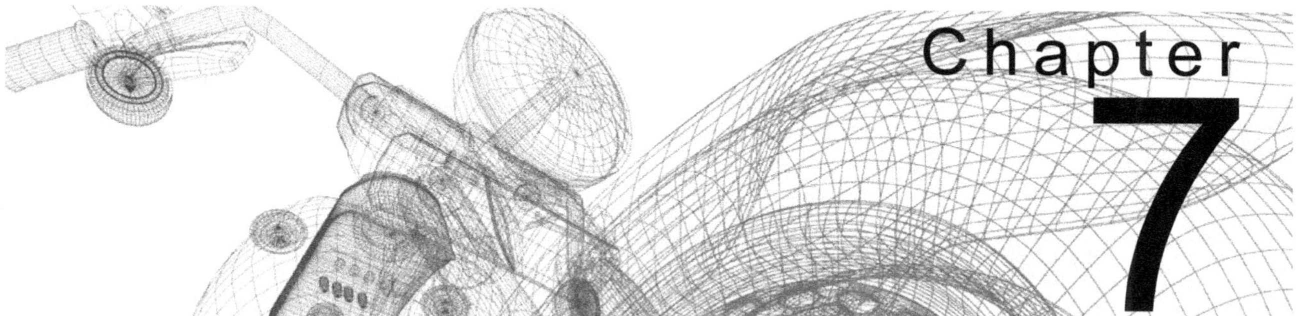

Analysis Tools

After you complete the modeling, you can run the Analysis tools on the model to verify that the intended design has been achieved.

Learning Objectives in this Chapter

- Learn to use Draft Analysis to check draft angles.
- Create Thread and Tap features.
- Learn to use Thread/Tap Analysis to review threads and taps in your model.
- Understand how to filter the model using the **Parameterization Analysis** tool.

7.1 Draft Analysis

While removing the mold, the key factor that determines whether the mold can be removed easily is the draft angle. You can use the **Draft Analysis** tool to check all of the draft angles in your model.

General Steps

Use the following general steps to run a Draft analysis:

1. Change the display settings and View mode.
2. Run the Draft Analysis.
3. Specify the mode.
4. Specify the display settings.
5. Specify the direction.
6. Complete the analysis.

Step 1 - Change the display settings and View mode.

The analysis is only displayed in the Shading with Material View mode. To change the View mode to **Shading with Material**, click (Shading with Material) in the View Mode toolbar, or select **View>Render Style>Shading with Material** in the menu bar.

Step 2 - Run the Draft Analysis.

Click (Draft Analysis) in the Analysis toolbar and select a face on the model.

The color of the model changes to display the analysis results, and the Draft Analysis and Draft Analysis.* dialog boxes open, as shown in Figure 7–1.

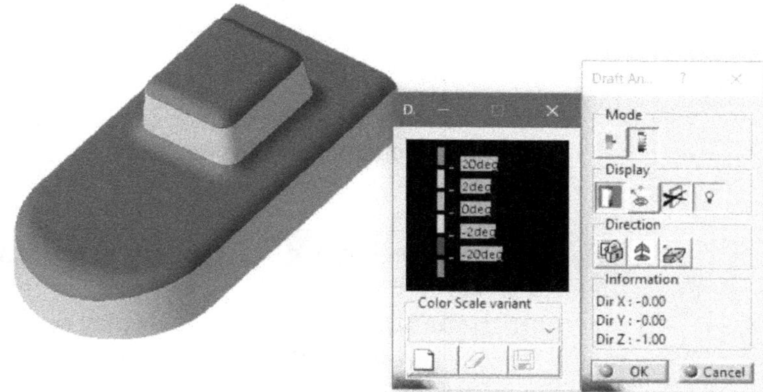

Figure 7–1

Step 3 - Specify the mode.

There are two different types of analysis modes: Quick Analysis mode (indicated by) and Full Analysis mode (indicated by), as shown in Figure 7–2.

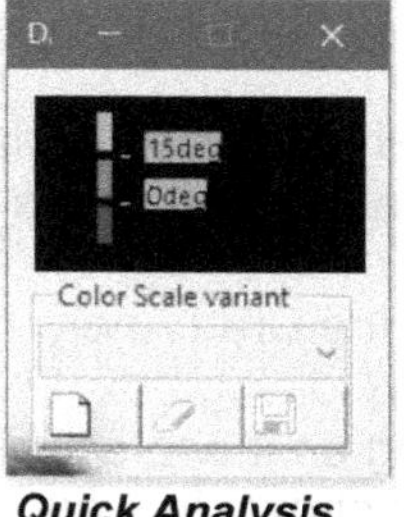

Quick Analysis mode is selected

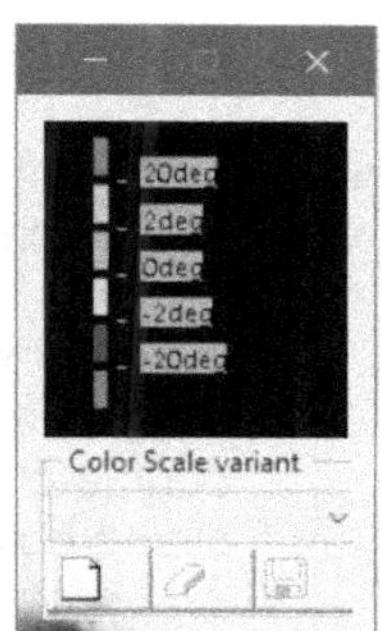

Full Analysis mode is selected

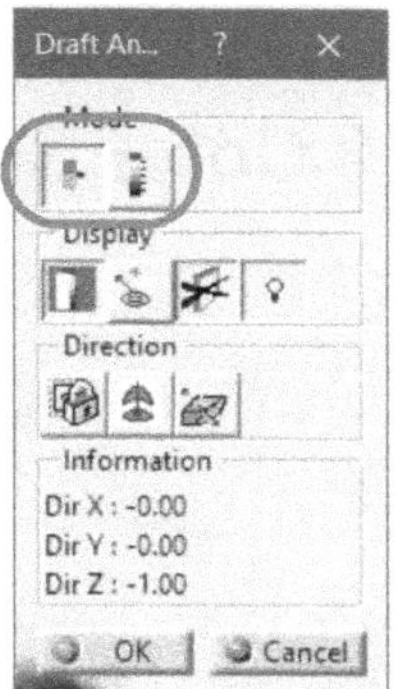

Figure 7–2

In the Quick Analysis mode, the analysis result can display in up to three different colors on the model. In the Full Analysis mode, the analysis result can display in up to six different colors on the model.

If the model only has one Draft angle, or if you want to analyze the model for each Draft angle, you can use the Quick Analysis mode.

If the model has more than one Draft angle, and all of the drafted faces are to be analyzed in one step, you can use the Full Analysis mode.

Color Scale Variant enables you to create, delete, and save customized configurations of the Draft Analysis display.

Step 4 - Specify the display settings.

Use the tools in the display section in the Draft Analysis dialog box to better understand and clarify your results, as shown in Figure 7–3.

[icon] highlights representations on the model. [icon] controls the brightness of the model.

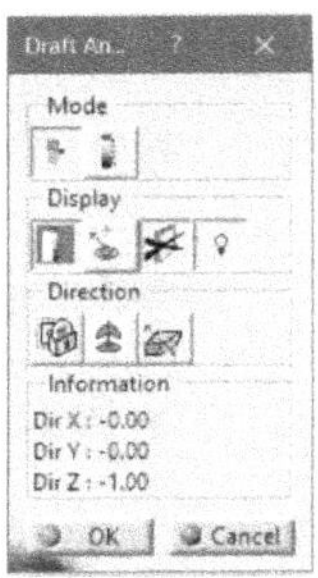

Figure 7–3

Color Scale

The Draft Analysis result displayed on the model depends on which scale values and colors are used in the Draft Analysis.* dialog box. In the Draft Analysis dialog box, click [icon] to open the Draft Analysis.* dialog box. The color can be changed by double-clicking on it and selecting a different color in the Color dialog box, as shown in Figure 7–4.

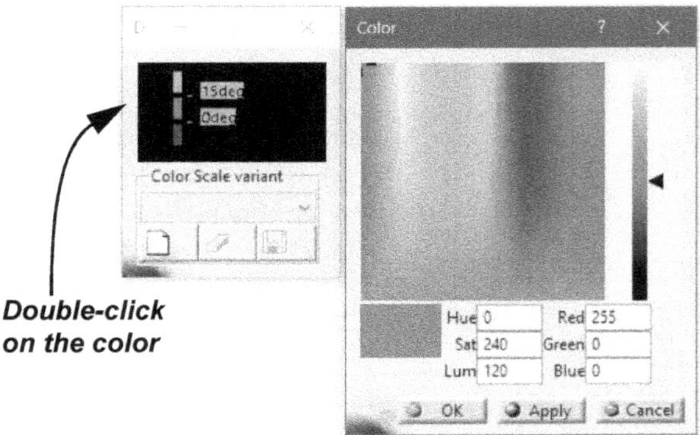

Figure 7–4

The default scale values increase linearly. However, it is possible to modify the scale value by double-clicking on it and entering the required value in the Edit dialog box, as shown in Figure 7–5. When the scale value is modified, a green frame displays on the scale value. To use a linear value, right-click on the value and select **Unfreeze**.

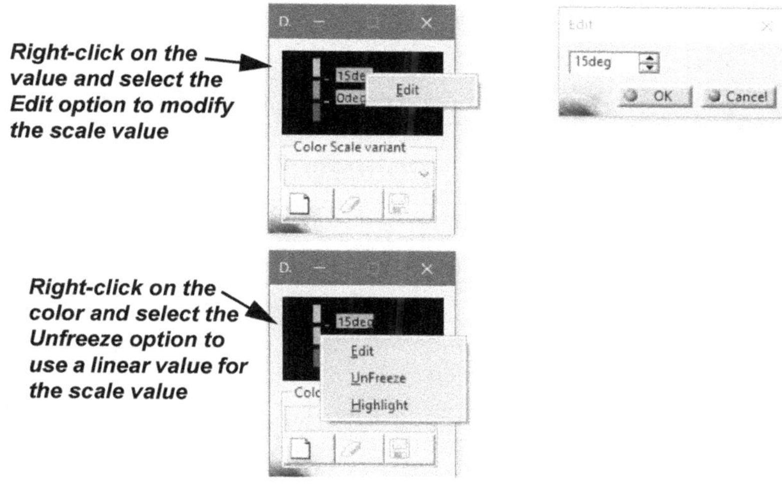

Right-click on the value and select the Edit option to modify the scale value
15deg
0deg
Edit
Color Scale variant
Edit
15deg
OK
Cancel
Right-click on the color and select the Unfreeze option to use a linear value for the scale value
15deg
Edit
UnFreeze
Highlight

Figure 7–5

On The Fly

If you click [icon] in the Draft Analysis dialog box, the analysis result displays for any location in the model. Three arrows display on the model, as shown in Figure 7–6.

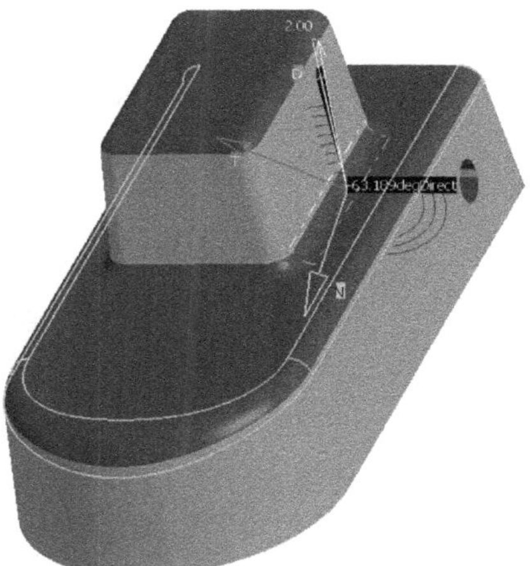

Figure 7–6

The arrows are described as follows:

Type	Description
Red Arrow	Draft direction.
Blue Arrow	Tangent direction.
Green Arrow	Normal direction.

A cone is attached to the Draft direction arrow, which depends on the maximum value of the Draft analysis scale. This cone (shown in Figure 7–7) can be used to compare different Draft angles with the maximum value of the Draft analysis scale.

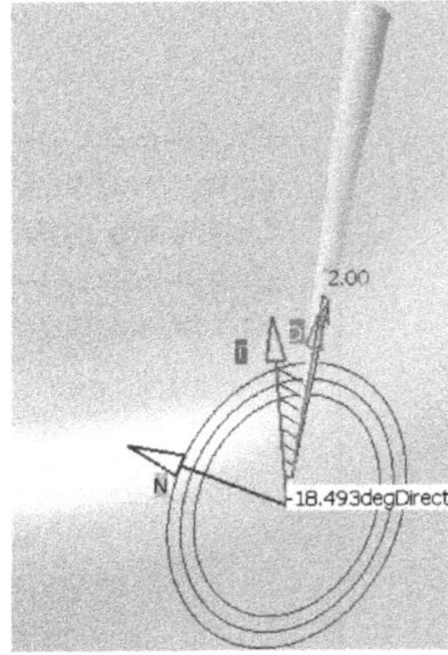

Figure 7–7

If you right-click on the draft direction arrow, the options shown in Figure 7–8 display.

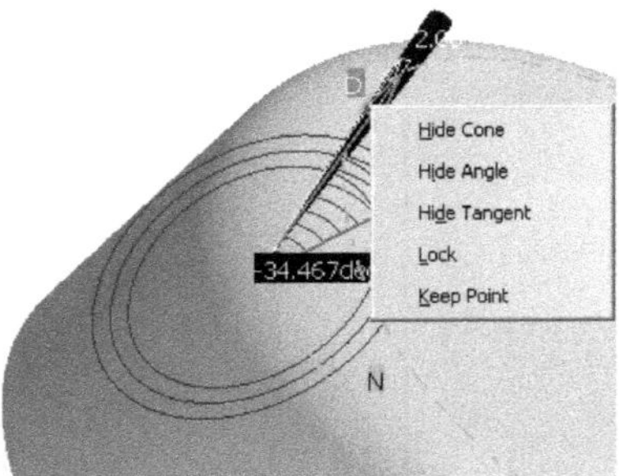

Figure 7–8

They are described as follows:

Options	Description
Hide Cone	Hides the cone.
Hide Angle	Hides the angle.
Hide Tangent	Hides the circles that show the tangent plane.
Lock	Locks the position.
Keep Point	Creates a point for the selected location.

Step 5 - Specify the direction.

In the Draft Analysis dialog box, in the *Direction* area, there are three options that control the reference Draft direction. The Draft analysis results are generated according to the position of the global axis system. When you click [icon], the compass snaps to the origin of the global axis system. To use a different reference Draft direction, manipulate the compass. The results of the analysis change according to the position of the compass. You can also lock the position of the compass by clicking [icon]. To change the draft direction, click [icon], as shown in Figure 7–9.

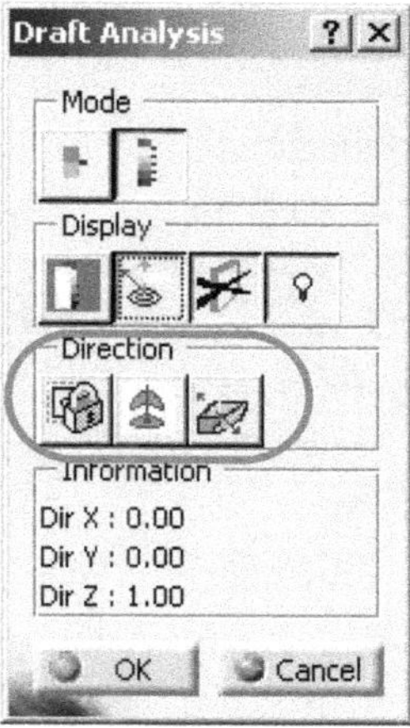

Figure 7–9

Step 6 - Complete the analysis.

To complete the analysis, click **OK**. The analysis result is saved in the specification tree, as shown in Figure 7–10.

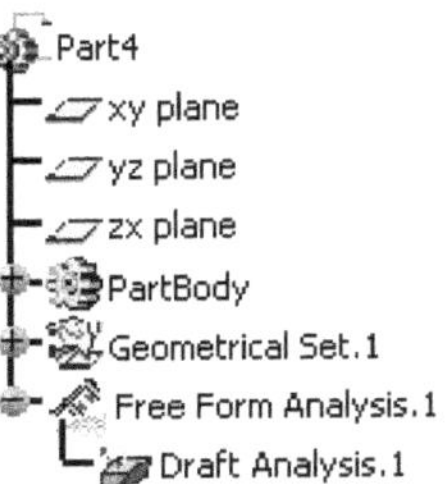

Figure 7–10

Having a smaller 3D accuracy setting enables you to have better visualization while zooming into the model, but it affects the performance of your system. There are two different options: **Proportional** and **Fixed**. Select the **Proportional** option if you are working on an area that is not smaller than the overall model. Select the **Fixed** option if the working surface area is too small when compared to the overall size of the model.

To change the 3D accuracy settings, select **Tools>Options> General>Display** and select the *Performances* tab, as shown in Figure 7–11.

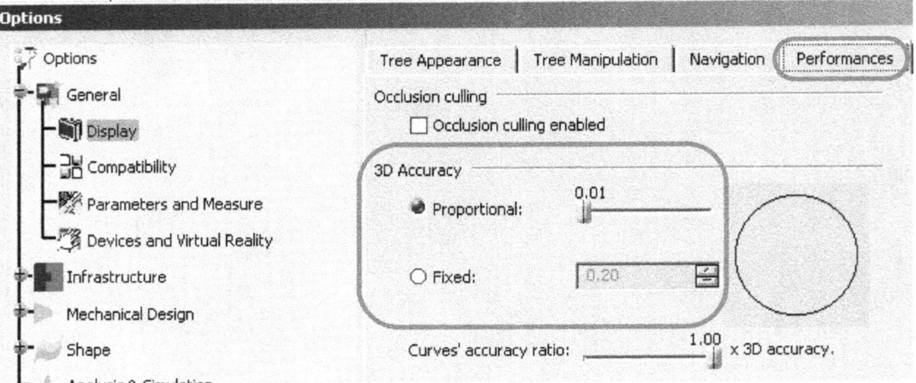

Figure 7–11

7.2 Threads and Taps

You can create Thread and Tap features on cylindrical surfaces. These features are only used to simulate a Helical Groove. They are non-solid features and their purpose is to store the Thread and Tap information, which is then shown on a drawing. The actual Groove geometry is not created.

General Steps

Use the following general steps to create a Thread/Tap feature:

1. Open the Thread/Tap Definition dialog box.
2. Select the face(s) to be threaded or tapped.
3. Specify the Thread type and depth.
4. Complete the feature.

Step 1 - Open the Thread/Tap Definition dialog box.

Click (Thread/Tap). The Thread/Tap Definition dialog box opens as shown in Figure 7–12.

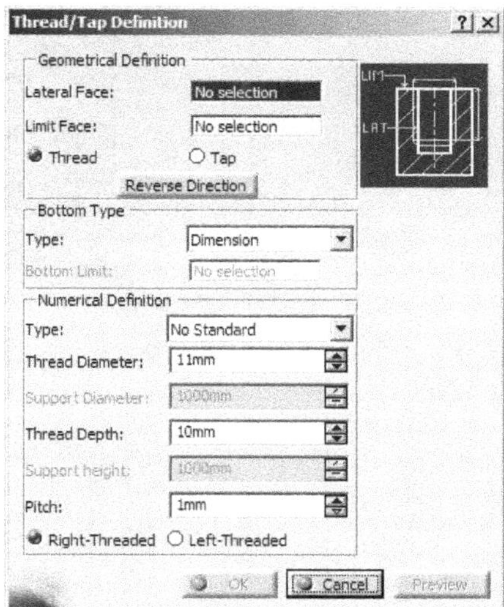

Figure 7–12

Step 2 - Select the face(s) to be threaded or tapped.

Select a lateral face (cylindrical surface) to place the Threads, and a limit face to define the start of the Threads.

Step 3 - Specify the Thread type and depth.

You can apply any of the standard Threads loaded into CATIA. Alternatively, you can create a special, non-standard Thread. The depth of the Thread is calculated from the limit face to the specified Thread depth.

Step 4 - Complete the feature.

Click **OK** to complete the feature. The Thread displays in the specification tree. When you select the Thread feature in the specification tree, it is also highlighted on the model, as shown in Figure 7–13.

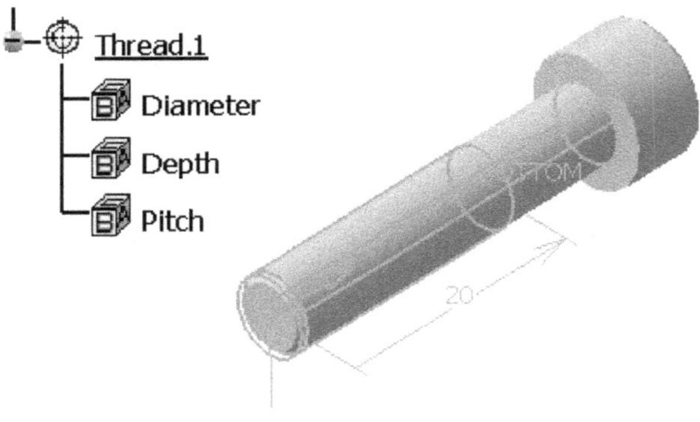

Figure 7–13

7.3 Thread/Tap Analysis

Since Threads and Taps are not displayed as solid geometry, it can sometimes be difficult to keep track of them. You can use the Thread/Tap Analysis to explore the Threads/Taps in your model.

General Steps

Use the following general steps to run a Thread/Tap Analysis:

1. Open the Thread/Tap Analysis dialog box.
2. Run the Thread/Tap Analysis.

Step 1 - Open the Thread/Tap Analysis dialog box.

Click (Thread/Tap Analysis) in the Analysis toolbar. The Thread/Tap Analysis dialog box opens as shown in Figure 7–14. The *Numerical Analysis* area reports the number of Thread and Tap features that are present in the model. Any Hole features that have Thread parameters defined are included in the reported Taps.

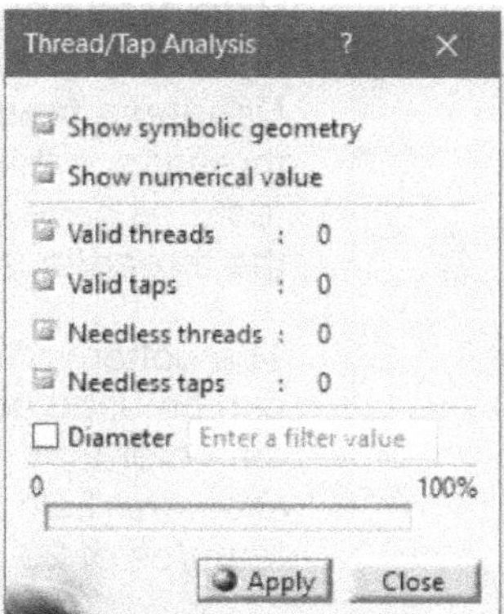

Figure 7–14

Step 2 - Run the Thread/Tap Analysis.

To run the analysis, click **Apply**. By default, the system displays a symbolic surface and parameter information for each Thread or Tap on the model, as shown in Figure 7–15.

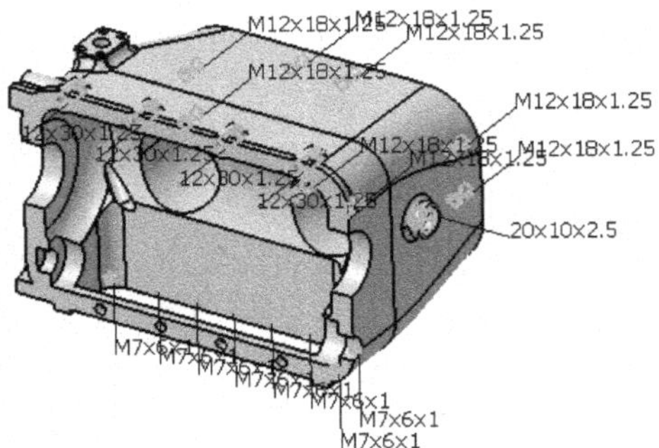

Figure 7–15

The top of the Thread/Tap Analysis dialog box contains the **Show symbolic geometry** and **Show numerical value** options. These options enable you to control the display of the symbolic surface and parameter information, respectively.

The middle of the dialog box contains the **Valid threads** and **Valid taps** options. These options give a count of the thread/taps that have no issues. Additionally, the **Needless threads** and **Needless taps** options. These will give a count of the thread/taps that have become insignificant because other features have been created that take up the space consumed by the thread/taps.

The bottom of the dialog box contains the **Diameter** option. This can be used as a filter to only display the Thread/Taps with a diameter that you specify. For example, if you enter **20** in the *Diameter* field, as shown in Figure 7–16, only the Thread or Tap features of 20 display.

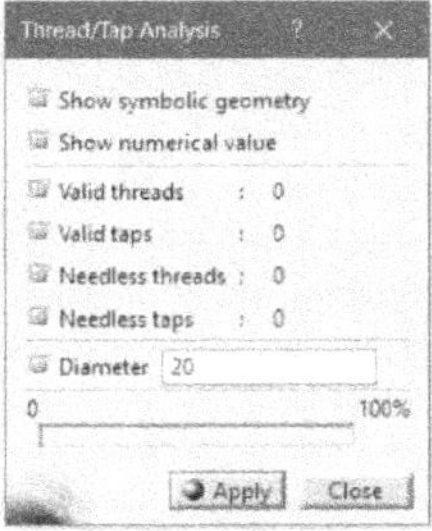

Figure 7–16

7.4 Parameterization Analysis

In a complex model with several features, it can become difficult to manage and investigate the specification tree. The **Parameterization Analysis** tool can filter the model and locate specific features in the tree. For example, you can search for fully constrained sketches, under-constrained sketches, and failed features in a model.

General Steps

Use the following general steps to run a Parameterization Analysis:

1. Open the Parameterization Analysis dialog box.
2. Run the Parameterization Analysis.

Step 1 - Open the Parameterization Analysis dialog box.

Select **Tools>Parameterization Analysis** in the menu bar, as shown in Figure 7–17.

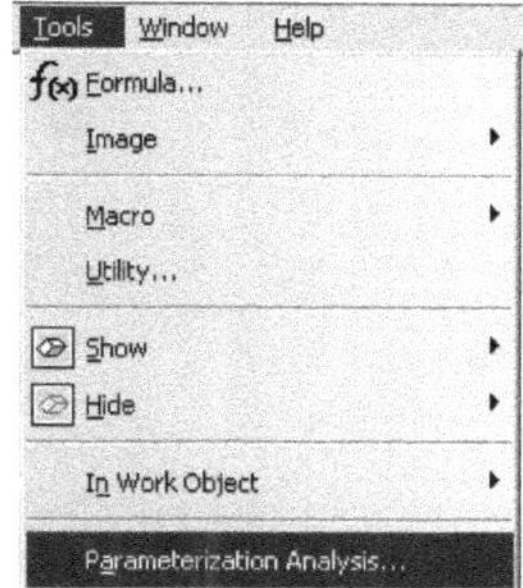

Figure 7–17

The Parameterization Analysis dialog box opens as shown in Figure 7–18.

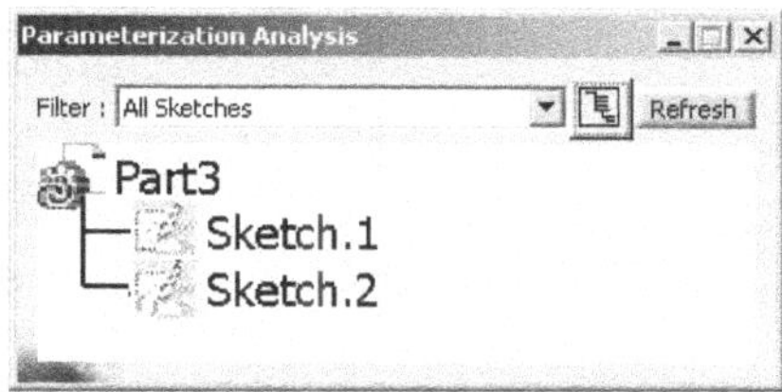

Figure 7–18

The specification tree is shown in Figure 7–19.

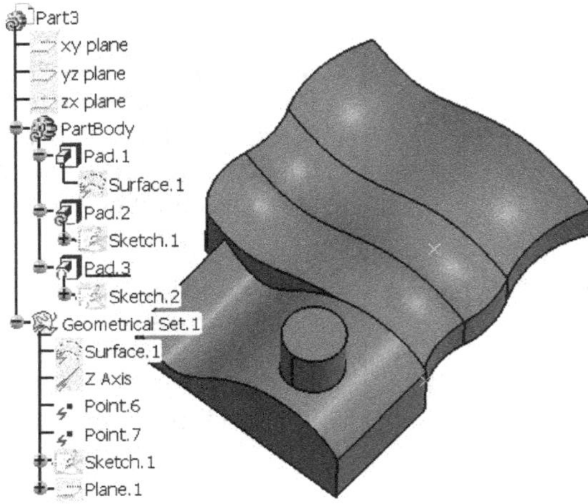

Figure 7–19

Step 2 - Run the Parameterization Analysis.

In the Parameterization Analysis dialog box, select a filter type in the Filter drop-down list, as shown in Figure 7–20.

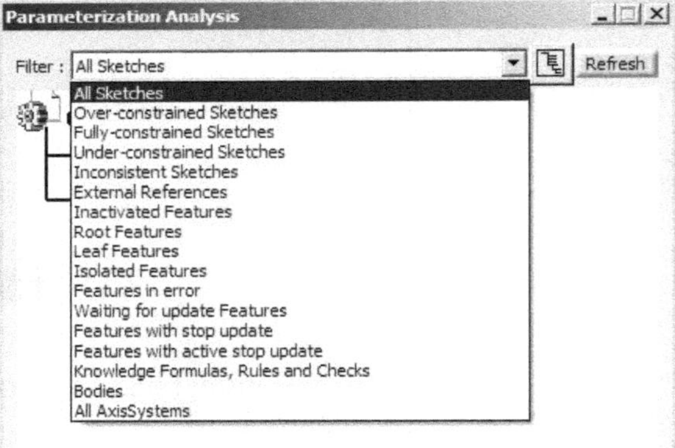

Figure 7–20

The following options are available in the Filter drop-down list.

- All Sketches
- Over-constrained Sketches
- Fully-constrained Sketches
- Under-constrained Sketches

- Inconsistent Sketches
- External References
- Inactivated Features
- Root Features
- Leaf Features
- Isolated Features
- Features in error
- Waiting for update Features
- Features with stop update
- Features with active stop update
- Knowledge Formulas, Rules and Checks
- Bodies
- All AxisSystems

The Parameterization Analysis dialog box updates according to your filter selection. An example is shown in Figure 7–21.

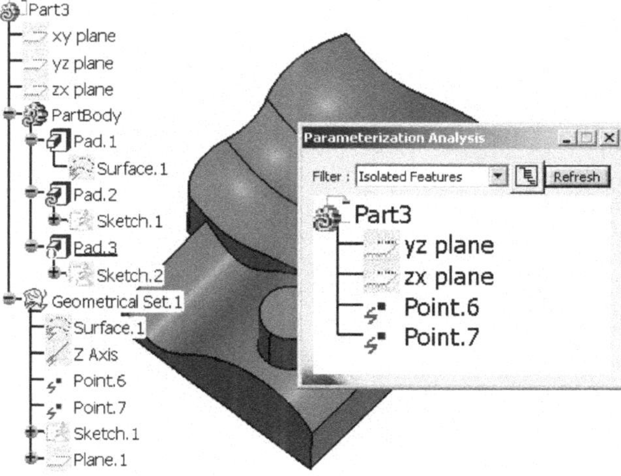

Figure 7–21

To display the body structure in the same order as in the specification tree, click (Displays body structure), as shown in Figure 7–22.

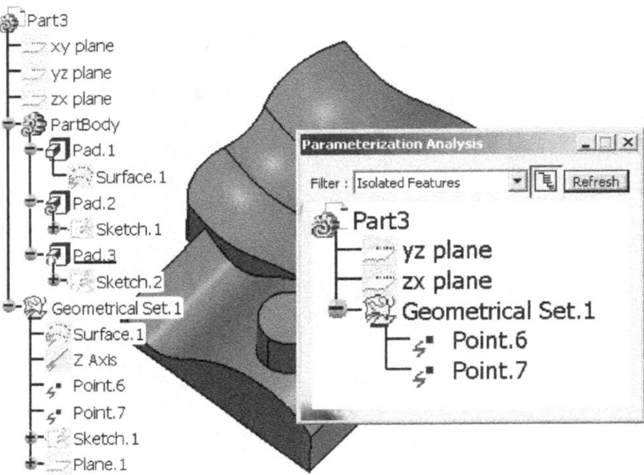

Figure 7–22

Practice 7a

Draft Analysis

Practice Objective

- Perform a Draft Analysis.

In this practice, you will perform a Draft analysis on the model shown in Figure 7–23, and verify that the part is correctly drafted.

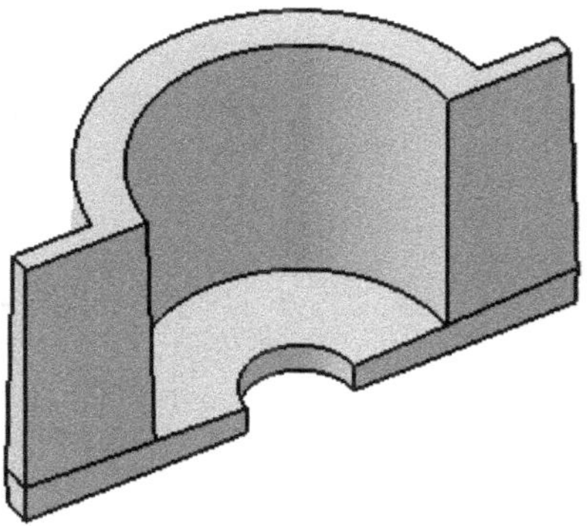

Figure 7–23

Task 1 - Open the part.

1. Open **Draft_Analysis.CATPart**. The model displays as shown in Figure 7–24.

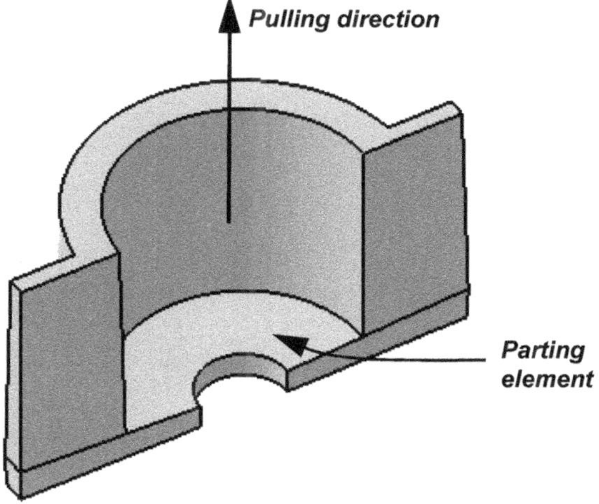

Figure 7–24

Task 2 - Change the View mode.

1. In the View mode toolbar, click (Shading with Material) or select **View>Render Style>Shading with Material**.

Task 3 - Perform a Draft analysis.

1. In the Analysis toolbar, click (Draft Analysis) and select one of the faces of the model. The analysis result displays on the model, as shown in Figure 7–25.

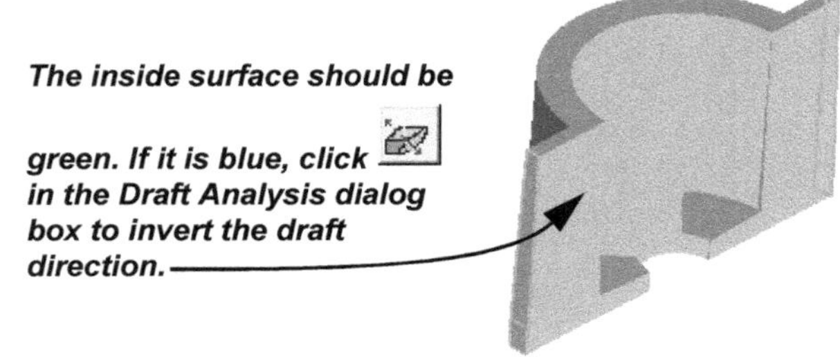
The inside surface should be green. If it is blue, click in the Draft Analysis dialog box to invert the draft direction.

Figure 7–25

2. In the Draft Analysis dialog box, click to toggle off the light effect.

3. In the Draft Analysis toolbar, ensure that (Quick Analysis mode) is selected. The Draft Analysis and Draft Analysis.1 dialog boxes open as shown in Figure 7–26.

If you do not see the Draft Analysis.1 dialog box, click .

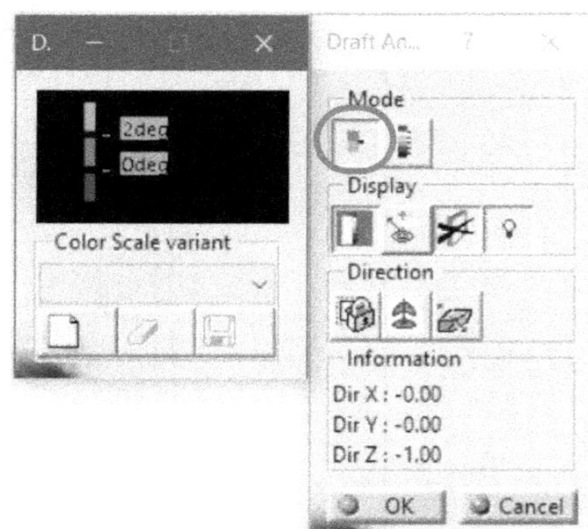
2deg
0deg
Color Scale variant
Mode
Display
Direction
Information
Dir X : -0.00
Dir Y : -0.00
Dir Z : -1.00
OK
Cancel

Figure 7–26

Note that your images will vary slightly from those in this section, depending on your model's orientation and where you select.

4. In the *Display* area, click [icon], and drag the cursor over the model. In Figure 7–27, note that the draft direction is not pointing to the right.

   If your results are the inverse of those shown in Figure 7–27, click [icon] in the Draft Analysis dialog box to invert the draft direction.

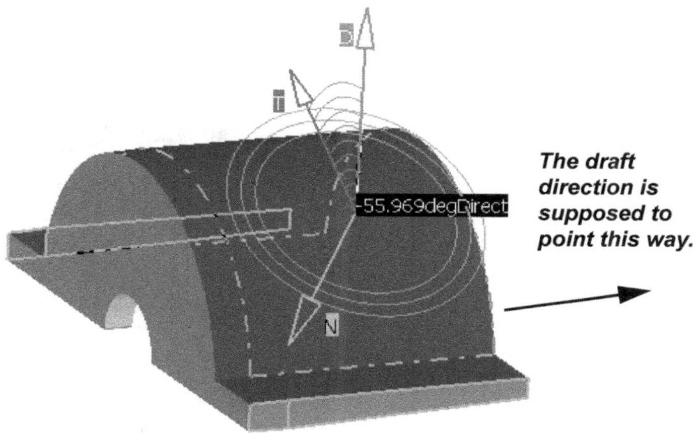

D
T
-55.969degDirect
N
The draft direction is supposed to point this way.

Figure 7–27

5. In the Draft Analysis dialog box, click [icon]. The compass will snap to the origin of the global axis system.

6. Locate the compass, as shown in Figure 7–28.

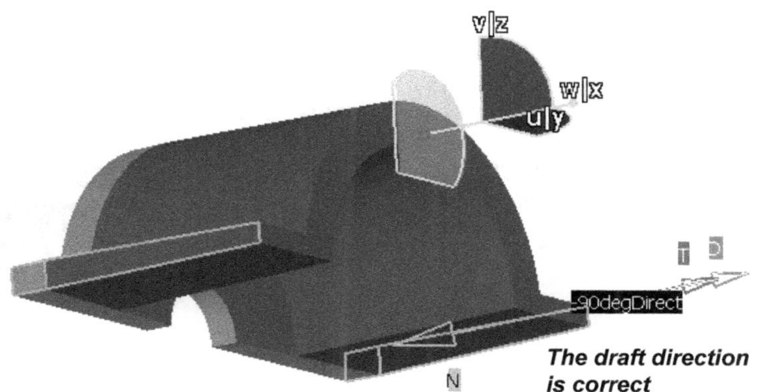

v|z
w|x
u|y
T
D
-90degDirect
N
The draft direction is correct

Figure 7–28

7. In the Draft Analysis dialog box, click [icon] to lock the position of the compass.

Design Considerations

Both sides of the part are drafted using **1deg** draft angle. To display the drafted faces with **1deg**, the scale values need to be modified.

8. Double-click on **0deg**. The Edit dialog box opens as shown in Figure 7–29. In the Edit dialog box, enter **0.25**. The colors of the model update automatically.

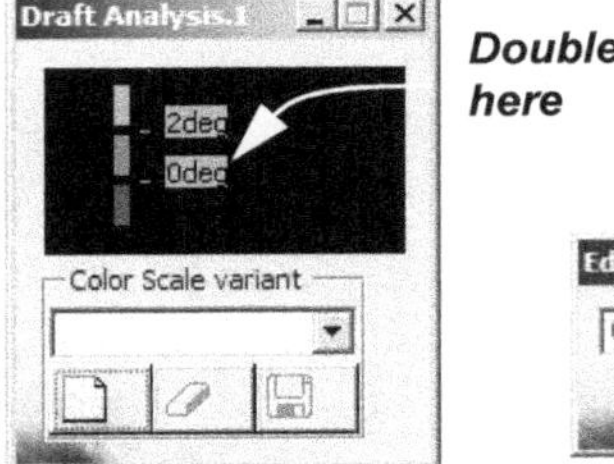

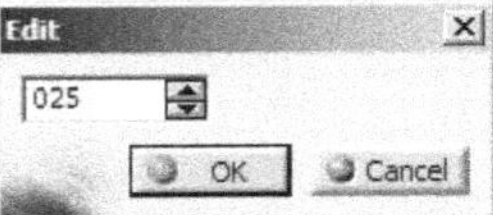

Figure 7–29

9. All of the red faces displayed on the model have a draft angle between 0.25deg and 2deg. This means that all of the red faces are drafted with a 1deg angle value.

10. Explore the model to note the faces that display in red.

    The colors on the model might disappear if you select in the display background. To display the results again, clear

     and select any surface on the model.

11. Change the scale values as shown in Figure 7–30. Change the *0.25deg* value to **-1.5deg** and then change the *2deg* value to **-0.25deg**.

Ensure that you edit the values in the order listed in Step 11.

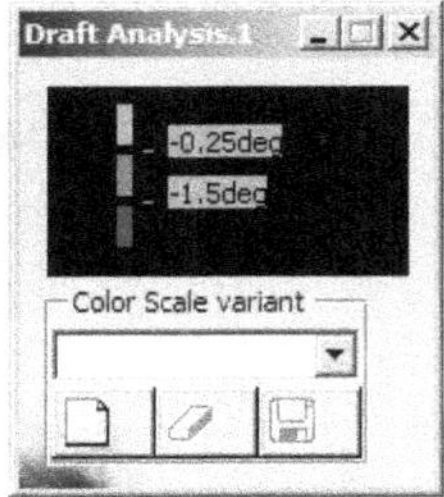

Figure 7–30

12. All of the red faces displayed on the model have a draft angle between -1.5deg and -0.25. This means all of the red faces are drafted with a -1deg angle value.

13. In the Draft Analysis toolbar, click (Full Analysis mode). The Draft Analysis.1 dialog box displays as shown in Figure 7–31.

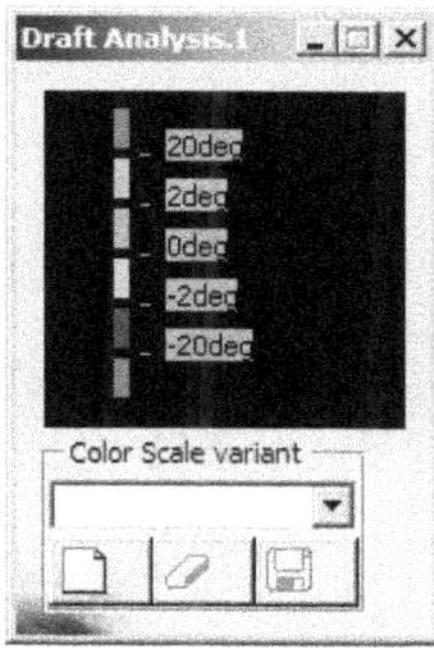

Figure 7–31

14. Edit the values as follows:

- *0deg:* **0.25**
- *2deg:* **0.75**
- *20 deg:* **1.25**
- *-2deg:* **-.5**
- *-20deg:* **-1.25**

15. The Draft Analysis dialog box displays as shown in Figure 7–32.

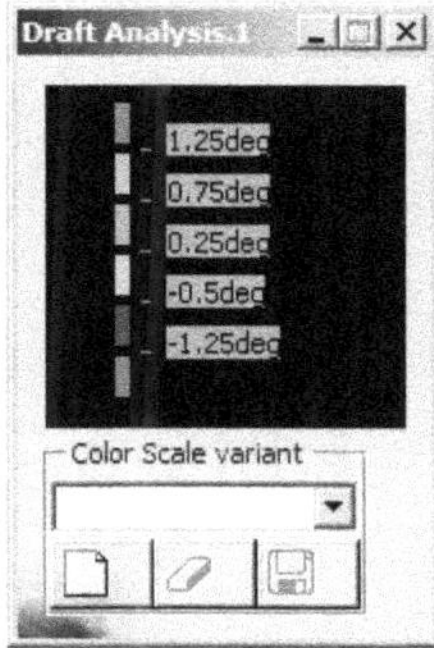

Figure 7–32

16. Double-click on the red color, which is the last color on the scale. The Color dialog box opens as shown in Figure 7–33.

17. Change the color to pink.

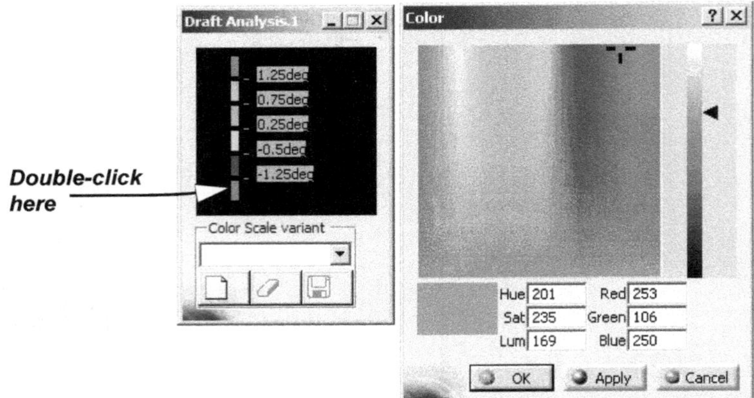

Figure 7–33

18. Click **OK**. The model displays as shown in Figure 7–34.

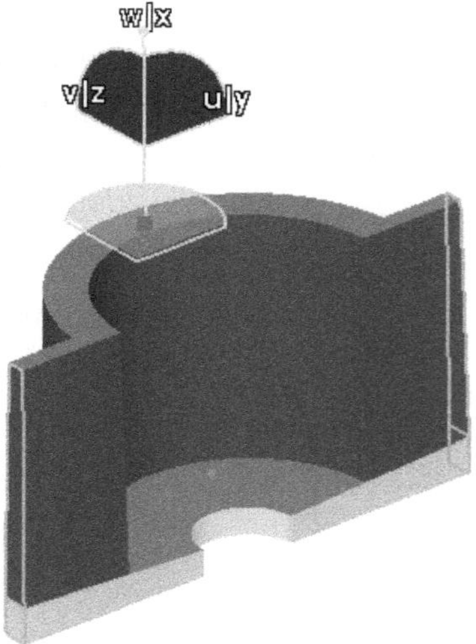

Figure 7–34

19. Explore all of the faces and the colors of the model. The part is supposed to be drafted with 1deg draft angle. Verify that the part has been drafted correctly. If not, try to determine which faces need to be drafted.

20. Save and close the model.

Practice 7b

Creating Threads and Taps

Practice Objectives

- Create a Thread.
- Create a Tap.
- Modify a Hole to include a Tap.

In this practice, you will use the **Thread/Tap** tool to add Threads and Taps to the model shown in Figure 7–35.

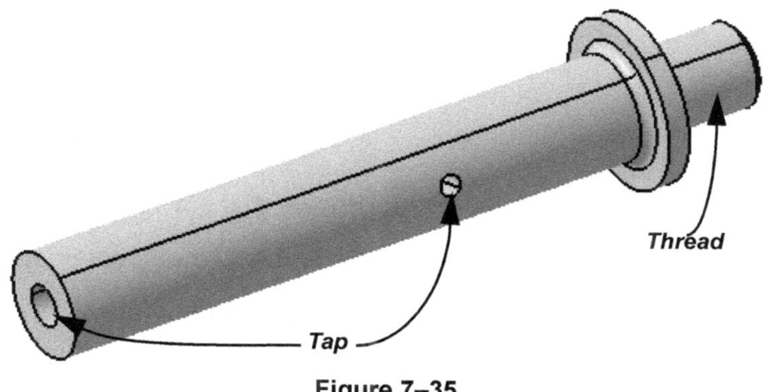

Figure 7–35

Task 1 - Open the part.

1. Open **ThreadTap.CATPart**.

Task 2 - Create a thread.

[icon] can be found in the Dress-Up Features toolbar.

1. Click [icon] (Thread/Tap) to open the Thread/Tap Definition dialog box.

2. Select geometry for the lateral face and limit face as shown in Figure 7–36.

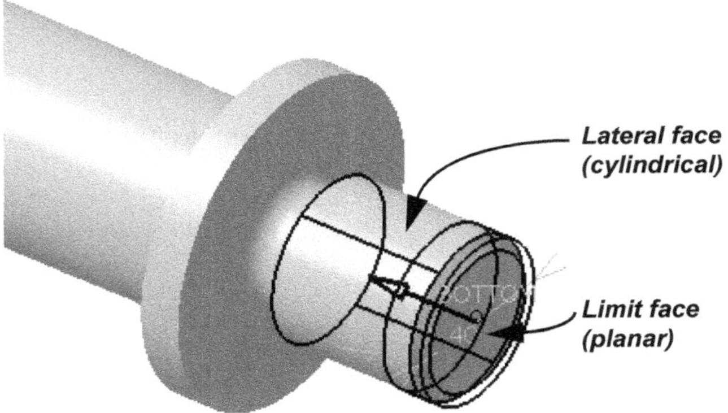

Figure 7–36

3. Ensure that the **Thread** option is selected.

4. Enter the following parameter values:

   - *Type:* **No Standard**
   - *Thread Diameter:* **40mm**
   - *Thread Depth:* **40mm**
   - *Pitch:* **5mm**
   - Select **Right-Threaded**.

5. Click **OK** to complete the Thread feature. Note that there is no visual representation for the Thread, but the information is stored in the specification tree, as shown in Figure 7–37.

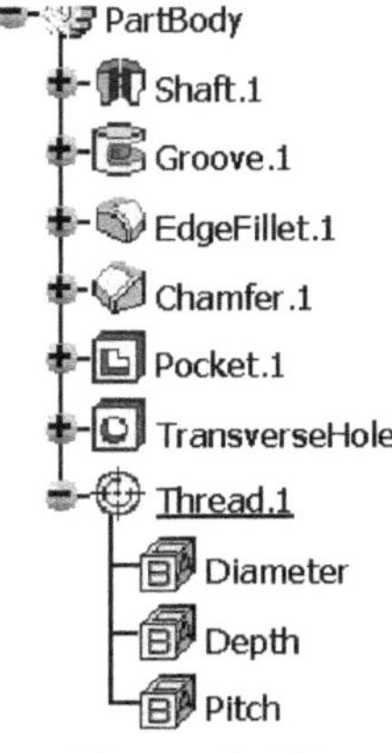

Figure 7–37

6. Rename the *Thread.1* feature as **ShaftThread**.

Task 3 - Create a tap.

1. Click [icon] (Thread/Tap).
2. Ensure that the **Tap** option is selected.
3. Select geometry for the lateral face and limit face, as shown in Figure 7–38.

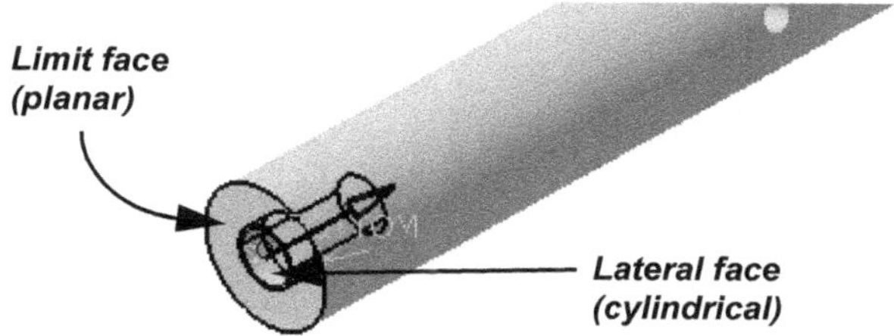

Figure 7–38

4. In the Type drop-down list, select **Metric Thick Pitch**. The Feature Definition Error dialog box opens when this selection is made, as shown in Figure 7–39.

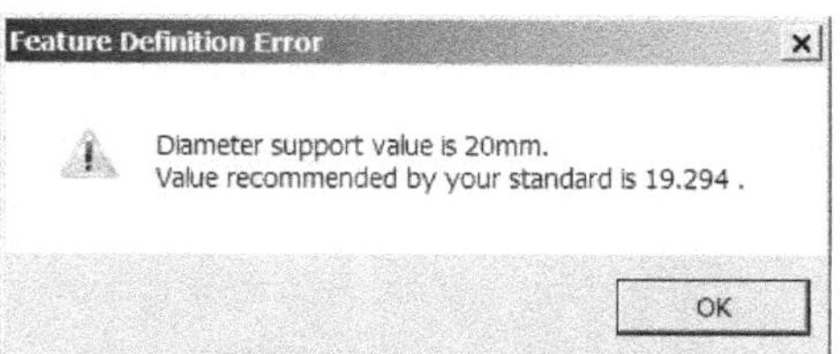

Figure 7–39

Design Considerations

The Feature Definition Error dialog box provides an automatic reference to ISO standards. The recommended value of 19.294mm is the ISO standard for the minor diameter of the M22 thread/tap. Because the diameter of the Pocket feature is 20mm, the M22 Thread Description is best suited for this application.

5. Click **OK** to close the dialog box. The system automatically selects the **M22** standard for the Thread Description.
6. Make the following selections:
   - *Thread depth:* **40mm**
   - Select **Right-Threaded**.

The Thread/Tap Definition dialog box opens as shown in Figure 7–40.

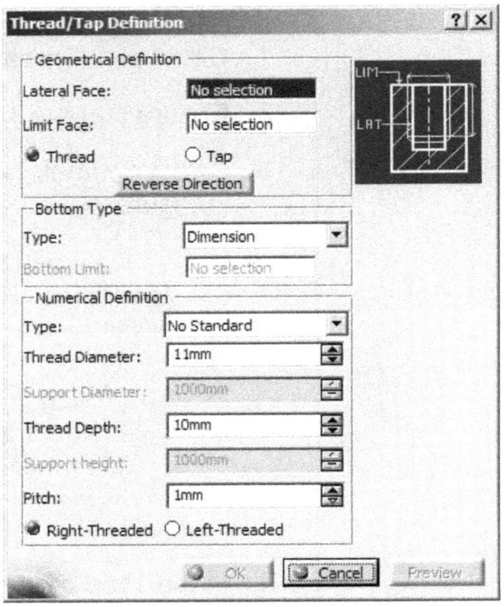

Figure 7–40

7. Complete the Tap feature and rename the Thread.2 feature as **BaseTap**.

Task 4 - Modify a hole to include a tap.

Another method of defining a Tap is through the Hole Definition dialog box.

1. Double-click on the TransverseHole feature to open the Hole Definition dialog box.
2. Select the *Thread Definition* tab and select the **Threaded** option.
3. Enter the following parameter values:
   - *Type:* **Metric Thick Pitch**
   - *Thread Description:* **M12**
   - Select **Left-Threaded**.
4. To define the thread depth, right-click on the *Thread Depth* field and select **Edit Formula**.

5. With the Formula Editor dialog box open, select the **45mm** dimension shown in Figure 7–41. This will set the thread depth equal to the hole depth.

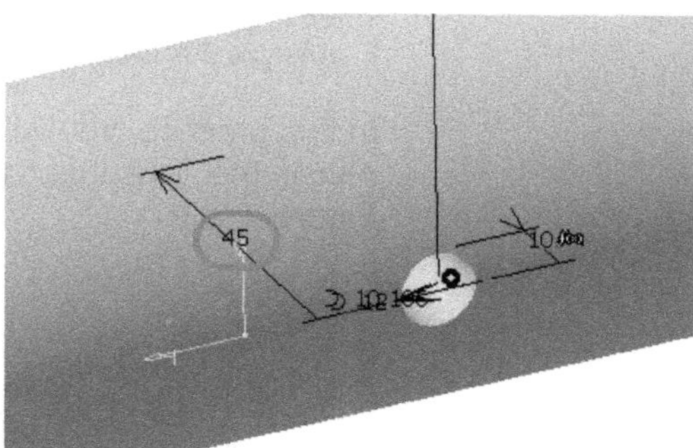

Figure 7–41

6. In the Formula Editor dialog box, click **OK** to complete the formula. The Hole Definition dialog box opens as shown in Figure 7–42.

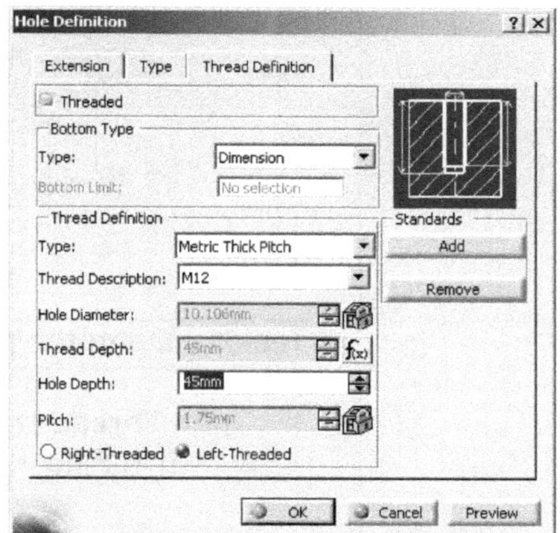

Figure 7–42

7. Click **OK** to complete the Tap feature.

Design Consideration

Rather than creating a Pocket and applying a Tap, you can create a threaded hole using the Hole Definition dialog box. This reduces the model feature count. Additionally, the **Thread Description** option in the Hole Definition dialog box automatically resizes the Hole diameter to the ISO standard minor-diameter for the selected Thread Description.

8. Save and close the file.

Practice 7c

Thread/Tap Analysis

Practice Objective

- Analyze the Taps and Threads that are in a model.

In this practice, you will use the **Thread/Tap Analysis** tool to review the Taps that have been applied to the part shown in Figure 7–43.

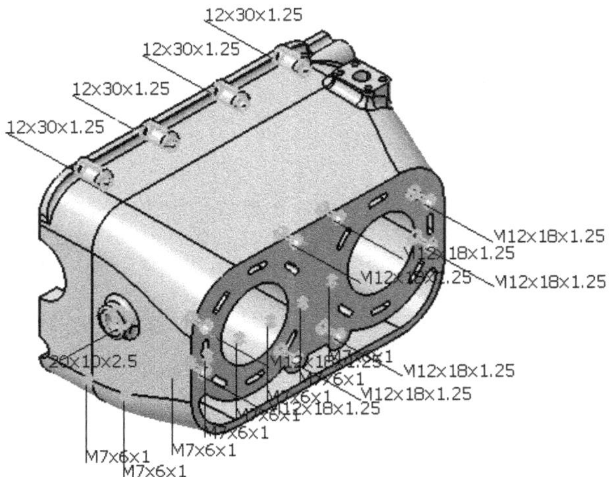

Figure 7–43

Task 1 - Open the part.

1. Open **ThreadAnalysis.CATPart**. The model displays as shown in Figure 7–44.

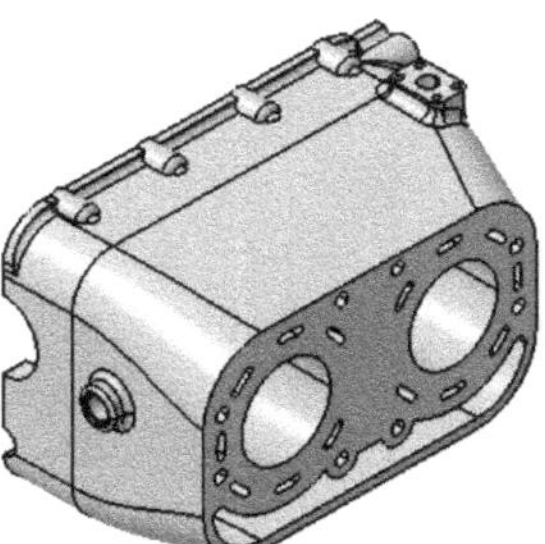

Figure 7–44

Although Tap features are present in the model, there is no visual indication that they are present when reviewing the geometry.

Task 2 - Perform a Thread/Tap Analysis.

1. In the Analysis toolbar, click (Thread/Tap Analysis).
2. The Thread/Tap Analysis dialog box opens as shown in Figure 7–45. The number of Threads and Taps display in the dialog box. By default, the **Show symbolic geometry** and **Show numerical value** options are selected.

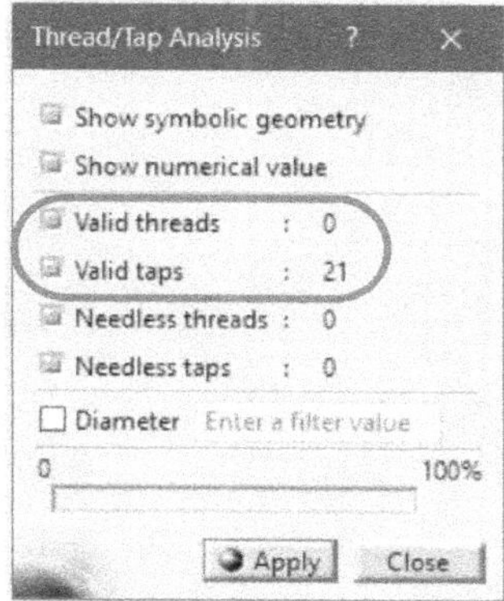

Figure 7–45

3. Click **Apply**. The Tap and Thread information displays on the model. Since the **Thread/Tap Analysis** options were set to display both geometry and values, each Tap is highlighted and the Tap information displays, as shown in Figure 7–46.

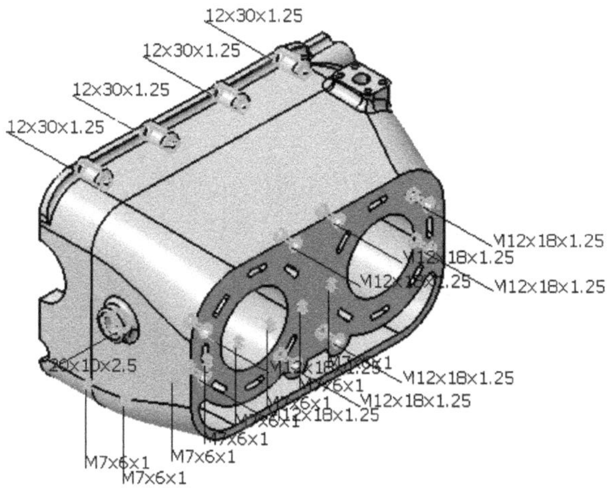

Figure 7–46

Task 3 - Modify the tap analysis parameters.

In this task, you will modify the parameters in the Thread/Tap Analysis dialog box to locate specific taps on the model.

1. Select **Diameter**. This option enables you to specify the diameter of the Tap or Thread to report.

2. In the *Value* field, enter **7** and click **Apply**. The model displays as shown in Figure 7–47.

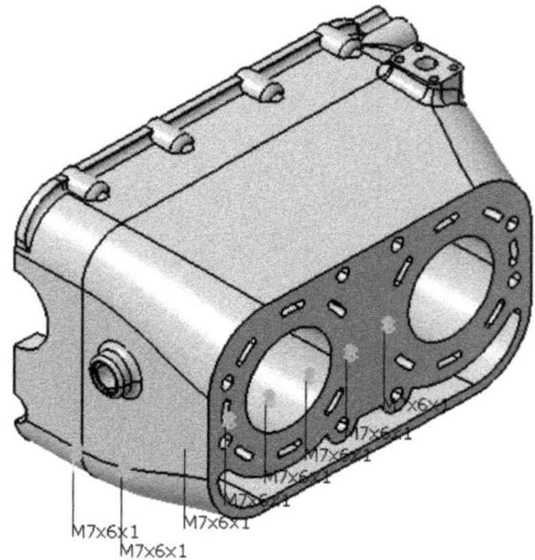

Figure 7–47

3. Close the Thread/Tap Analysis dialog box.

4. Close the file. Since no modifications were made, the model does not need to be saved.

Practice 7d

Parameterization Analysis

Practice Objective

- Perform a Parameterization Analysis.

In this practice, you will perform a parameterization analysis on the model shown in Figure 7–48.

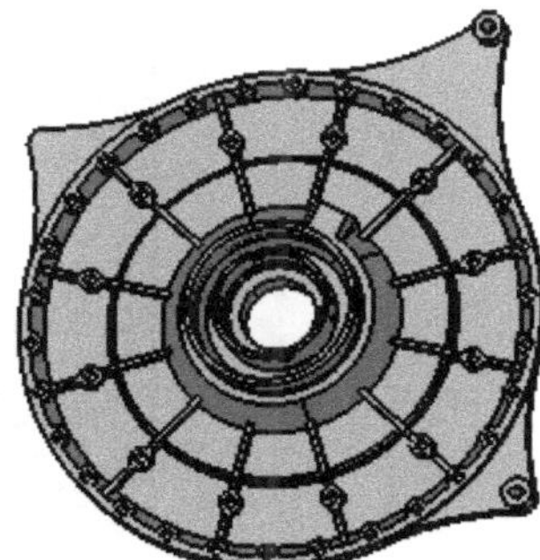

Figure 7–48

Task 1 - Open the part.

1. Open **Aft_Cover.CATPart**. The model displays as shown in Figure 7–49.

Figure 7–49

Task 2 - Perform a Parameterization Analysis.

1. Select **Tools>Parameterization Analysis**. The Parameterization Analysis dialog box opens. The **All Sketches** option is the default filter. This option displays all of the sketches that currently exist in the model.

2. In the Filter drop-down list, select the **Fully-constrained sketches** option to display the fully constrained sketches, as shown in Figure 7–50. The Parameterization Analysis dialog box only lists the sketches that are fully constrained.

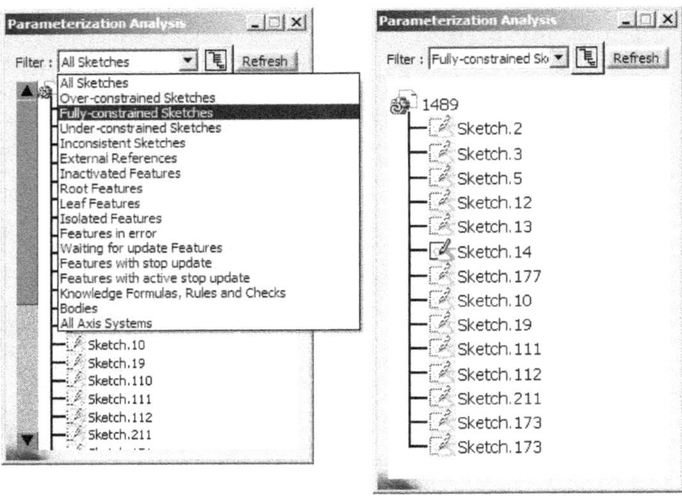

Figure 7–50

3. In the Filter drop-down list, select the **Over-constrained sketches** option to display the over-constrained sketches, as shown in Figure 7–51.

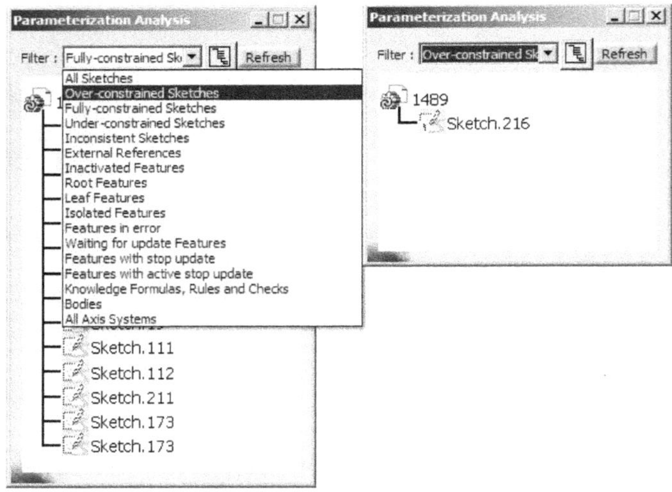

Figure 7–51

4. To locate the over-constrained sketch, right-click on **Sketch.216** and select **Center graph**, as shown in Figure 7–52.

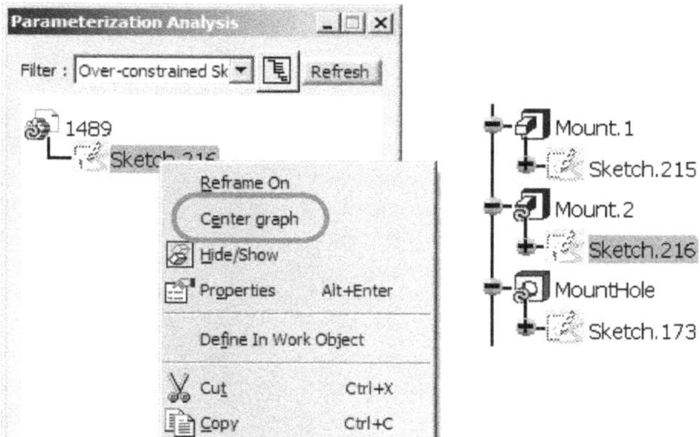

Figure 7–52

5. Double-click on **Sketch.216** to enter the Sketcher workbench.

6. Delete the dimension shown in Figure 7–53, and exit the Sketcher workbench.

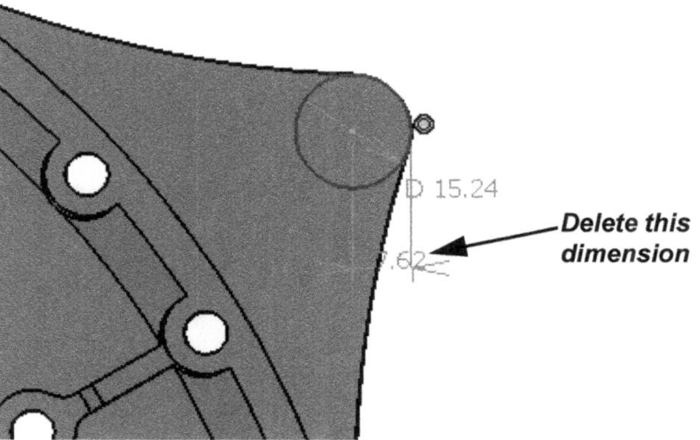

Figure 7–53

7. The Update Diagnosis: Sketch.216 dialog box opens, indicating that the profile used for Mount.1 is not a closed profile.

Design Considerations

The focus of this practice is to show you how to use the **Parameterization Analysis** tool. The problems in the model will not be fixed.

8. Click **Close**.

9. Run the Parameterization Analysis to display the over-constrained sketches. There are no over-constrained sketches in the specification tree, as shown in Figure 7–54.

Figure 7–54

10. In the Filter drop-down list, select **Waiting for update Features**, as shown in Figure 7–55.

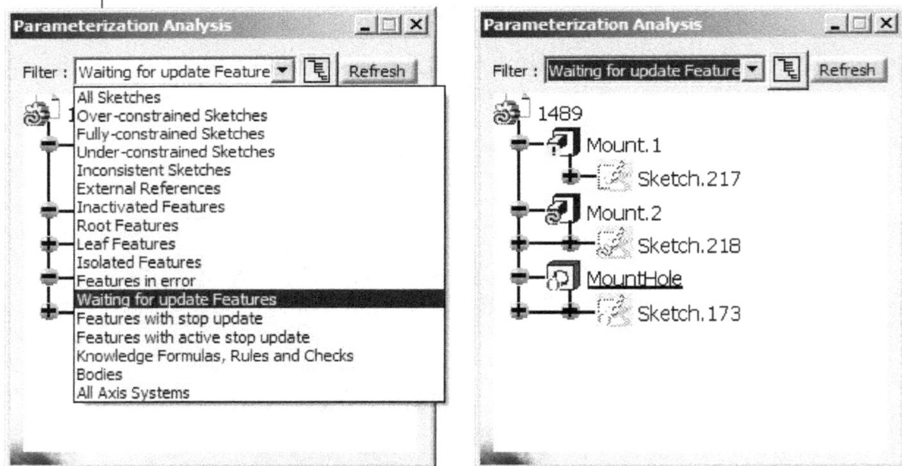

Figure 7–55.

11. To display the body structure in the same order as in the specification tree, click [icon] (Display the body structure). In the Parameterization Analysis dialog box, the body structure display changes as shown in Figure 7–56.

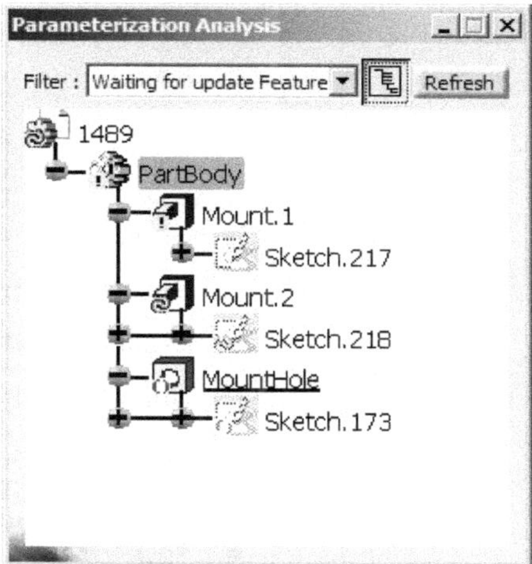

Figure 7–56

12. Save and close the file.

Chapter Review Questions

1. The **Draft Analysis** tool checks all of the draft angles in your model.
    a. True
    b. False
2. To display draft analysis results, the display mode has to be set to_____.
    a. Shading
    b. Shading with Edges
    c. Shading with Material
    d. Shading with Edges and Hidden Edges
3. Thread and Tap features create solid geometry to represent threaded cylinders or tapped holes.
    a. True
    b. False
4. What does the limit face do when defining a thread?
    a. Defines the start of the thread.
    b. Defines the end of the thread.
    c. Defines the pitch of the thread.
    d. None of the above.
5. You can use Thread/Tap Analysis to investigate the Thread and Tap features in the model.
    a. True
    b. False
6. The **Parameterization Analysis** tool can be used to filter the specification tree to locate specific features. You can filter for:
    a. Fully-constrained Sketches
    b. Isolated Features
    c. External References
    d. All of the above.

Multi-Model Links

You can reuse an existing design by copying and pasting a part body from one part to another part. If a geometry link is required between the part bodies, you can use special Paste options. The geometry link can be valuable when changes to the source part are expected.

Learning Objectives in this Chapter

- Understand the difference between Paste and Paste Special.
- Learn about the various Paste Special options.
- Use links to create references to other documents.
- Use Publications to identify and select externally linked elements.
- Review the best practices for managing links.

8.1 Reuse of Geometry

Geometry created in a part can be reused in the same part file or another file. You can copy many types of elements, including:

- Sketches
- Solid features
- Wireframe and Surface features
- Part Bodies
- Geometrical Sets
- Ordered Geometrical Sets

You can copy these features into the same or another part file. When you use the standard **Paste** command, the copy includes all of the parameters and information, without a link to the original geometry. When you use the **Paste Special** command, you can create the copy with or without a link to the original element, and with or without all of the specifications.

Advantages

- Copying and pasting geometry reduces re-work time, because you can use preexisting data to create similar parts.
- By preserving links between the original geometry and the copy, you can update multiple parts by only modifying one part.
- By severing links, you can create variations of a part while preserving the original features and dimensions.

Disadvantages

- If you create a copy without a link to the original, you cannot update the copy to reflect changes to the original.
- If you want to modify linked geometry, the referenced file must be available and loaded into CATIA.

8.2 Copy and Paste Special

Regular **Copy** and **Paste** options work well if you require a non-associative copy of a part body from another part. If you want to have a geometrical link between the source part body and the target part, you can use the **Paste Special** option.

General Steps

Use the following general steps to copy a body from one model and paste it into a second model with an external link.

1. Copy a body from the first model.
2. Paste the body into the second model using the **Paste Special** option.

Step 1 - Copy a body from the first model.

To copy a body from one model to another, select the body to be copied and select **Edit>Copy**, as shown in Figure 8–1.

Figure 8–1

Step 2 - Paste the body into the second model using the Paste Special option.

Activate the model in which you want to paste the body and select **Edit>Paste Special**. The Paste Special dialog box opens as shown in Figure 8–2.

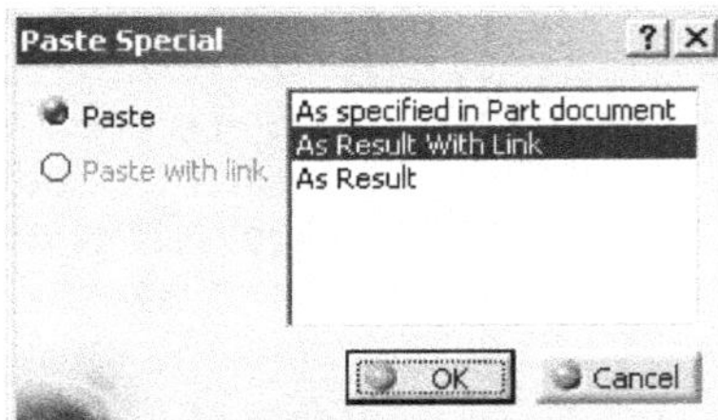

Figure 8–2

You can paste the body into the new document using one of the following options:

- As specified in Part document
- As Result With Link
- As Result

As Specified in Part Document

You can use this option to paste the body with its design specifications into the target document. When you use this option, each copied element displays in the specification tree as part of the pasted body. Two bodies are copied into a document, as shown in Figure 8–3. **Body.2** is pasted using **AsResult**, and Body.3 is pasted using **As Specified in Part Document**.

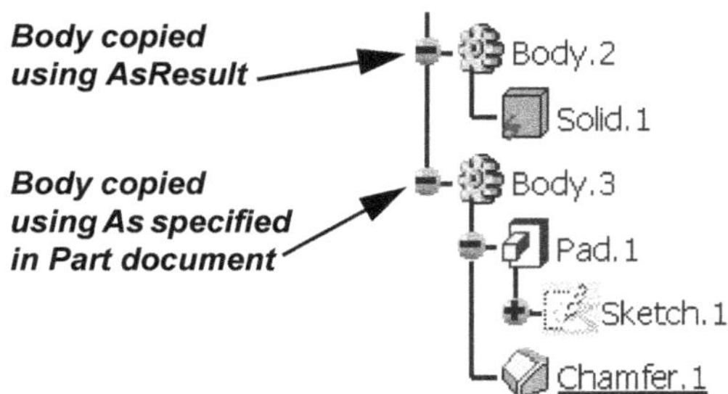

Figure 8–3

As Result With Link

You can use this option to paste the body without its design specifications and to maintain a link between the original and the copy. This means that if the original is modified, the copy can be updated to reflect the changes.

The body in Figure 8–4 is copied from another document and displays as Solid.1 in the specification tree.

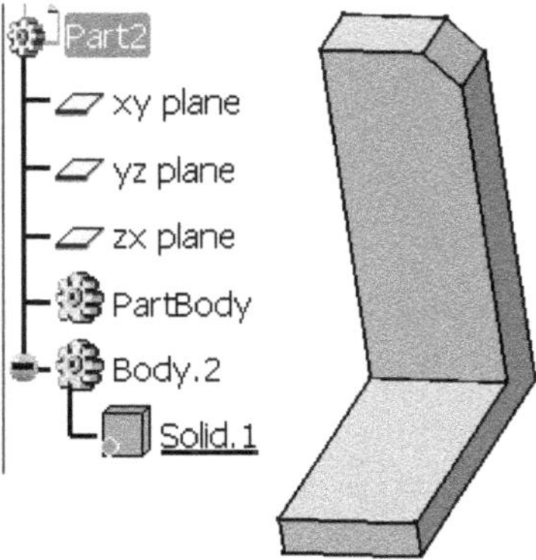

Figure 8–4

If the original body is modified, a red **X** displays in the specification tree to the left of the copied body (Solid.1), as shown in Figure 8–5. This red **X** indicates that changes have been made to the original body and that the copied element must be updated to display these changes.

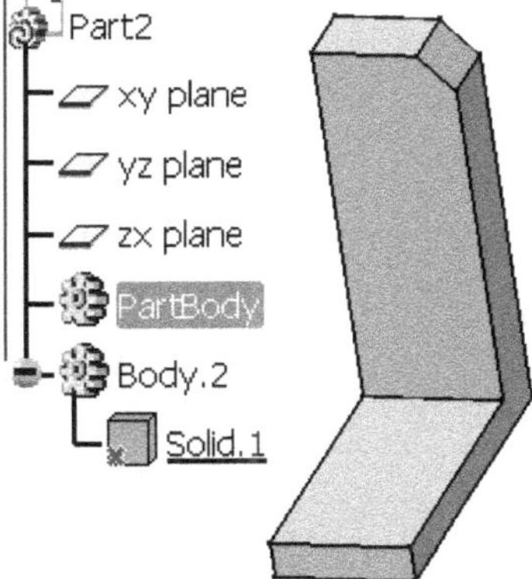

Figure 8–5

To update the file, click [update icon] or select **Edit>Update**. Figure 8–6 shows the copied document after it has been updated. The symbol to the left of Solid.1 in the specification tree has returned to its original form.

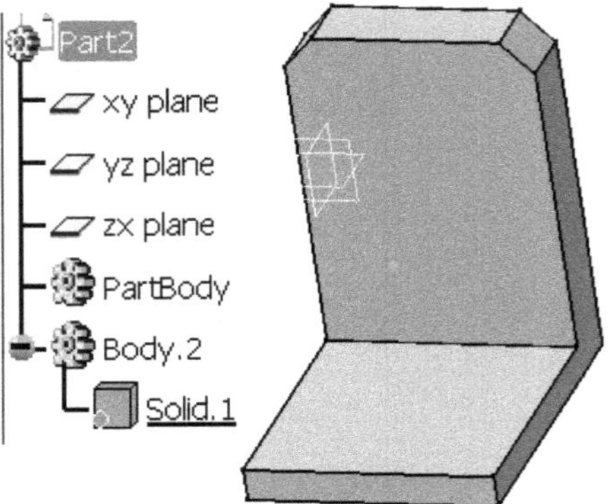

Figure 8–6

You can restrict the ability of elements to be linked between models. Select **Tools>Options>Infrastructure>Part Infrastructure**. Select the *General* tab, and select the **Restrict external selection with link to published elements** option. By doing so, you enable only published elements to be pasted with a link between models. If you select this option and then attempt a paste using the **As Result With Link** option, the error message shown in Figure 8–7 opens.

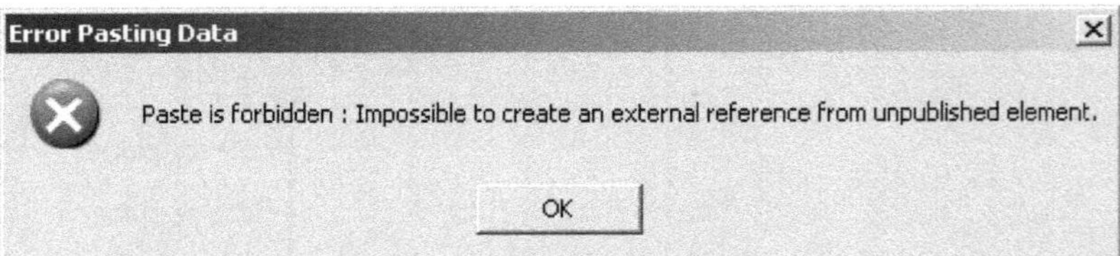

Figure 8–7

As Result

You can use this option to paste the body without its design specifications and without making a link between the source and target documents. When you use this option, one element is added to the specification tree of the target document, regardless of the number of elements copied. This option is useful if you do not plan to make changes to the element, and it simplifies the display of the specification tree. The copied items display in the specification tree as solid.***x*** (where ***x*** indicates the number of that particular element inserted into the model), as shown in Figure 8–8.

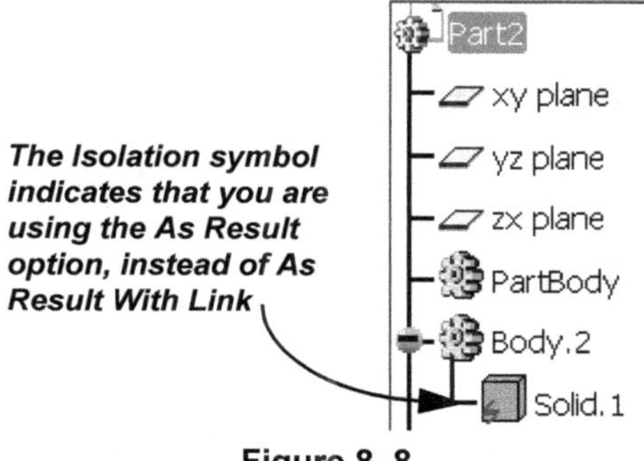

The Isolation symbol indicates that you are using the As Result option, instead of As Result With Link
Part2
xy plane
yz plane
zx plane
PartBody
Body.2
Solid.1

Figure 8–8

Referenced Geometry Symbols

The referenced geometry link status symbols are described as follows:

Link Status Symbol	Description
Solid.1	Copied geometry is up-to-date.
Solid.1	Pointed document has been found but not loaded.
Solid.1	Source geometry has been modified. Target body is not up-to-date.
Solid.1	Source geometry has been deleted or pointed document not found.
Solid.1	External link has been isolated.

8.3 External Links

You can create references to other documents to ensure that designs are consistent. As the number of documents increases, it becomes difficult to remember where information in a document is being read from. You can use the Links dialog box to manage external links in documents.

*To only display the links of one body in the document, select the required body, and select **Edit>Links**.*

To open the Links dialog box, select **Edit>Links**. The dialog box contains two tabs: *Links* and *Pointed Documents*. In the Links dialog box, you can review the external references of an entire document or of just one body in the document.

Links Tab

The *Links* tab lists all of the external references in the selected element. Select a link in the window to display its full path at the bottom of the dialog box, as shown in Figure 8–9.

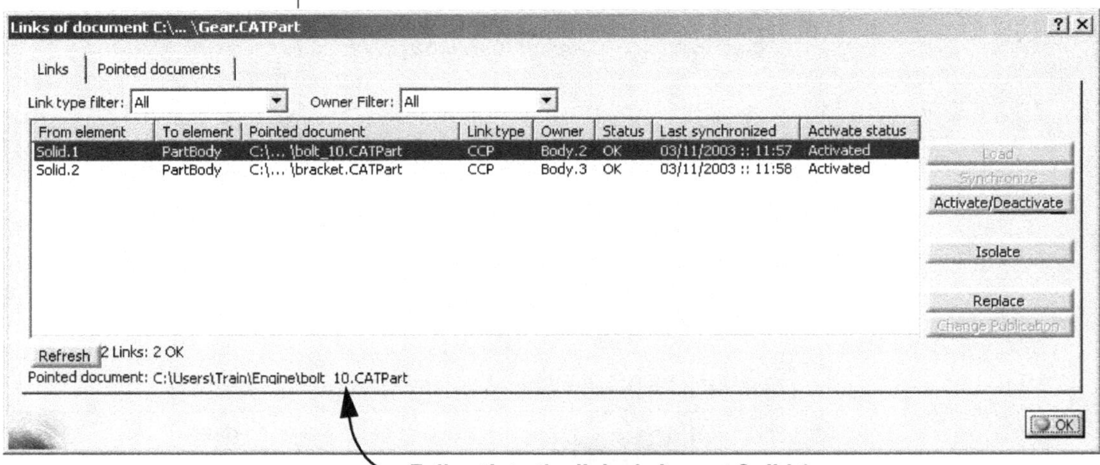

Figure 8–9

The columns in the Links dialog box are described as follows:

Column	Description
From element	The referenced element.
To element	The referencing element.
Pointed document	The document containing the referenced element.
Link type	The type of reference (i.e., Instance, Import, CCP, etc.).
Owner	The body to which the link belongs, in the current body.
Status	Can be shown as: • **OK** • **Not synchronized** • **Reference not found** • **Document not found** • **Document not loaded** • **Isolated**
Last synchronized	Time and date link was last updated to the original copied element.
Activate status	The status of the link (activated or deactivated).

If the document you are reviewing has a number of external references, try using the Filter drop-down lists to find the required reference. You can filter the information by Link type and/or Owner.

To manage links, use the following icons on the right side of the tab:

- Load
- Synchronize
- Activate/Deactivate
- Isolate
- Replace
- Change Publication

You can click **Load** to bring a document containing an external linked element into session. The **Load** function only loads body information. It does not actually open the body. If a document is **not loaded** as shown in Figure 8–10, it means that the reference body is not in session. CATIA is displaying the last known configuration of that body. Changes made to the linked element are not displayed in the body until the referenced document is loaded.

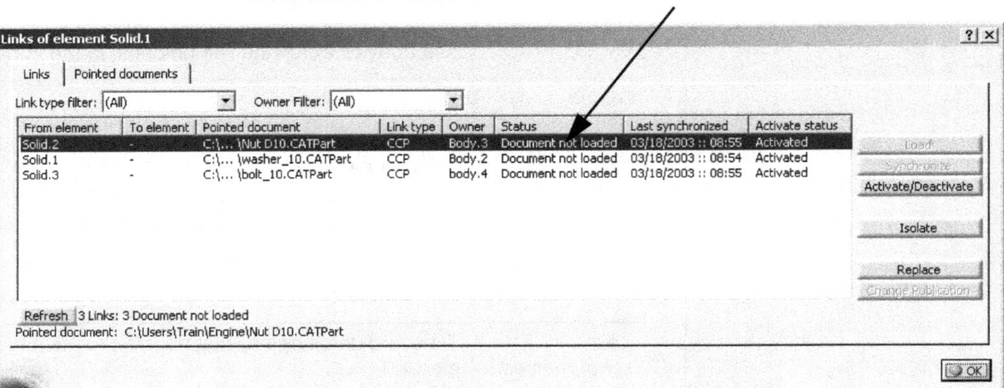

Figure 8–10

A link is also synchronized when the body is updated, as long as the linked documents are loaded and the link is active.

You can click **Synchronize** to update a link. If you make a change in the linked element, the copied element in the current document must be synchronized to the referencing document so that the changes are reflected. **Synchronize** is only available if the highlighted link needs to be updated. If a link requires synchronization, its Status is **Not synchronized**, as shown in Figure 8–11. Once a link has been synchronized, its Status changes to **OK**.

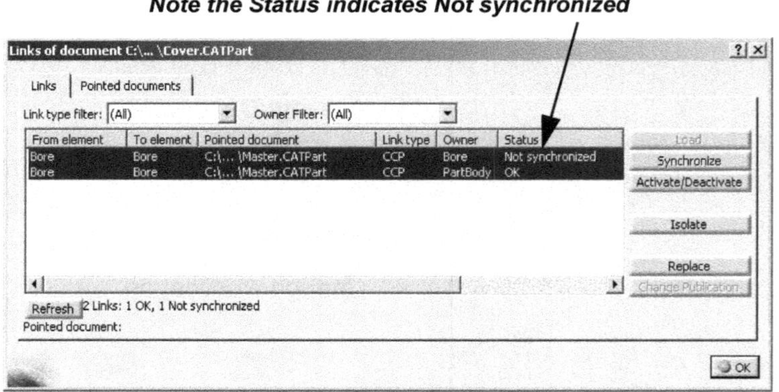

Figure 8–11

The other buttons in the dialog box are described as follows:

Button	Description
Activate/Deactivate	Activates or deactivates a link. Deactivation of a link temporarily breaks the association between the copied element and its reference. This prevents the element from synchronizing with the reference document while the body is being updated. To reactivate a link, click the button again.
Synchronize	Displays if changes are made to the reference document while the link was deactivated.
Isolate	Removes the link between the referenced document and the current document. Once a link is isolated, it no longer displays in the dialog box and cannot be re-linked. To re-create a link, you must copy the referenced element again and delete the element that was isolated.
Replace	Replaces the selected link with a new link. Click this button to open the replacing document. When replacing one document with another, remember that the replacing elements must be compatible with the original (i.e., you cannot replace a circular element with a linear element). Additionally, you cannot replace a document with a document of the same name. It is recommended that you replace a document with a copy of a body that was created using **File>Save As**. This ensures that the references in the old document update correctly to the new document.
Change Publication	Replaces the selected publication with a new one. Click this button and then select a new published element to replace the existing one. Update the model to display the changes. To use this option, the link must exist between parts and not in the context of an assembly. You can use this option to change only one link at a time.

Pointed Documents Tab

The *Pointed Documents* tab displays additional information on the document that contains the referenced elements. Select a reference in the *Pointed Document* column to display a preview of the referenced document, as shown in Figure 8–12.

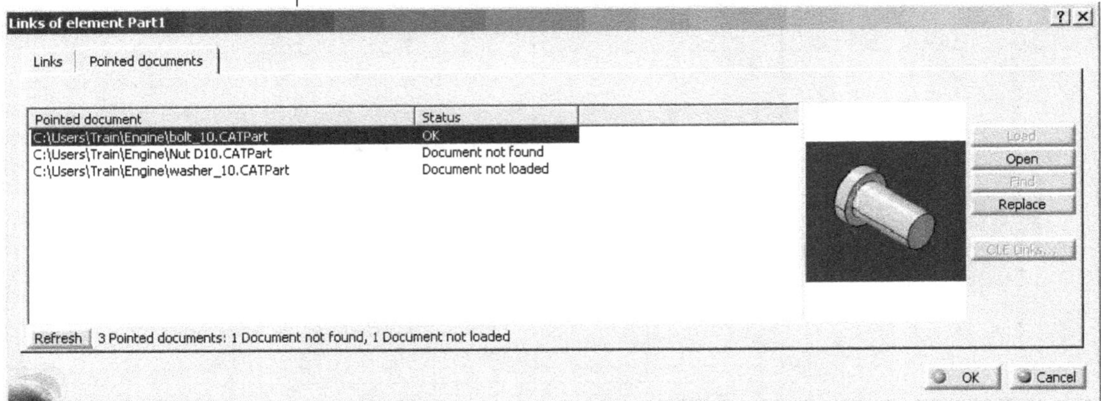

Figure 8–12

Use the following icons on the right side of the tab to help manage the documents that contain the referenced elements:

- **Load**
- **Open**
- **Find**
- **Replace**

You can click **Load** to bring the selected document into session. Loading a document from this tab is the same as loading it from the *Links* tab. If changes have been made to any elements in the reference document, those elements need to be synchronized in the *Links* tab.

If you want to open the selected document and make it the active document in the session, you can click **Open**. This option is useful in locating the original file quickly if changes need to be made.

You can click **Find** to locate broken links. When you do so, the File Selection dialog box opens and you can browse to any missing documents. A document might be missing if it has been moved from the folder from which CATIA last opened it, or if it has been renamed.

For example, the second document shown in Figure 8–13 has a Status of **Document not found**.

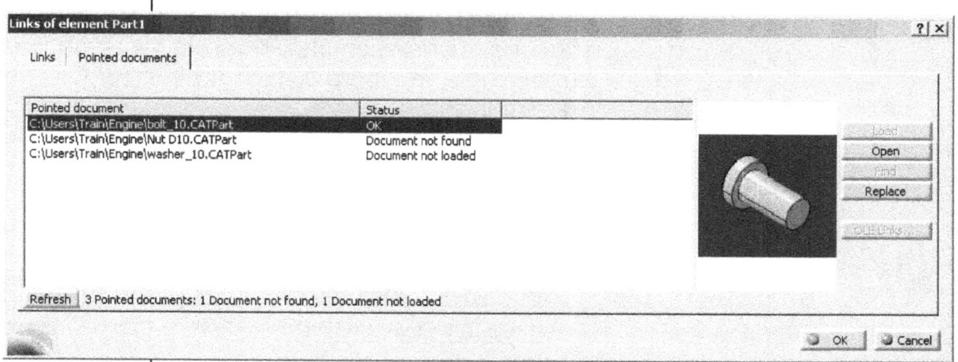

Figure 8–13

The path shown is no longer the correct path to the file, which was moved from this location. Click **Find**, browse to the new location of the file and update the link. The Status changes to **OK**.

Replace in the *Pointed Documents* tab is similar to the one in the *Links* tab, except that it re-routes all of the referenced elements from the original file to the new file. If you click **Replace** in the *Links* tab, only the selected link is re-routed to the new document.

Re-establishing Broken Links

The are three reasons for links between parts becoming broken:

- The part has been renamed.
- The part has been moved to another folder.
- The part has been deleted.

When you open a product file that has a broken link, a warning message opens as shown in Figure 8–14.

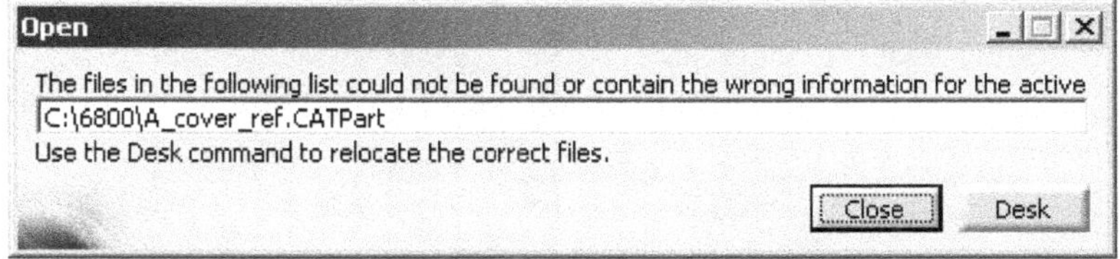

Figure 8–14

There are two different ways to locate the missing file:

- Click **Desk**.
- Select **Edit>Links**.

If you click **Desk**, the Desk window opens, displaying the structure of the assembly. The file in red is the file that is missing. For example, in Figure 8–15 **A_cover_ref.CATPart** is the file that is missing.

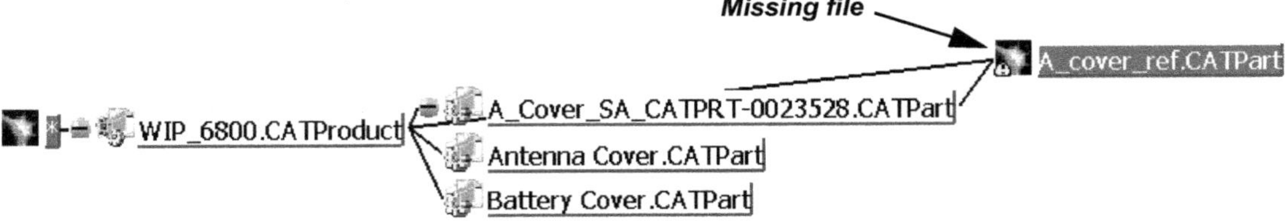

Figure 8–15

To re-establish the link, right-click on the missing file, and select **Find**, as shown in Figure 8–16.

Figure 8–16

In the File Selection dialog box, select the missing file and click **Open**, as shown in Figure 8–17.

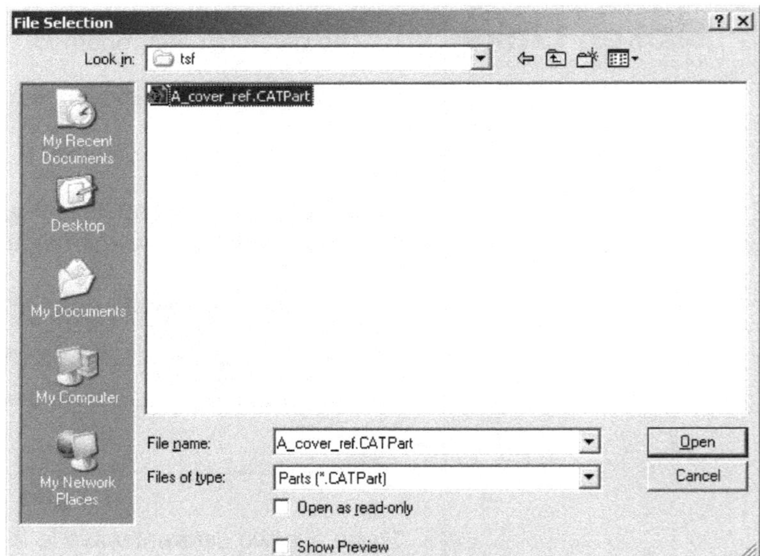

Figure 8–17

The color of the file changes to white, as shown in Figure 8–18.

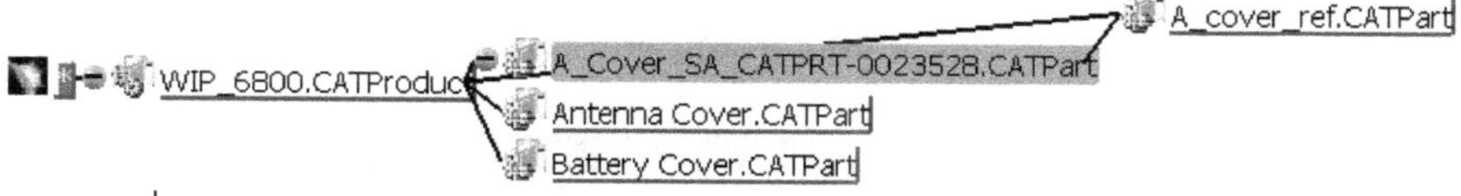

Figure 8–18

The second way to re-establish the link is by selecting **Edit>Links**. In the Open dialog box, click **Close**, as shown in Figure 8–19.

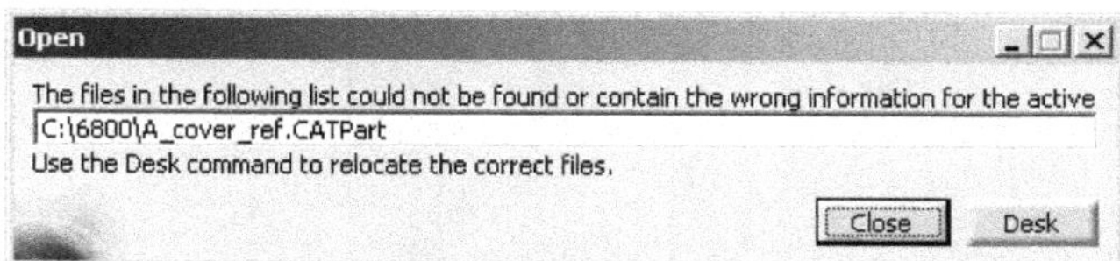

Figure 8–19

In the menu bar, select **Edit>Links**. In the Links dialog box, select the *Pointed documents* tab.

The Status of the **A_Cover_ref.CATPart** is **Document not found** as shown in Figure 8–20.

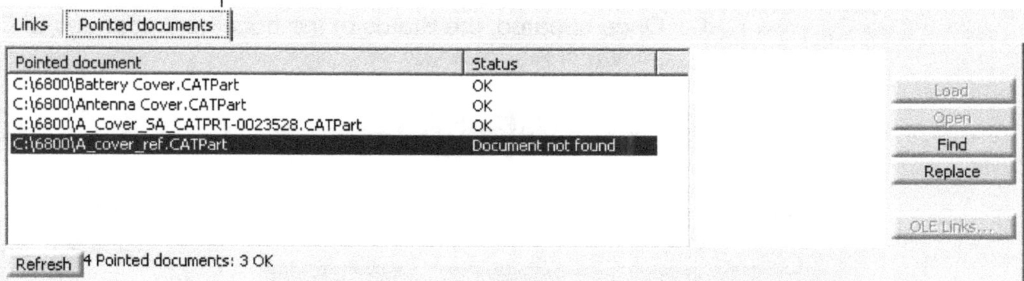

Figure 8–20

You can click **Find** to locate broken links. When you do so, the File Selection dialog box opens as shown in Figure 8–21. In this dialog box, you can browse to the new location of the missing document, and update the link.

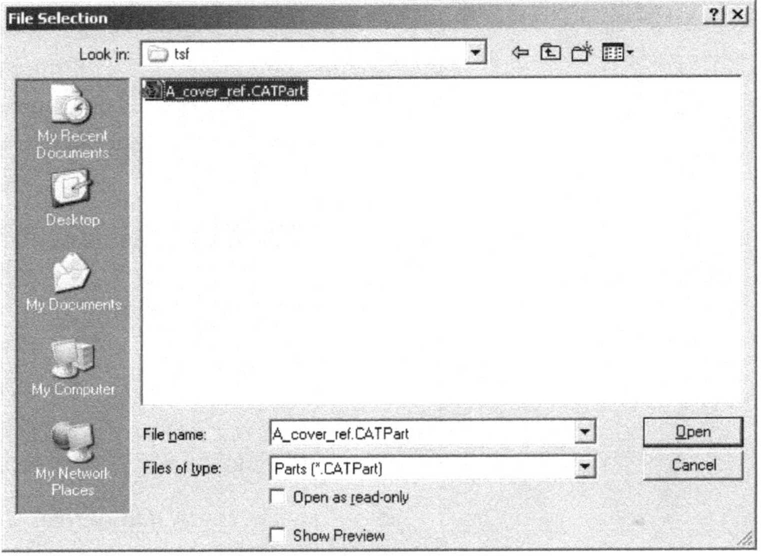

Figure 8–21

Once updated, the Status of the document changes to **OK**, as shown in Figure 8–22.

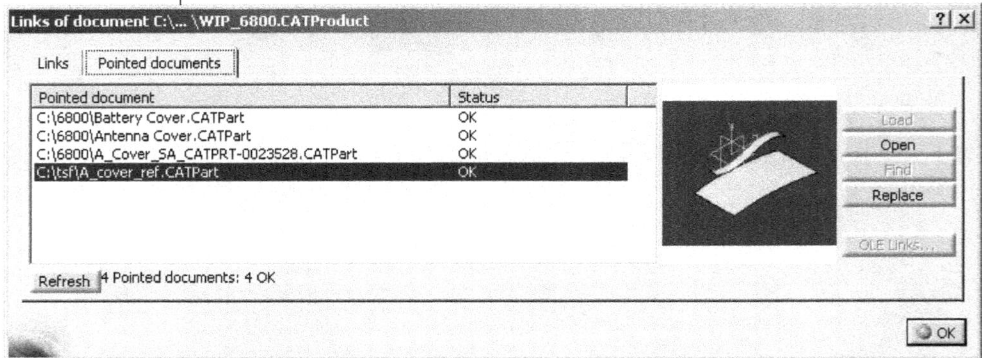

Figure 8–22

If the document is renamed, you must click **Replace** to re-link the file. It is similar to **Find**.

8.4 Publications

A publication is an organizational and reference management tool that you can use to identify and select elements that are externally referenced. When an element is published, it is added to a new Publications branch in the specification tree. You can then rename it, so that it can be easily identified and selected by other designers.

For example, the dashboard surface for an automobile has been published in the DashSkel component shown in Figure 8–23. This publication can then be referenced externally by any of the dashboard components, such as the HVAC vent bezel or the storage compartment lid, to define the shape of these components.

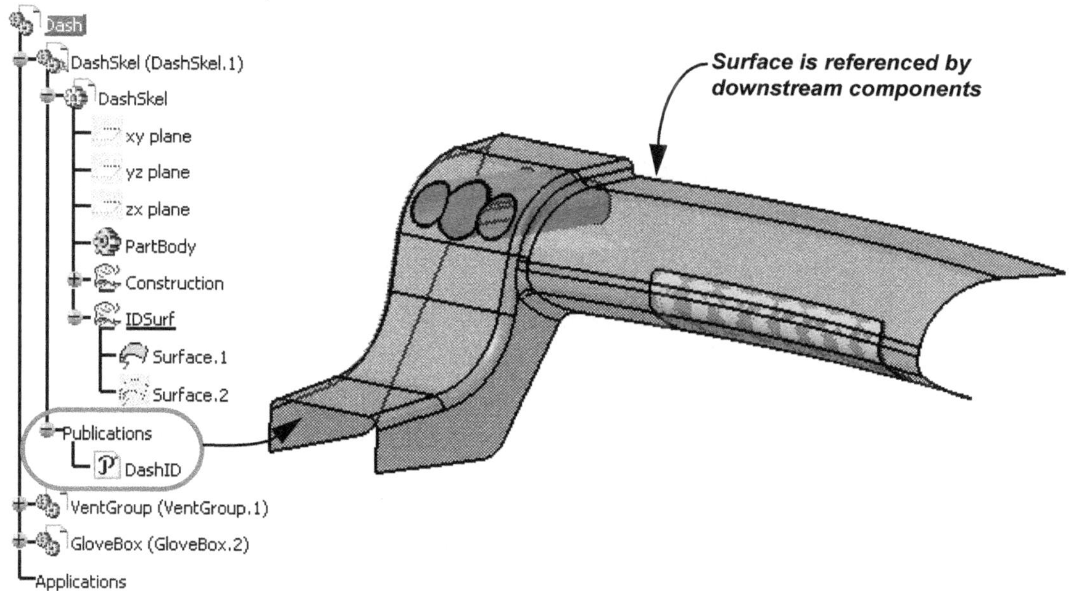

Figure 8–23

Creating this contextual link between elements helps to ensure that the shape of the dashboard components always matches the design intent defined by the styling department that created the published surface. The use of publications in performing this operation is similar to a controlling mechanism that defines which geometry can be externally referenced, and facilitates its selection by placing it in a separate branch in the tree.

Another benefit of publishing data is seen during integration with a data management system, such as LCA, VPM, or SmarTeam. During the lifecycle process of data creation, links can become disconnected from their references for a number of reasons. The use of publications places the geometry at a higher level of importance by giving the Publication feature its own UUID. Therefore, the publication is viewed with the same weight as an actual part file. This facilitates the management of links through the use of publications.

You can publish the following types of elements:

- Reference elements, such as Points, Planes, Lines, and Splines
- Features
- Sketches
- Bodies
- Surfaces
- Parameters
- Sub-elements, such as faces, edges, and axes

Many companies enforce a design standard that requires the publication of any element that is going to be externally referenced. This is to ensure that no undesired parent-child relationships are developed.

There are two ways in which reference selections can be made:

- External References
- Constraint Creation

External References

The options that control the use of publications for external references are highlighted in Figure 8–24. To use these options, select **Tools>Options>Infrastructure>Part Infrastructure** and select the *General* tab.

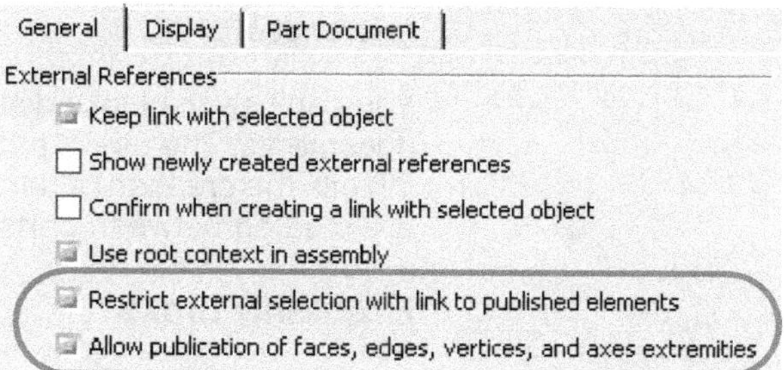

Figure 8–24

The highlighted options are as follows.

Option	Description
Restrict external selection with link to published elements	When this option is selected, external references can only be developed by selecting a published element.
Allow publication of faces, edges, vertices, and axes extremities	You must select this option to publish individual sub-elements of features, such as the face, edge, or vertex of a Pad. When this option is disabled, sub-elements cannot be published, thus restricting users from making boundary representation selections.

8.5 Best Practices

Link Management

You must create references to other documents to ensure that designs are consistent. As the number of documents increases, it is difficult to remember where information in a document is being read from. Avoid creating any unnecessary external references.

You can use the Links dialog box to manage external links in documents. The use of publications to create external references inhibits the creation of unnecessary links, and only required links are created between parts.

Breaking Links

After the model is finalized, you must isolate all of the external references that were created during modeling of the part. Doing so ensures that if one of the referencing models is used and modified in a different assembly, the final model is not impacted by the changes.

PDM Considerations

Use of one of the many available PDM systems can be key in keeping a project organized. The following features of PDM systems help avoid some of the pitfalls associated with collaborative work:

- They can track and store revisions of the CATIA data.
- They can ensure that files are not accidentally overwritten or deleted.
- They provide a permission structure that ensures that model geometry is not accidentally modified by other users.

Practice 8a

Paste Special Options

Practice Objective

- Understand the differences between the Paste Special options.

In this practice, you will use the three **Paste Special** options to copy part bodies from one CATPart to another. You will see the different results produced by the three **Paste Special** options:

- **As specified in Part document**
- **As Result With Link**
- **As Result**

The completed model displays as shown in Figure 8–25.

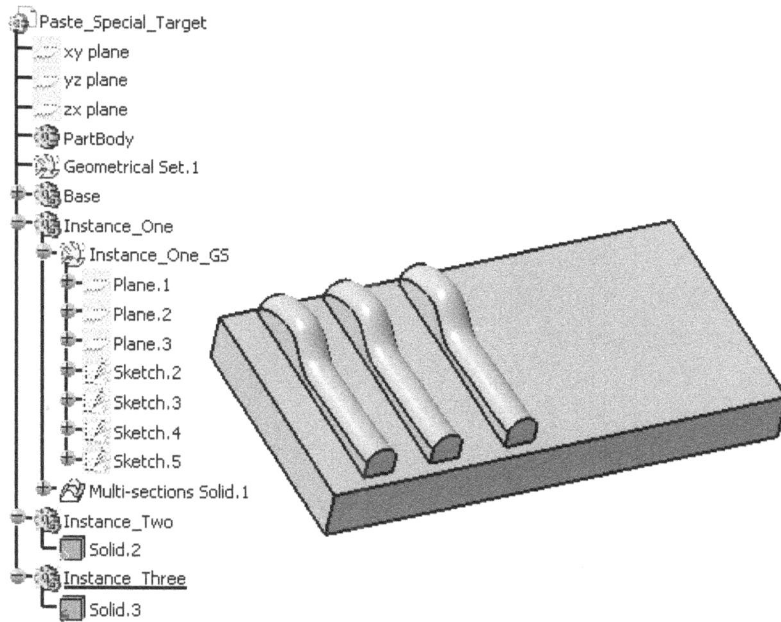

Figure 8–25

Task 1 - Open the part from which to copy the part bodies.

1. Open **Paste_Special_Original.CATPart**. The model contains a PartBody named **Base**, as well as three copies of a Multi-sections Solid feature, as shown in Figure 8–26.

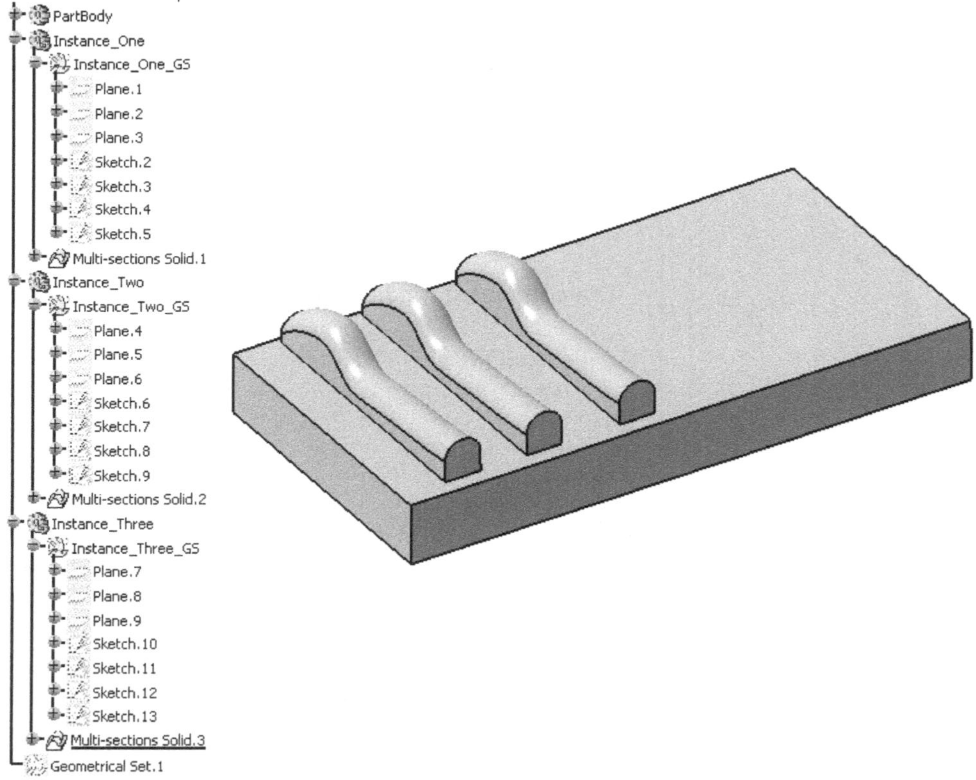

Figure 8–26

Task 2 - Paste using the As specified in Part document option.

1. Select the **Instance_One** body and select **Edit>Copy**.
2. While keeping the **Paste_Special_Original.CATPart** window open, open **Paste_Special_Target.CATPart**. The model contains a base part body, as shown in Figure 8–27.

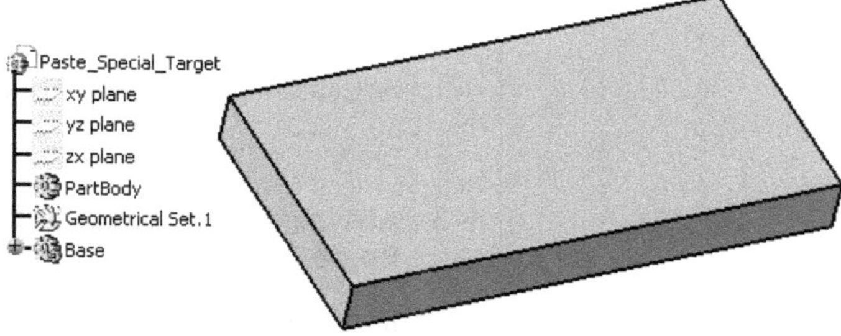

Figure 8–27

3. Select **Edit>Paste Special**. The Paste Special dialog box opens as shown in Figure 8–28.

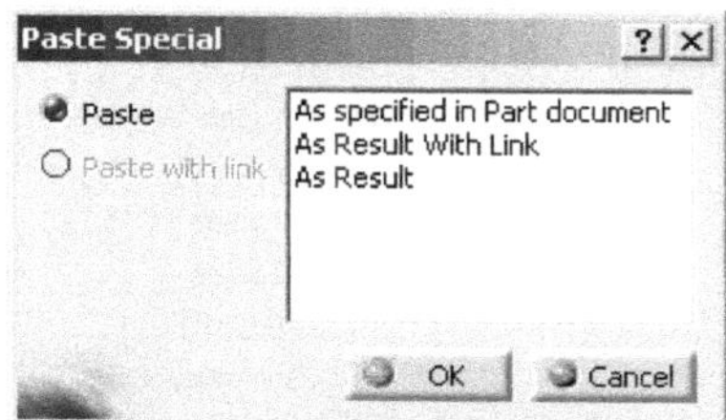

Figure 8–28

4. Select the **As specified in Part document** option and click **OK**.

5. Expand the new **Instance_One** body. The body contains a copy of the features that were selected in the referenced model, as shown in Figure 8–29.

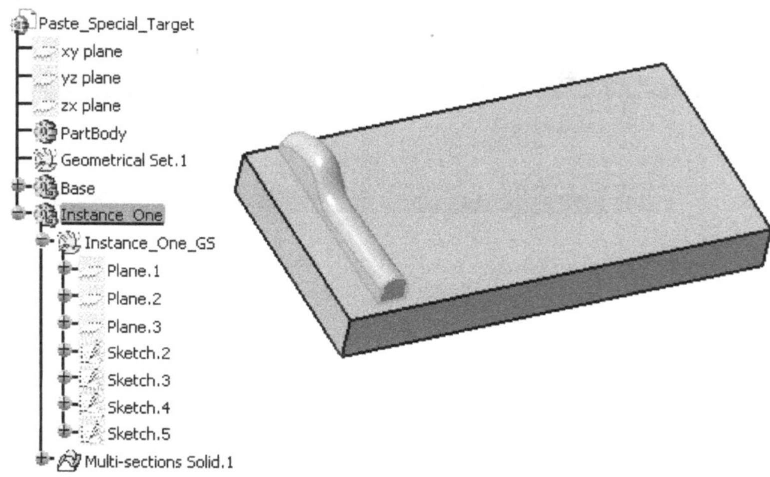

Figure 8–29

Task 3 - Paste using the As Result With Link option.

1. Activate the **Paste_Special_Original.CATPart** window.
2. Copy the **Instance_Two** body.
3. Activate **Paste_Special_Target.CATPart** and select **Edit> Paste Special**.
4. In the Paste Special dialog box, select **As Result With Link**.
5. Click **OK**. The new body is added, as shown in Figure 8–30. The **As Result With Link** option places a linked solid feature into the new body.

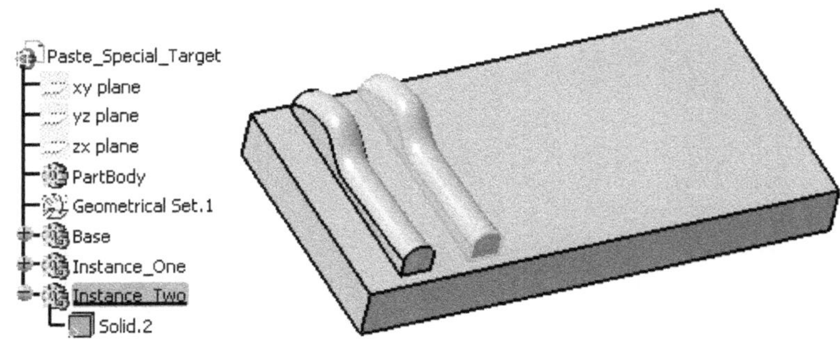

Figure 8–30

Task 4 - Investigate the links.

1. Select **Edit>Links**. The Links dialog box opens as shown in Figure 8–31.

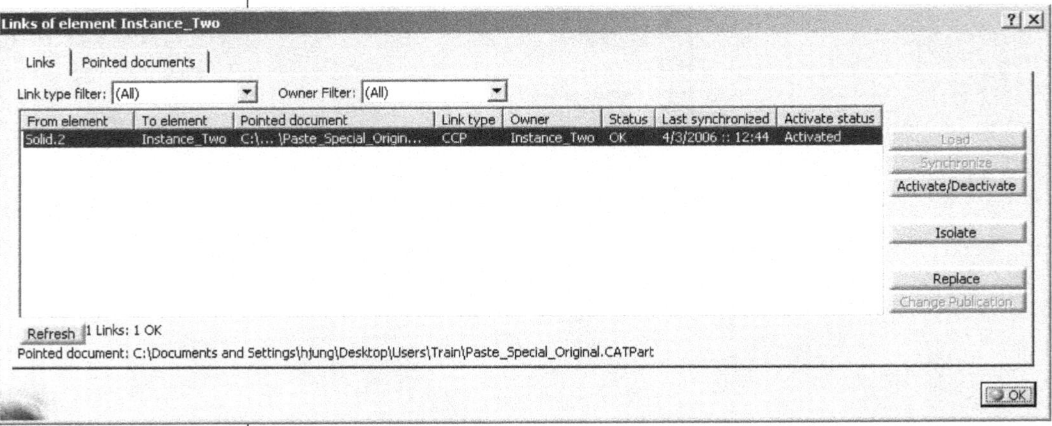

Figure 8–31

Design Considerations

This dialog box indicates any links that exist in the model. The system shows that the **Solid.2** element is linked to the **Instance_Two** element in the **Paste_Special_Original.CATPart** model. The dialog box also indicates that this link is **Activated** and has an **OK** Status.

2. Close the Links dialog box.

Task 5 - Paste using the As Result option.

1. Activate **Paste_Special_Original.CATPart** and copy the **Instance_Three** body.
2. Perform a **Paste Special** in **Paste_Special_Target.CATPart**.
3. In the Paste Special dialog box, select the **As Result** option.
4. Click **OK**. The new body is added, as shown in Figure 8–32. This time, an isolated solid is added to the body.

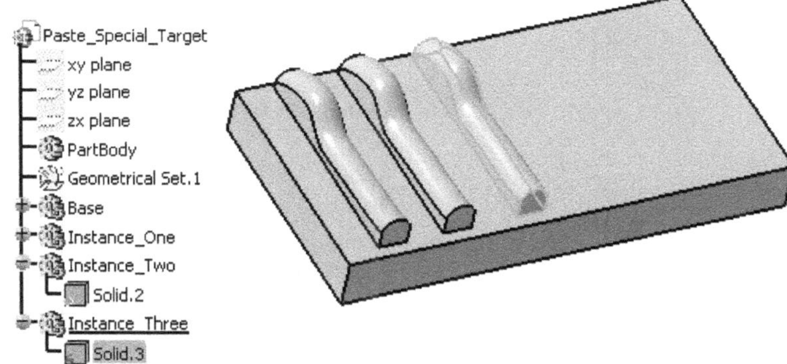

Figure 8–32

5. Compare the results among the three instances that were copied.
6. Save all of the models and close the windows.

Practice 8b

Multi-Model Links

Practice Objective

- Copy geometry between part models while keeping the link.

In this practice, you will create a link between a cover and a bushing using the **As Result With Link** option. You will also synchronize the parts shown in Figure 8–33. You will see how the linked components interact when dimensions are changed.

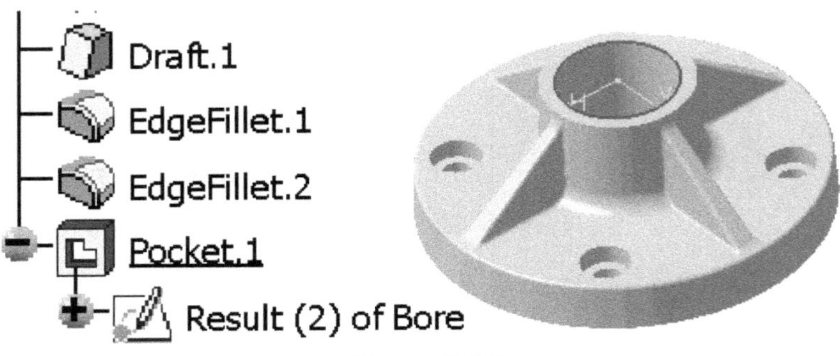

Figure 8–33

Task 1 - Set the required options.

1. Open the Options dialog box and select **Infrastructure>Part Infrastructure**. In the *General* tab, select **Restrict external selection with link to published elements**, as shown in Figure 8–34.

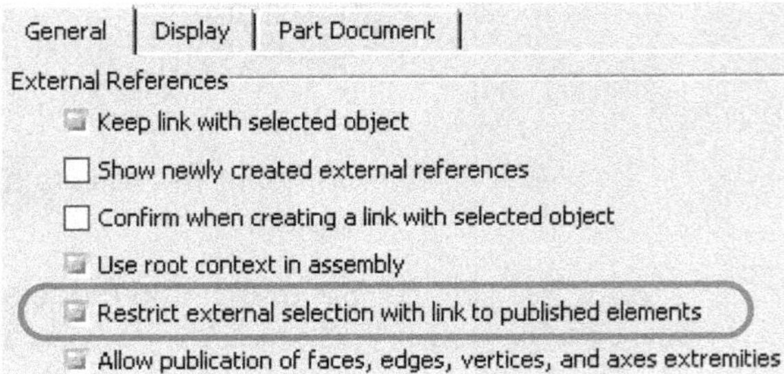

Figure 8–34

2. Select the *Display* tab.

3. Select **Parameters** and **Relations**, as shown in Figure 8–35.

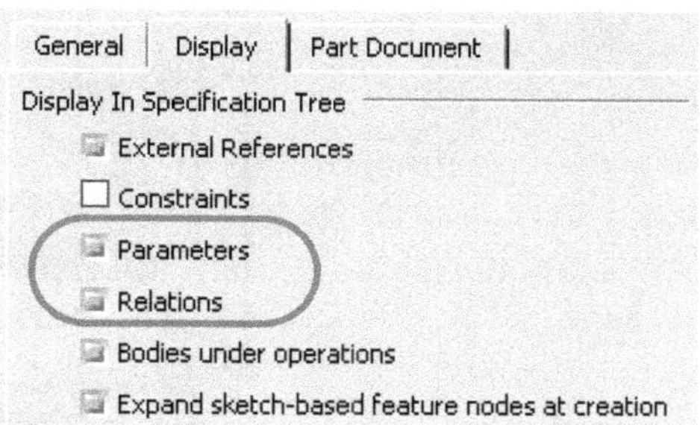

Figure 8–35

4. Click **OK**.

Task 2 - Open a part file.

1. Open **Master.CATPart** from the *MultiModelLinks* folder. The model contains three sketches and two published geometries, as shown in Figure 8–36. The Bore and the Bushing sketches are the published geometries. The **Bore1** sketch is a copy of Bore, but it is not published.

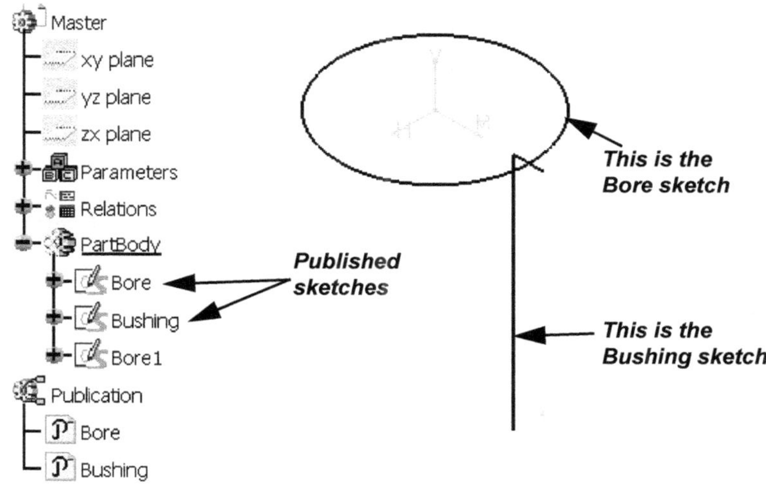

Figure 8–36

2. Double-click on the **Clearance** parameter. The Edit Parameter dialog box opens.

3. Change the parameter value to **20mm**, as shown in Figure 8–37.

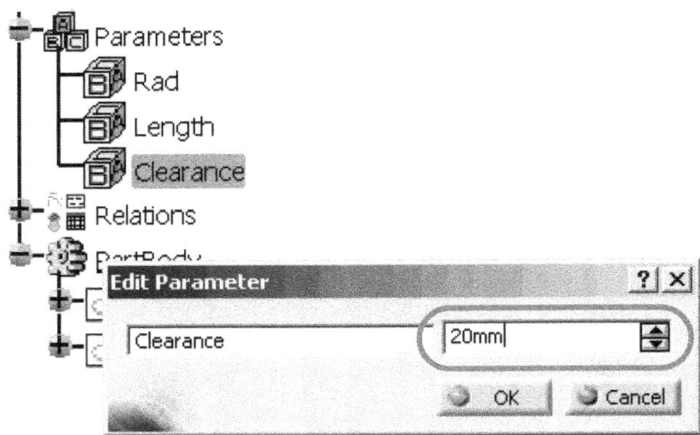

Figure 8–37

The Bushing sketch updates, as shown in Figure 8–38.

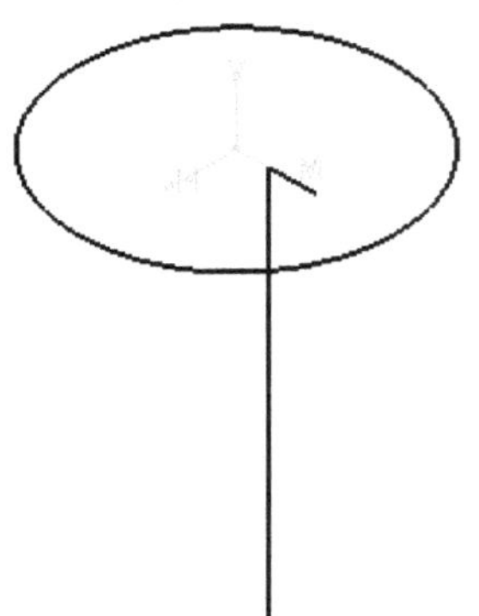

Figure 8–38

4. Change the **Clearance** parameter value to **4mm**, as shown in Figure 8–39.

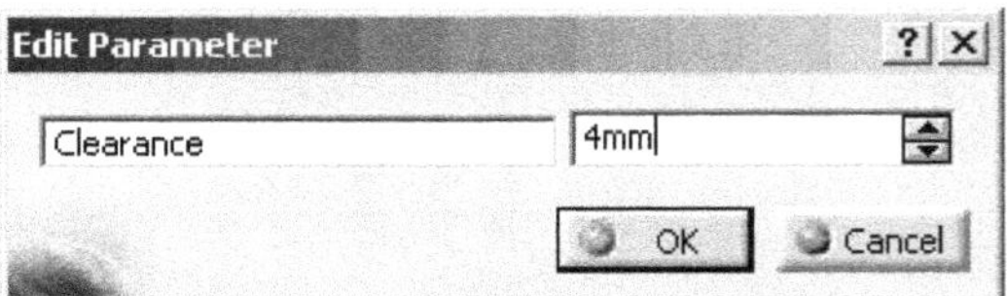

Figure 8–39

The Bushing sketch updates, as shown in Figure 8–40.

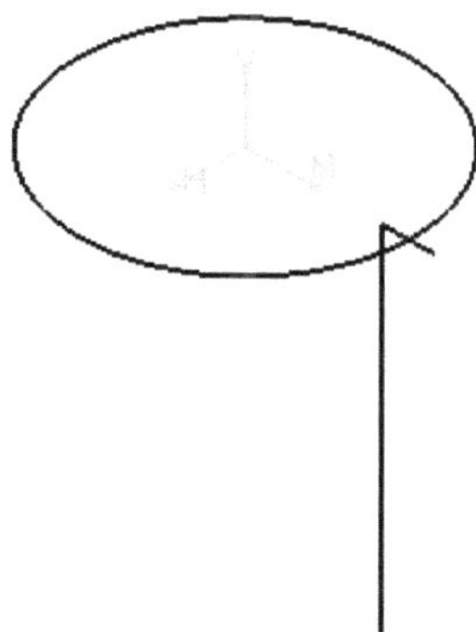

Figure 8–40

Task 3 - Open a part file.

1. Keep the Master part open. Open **Cover.CATPart** from the *MultiModelLinks* folder. The model displays as shown in Figure 8–41.

Figure 8–41

2. Select **Edit>Links** to verify whether the part has any external links. A message box opens indicating that the part does not have external links, as shown in Figure 8–42.

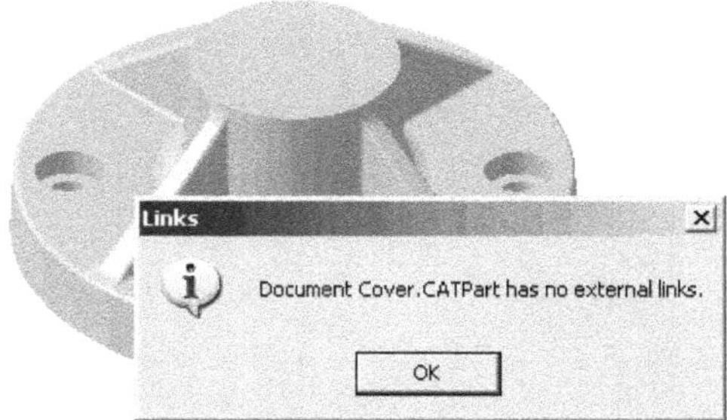

Figure 8–42

Task 4 - Copy and paste a sketch between parts.

1. Activate the Master part window.
2. In the specification tree, right-click on the **Bore1** sketch and select **Copy**, as shown in Figure 8–43.

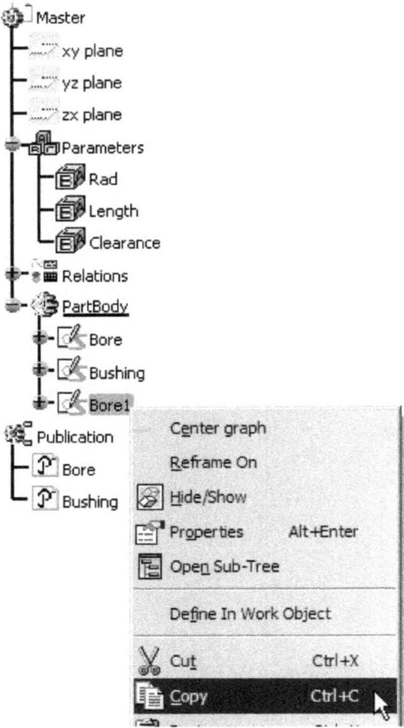

Figure 8–43

3. Activate the Cover part window.

4. Right-click on the **PartBody** and select **Paste Special**, as shown in Figure 8–44.

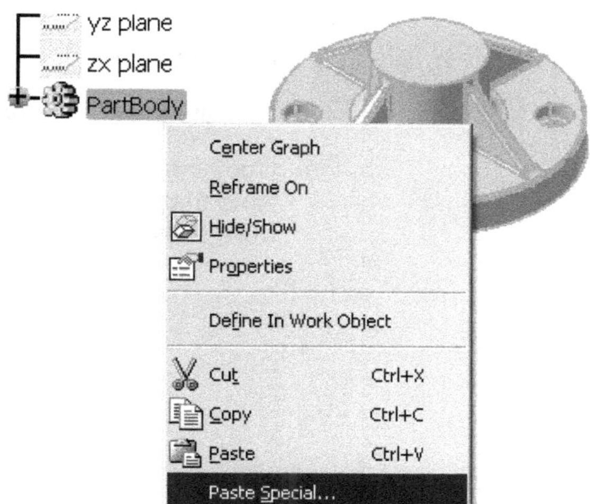

Figure 8–44

5. In the Paste Special dialog box, select the **As Result With Link** option, as shown in Figure 8–45.

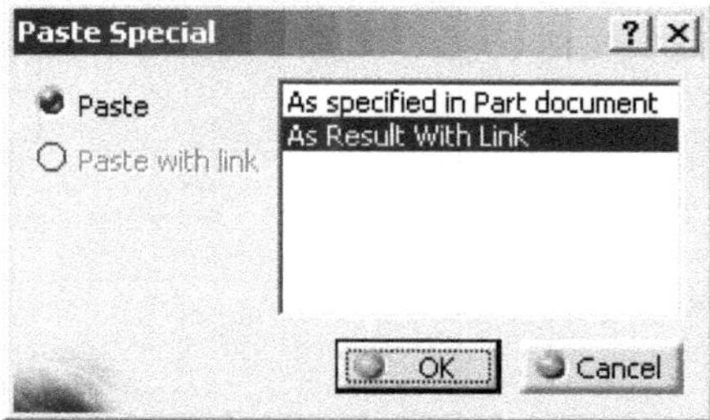

Figure 8–45

6. Click **OK**. An Error dialog box opens as shown in Figure 8–46.

Figure 8–46

Design Considerations

Use of published elements restricts external reference creation. The Bore1 sketch is not published. That is why the Copy/Paste has failed.

7. Close the Error dialog box.
8. Activate the Master part window.
9. Copy the Bore published geometry, as shown in Figure 8–47. Note that when the Bore published element is selected, the Bore sketch is highlighted as well.

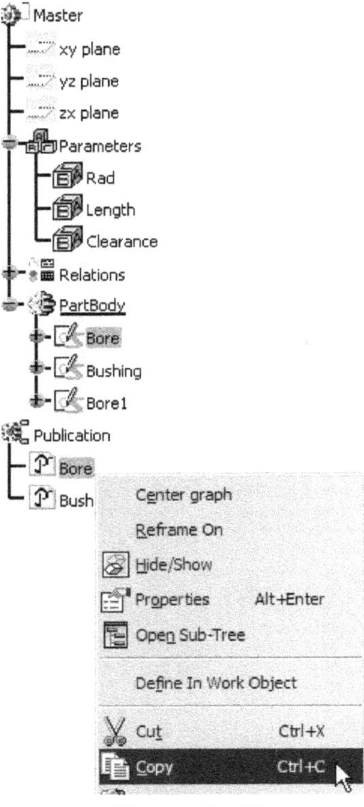

Figure 8–47

10. Activate the Cover part window.
11. Paste the Bore sketch into the PartBody using the **As Result With Link** option.

Design Considerations

The pasted sketch displays as a result in the specification tree. The green symbol shown in Figure 8–48 indicates that this sketch maintains a link with the original sketch.

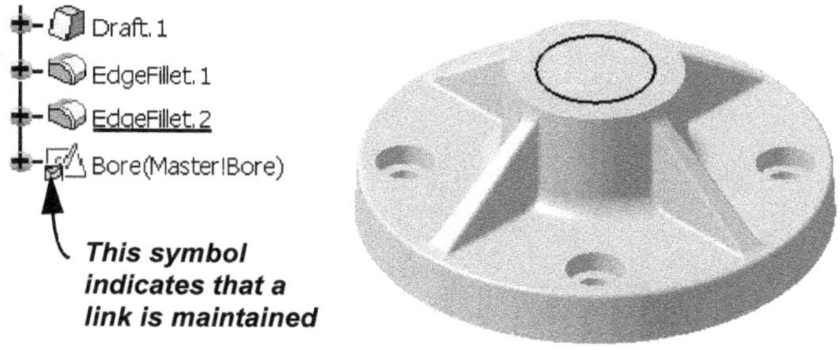

Figure 8–48

12. Investigate the resulting links by selecting **Edit>Links.** The Links dialog box shown in Figure 8–49 indicates that this part has two links. One link is to the part body of the Master part and one is to the published element that has been copied and pasted using one of the **Paste Special** options.

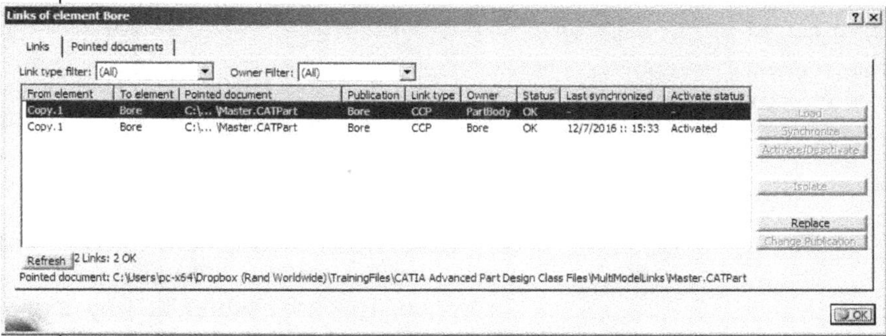

Figure 8–49

13. Select the *Pointed Documents* tab, as shown in Figure 8–50, to display the file path and part filename from which the linked geometry originates.

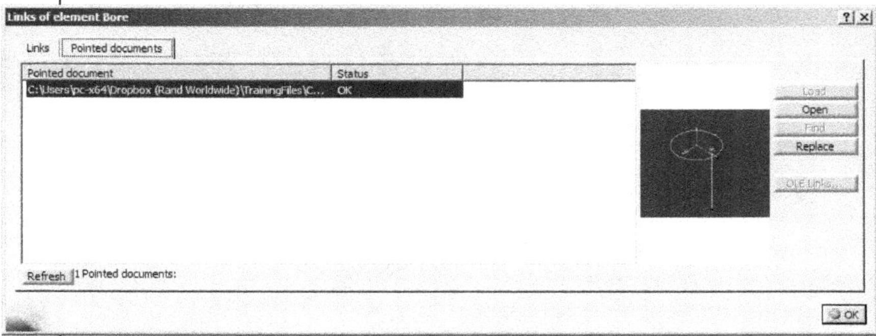

Figure 8–50

14. Click **OK**.

Task 5 - Create geometry from a pasted sketch.

1. Select the pasted sketch and create the Pocket feature shown in Figure 8–51.

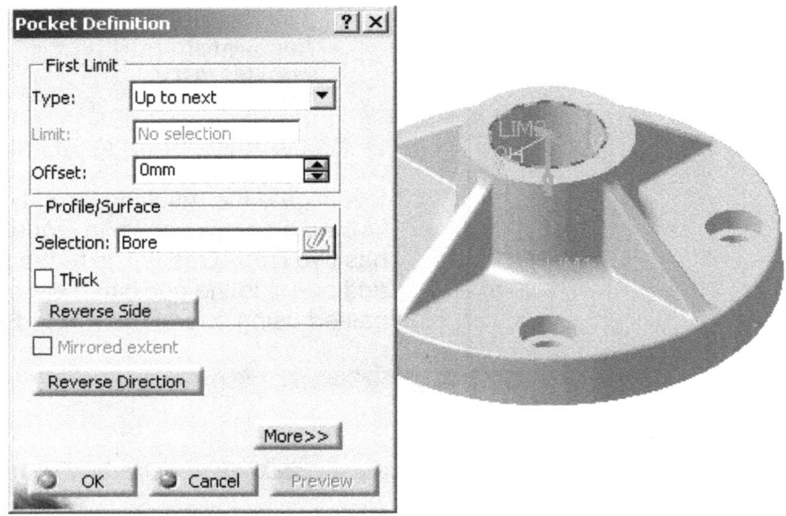

Figure 8–51

Design Considerations

The Cover part model is now linked to **Master.CATPart**. When saving models that have external links, you must use the **Save All** option. This will ensure that any changes are saved to all of the models and that no links are lost or severed.

2. Use the **Save All** option to save **Cover.CATPart** and then close the window. Leave the Master part file open.

Task 6 - Open a part file.

1. Open **Bushing.CATPart**. The model does not contain any geometry. It displays as shown in Figure 8–52.

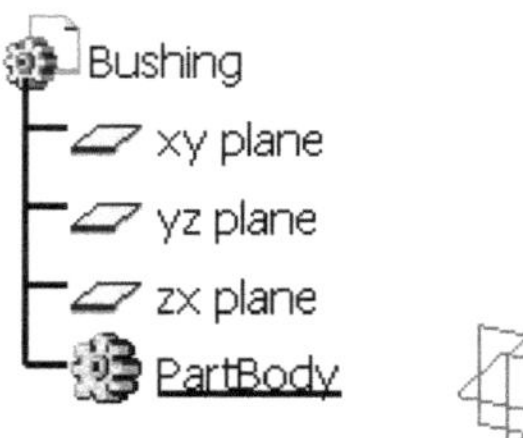

Figure 8–52

2. Copy and paste the Bushing published geometry into the Bushing part file using the **As Result With Link** option. The resulting geometry displays as shown in Figure 8–53.

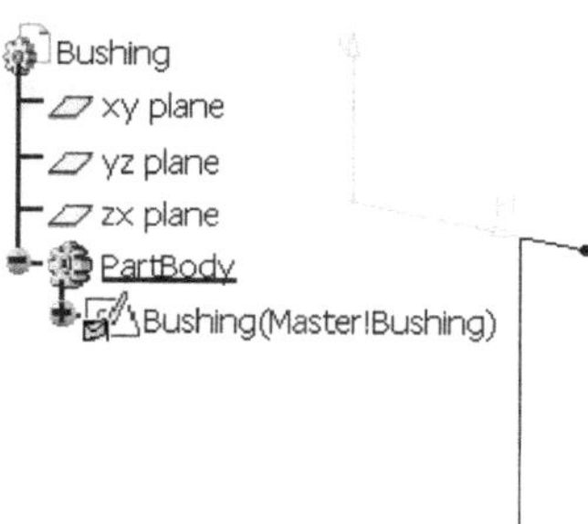

Figure 8–53

3. Create a thick profiled Shaft feature from the pasted sketch, as shown in Figure 8–54.

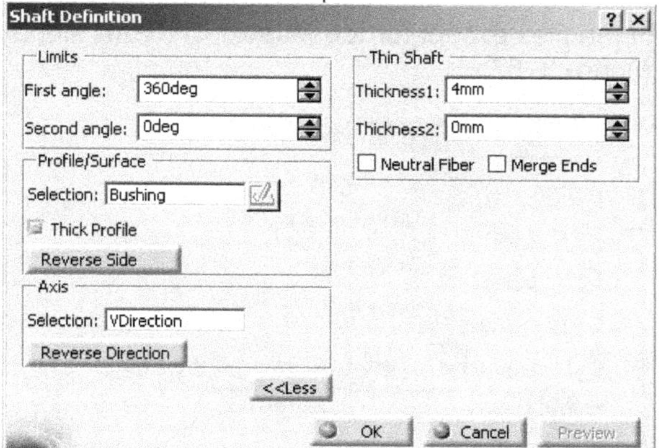

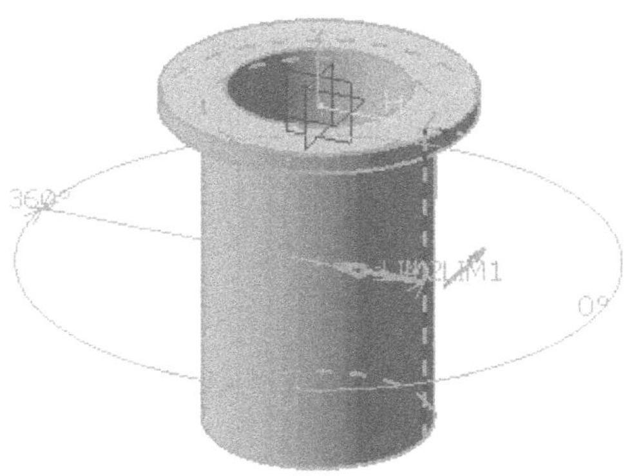

Figure 8–54

The completed bushing part displays as shown in Figure 8–55.

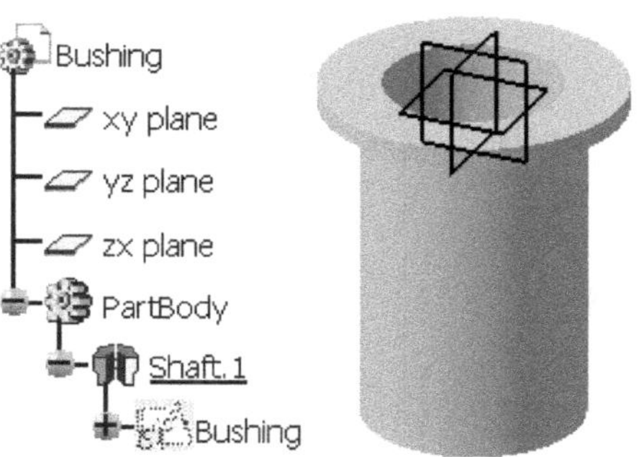

Figure 8–55

4. Note the resulting links, as shown in Figure 8–56.

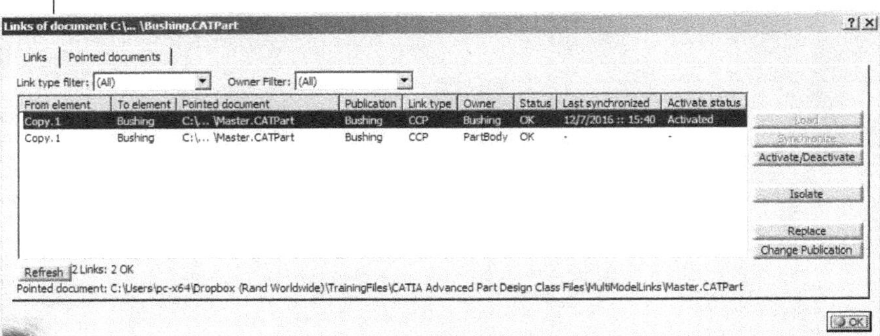

Figure 8–56

5. Save the Bushing part.

Task 7 - View the link status.

1. Close all of the files except for the **Master.CATPart** file, as shown in Figure 8–57.

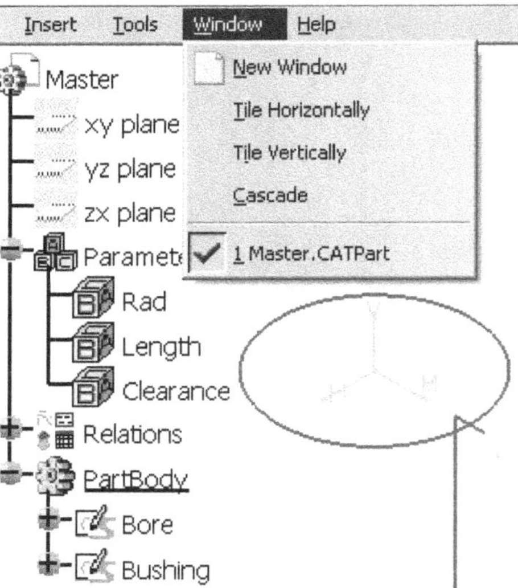

Figure 8–57

2. Change the radius of the Bore sketch by changing the value of the **Rad** parameter to **30mm**, as shown in Figure 8–58.

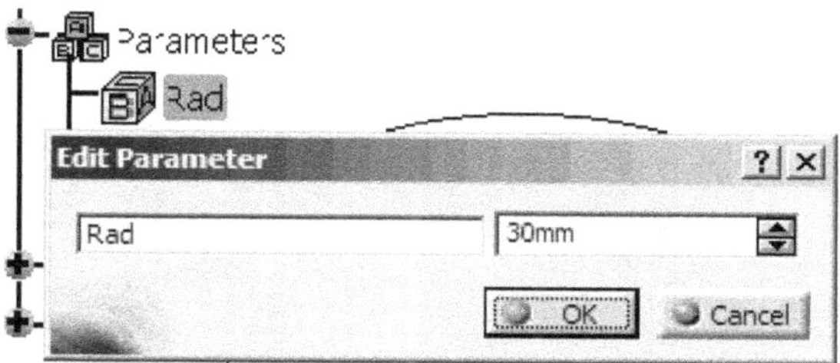

Figure 8–58

3. Save the Master part and close the file.

4. Open **Cover.CATPart**. Show the Bore Sketch under the **Pocket.1** feature. The model displays as shown in Figure 8–59.

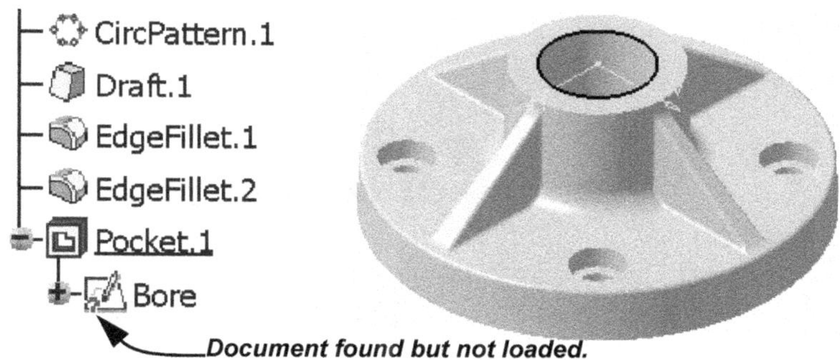

Figure 8–59

5. Note the symbol for the sketch that has been pasted using the **As Result With Link** option.

Design Considerations

You have closed **Master.CATPart** and opened **Cover.CATPart**. The application recognizes that a link to another document (**Master.CATPart**) exists, but that document has not been loaded. This status is indicated by .

6. Investigate the links by selecting **Edit>Links**. The Status column indicates **Document not loaded**, as shown in Figure 8–60.

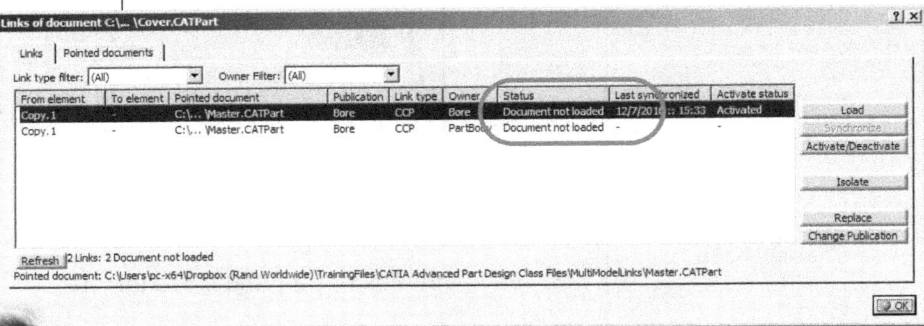

Figure 8–60

7. Click **Load** to load the information from the pointed document. Note that this does not open the pointed document, but only loads the information from the pointed document.

8. Note the *Status* column, as shown in Figure 8–61.

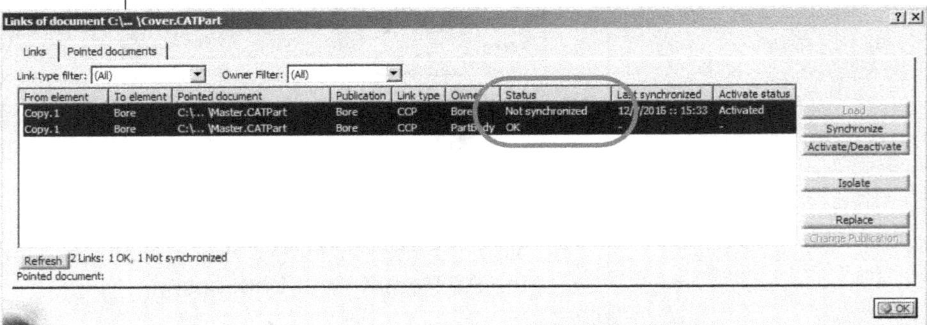

Figure 8–61

9. Click **OK**.

Design Considerations

Now that you have loaded the information from the pointed document; the application recognizes that changes have been made (you changed the Rad parameter of **Master.CATPart** to **30mm**) and that the result of the **Paste Special** element is not up to date. The **Cover.CATPart** displays in red, indicating that an update is required. The linked result icon displays as (Yellow P), as shown in Figure 8–62, indicating that the pointed document has been modified and the target geometry is not up to date. The copied element is a published element, and that is why the P letter displays on the icon.

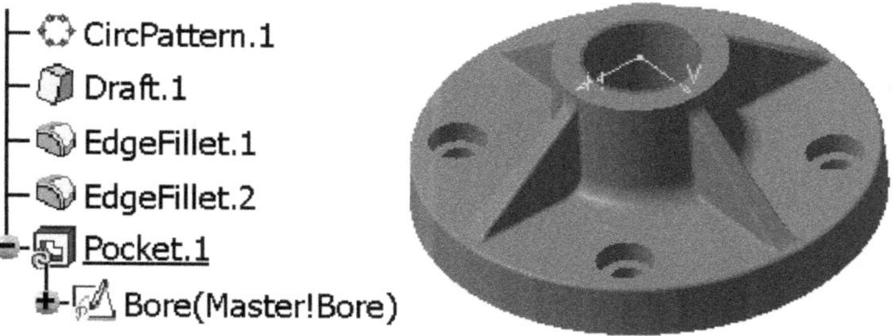

Figure 8–62

10. Click to update the model. The model updates with the changes made to the pointed document and the symbol indicates that the result is up to date, as shown in Figure 8–63.

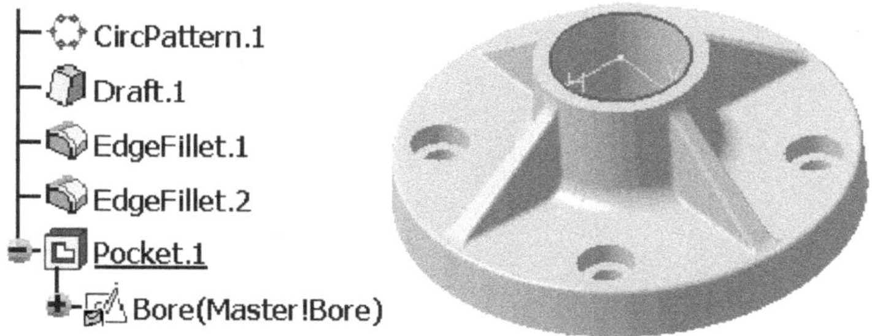

Figure 8–63

Task 8 - Update links.

In this task, you will open the Bushing part for updating. Since the pointed document will already be in session, all that is required is an update of the target document.

1. Open **Bushing.CATPart**. The part displays as shown in Figure 8–64.

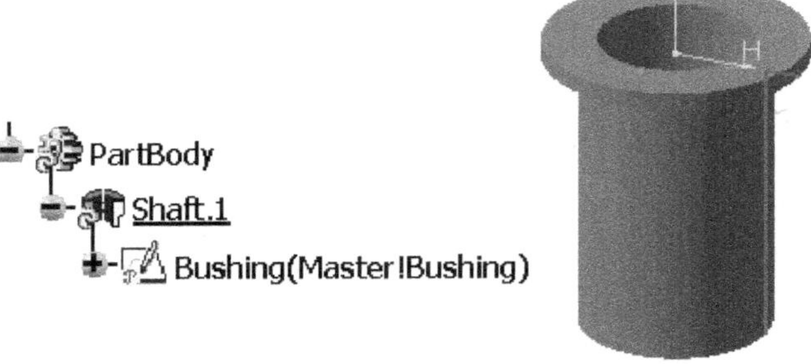

Figure 8–64

2. Click [icon]. The model updates to reflect the changes made to the pointed document. The model displays as shown in Figure 8–65.

Figure 8–65

This practice shows you that design intent can be captured in a single *.CATPart file, and that information can be used to drive the geometry of any number of part files using the **Paste Special** and **As Result With Link** options.

3. In the Links dialog box, select the *Pointed documents* tab. Note that the status of the link is **OK**, as shown in Figure 8–66.

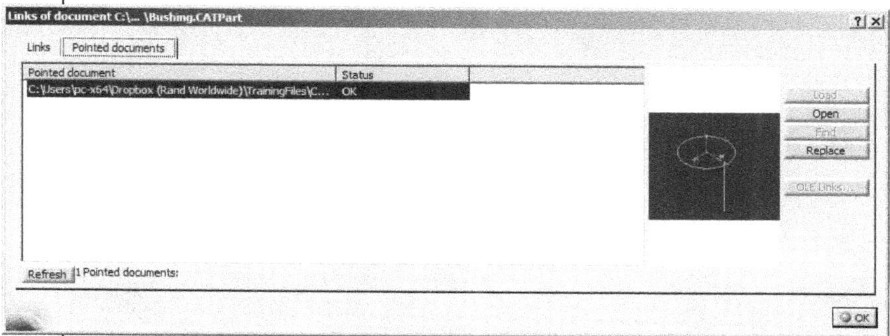

Figure 8–66

4. Save the Bushing file.

5. If time permits, leave the files open and continue with the next practice, otherwise, save and close all files.

Practice 8c

Managing Multi-Model Links

Practice Objective

- Manage multi-document link.

In this practice, you will use the bushing shown in Figure 8–67 to explore and manage multi-model linking by editing linked parts in an assembly and using the **Isolate** command.

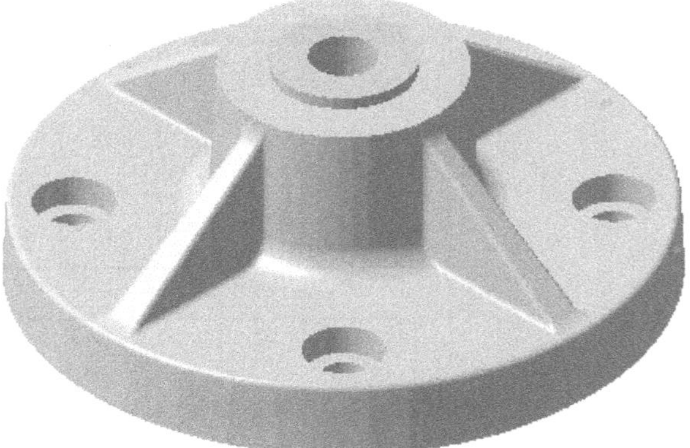

Figure 8–67

Task 1 - Open the assembly.

1. Open **FrontCover.CATProduct** from the *MultiModelLinks* folder. The assembly displays as shown in Figure 8–68.

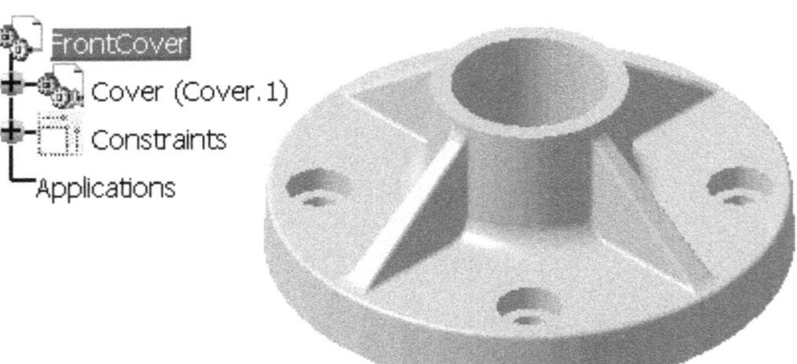

Figure 8–68

2. Assemble **Bushing.CATPart** using a coincidence and contact constraint, as shown in Figure 8–69.

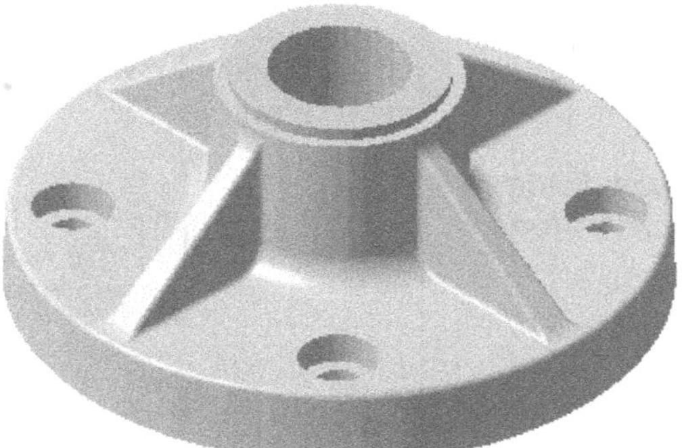

Figure 8–69

3. Note the links to the product file, as shown in Figure 8–70.

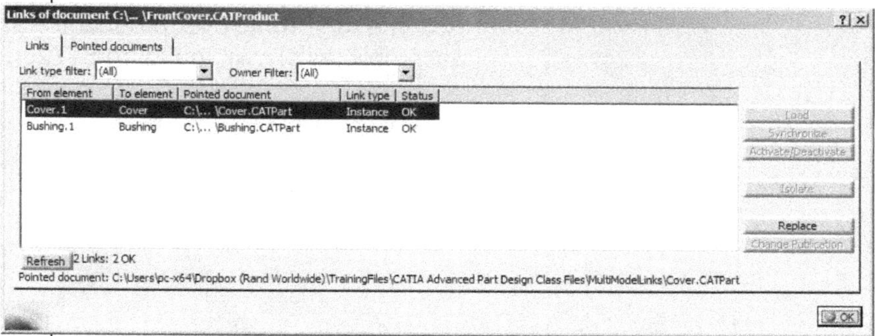

Figure 8–70

A product file points to each part and/or product that is assembled into the product file.

4. Click **OK**.

Task 2 - Modify the pointed document.

1. Open **Master.CATPart**.

2. Modify the **Rad** parameter to **15mm**, as shown in Figure 8–71.

*If the Warnings dialog box opens, click **Close**.*

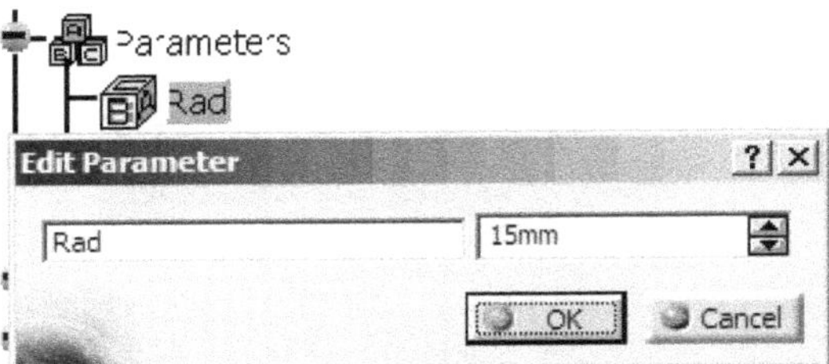

Figure 8–71

3. Save the Master part.

4. Activate the FrontCover product file and update the assembly, as shown in Figure 8–72.

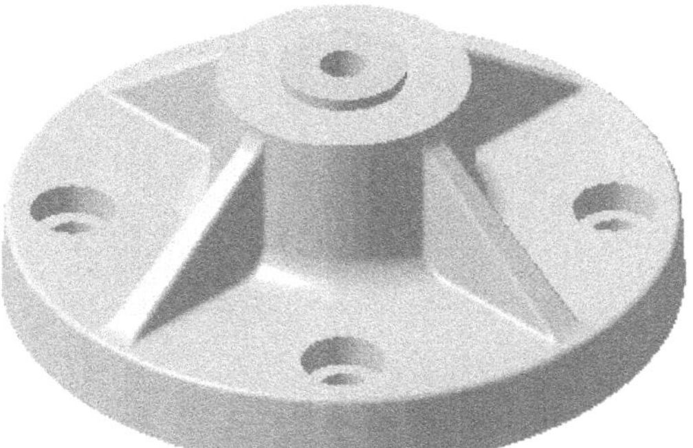

Figure 8–72

Design Considerations

The product file does not directly point to the Master part. However, the Master part controls the individual parts through the part-to-part links established in the previous practice. Using the **Paste Special** and **As Result With Link** options is a great method for sharing information between parts, and for capturing assembly design intent. In the following steps, you will see how the clearance between two parts can be controlled using this technique.

5. Rotate the product so that you can see the clearance between the two parts, as shown in Figure 8–73.

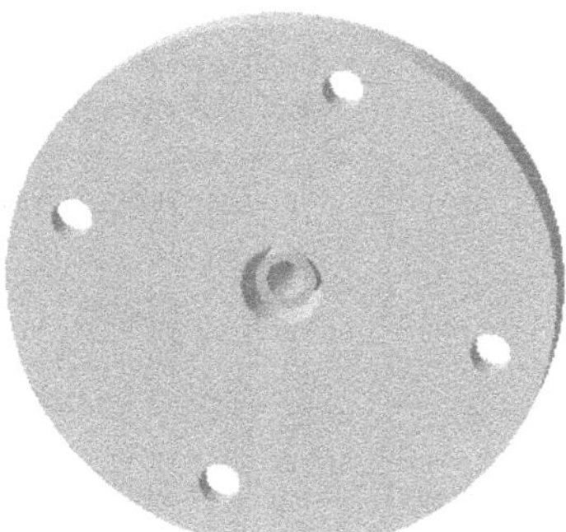

Figure 8–73

6. Activate the **Master.CATPart** window and modify the **Clearance** parameter to **0.5mm**, as shown in Figure 8–74.

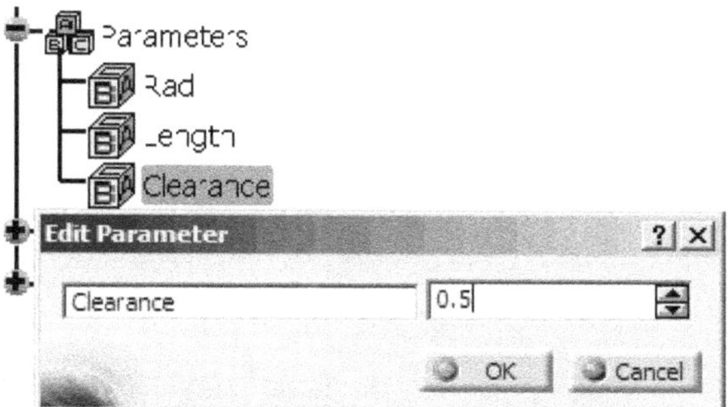

Figure 8–74

7. Activate and update the **FrontCover.CATProduct** window. Note the updated clearance between the parts, as shown in Figure 8–75.

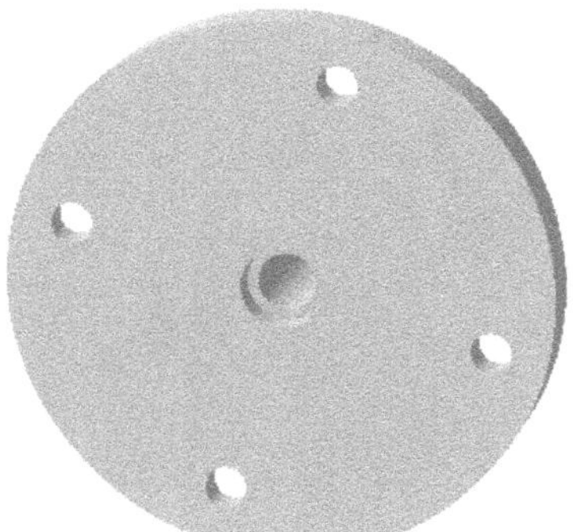

Figure 8–75

Task 3 - Manage links.

Design Considerations

Using the **As Result With Link** option can be a valuable technique in the early stages of a design, as changes made to the Master part will be reflected in the parts that point to it. However, as the design matures and the final component configuration has been achieved, links to the pointed document can be isolated as required. Keep in mind that once a link has been isolated, it cannot be re-established.

1. Open **Bushing.CATPart** in a separate window.
2. Open the Links dialog box. It will display as shown in Figure 8–76.

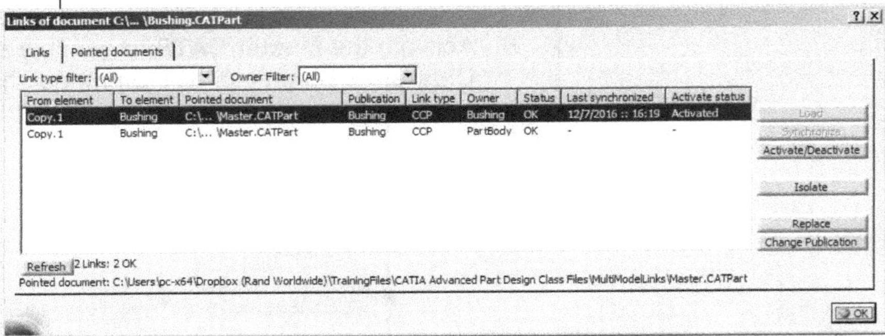

Figure 8–76

3. Isolate the link by selecting the first line and clicking **Isolate**. The *Status* column indicates that this link is now **Isolated**, as shown in Figure 8–77.

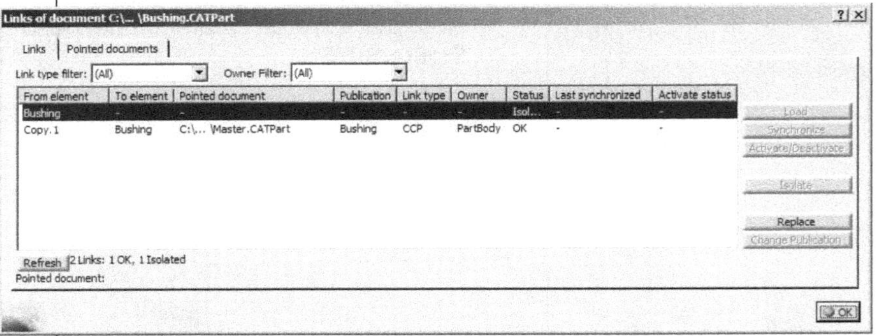

Figure 8–77

4. Click **OK**.

5. Select **Edit>Links.** A message box opens, indicating that this part does not have external links, as shown in Figure 8–78.

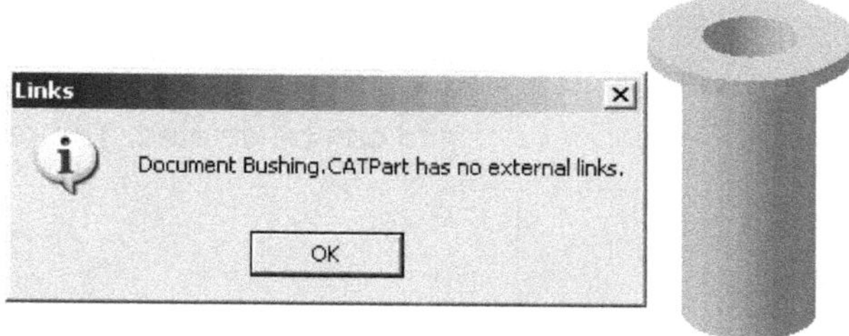

Figure 8–78

6. Open **Cover.CATPart** in a separate window.
7. Right-click on the link and isolate it, as shown in Figure 8–79.

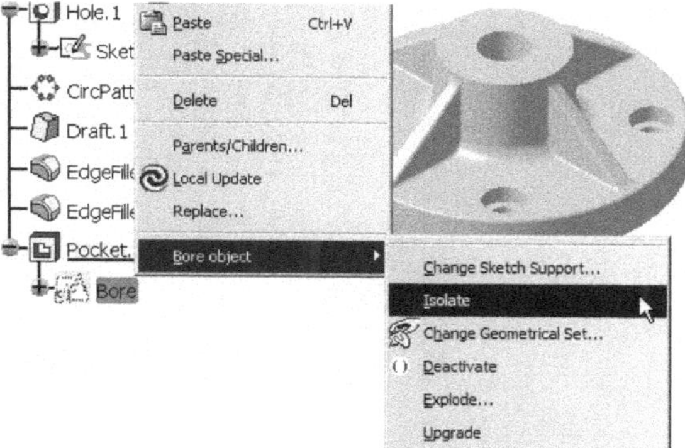

Figure 8–79

8. Investigate the links for the Cover part, as shown in Figure 8–80.

Figure 8–80

9. Save and close all of the part files.

Design Considerations

Use of multi-model links is an effective method of communicating design intent between parts. Once the design is finalized and the links between parts are isolated, models can act as independent part files. You can reuse these files in other designs without being concerned about maintaining the multi-model links. At this stage in the design, the **Master.CATPart** is no longer required and can be deleted. The result is shown in Figure 8–81.

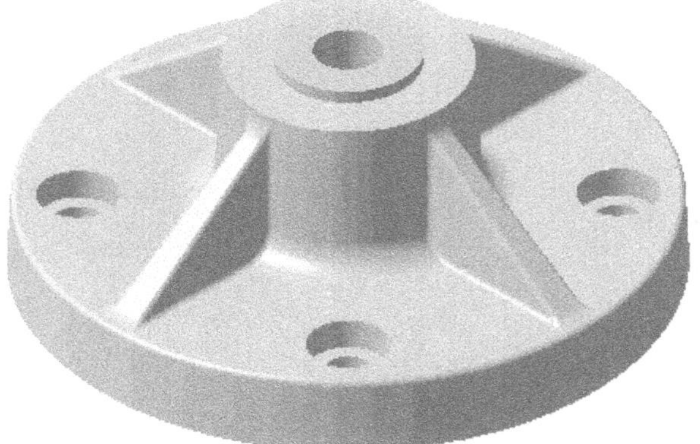

Figure 8–81

10. Save the assembly and close the file.

Chapter Review Questions

1. Which of the following can be copied in a part?
    a. Sketches
    b. Part Bodies
    c. Solid Features
    d. Geometrical Sets
    e. All of the above
2. Which of the following are advantages of copying and pasting?
    a. Copying and pasting geometry reduces re-work time because you can use pre-existing data to create similar parts.
    b. By preserving links between the original geometry and the copy, you can update multiple parts by only modifying one part.
    c. By severing links, you can create variations of a part while preserving the original features and dimensions.
    d. All of the above.
3. When using **Paste Special**, what does the **As Result** option do?
    a. Pastes the body with its design specifications into the target document.
    b. Pastes the body without its design specifications and maintains a link between the original and the copy.
    c. Pastes the body without its design specifications and without making a link between the source and target documents
    d. None of the above.
4. The Links dialog box lists the external references of an entire document or only one body in the document.
    a. True
    b. False

5. A change to a linked element in a document that is not loaded, is automatically updated in the copied element of the current document.

    a. True

    b. False

6. Under which circumstances could links between parts be broken?

    a. The part has been renamed.

    b. The part has been moved to another folder.

    c. The part has been deleted.

    d. All of the above.

7. One method for reusing a group of elements that are externally referenced is to create a _____?

    a. Document

    b. Guide

    c. Publication

    d. None of the above.

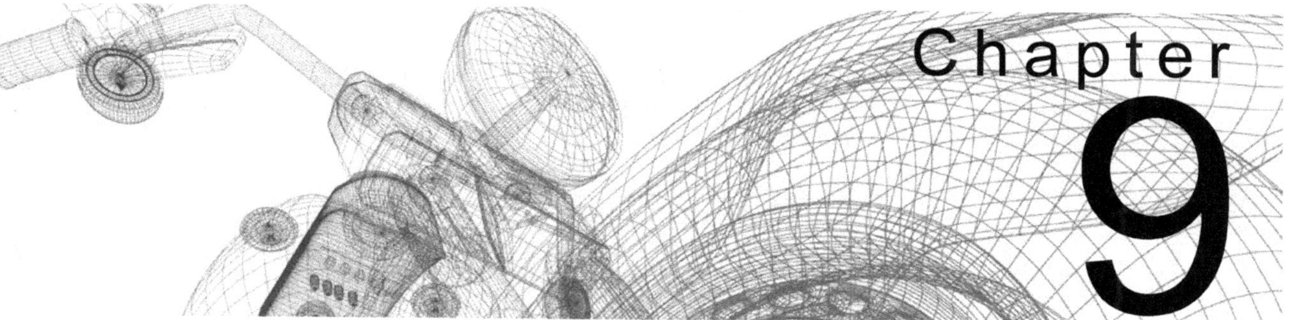

Boolean Operations

Boolean operations in CATIA V5 are powerful design tools. The ability to combine feature-based modeling with boolean operations enables the creation of robust geometry. You can work with various bodies in a single part file. This provides flexibility in design scenarios, promotes concurrent engineering, and enables viewing and manipulation of multiple model states.

Learning Objectives in this Chapter

- Learn how to create and use multiple bodies in a part.
- Understand how multiple bodies can be used to both organize your model geometry and to facilitate boolean operations.
- Understand boolean operations.
- Understand 3D constraints.

9.1 Creation of Bodies

You can create and use multiple bodies in a CATPart file. This makes it easy to create the structure and organize groups of features.

Advantages include:

- You can improve model organization by grouping features in separate bodies with respect to their function or position.
- You can create each body in a separate part file and then paste it into the finished model. Using this feature, a number of designers working concurrently can build a model.
- A single part file can contain and display a variety of model states (i.e., cast and machined state).

General Steps

Use the following general steps when working with part bodies:

1. Insert the bodies.
2. Rename the bodies.
3. Create the features.

Step 1 - Insert the bodies.

Select **Insert>Body**. Inserted bodies display as shown in Figure 9–1.

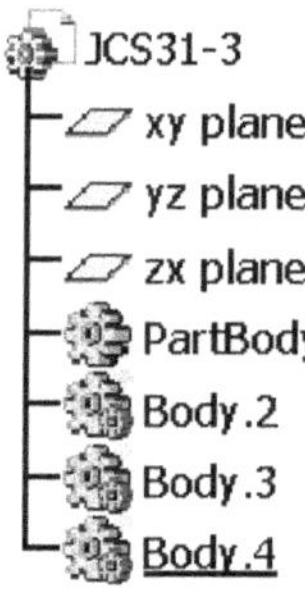

Figure 9–1

To add an existing feature to a part body, select the feature, right-click, and select **Insert in new**, as shown in Figure 9–2.

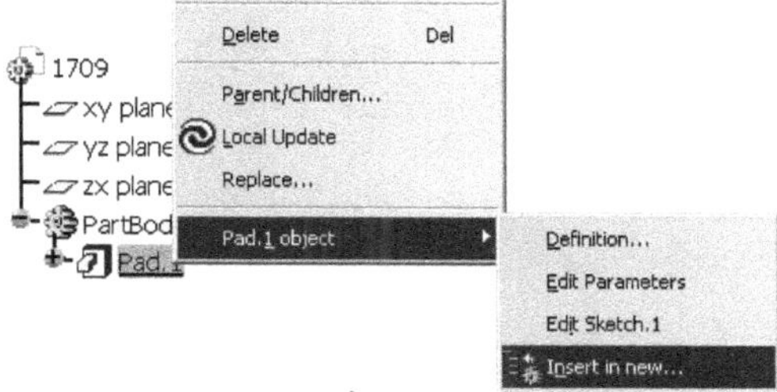

Figure 9–2

The feature is added to a new body and automatically assembled to the PartBody using the **Assemble Boolean** operation, as shown in Figure 9–3.

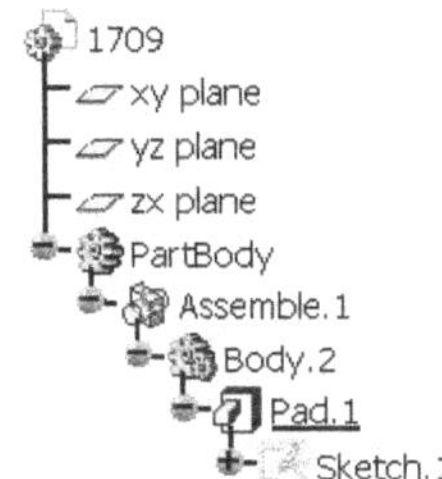

Figure 9–3

Step 2 - Rename the bodies.

It is considered good practice to rename new bodies. Doing so results in better organization, as shown in Figure 9–4.

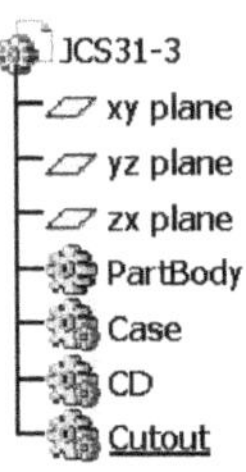

Figure 9–4

Give each body a meaningful name that is easily recognizable by other users.

Step 3 - Create the features.

Activate the appropriate body by selecting the body, right-clicking, and selecting **Define In Work Object**, as shown in Figure 9–5. You can now create features in the body.

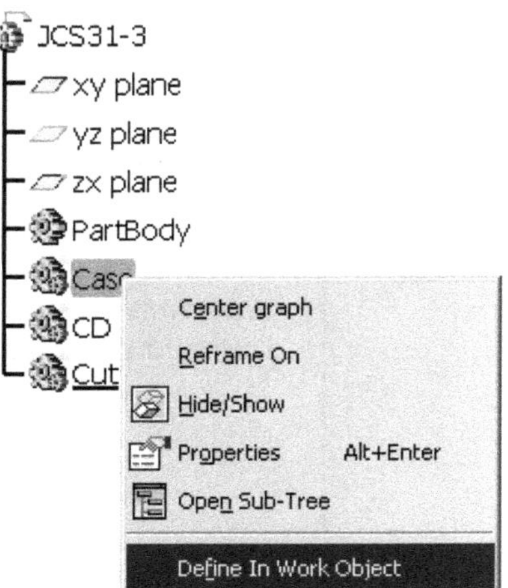

Figure 9–5

9.2 Feature Organization

Using various bodies not only facilitates boolean operations, but helps keep the part geometry organized. Consider the example shown in Figure 9–6. The specification tree depicts a cast part. The Casting body contains all of the bodies and features required to create the cast geometry. The MachiningOperations body lists all of the bodies and features required to achieve post-machining geometry.

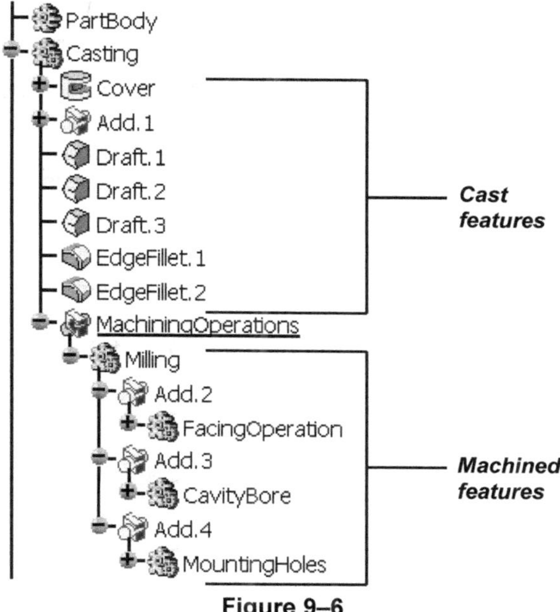

Figure 9–6

PartBody

A PartBody can only be used as the operand, not the operator.

Geometrical Set

It is suggested that you insert a geometrical set for each body. This helps in better organization of the features of the model. All of the sketches and wireframe elements can be stored under the geometrical set(s).

As the part becomes more complex, it is more difficult to keep track of the features. If there are several designers working on the same model, all of the designers can use the geometrical set(s) to understand how the model is built. Use of geometrical sets also makes it easier to find the required sketches and wireframe elements to make the required modifications.

Axis System

You must create an axis system for each body. All of the elements and features for a body should be referenced by its axis system. If you need to move a body, you can do so easily by changing the position of its axis system.

Design Considerations

While designing the bodies, you must ensure that the features do not reference the other bodies before the boolean operations, unless it is required. If the reference body is deleted, moved, or modified, the children of the reference body are most likely to cause an update failure. Therefore, you must ensure that non-required external links to the other bodies are isolated.

Activate and Deactivate

You can deactivate individual part bodies to reduce update time, and to display a model in various states. The models in Figure 9–7 are shown in a cast pre-machined state (MachiningOperations deactivated) and in a post-machined state.

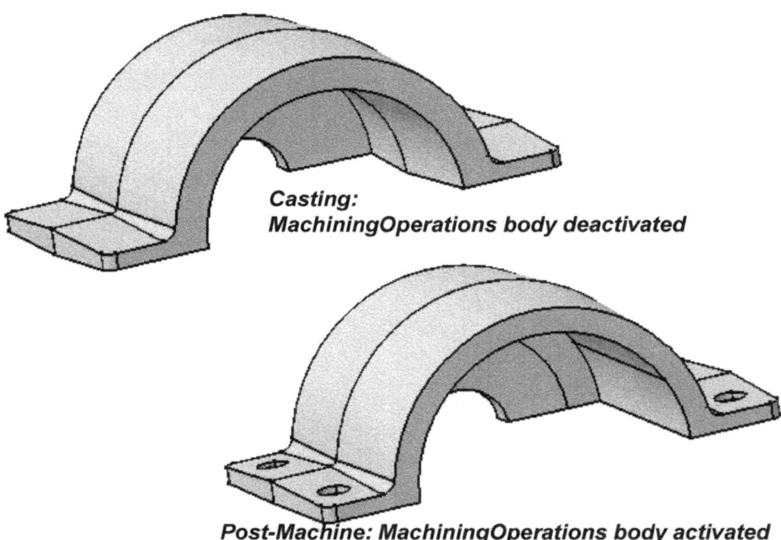

Figure 9–7

Hide and Show

Hiding bodies might be a convenient method of simplifying the display of a complex model. You can only hide bodies independently if they have not been used in a boolean operation.

Color

To differentiate between bodies, it is suggested that you apply different colors for each body. You can do this by adjusting the graphic properties for each body.

Geometry Display Options

You can control the display of the model based on the activated body or geometrical set by using the settings in the Options dialog box. To open the Options dialog box, select **Tools >Options**. Expand **Infrastructure>Part Infrastructure** and select the *Display* tab. The **Only the current operated solid** and **Only current body** options are shown in Figure 9–8. These options enable the designer to focus on the geometry of the active body or geometrical set, and are useful for organizing the display of a complex, multi-body part.

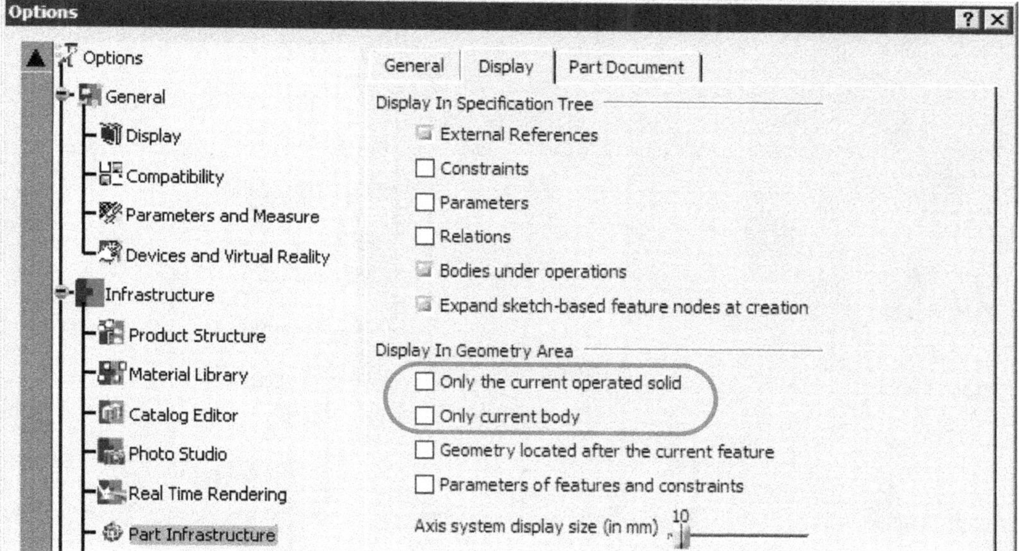

Figure 9–8

The options are also located in the Tools toolbar, as shown in Figure 9–9.

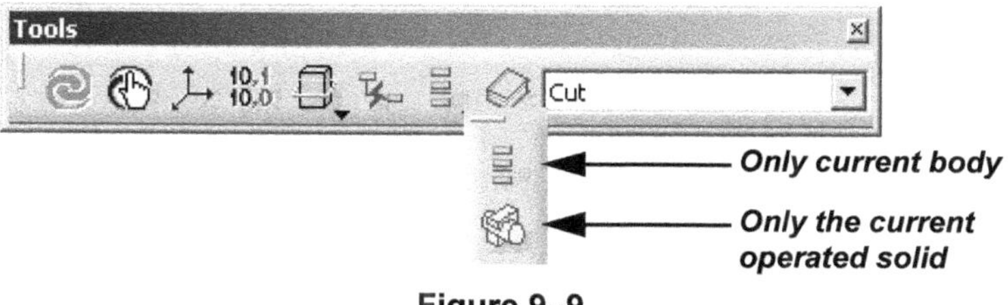

Figure 9–9

Only the Current Operated Solid

When you select this option, all of the bodies and geometrical sets display, except for any parent bodies. For example, consider the scenario shown in Figure 9–10. With Body.3 activated, all of the features in the parent Body.2 are not displayed. However, all of the features of **Body.3**, **Body.4**, **Geometrical Set.1**, and **Body.5** are visible.

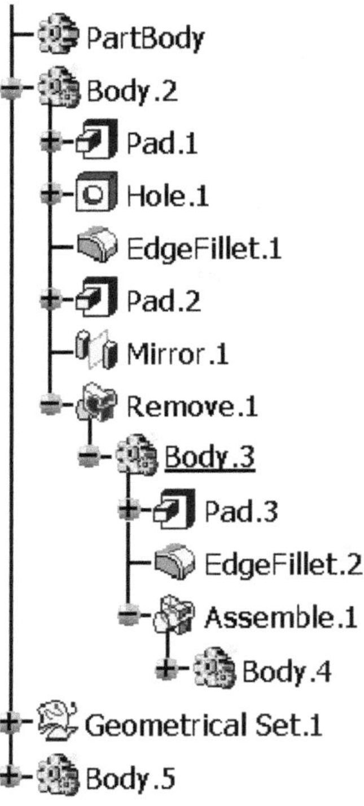

Figure 9–10

Only Current Body

When you select this option, only the geometry of the active geometrical set or solid body displays. Any bodies that are located beneath the active body (through a **Boolean** operation) are also displayed. If you consider the same scenario shown in Figure 9–10, if the **Only current body** option is selected, only the geometry of **Body.3** and **Body.4** would be visible. Since **Geometrical Set.1** and **Body.5** do not belong to **Body.3**, they would be hidden.

9.3 Boolean Operations

The Boolean Operations toolbar and the names of all of the boolean operation icons are shown in Figure 9–11.

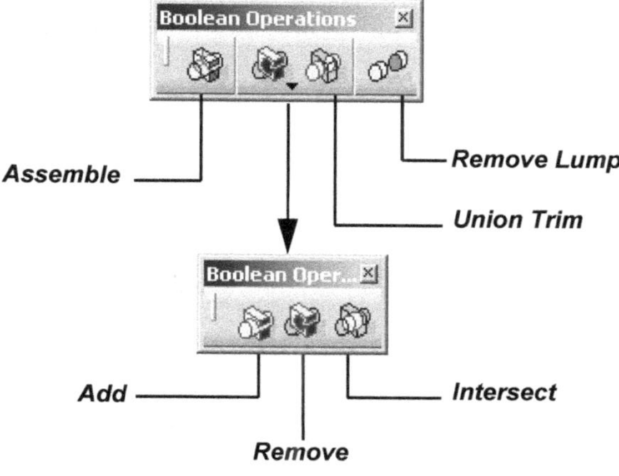

Figure 9–11

The following types of boolean operations are discussed, using the example model shown in Figure 9–12:

- Assemble
- Add
- Remove
- Intersect
- Union Trim
- Remove Lump

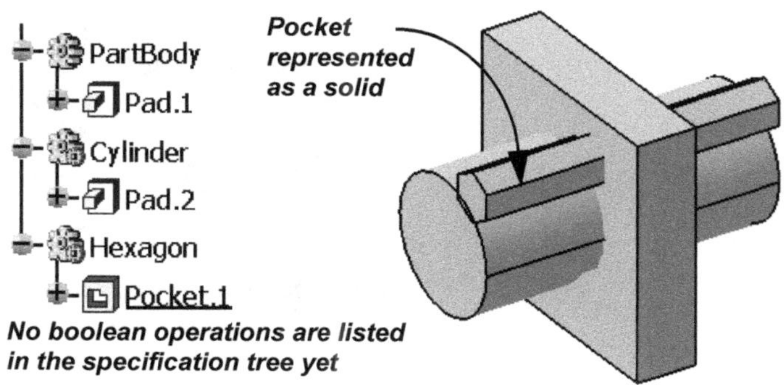

Figure 9–12

Assemble

(Assemble) assembles the selected body into another body. Because the features are assembled, they are not altered in any way. For example, **Pad.2** of the Cylinder body results in the addition of geometry to the PartBody, and **Pocket.1** of the Hexagon body results in the removal of geometry from the PartBody, as shown in Figure 9–13 and Figure 9–14.

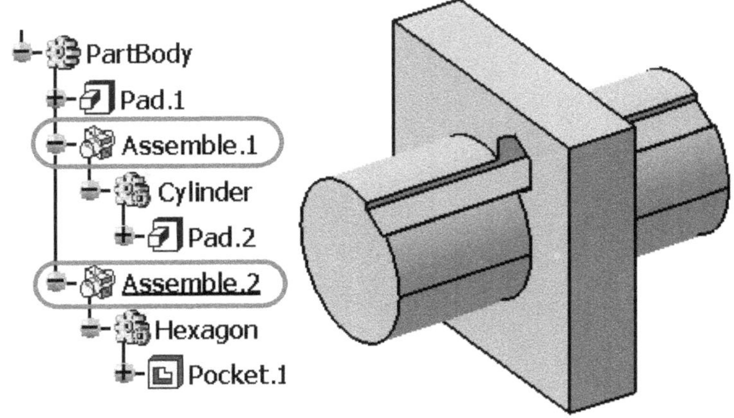

Figure 9–13

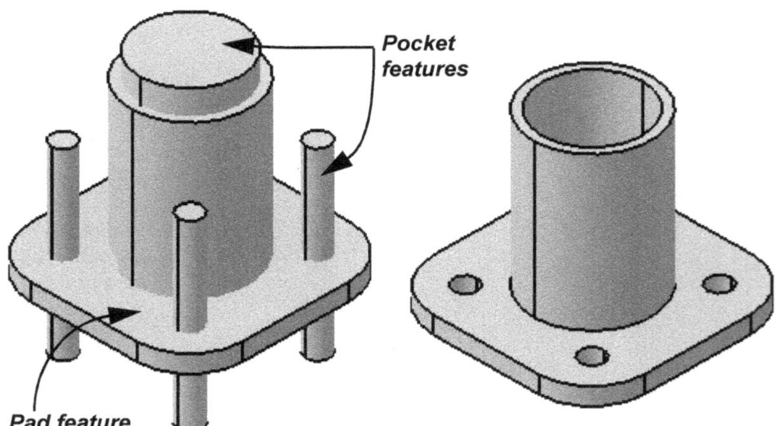

Figure 9–14

Add

(Add) considers all of the features of a body to be additive. Therefore, both the Pad and Pocket features from the original bodies add material to the PartBody, as shown in Figure 9–15.

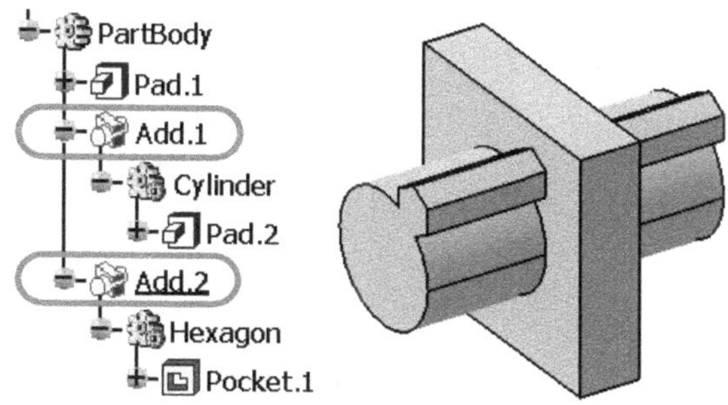

Figure 9–15

Remove

(Remove) considers all of the features of a body to be subtractive. Therefore, both the Pad and Pocket features from the original bodies remove material from the PartBody, as shown in Figure 9–16 and Figure 9–17.

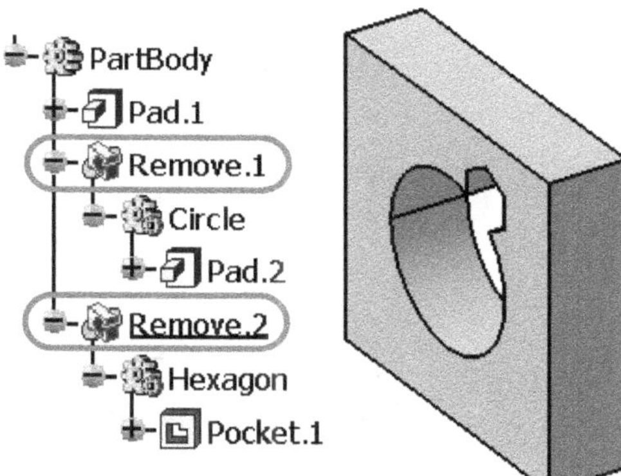

Figure 9–16

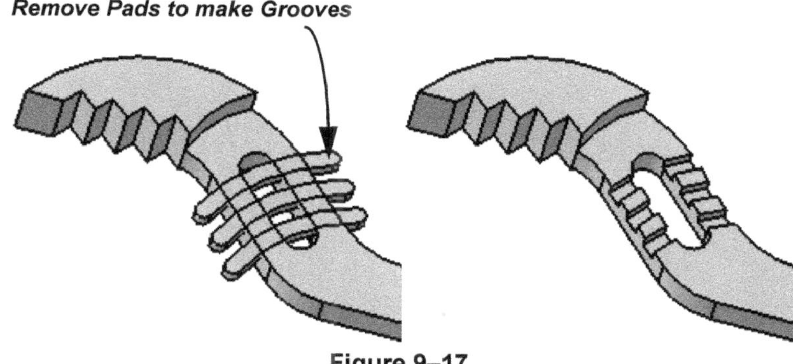

Figure 9–17

Intersect

The result of an (Intersect) is the shared volume between the two bodies. For example, if the Cylinder body were intersected with the PartBody, the result would display as shown in Figure 9–18.

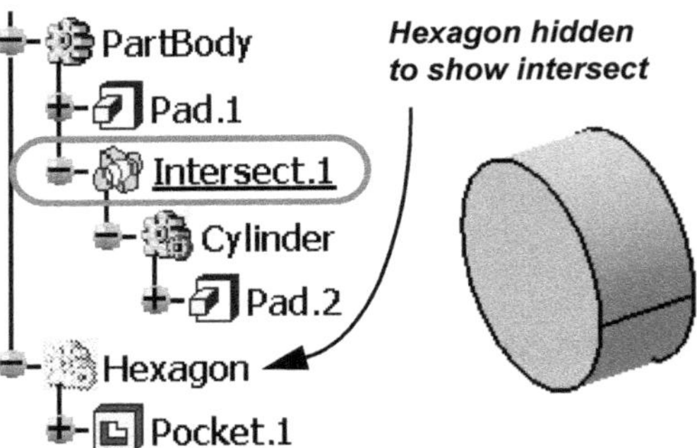

Figure 9–18

In another example, an engine block model located in **Body1** is intersected with the geometry of a transmission interface located in **Body2**. The resulting intersection displays as shown in Figure 9–19.

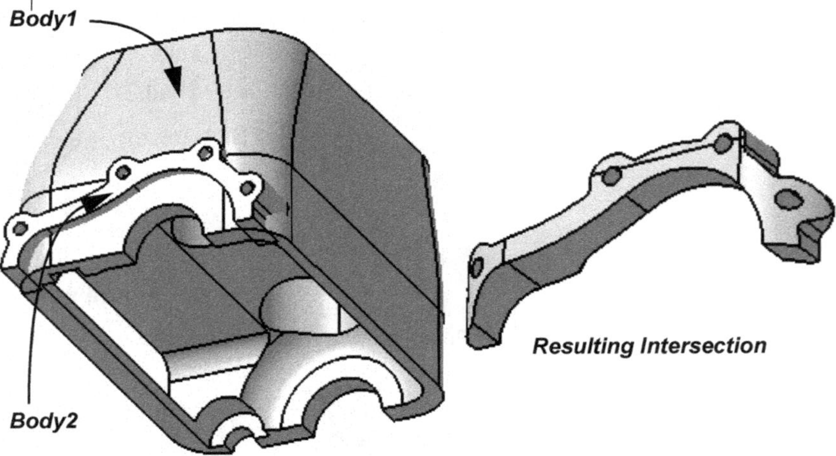

Figure 9–19

Union Trim

(Union Trim) is similar to an **Add** operation, with the ability to remove or keep selected faces on the two bodies. For example, if you select to remove the faces from the frame and circle geometry, the resulting geometry displays as shown in Figure 9–20.

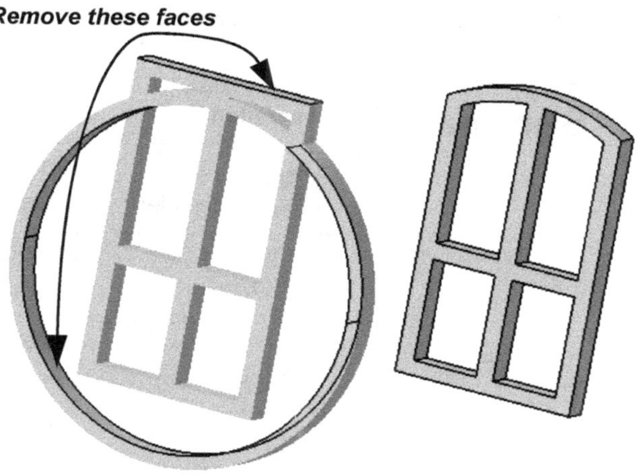

Figure 9–20

Remove Lump

(Remove Lump) removes growths and gaps and reshapes the body by selecting faces that you can remove and keep. The example models demonstrate the **Remove Lump** operation, as shown in Figure 9–21 and Figure 9–22.

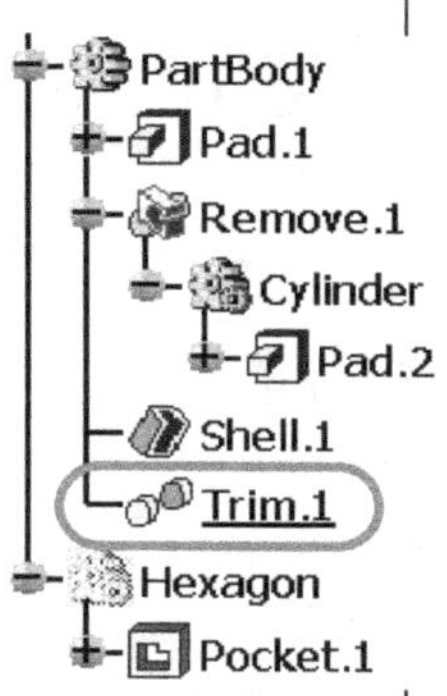

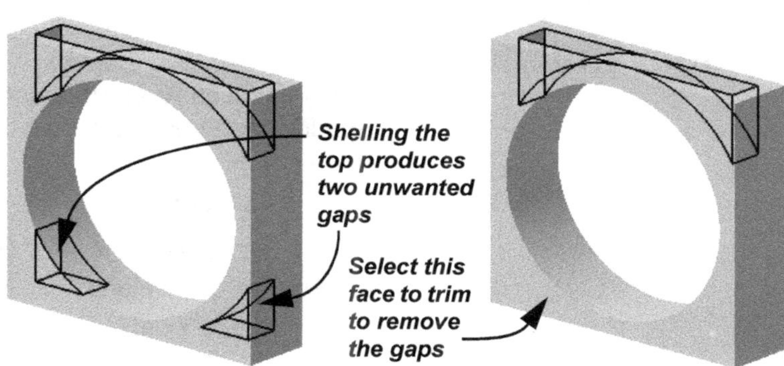

Figure 9–21

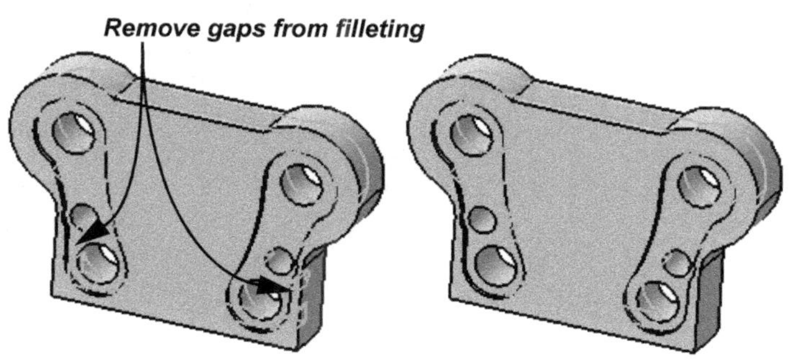

Figure 9–22

Boolean Operation Summary

The different types of Boolean operations and their results are described as follows:

Operation	Result
(Assemble)	Pocket = Pocket Pad = Pad
(Add)	Pocket = Pad Pad = Pad
(Remove)	Pocket = Pocket Pad = Pocket
(Intersect)	Shared volume.
(Union Trim)	Select faces to keep and/or remove (adds part of selected body).
(Remove Lump)	Reshape a body by selecting faces to remove and/or keep.

Naming Conventions

When you perform a Boolean operation, the original body is represented by the Boolean feature in the top level in the specification tree. For example, when **CutOut** is added to the PartBody using an **Assemble** operation, **Assemble.1** displays in the specification tree, as shown in Figure 9–23.

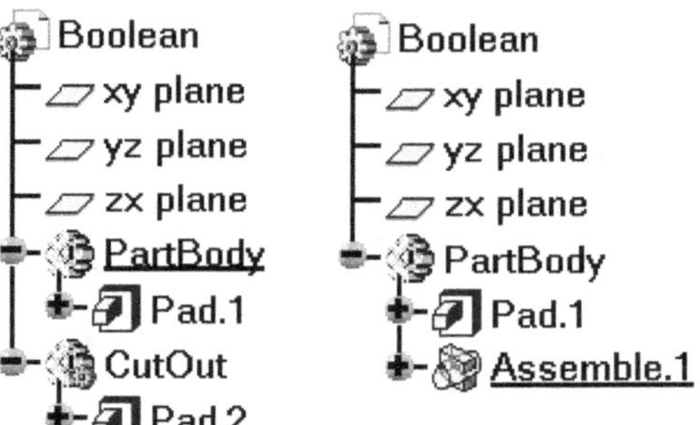

Figure 9–23

To simplify the location of bodies in the tree and make the model easier to understand for other designers, you must rename the Boolean feature after the body that was operated on. For example, the Boolean feature from the previous example could be renamed as **CutOut (Assemble)**, as shown in Figure 9–24.

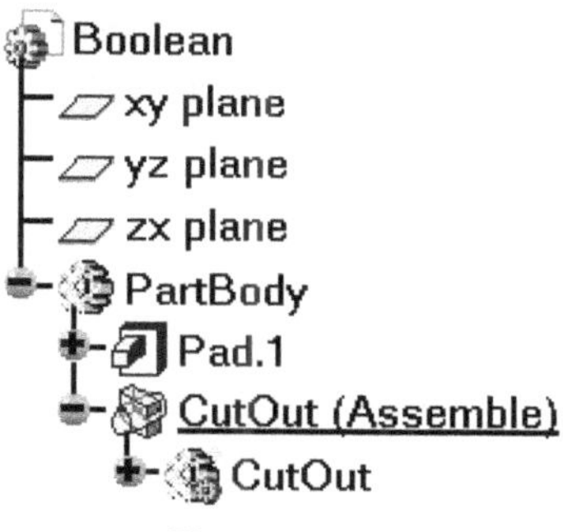

Figure 9–24

Advantages

The advantages of using Boolean operations include the following:

- Increases flexibility in the combination of part bodies and their geometry.
- Provides an extension of parametric, feature-based modeling practices.
- Can simulate core injection molding, cavity injection molding, and machining operations.
- Improves modeling and system performance when working with complex models that have a large number of features.

Disadvantages

The disadvantages of using Boolean operations include the following:

- Cannot use PartBody as an operator.
- Requires strategic planning on the position and structure of features in the model.
- Using bodies with features that are tangent to each other can result in geometric instabilities.

9.4 3D Constraints

Copied features can be positioned relative to other geometry using 3D constraints. This is useful if geometry is reused in a different location or orientation than the original.

3D constraints can only be applied to copies that do not have stored history. Therefore, features created with the **As Result** and **As Result with Link** options can be positioned in space in this manner. 3D constraints have the same appearance as sketch constraints, as shown in Figure 9–25.

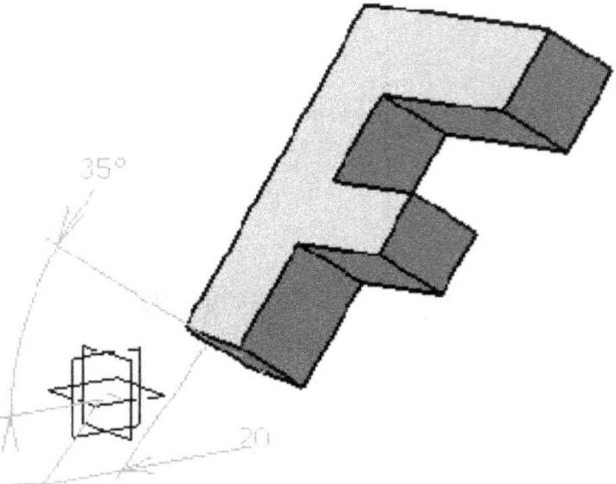

Figure 9–25

If a constraint is created on or between features with design history, the constraint becomes a reference that reflects the dimension without letting the dimension be changed. References are denoted by parentheses around the value, as shown in Figure 9–26.

Figure 9–26

Eight 3D constraint types can be created. These constraints are similar to Sketcher constraints, but they are used to constrain 3D geometry rather than sketched elements.

- Fix
- Length
- Distance
- Angle
- Coincidence
- Tangency
- Parallel
- Perpendicular

To create a 3D constraint, use  or .

Constraints Defined in Dialog Box

(Constraints Defined in Dialog Box) is available after one or more elements have been selected. You can click this icon to open a dialog box containing the types of constraints available for the group of elements that were selected. The dialog box opens as shown in Figure 9–27.

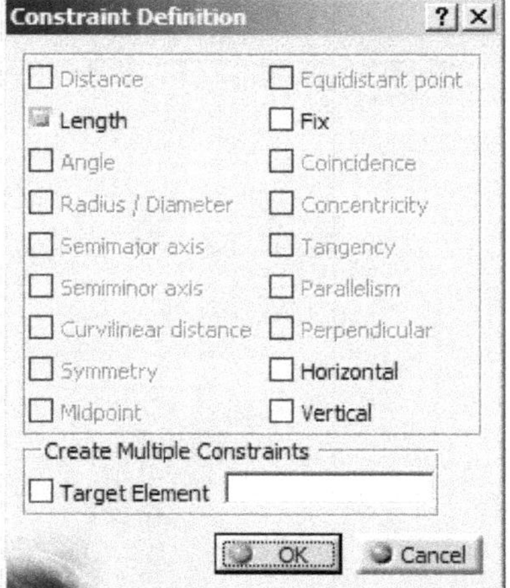

Figure 9–27

Constraint

(Constraint) automatically determines a default constraint type based on the types of elements selected. Select the constraint to accept the default constraint type. To change the constraint type, right-click on the constraint and select the constraint type, as shown in Figure 9–28.

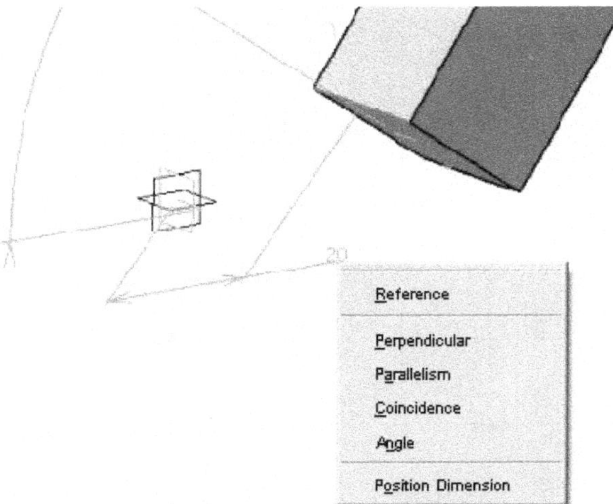

Figure 9–28

Practice 9a

Boolean Operations Overview

Practice Objective

- Review the Boolean operations of a model.

In this practice, you will open a part file of a cast/machined part. The features are organized by using casting and machining operations. Boolean operations have been used to achieve the final part geometry, and inherently provide flexibility in terms of viewing different states of the model.

Task 1 - Open the part and investigate the boolean operations.

1. Open **Cover.CATPart** from the *Boolean* directory. The model displays as shown in Figure 9–29.

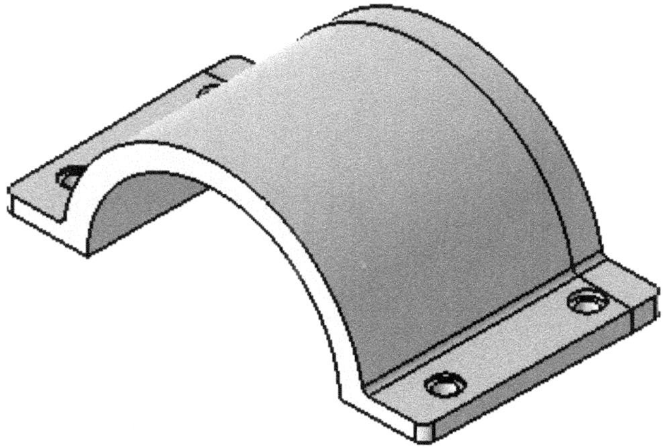

Figure 9–29

2. In the specification tree, note that no geometry has been created in the PartBody. When using **Boolean** operations, you must ensure that no geometry is created in the PartBody. This provides more flexibility in that the PartBody can only be used as the operand, and not the operator (i.e., a PartBody cannot be removed from an inserted body).

3. Expand the specification tree and note the features listed under the **Casting** body, as shown in Figure 9–30.

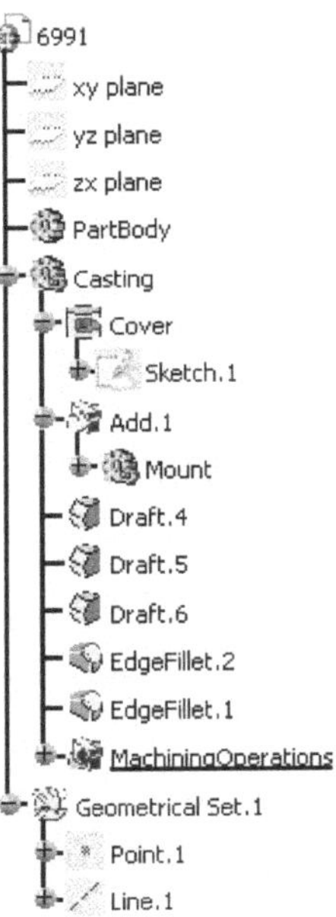

Figure 9–30

4. Expand the **MachiningOperations** feature and note the bodies and features listed.

Task 2 - Deactivate a body.

1. Deactivate the **MachiningOperations** feature and note the casting geometry, as shown in Figure 9–31.

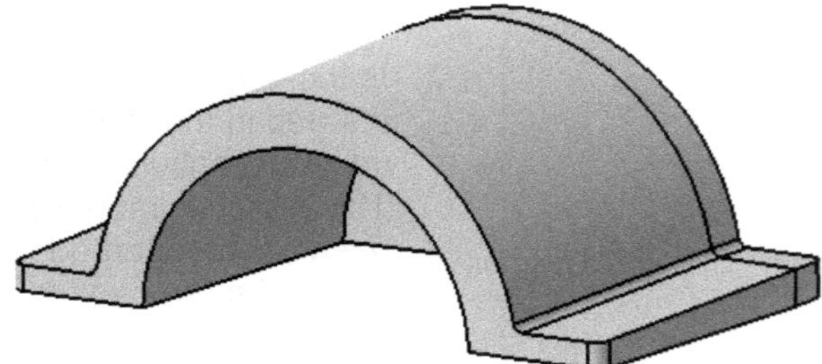

Figure 9–31

2. Activate the **MachiningOperations** feature.

3. Save the part and close the window.

Practice 9b

Boolean Operations

Practice Objective

- Model using Boolean operations.

In this practice, you will create a part file and structure the part by creating the required bodies. Geometry is created in the appropriate bodies, and **Boolean** operations are used to achieve the final configuration.

Task 1 - Create a new part.

1. Create a new part file called **JCS31-3**. Ensure that the **Enable hybrid design** option is cleared.

Task 2 - Insert bodies.

1. Select **Insert>Body** to insert a body. Repeat the operation two more times.
2. Rename the three new bodies as **Case**, **CD**, and **Cutout**, as shown in Figure 9–32.

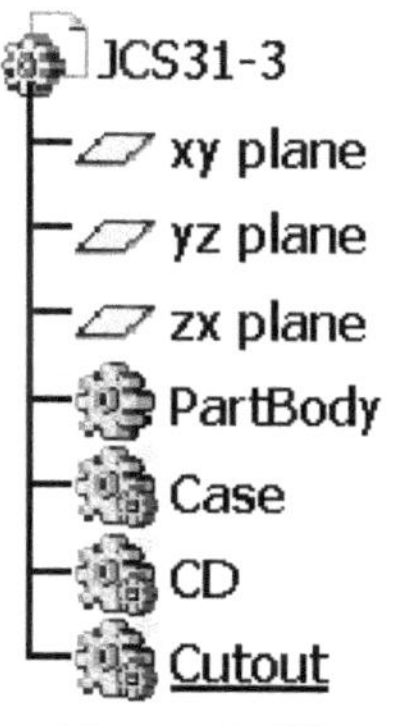

Figure 9–32

3. Ensure that the units are set to **Millimeter** (mm).
4. Define the **Case** body as the In Work Object.

Task 3 - Create a Pad feature.

1. Select the **xy plane** as the sketch support and activate the Sketcher workbench.
2. Sketch a rectangle. Define the symmetry with the vertical and horizontal axes and create two dimensions with the values, as shown in Figure 9–33.

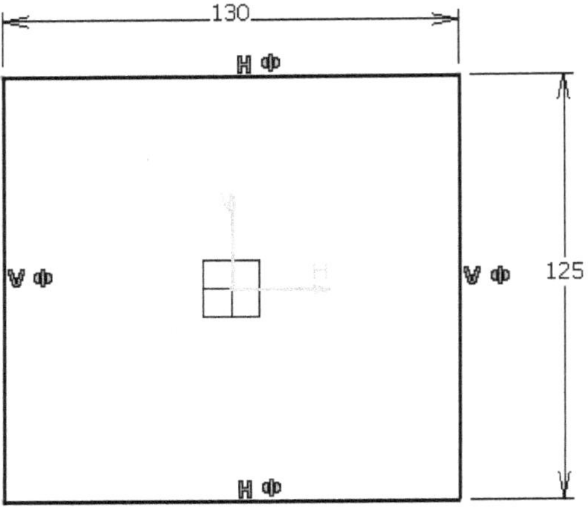

Figure 9–33

3. Exit Sketcher.
4. Create a Pad. In the *Length* field, enter **4**. Ensure that the directional arrow points up, as shown in Figure 9–34.

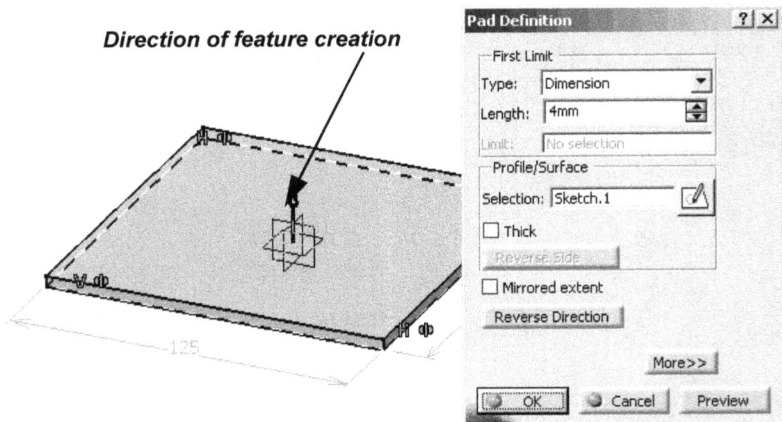

Figure 9–34

Task 4 - Create a reference plane.

1. Create a reference plane offset from the xy plane by **2.5**. Ensure that the directional arrow points up, as shown in Figure 9–35.

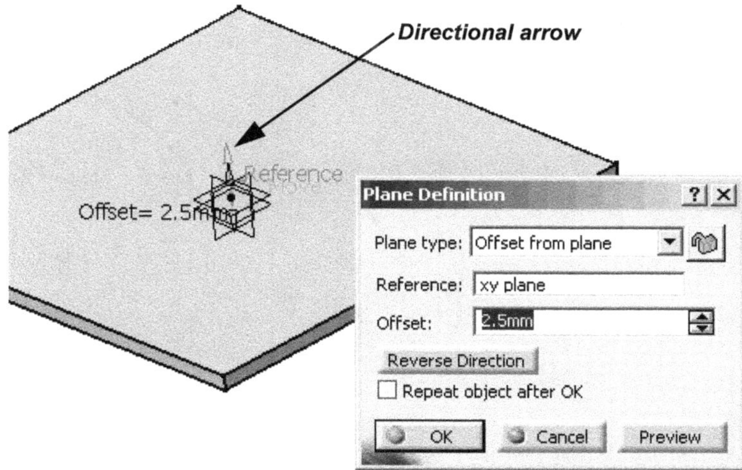

Figure 9–35

2. Rename the plane as **CDPlane**.

3. Define the **CD** body as the Work Object. The specification tree displays as shown in Figure 9–36.

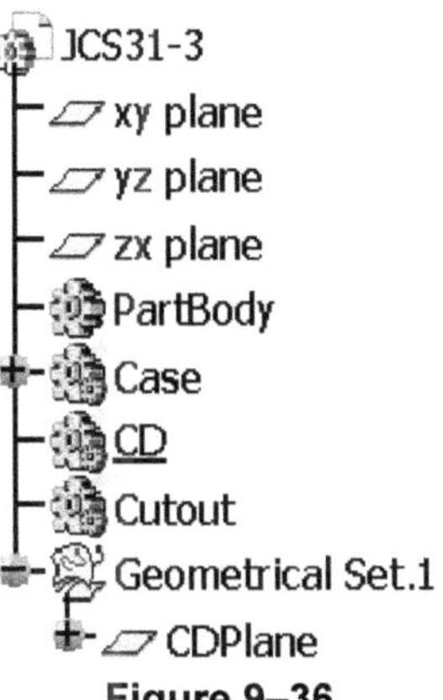

Figure 9–36

4. Hide the **Case** body.

Task 5 - Create a sketch.

1. Select **CDPlane** and activate the Sketcher workbench.
2. Create two circles. Ensure that the centers of the circles are located at the origin of the sketch and dimensioned as shown in Figure 9–37. Create the smaller circle first and then the larger circle.

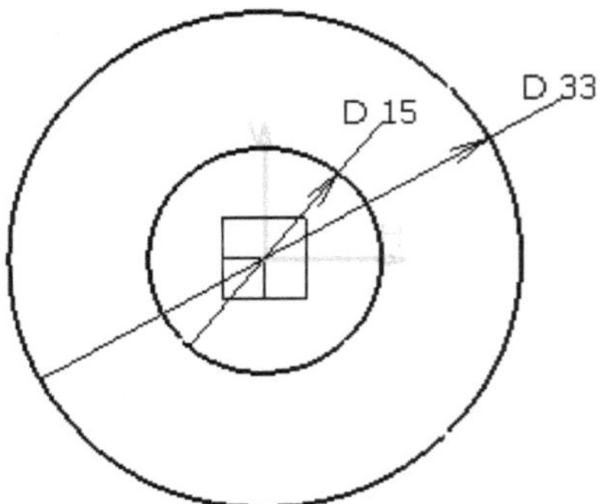

Figure 9–37

3. Sketch a third circle and dimension it as **120**, as shown in Figure 9–38.

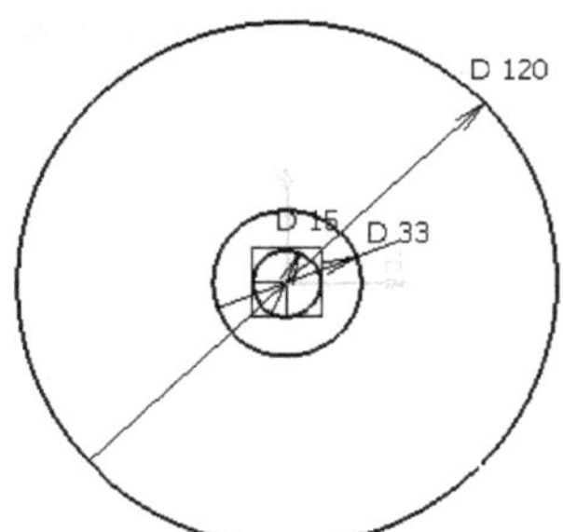

Figure 9–38

4. Exit the Sketcher workbench.

Task 6 - Create a Multi-pad.

1. Click to create a Multi-pad.
2. In the *Domain* area, select **Domain 1**. The large circle and the middle circle are highlighted.

3. In the *First Limit* area, in the *Length* field, enter **1.5**.
4. In the *Second Limit* area, in the *Length* field, enter **4**, as shown in Figure 9–39.

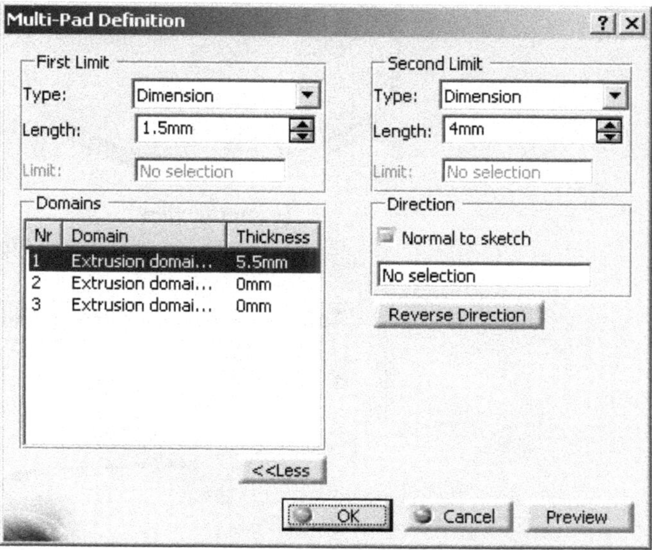

Figure 9–39

5. In the *Domain* area, select **Domain 2**. The middle circle and the small circle are highlighted.
6. In the *First Limit* area, in the *Length* field, enter **1.0**.
7. In the *Second Limit* area, in the *Length* field, enter **4**.
8. Ensure that the direction of feature creation points down, as shown in Figure 9–40.

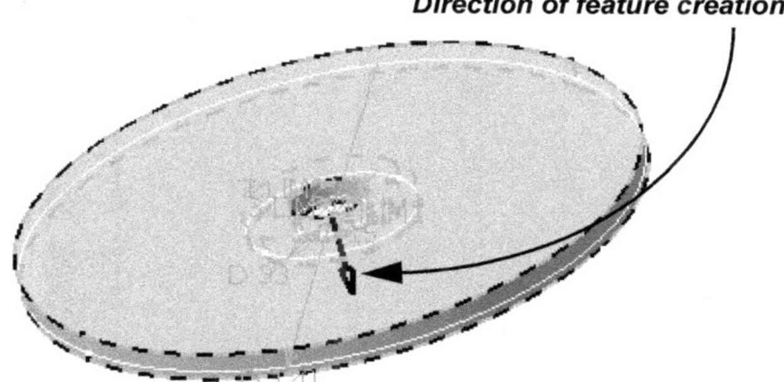

Figure 9–40

9. Click **OK**. The Multi-pad feature displays as shown in Figure 9–41.

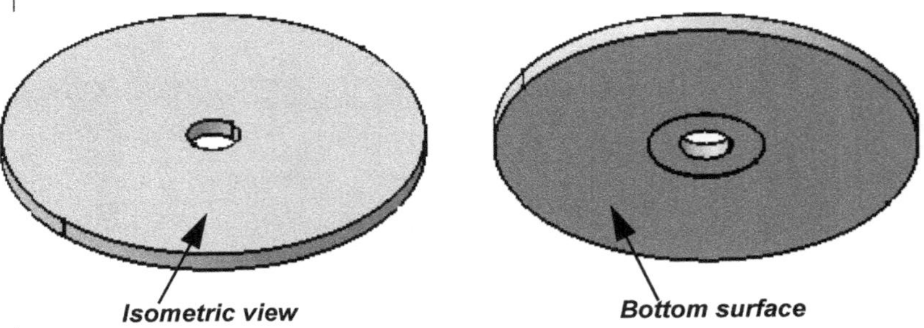

Figure 9–41

Task 7 - Create an Edge Fillet.

1. Create a **0.5** Edge Fillet on the edge shown in Figure 9–42.

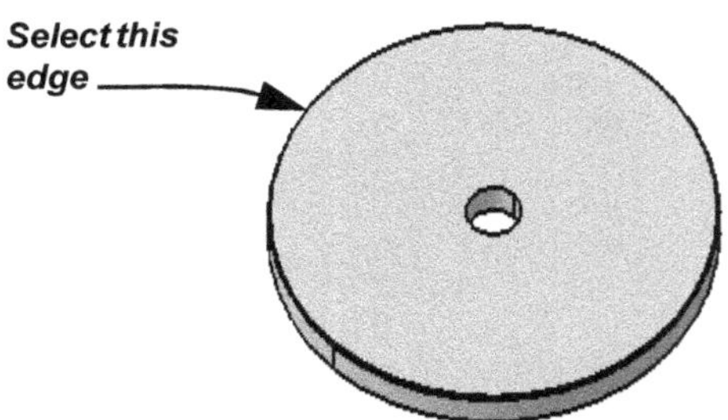

Figure 9–42

2. Define the **Case** body to be the Work Object. The specification tree displays as shown in Figure 9–43.

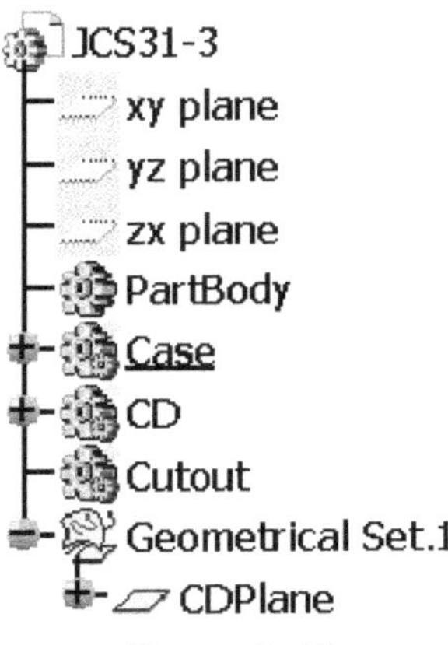

Figure 9–43

*You might need to display the Boolean Operations toolbar to use the **Remove** icon.*

Task 8 - Perform a Boolean operation.

1. Select the background of the display to clear **Case** body.
2. In the Boolean Operations toolbar, click 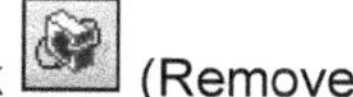 (Remove).
3. Select the CD body. The Remove dialog box opens as shown in Figure 9–44.

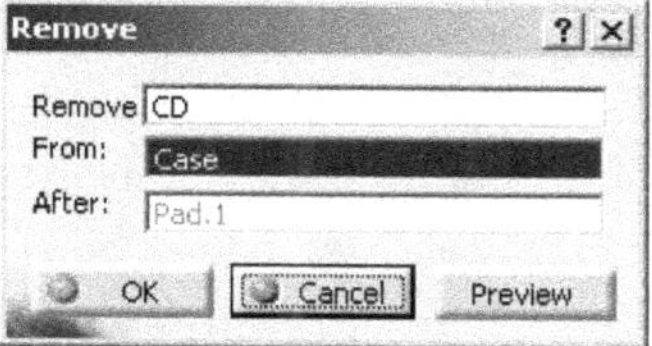

Figure 9–44

4. Click **OK** to complete the operation.
5. Click . The model displays as shown in Figure 9–45.

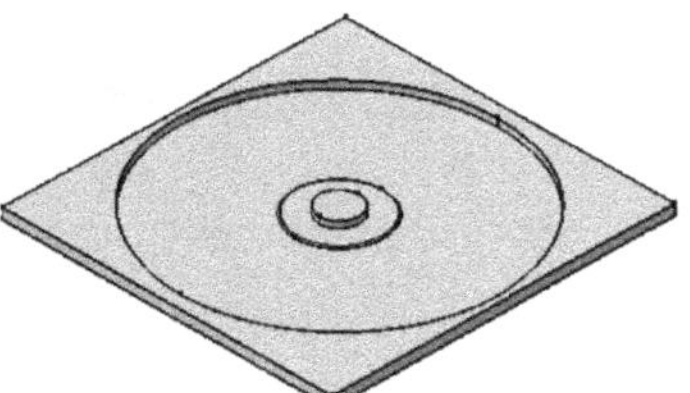

Figure 9–45

Task 9 - Create cutout geometry.

1. Define **Cutout** body as the Work Object.
2. Select the top surface as shown in Figure 9–46, and enter the Sketcher workbench.

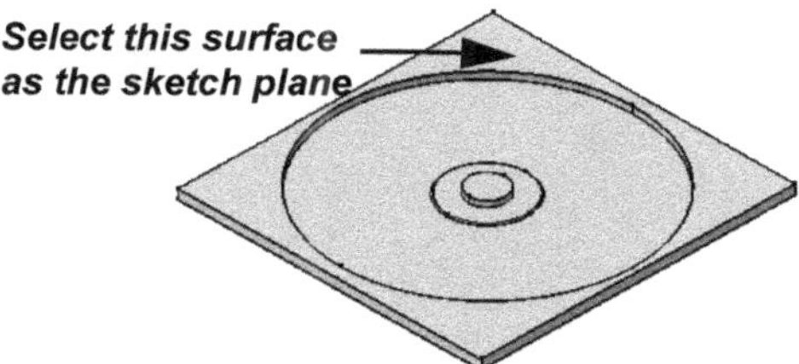

Figure 9–46

The sketch view displays as shown in Figure 9–47.

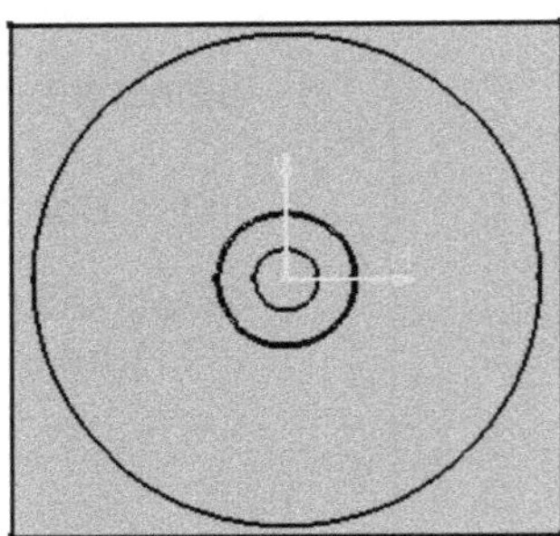

Figure 9–47

3. Double-click on (Offset) and offset the three edges shown in Figure 9–48 by **1** to the inside of the geometry.

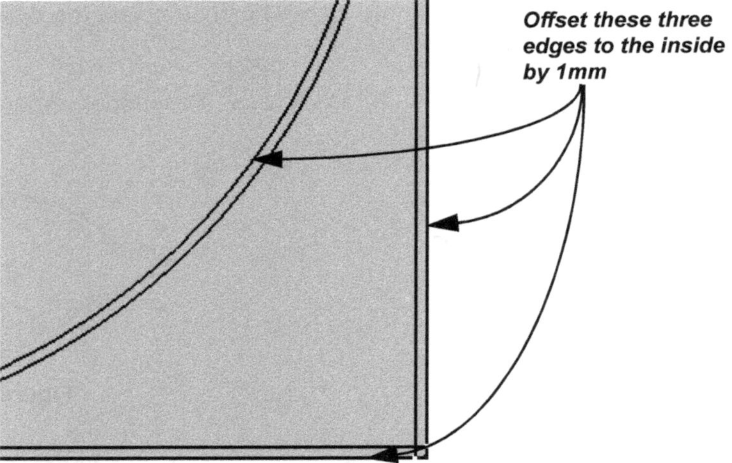
Offset these three edges to the inside by 1mm

Figure 9–48

4. Sketch a horizontal and a vertical line. Dimension the horizontal line by **55** and the vertical line by **45**, as shown in Figure 9–49.

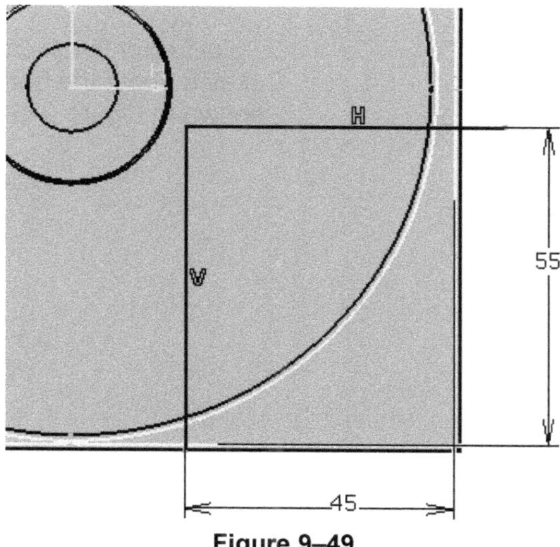

Figure 9–49

5. Click [icon] to create the sketch geometry shown in Figure 9–50.

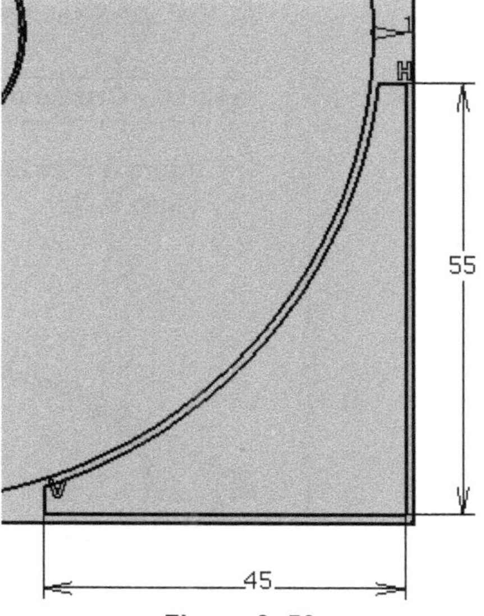

Figure 9–50

6. Select all of the sketch geometry and use [mirror icon] to mirror the sketch about the horizontal axis. The sketch displays as shown in Figure 9–51.

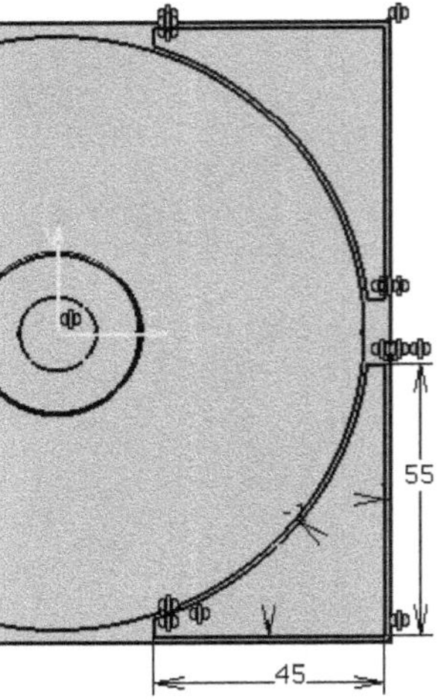

Figure 9–51

7. Exit the Sketcher workbench.

Task 10 - Create solid geometry.

1. Create a Pad **2mm** in length in the direction shown in Figure 9–52.

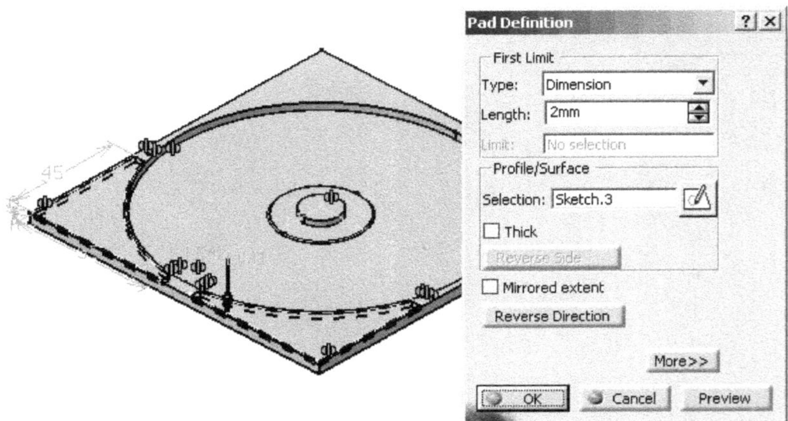

Figure 9–52

2. Mirror the Pad feature about the yz plane. The model and the specification tree display as shown in Figure 9–53.

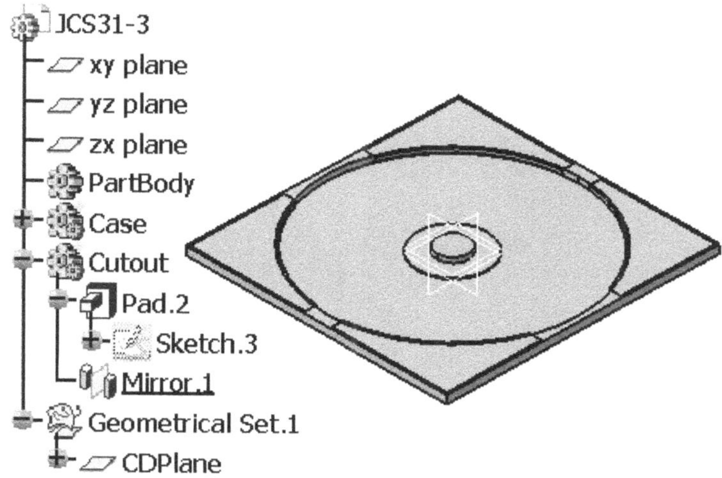

Figure 9–53

3. Define the **Case** body as the Work Object, and clear the **Case** body by selecting the background of the display.

4. Click (Remove) to remove the **Cutout** body from the **Case** body. The model displays as shown in Figure 9–54.

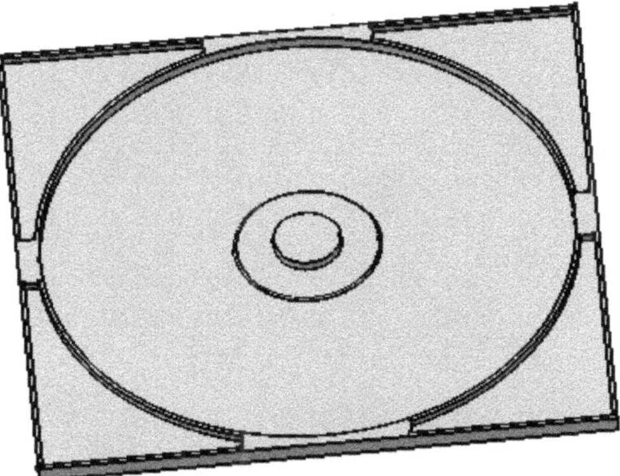

Figure 9–54

Task 11 - Create a sketch.

1. Select the planar surface shown in Figure 9–55 and activate the Sketcher workbench.

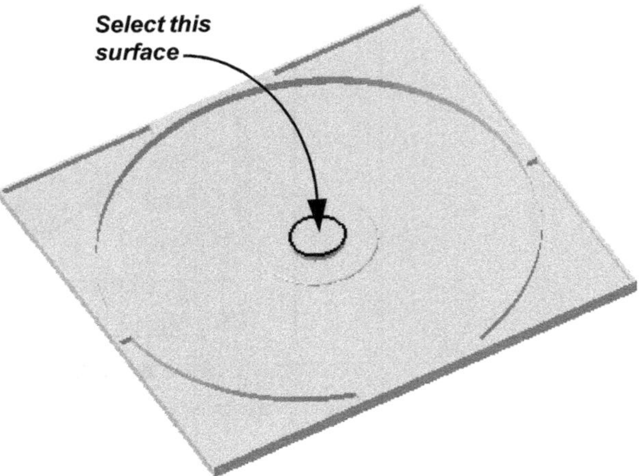

Figure 9–55

2. Use [icon] to offset the circular edge to the inside by **1**, as shown in Figure 9–56.

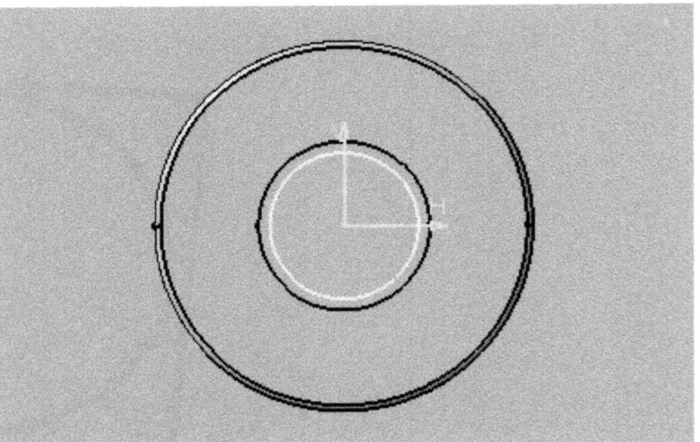

Figure 9–56

3. Create a Pocket feature **2.5** deep using the sketch you just created. The Pocket feature displays as shown in Figure 9–57.

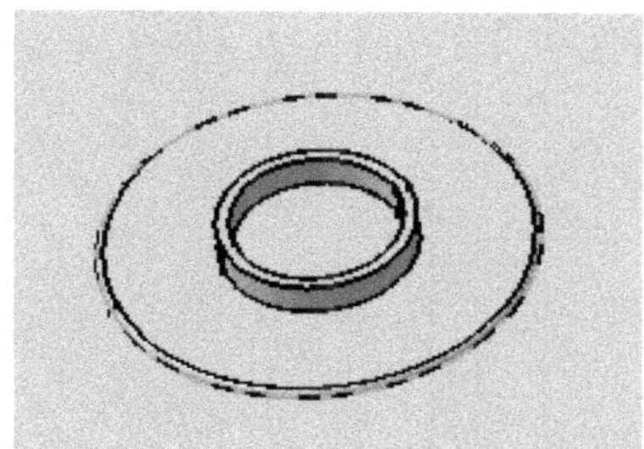

Figure 9–57

4. Save the model as **JCS31-3** to the *Boolean* directory, but do not close the file.

Task 12 - Cut and paste a body.

1. Open **CenterCutOut.CATPart** from the *Boolean* directory.
2. Copy the **CenterCutOut** body as shown in Figure 9–58.

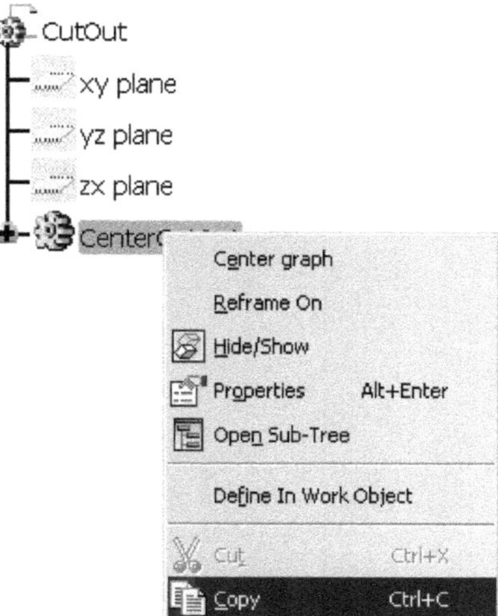

Figure 9–58

3. Activate the **JCS31-3** window.

4. Paste **CenterCutOut** body into the top-most level of the specification tree, as shown in Figure 9–59.

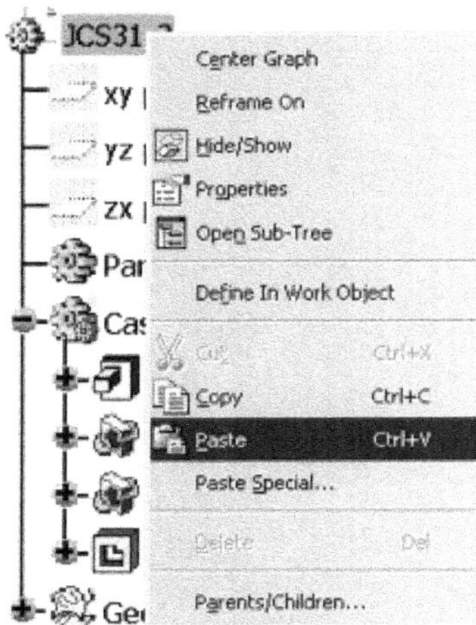

Figure 9–59

The body displays at the bottom of the specification tree.

5. Zoom in and note the pasted geometry, as shown in Figure 9–60.

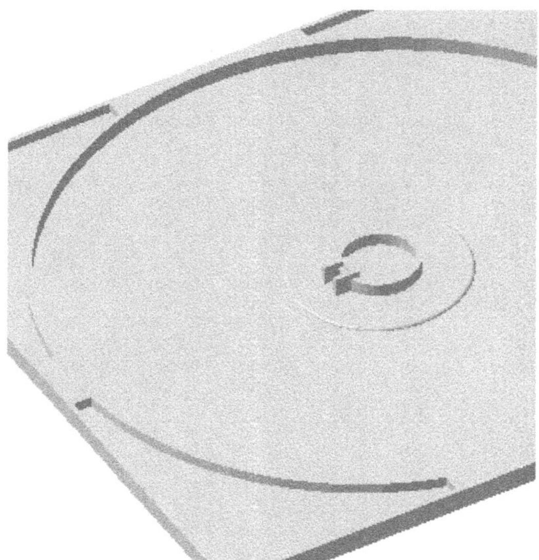

Figure 9–60

Task 13 - Create a pattern.

1. Select the Pad feature under the pasted **CenterCutOut** body, as shown in Figure 9–61, and click [icon].

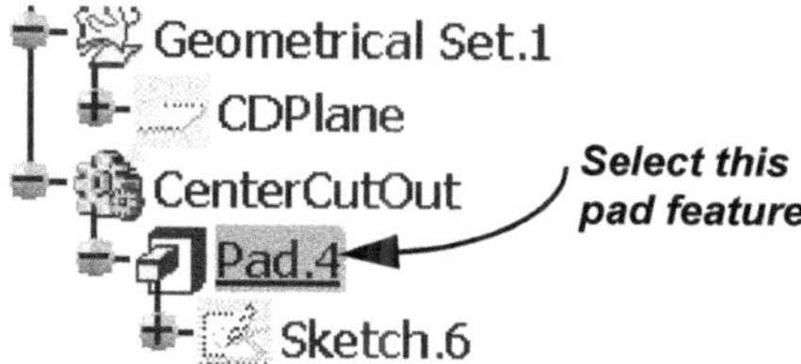

Figure 9–61

2. Specify the pattern using the following values:

   - *Parameters:* **Complete crown**
   - *Instance(s):* **3**
   - *Reference element:* as shown in Figure 9–62

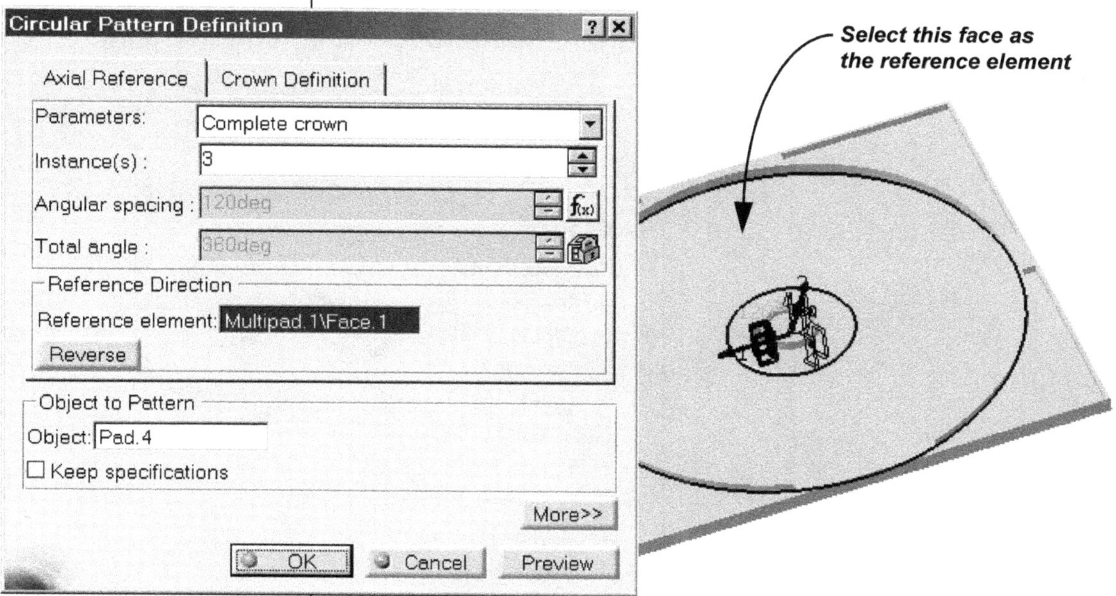

Figure 9–62

3. Click **OK**. The pattern displays as shown in Figure 9–63.

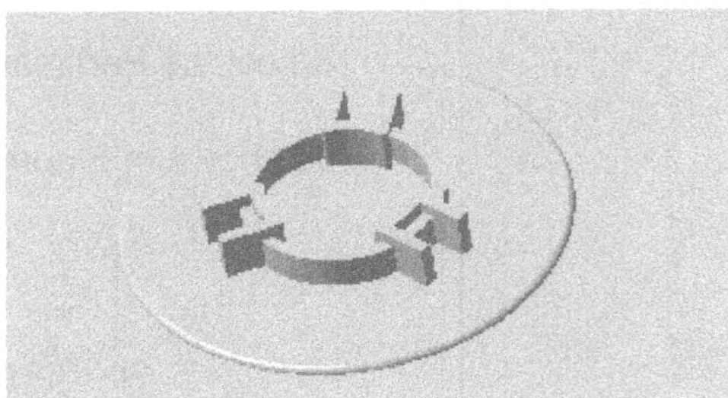

Figure 9–63

4. Remove the **CenterCutOut** body from the **Case** body. The model and the specification tree display, as shown in Figure 9–64.

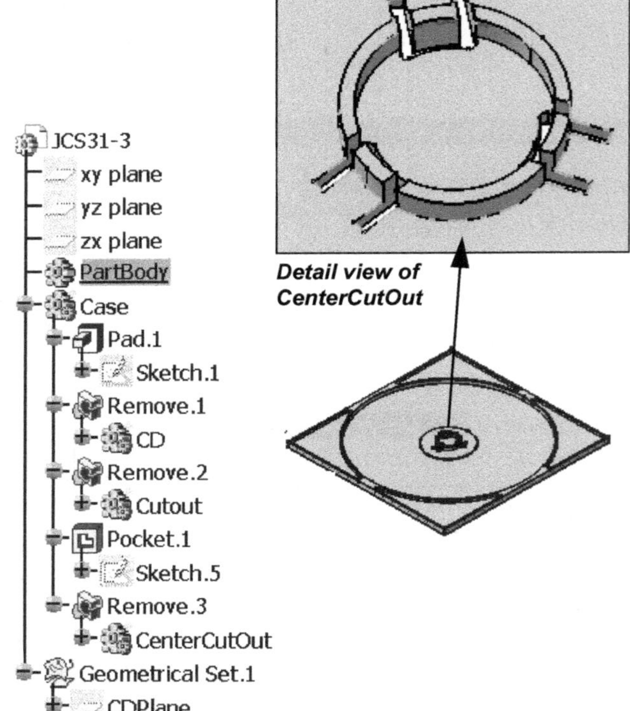

Figure 9–64

5. Save the model and close the file.

Practice 9c

3D Constraints

Practice Objective

- Use 3D constraints to position the copied geometry.

In this practice, you will use the geometry of a flange that has been constructed in a separate part file to develop the ends of a right-angled pipe. You will copy and paste the flange twice into the part file, and use constraints to position the new geometry. Boolean operations will be used to assemble the flanges and pipe. The final result is shown in Figure 9–65.

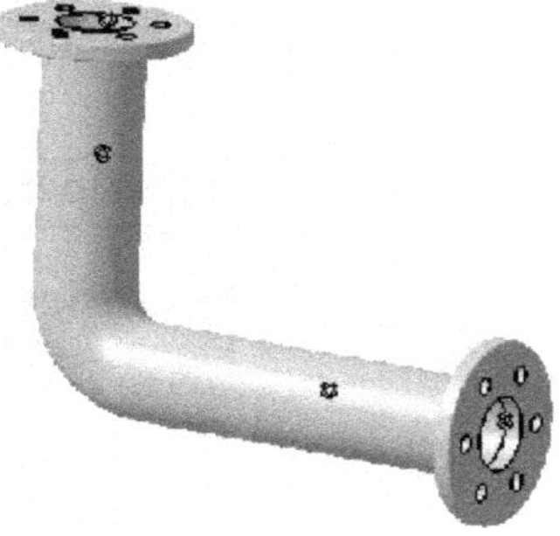

Figure 9–65

Task 1 - Set display options.

1. Open the Options dialog box, and select **Infrastructure>Part Infrastructure**. In the *Display* tab, select **Constraints**, as shown in Figure 9–66.

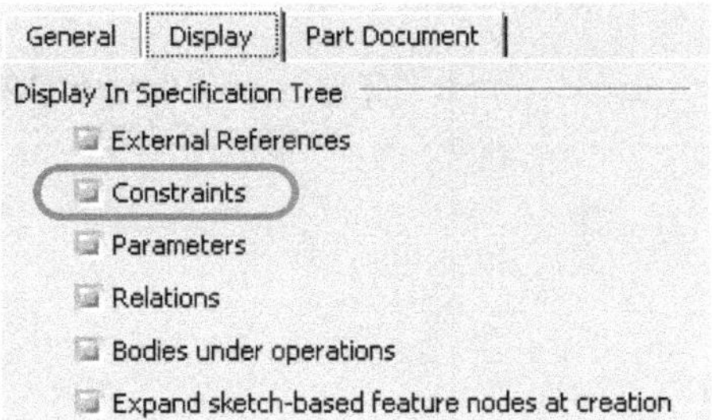

Figure 9–66

2. Select the *General* tab and clear the **Restrict external selection with link to published elements** option, as shown in Figure 9–67.

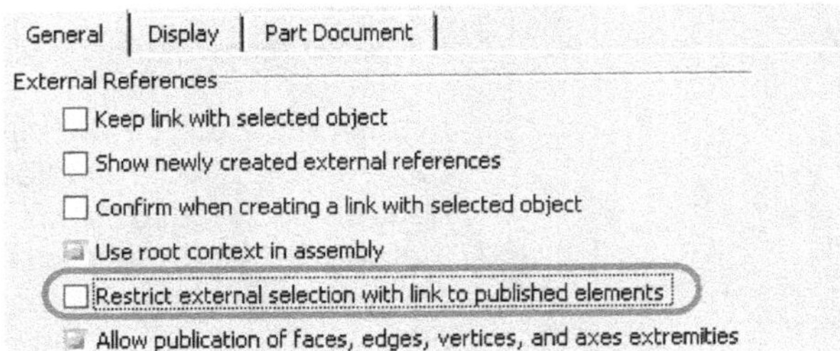

Figure 9–67

3. Click **OK**.

Task 2 - Open the existing pipe and flange files.

1. Open **Pipe.CATPart**. The part displays as shown in Figure 9–68.

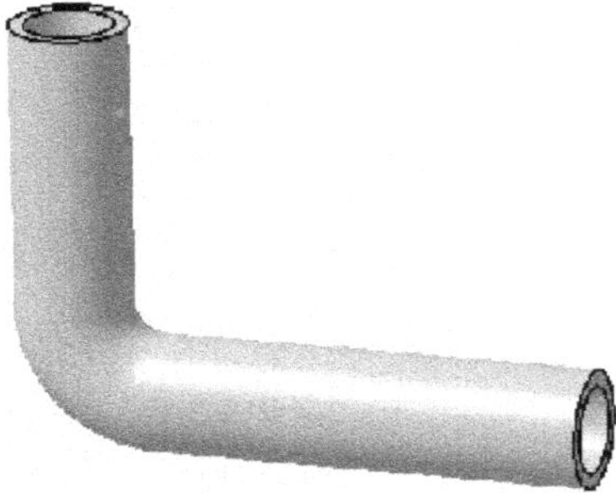

Figure 9–68

2. Open **Flange.CATPart**. The part displays as shown in Figure 9–69.

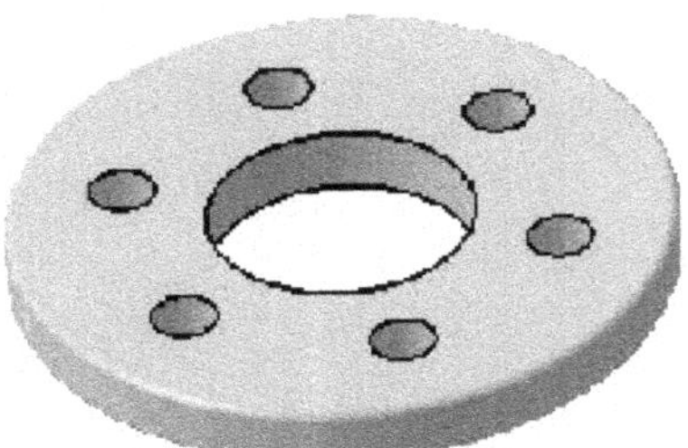

Figure 9–69

Task 3 - Copy the flange into the pipe file.

1. In the Flange part window, right-click on the **PartBody**, and select **Copy**.
2. Activate the Pipe part window and select **Edit>Paste Special**.
3. Select **As Result with Link**.
4. Click **OK**. The part displays as shown in Figure 9–70.

Figure 9–70

Task 4 - Position the flange on the end of the pipe with 3D constraints.

1. Press and hold <Ctrl> and select the top of the flange and the end of the pipe, as shown in Figure 9–71.

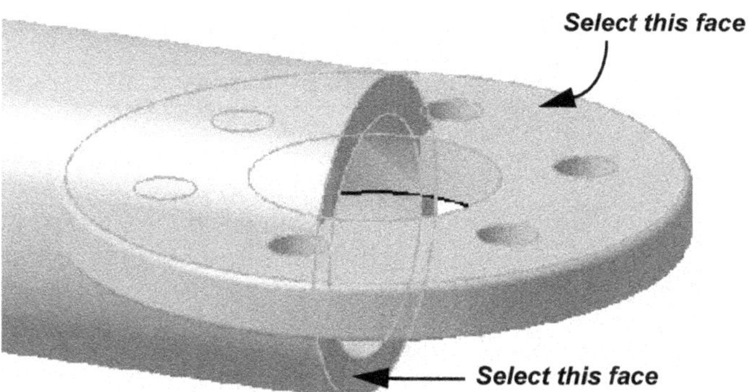

Figure 9–71

2. Click to create a constraint.

3. Select **Coincidence** in the list. The flange moves, as shown in Figure 9–72.

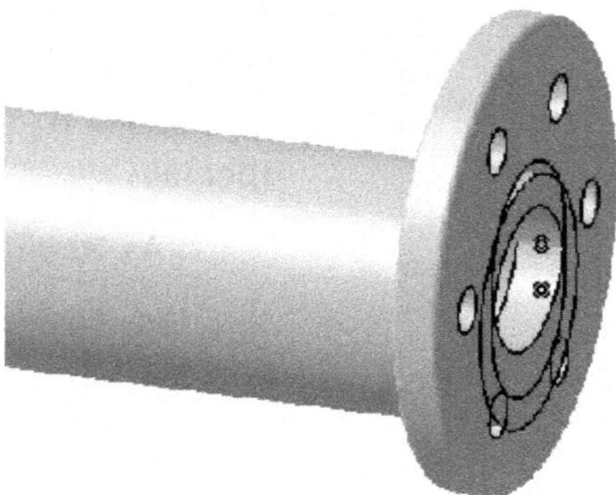

Figure 9–72

4. In the specification tree, expand the **Constraints** branch to display the Coincidence constraint, as shown in Figure 9–73.

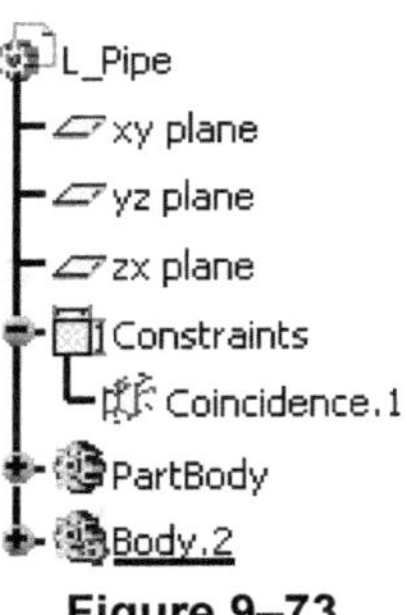

Figure 9–73

Task 5 - Modify a 3D constraint.

By default, the Coincidence constraint will set a normal vector for both faces to point in the same direction. To have the flange mate with the end of the pipe, you must modify the Coincidence constraint and set the normal directions to be opposite.

1. Double-click on the Coincidence constraint.
2. In the Definition dialog box, click **More**.
3. In the **Orientation** menu, select **Opposite**.

4. Click **OK**. The part updates, as shown in Figure 9–74.

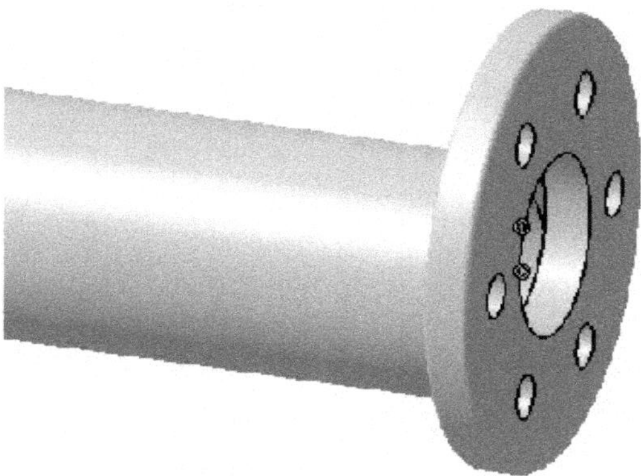

Figure 9–74

Task 6 - Align the axis of the flange with the axis of the pipe.

1. Click [icon] to create a new constraint.
2. Click the inner cylindrical surface of the flange. Note that the central axis of the flange is selected.
3. Click the inner cylindrical surface of the pipe to select the central axis.
4. CATIA automatically selects a Distance constraint. To change this to a Coincidence, right-click on the constraint and select **Coincidence**, as shown in Figure 9–75.

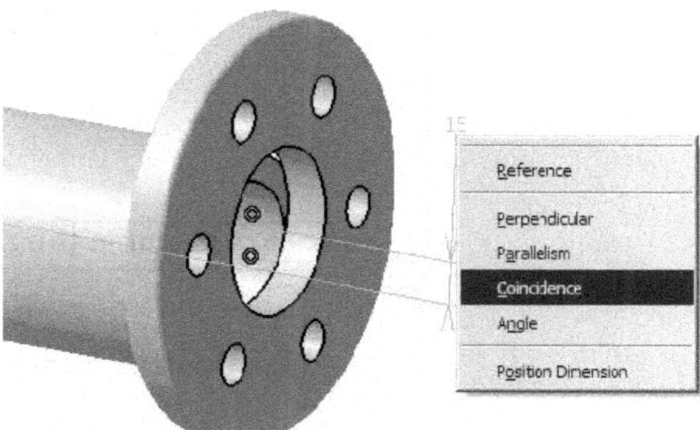

Figure 9–75

The flange moves to a coaxial position with the pipe, as shown in Figure 9–76.

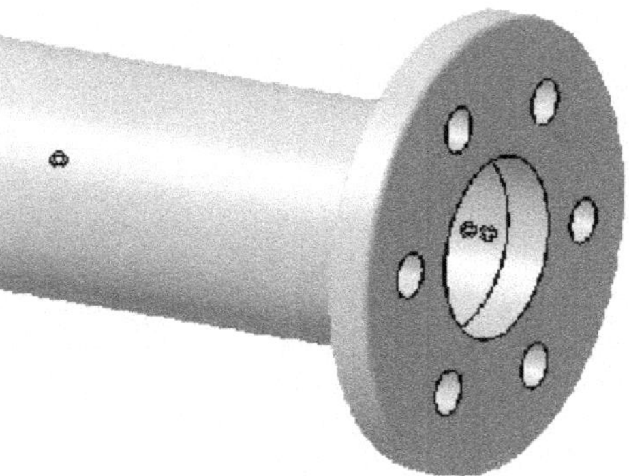

Figure 9–76

Task 7 - Paste and position another flange into the pipe file.

1. Repeat Tasks 2 to 6 to place another flange on the other end of the pipe. The required result is shown in Figure 9–77.

Figure 9–77

Task 8 - Assemble the flanges to the pipe.

1. In the Boolean Operations toolbar, click (Assemble).
2. Select **Body.2** and select the **PartBody**.
3. Click **OK**. The flange will be assembled into the pipe.

4. Repeat the **Assemble** operation to assemble **Body.3** into the **PartBody**. The part displays as shown in Figure 9–78.

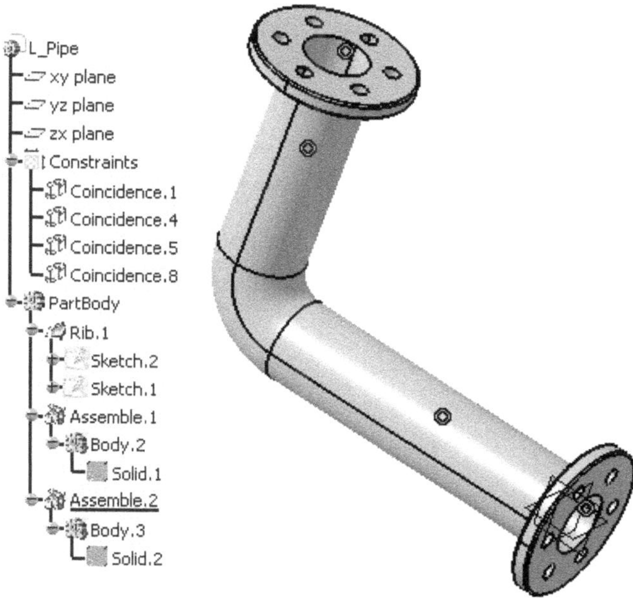

Figure 9–78

5. Use **Save All** to save both models and close all of the windows.

Practice 9d (Optional) Importing Bodies

Practice Objective

- Work with multiple bodies.

In this practice, you will use the geometry of existing parts to design an air vent for the passenger side dash of an automobile. The known geometry includes the curved surface of the dash, the general shape of the vent, and the size and configuration of the air flow slots, as shown in Figure 9–79.

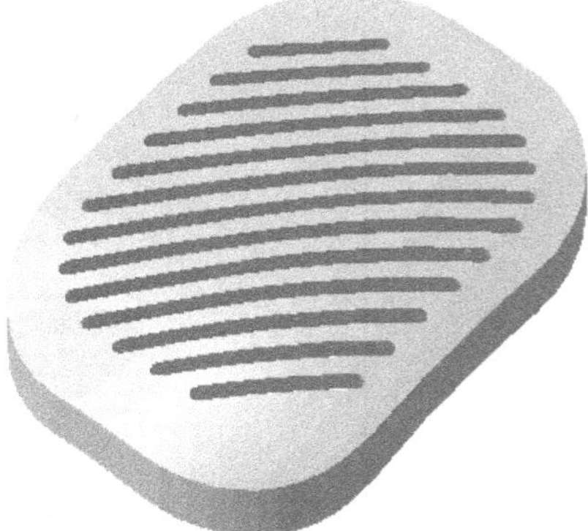

Figure 9–79

Task 1 - Open the part.

1. Select **File>Open** and simultaneously select **Dash.CATPart**, **Grill.CATPart**, and **VentShape.CATPart** from the *Boolean* directory using <Ctrl>.
2. Activate the window of each part to display the three part files as shown in Figure 9–80.

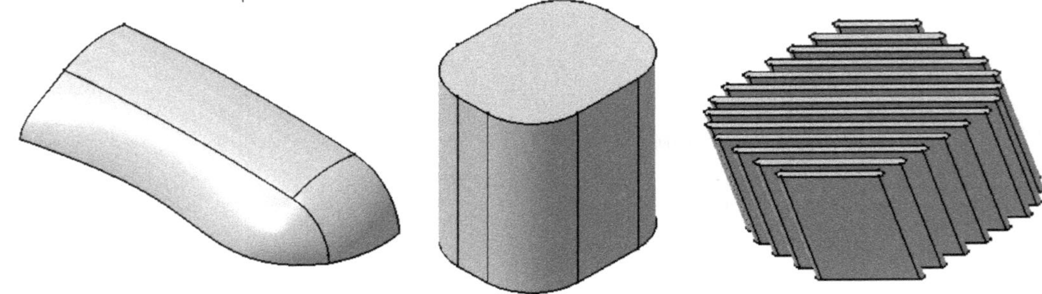

Figure 9–80

Task 2 - Create a new part file.

1. Activate the **Dash.CATPart** window.
2. Select **File>Save As**. Save it in the *Boolean* directory and enter **VentGrill** as the name.
3. In the Tools toolbar, click [icon]. The Axis System Definition dialog box opens as shown in Figure 9–81.

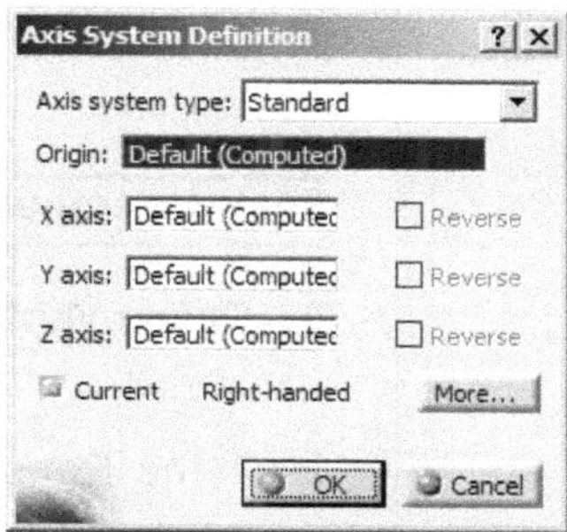

Figure 9–81

4. Click **OK** to accept the default axis definition settings.

Task 3 - Copy a body.

1. Activate the **VentShape.CATPart** window.
2. Copy the **VentShape** body shown in Figure 9–82.

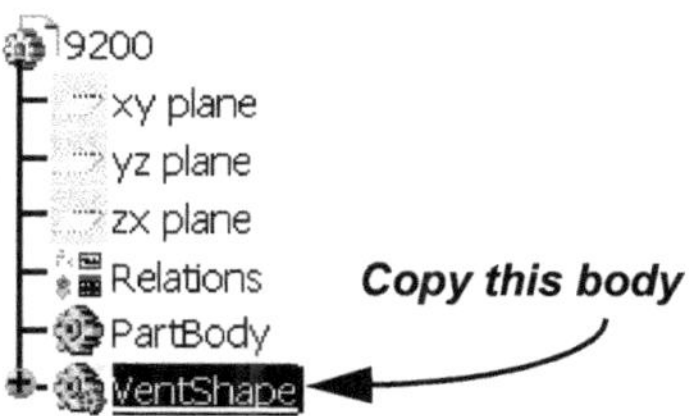

Figure 9–82

3. Activate **VentGrill.CATPart** and paste the **VentShape** body into the top-most level. The model displays as shown in Figure 9–83.

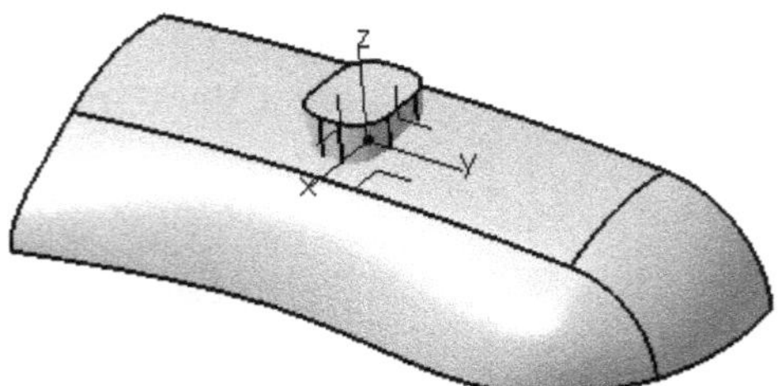

Figure 9–83

Task 4 - Translate a body.

1. Define **VentShape** body as the Work Object.
2. In the Transformations toolbar, click (Translation).
3. In the Question window, click **Yes**, as shown in Figure 9–84.

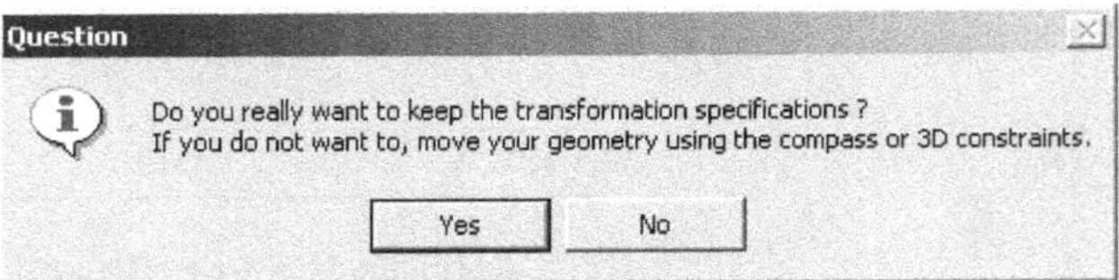

Figure 9–84

4. In the Translate Definition dialog box, expand the **Vector Definition** drop-down list and select **Coordinates**.
5. In the *X* field, enter **40** and in the *Y* field, enter **260**, as shown in Figure 9–85.

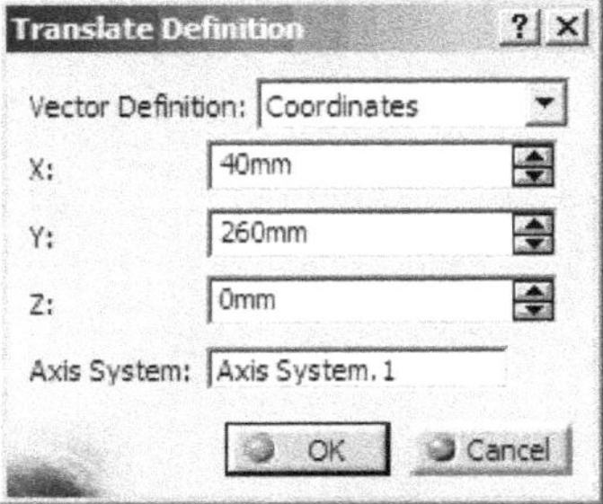

Figure 9–85

6. Click **OK**. The model displays as shown in Figure 9–86.

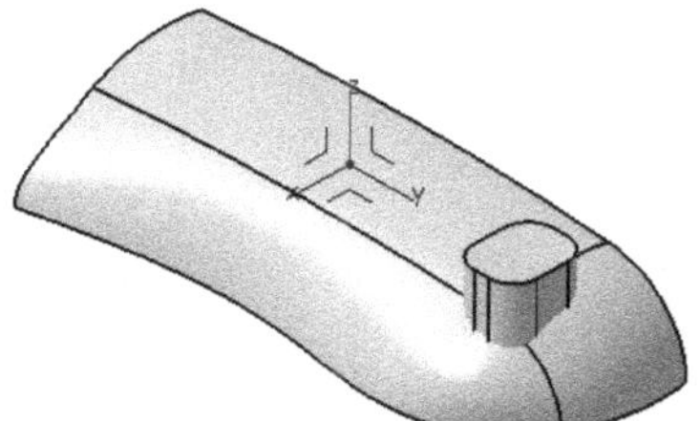

Figure 9–86

Task 5 - Manipulate geometry with another body.

1. In the Boolean Operations toolbar, expand the Boolean Operations flyout, click (Intersect). The Intersect dialog box opens.
2. In the *Intersect* field, select the **Dash** body. In the *To* field, **VentShape** should be selected automatically, and in the After field, **Translate.1** should be selected automatically as shown in Figure 9–87.

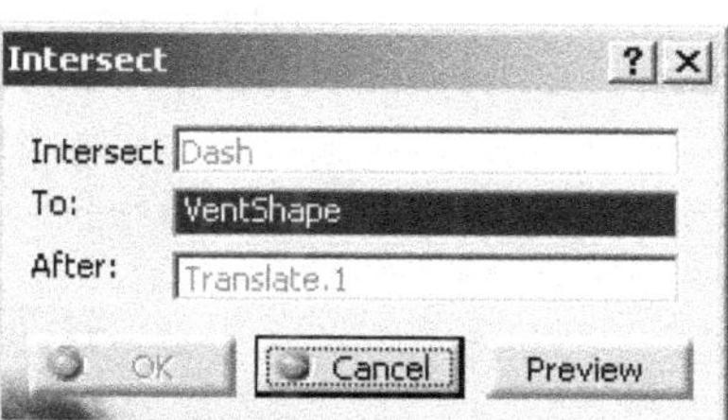

Figure 9–87

3. To complete the operation, click **OK**.
4. In the specification tree, hide **Group-DashGeom**. The model displays as shown in Figure 9–88.

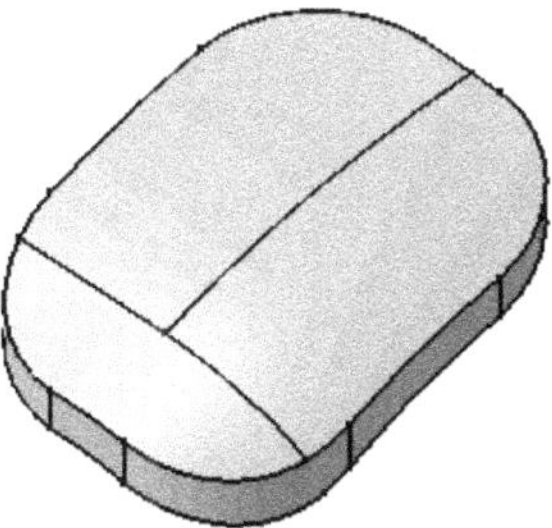

Figure 9–88

Task 6 - Create a Shell feature.

1. Click (Bottom View). The model displays as shown in Figure 9–89.

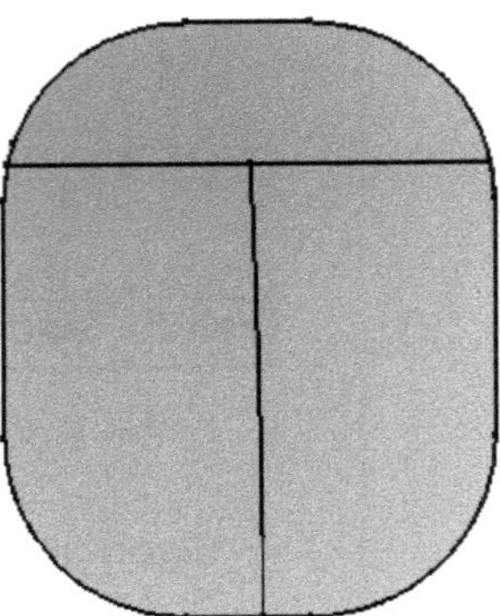

Figure 9–89

2. Click . The Shell Definition dialog box opens.
3. Select the face as shown in Figure 9–90. All of the tangent faces will be selected automatically.
4. In the Shell Definition dialog box, in the *Default outside thickness* field, enter **4**.

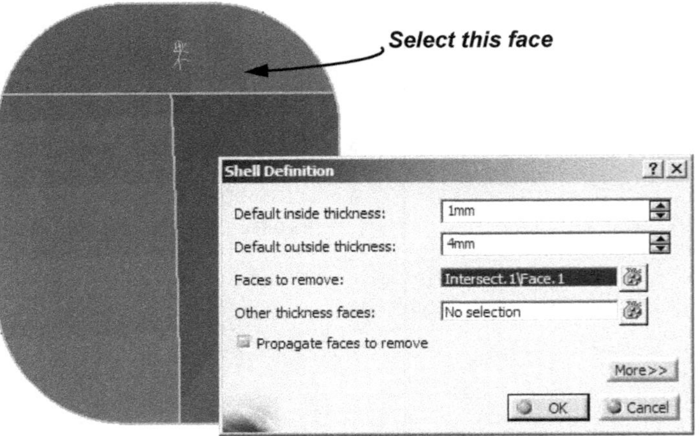

Figure 9–90

5. Click **OK**. The model displays as shown in Figure 9–91.

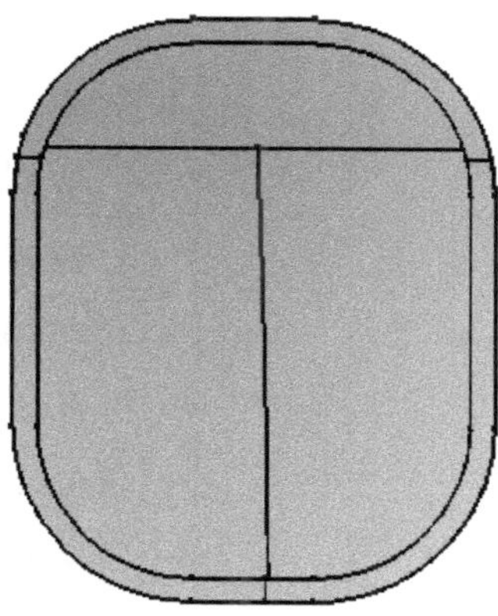

Figure 9–91

6. Click .

Task 7 - Import a body with link.

1. Activate the **Grill.CATPart** window and copy the **GrillSlots** Publication shown in Figure 9–92.

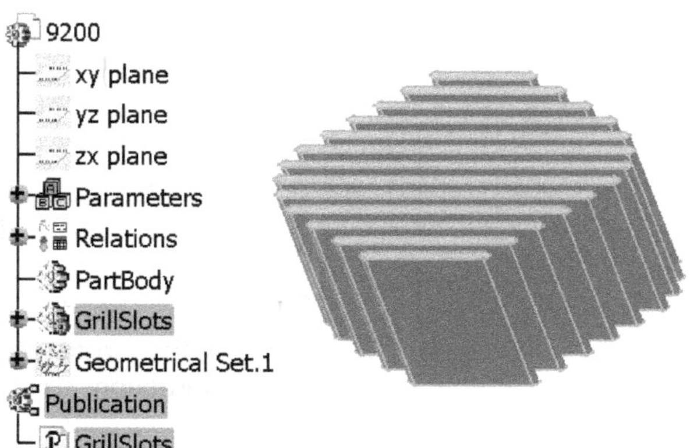

Figure 9–92

2. Activate the **VentGrill.CATPart** window.

3. Insert the **GrillSlots** body using **Paste Special**, as shown in Figure 9–93.

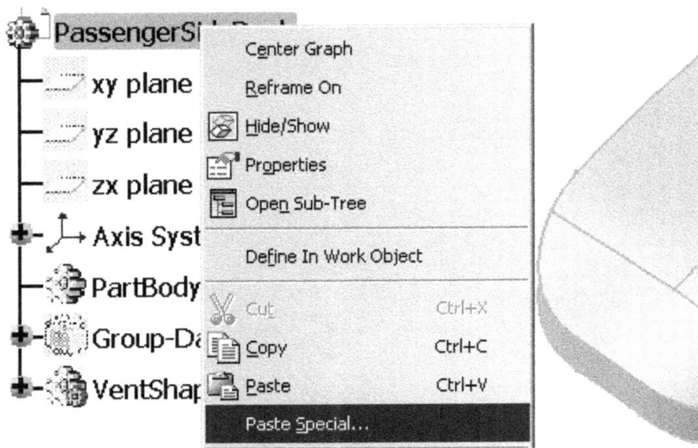

Figure 9–93

4. In the Paste Special dialog box, select **As Result With Link**, as shown in Figure 9–94, and click **OK**.

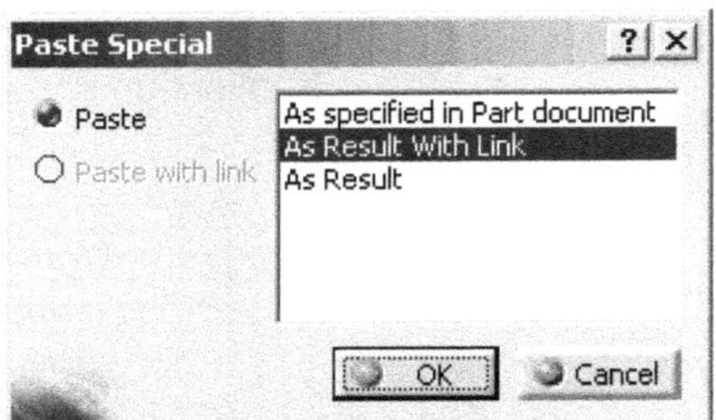

Figure 9–94

5. Click **Yes** in the Question dialog box.

6. Translate the **GrillSlots** body by **40** in the *X* direction and **260** in the *Y* direction, as shown in Figure 9–95.

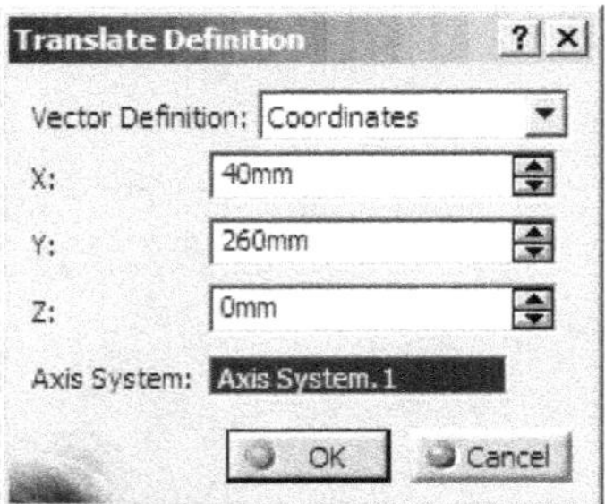

Figure 9–95

7. Click **OK**. The model displays as shown in Figure 9–96.

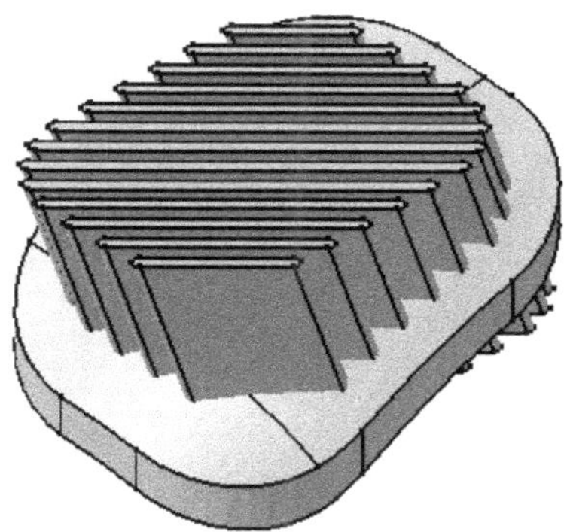

Figure 9–96

8. Define **VentShape** to be the Work Object.

9. Use the Boolean **Remove** operation to remove the **GrillSlots** body, as shown in Figure 9–97.

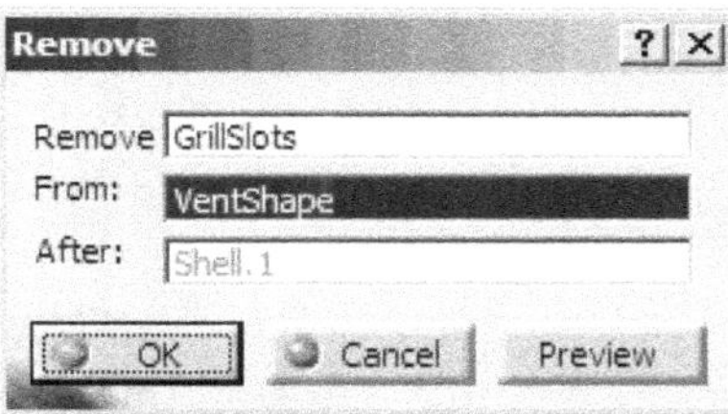

Figure 9–97

10. Click **Yes** in the Warning dialog box.

11. Click **OK**. The model displays as shown in Figure 9–98.

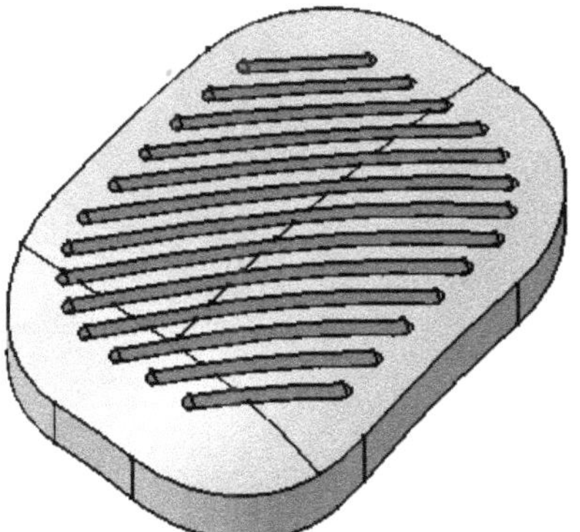

Figure 9–98

Design Considerations

This practice shows you the power of combining multi-body technique, boolean (**Intersect** and **Remove**), and feature-based (**Shell**) operations to achieve the required part geometry. Concurrent engineering is promoted using **Paste Special** when importing the **GrillSlots** body. An engineer might still need to make changes to the **GrillSlots** due to the results of some maximum air flow calculations. If changes are made to the **Grill** part model (i.e., slots become wider), then those changes are automatically propagated to the **VentGrill** part. This results in a fully defined, up-to-date part.

12. Save the part and close the file.

Chapter Review Questions

1. What are the advantages of using multiple bodies in a model?
   a. You can improve model organization by grouping features in separate bodies with respect to their function or position.
   b. You can create each body in a separate part file and then paste it into the finished model.
   c. A single part file can contain and display a variety of model states.
   d. All of the above.
2. You must always create an axis system for a body so that If you need to move a body, you can do so easily by changing the position of the axis system.
   a. True
   b. False
3. You can Deactivate individual part bodies to reduce update time and display a model in various states.
   a. True.
   b. False
4. Which of the following is NOT a Boolean Operation?
   a. Assemble
   b. Intersect
   c. Divide
   d. Remove
5. When using the **Add** boolean operator, the software combines the bodies. Therefore, any pad features add material and any pocket features remove material.
   a. True
   b. False

6. Which of the following are advantages of using Boolean operations?
    a. Increases flexibility in the combination of part bodies and their geometry.
    b. Provides an extension of parametric, feature-based modeling practices.
    c. Requires strategic planning on the position and structure of features in the model.
    d. Improves modeling and system performance when working with complex models that have a large number of features.
    e. All of the above.

Feature Failure Resolution

Feature failures can be caused by incorrect selections or settings. Failures can also occur when a part is changed and updated. For update failures, the problem might not be with the feature itself, but with another feature that it relies on. By becoming familiar with the software, you can efficiently resolve these failures.

Learning Objectives in this Chapter

- Learn how features fail during creation.
- Understand the methods used to resolve failures.
- Learn how models can fail on update.
- Understand the methods used to resolve the failures.

10.1 Failures During Feature Creation

Features can fail during creation because the incorrect options have been set or inappropriate elements have been selected. In such cases, you might have to modify the geometry of the feature. You must resolve the failure before you continue with the feature creation.

General Steps

Use the following general steps to resolve failures:

1. Read the failure messages.
2. Investigate the failure.
3. Modify the geometry.

Step 1 - Read the failure messages.

During feature creation, if the selected geometry is not suitable for the feature, a Feature Definition Error dialog box opens as shown in Figure 10–1.

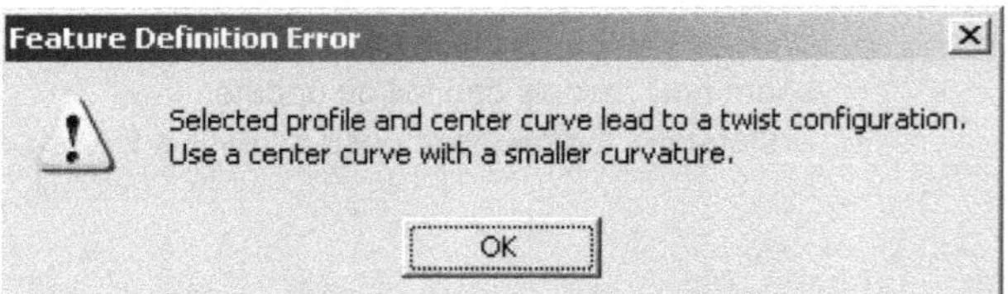

Figure 10–1

Step 2 - Investigate the failure.

When features fail, you can modify and correct them instead of deleting and reconstructing them. An example is shown in Figure 10–2. A Rib feature creation has failed because its profile overlaps during the solid creation. A message box opens describing the error.

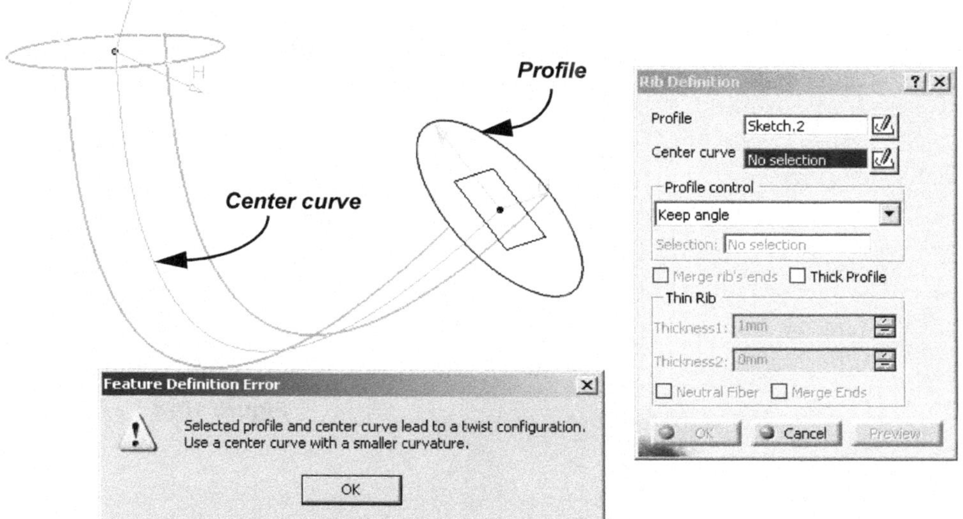

Figure 10–2

Step 3 - Modify the geometry.

Based on the error message, perform the required modifications to resolve the failure. This might require changes to the immediate feature or changes to the supporting geometry used to build the feature. If a sketch is the cause of the problem, use the **Sketch Analysis** tool to verify that any problems with the sketch have been resolved.

In Figure 10–2, the failure could be resolved by reducing the curvature of the center curve, or by reducing the diameter of the profile.

Figure 10-3 shows the center curve with a lower curvature.

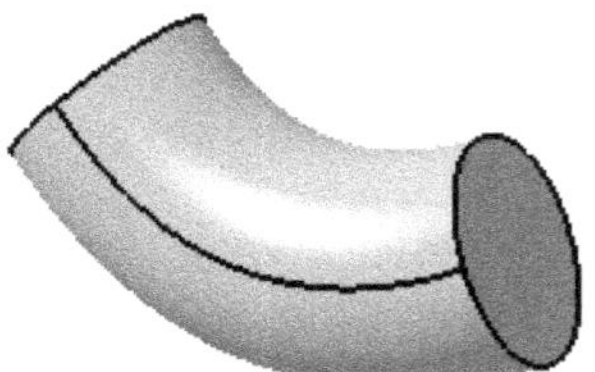

Figure 10–3

In Figure 10–4, the diameter of the profile is changed to a smaller size.

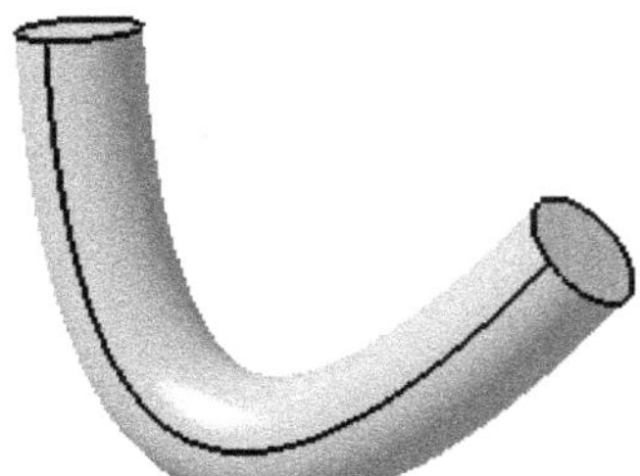

Figure 10–4

10.2 Resolution of Update Failures

When you update a model, failures can occur for a variety of reasons (i.e., geometry cannot be created due to invalid or missing references, dimensional changes result in geometry that cannot be calculated, etc.). The failed feature displays in the specification tree with a yellow warning sign. Until it is fixed, the children of the feature display with an update sign, as shown in Figure 10–5. When a failure occurs, you must resolve the failure before continuing.

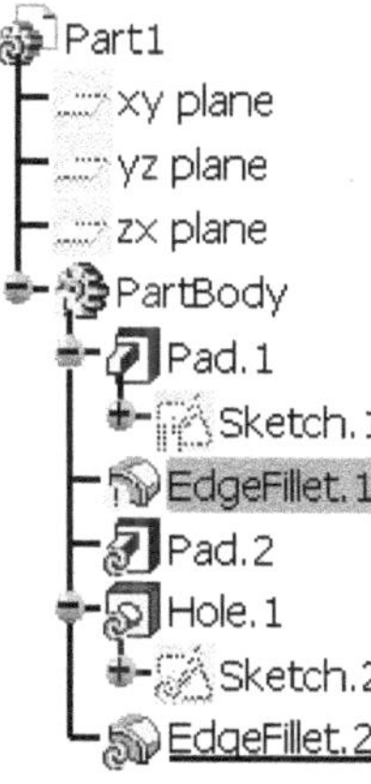

Figure 10–5

General Steps

Use the following general steps to resolve failures:

4. Investigate the failure.
5. (Optional) Undo the changes.
6. Resolve the failure.

Step 4 - Read the failure messages.

Investigate the geometry and try to understand what might have caused the failure. There are several reasons that might cause the Update failure, such as:

- Update Cycle
- Links
- Boundary Representations

Update Cycle

The creation order of the features can cause the feature failures. The features should reference each other in one direction. An example is shown in Figure 10–6. **Pad.1** is the base feature of the model and is created using the **Dimension** option. **Point.1** is created using the **On plane** option. This point is referenced by the top face of the **Pad.1** feature. **Point.2** and **Point.3** are created using **Point.1** as the reference point. **Spline** is created using these three reference points and **Plane.1** is created with the **Normal to curve** option. The Parents and Children relation for **Plane.1** is shown in Figure 10–7.

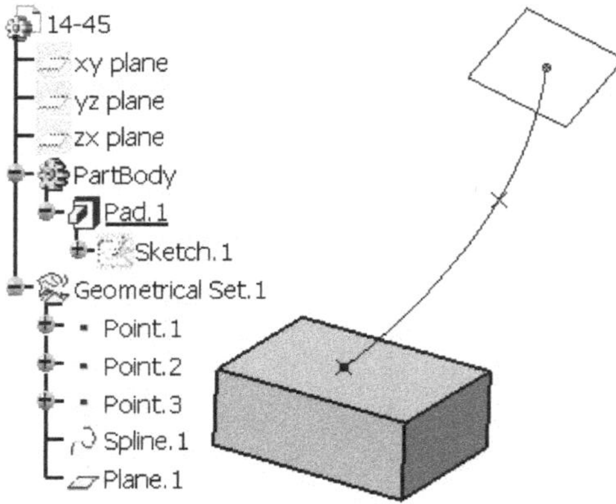

Figure 10–6

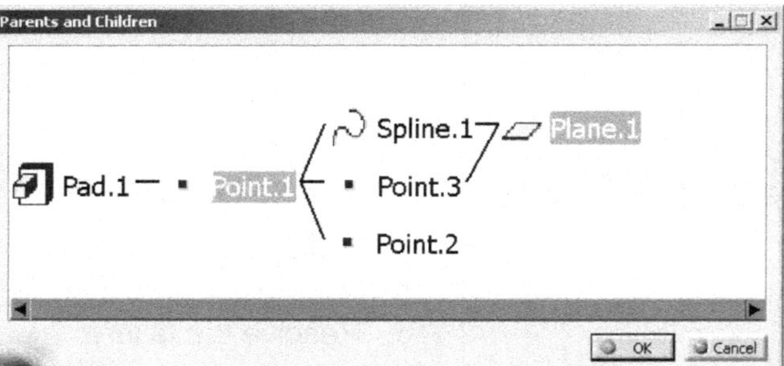

Figure 10–7

If you change the limit type of **Pad.1** from *Dimension* to **Up to surface**, as shown in Figure 10–8, using **Plane.1** as the limiting element, an Update cycle error occurs. This is because **Plane.1** is created using **Point.1**, and **Point.1** is created using the face of the Pad feature. This means that the two features are referencing each other in an endless cycle.

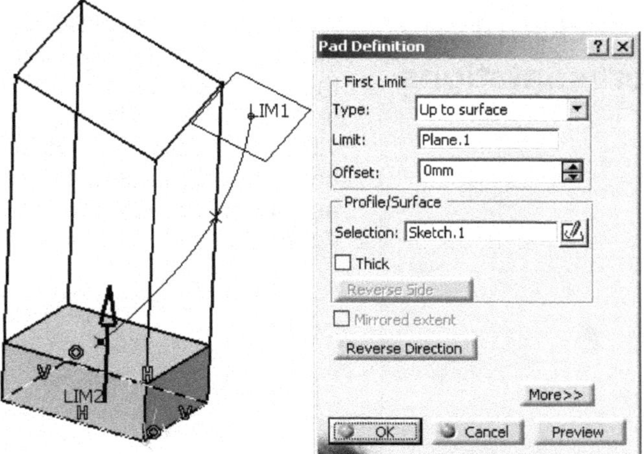

Figure 10–8

The Update cycle error is shown in Figure 10–9.

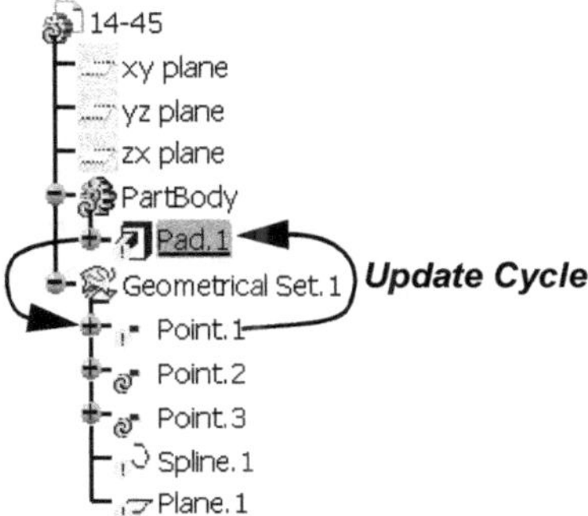

Figure 10–9

To resolve this error, check the Parent-Child relationship of the features. When you find the feature(s) causing the problem, you can modify or isolate them.

Links

Links are commonly established between parts. You can create links in the Assembly workbench using contextual design, or in the Part Design workbench using the **Paste Special** option. If the referencing part is moved or renamed, the link breaks and the feature fails. You can re-establish the links if they are required. If not, you can isolate and remove the links.

Boundary Representations

A boundary representation refers to the selection of any sub-element when defining references for a feature. This means that a feature in the specification tree is not directly referenced. Instead, an entity belonging to the feature, such as the edge or vertex of a solid, is selected. The EdgeFillet feature uses the boundary representation (selecting an edge of a solid). CATIA assigns a name for the selected sub-elements, as shown in Figure 10–10.

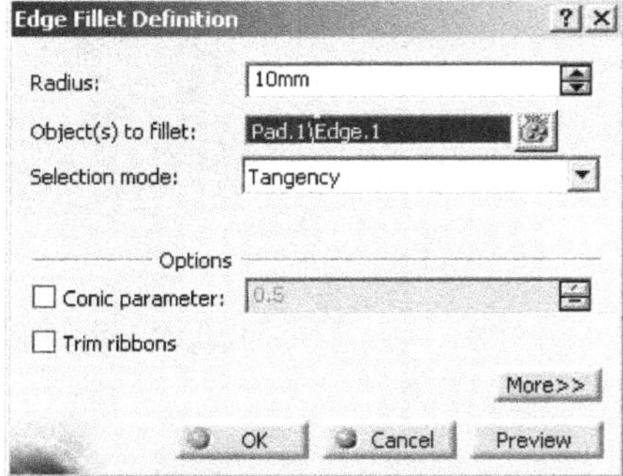

Figure 10–10

Even if a circular profile of a Pad feature is deleted and a new profile is created that is identical to the previous one, the feature fails. This is because CATIA generates a new name for the selected edge, and the EdgeFillet feature fails in finding the reference edge. It is recommended that you use the **Replace** command while changing the existing profile with a new one. If it is possible, try to avoid using the boundary representations. Instead, you must try to create the reference elements (Points, Lines, Planes, Splines, Extracts, etc.)

The Update Diagnosis dialog box provides information on why a feature has failed. Therefore, the content in the Update Diagnosis dialog box is dependent on the error that caused the problem. The items listed under the feature provide you with notes to help determine why the feature could not be created. Select one item at a time to review the information in the lower frame of the window. Items with yellow warning signs indicate errors. In general, warnings provide solutions, while errors explain why the current combination of references and values failed.

In Figure 10–11, the model was created using a Pad and an EdgeFillet feature. The profile for the Pad feature is circular. The edge of the Pad feature is used to create the EdgeFillet feature.

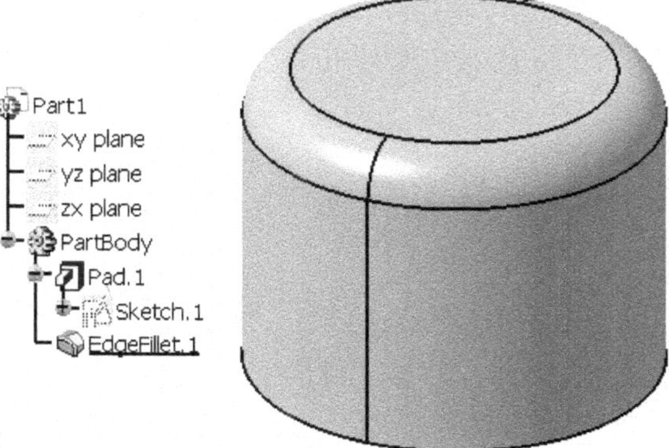

Figure 10–11

If the profile of the Pad feature is changed to a rectangular profile, the EdgeFillet feature fails, because it cannot find the referencing edge, as shown in Figure 10–12.

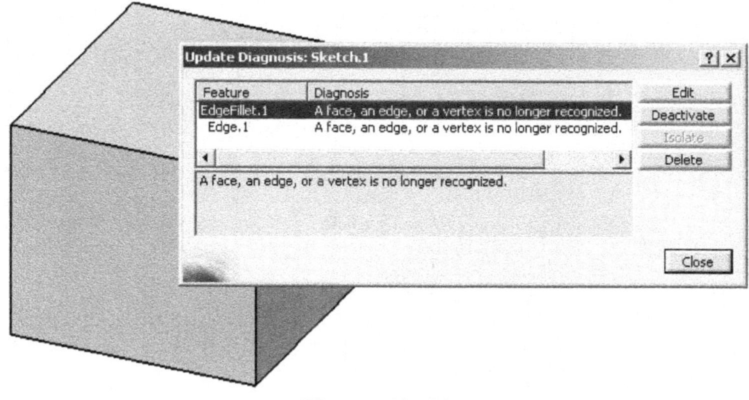

Figure 10–12

The options in the Update Diagnosis dialog box are described as follows:

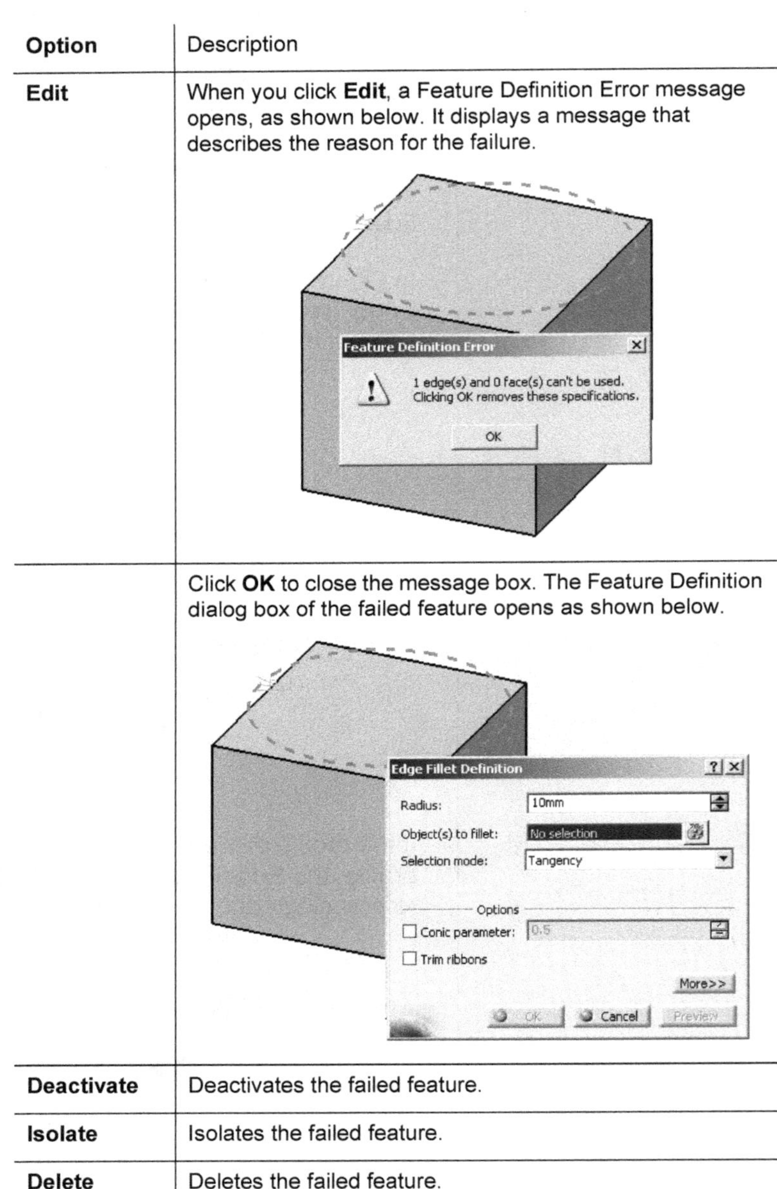

Option	Description
Edit	When you click **Edit**, a Feature Definition Error message opens, as shown below. It displays a message that describes the reason for the failure.
	Click **OK** to close the message box. The Feature Definition dialog box of the failed feature opens as shown below.
Deactivate	Deactivates the failed feature.
Isolate	Isolates the failed feature.
Delete	Deletes the failed feature.

Step 5 - (Optional) Undo the changes.

You can undo the changes that you have made to the model. The model then automatically updates and returns to its pre-failure state.

Step 6 - Resolve the failure.

Once you have investigated the reason for the failure, the next step is to resolve it. After investigation, perform the required modifications to resolve the failure. This might require making changes to the immediate feature, re-establishing links, isolating links, re-ordering the features, replacing the profiles, etc.

Practice 10a Update Cycle

Practice Objective

- Resolve Update Cycle failures.

In this practice, you will make the modifications to the model shown in Figure 10–13. The feature you are modifying will cause Update cycle failures that must be resolved using a different approach.

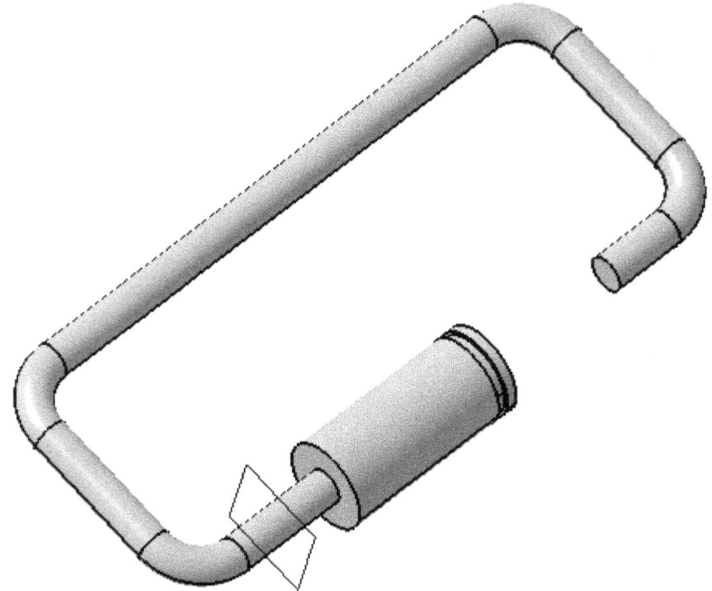

Figure 10–13

Task 1 - Open the part.

1. Open **SP-hook.CATPart**.
2. Investigate the model features.

Task 2 - Modify the Pad.1 feature.

1. Double-click on **Pad.1**.
2. In the Pad Definition dialog box that opens, expand the Type drop-down list and select **Up to Surface**. For the *Limit*, select **Plane.1**. The dialog box and model display as shown in Figure 10–14.

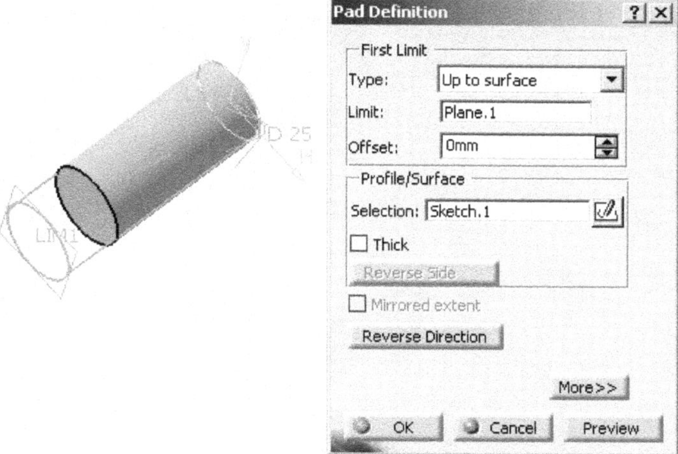

Figure 10–14

3. Click **OK**. The Feature Definition Error dialog box opens as shown in Figure 10–15.

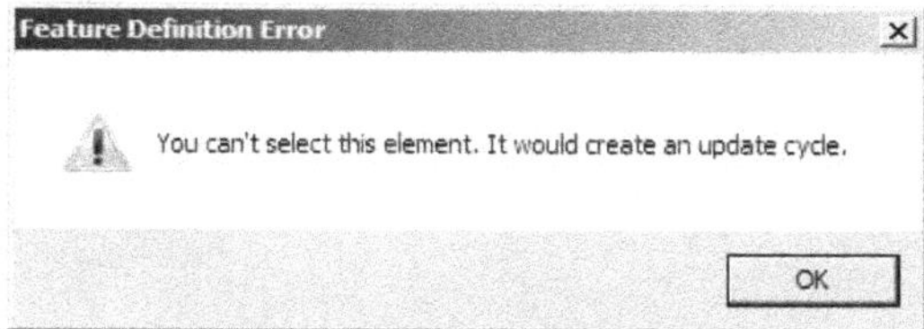

Figure 10–15

The error message indicates that there is an update cycle problem. There are two features that need to be investigated: **Pad.1** and **Plane.1**.

Task 3 - Investigate the error.

In this task, you will investigate the Parent-Child relation of **Plane.1**. This will help you to see what is causing the problem.

1. Click **OK** in the Feature Definition Error dialog box.
2. Click **Cancel** in the Pad Definition dialog box.
3. Right-click on **Plane.1** and select **Parents/Children**, as shown in Figure 10–16.

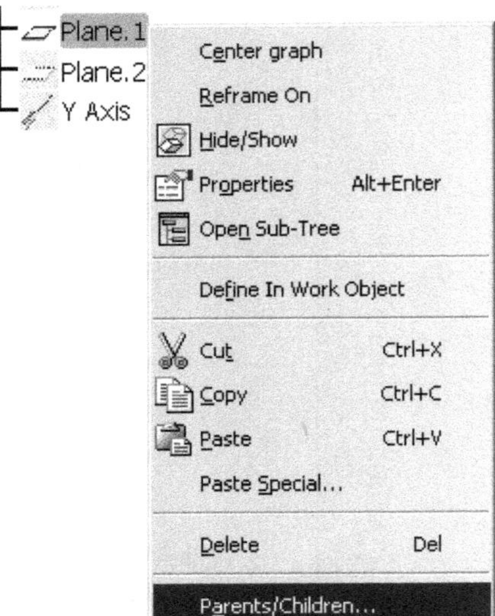

Figure 10–16

The Parents and Children dialog box opens as shown in Figure 10–17.

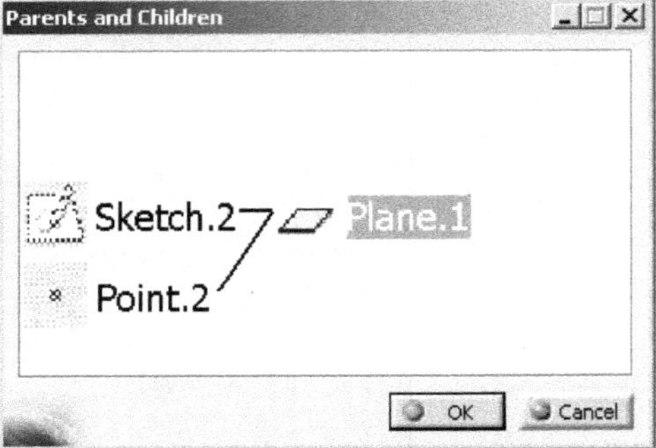

Figure 10–17

4. In the Parents and Children dialog box, double-click on **Sketch.2**, as shown in Figure 10–18.

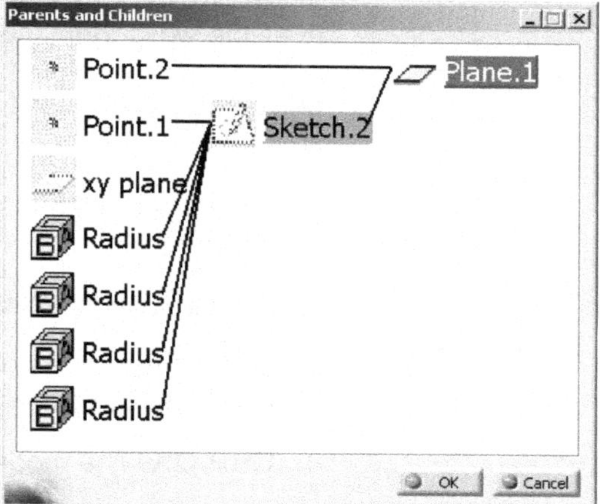

Figure 10–18

5. In the Parents and Children dialog box, double-click on **Point.1**, as shown in Figure 10–19.

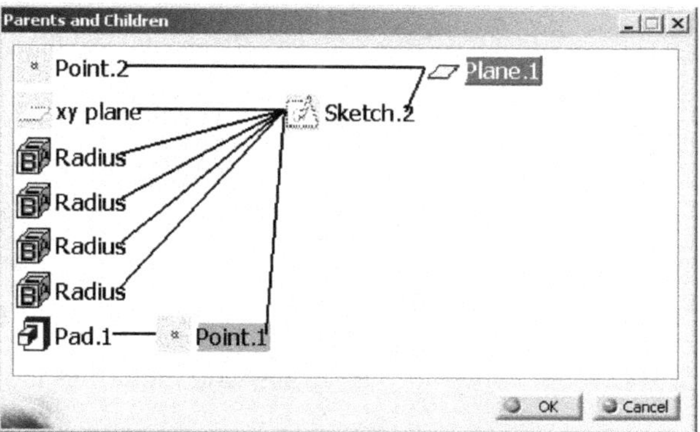

Figure 10–19

As you can see, **Pad.1** is one of the parents of **Plane.1**. The two features are referencing each other in an endless cycle. To resolve this issue, there are three options: extending the Pad by using a bigger dimension, creating a new reference plane which is not related to **Pad.1**, or isolating **Plane.1**.

6. Close the Parent and Children dialog box.

Task 4 - Resolve the update cycle.

In the previous Task, the error was investigated and three possible ways to fix the problem were indicated. In this practice only one of the solutions will be applied. However, if time permits, you can also try resolving the problem using the other solutions.

1. In the specification tree, right-click on **Plane.1** and select **Isolate**.
2. Double-click on **Pad.1**.
3. In the Type drop-down list, select **Up to Surface**. For the *Limit*, select **Plane.1**.
4. Click **OK**. The model updates as shown in Figure 10–20.

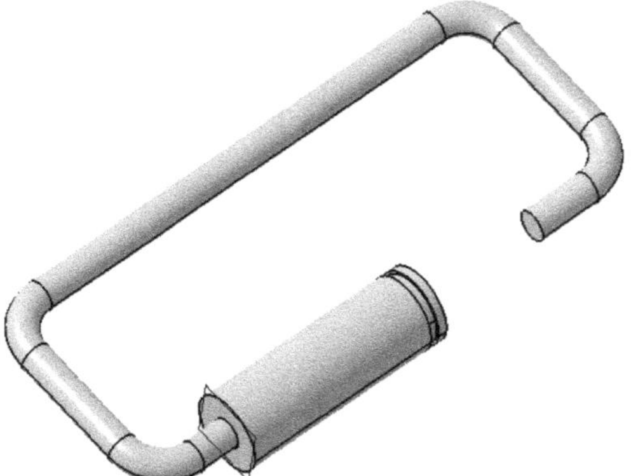

Figure 10–20

5. Save and close the file.

Practice 10b

Update Failures

Practice Objectives

- Re-establish links.
- Resolve update failures.
- Resolve feature failures.

In this practice, you will fix the links of a product and modify an existing model. The completed model displays as shown in Figure 10–21.

Figure 10–21

Task 1 - Open the assembly.

1. Open **Bike.CATProduct** from the *Bike* folder. The model and the Open dialog box display, as shown in Figure 10–22.

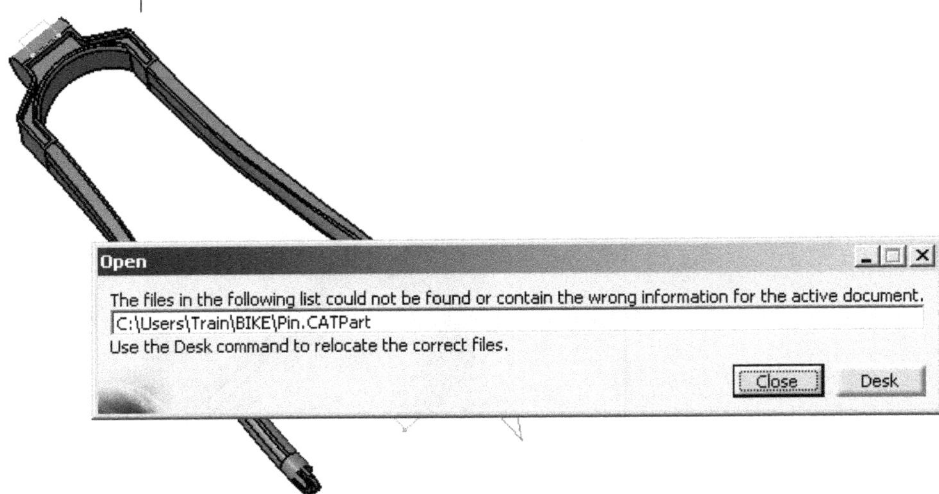
Open
The files in the following list could not be found or contain the wrong information for the active document.
C:\Users\Train\BIKE\Pin.CATPart
Use the Desk command to relocate the correct files.
Close
Desk

Figure 10–22

The Open dialog box indicates that the **Pin.CATPart** file is not found. The model displays in red, indicating that it needs to be updated. However, the links need to be fixed first.

Task 2 - Fix the broken link.

In this task, you will re-establish the broken link.

1. Click **Desk**. The Desk window opens as shown in Figure 10–23.

Bike.CATProduct
Pin.CATPart
Seatstay_swingarm.CATPart

Figure 10–23

You must re-locate the name of the model that displayed in red.

2. Right-click on **Pin.CATPart**, and select **Find**, as shown in Figure 10–24.

Figure 10–24

3. The File Selection dialog box opens.

4. Browse to the *Bike* folder.

5. Highlight **Pin-2.CATPart** as shown in Figure 10–25, and click **Open**.

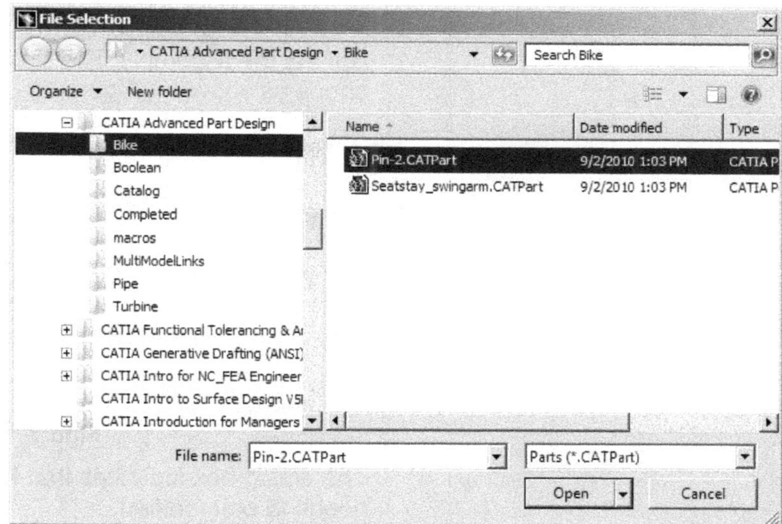

Figure 10–25

6. Close the Desk window.

Task 3 - Resolve the update failure.

In this task, you will resolve the update failure.

1. The **Pin** displays as shown in Figure 10–26.

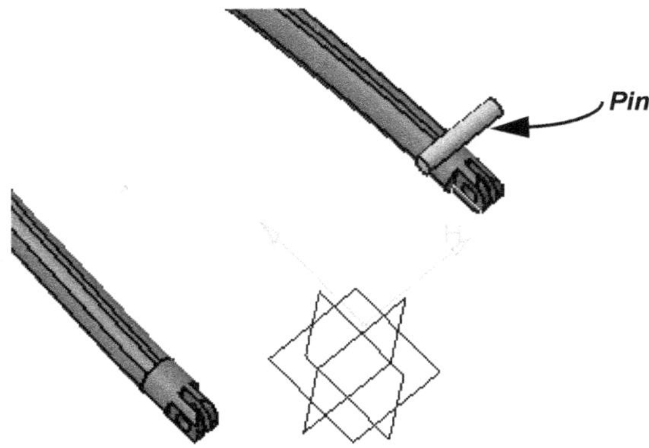
Pin

Figure 10–26

2. Update the assembly. The Update Diagnosis: Bike dialog box opens as shown in Figure 10–27.

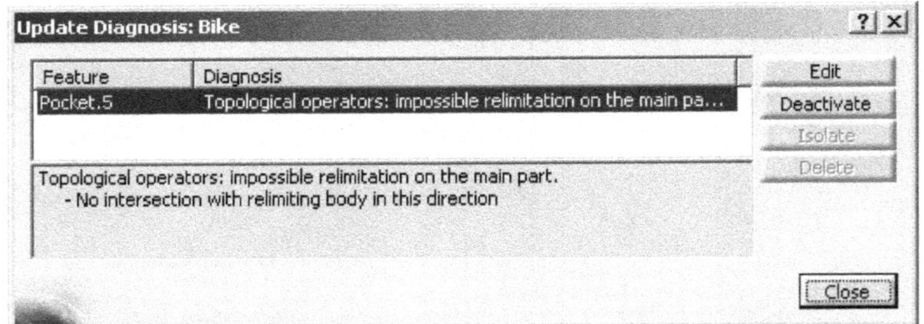
Update Diagnosis: Bike
Feature
Diagnosis
Pocket.5
Topological operators: impossible relimitation on the main pa...
Edit
Deactivate
Isolate
Delete
Topological operators: impossible relimitation on the main part.
- No intersection with relimiting body in this direction
Close

Figure 10–27

The dialog box indicates that **Pocket.5** is the feature that needs to be modified.

3. Click **Edit**. The Feature Definition Error dialog box opens as shown in Figure 10–28.

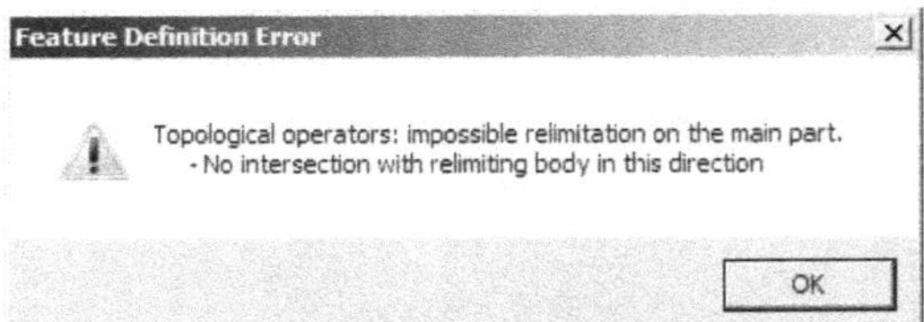
Feature Definition Error
Topological operators: impossible relimitation on the main part.
- No intersection with relimiting body in this direction
OK

Figure 10–28

4. Click **OK** to close the dialog box. The Pocket Definition dialog box opens as shown in Figure 10–29.

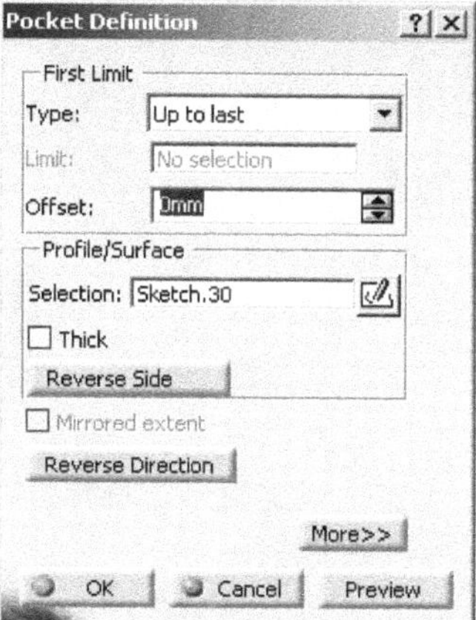

Figure 10–29

5. Click [icon] to enter the Sketcher workbench. The profile is the projection of the **Pin** section. As you can see in Figure 10–30, it is not intersecting the part.

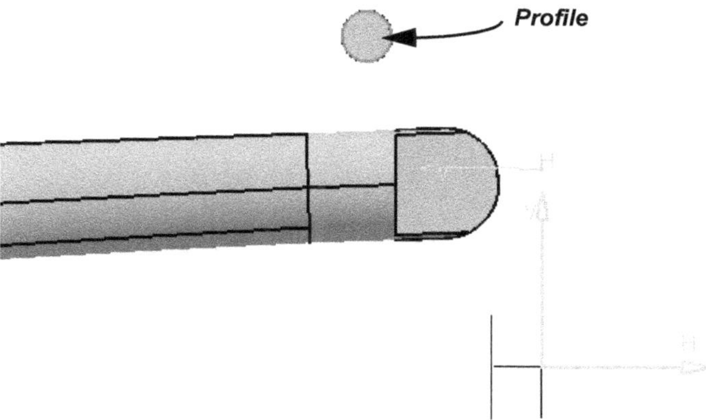

Figure 10–30

6. Exit the Sketcher workbench and close all of the dialog boxes.

7. Activate the assembly.

8. Create a Coincidence constraint between the **Pin** and the **Seatstay Swingarm** components, as shown in Figure 10–31.

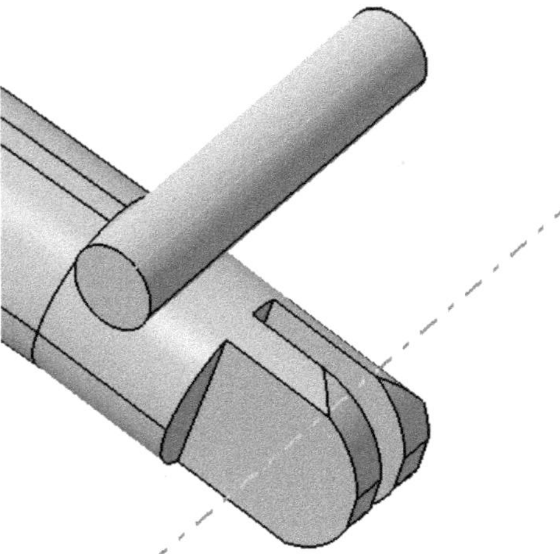

Figure 10–31

9. Update the assembly. The update failure is resolved.

10. Hide the **Pin** component. The model displays as shown in Figure 10–32.

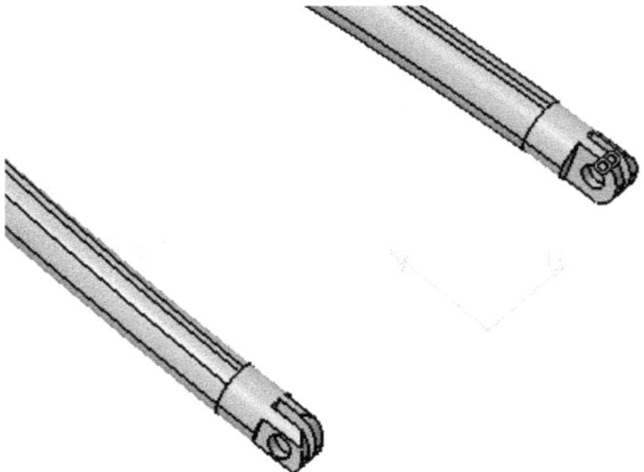

Figure 10–32

Task 4 - Create a Pocket.

In this task, you will create a Pocket.

1. Activate the PartBody of the **Seatstay Swingarm** component.

2. Click (Pocket) and select the sketch named **Pocket**. The Feature Definition Error dialog box opens as shown in Figure 10–33.

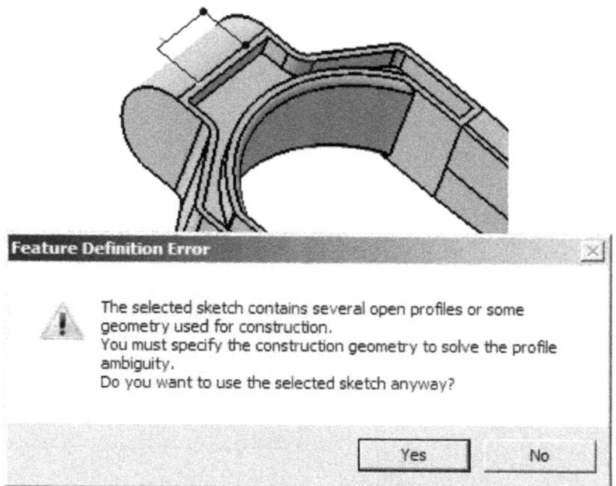

Figure 10–33

The error message indicates that there is a problem with the sketch.

3. In the Feature Definition Error dialog box, click **Yes**.

4. Click to enter the Sketcher workbench in the Pocket Definition dialog box. The profile displays as shown in Figure 10–34.

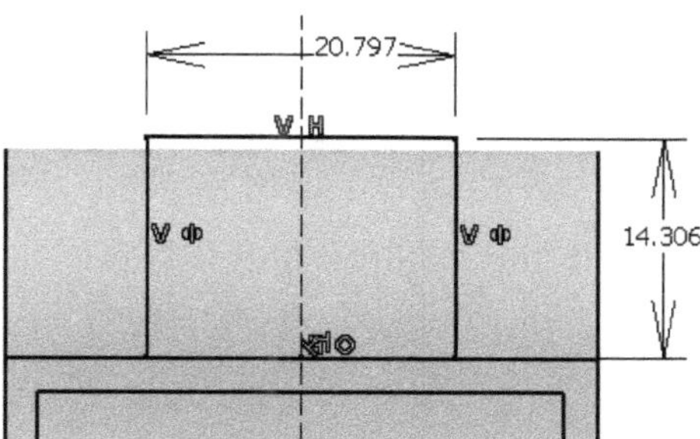

Figure 10–34

5. Click (Sketch Analysis). The Sketch Analysis dialog box opens as shown in Figure 10–35.

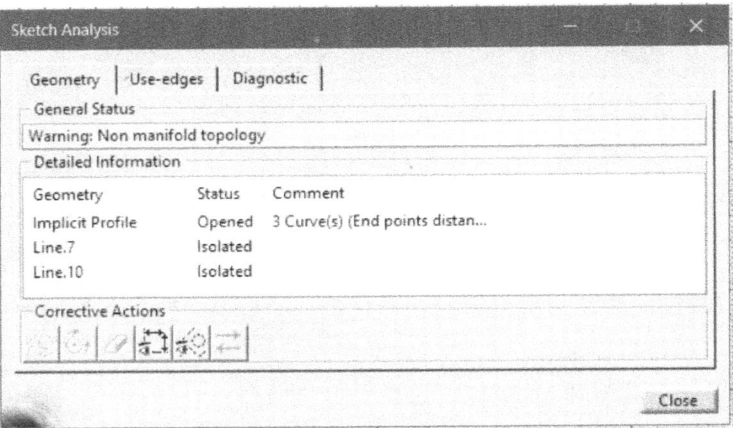

Figure 10–35

There are two lines at the same location that cause an open profile. One of the lines needs to be deleted.

6. Delete **Line.10**. The Sketch Analysis dialog box is updated, as shown in Figure 10–36. Now there are no problems with the profile.

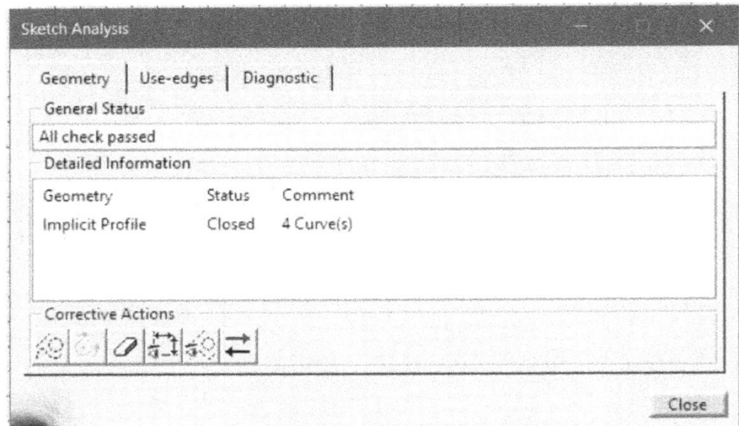

Figure 10–36

7. Close the Sketch Analysis dialog box.

8. Exit the Sketcher workbench.

9. *Create a Pocket with the following selection:*

   - *Type:* **Dimension**
   - *Depth:* **8 mm**

   The model displays as shown in Figure 10–37.

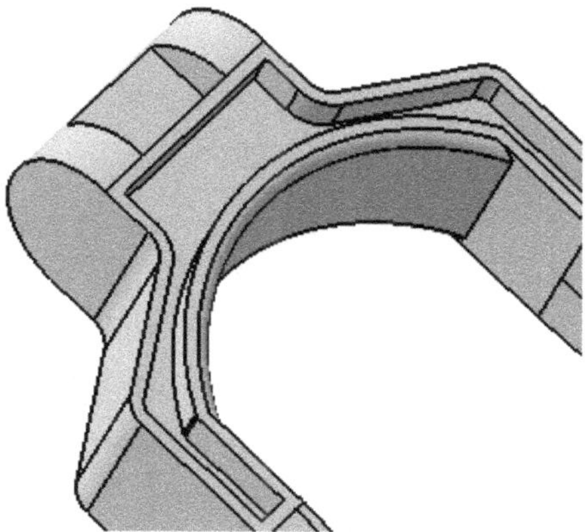

Figure 10–37

10. Save and close the files.

Chapter Review Questions

1. In general to resolve a failure, you:
    a. Read the failure message.
    b. Investigate the failure.
    c. Modify the geometry.
    d. All of the above.
2. If a sketch causes a failure, you can use the _______ to verify that any problems have been resolved.
    a. **Sketch Diagnosis** tool.
    b. **Sketch Resolve** tool.
    c. **Sketch Analysis** tool.
    d. None of the above.
3. Models can fail during creation or after modifications have been made.
    a. True
    b. False
4. The feature creation order is not relevant to feature failures.
    a. True
    b. False

5. What does the yellow icon next to the EdgeFillet.1 (shown in Figure 10–38) indicate?

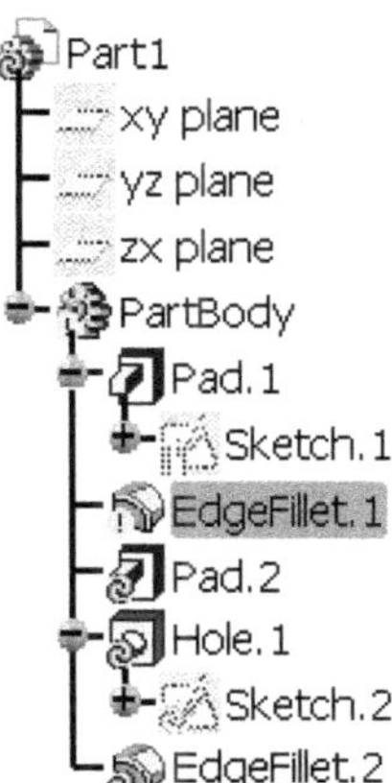

Figure 10–38

   a. The feature needs to be updated.
   b. The feature has failed.
   c. The feature has a failed child.
   d. None of the above.

Additional Features

When you import files from a different CAD system using neutral file formats (STP or IGES), feature history is not available for the model. The features introduced in this chapter can be used to modify models that do not have history and complex CATIA models.

Learning Objectives in this Chapter

- Learn how to use the Thickness feature to add material to the faces of a model.
- Remove faces from CATParts or imported data.
- Replace a model face with another face or surface.

11.1 Thickness

The Thickness feature adds material to the specified face(s) of a model. When the face(s) are thickened, the Thickness feature is added to the specification tree. In Figure 11–1, the four faces of the Pad are thickened using the Thickness feature.

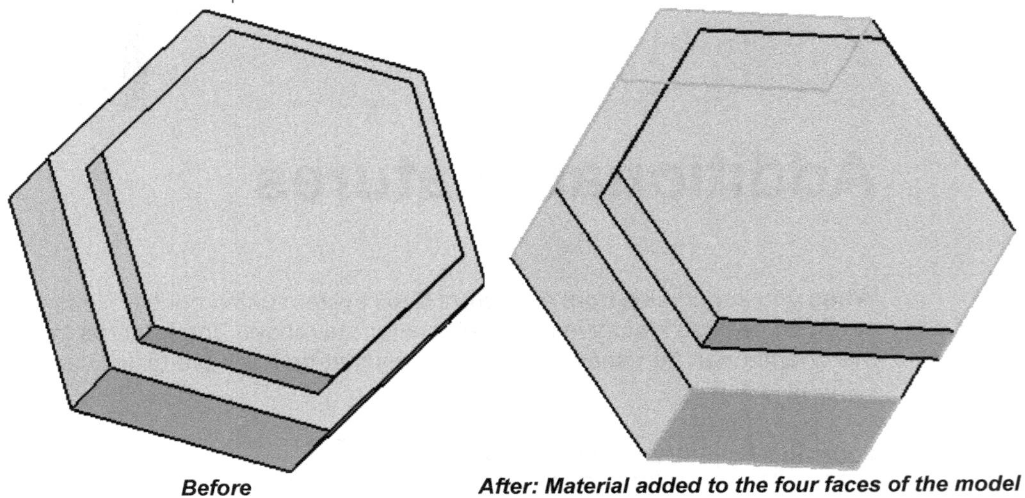

Before

After: Material added to the four faces of the model

Figure 11–1

General Steps

Use the following general steps to add material on the face(s):

1. Open the Thickness Definition dialog box.
2. Select the face(s) to which to add material.
3. Complete the feature.

Step 1 - Open the Thickness Definition dialog box.

Click (Thickness). The Thickness Definition dialog box opens as shown in Figure 11–2.

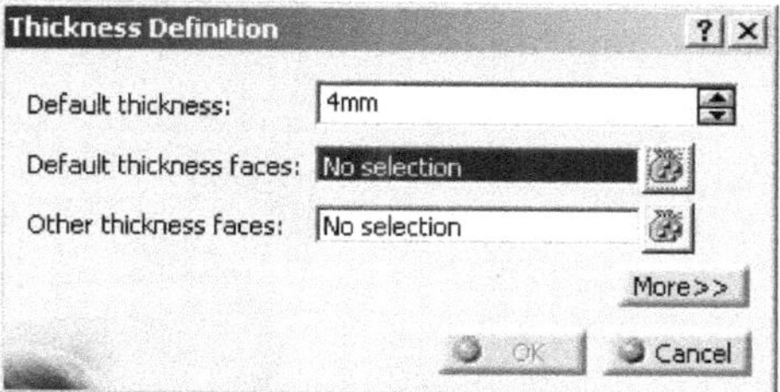

Figure 11–2

Step 2 - Select the face(s) to which to add material.

When you select a face, the faces that are tangent to the selected face are also selected automatically. It is also possible to apply different thickness values to different faces. To do so, select the *Other thickness faces* field and select the faces of the model. The values for each selected face display on the model, as shown in Figure 11–3.

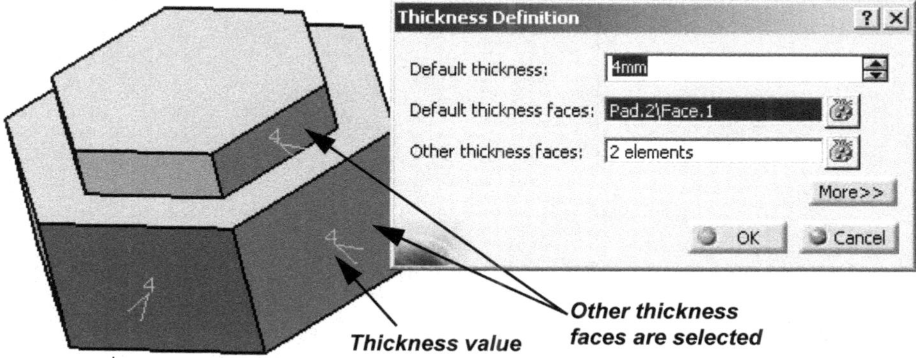

Figure 11–3

You can change the values by double-clicking on the thickness value that displays on the model and entering the required dimension in the Parameter Definition dialog box that opens, as shown in Figure 11–4.

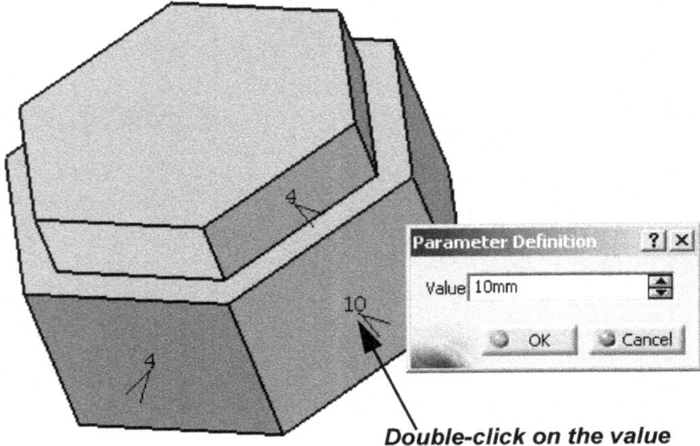

Figure 11–4

Step 3 - Complete the feature.

Click **OK** to complete the feature. The Thickness feature displays in the specification tree.

11.2 Face Removal

This feature removes the selected faces of a model, whether it is a CATPart or imported data. In Figure 11–5, the interior face of the model is removed using the Remove Face feature.

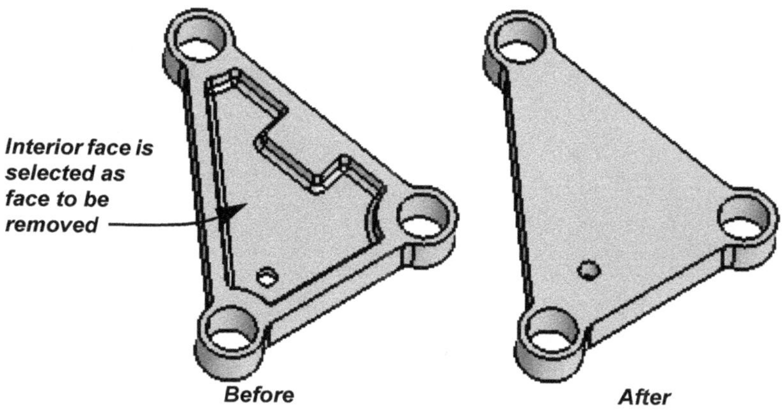

Figure 11–5

General Steps

Use the following general steps to remove face(s):

1. Open the Remove Face Definiton dialog box.
2. Select the face(s) to remove.
3. Complete the feature.

Step 1 - Open the Remove Face Definiton dialog box.

Click (Remove Face). The Remove Face Definition dialog box opens as shown in Figure 11–6.

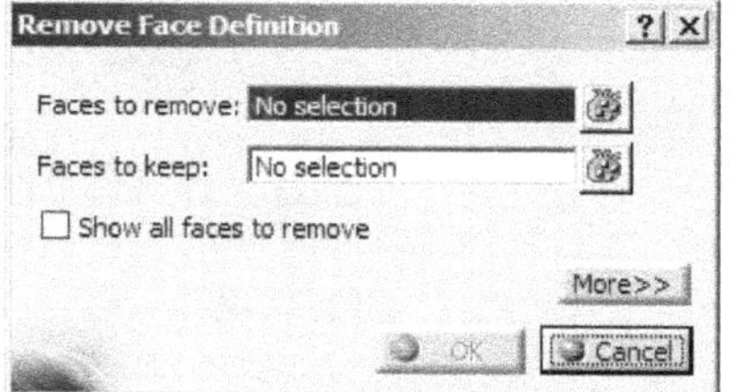

Figure 11–6

Step 2 - Select the face(s) to remove.

Select the face(s) to remove and/or keep on the model. To enable the selection to be cleared, you can right-click in the *Faces to remove* field and select **Clear selection**, as shown in Figure 11–7. To highlight all of the faces that are tangent to the selection, select **Tangency Propagation**. To preview the selection, in the Remove Face Definition dialog box, select the **Show all faces to remove** option.

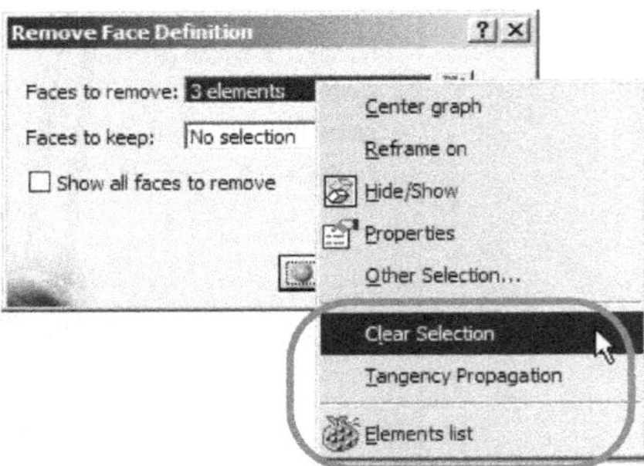

Figure 11–7

When you have selected than one face, the *Faces to Remove* field changes to list the number of faces selected, rather than listing the individual faces.

To display a list of the individual elements that have been selected, right-click and select **Elements list**, which opens the dialog box shown in Figure 11–8. You can also use this dialog box to remove or replace any of the selected elements.

Figure 11–8

Step 3 - Complete the feature.

Click **OK** to complete the feature. The Remove Face feature displays in the specification tree.

11.3 Face Replacement

You can use the Replace Face feature to replace a face of the model with a different surface or face of the model. When you replace a face, the Replace Face feature is added to the specification tree. In Figure 11–9, the face of the model is replaced with a surface.

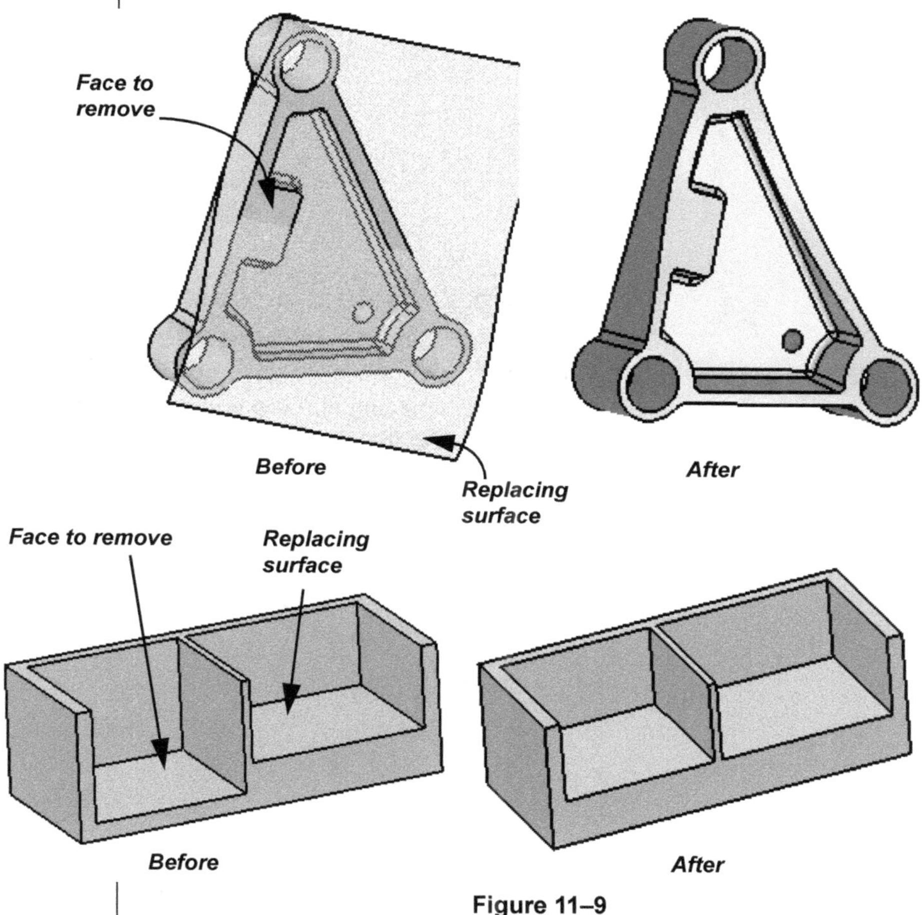

Figure 11–9

General Steps

Use the following general steps to replace the face(s):

1. Open the Replace Face Definiton dialog box.
2. Select a replacing surface and a face to remove.
3. Complete the feature.

Step 1 - Open the Replace Face Definiton dialog box.

Click (Replace Face). The Replace Face Definition dialog box opens as shown in Figure 11–10.

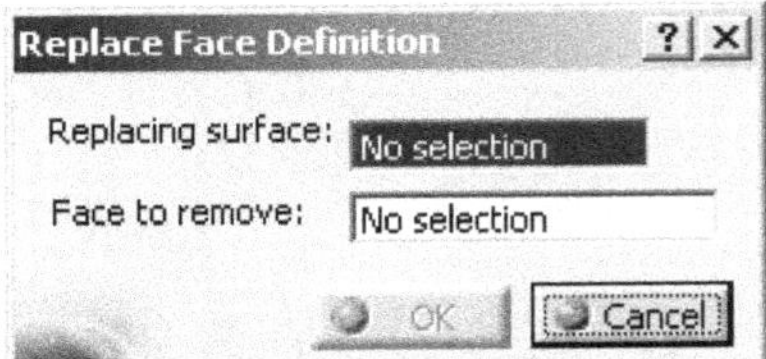

Figure 11–10

Step 2 - Select a replacing surface and a face to remove.

Select a replacing surface and a face to remove. Verify that the material direction is toward the model, as shown in Figure 11–11.

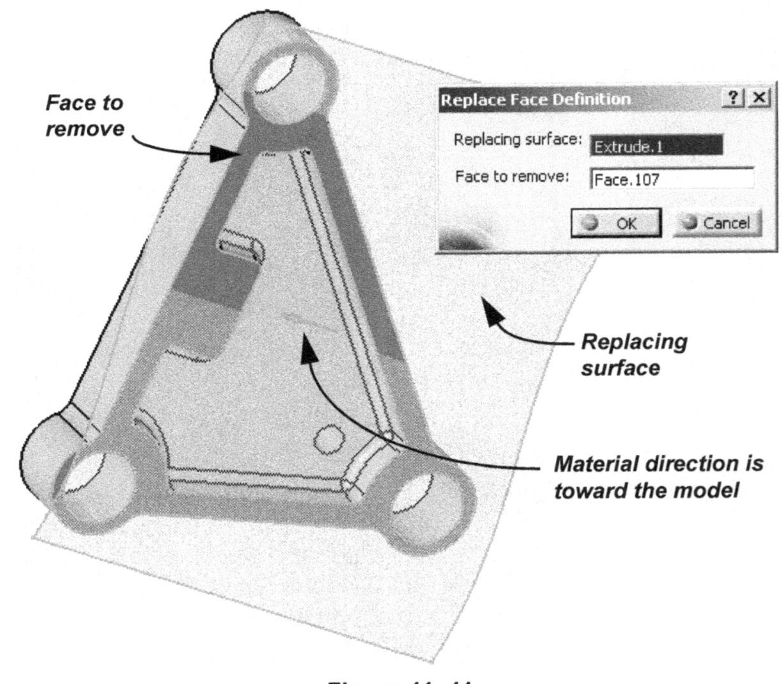

Figure 11–11

Only a planar face of the model can be used as the Replacing surface.

Step 3 - Complete the feature.

Click **OK** to complete the feature. The Replace Face feature displays in the specification tree.

Practice 11a Thickness

Practice Objective

- Use the Thickness feature.

In this practice, you will create a molded model for a finished part. You will add material to the faces of the model using the Thickness feature. The completed model displays as shown in Figure 11–12.

Figure 11–12

Task 1 - Open the part.

1. Open **Link10205.CATPart**. The model displays as shown in Figure 11–13.

Figure 11–13

Task 2 - Copy and paste the PartBody.

In this task, you will copy the **Completed Model** PartBody and paste it under a body using the **Paste Special** option. This way, it is possible to create a link between the original and the molded part. For example, if the completed model is modified, the molded part will be updated automatically according to the changes.

1. Copy the **Completed Model** PartBody.
2. In the specification tree, right-click on the **Link_10205** branch and select **Paste Special**.
3. Select the **As Result With Link** option.
4. Click **OK**.
5. Rename the Body as **Molded Model**, as shown in Figure 11–14.

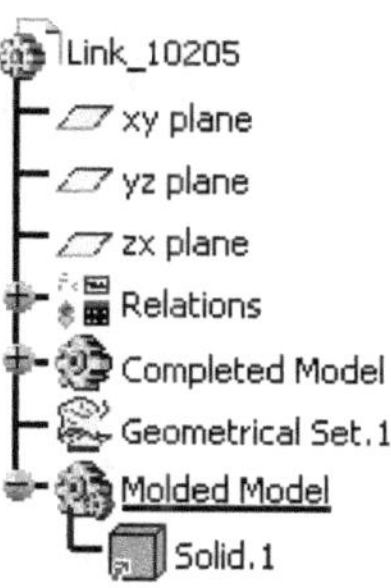

Figure 11–14

6. Hide the **Completed Model** PartBody.

Task 3 - Create Thickness.

In this task, you will add additional material on the faces that will be machined.

1. In the Dress-Up Feature toolbar, click (Thickness). The Thickness Definition dialog box opens as shown in Figure 11–15.

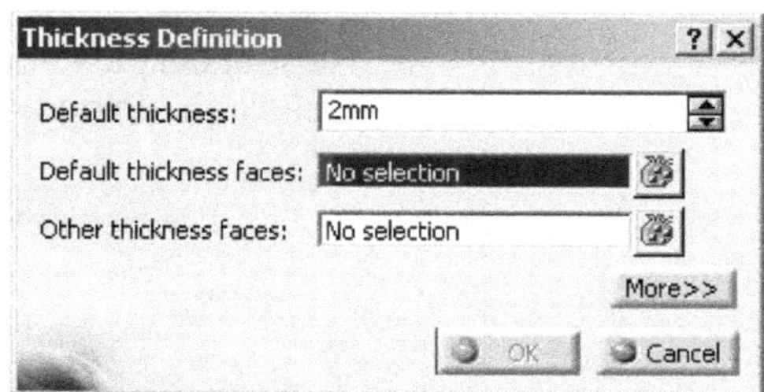

Figure 11–15

2. Select the top and bottom faces of the model to add **2mm** of material, as shown in Figure 11–16.

3. Select the *Other thickness faces* field and select the holes.

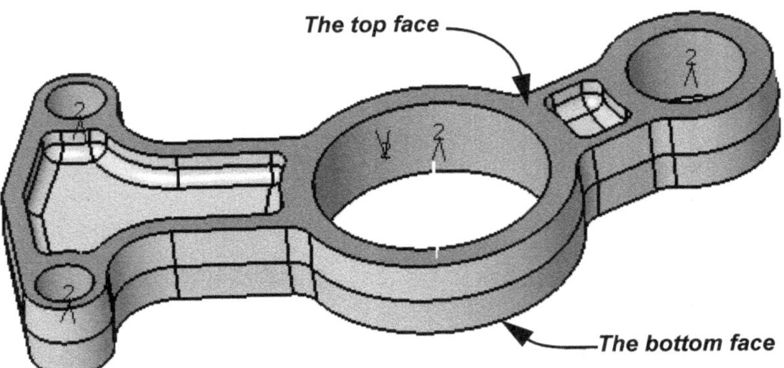

Figure 11–16

4. Double-click on the thickness value of the hole shown in Figure 11–17. The Parameter Definition dialog box opens as shown in Figure 11–17.

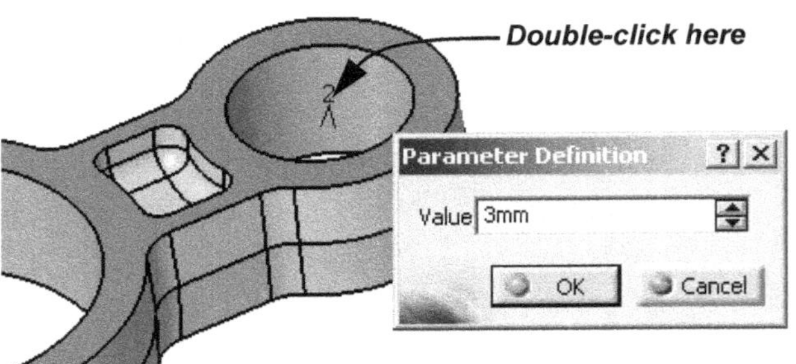

Figure 11–17

5. In the *Value* field, enter **3mm** and click **OK**.

6. Repeat Steps 4 and 5 for the rest of the holes. The Thickness Definition dialog box opens as shown in Figure 11–18.

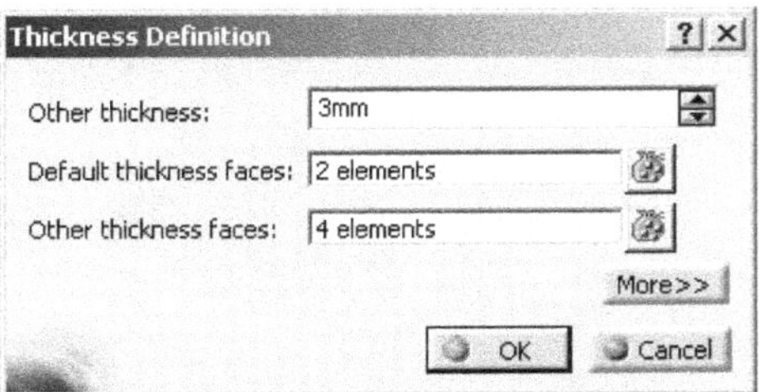

Figure 11–18

7. Click **OK** to complete the feature. The model displays as shown in Figure 11–19.

Figure 11–19

Task 4 - Create Draft.

In this task, you will draft the Holes to ease the process of removing the mold.

1. Click (Draft) and then click **More**.
2. Make the following selections, as shown in Figure 11–20:
   - *Angle:* **3deg**
   - *Face(s) to draft:* The faces of the four holes
   - *Neutral Element:* **yz plane**
   - Select **Parting = Neutral**.
   - Select **Draft both sides**.

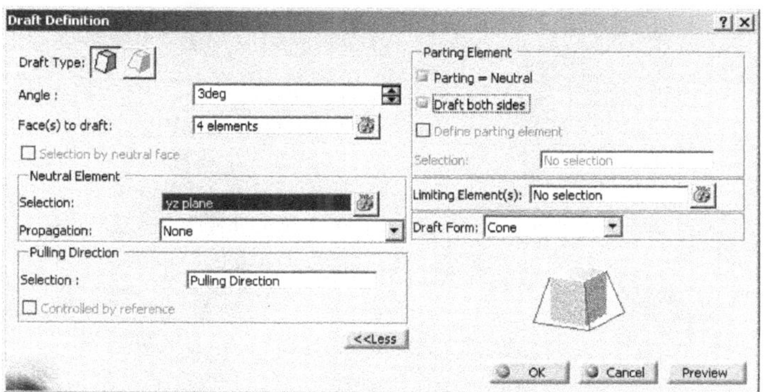

Figure 11–20

3. Click **OK** to complete the feature. The model displays as shown in Figure 11–21.

Figure 11–21

4. Right-click on the **Molded** model and select **Properties**. The Properties dialog box opens.

5. In the Properties dialog box, select the *Graphic* tab, and set the *Transparency* value to **150**, as shown in Figure 11–22.

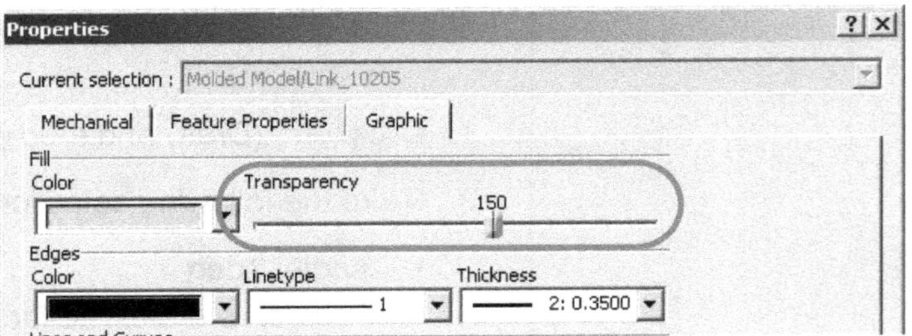

Figure 11–22

6. Show the **Completed Model** PartBody. The model displays as shown in Figure 11–23.

7. Save and close the model.

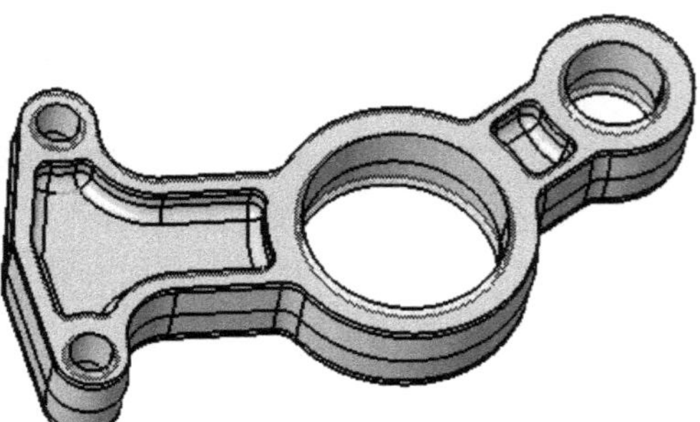

Figure 11–23

Practice 11b Remove Face

Practice Objective

- Create a Remove Face feature.

In this practice, you will modify an imported part to prepare for the FEA analysis. To mesh the part homogeneously, the Fillets and Holes need to be removed from the model. The completed model displays as shown in Figure 11–24.

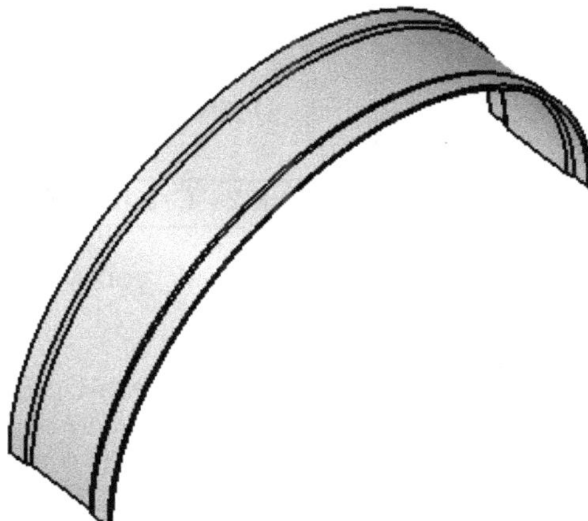

Figure 11–24

Task 1 - Open the part.

1. Open **Stator_Band.stp**. The Stator_Band.stp message box opens as shown in Figure 11–25 indicating that the part has been opened successfully.

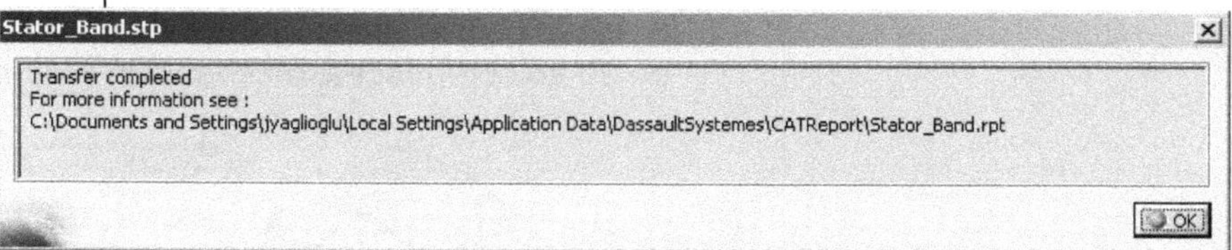

Figure 11–25

2. Click **OK**. The model displays as shown in Figure 11–26.

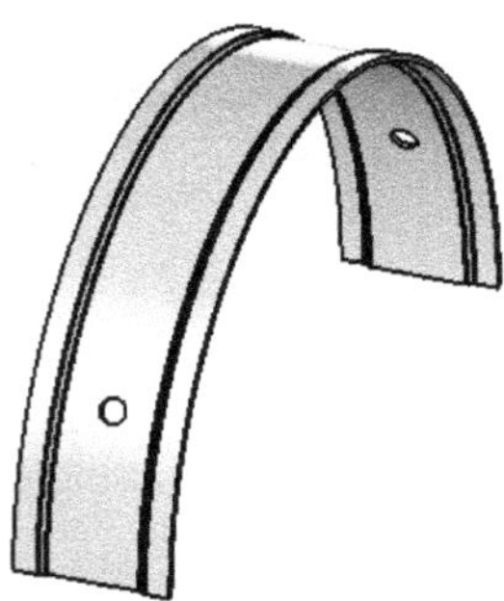

Figure 11–26

3. Define the **PartBody** as the In Work Object.

Task 2 - Create a Remove Face Feature.

In this task, you will remove the Fillets and the Holes.

1. In the Dress-Up Feature toolbar, click (Remove Face). The Remove Face Definition dialog box opens as shown in Figure 11–27.

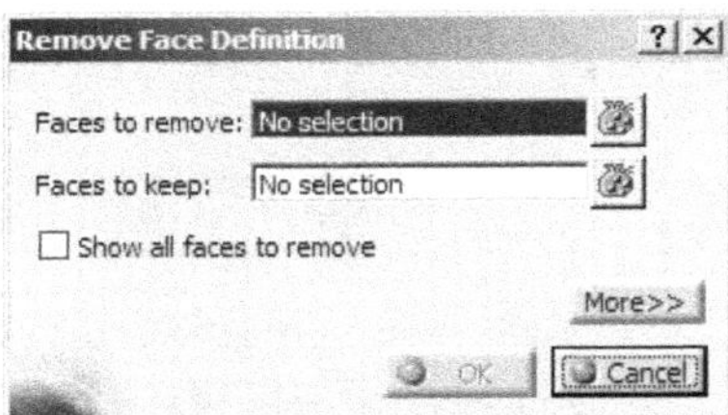

Figure 11–27

2. Select all of the faces of the Fillets and Holes. There should be 20 selected faces, as shown in Figure 11–28.

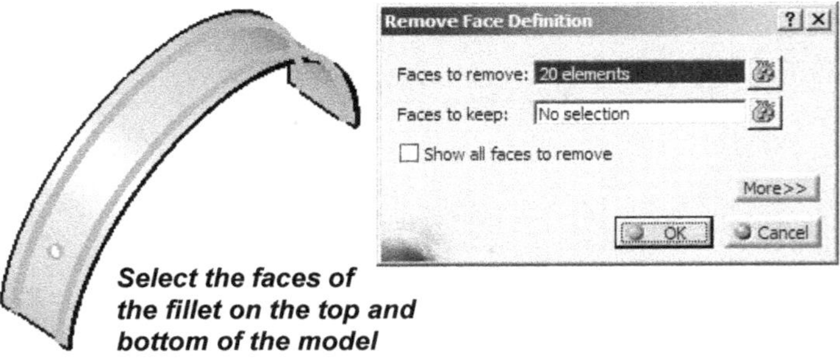

Figure 11–28

3. Click **OK** to complete the feature. The model displays as shown in Figure 11–29.

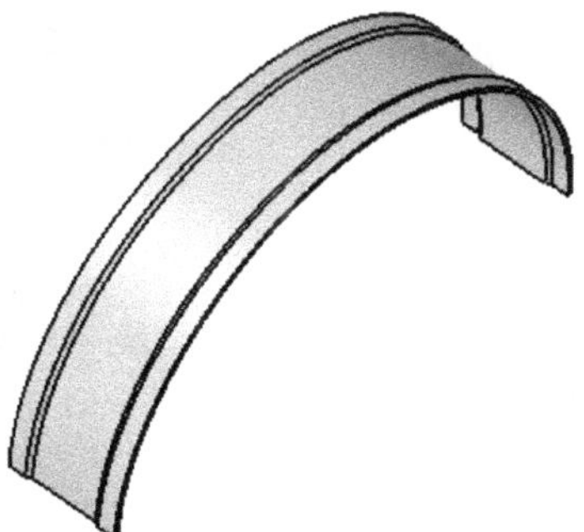

Figure 11–29

4. Save and close the model.

Practice 11c Replace Face

Practice Objectives

- Create a Replace Face feature.
- Create a Remove Face feature.

In this practice, you will modify an imported part using the Replace Face and Remove Face features. The completed model displays as shown in Figure 11–30.

Figure 11–30

Task 1 - Open the part.

1. Open **Replace_face.stp**. The Replace_face.stp message box opens as shown in Figure 11–31 indicating that the part has been opened successfully.

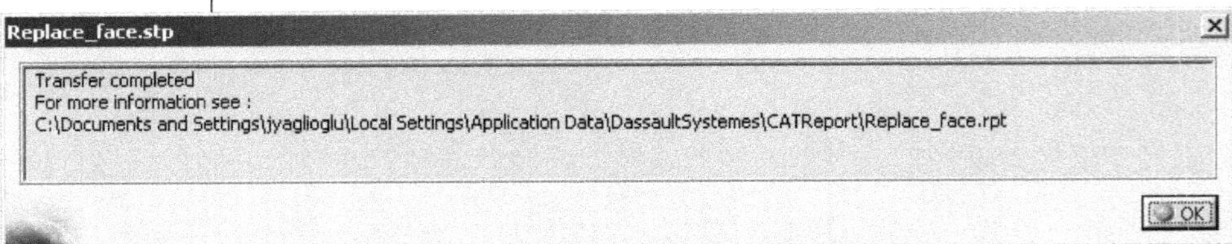

Figure 11–31

2. Click **OK**. The model displays as shown in Figure 11–32.

Figure 11–32

3. Define the **PartBody** as the In Work Object.

Task 2 - Create a Replace Face Feature.

1. In the Dress-Up Feature toolbar, click (Replace Face). The Replace Face Definition dialog box opens as shown in Figure 11–33.

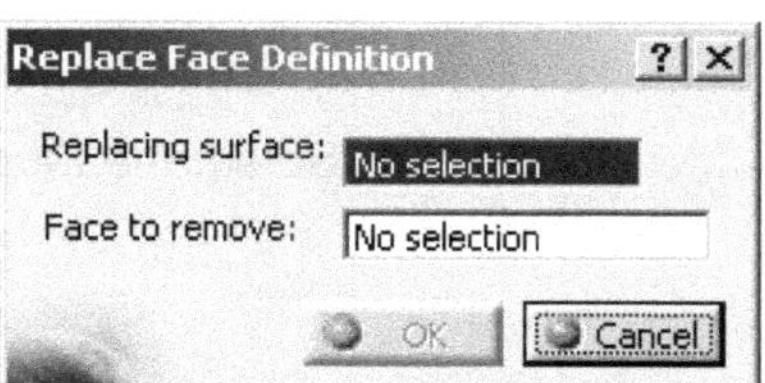

Figure 11–33

2. Select the face that defines the Replacing surface and the Face to remove, as shown in Figure 11–34.

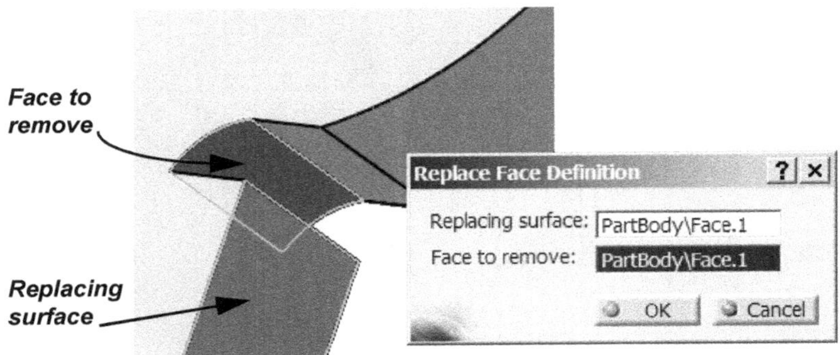

Figure 11–34

3. Click **OK** to complete the feature. The model displays as shown in Figure 11–35.

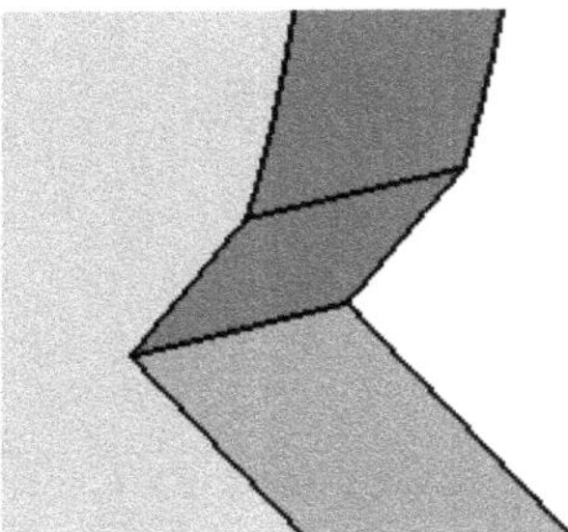

Figure 11–35

Task 3 - Create a Remove Face Feature.

1. In the Dress-Up Feature toolbar, click (Remove Face).
2. Select the face of the model, as shown in Figure 11–36.

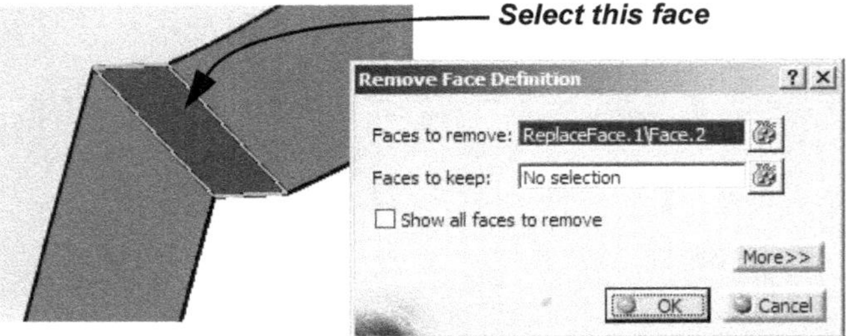

Figure 11–36

3. Click **OK**. The model displays as shown in Figure 11–37.

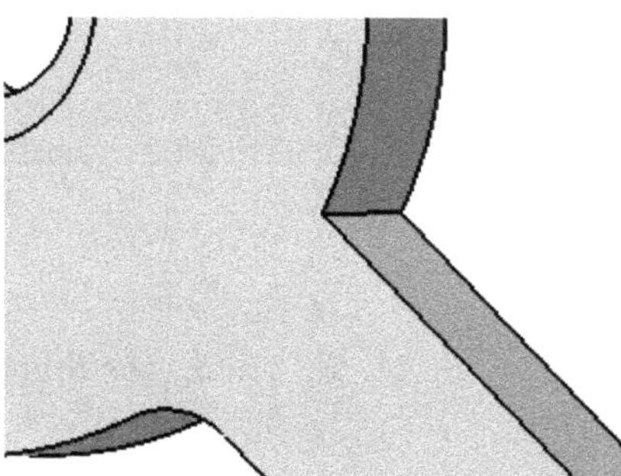

Figure 11–37

4. Create a **10mm** Edge Fillet, as shown in Figure 11–38.

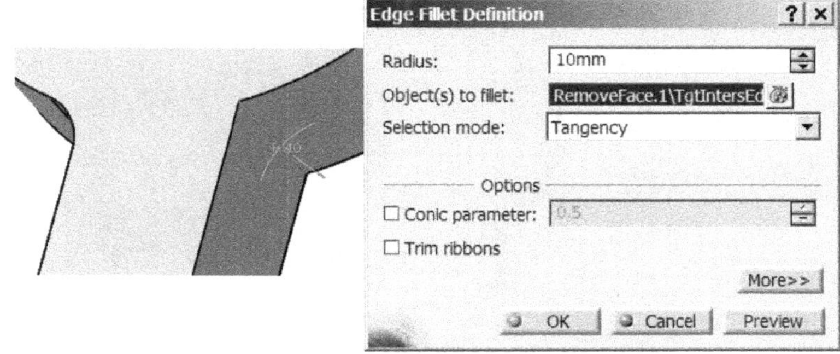

Figure 11–38

5. Click **OK**. The model displays as shown in Figure 11–39.

Figure 11–39

6. Save and close the model.

Chapter Review Questions

1. You can add material to specified faces of a model using the Thickness feature.
   a. True
   b. False
2. Thickness features add the same thickness to all of the selected faces.
   a. True
   b. False
3. **Remove Face** is used to remove pocket features from the model.
   a. True
   b. False
4. You substitute one surface for another using _____.
   a. **Remove Face**
   b. **Switch Face**
   c. **Swap Face**
   d. **Replace Face**
5. When replacing a surface, it is important that _____.
   a. The replacing surface is planar.
   b. The material direction is toward the model.
   c. The replacing surface falls within the boundary of the face to be removed.
   d. All of the above.

Knowledge Templates

Reuse of existing information saves time and ensures consistency. This chapter introduces two types of knowledge templates: PowerCopy and UserFeature. The PowerCopy template enables you to use features in other documents, and provides more control over the placement of data than simply copying and pasting. UserFeature templates are similar in function. However, use of the UserFeature template results in a single representative feature, whereas the PowerCopy template can result in a group of features.

Learning Objectives in this Chapter

- Understand knowledge templates.
- Create a PowerCopy.
- Learn how to use a PowerCopy and a UserFeature in other models.
- Create a UserFeature.

12.1 Knowledge Templates

A knowledge template is a replication tool that you can use to create a sequence of features automatically. To be successfully created, features must possess the ability to locate new references. The references must correspond to those used when the geometry was originally created. In this way, previously-created geometry can be adapted to a new design that is similar in context.

Knowledge templates can be used for a variety of applications, including:

- Adding frequently created features to a part. These features can be modified to apply to the design intent and context of the new part.
- Adding a complete and validated sequence of features to a part. Once positioned in the new part, these features are ready to use and do not require modification.
- Creating a series of customized features for a specific field of activity.

This chapter introduces the two types of knowledge templates in CATIA V5. These templates are as follows

Knowledge Template	Description	**Result**	Applications
PowerCopy	Copies a selection of features and parameters from the source model into a template that can be applied to target part models.	Copies the entire list of features into the target model. Features have an identical behavior to the original features, and can be modified.	Redundant creation of features that require modification in the target model.
UserFeature	Copies a selection of features and parameters from the source model into a template that can be applied to target part models. This type of knowledge template requires a Product Knowledge Template (PKT) license.	Places a single feature into the target model that contains the geometry of all of the selected features. Only published parameters can be modified.	Redundant creation of features that do not require modification in the target model.

12.2 Creation of a PowerCopy

PowerCopies can be very useful when a feature or group of features is required in several models. Rather than recreate the same features in each model, you can create them once and then use PowerCopy to copy the original feature(s) into another model. Unlike the **Paste** option, you can also control the referencing features and dimensions while placing the feature(s).

Carefully consider which references to select when you create features for a PowerCopy. Consider the following tips:

- When creating sketches, try to constrain the sketch to edges and faces rather than to reference planes. This technique makes it easier to place the PowerCopy, because some reference planes might no longer exist.
- Avoid constraining features that you plan to use in a PowerCopy with respect to the Horizontal-Vertical (H-V) absolute axis. This is because the origin and orientation of the absolute axis cannot be controlled. Therefore, the results of placing the PowerCopy are unreliable.
- Avoid using projections and intersections in a sketch that you plan to use in a PowerCopy.
- Ensure that your sketch is ISO-constrained, (i.e., the sketched entities are green) so that the results of the PowerCopy are as expected.

General Steps

Use the following general steps to create a PowerCopy:

1. Start the creation of the PowerCopy.
2. Add features to the PowerCopy.
3. Rename the features.
4. Set the variable parameters, if required.
5. Set an icon or preview for the PowerCopy.
6. Complete the PowerCopy.

Step 1 - Start the creation of the PowerCopy.

Once all of the features for the PowerCopy have been created, save the model.

You cannot create a PowerCopy in a model with unsaved changes.

To open the PowerCopy Definition dialog box and select **Insert> Knowledge Templates> PowerCopy**, as shown in Figure 12–1.

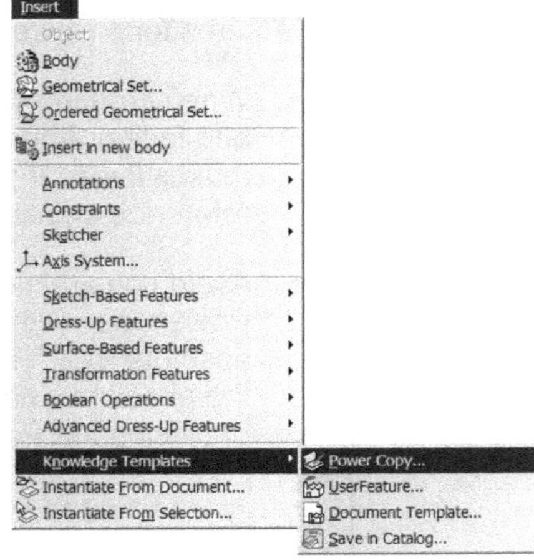

Figure 12–1

The PowerCopy Definition dialog box opens as shown in Figure 12–2.

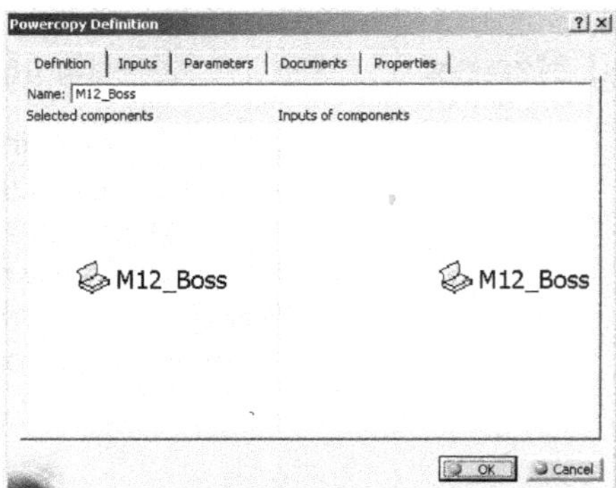

Figure 12–2

In the *Name* field, enter a descriptive name for the PowerCopy and press <Enter>.

Step 2 - Add features to the PowerCopy.

To begin adding features to the PowerCopy, select the *Definition* tab in the PowerCopy Definition dialog box.

If you accidentally select a feature you do not want to include in the PowerCopy, select the feature again in the specification tree to remove it.

A PowerCopy can contain a variety of features, such as geometric features, formulas, and constraints. To add a feature to a PowerCopy, select it in the specification tree. Once selected, the feature displays in the *Components* area in the PowerCopy Definition dialog box. Any references used when the feature was created are listed in the *Inputs of components* area, as shown in Figure 12–3.

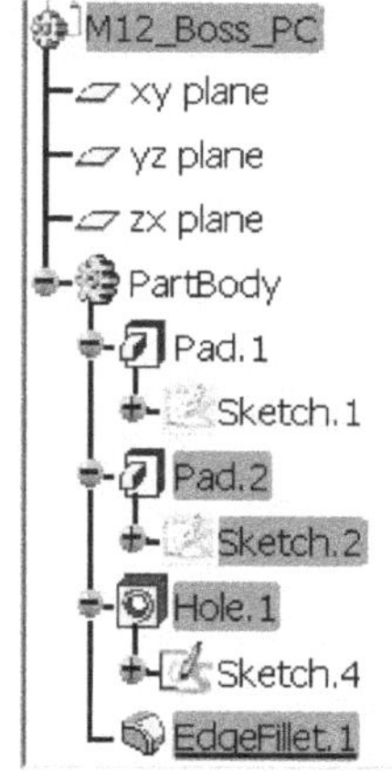

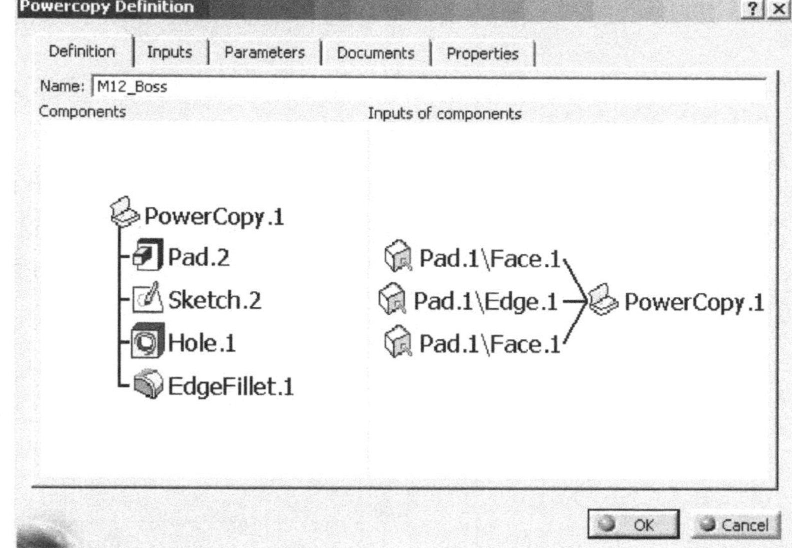

Figure 12–3

These references are used as inputs when the PowerCopy is placed in another model.

Try not to add a large number of features to the PowerCopy. This avoids complications in the PowerCopy and problems that could occur when placing the PowerCopy later.

Step 3 - Rename the features.

Once you finish adding the features to the PowerCopy, it is a good idea to enter descriptive names for the features. This makes it easier to place the PowerCopy later.

To rename an input, select the *Input* tab. Select the feature in the Inputs window and enter a new name in the *Name* field at the bottom of the dialog box. The original name of the feature remains in brackets in the Inputs window, as shown in Figure 12–4.

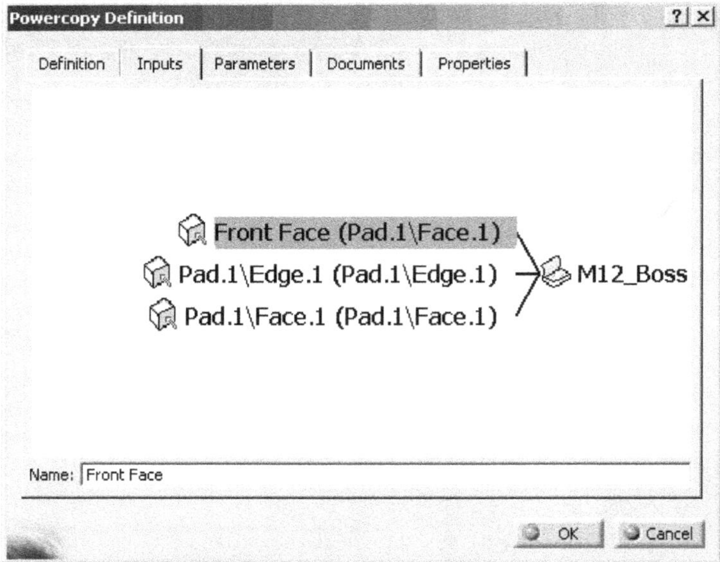

Figure 12–4

Step 4 - Set the variable parameters, if required.

Select the *Parameters* tab to define which parameter values you want to be variable when you are placing the PowerCopy feature. You can change the value of a variable parameter to suit the model in which it is placed.

To create a modifiable parameter, select the parameter and select the **Published** option. The *Name* field displays. Enter a descriptive name for the feature. This name can be used when the PowerCopy is placed in the new model.

The remaining values associated with the PowerCopy are not published. Therefore, their values are not modifiable during placement.

For example, the parameter selected in Figure 12–5 is published. This parameter is now variable.

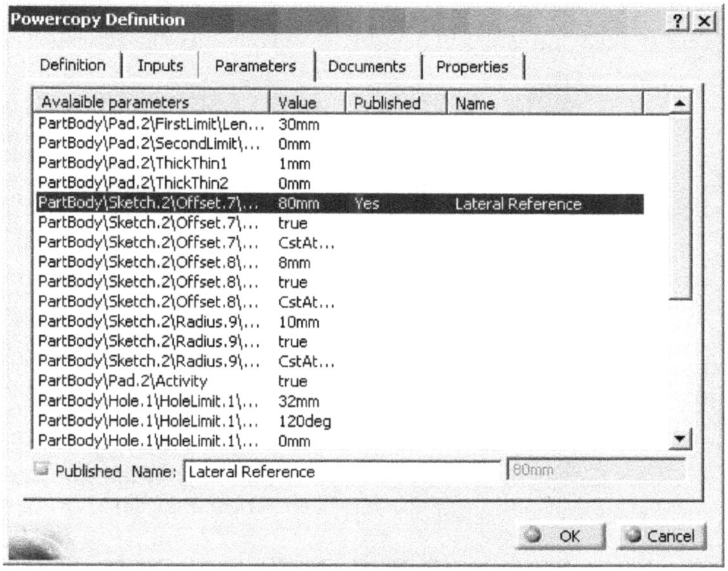

Figure 12–5

Step 5 - Set an icon or preview for the PowerCopy.

Select the *Properties* tab and select an icon by which you can identify the PowerCopy in the specification tree. Click  to expand the flyout of commonly selected icons, as shown in Figure 12–6.

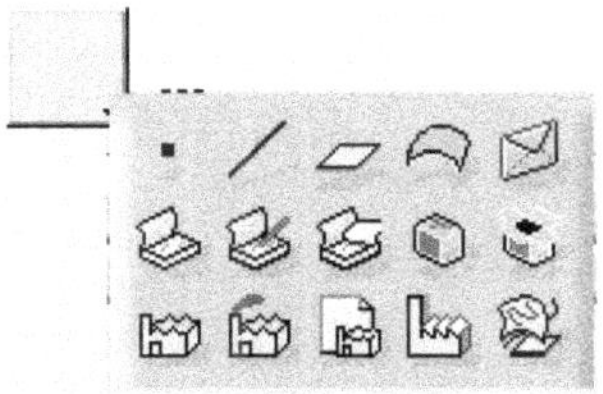

Figure 12–6

The selected icon is shown in Figure 12–7.

You can also browse through all of the icons loaded in your CATIA session by clicking ··· *.*

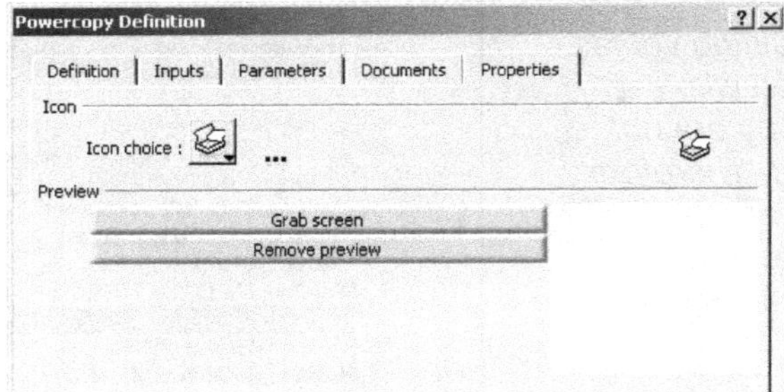

Figure 12–7

Preview

You can use the *Properties* tab to create a preview that is stored with the PowerCopy Definition. To create a preview, set up the model display according to how you want it to display in the preview. Select **View>Specifications** or **View>Compass** to clear the display of the specification tree and compass as required. Then click **Grab screen** to take a screen shot.

This screen shot is used as the preview, as shown in Figure 12–8.

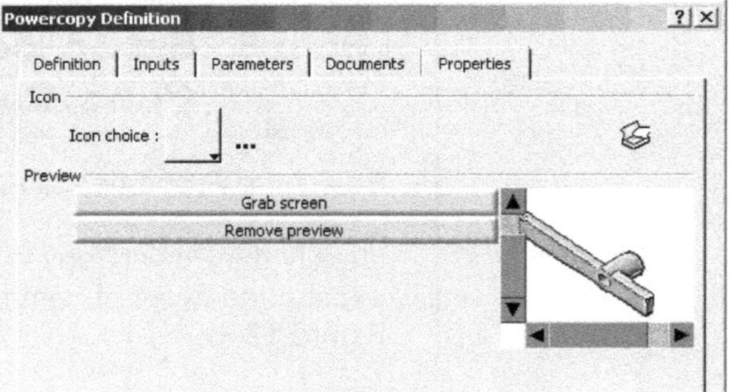

Figure 12–8

Click **Remove preview** to remove the preview.

Step 6 - Complete the PowerCopy.

Once you have completed the PowerCopy Definition, click **OK** to close the dialog box.

12.3 Instantiation of a PowerCopy

Once a PowerCopy has been created, you can use it in other models. You can modify any variable parameters to suit the new model.

General Steps

Use the following steps to instantiate the PowerCopy.

1. Select the PowerCopy to be instantiated.
2. Place the PowerCopy.
3. Change the parameters and complete the instantiation.

Step 1 - Select the PowerCopy to be instantiated.

The document containing the PowerCopy must be closed (i.e., not in session) when it is being inserted into another document.

In the target model (where you are placing the PowerCopy), select **Insert>Instantiate From Document**, as shown in Figure 12–9.

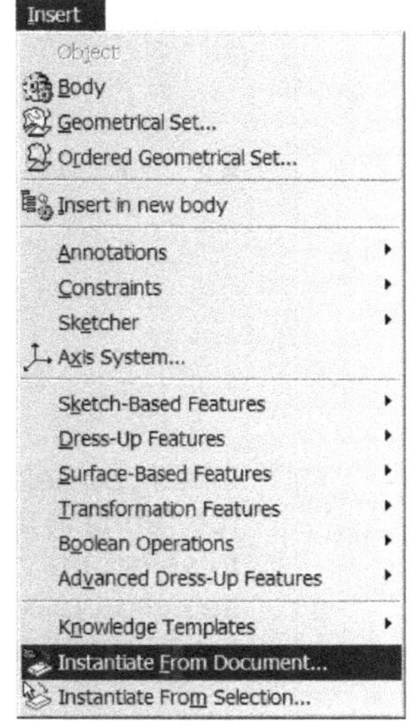

Figure 12–9

In the File Selection dialog box, navigate to the document containing the PowerCopy, and click **Open** to begin inserting the object.

Step 2 - Place the PowerCopy.

When you select a document to open, the Insert Object dialog box opens as shown in Figure 12–10. In the Reference drop-down list, select the correct PowerCopy (if more than one exists in the source document).

You can also specify the destination of the geometry by selecting **Inside** or **After** in the Destination drop-down list. In the *Reference* field, you can define the geometrical set or PartBody in which the features can be located.

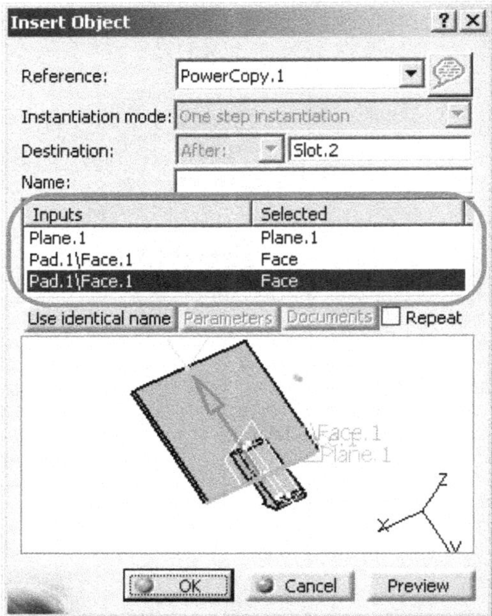

Figure 12–10

Once you select the PowerCopy to reference, CATIA highlights a reference in the *Inputs* column in the dialog box and waits for you to select the corresponding feature in the new model. This selection process is repeated until all of the references have been selected and the PowerCopy is successfully positioned.

At this point, you can display the PowerCopy with the model by clicking **Preview**.

A slide cover and clip being inserted onto the end of the bed are shown in Figure 12–11. The references indicated on the model are selected to correspond to the references listed as inputs in the dialog box.

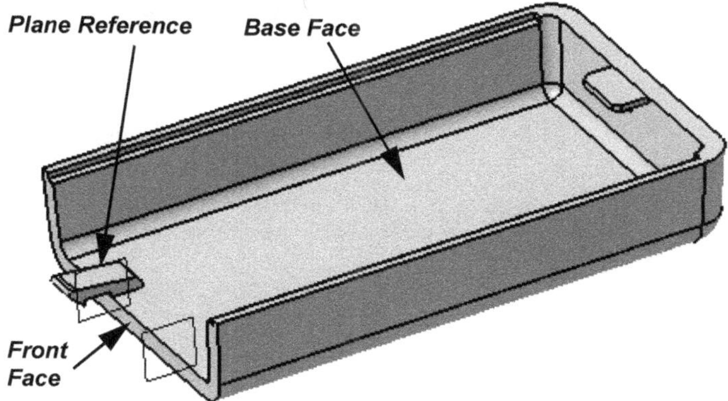

Figure 12–11

If the name of the reference in the target model is the same as in the source model, you can also place references by clicking **Use identical name**. CATIA automatically places the reference by matching the reference name in the PowerCopy to the reference name in the new model. For example, the **Plane.1** listed in the dialog box uses the **Plane.1** in the model as a reference for placement, as shown in Figure 12–12.

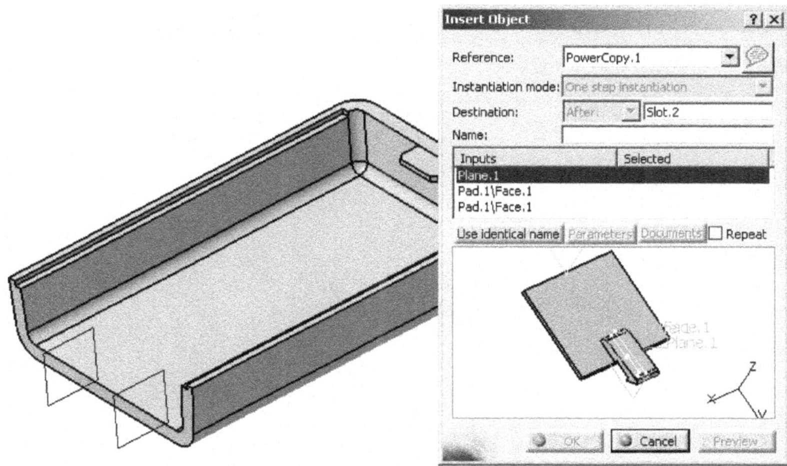

Figure 12–12

Once instantiated, each feature of a PowerCopy becomes a separate feature and is no longer linked to the original PowerCopy.

If you place more than one of the same object, you can select the **Repeat** option to save time. Once you complete placing the PowerCopy, the dialog box remains open to place another one.

Step 3 - Change the parameters and complete the instantiation.

If any parameters have been published with the PowerCopy, **Parameters** is available. Click it to open the Parameters dialog box. Any modifiable parameters are listed with the default values, as shown in Figure 12–13.

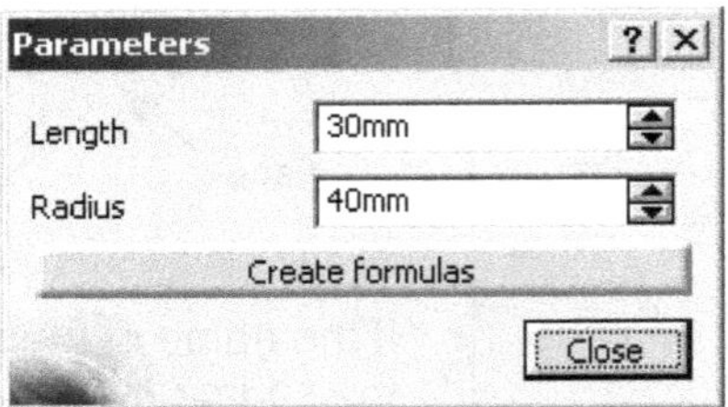

Figure 12–13

Click **Create formulas** to automatically create a formula for any parameter in the model with the same name as a parameter in the PowerCopy. When the PowerCopy is instantiated in a model with the parameter of the same name and you click **Create formulas**, the length of the rectangular box is automatically driven by the new value.

Once the PowerCopy is placed correctly in the model, click **OK** to complete the instantiation.

12.4 Creation of UserFeatures

The process of creation and instantiation of a UserFeature is similar to that of a PowerCopy. The difference between the two Knowledge Templates is in the result. While a PowerCopy adds all of the copied features to the target model, the UserFeature only adds geometry as a single feature in the specification tree. This feature cannot be modified. Only parameters that have been published during feature creation can be changed. To use this feature, you must have a PKT (Product Knowledge Template) license.

Creating a UserFeature

To create a UserFeature, select **Insert>Knowledge Templates>UserFeature**. The UserFeature Definition dialog box opens as shown in Figure 12–14.

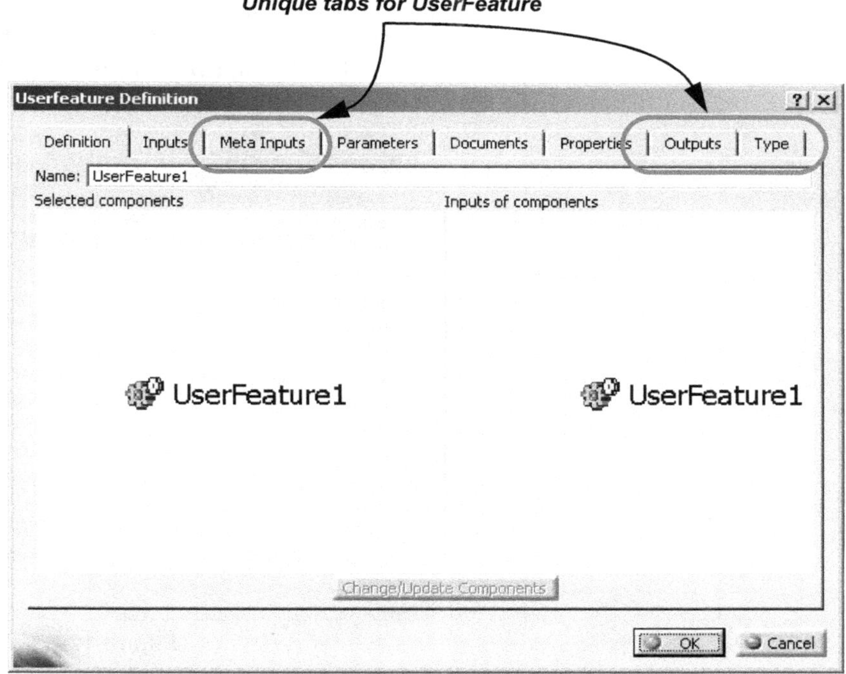

Figure 12–14

You can create a UserFeature using the methods described for a PowerCopy. The UserFeature Definition dialog box is identical to the PowerCopy Definition dialog box, except for three additional tabs: *Meta Inputs*, *Outputs*, and *Type*.

Meta Inputs Tab

You can use meta inputs to instantiate entire parts or part bodies efficiently. Using meta inputs, CATIA automatically assigns all of the inputs when instantiating. Meta inputs are only available with a Product Knowledge Template license.

Outputs Tab

You can use the *Outputs* tab to define features that are carried forward when the UserFeature is instantiated in another model. For example, you could use the *Outputs* tab if you added a Pad feature, but only wanted the sketch used by the Pad to be brought into the new model.

Select the *Outputs* tab to specify an output, as shown in Figure 12–15, and select the Main Result in the list. To add a feature to the output, click **Add** and then select a feature in the specification tree or model. Any feature that has been added can be removed using **Remove**. To replace the default Main Result with a different feature, click **Replace**.

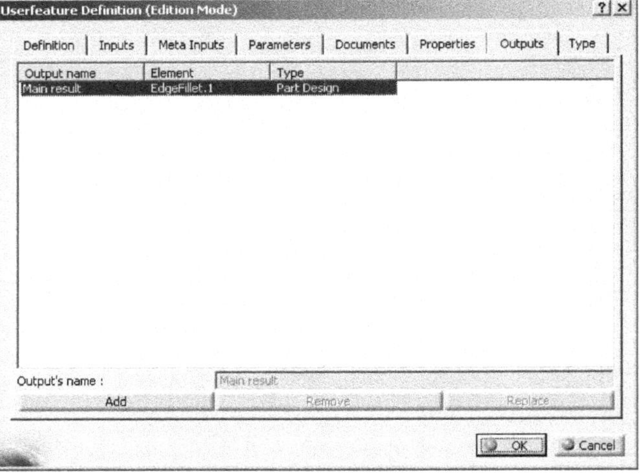

Figure 12–15

Type Tab

When a UserFeature is instantiated in a new model, it displays as a single entry in the specification tree, although it might contain a variety of features. The *Type* tab enables you to define a type that you can associate with the UserFeature so that it can be located when performing a search. For example, you could associate the type Pad with the UserFeature so that it can be located when searching for Pads. The *Type* tab displays as shown in Figure 12–16.

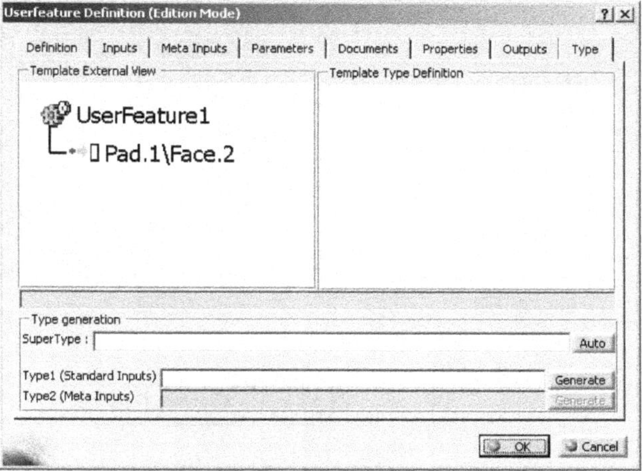

Figure 12–16

Instantiating a UserFeature

You can instantiate UserFeatures in another model using the same method as for a PowerCopy.

The result of a UserFeature instantiation displays as a single feature in the specification tree, as shown in Figure 12–17. The only parts of a UserFeature that can be modified are the parameters that have been published.

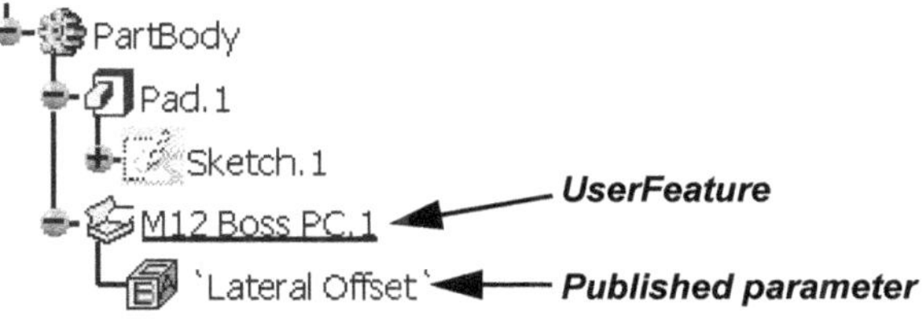

Figure 12–17

Practice 12a PowerCopy Creation

Practice Objective

- Instantiate a PowerCopy.

In this practice, you will instantiate a PowerCopy twice, as shown in Figure 12–18.

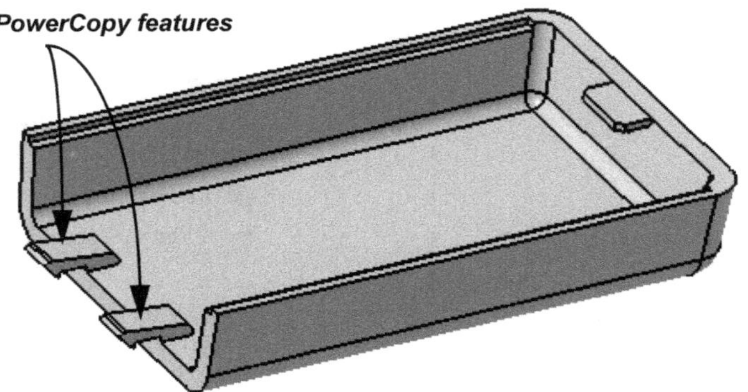

Figure 12–18

Task 1 - Open the part.

1. Open **Clip.CATPart**. The part displays as shown in Figure 12–19.

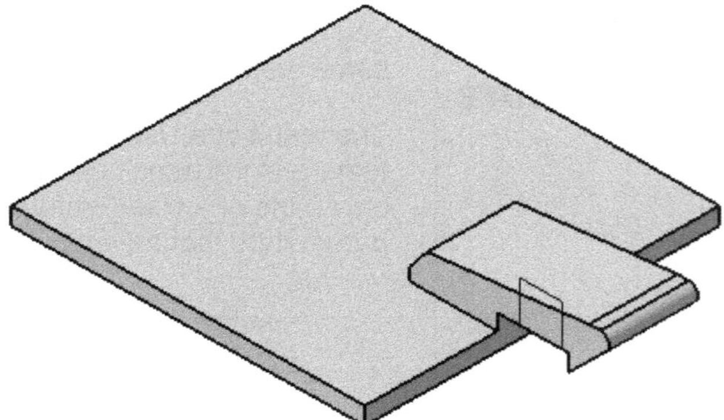

Figure 12–19

Task 2 - Explain the geometry of the PowerCopy.

Design Considerations

This model was created as a source model of the PowerCopy so that you can insert the geometry of the clip into other models using similar references. The PowerCopy Geometry and Support Geometry are shown in Figure 12–20.

Support Geometry

The support geometry consists of the following:

- **Pad.1:** Pad.1 was created so that you can select appropriate sketcher references when creating **Sketch.2**.
- **Plane.1:** Plane.1 was used as a sketching plane for **Sketch.2**.

Each time this PowerCopy is placed, a plane or a planar surface must be selected as the new sketch plane for **Sketch.2**.

PowerCopy Geometry

The PowerCopy consists of the following three features:

- **Pad.2** (and **Sketch.2**)
- **Chamfer.1**
- **EdgeFillet.1**

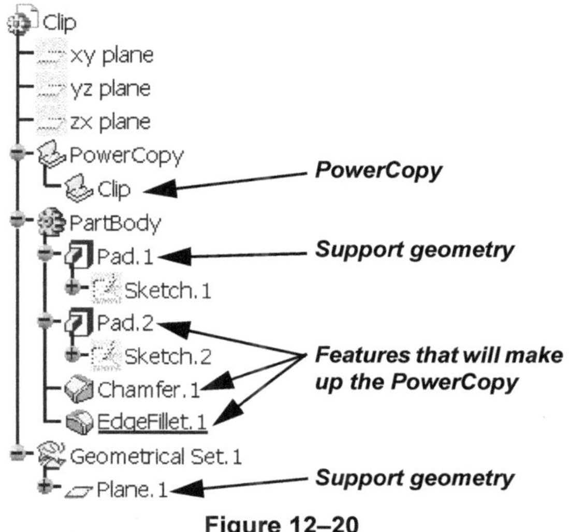

Figure 12–20

2. Close the file.

Task 3 - Instantiate a PowerCopy.

1. Open **SlideCover.CATPart**. The model displays as shown in Figure 12–21.

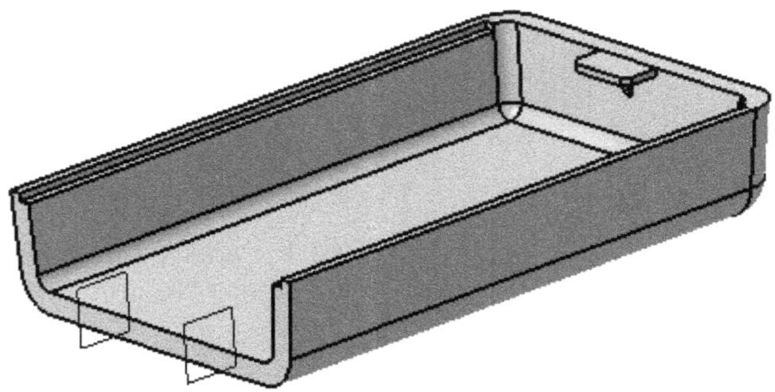

Figure 12–21

2. Select **Insert>Instantiate From Document**.

3. Select **Clip.CATPart** from the training files directory. The Insert Object dialog box opens as shown in Figure 12–22.

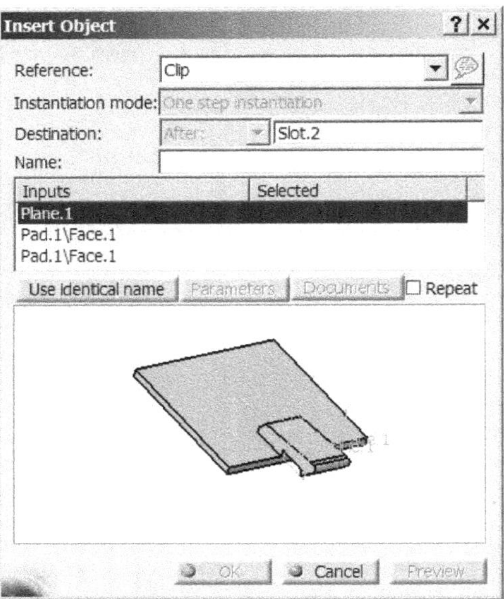

Figure 12–22

Design Considerations

The *Inputs* area in the dialog box lists the references required to place the PowerCopy. The **Plane.1** input is highlighted. You must select a reference that corresponds to **Plane.1**.

4. Select **Plane.1** for the plane placement reference, as shown in Figure 12–23.

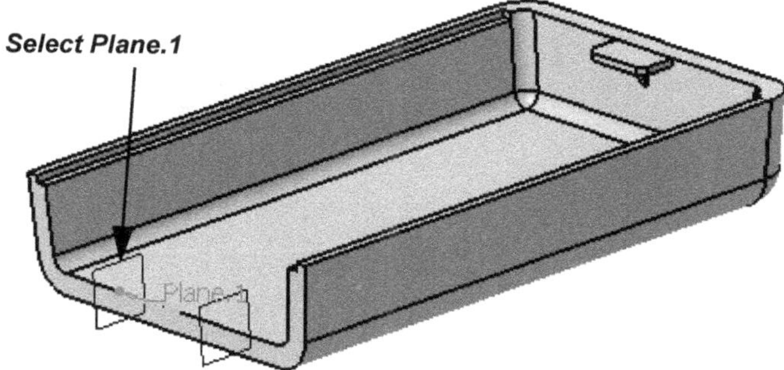

Figure 12–23

5. You must select a planar surface as the next placement reference. Select the top surface of the model, as shown in Figure 12–24.

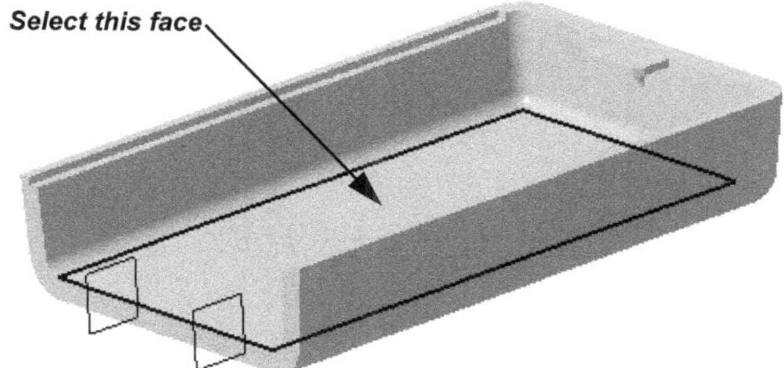

Figure 12–24

6. Select a planar surface as the third and final required placement reference. Select the end surface of the model, as shown in Figure 12–25.

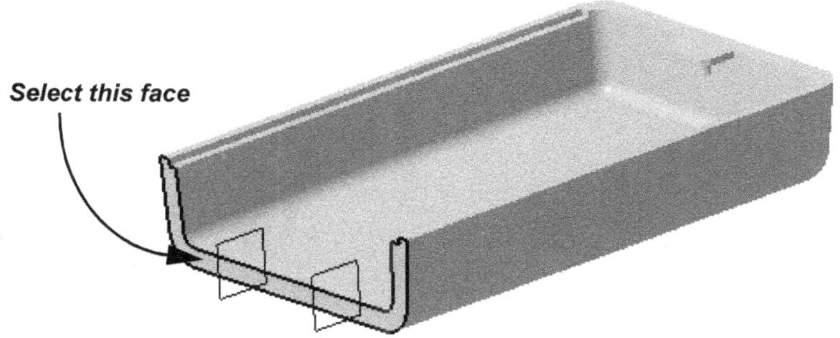

Figure 12–25

Design Considerations

The *Inputs* area in the Insert Object dialog box indicates that all of the inputs have a corresponding reference selected, as shown in Figure 12–26. The PowerCopy can now be placed successfully.

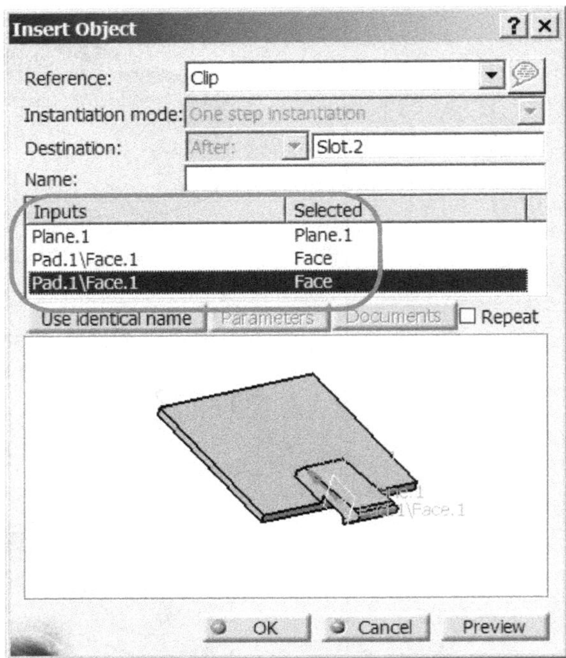

Figure 12–26

7. Click **OK** to complete the instantiation of the Clip PowerCopy. The model displays as shown in Figure 12–27.

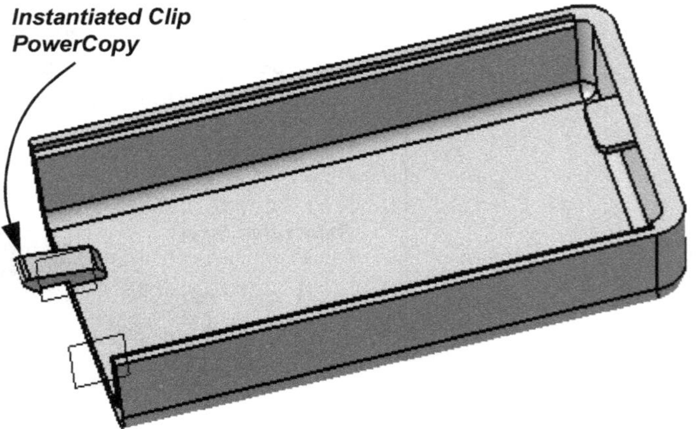

Figure 12–27

Task 4 - Instantiate another instance of the Clip PowerCopy.

1. Select **Insert>Instantiate From Document** and select **Clip.CATPart** to instantiate another instance of the Clip PowerCopy.

2. Select **Plane.2** as the corresponding plane reference, as shown in Figure 12–28.

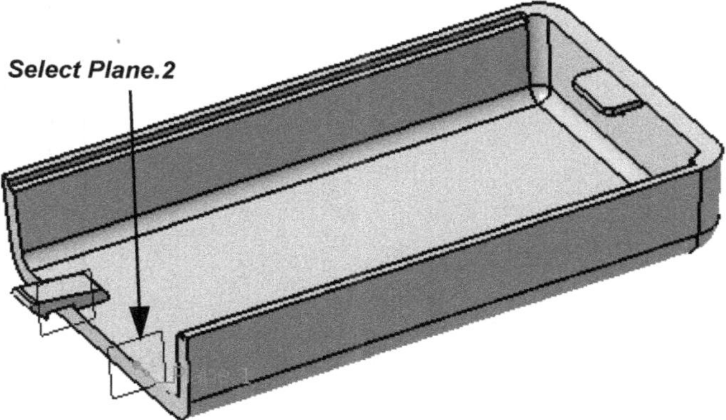

Figure 12–28

3. Select the appropriate placement references to instantiate another instance of the Clip PowerCopy. (Hint: The same surfaces as before.) The completed model displays as shown in Figure 12–29.

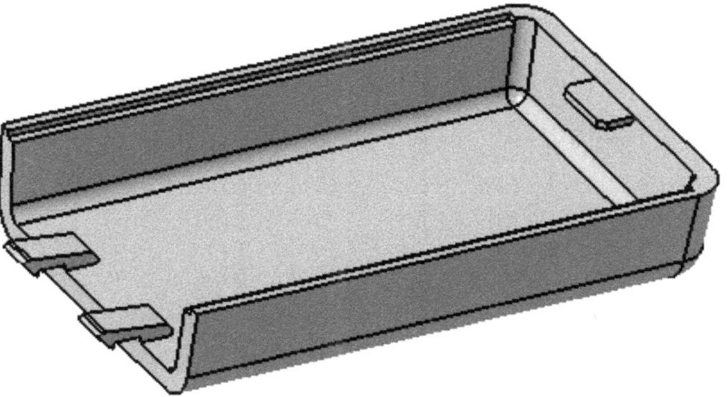

Figure 12–29

Design Considerations

Expand the specification tree to displays the feature list. In Figure 12–30, note that the features that make up the Clip PowerCopy are listed as separate, modifiable features.

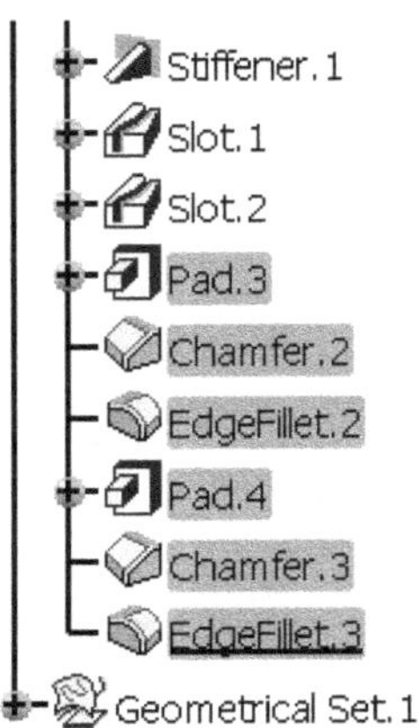

Figure 12–30

4. Save the model and close the file.

Practice 12b Working with PowerCopies

Practice Objectives

- Create features for a PowerCopy.
- Instantiate a PowerCopy from a Document.

In this practice, you will create features for a PowerCopy, create the Powercopy, and then instantiate it four times from a document. An example of Powercopy features is shown in Figure 12–31.

Figure 12–31

Task 1 - Open the part.

1. Open **Lid.CATPart**. The model displays as shown in Figure 12–32.

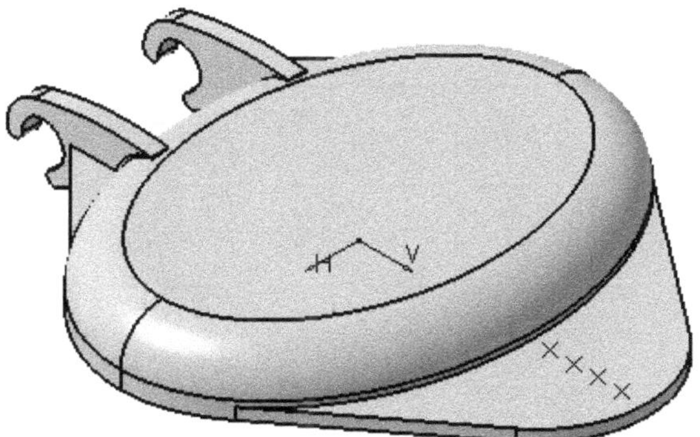

Figure 12–32

Design Considerations

The **Lid** part has a sketch called **GripLocation**, which consists of four sketch points. These points provide a location reference for the PowerCopy that you will create. The PowerCopy will consist of a Pad and a Tritangent Fillet, which represent the thumb grip texture on the pull-tab of the **Lid Pad**. One instance of the **Grip** PowerCopy is shown in Figure 12–33. The location of the grip is defined by one of four sketch points. In this practice, four grip PowerCopies are instantiated (one per sketch point).

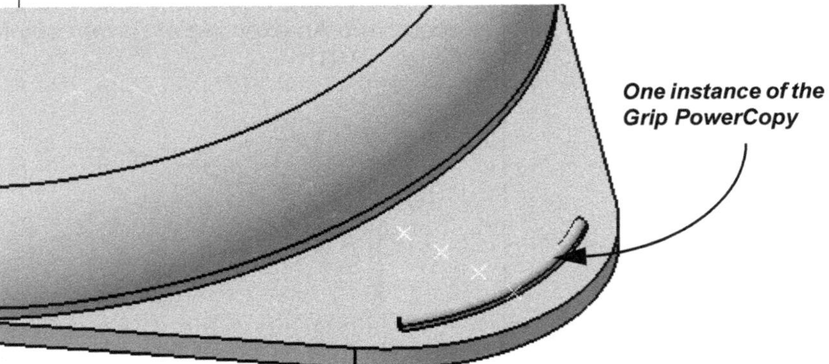

Figure 12–33

2. Leave the **Lid.CATPart** file open.

Task 2 - Create a part file.

In this task, you will create a new part file and create the features for the **Grip** PowerCopy.

1. Create a new part file and save it in the training files directory with the name **LidGrip**.
2. Create a sketch on the xy plane and sketch a single sketch point that is 5mm away from the sketch origin, as shown in Figure 12–34.

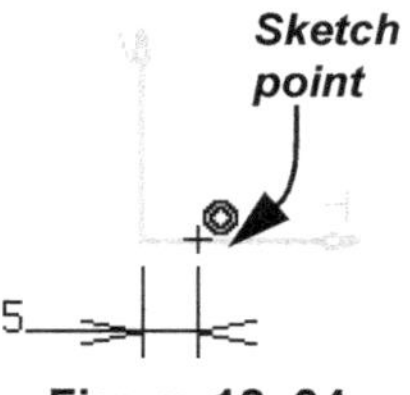

Figure 12–34

3. Exit the Sketcher workbench.

4. Hide the xy, yz, and zx planes, as shown in Figure 12–35.

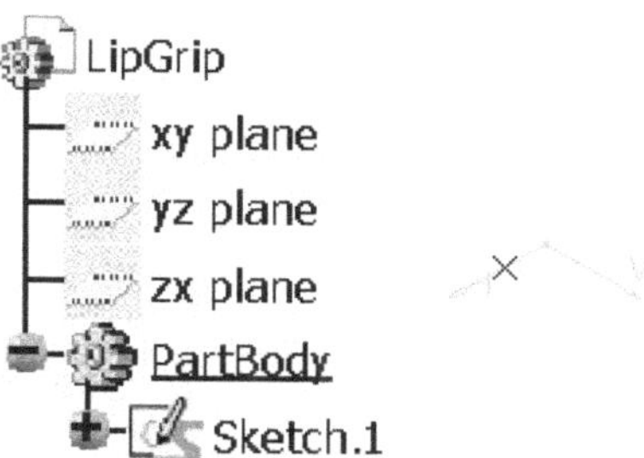

Figure 12–35

5. Create another sketch on the xy plane (select the xy plane in the specification tree).

Design Considerations

The reference planes are hidden so that you cannot select them for dimensional references. For this PowerCopy creation, all dimensional references and constraints should be to the sketch point of **Sketch.1**.

6. Create a horizontal axis, 20mm long and equidistant with respect to the sketch point, as shown in Figure 12–36.

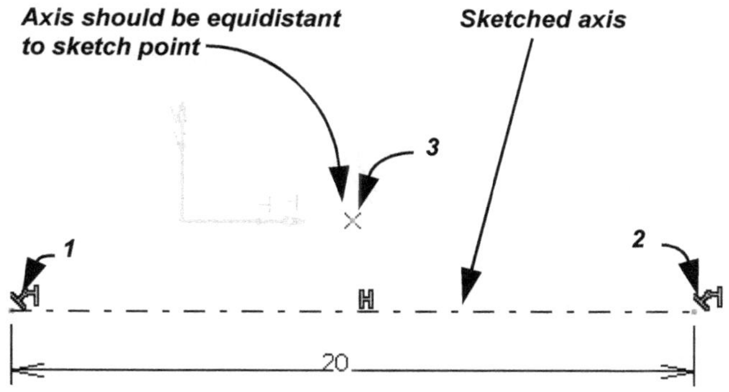

To create the equidistant constraint, hold <Ctrl> and select points 1, 2 and 3. Select the Constraints Defined in Dialog Box option from the Constraints toolbar.

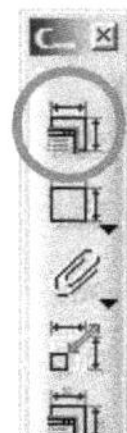

Figure 12–36

7. Sketch an R20 arc, passing through the sketch point (**Sketch.1**), with the end points at each end of the axis, as shown in Figure 12–37.

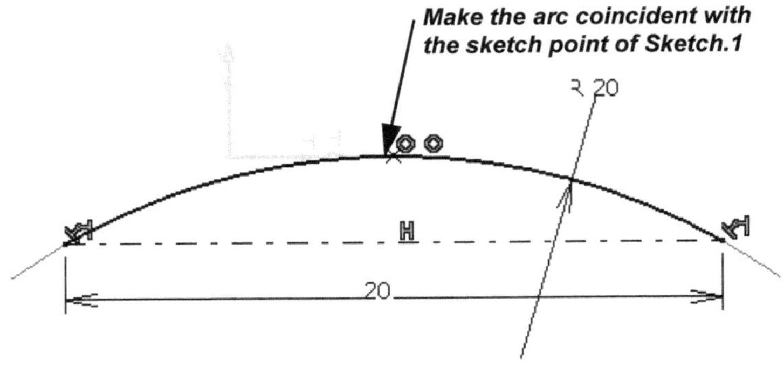

Figure 12–37

8. Create a Thick Pad with the parameters shown in Figure 12–38.

   - *Length:* **1**
   - Select **Thick**.
   - *Thickness1:* **1**
   - Select **Neutral Fiber**.

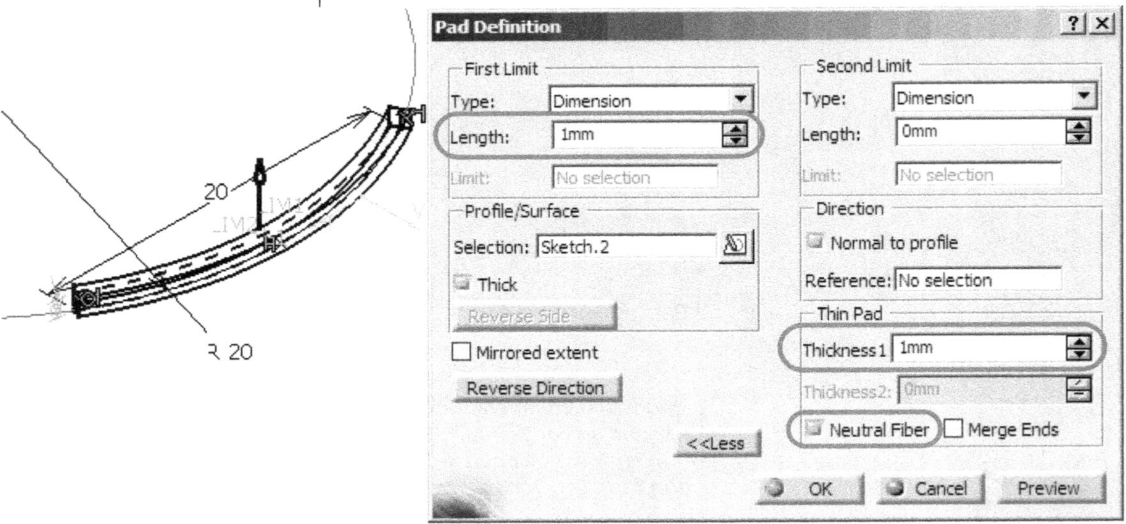

Figure 12–38

Task 3 - Create a Tritangent Fillet.

1. Create the Tritangent Fillet shown in Figure 12–39.

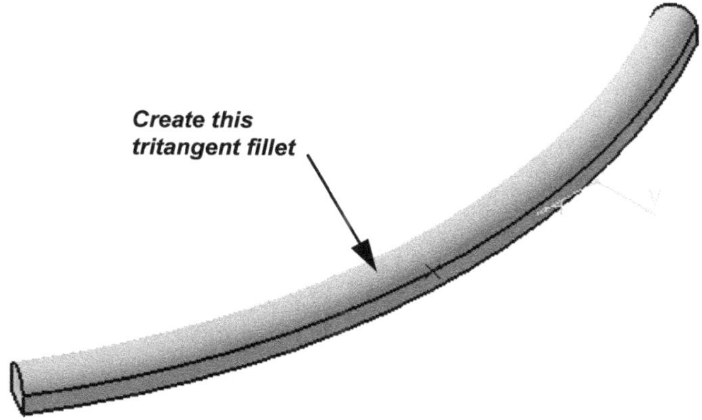

Figure 12–39

Design Considerations

Consider the references that you selected to create the Pad:

- The xy plane was selected as a sketching plane.
- All dimensional references and constraints for the Pad have been created to the sketched point of **Sketch.1**.

The Pad only references two elements: the xy plane and the sketched point. Therefore, only two references are required to place a PowerCopy of the Pad. The Tritangent Fillet only references the Pad.

Task 4 - Create a PowerCopy.

1. Select **Insert>Knowledge Templates>PowerCopy**.
2. Define the PowerCopy with the following parameters:
   - *Name:* **Grip**
   - *Selected components:* **Pad.1**, **Sketch.2**, and **TritangentFillet.1**

3. Select the *Inputs* tab and rename the following inputs, as shown in Figure 12–40:

   - *xy plane:* **PlacementPlane**
   - *Sketch.1:* **LocationPoint**

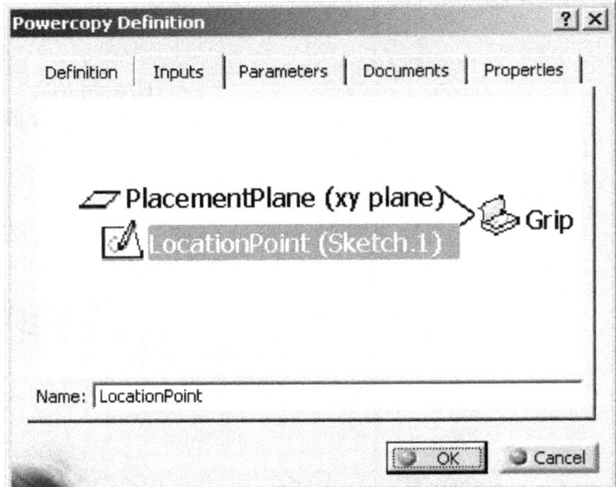

Figure 12–40

4. Select the *Parameters* tab. Publish and rename the following parameters, as shown in Figure 12–41:

   - *PartBody\Sketch.2\ ... \Length\20mm:* **Length**
   - Select **Publish Name**.
   - *PartBody\ Sketch.2\ ... \Radius\20mm:* **Radius**
   - Select **Publish Name**.

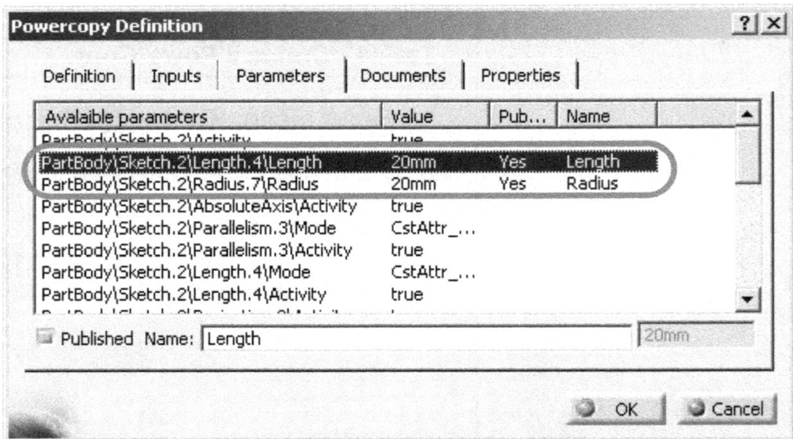

Figure 12–41

5. Click **OK** to complete the **Grip** PowerCopy creation. The model displays as shown in Figure 12–42.

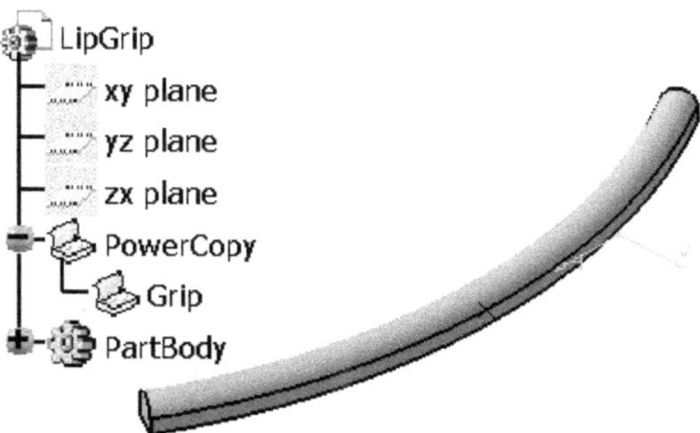

Figure 12–42

Design Considerations

You can publish any parameter of a feature included in a PowerCopy. By publishing a parameter, you can change its value at the time of instantiation.

6. Save and close the file.

Task 5 - Instantiate a PowerCopy.

1. If not already active, activate **Lid.CATPart**.

2. Select **Insert>Instantiate from Document** and open the **LidGrip.CATPart** model. The Insert Object dialog box opens as shown in Figure 12–43.

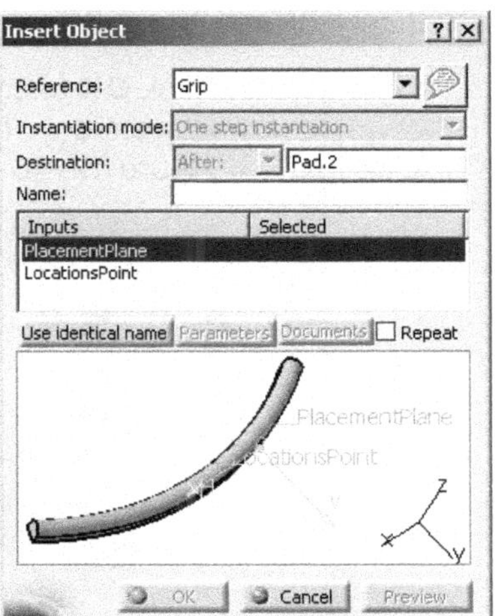

Figure 12–43

3. Select the surface shown in Figure 12–44 as the **PlacementPlane** reference.

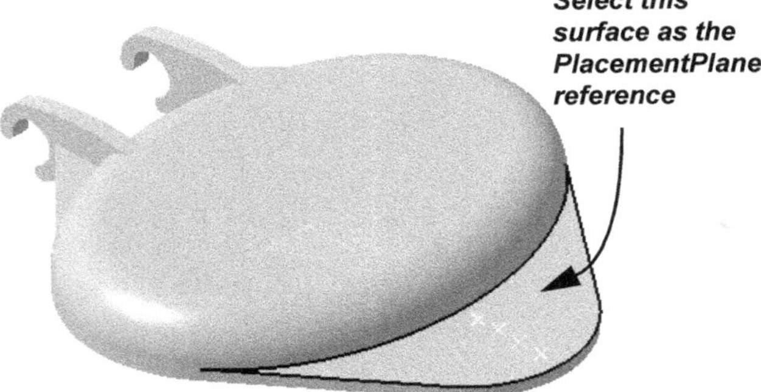
Select this surface as the PlacementPlane reference

Figure 12–44

4. Select the sketch point shown in Figure 12–45 as the LocationPoint reference.

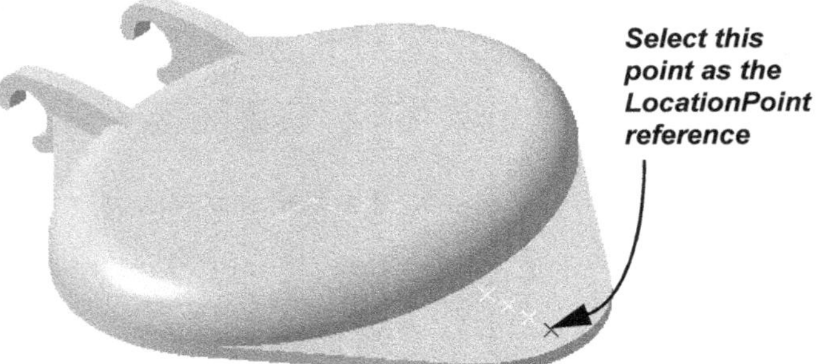
Select this point as the LocationPoint reference

Figure 12–45

1. Click **OK** to complete the instantiation of the **LidGrip** PowerCopy. The **Lid** model displays as shown in Figure 12–46.

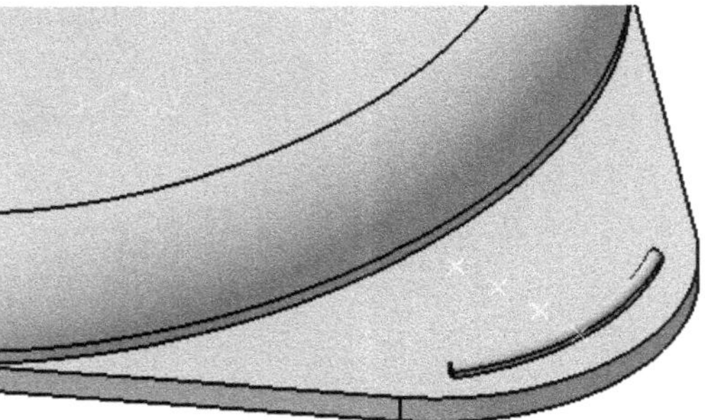

Figure 12–46

Task 6 - Instantiate a PowerCopy.

1. Instantiate an instance of the **LidGrip** PowerCopy by selecting **Insert>Instantiate From Document**.

2. Since you are instantiating three instances of the **LidGrip** PowerCopy, make the following selections, as shown in Figure 12–47:

   - *Reference:* **Grip**
   - Select **Repeat**.

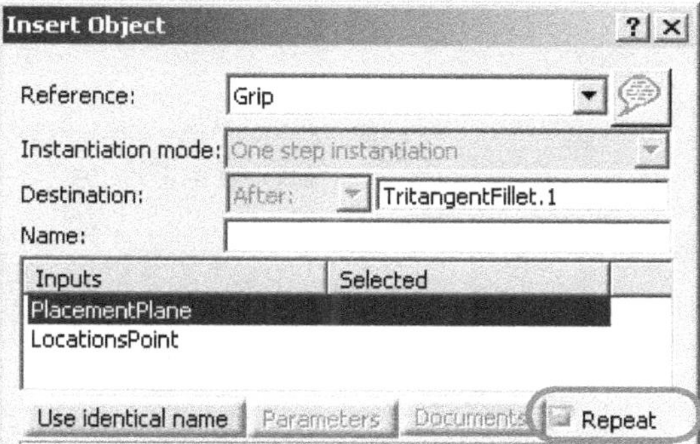

Figure 12–47

3. Use the appropriate references to instantiate the PowerCopy, as shown in Figure 12–48.

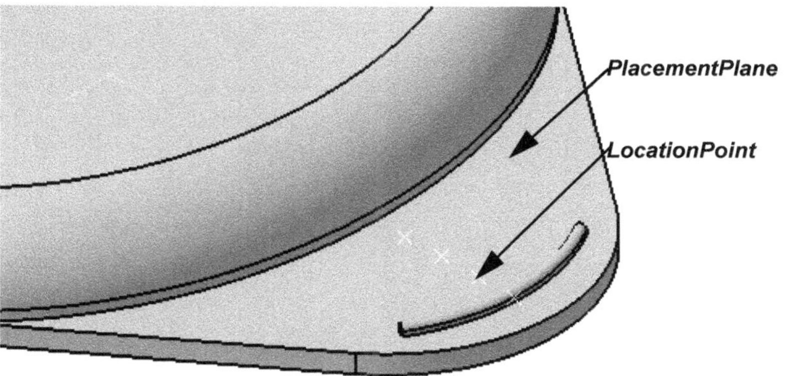

Figure 12–48

4. Click **Parameters**. In the Parameters dialog box, make the following changes, as shown in Figure 12–49:

   - *Length:* **25**
   - *Radius:* **30**

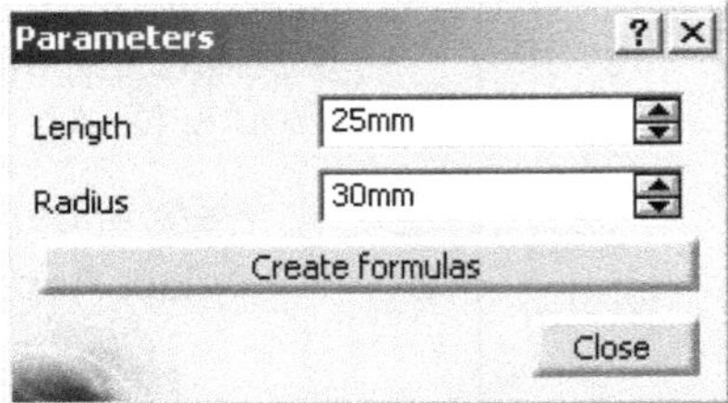

Figure 12–49

5. Click **Close** and **OK**. The **LidGrip** PowerCopy displays as shown in Figure 12–50.

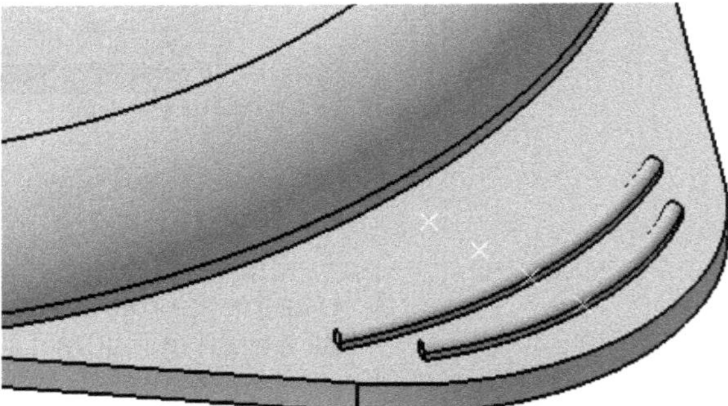

Figure 12–50

6. Place the second instance of the **LidGrip** PowerCopy using the appropriate references and the parameter values shown in Figure 12–51.

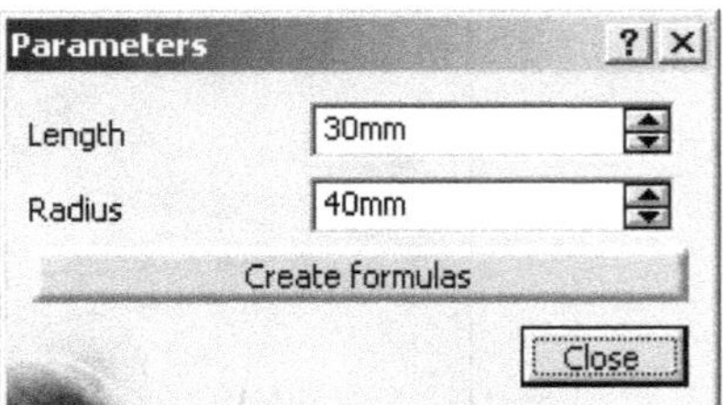

Figure 12–51

7. The second instance of the **LidGrip** PowerCopy displays as shown in Figure 12–52.

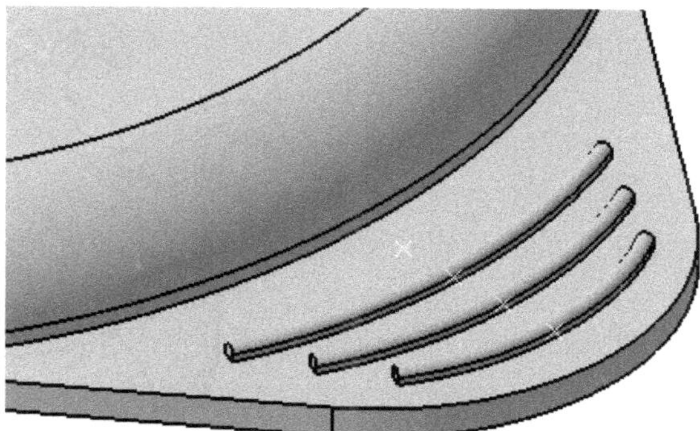

Figure 12–52

8. Instantiate the third instance using the parameter values shown in Figure 12–53.

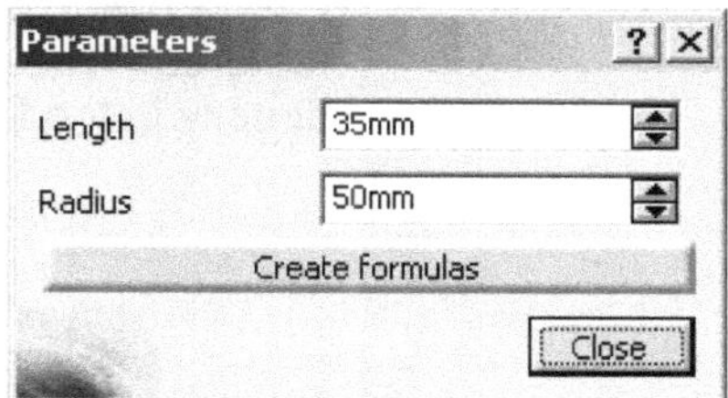

Figure 12–53

The third instance of the **LidGrip** PowerCopy is shown in Figure 12–54.

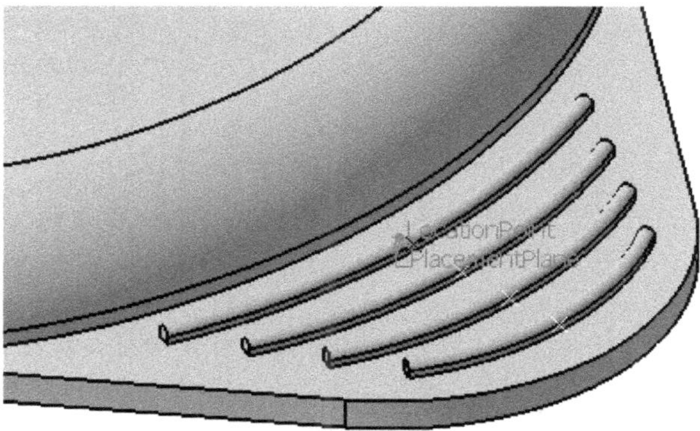

Figure 12–54

9. Click **OK** and **Cancel**. The completed model displays as shown in Figure 12–55.

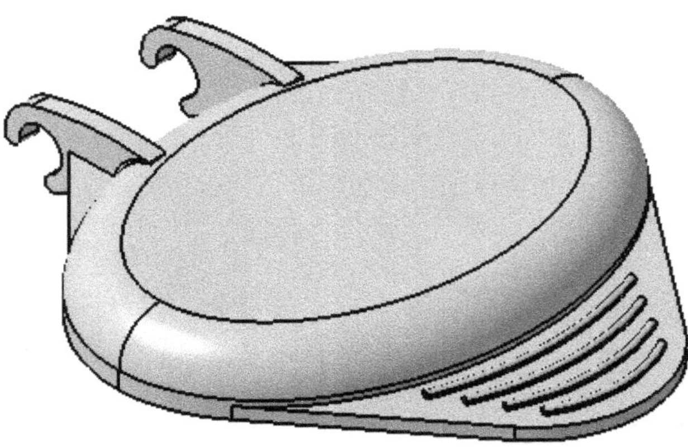

Figure 12–55

10. Expand the specification tree as shown in Figure 12–56. Each PowerCopy has recreated a set of Pad and Fillet features. These features behave as if they were created directly in the **Lid** model.

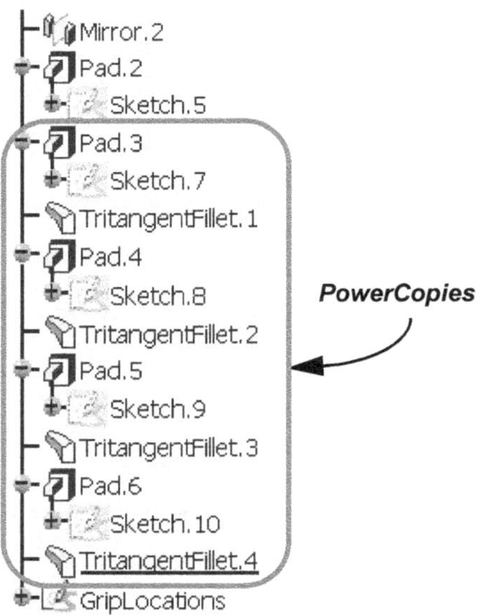

Figure 12–56

11. Save the model and close the file.

Chapter Review Questions

1. Which of the following is true of Knowledge Templates?.
   a. Features must possess the ability to locate new references.
   b. References must correspond to those used when the geometry was originally created.
   c. Previously-created geometry can be adapted to a new design that is similar in context.
   d. All of the above.
2. A PowerCopy copies a selection of features and parameters from the source model into a template that can be applied to target part models.
   a. True
   b. False
3. Creating a PowerCopy is the same as using the **Paste** option.
   a. True
   b. False
4. Parameters can be set as variable so they can be changed when placing a PowerCopy.
   a. True
   b. False
5. A PowerCopy can only be used in the model in which it has been created.
   a. True
   b. False
6. A UserFeature adds all of the copied features to the target model.
   a. True
   b. False

Part Design Tables

You can use part design tables to create multiple versions of a part using a single file. A part design table uses model parameters to create a variety of design configurations for a specific model. A part design table is very useful for creating a series of models that have a similar geometric shape, but come in a variety of sizes.

Learning Objectives in this Chapter

- Prepare a model for use with design tables.
- Learn to rename parameters and Create formulas.
- Create and manipulate design tables.

13.1 Preparation of a Model

When creating a design table, you must first prepare your model by adding parameters to it. An example of a design table is shown in Figure 13–1.

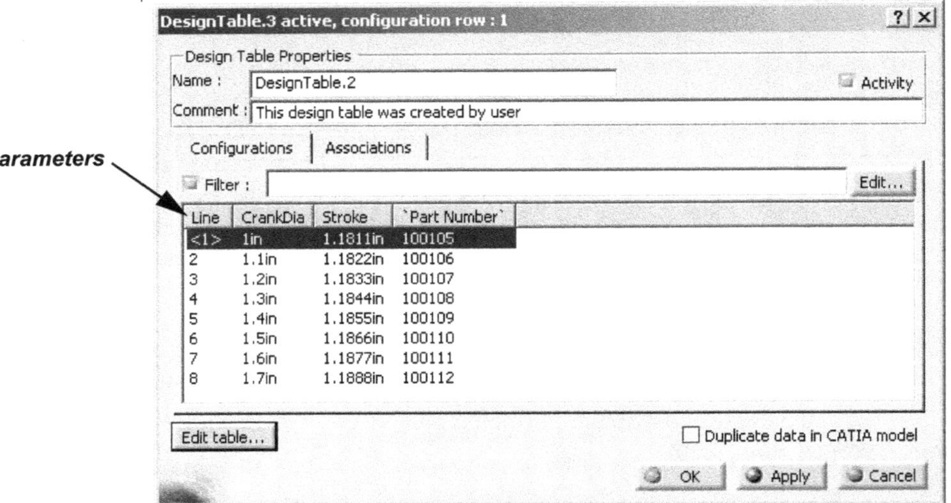

Figure 13–1

You can prepare your model for use in a design table with the following methods:

- Rename parameters
- Create formulas

Rename Parameters

CATIA creates a model parameter for every entity in a model (e.g., dimensions, features, etc.). Even the list of model parameters for a simple model can be difficult to search through. When preparing your model, carefully consider which model parameters to use in the table. Use descriptive names to rename these parameters. Renamed parameters are easier to locate when you create the table, and are helpful to users who are unfamiliar with the model.

To rename parameters, click f(x) (Formula) and select the part in the display. The Formulas dialog box opens and the part dimensions display on the model, as shown in Figure 13–2.

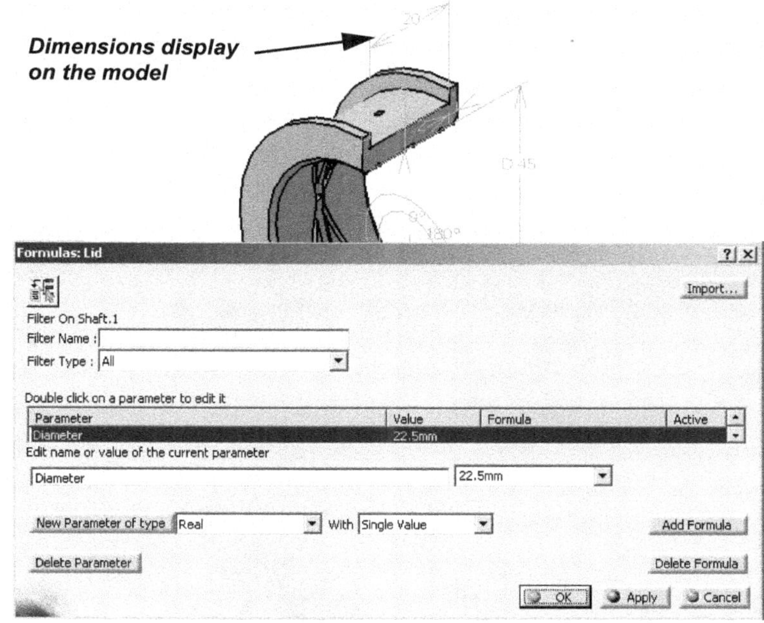

Figure 13–2

Rename the parameters using the Formulas dialog box.

The dialog box used to select parameters for a design table is shown in Figure 13–3. The graphic on the left lists all of the parameters in the model, which you can display by selecting **All** in the Filter Type drop-down list. The graphic on the right shows only the parameters that have been renamed for use in the design table. You can see these parameters by selecting **Renamed parameters** in the Filter Type drop-down list.

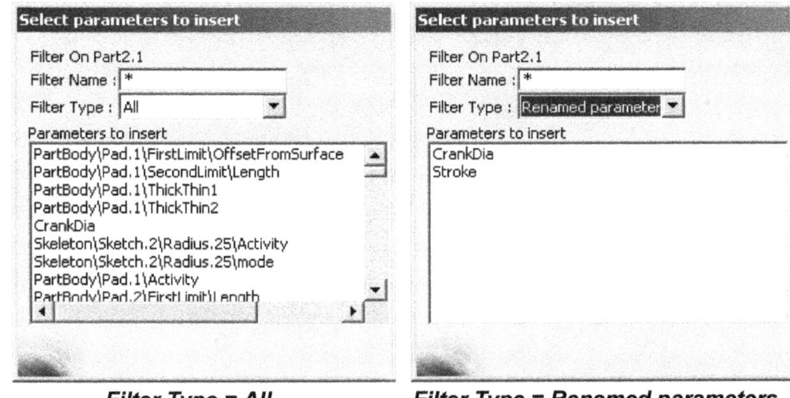

Filter Type = All ***Filter Type = Renamed parameters***

Figure 13–3

Create Formulas

You can use formulas to simplify the design table. To create a formula, click **Add Formula**. You can use formulas to control multiple features and dimensions using a single model parameter. Formulas reduce the number of parameters that need to be added to the design table to drive the design intent. As a result, the design table is easier to understand and modify.

13.2 Creation of a Part Design Table

Once you finish setting up your model, you can create the design table. Part design tables are useful for creating a series of models that have a similar geometric shape, but come in a variety of sizes.

For example, the bolt shown in Figure 13–4 comes in a number of different sizes. Rather than recreate the bolt using separate part files, you can create a design table of the bolt. You can then use the design table to create multiple versions of the bolt using a single part file.

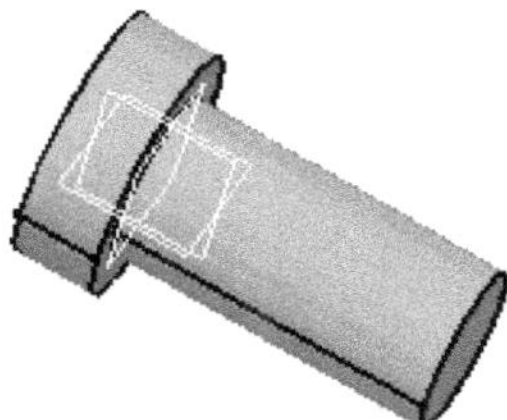

Figure 13–4

General Steps

Use the following general steps to create a part design table:

1. Start the creation of the design table.
2. Specify a creation method and enter the parameters.
3. Define the parameter values.
4. Retrieve a configuration.

Step 1 - Start the creation of the design table.

Click (Design Table) in the Knowledge toolbar. The Creation of a Design Table dialog box opens as shown in Figure 13–5.

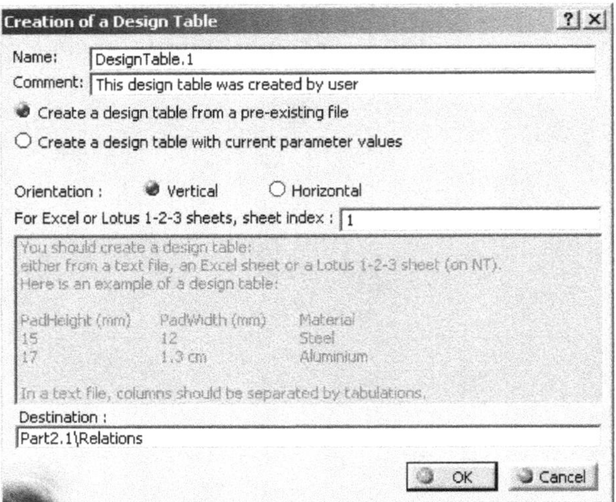
Creation of a Design Table
Name: DesignTable.1
Comment: This design table was created by user
Create a design table from a pre-existing file
Create a design table with current parameter values
Orientation : Vertical Horizontal
For Excel or Lotus 1-2-3 sheets, sheet index : 1
You should create a design table:
either from a text file, an Excel sheet or a Lotus 1-2-3 sheet (on NT).
Here is an example of a design table:
PadHeight (mm) PadWidth (mm) Material
15 12 Steel
17 1.3 cm Aluminium
In a text file, columns should be separated by tabulations.
Destination :
Part2.1\Relations
OK
Cancel

Figure 13–5

Enter a name and descriptive comment for the design table.

Step 2 - Specify a creation method and enter the parameters.

In the Creation of a Design Table dialog box, select one of the following creation methods for the design table:

- Create a design table from an existing file.
- Create a design table with current parameters.

Create a Design Table From a Pre-Existing File

This method uses data from an existing design table to configure the model. Select this option if configurations of your design table are similar to one already created, or the configurations for your design table have been specified in an external file, such as an Excel spreadsheet.

How To: Create a Design Table from an Existing File

1. Select **Create a design table from a pre-existing file** and click **OK**.
2. The File Selection dialog box opens. Select the Excel spreadsheet.
3. The Automatic associations dialog box opens as shown in Figure 13–6. Click **Yes** to automatically create the association or **No** to manually create the association.

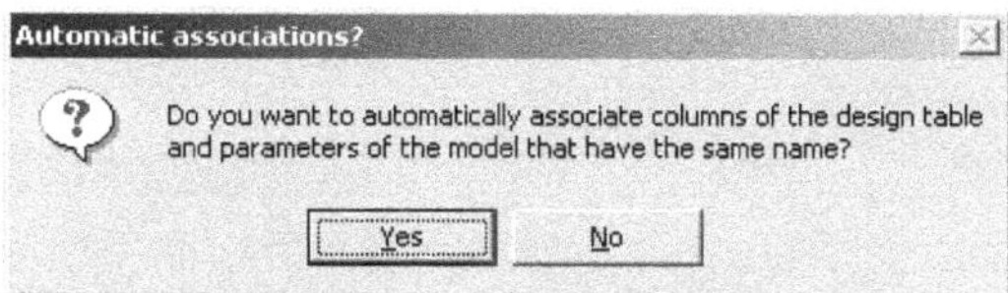

Figure 13–6

The Excel file is linked to the part file. This link must be managed as you would any other linked document in CATIA.

Associating Parameters

When a parameter is associated with a column heading, the column controls the value of the parameter for a given configuration.

Select the *Associations* tab to display a list of unassociated column headings, as shown in Figure 13–7.

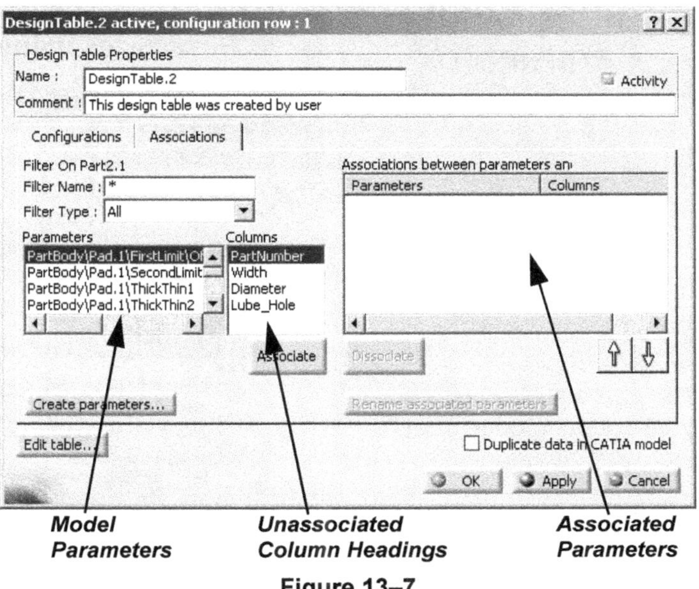

Figure 13–7

Before you complete the design table, you must create an association between any unassociated heading and a model parameter. Select an unassociated column heading in the *Columns* field and a parameter in the *Parameter* field and click **Associate**. The parameter and heading are added to the *Associated Parameters* field on the right in the dialog box.

If a parameter for the column heading does not exist, it can be created using **Create parameters**. The message box shown in Figure 13–8 opens. You can use it to add a new parameter to the model.

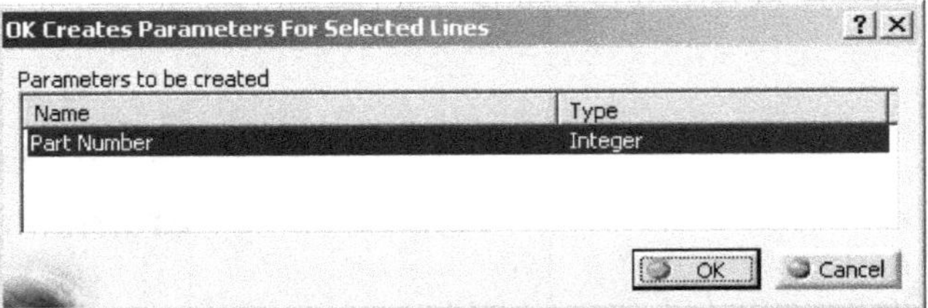

Figure 13–8

Create a Design Table With Current Parameters

This method creates a new Excel spreadsheet for the design table.

How To: Create a Design Table with Current Parameter Values

1. Select **Create a design table with current parameter values** and click **OK**.
2. In the Select parameters to insert dialog box, select the parameters to insert into the design table shown in Figure 13–9. In the Filter Type drop-down list, select **Renamed parameters** to list the parameters you renamed for use in the design table.

Although a model can have multiple design tables, parameters can only be added to one design table per model.

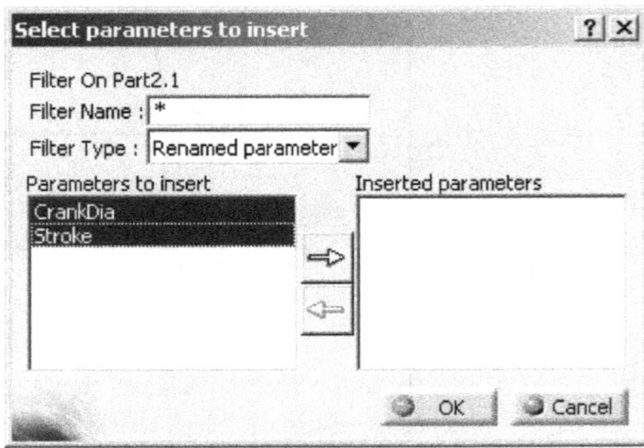

Figure 13–9

3. Click to insert the parameters and click **OK**. The Save As dialog box opens.
4. In the Save As dialog box, in the *File Name* field, enter a name for the Excel spreadsheet and save it on your computer.

Step 3 - Define the parameter values.

Once you have selected the parameters for the design table, you must specify parameter values for each configuration of the model.

How To: Specify Parameter Values

1. Click **Edit table**. The design table opens in Excel.
2. Enter parameter values for each configuration of the model, as shown in Figure 13–10.

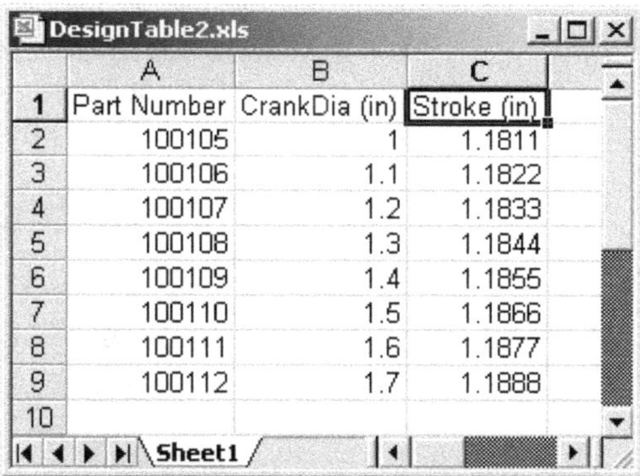
DesignTable2.xls

	A	B	C
1	Part Number	CrankDia (in)	Stroke (in)
2	100105	1	1.1811
3	100106	1.1	1.1822
4	100107	1.2	1.1833
5	100108	1.3	1.1844
6	100109	1.4	1.1855
7	100110	1.5	1.1866
8	100111	1.6	1.1877
9	100112	1.7	1.1888
10			

Sheet1

Figure 13–10

3. Save the spreadsheet and close Excel. The Knowledge Report dialog box opens, confirming that the design table has been synchronized, as shown in Figure 13–11.

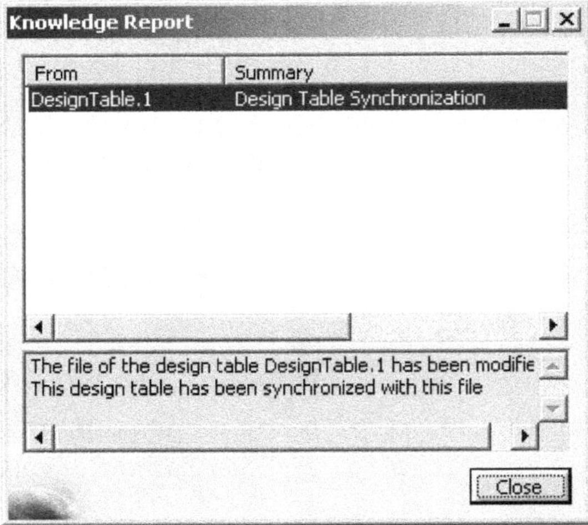

Figure 13–11

4. Close the Knowledge Report dialog box.
5. The DesignTable dialog box updates with the new information, as shown in Figure 13–12.

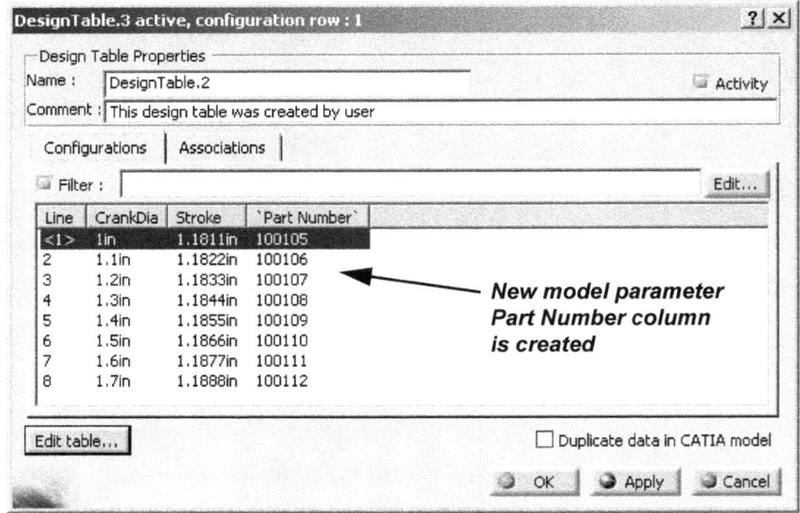

Figure 13–12

If any new columns were added to the spreadsheet while editing, they must be associated with model parameters before they display in the DesignTable dialog box.

Step 4 - Retrieve a configuration.

Each row in the design table represents a different configuration of the part model.

How To: Retrieve a Configuration into CATIA

1. Select the configuration from the design table.
2. Click **OK**. The features affected by the change in configuration are highlighted in red.
3. Click to update the model with the new configuration.

Practice 13a Parameter Setup

Practice Objectives

- Rename model parameters for use in design tables.
- Establish formulas to control feature deactivation.

In this practice, you will create a design table using formulas and renamed parameters.

Task 1 - Open the part.

1. Open **B121463_Bushing.CATPart**. The model displays as shown in Figure 13–13.

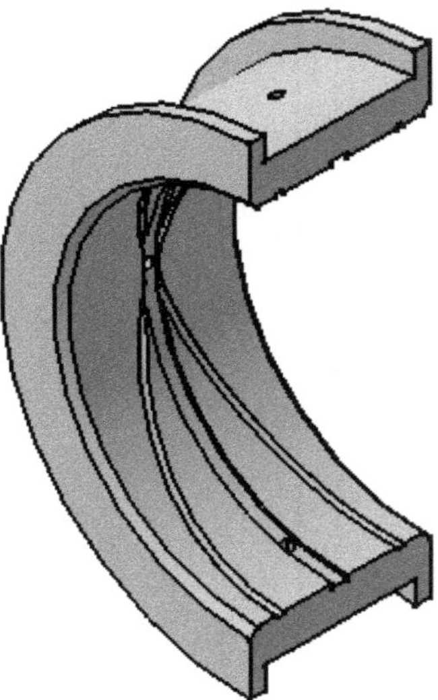

Figure 13–13

Task 2 - Rename parameters for use in the design table.

1. Click (Formula) and select the part in the display. The Formulas dialog box opens and the PartBody dimensions display on the model.

2. In the model, select the D45 dimension and rename its parameter as **Diameter**, as shown in Figure 13–14.

3. Click **Apply** to complete the change.

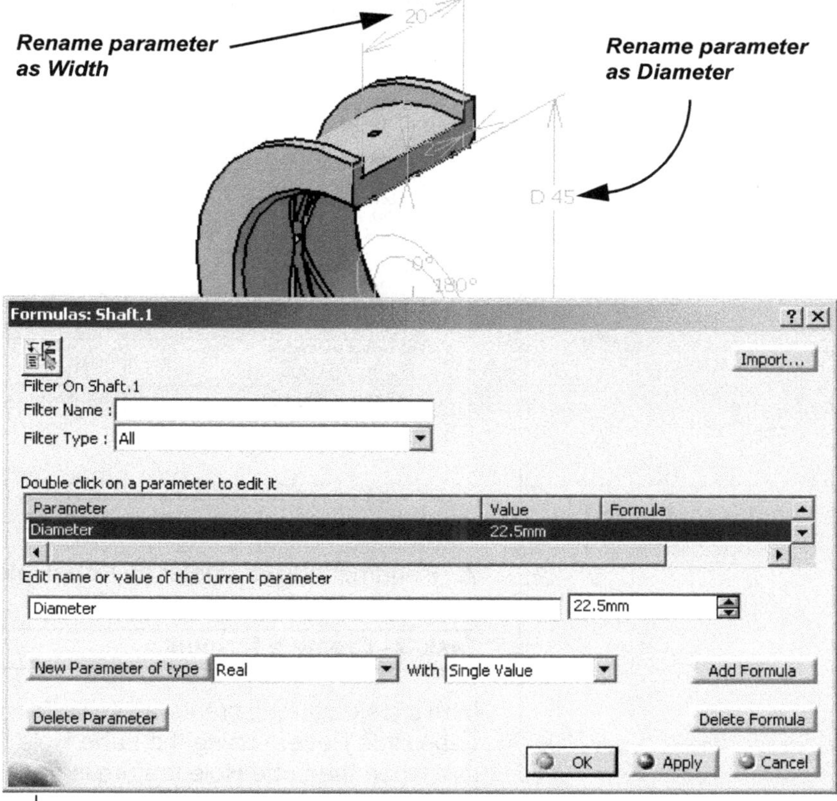

Figure 13–14

4. Rename the 20 dimension parameter as **Width** and click **Apply**.

5. In the specification tree, select the **Lube-Hole** feature.

6. In the Formulas dialog box, scroll down to the end of the parameters list to locate the default system parameter **PartBody\Lube Hole\Activity**, as shown in Figure 13–15. Ensure that you select the last Activity parameter.

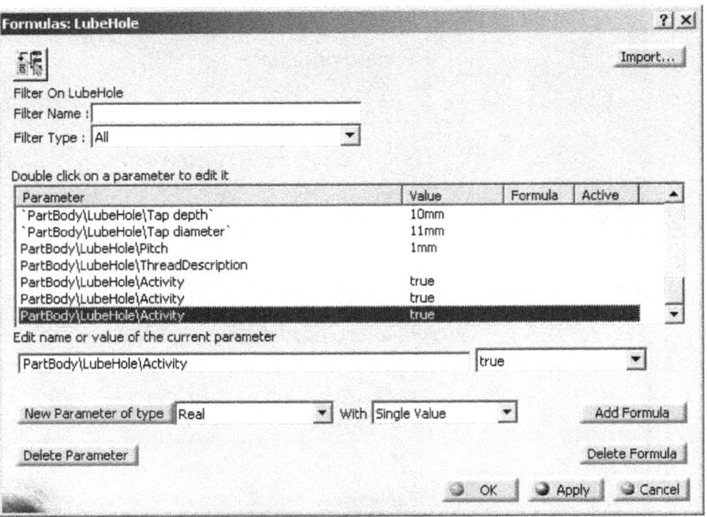

Figure 13–15

7. Rename this parameter as **LubeHole**.

Task 3 - Create a formula.

In this task, you will create a simple formula that controls the Lube Hole Pattern using the Lube Hole feature. This ensures that when the Lube Hole feature is deactivated, the pattern is also deactivated.

1. In the specification tree, select the **Lube Hole Pattern**.
2. In the Formulas dialog box, select **PartBody\LubeHolePattern\Activity** and click **Add Formula**.
3. Set the value of *PartBody\Lube Hole Pattern\Activity* equal to the **LubeHole** parameter, as shown in Figure 13–16.

Double-click on ***LubeHole*** *from the Members of Renamed parameters list, to add it to the formula box.*

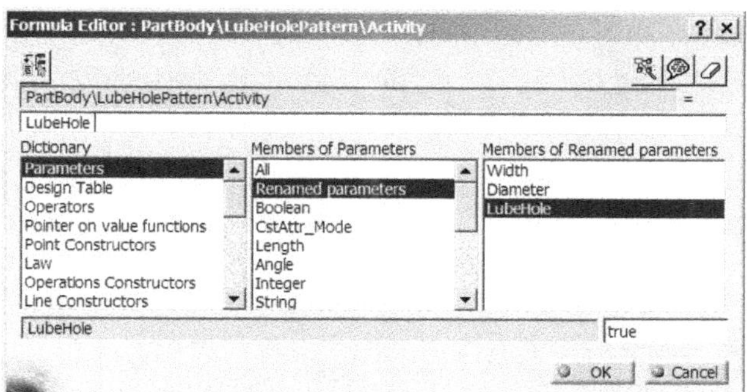

Figure 13–16

4. Click **OK** to close the Formula Editor dialog box. The Formulas dialog box opens as shown in Figure 13–17.

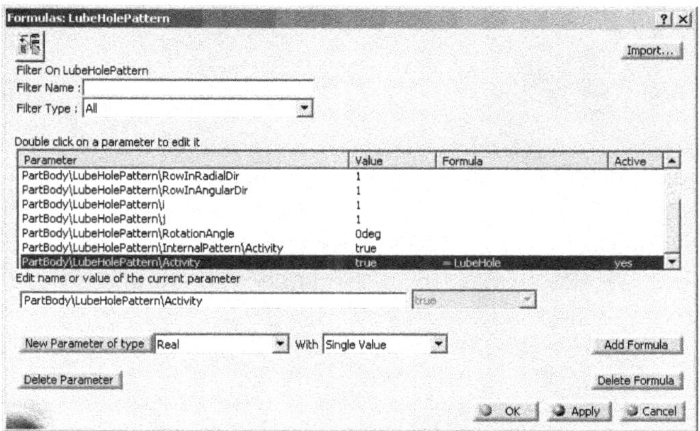

Figure 13–17

5. Click **OK** to close the Formulas dialog box.

Task 4 - Test the formula.

1. Deactivate the **Lube Hole** feature.

2. Clear the **Deactivate aggregated elements** option. The Deactivate dialog box opens as shown in Figure 13–18.

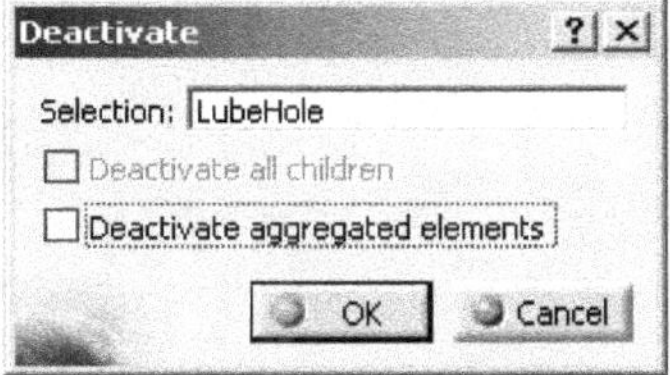

Figure 13–18

3. Click **OK**.

4. Although the children and aggregated elements are not deactivated, no pattern instances display on the model. The formula ensures that the pattern instances are all deactivated when the Lead feature is deactivated. The model displays as shown in Figure 13–19.

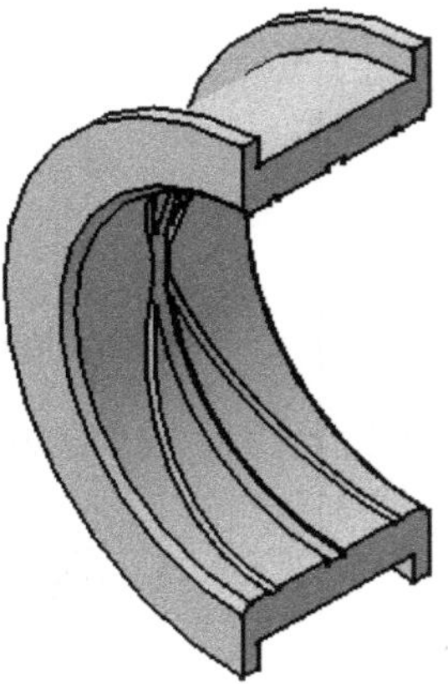

Figure 13–19

5. Activate the Lube Hole feature and save the model. This model is used in the next practice.

Practice 13b Design Table I

Practice Objectives

- Create a design table.
- Use Excel to edit the design table.
- Retrieve configurations of the design table.

In this practice, you will create a number of design configurations for the bushing model using a design table. You will then retrieve a configuration from the design table into the model.

Task 1 - Create a design table for the B121463 Bushing.

1. Ensure that the **B121463_Bushing.CATPart** model is open.

   If you did not complete the last practice, open **B121463_Bushing.CATPart** from the *Completed* directory instead.

2. Click (Design Table) to create a design table. The Creation of a Design Table dialog box opens as shown in Figure 13–20.

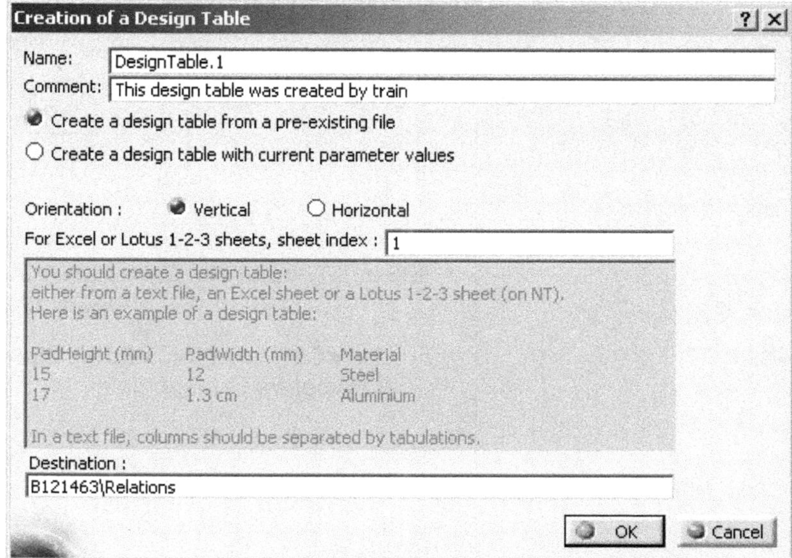

Creation of a Design Table
Name: DesignTable.1
Comment: This design table was created by train
Create a design table from a pre-existing file
Create a design table with current parameter values
Orientation : Vertical Horizontal
For Excel or Lotus 1-2-3 sheets, sheet index : 1
You should create a design table:
either from a text file, an Excel sheet or a Lotus 1-2-3 sheet (on NT).
Here is an example of a design table:
PadHeight (mm) PadWidth (mm) Material
15 12 Steel
17 1.3 cm Aluminium
In a text file, columns should be separated by tabulations.
Destination :
B121463\Relations
OK
Cancel

Figure 13–20

3. Select **Create a design table with current parameter values**.

4. In the *Name* field, enter **B121463 Bushing**.

5. Click **OK**. The Select parameters to Insert dialog box opens as shown in Figure 13–21.

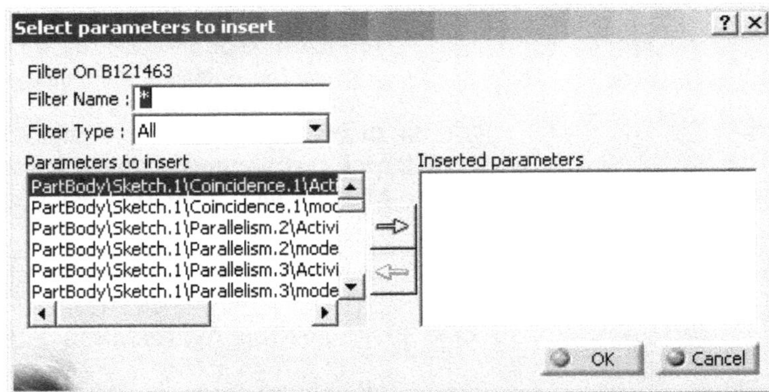

Figure 13–21

6. In the Filter Type drop-down list, select **Renamed parameters** as shown in Figure 13–22.

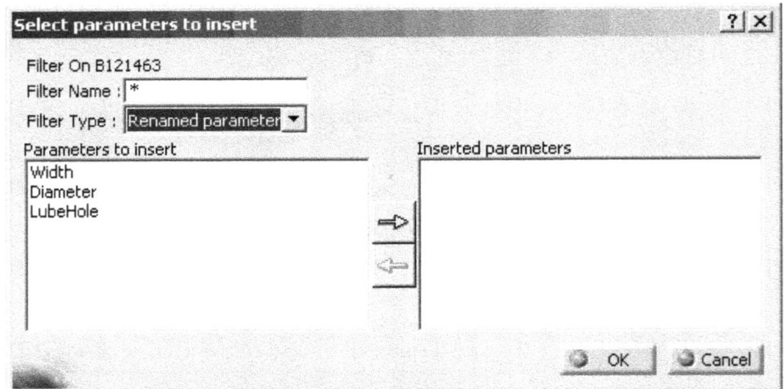

Figure 13–22

7. Use <Ctrl> to select **Width**, **Diameter**, and **LubeHole** in the *Parameters to Insert* field.

8. Click [icon] to add these parameters to the *Inserted parameters* field. The Select parameters to insert dialog box opens as shown in Figure 13–23.

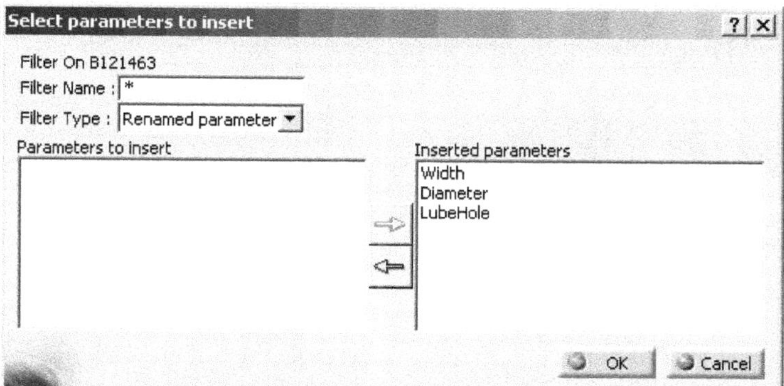

Figure 13–23

9. Click **OK** and save the design table information as **B121463 Bushing.xls**. The dialog box shown in Figure 13–24 opens.

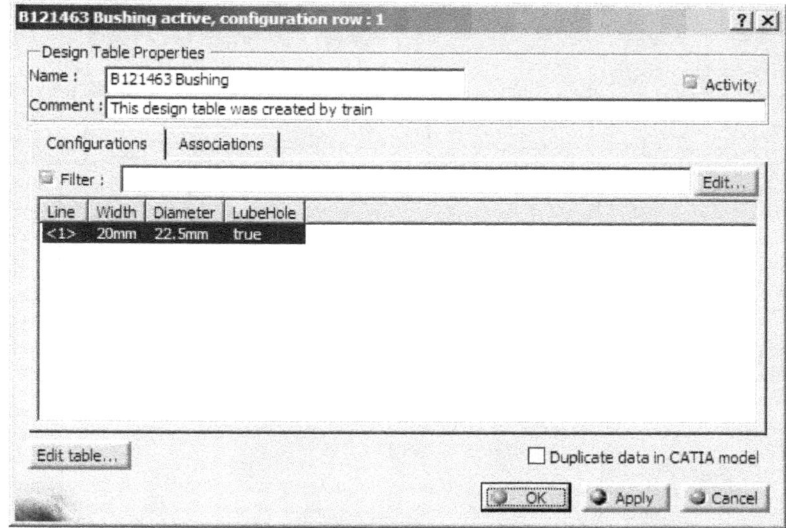

Figure 13–24

Task 2 - Edit the design table using Excel.

1. To open the table in Excel, click **Edit table**. Note that your version of Excel might look slightly different.

2. Insert a new column by right-clicking on column A, and selecting **Insert**, as shown in Figure 13–25.

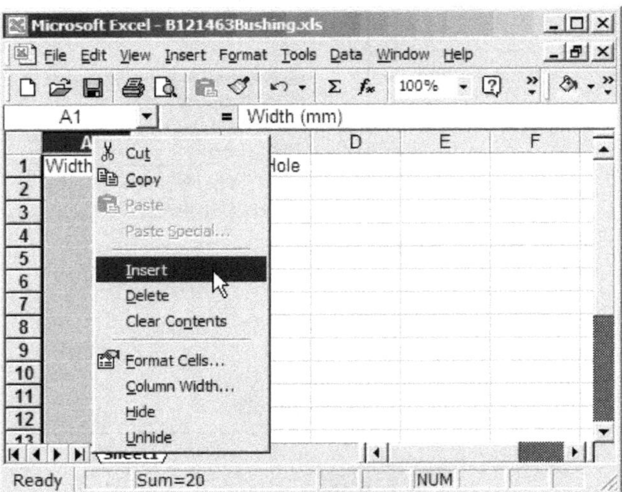

Figure 13–25

3. In cell *A1*, enter **PartNumber**.

4. In cell *A2*, enter **B121463**.

5. In cell *A3*, enter **B121464** as shown in Figure 13–26.

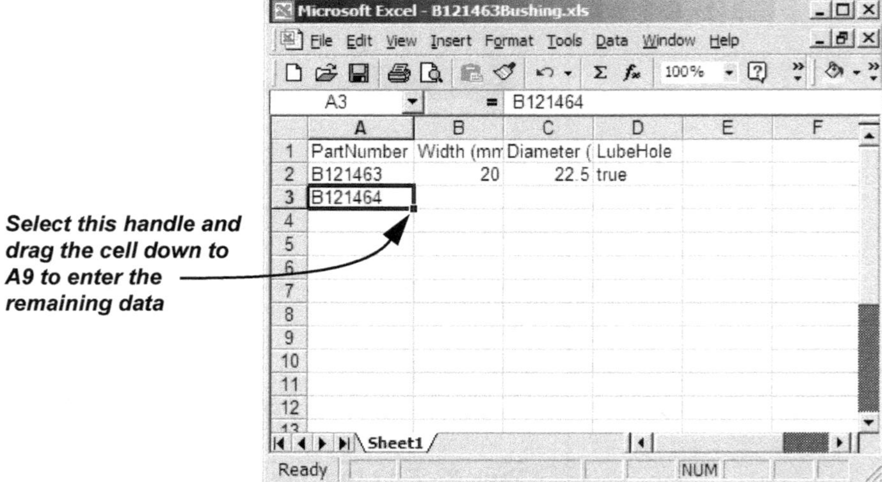
Select this handle and drag the cell down to A9 to enter the remaining data

Figure 13–26

6. Fill out the Excel spreadsheet, as shown in Figure 13–27.

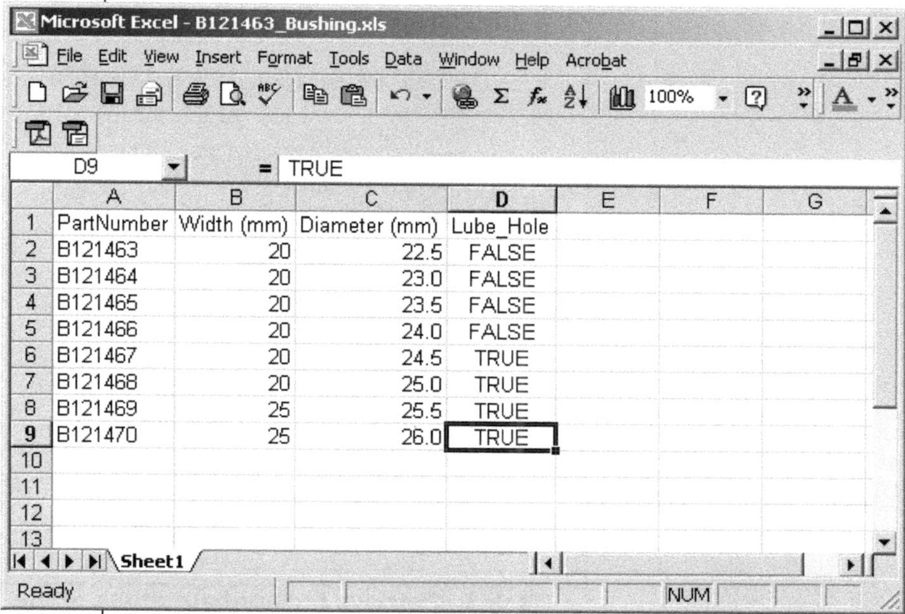

	A	B	C	D
1	PartNumber	Width (mm)	Diameter (mm)	Lube_Hole
2	B121463	20	22.5	FALSE
3	B121464	20	23.0	FALSE
4	B121465	20	23.5	FALSE
5	B121466	20	24.0	FALSE
6	B121467	20	24.5	TRUE
7	B121468	20	25.0	TRUE
8	B121469	25	25.5	TRUE
9	B121470	25	26.0	TRUE

Figure 13–27

7. Save and close the spreadsheet. The dialog box shown in Figure 13–28 opens. The design table has been synchronized with the part model.

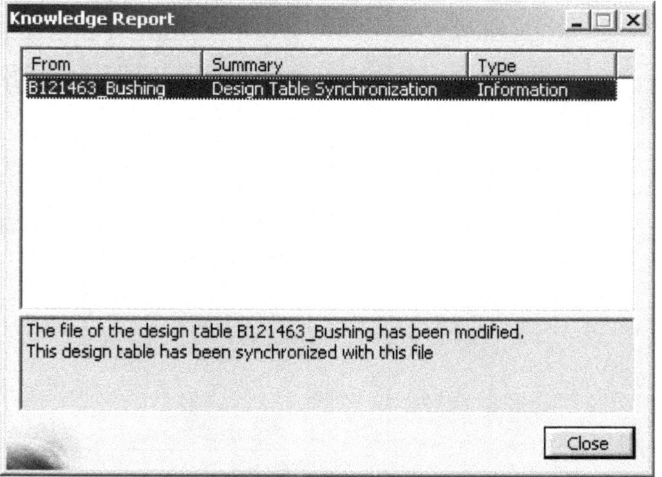

Figure 13–28

8. Click **Close**. The design table opens as shown in Figure 13–29. Note that the *PartNumber* column is not displayed in the table.

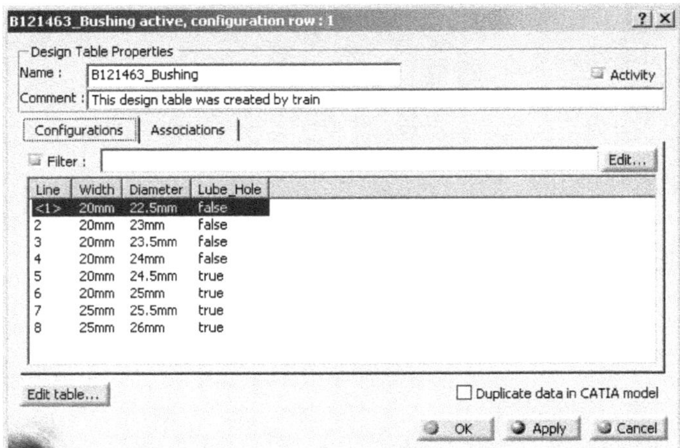

Figure 13–29

Task 3 - Retrieve the configurations of the design table.

1. Select the *Associations* tab. Scroll to the bottom of the parameters window. In the list, select **B121463\PartNumber** as shown in Figure 13–30.

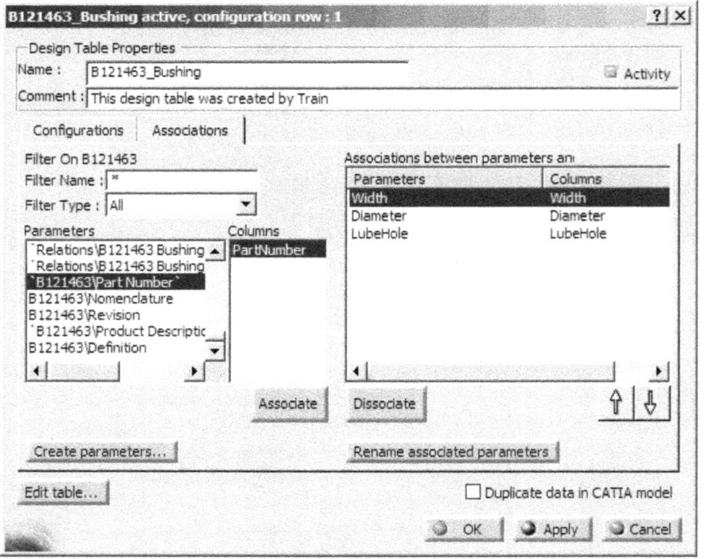

Figure 13–30

2. To associate the parameter with the *PartNumber* column, click **Associate**.

3. Use to move the parameter to the top of the list, as shown in Figure 13–31.

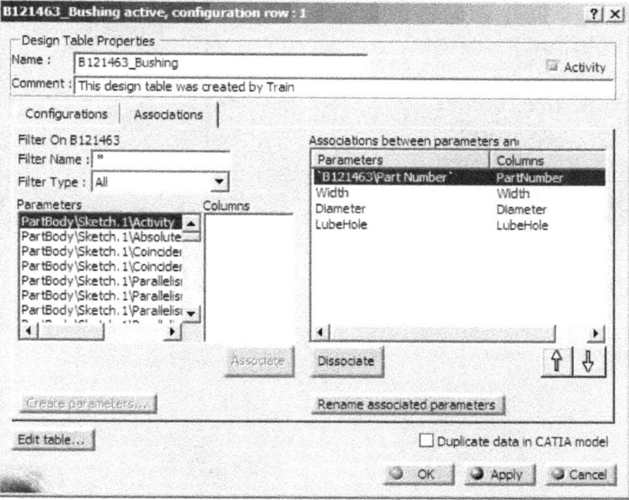

Figure 13–31

4. Select the *Configurations* tab. Verify that the **B121463** Part Number is selected, as shown in Figure 13–32.

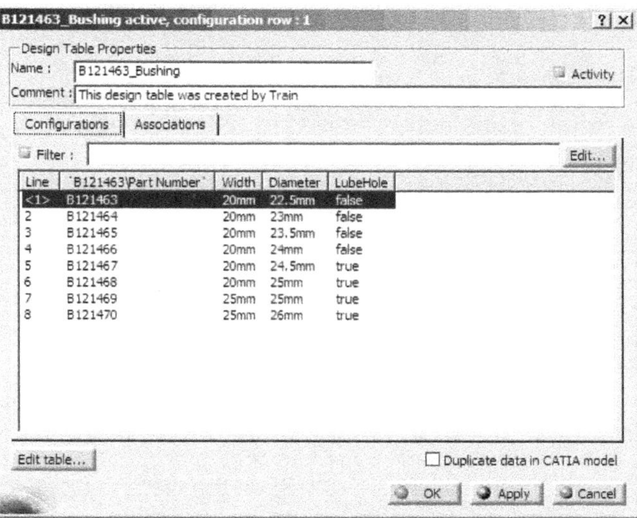

Figure 13–32

5. Click **OK**.

*To display the design table in the specification tree, relations must be shown. To do this, select **Tools>Options>Infrastructure>Part Infrastructure**, select the Display tab, and then select **Relations** in the Display In Specification Tree area.*

6. The model and specification tree display as shown in Figure 13–33. Note that the LubeHole and LubeHolePattern features are deactivated.

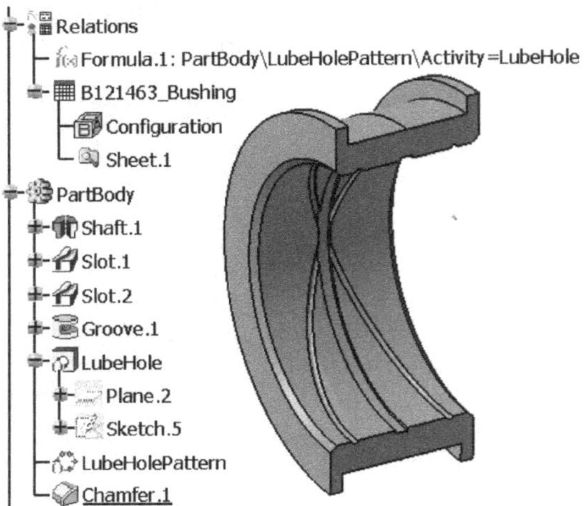

Figure 13–33

7. In the specification tree, under **Relations**, double-click on **B121463 Bushing** twice to open the design table.

8. Select part number **121470** (line 8) and click **OK**. The model updates with the design table values for **121470**, as shown in Figure 13–34.

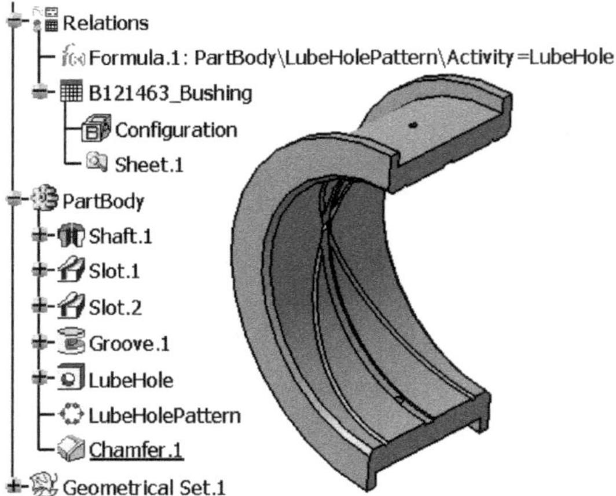

Figure 13–34

9. Save the file and close the window.

Practice 13c

(Optional) Design Table II

Practice Objective

- Create a design table without instructions

In this practice, you will create a number of design configurations for the **L-Bracket** model using a design table without instructions.

Task 1 - Create a design table for the L-Bracket.

In this task, you will create a design table for the **L-Bracket** model.

1. Open **L-Bracket.CATPart**. The model display as shown in Figure 13–35.

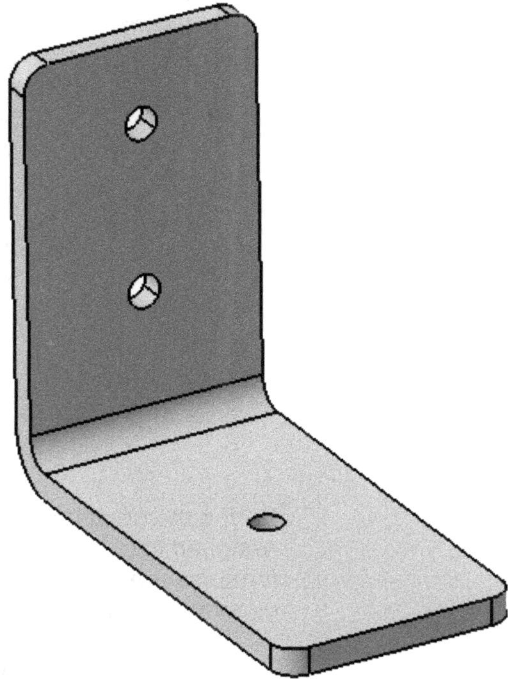

Figure 13–35

The following parameters have already been renamed, as shown in Figure 13–36.

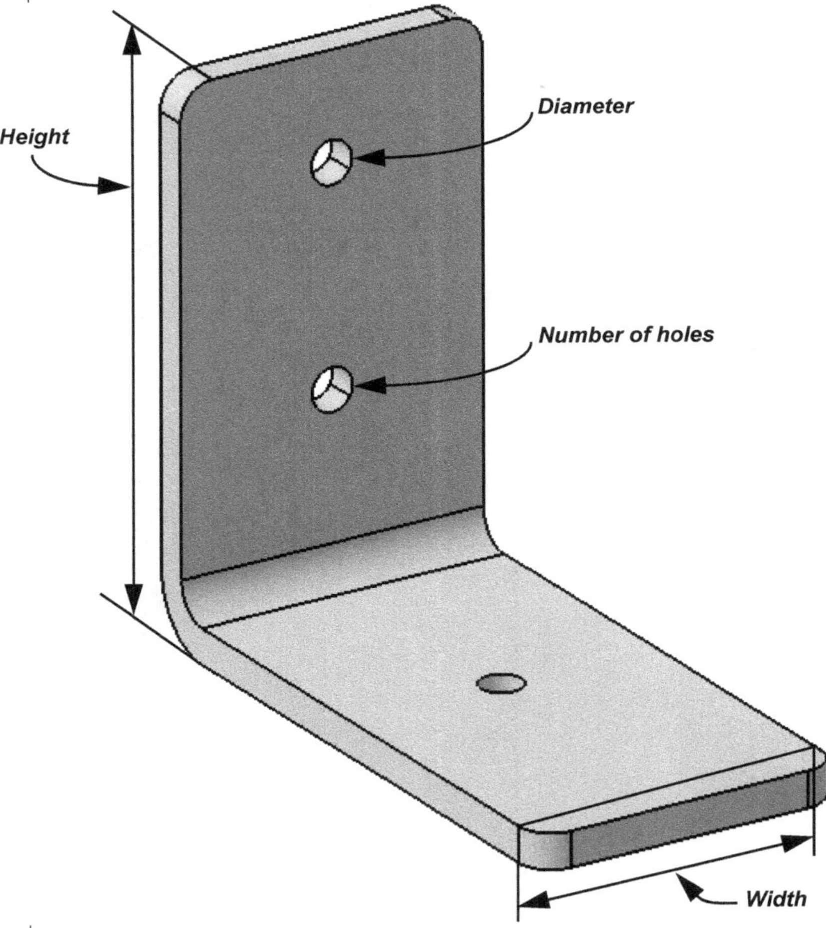

Figure 13–36

During the creation of the part, some of the formulas are assigned to control the positions of **Hole.1** and **Hole.2**. The other formulas are used to make the diameter of **Hole.2** equal to the diameter of **Hole.1**.

2. Create a design table for 9 different configurations of the **L-Bracket**. The values are listed in the table shown in Figure 13–37 below, with the initial values in the first row.

	A	B	C	D	E
1	PartNumber	Height (mm)	Width (mm)	Diameter (mm)	\`Number-of holes\`
2	B145	125	75	10	2
3	B146	135	75	10	2
4	B147	145	75	10	2
5	B148	155	75	10	2
6	B149	175	75	10	3
7	B150	185	100	15	3
8	B151	195	100	15	3
9	B152	240	100	15	4
10	B153	260	100	15	4

Figure 13–37

3. Open various instances to verify that the design table is functioning correctly.

4. Save the model and close the window.

Chapter Review Questions

1. You can prepare a model for use in a design table by renaming parameters or creating formulas.
   a. True
   b. False
2. CATIA creates a model parameter for every entity in a model, including dimensions and features.
   a. True
   b. False
3. How do formulas simplify a design table?
   a. Formulas can control multiple features and dimensions with a single parameter.
   b. Formulas reduce the number of parameters that need to be added to the design table to drive the design intent.
   c. Formulas make the design table easier to understand and modify.
   d. All of the above.
4. Part design tables are useful for creating a series of models that have a similar geometric shape, but come in a variety of sizes.
   a. True
   b. False
5. Design tables are unique to each design and cannot be stored in external files for reuse.
   a. True
   b. False

Catalogs

You can use catalogs to browse through CATIA's library of industry-standard parts, or to create custom libraries for company-specific parts. This chapter focuses on creating and working with custom catalogs.

Learning Objectives in this Chapter

- Understand the use of custom catalogs.
- Create custom catalogs.
- Learn how to insert a Power Copy into a catalog.
- Create Part Family catalogs.

14.1 Catalogs

CATIA V5 comes with a library of industry-standard fasteners and common parts. These parts are stored in catalogs, which provide quick access to predefined parts.

Custom catalogs can be defined to store additional predefined CATIA elements, industry-specific parts, and company-specific parts. You can use structured custom catalogs to store and find common parts. This increases consistency and efficiency. Catalogs can also contain many CATIA elements, including:

- PowerCopies
- Geometrical Sets
- Sketches
- 2D elements
- UserFeatures
- PartBodies
- Parameters
- Design tables

14.2 Creation of a Catalog

You can use CATIA V5 to create your own part catalogs based on company-specific requirements.

General Steps

Use the following general steps to create a catalog:

1. Open the Catalog Editor workbench.
2. Add a new chapter.
3. Add a new family.
4. Add a link to another catalog, if required.

Step 1 - Open the Catalog Editor workbench.

Select **File>New**. In the New dialog box, select **CatalogDocument**, as shown in Figure 14–1.

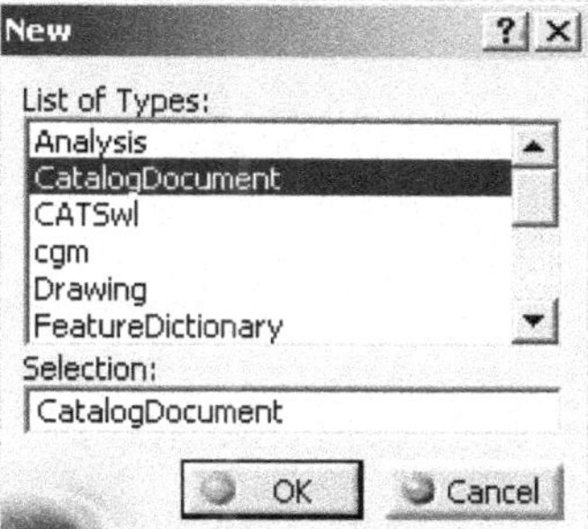

Figure 14–1

The new catalog opens as shown in Figure 14–2.

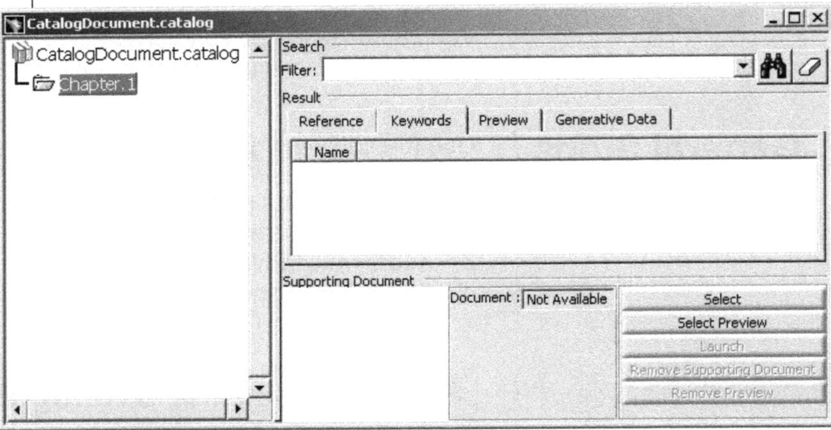

Figure 14–2

To rename the catalog, save the file with a new name. You might need to double-click on **CatalogDocument1.catalog** for the name change to take effect.

Step 2 - Add a new chapter.

A chapter is a collection of related chapters and/or families of parts in the catalog.

How To: Add a Chapter

The active level is indicated by the blue highlighted text. You can change the active level by double-clicking.

1. Activate the top-level chapter that you want the new chapter to follow.
2. Click (Add Chapter). The Chapter Definition dialog box opens as shown in Figure 14–3.

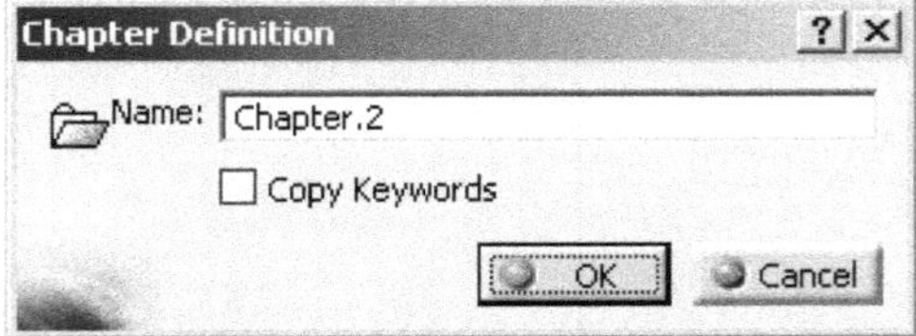

Figure 14–3

3. Enter the name of the chapter and click **OK**. The catalog opens with the new chapter in the tree, as shown in Figure 14–4.

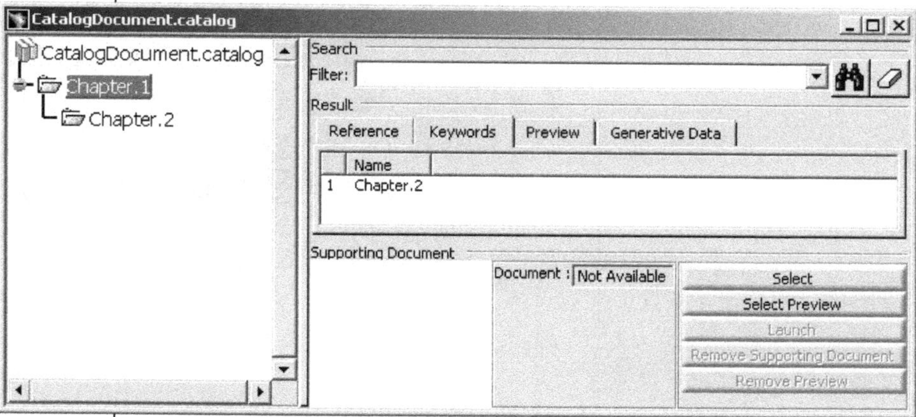

Figure 14–4

To rename a chapter, right-click on the chapter and select **Chapter.* object>Definition**.

Step 3 - Add a new family.

A family contains the related components that are added into and accessed from the catalog.

How To: Add a Family

Activate the chapter by double-clicking on it. The active chapter is indicated by the blue highlighted text.

1. Activate the chapter to which you want to add the family.
2. Click (Add Family). The Component Family Definition dialog box opens as shown in Figure 14–5.

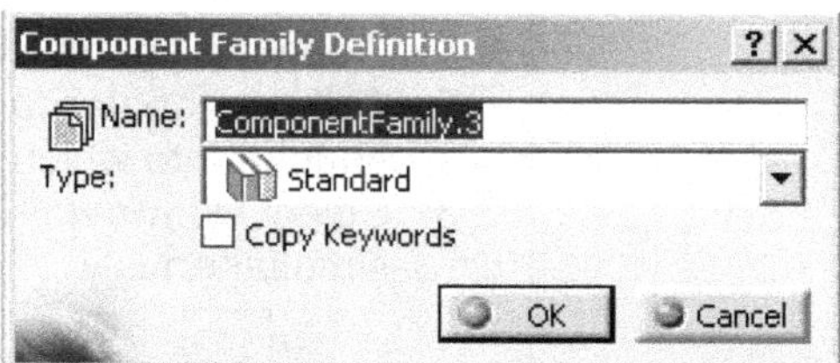

Figure 14–5

3. In the *Name* field, enter the Family name. In the Type drop-down list, select the *Family type*. In the specification tree, the catalog displays with the new **ComponentFamily.3** family, as shown in Figure 14–6.

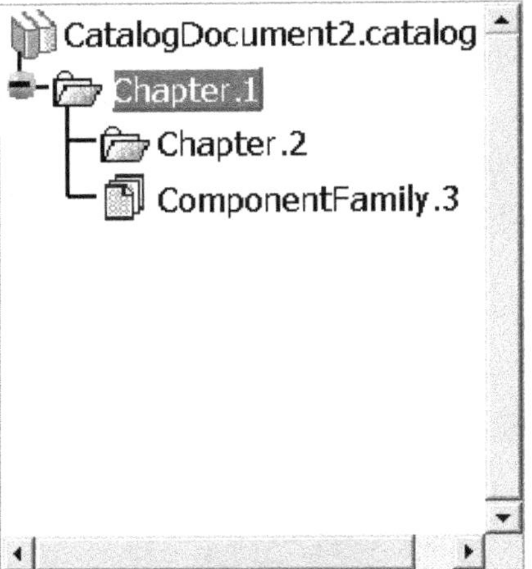

Figure 14–6

4. Use (Add Component) to activate the component family and add components as required.

Step 4 - Add a link to another catalog, if required.

You can generate links between catalogs, so that you can access a variety of catalog structures and objects from within a single, top-level catalog.

How To: Add a Link to a Catalog

1. Open the source catalog to be accessed by the link.
2. Activate the window of the target catalog. Activate the chapter into which the link is to be added.
3. Select **Window>Tile Horizontally** to display both catalogs simultaneously.
4. Click (Add link to other catalog).

5. Select the chapter or family that you want to link to from the source catalog. This link displays under the activated chapter. For example, a link to the PowerCopies chapter of another catalog is added beneath **Chapter.2**, as shown in Figure 14–7.

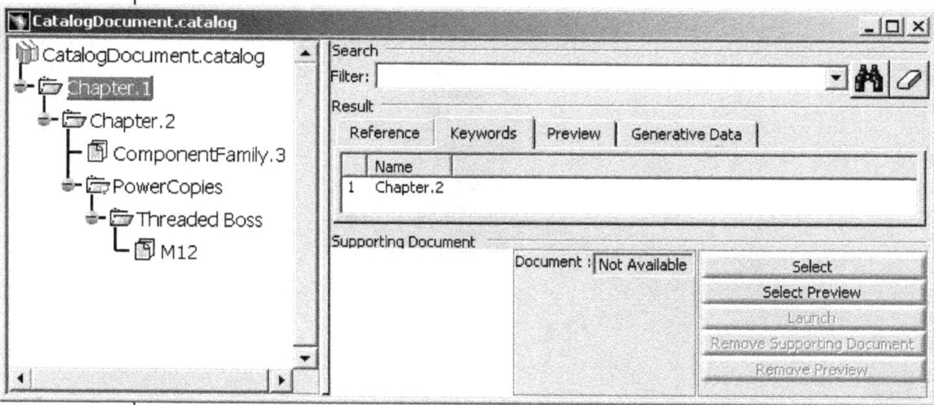

Figure 14–7

The *Reference* tab displays the linked folder and with **External** chapter as its Type. The arrow on the folder icon, , indicates a link. Other catalog creation options are described as follows:

Option	Description
(Add Keyword)	Adds keywords to chapters so you can find those chapters through a search. Keyword types can be integer, string, boolean, or angle.
(Add Component)	Adds a component to the current family.
Reorder	Re-orders chapters, families, and components in the specification tree.
(Add Part Family)	Adds a family to a chapter that refers to a Part file that has different parameter values managed by a design table.
(Add Part Family Components)	Adds components in a design table to an existing part family.

14.3 Cataloging a PowerCopy

You can insert a PowerCopy into a catalog from the document in which it was created. Activate the document with the PowerCopy and select **Insert>Knowledge Templates>Save in Catalog**, as shown in Figure 14–8.

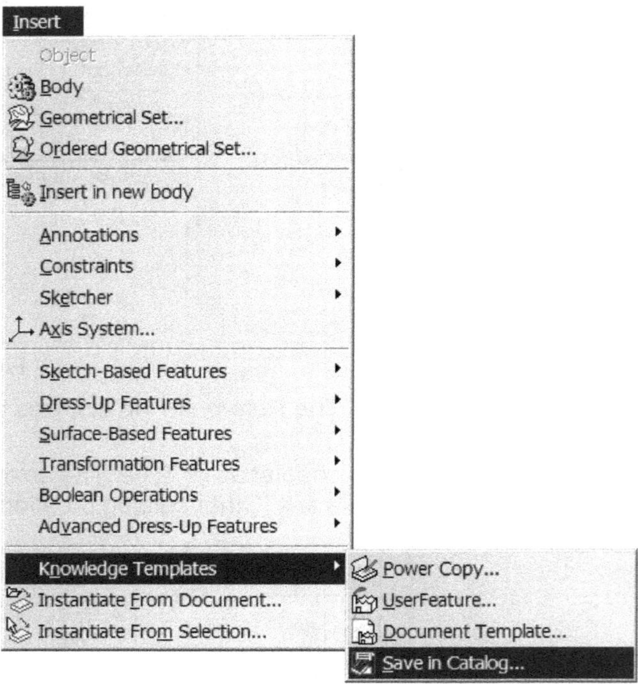

Figure 14–8

The Catalog save dialog box opens as shown in Figure 14–9.

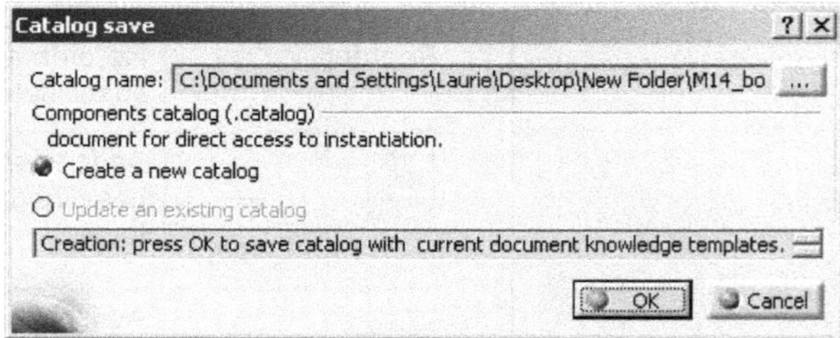

Figure 14–9

The **Create a new catalog** option is selected by default. If you want to add the PowerCopy to an existing catalog, click ... and browse to the catalog file. Click **OK** to finish.

CATIA automatically creates a chapter in the selected catalog that contains a family with the **PowerCopy** component, as shown in Figure 14–10.

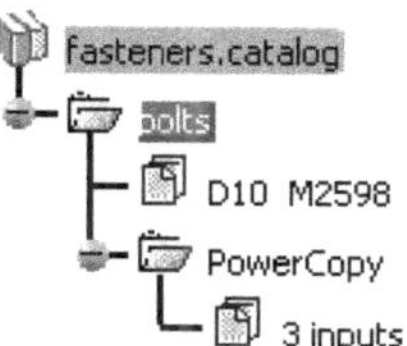

Figure 14–10

If you want to change the default name of the chapter containing the PowerCopy, right-click on the chapter and select **PowerCopy Object>Definition**. Enter the new name. The family name for the PowerCopy can be changed using the same technique.

Instantiate a PowerCopy from the Catalog

A PowerCopy is instantiated into a document similar to other cataloged features.

How To: Instantiate a PowerCopy from a Catalog

1. Click (Catalog Browser).
2. Locate the catalog that contains the PowerCopy by clicking , and browse to the PowerCopy.
3. Double-click on the required PowerCopy to open the Insert Object dialog box.
4. Place the PowerCopy using the method described earlier.

14.4 Creating Part Family Catalogs

Once you create the design table, you can add it to a catalog where you can retrieve the different configurations as separate part files.

General Steps

Use the following steps to add a design table to a catalog:

1. Create a new catalog.
2. Add a part family.
3. Complete the catalog and save the file.
4. Retrieve a configuration.

Step 1 - Create a new catalog.

You can add a part design table to a new catalog or an existing one. It is recommended that you become familiar with any existing catalog document structure before creating new catalog documents.

How To: Create a New Catalog

1. Select **File>New**. In the New dialog box, select **CatalogDocument**.
2. To rename the catalog, save the file with a new name. To rename the chapter, right-click on it and select **Chapter.1 object>Definition**. The catalog displays as shown in Figure 14–11.

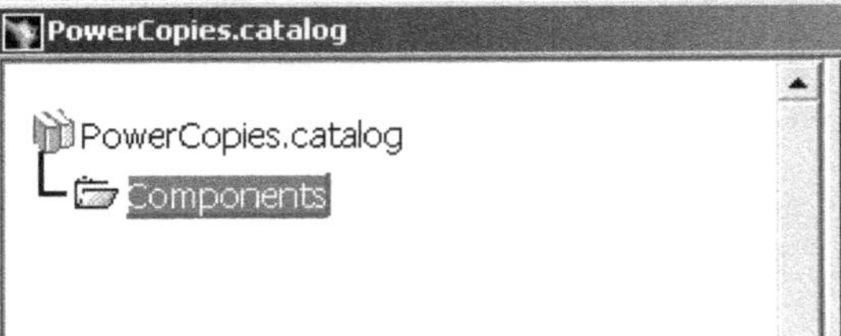

Figure 14–11

Step 2 - Add a part family.

Click [icon] to add a part family. The Part Family Definition dialog box opens as shown in Figure 14–12.

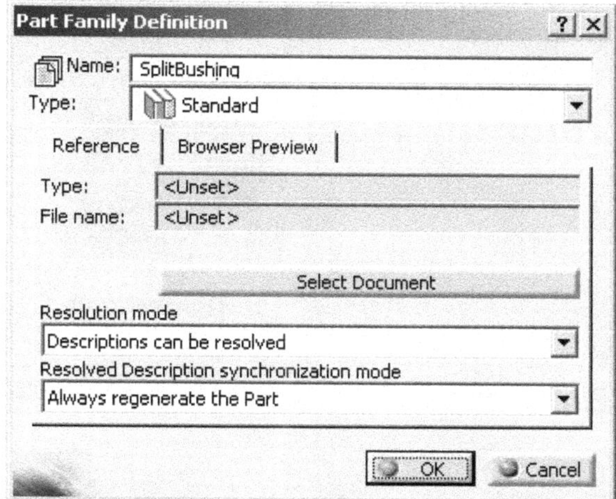

Figure 14–12

Enter a name for the part family. Click **Select Document** to browse to the part file containing the design table.

Once selected, the file displays in the *File Name* field in the Part Family Definition dialog box. Click **OK**. The document is loaded into the catalog, as shown in Figure 14–13.

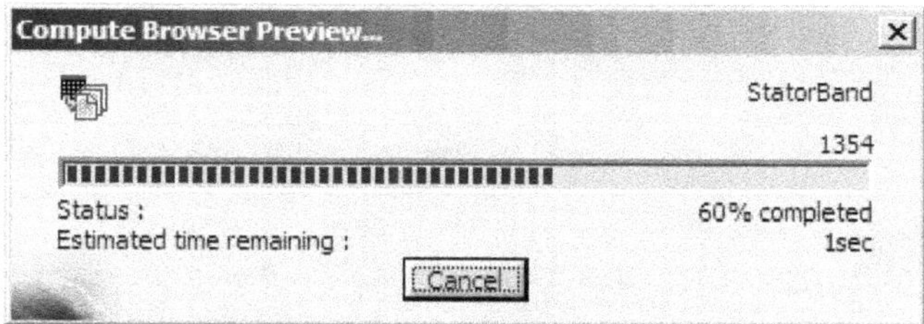

Figure 14–13

When the document finishes loading, activate the **PartFamily** in the specification tree. The configurations display in the table on the right. Select the *Preview* tab to display all of the configurations of the part, as shown in Figure 14–14.

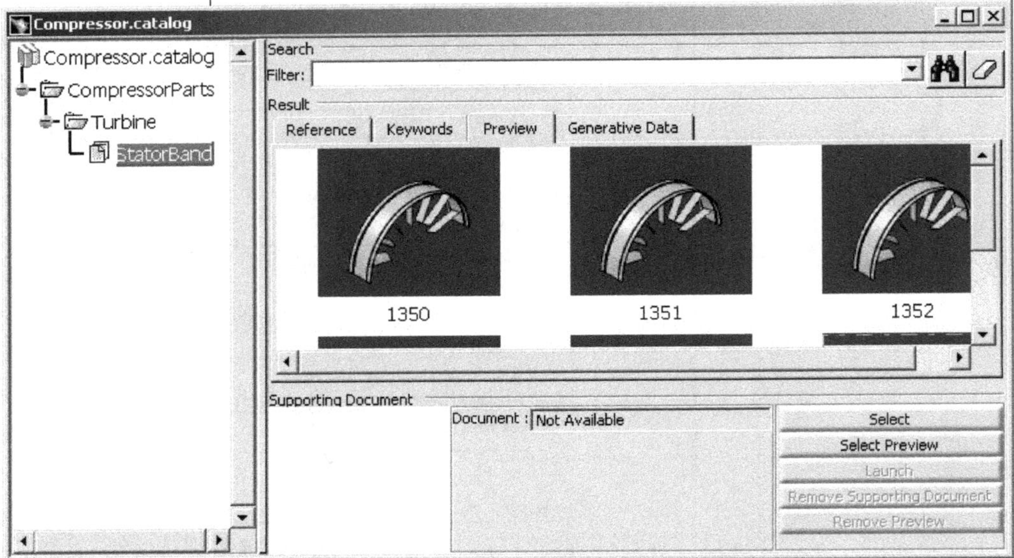

Figure 14–14

The tabs in the CatalogDocument dialog box are described as follows:

Tab	Description
Reference	Lists the name, type, and file location of each configuration.
Keywords	Displays each configuration and its set of parameter values defined in the design table.
Preview	Provides a preview image of each configuration.
Generative Data	Stores queries using . The queries filter out specific configurations from a design table and are listed in the *Generative Definitions* field. The results of a selected query display in the *Generated Components* field.

Step 3 - Complete the catalog and save the file.

Once you finish adding a part family to the catalog, you should resolve each configuration. Right-click on the part family in the tree and select *.**object>Resolve**, as shown in Figure 14–15.

Figure 14–15

Resolving enables you to verify that the design table does not contain any errors and that each configuration produces a usable model. If no errors are found, the *Type* column in the *Reference* tab updates to **Resolved part family configuration**, as shown in Figure 14–16.

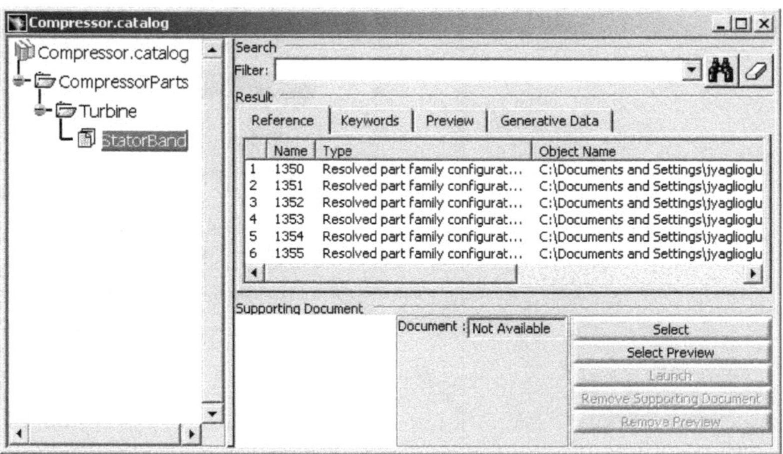

Figure 14–16

The catalog now contains links to each configuration. To set the path where the resolved components are dumped, select **Tools> Options>Infrastructure>Catalog Editor**. This is important if the catalog is going to be used by other designers. Anyone instantiating these resolved components must have access to this directory. You can see this if you select **Edit>Links** before and after resolving a part family.

Save the file and close the window.

Step 4 - Retrieve a configuration.

You can now retrieve configurations of the part model using the Catalog Browser.

How To: Retrieve a Part Configuration

1. Open the part or product file to which you want to retrieve the part configuration.
2. Click (Catalog Browser) to open the Catalog Browser.
3. Expand the Current drop-down list, select the catalog containing the part family. If the catalog is not available, click and browse to the catalog.
4. Browse through the catalog tree to locate the required configuration. Use filters to reduce the amount of data to search through.
5. Click to open the Filter dialog box, as shown in Figure 14–17.

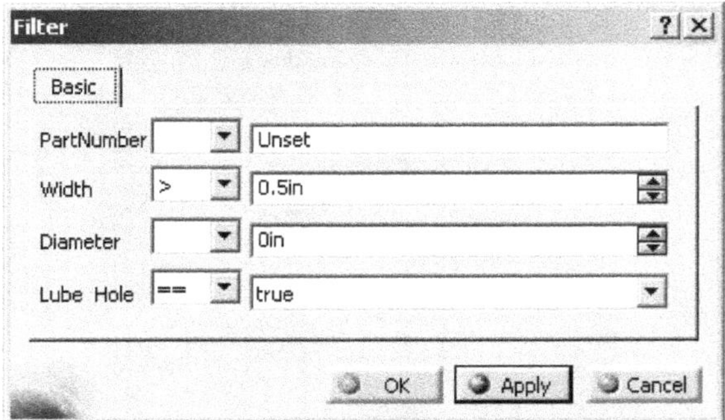

Figure 14–17

For example, to display parameters with a value larger than **0.5** for the Width parameter and a value of **true** for the **Lube Hole** parameter, select **Width>0.5** and **Lube Hole == true** in the *Filter* fields.

6. Once you locate the required configuration, double-click on the configuration to retrieve it into CATIA. The Catalog window opens, in which you can confirm your selection.

Practice 14a Catalogs

Practice Objectives

- Create a catalog.
- Add elements to a catalog.
- Link from one catalog to another.

In this practice, you will create the structure for a catalog. The parts are added to the catalog. Finally, you will generate a new catalog and create a link from the first catalog to the new one. The completed catalogs display as shown in Figure 14–18.

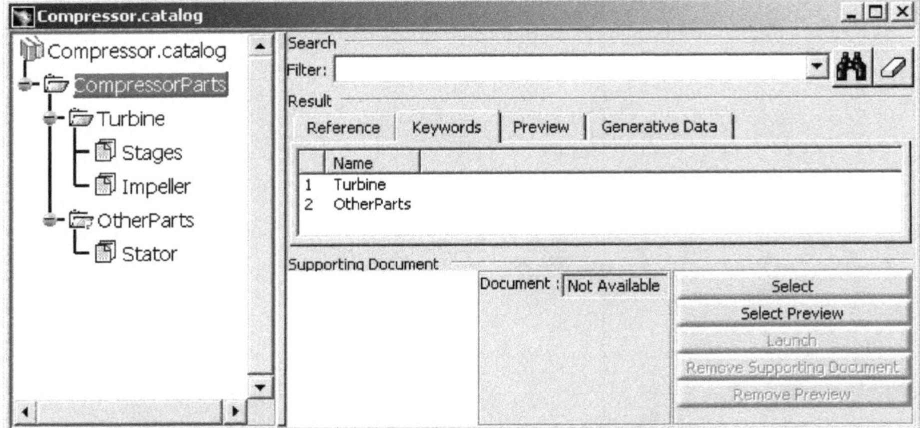

Figure 14–18

Task 1 - Create a new catalog.

1. Select **File>New**. In the New dialog box, select **CatalogDocument**.
2. Click **OK**.
3. Save the file in the *Turbine* directory as **Compressor.catalog**.
4. In the specification tree, right-click on **Chapter.1** and select **Chapter.1 object>Definition** to rename **Chapter.1**. The Chapter Definition dialog box opens as shown in Figure 14–19.

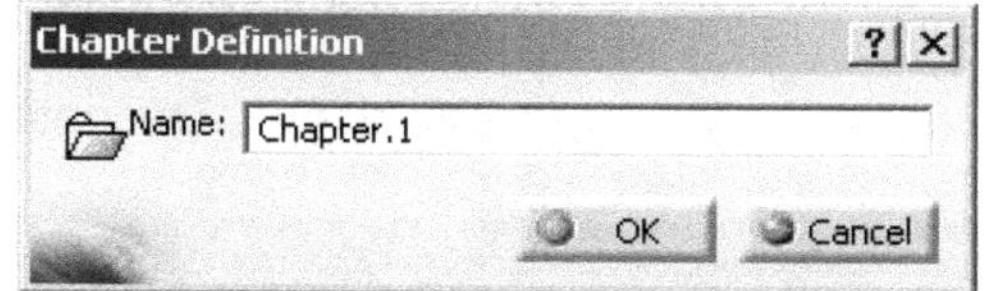

Figure 14–19

5. In the *Name* field, enter **CompressorParts**.
6. Click **OK**. The **Compressor** catalog displays as shown in Figure 14–20.

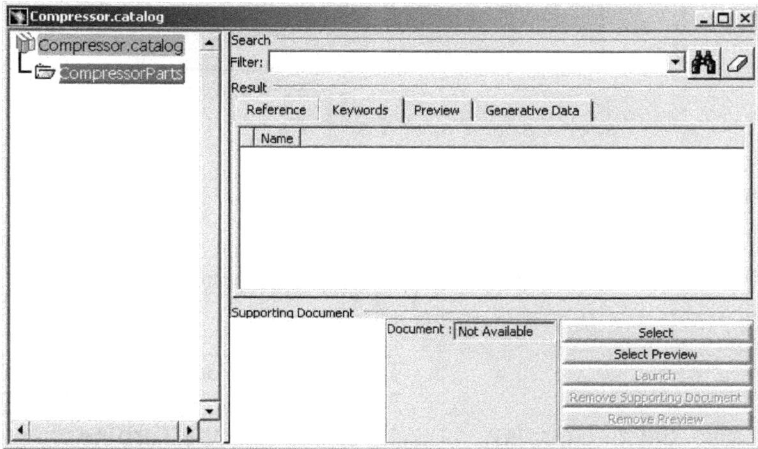

Figure 14–20

7. Save the catalog.

Task 2 - Add a chapter.

1. Ensure that the **CompressorParts** chapter is active by double-clicking on it in the specification tree (active chapters display in blue).
2. Click (Add Chapter). The Chapter Definition dialog box opens as shown in Figure 14–21.

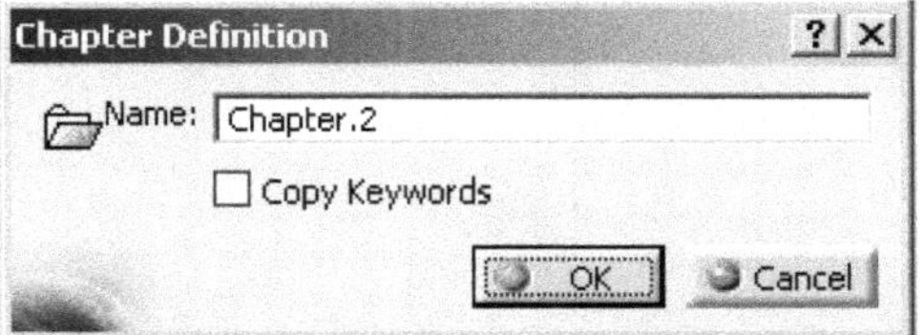

Figure 14–21

3. In the *Name* field, enter **Turbine**.

4. Click **OK**. The catalog displays as shown in Figure 14–22.

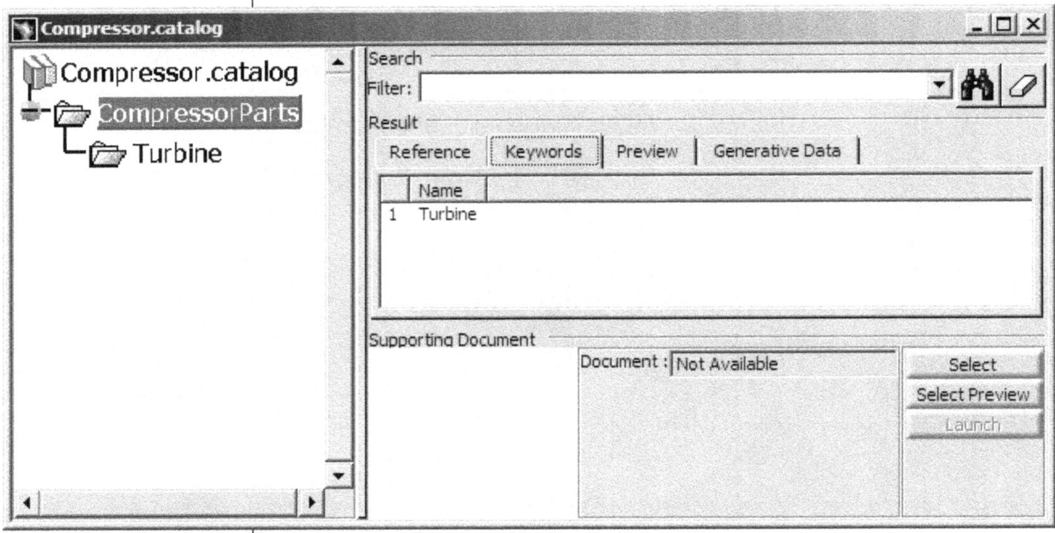

Figure 14–22

Task 3 - Add Families to a chapter.

Active chapters display in blue.

1. Ensure that the **Turbine** chapter is active. If not, activate it by double-clicking on it.

2. Click (Add Family). The Component Family Definition dialog box opens as shown in Figure 14–23.

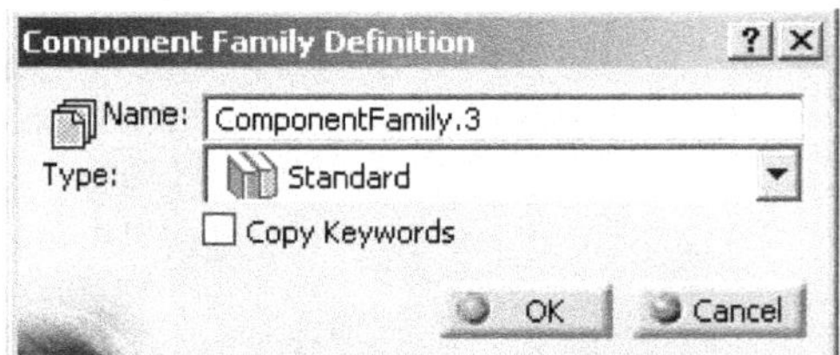

Figure 14–23

3. In the *Name* field, enter **Stages**.

4. Click **OK**. The catalog displays as shown in Figure 14–24.

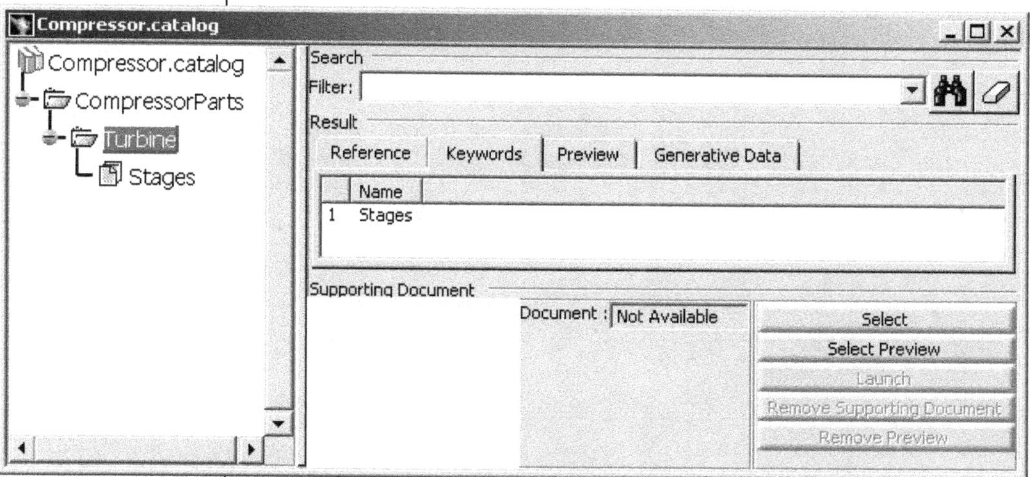

Figure 14–24

5. Add another family to the **Turbine** chapter. Change the name to **Impeller**. The *Compressor* catalog displays as shown in Figure 14–25.

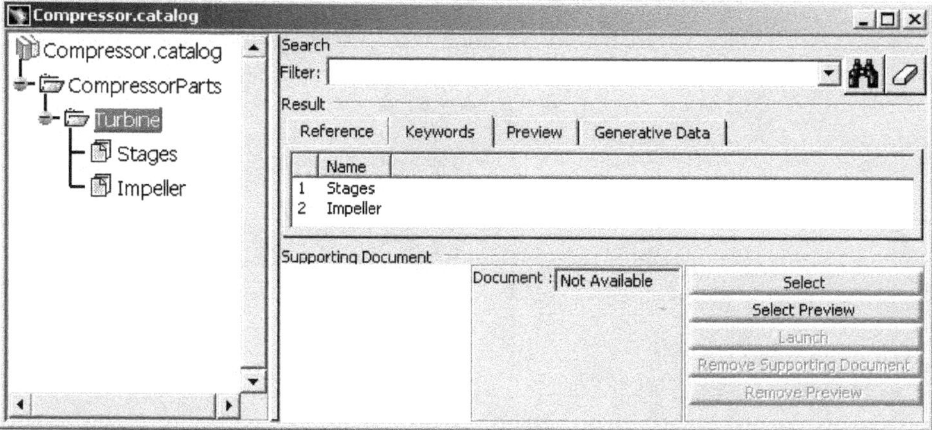

Figure 14–25

Task 4 - Add components to a family.

1. Activate the Stages family.

2. Click (Add Component). The Description Definition dialog box opens as shown in Figure 14–26.

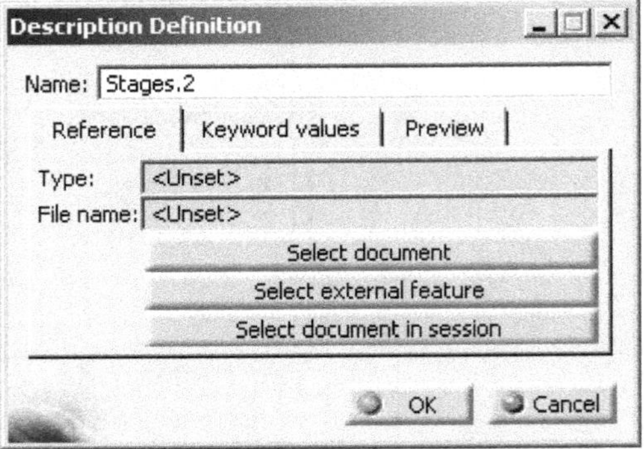

Figure 14–26

3. Rename the component as **1stStage**.

4. Click **Select document** and select **1stStage.CATPart** in the *Turbine* directory. The file path displays in the *File Name* field in the Description Definition dialog box as shown in Figure 14–27.

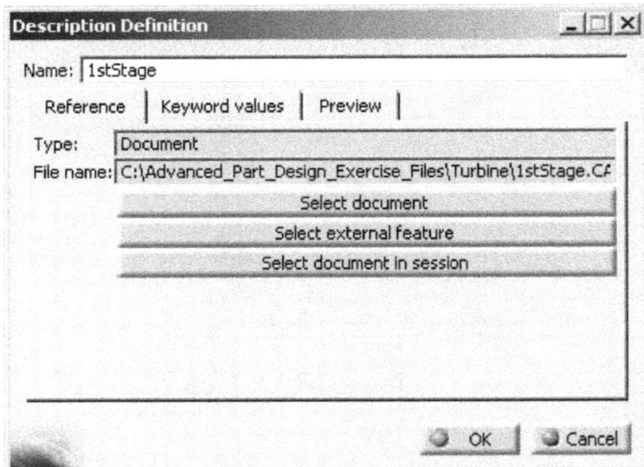

Figure 14–27

5. Click **OK**.

6. Repeat this procedure to add **2ndStage.CATPart** from the *Turbine* directory to the Stages family. The catalog displays as shown in Figure 14–28.

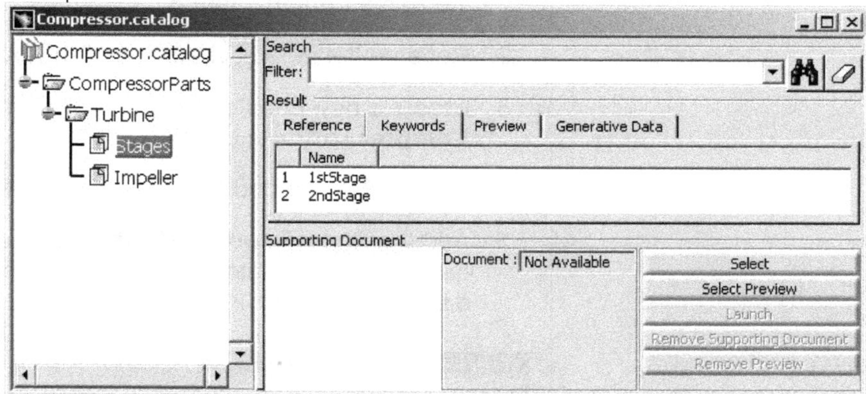

Figure 14–28

Note the paths to **1stStage.CATPart** and **2ndStage.CATPart** in the *Reference* tab.

7. Activate the Impeller family and add **Impeller.CATPart** from the *Turbine* directory. The **Compressor** catalog opens as shown in Figure 14–29.

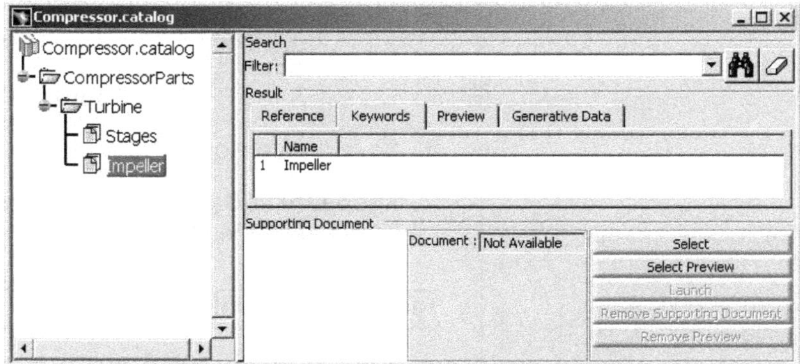

Figure 14–29

8. Save the catalog.

Task 5 - Create a new catalog.

1. Create a new catalog and save it in the *Turbine* directory with the name **LinkedCatalog**.
2. Rename the default chapter as **CompressorParts**.
3. Create a new chapter named **OtherParts** beneath the **CompressorParts** chapter.
4. Add a family named **Stator** beneath the **OtherParts** chapter.
5. Add the **StatorBand.CATPart** component from the *Turbine* directory to the Stator family. Once complete, the catalog displays as shown in Figure 14–30.

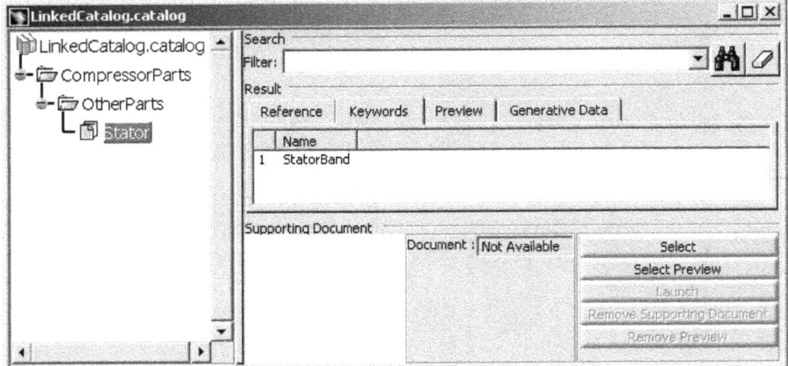

Figure 14–30

6. Save the catalog.

   Keep **LinkedCatalog** open, because this catalog will be linked to by the **Compressor** catalog.

Task 6 - Add a link to a chapter.

1. Activate the **Compressor** catalog.
2. Activate the **CompressorParts** chapter.
3. Click (Add link to another catalog).
4. Select the **OtherParts** chapter from **LinkedCatalog**.

A link is created in the **Compressor** catalog, as shown in Figure 14–31. Note that the *Type* column for **OtherParts** indicates that it is an **External** chapter.

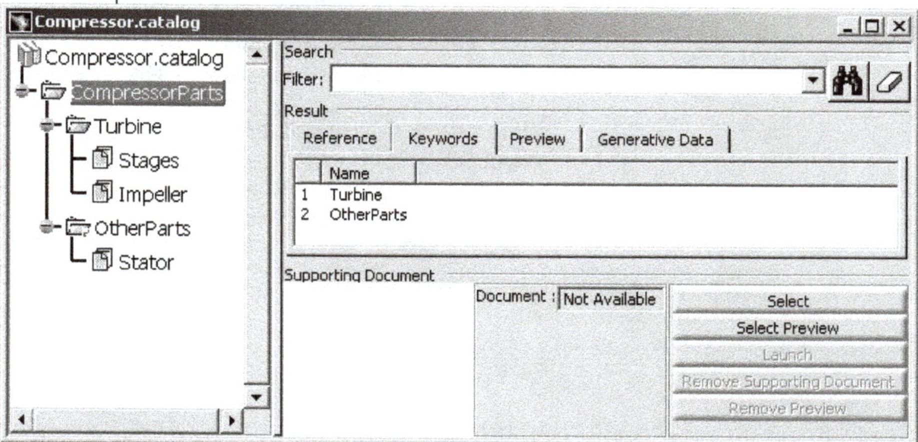

Figure 14–31

5. Save the catalogs and close the files.

Practice 14b PowerCopy in Catalogs

Practice Objectives

- Add a PowerCopy to a catalog.
- Insert the PowerCopy into a model using the catalog.

In this practice, you will add two instances of the **M12 Boss PowerCopy** to the model from the previous practice. These instances are added and then instantiated from an existing catalog. The completed model displays as shown in Figure 14–32.

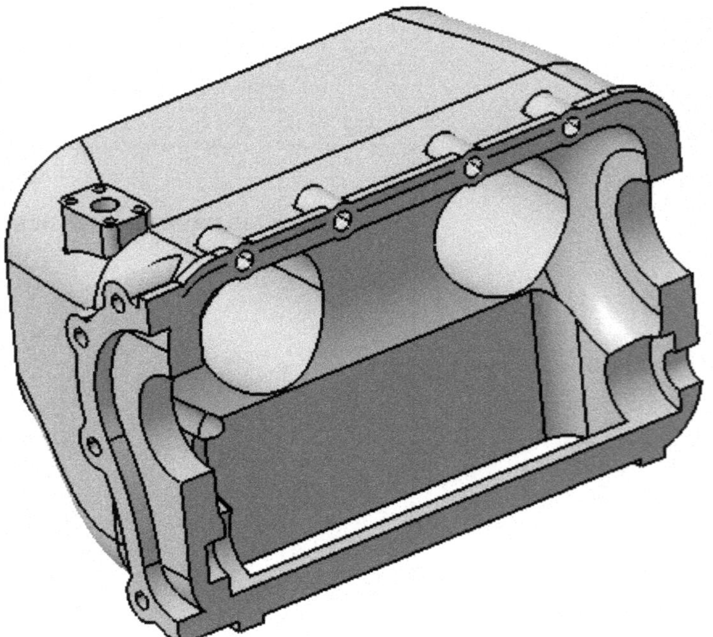

Figure 14–32

Task 1 - Open the part and investigate feature history.

1. Open the **M12-BossPC.CATPart** model. The model displays as shown in Figure 14–33.

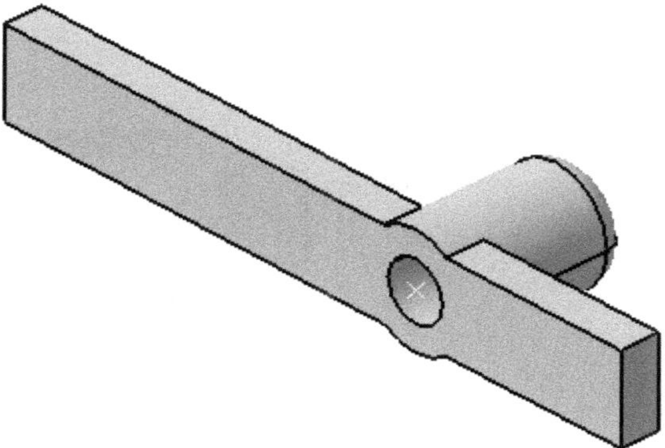

Figure 14–33

Task 2 - Investigate feature order.

1. Select **Edit>Scan or Define In Work Object**. Expand the drop-down list and select **Update**. The Scan dialog box displays as shown in Figure 14–34.

Figure 14–34

2. Click and replay the creation of the model by clicking . Note the feature order and possible references that have been generated. Note that **Point.1** was created before the boss (**Pad.2**).

3. Click to scan to the last feature and close the Scan dialog box.

Design Considerations

Point.1 was updated before **Pad.2**. All references for the boss are to **Point.1**, as shown in Figure 14–35. You should use a face and a point as references when locating circular PowerCopies. This technique uses the minimum amount of references, requires less constraining, and is less confusing than selecting several references.

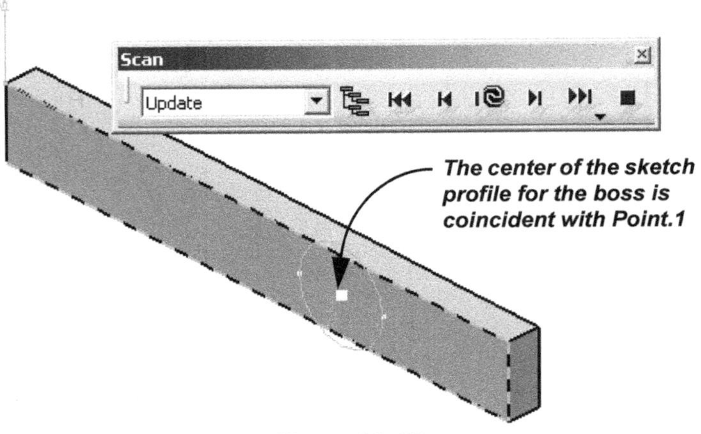

Figure 14–35

Task 3 - Investigate references of a PowerCopy.

1. In the specification tree, double-click on **M12 Boss** PowerCopy. The Powercopy Definition dialog box opens as shown in Figure 14–36.

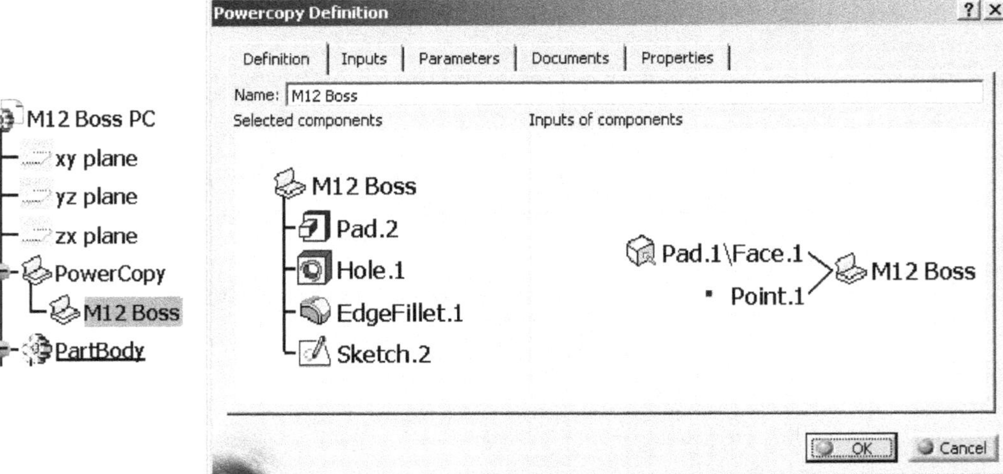

Figure 14–36

2. Select the *Inputs* tab. It lists the references required to place the PowerCopy into a model, as shown in Figure 14–37.

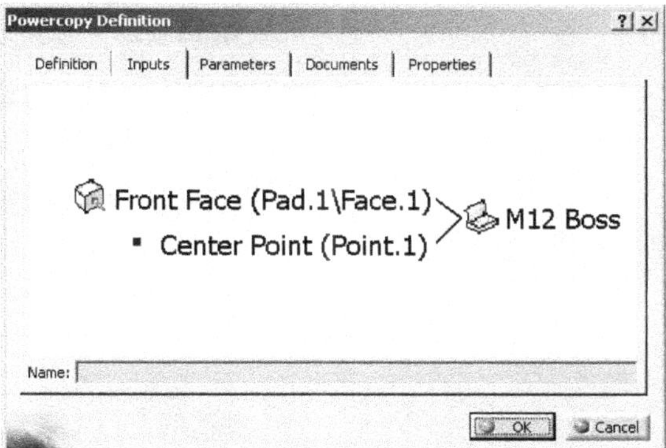

Figure 14–37

The references that are required to place the PowerCopy are:

- A face
- A reference point

3. Close the Powercopy Definition dialog box.

Design Considerations

In the next task, you will insert the PowerCopy into a catalog. You must always ensure that all changes to a document are saved before you insert a PowerCopy into a catalog. Although no changes have been made to the document, the **Scan** operation will indicate to CATIA that a **Save** needs to be performed.

4. Save the model.

Task 4 - Create a catalog for PowerCopies.

1. Select **Insert>Knowledge Templates>Save In Catalog**. The Catalog save dialog box opens as shown in Figure 14–38.

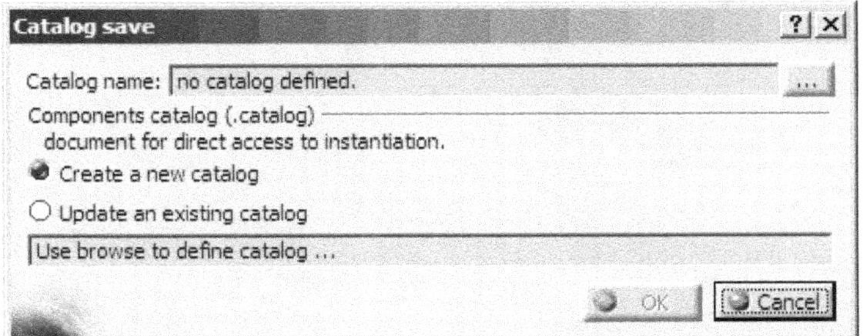

Figure 14–38

2. Click [...].

3. Save the catalog using **PowerCopies** as the name for the new catalog.

   The Catalog save dialog box opens as shown in Figure 14–39.

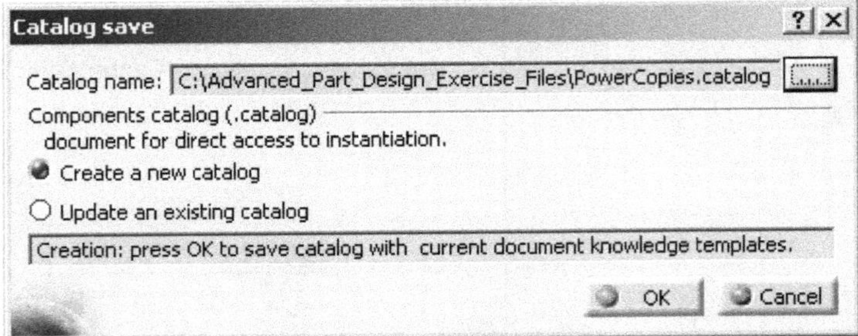

Figure 14–39

4. Click **OK** to complete the catalog save.

5. Close the **M12-BossPC** file.

Task 5 - Open the catalog file and rename the chapters.

1. Open **PowerCopies.catalog**. It displays as shown in Figure 14–40.

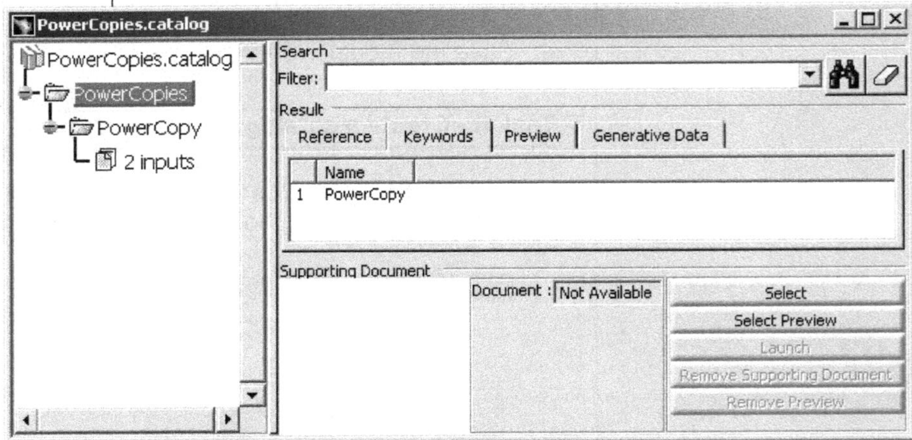

Figure 14–40

2. Rename the **PowerCopy** chapter as **Threaded Boss**, as shown in Figure 14–41.

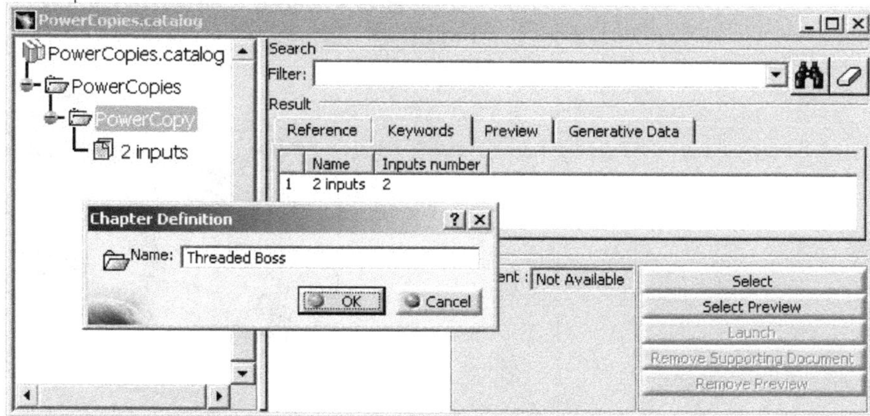

Figure 14–41

3. Rename *2 inputs* as **M12**, as shown in Figure 14–42.

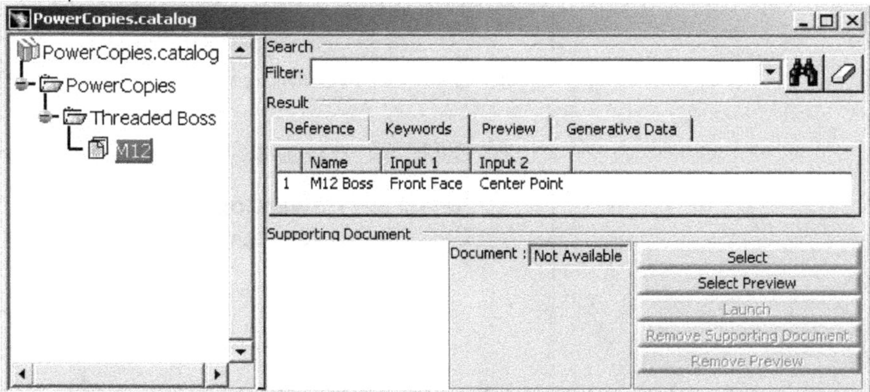

Figure 14–42

4. Save the catalog and close the window.

Task 6 - Open a part file.

1. Open **BlockLeft8c.CATPart**. The part displays as shown in Figure 14–43.

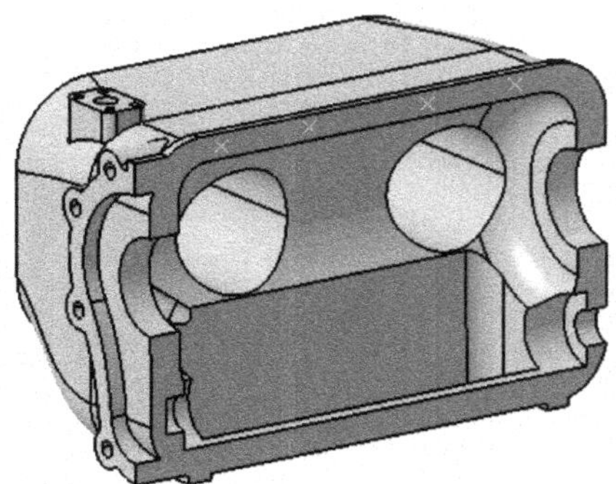

Figure 14–43

Task 7 - Instantiate PowerCopy features from the catalog.

1. Click (Catalog Browser) to open the Catalog Browser.
2. Click to browse to the **PowerCopies.catalog** file.
3. Select the **PowerCopies.catalog** file and click **Open**. The Catalog Browser opens as shown in Figure 14–44.

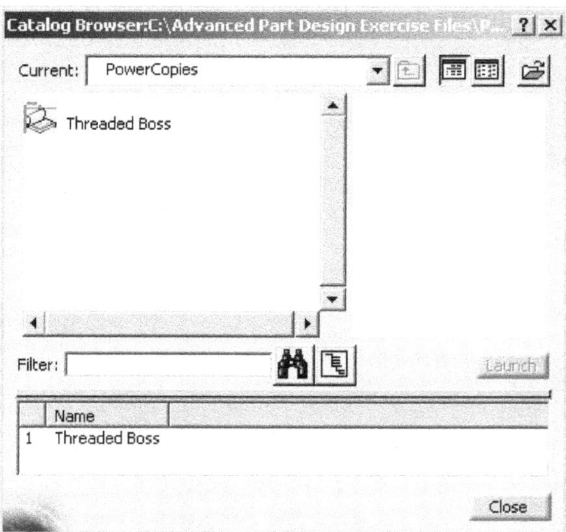

Figure 14–44

4. Navigate to the **M12 Boss** PowerCopy, as shown in Figure 14–45.

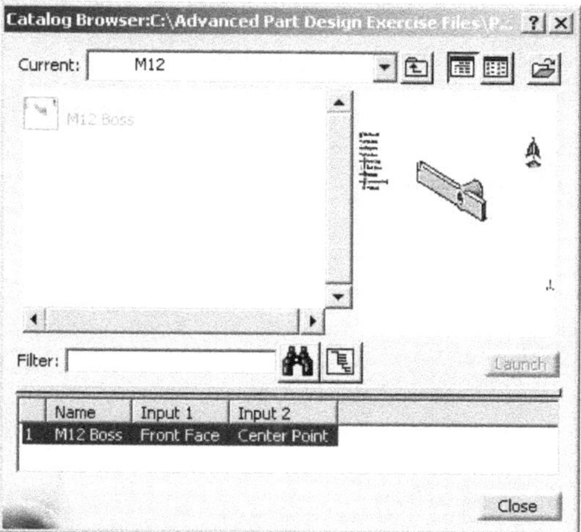

Figure 14–45

5. Double-click on the **M12** boss on the left side of the Catalog Browser to instantiate the PowerCopy.

6. Select the references shown in Figure 14–46 to locate the PowerCopy.

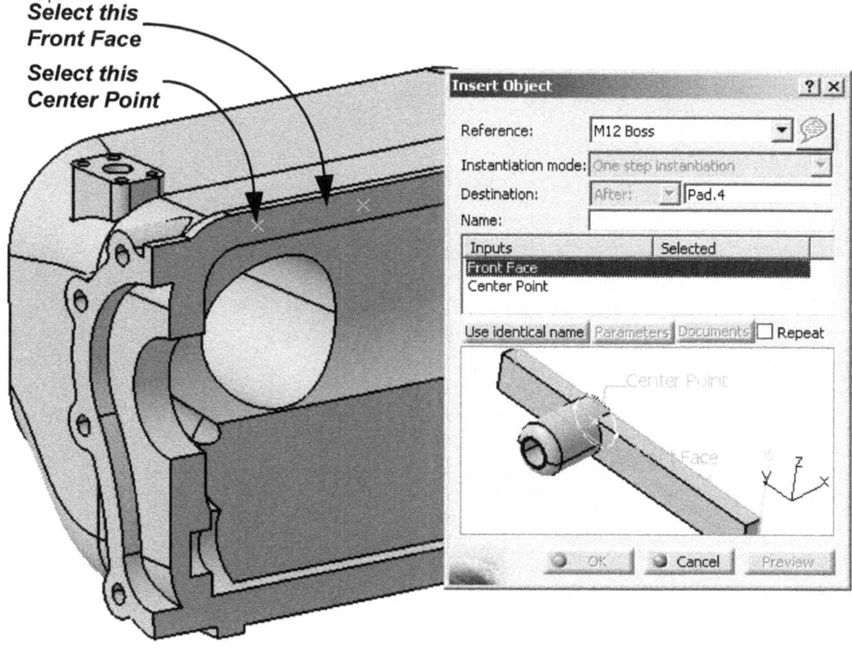

Figure 14–46

7. Click **Preview** to ensure that the placement of the PowerCopy is correct.

8. Since you are placing three more instances of the boss, select **Repeat**, as shown in Figure 14–47.

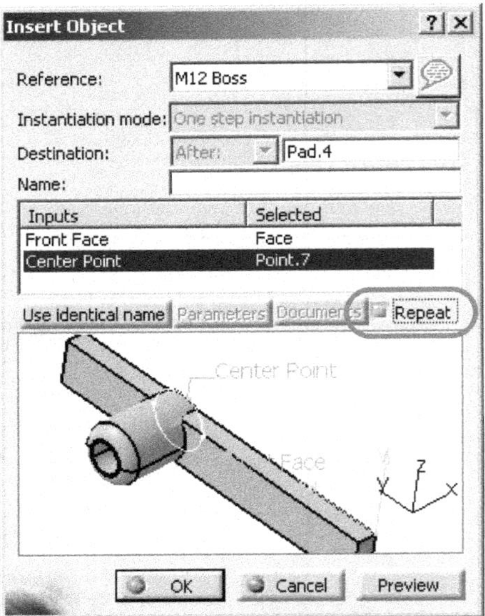

Figure 14–47

9. Click **OK**. The PowerCopy displays as shown in Figure 14–48.

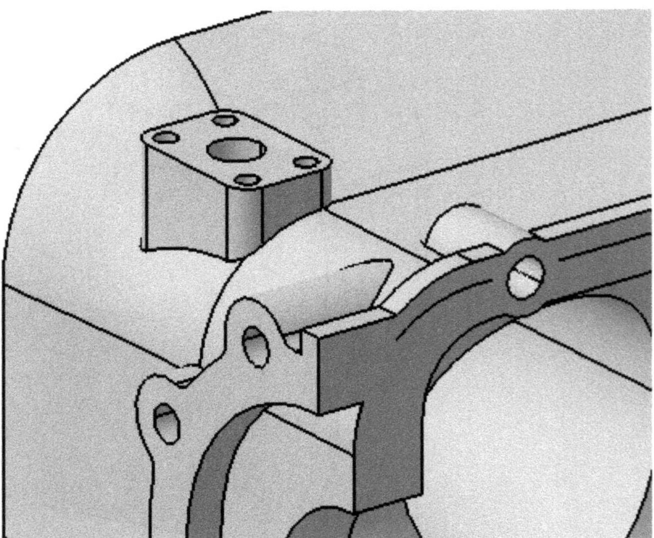

Figure 14–48

10. Note that the Insert Object dialog box stays active and that the **Front Face** is already listed as an input from the previous boss.

11. In the Insert Object dialog box, activate **Center Point** and select the reference point to place the next boss, as shown in Figure 14–49.

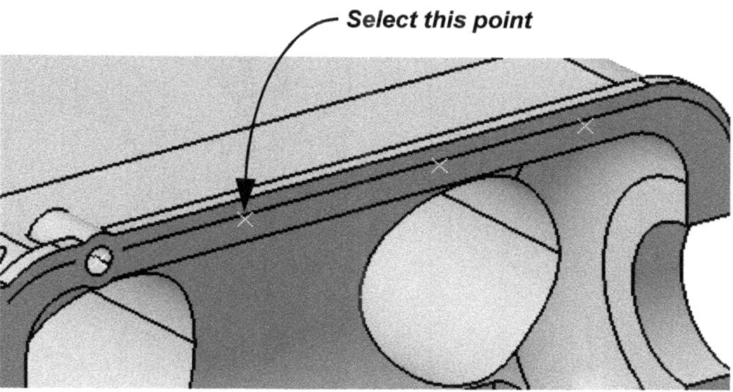

Figure 14–49

12. Click **Preview** to ensure that the placement of the PowerCopy is correct.

13. Click **OK**. Select the next point, as shown in Figure 14–50.

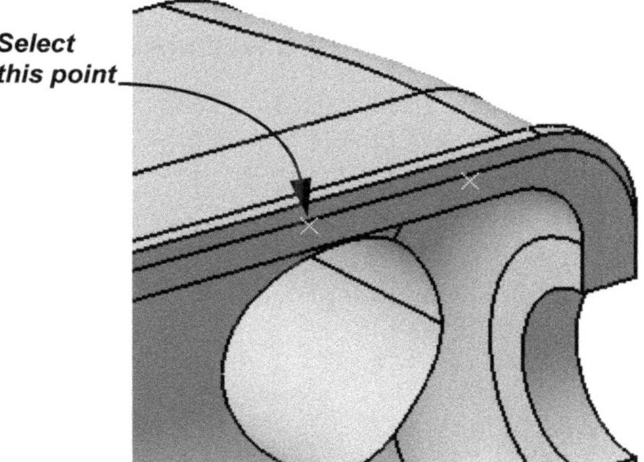

Figure 14–50

14. Click **Preview** to ensure that the placement of the PowerCopy is correct.

15. Click **OK**.

16. In the Insert Object dialog box, clear the **Repeat** option.

17. Place the final boss, as shown in Figure 14–51.

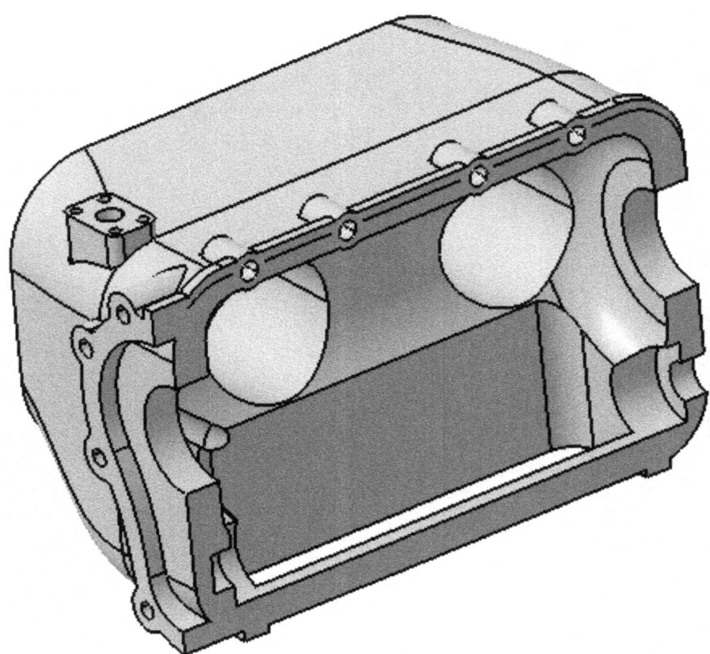

Figure 14–51

18. In the Catalog Browser, click **Close**.

19. Save the model and close the file.

Practice 14c

Using a Catalog

Practice Objectives

- Open a file from a catalog.
- Insert the PowerCopies into a model using a catalog.

In this practice, you will create an engine block using a catalog. You will open the start file from a catalog that is a template file. Then, you will insert all of the required sketches and solid features using a catalog. The completed model displays as shown in Figure 14–52.

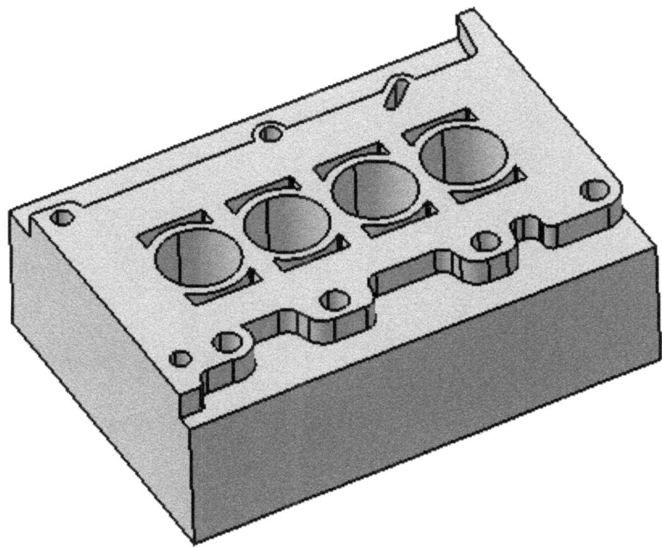

Figure 14–52

Task 1 - Create a new part.

1. Create a new part file.

Task 2 - Open the template file from a catalog.

In this task, you will open the template file that has all of the geometrical sets, using the Catalog Browser.

1. Click (Catalog Browser) to open the Catalog Browser.

2. Click [icon] to browse to the **Engine_block-JY.catalog** file in the *Catalog* directory, and then select the file.

3. Click **Open**. The Catalog Browser display as shown in Figure 14–53.

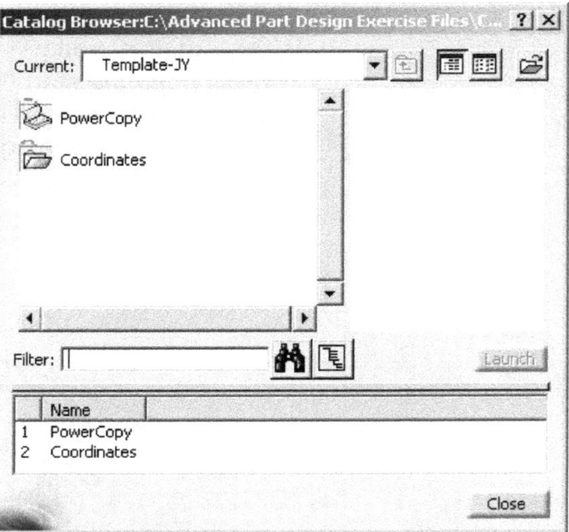

Figure 14–53

4. Navigate to the Coordinates as shown in Figure 14–54.

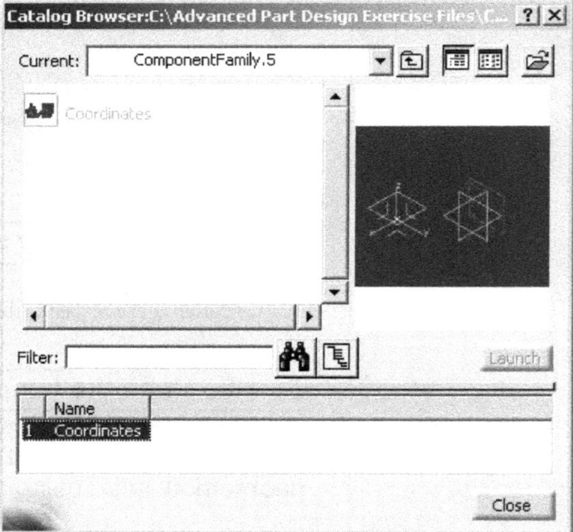

Figure 14–54

5. Right-click on **Coordinates** and select **Open As New Document**, as shown in Figure 14–55.

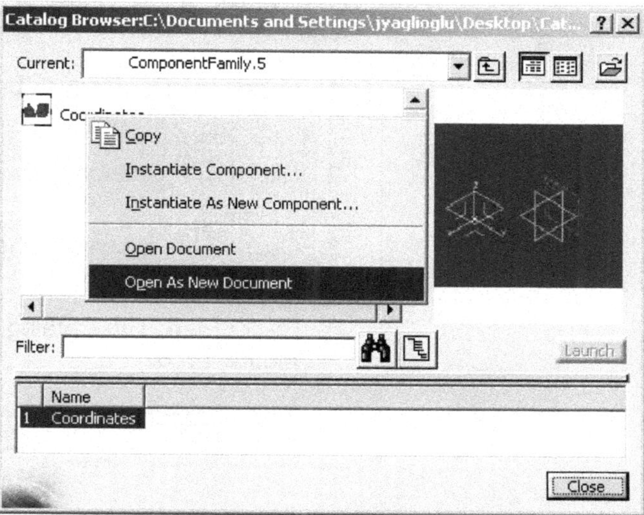

Figure 14–55

Design Considerations

Using the **Open As New Document** option makes the new file completely independent from the catalog file by assigning a new UUID (Universally Unique Identifier number).

Set the display to the Isometric View, and the template file displays as shown in Figure 14–56.

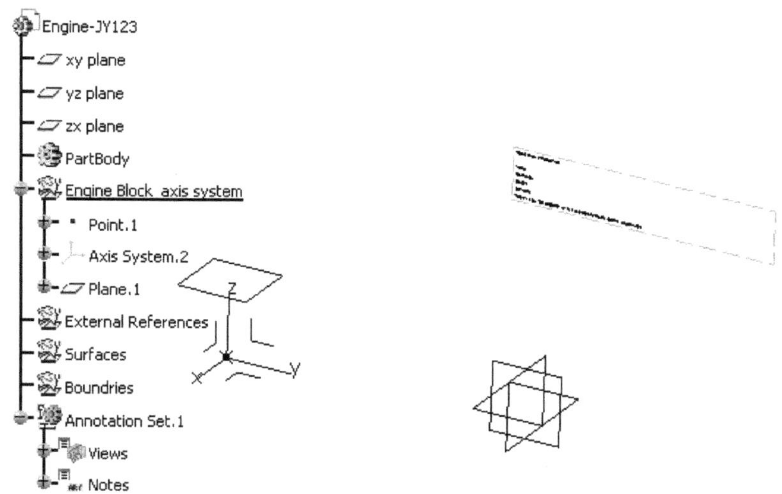

Figure 14–56

Task 3 - Insert the power copies from a catalog.

In this task, you will insert all of the required geometry using a catalog.

1. Define the PartBody to be the work object.

2. Click (Catalog Browser) to open the Catalog Browser.

3. Click to browse to the **Engine_block-JY.catalog** file in the *Catalog* directory.

4. Click **Open**. The Catalog Browser opens as shown in Figure 14–57.

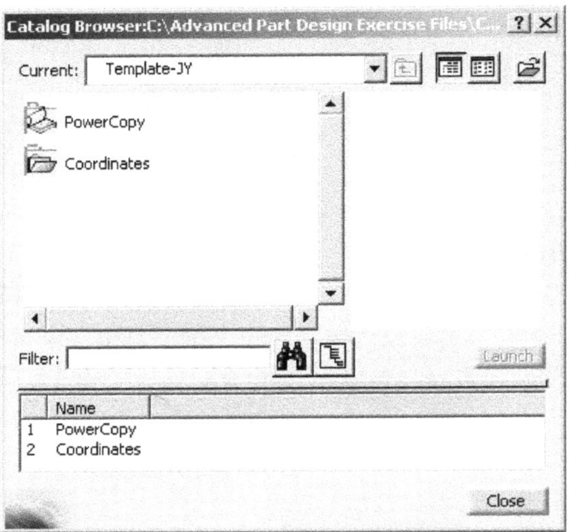

Figure 14–57

5. Navigate to the **Engine-pad** in the **PowerCopy** chapter, as shown in Figure 14–58.

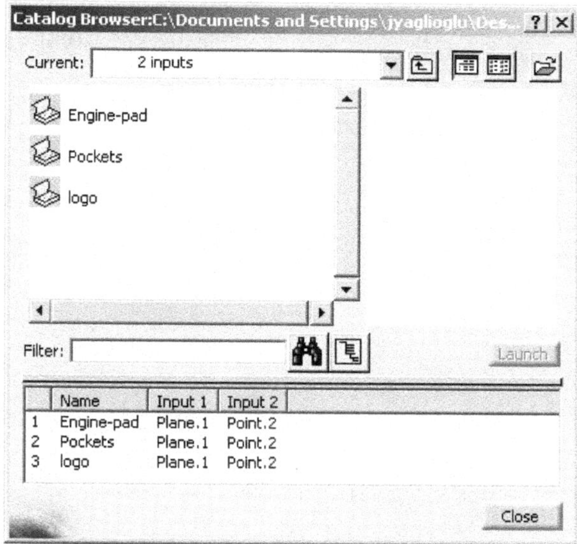

	Name	Input 1	Input 2
1	Engine-pad	Plane.1	Point.2
2	Pockets	Plane.1	Point.2
3	logo	Plane.1	Point.2

Figure 14–58

6. To instantiate the PowerCopy, double-click on the **Engine-pad** on the left on the Catalog Browser.

7. To locate the PowerCopy, select the references shown in Figure 14–59.

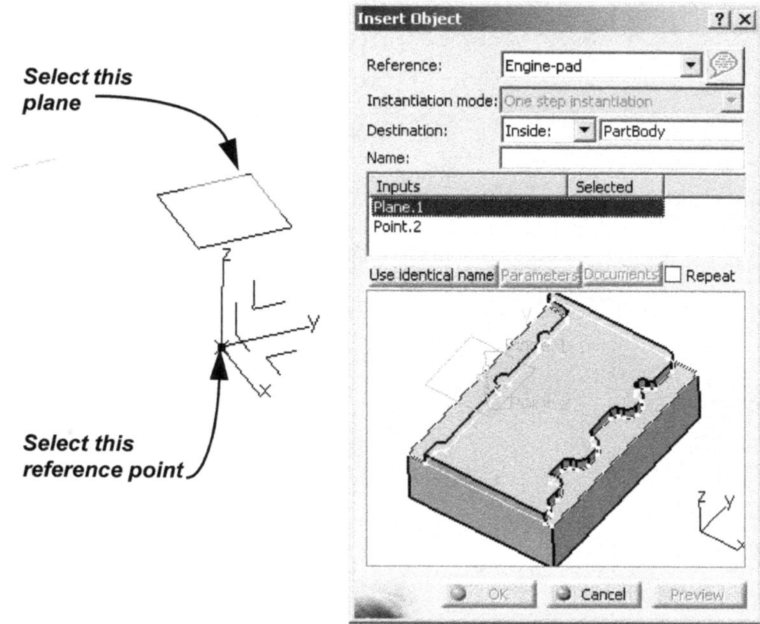

Figure 14–59

8. Click **Preview**. The preview displays as shown in Figure 14–60. Ensure that the placement of the PowerCopy is correct.

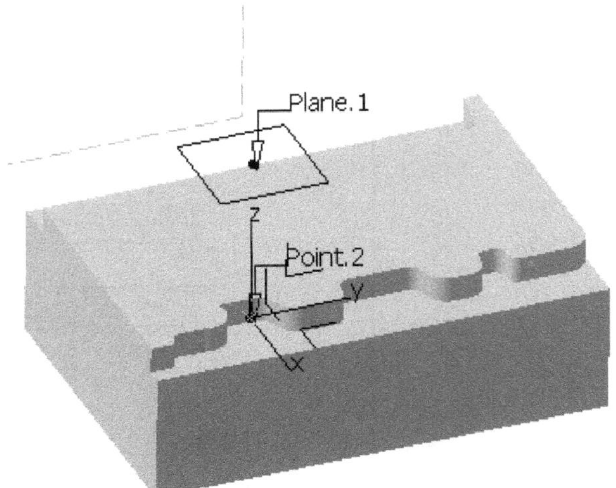

Figure 14–60

9. Click **OK**. Do not close the Catalog Browser.

10. Hide **Plane.1**, **Sketch.1**, and **Sketch.2**.

11. Define the **PartBody** to be the work object.

12. Double-click on the **Pockets** PowerCopy in the Catalog Browser dialog box.

13. Note the warning message that displays on the screen, as shown in Figure 14–61, indicating that the PowerCopy has three formulas and cannot be copied under the **PartBody**. These elements will be inserted in the **Relations** branch in the specification tree.

Warning : The destination PartBody can be chosen as destination of insertion of this template reference .
However these following elements will be inserted directly under another location:
Formula.1
Formula.2
Formula.3

Figure 14–61

14. To locate the PowerCopy, select the references shown in Figure 14–62.

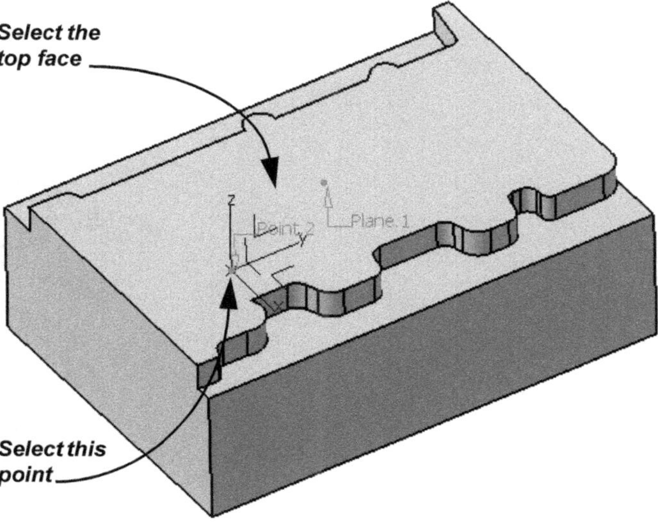

Figure 14–62

15. Click **OK**.

16. Close the Catalog Browser.

17. Hide **Point.1** and **Axis System**. The model displays as shown in Figure 14–63.

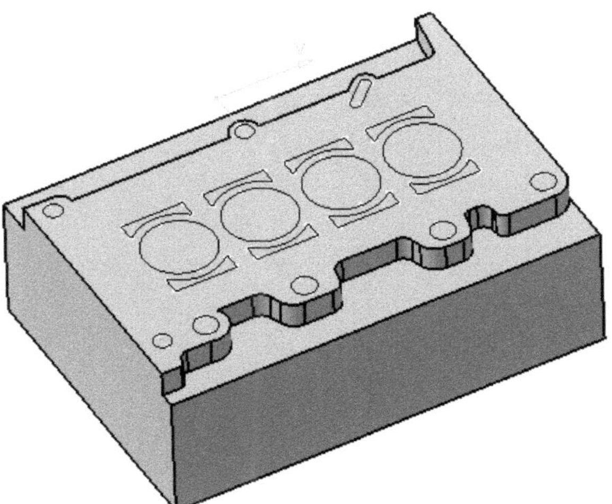

Figure 14–63

18. Using **Sketch.3**, create a Pocket with an **80mm** depth. The model displays as shown in Figure 14–64.

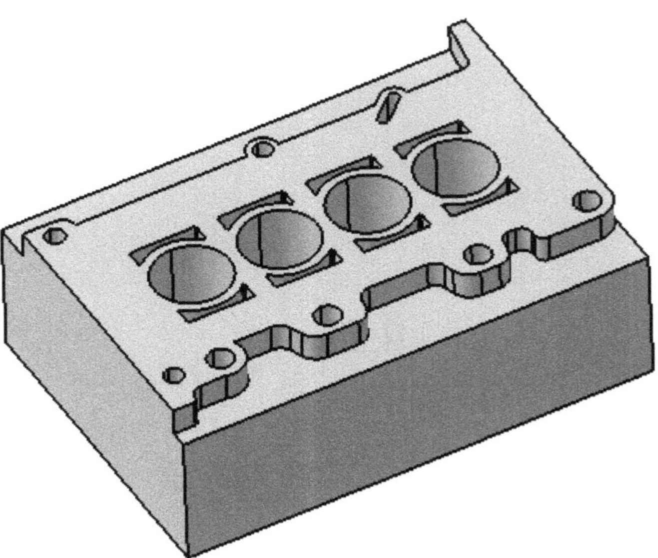

Figure 14–64

19. Save and close the file.

Practice 14d (Optional) Stator Band

Practice Objectives

- Create a Design Table.
- Add the Design Table to a catalog.

In this practice, you will create and add a design table to a new catalog. Begin this practice if time permits.

Task 1 - Open the part.

1. Open **StatorBand.CATPart** from the *Turbine* directory. The model displays as shown in Figure 14–65.

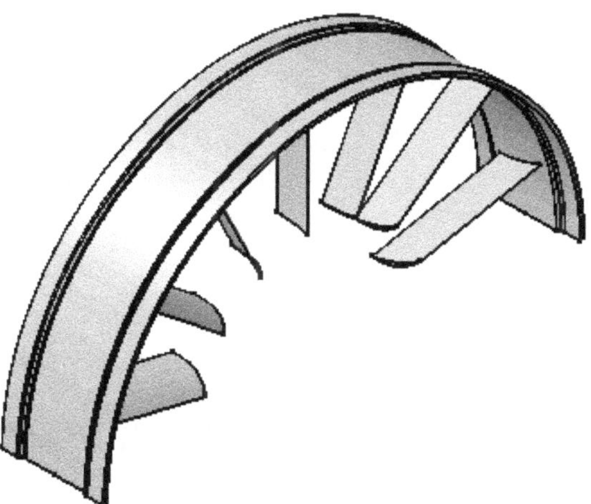

Figure 14–65

Task 2 - Create a design table.

1. Create a design table. Fill in the dialog box as shown in Figure 14–66.

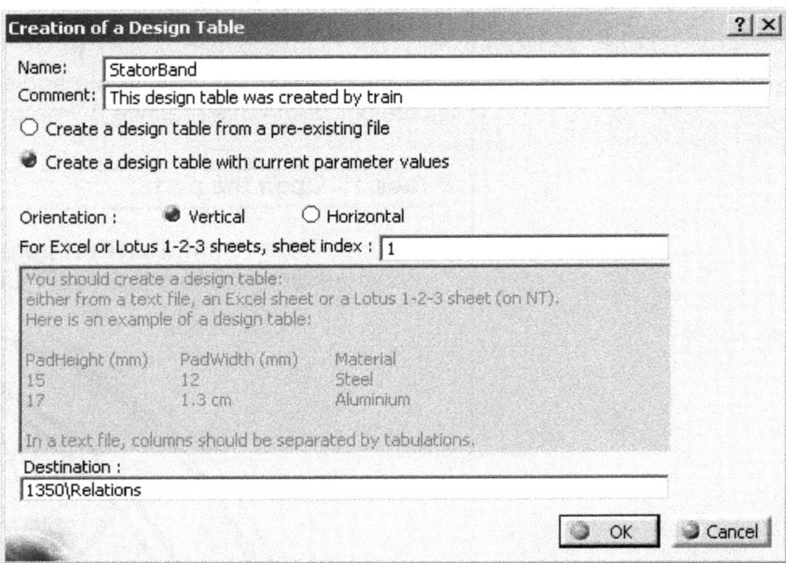

Figure 14–66

2. Insert the four parameters shown in Figure 14–67.

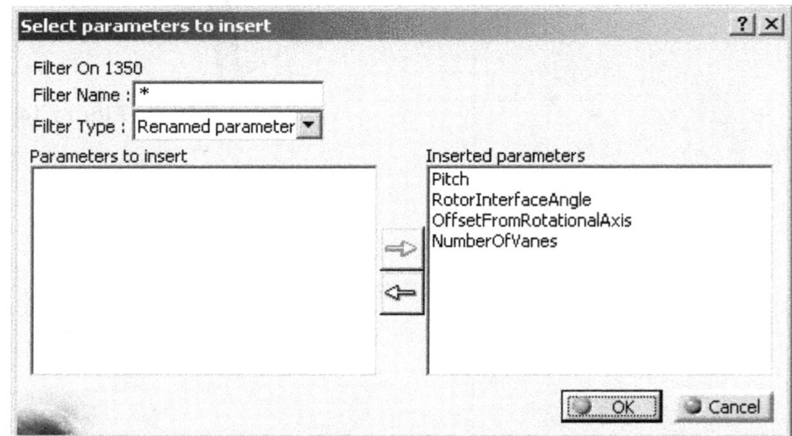

Figure 14–67

3. For the name of the Excel spreadsheet, enter **StatorBand**. Ensure that it is saved in the *Turbine* directory.

4. Click **Edit table**.

5. Add values to the Excel spreadsheet, as shown in Figure 14–68.

When creating a Part Number column in a design table, it is important that you label it "PartNumber", without a space between the two words. If you include a space, CATIA will not enable you to save it as a part family in a catalog.

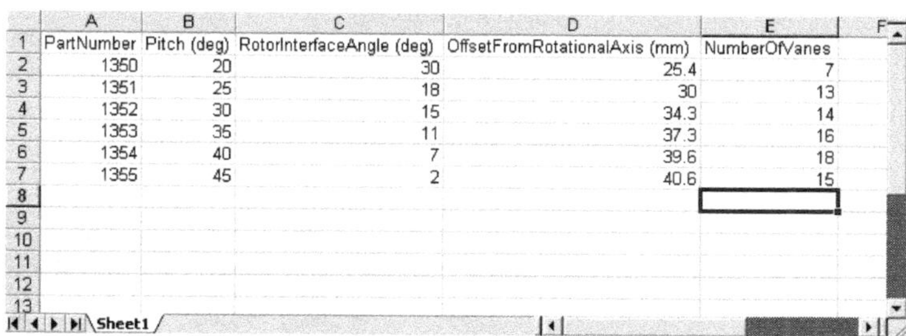

	A	B	C	D	E
1	PartNumber	Pitch (deg)	RotorInterfaceAngle (deg)	OffsetFromRotationalAxis (mm)	NumberOfVanes
2	1350	20	30	25.4	7
3	1351	25	18	30	13
4	1352	30	15	34.3	14
5	1353	35	11	37.3	16
6	1354	40	7	39.6	18
7	1355	45	2	40.6	15

Figure 14–68

6. Save and close the spreadsheet. Close any messages that display in Knowledge dialog boxes. The design table dialog box updates as shown in Figure 14–69.

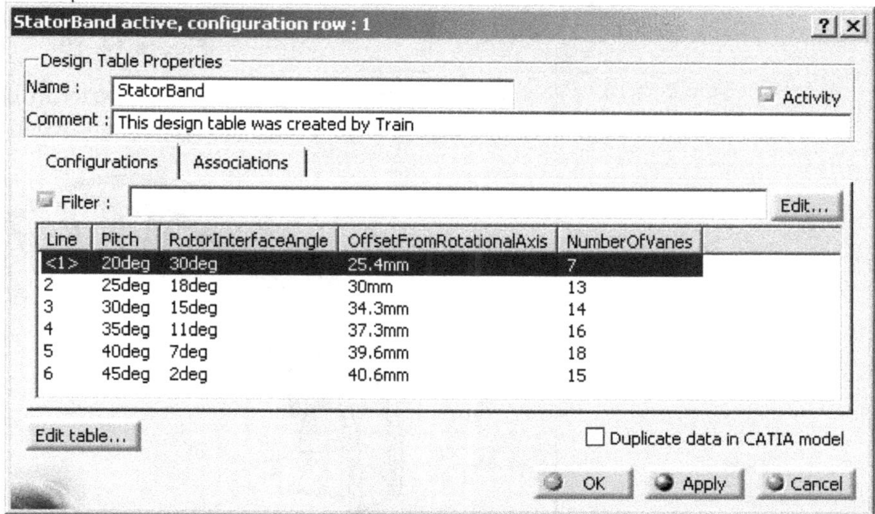

Figure 14–69

7. Select the *Associations* tab and create a parameter for the PartNumber. Ensure that the newly added parameter is re-ordered to display at the top of the list.

8. Select the *Configurations* tab. The dialog box opens as shown in Figure 14–70.

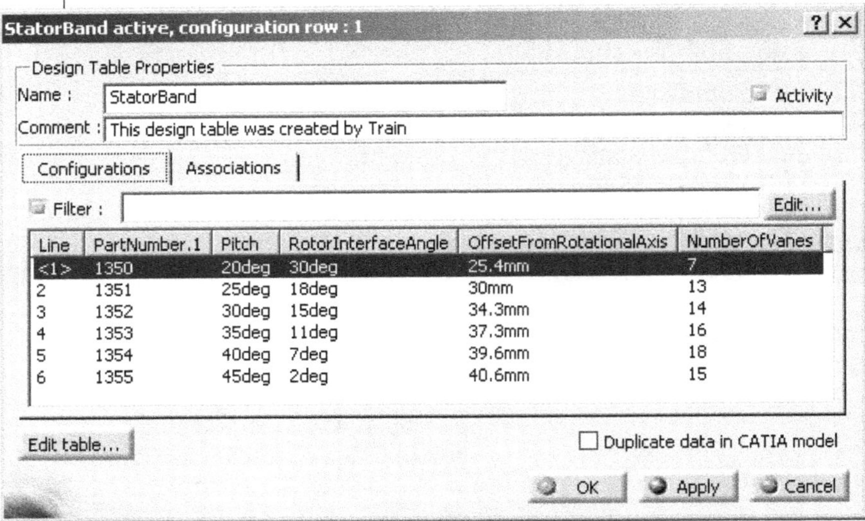

Line	PartNumber.1	Pitch	RotorInterfaceAngle	OffsetFromRotationalAxis	NumberOfVanes
<1>	1350	20deg	30deg	25.4mm	7
2	1351	25deg	18deg	30mm	13
3	1352	30deg	15deg	34.3mm	14
4	1353	35deg	11deg	37.3mm	16
5	1354	40deg	7deg	39.6mm	18
6	1355	45deg	2deg	40.6mm	15

Figure 14–70

9. Select the configuration with **PartNumber 1355** and click **Apply**. The model displays as shown in Figure 14–71.

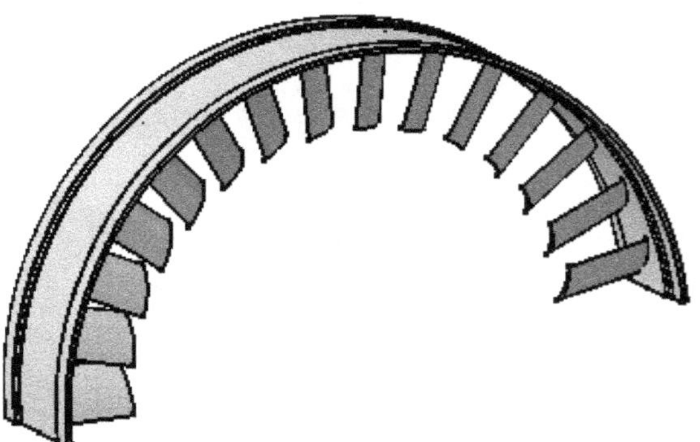

Figure 14–71

10. Open two other configurations in the part window to ensure that the parameter values are working correctly.

11. Reset the current model to **PartNumber 1350** and close the Design Table dialog box.

12. Save the model and close the file.

Task 3 - Add a design table to a catalog.

1. Open **Compressor.catalog** from the *Turbine* directory.

   If you did not complete the previous practice, open **TurbineComplete** from the *Completed* directory.

2. Activate the **Turbine** chapter.

3. Click (Add Part Family). The Part Family Definition dialog box opens as shown in Figure 14–72.

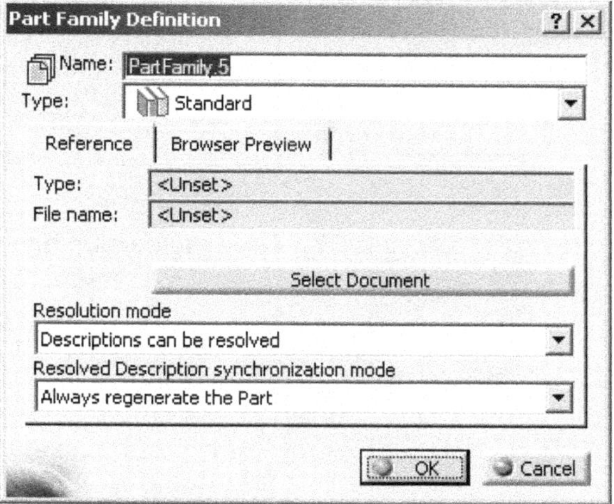

Figure 14–72

4. Enter **StatorBand** for the name.

5. Click **Select Document** and browse to the **StatorBand.CATPart** component in the *Turbine* directory.

6. Click **OK**. The system reads in each instance from the design table, as shown in Figure 14–73.

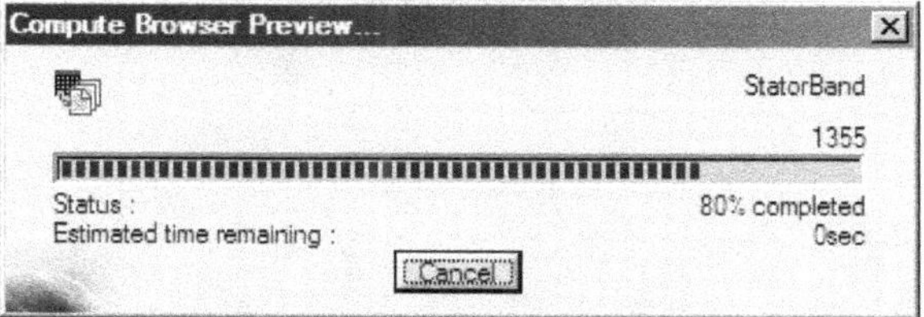

Figure 14–73

Once complete, the **Compressor** catalog displays as shown in Figure 14–74.

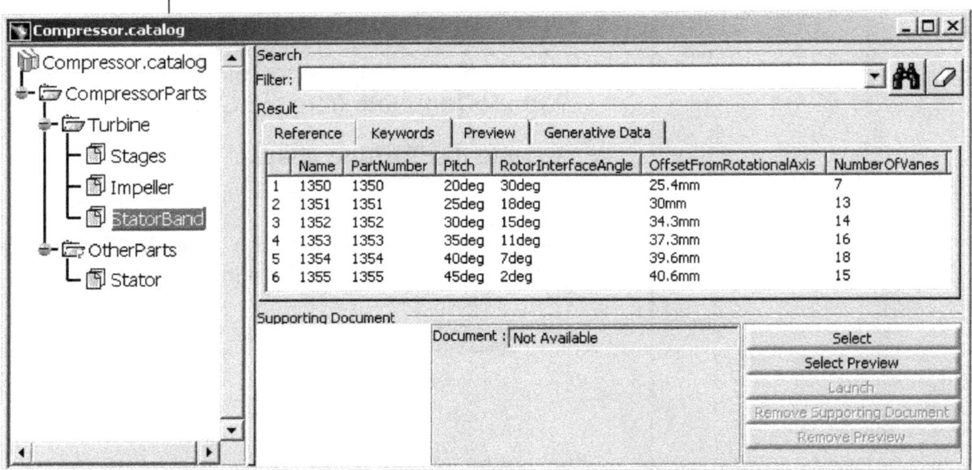

Figure 14–74

7. Save the catalog and close the file.

Chapter Review Questions

1. CATIA comes with standard catalogs and enables you to create custom catalogs.
   a. True
   b. False
2. Which of the following CATIA elements can be included in custom catalogs?
   a. PartBodies
   b. PowerCopies
   c. Sketches
   d. Parameters
   e. All of the above.
3. Catalogs are stored with the _____ extension.
   a. .cat
   b. .catalog
   c. .document
   d. None of the above.
4. A chapter is a collection of families of parts in a catalog.
   a. True
   b. False
5. You should resolve each configuration of a part family in a catalog to verify that the design table does not contain any errors and that each configuration produces a usable model.
   a. True
   b. False

Introduction to Automation

This chapter introduces tools in CATIA that you can use to automate the performance of redundant tasks. These tools speed up modeling in CATIA by recognizing groups of features and operations as a single object, such as a macro or a selection set. This chapter also introduces techniques to search for features in the specification tree.

Learning Objectives in this Chapter

- Learn how to use Macros to help automate your work.
- Understand how visual basic programs are structured.
- Explore the Visual Basic programming interface.

15.1 Macro Creation

A macro is a series of actions performed in CATIA that have been recorded into a single command. You can replace a string of regularly used menu selections with a macro.

General Steps

Use the following general steps to create a macro:

1. Record the macro.
2. Run the macro.

Step 1 - Record the macro.

The information in a macro is captured using a Visual Basic script. This script can be stored in the active CATPart document or as a separate file (*.CATVBS) in a macro library. This file can either be stored in the part file or in a macro library. If you store the file in a macro library, you can access the macro at any time. When the macro file is stored with the part file, it is only accessible when the referenced part file is open in CATIA.

To create a new macro, select **Tools>Macro>Start Recording**. The Record macro dialog box opens as shown in Figure 15–1.

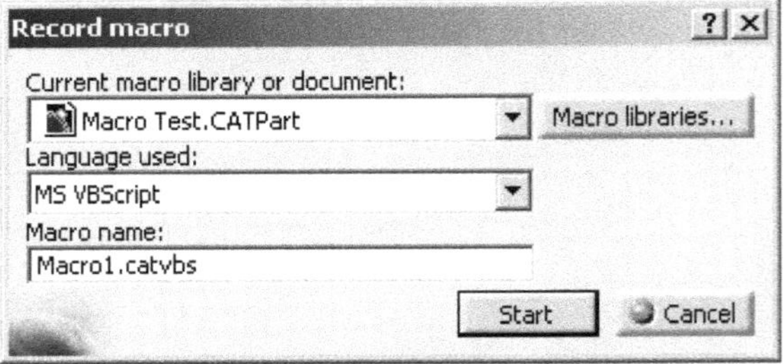

Figure 15–1

1. Select a document or macro library in which to store the recorded macro. By default, the system stores the macro in the current model.
2. Enter an appropriate macro name. For example, a macro used to create hole features can be named **holes.catvbs**.
3. Click **Start**. Each menu selection and keyboard entry you make is now recorded into the macro. To stop recording the macro, click [icon] in the **Stop Recording** menu.

Some menus cannot be recorded.

Step 2 - Run the macro

1. Select **Tools>Macro>Macros**. The Macros dialog box opens as shown in Figure 15–2.

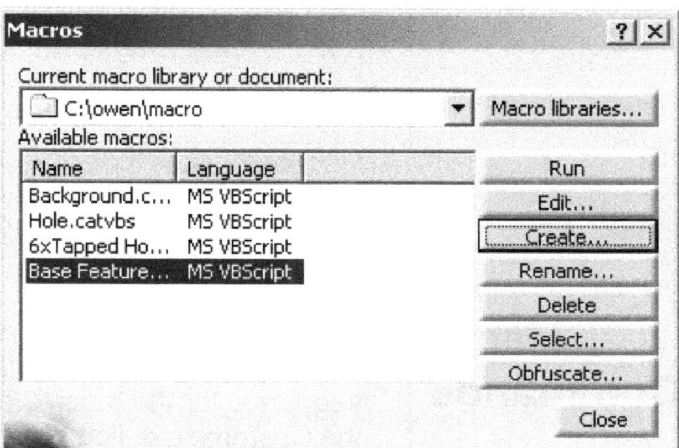

Figure 15–2

2. Select the macro to be run and click **Run**. The options for the Macros dialog box are described as follows:

Option	Description
Current macro library or document	Lists the locations in which the macros are stored. If a macro library is not listed in the drop-down list, browse to it by clicking **Macro libraries**.
Available macros	Lists macros stored under the current macro location. Actions can be performed on a macro by selecting it from the list and clicking one of the following buttons:
Run	Runs the selected macro.
Edit	Edits the selected macro. The Visual Basic script displays in a Macros Editor.

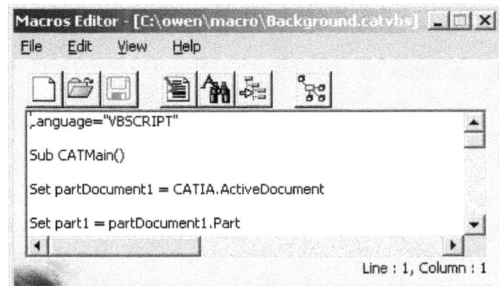

	Create	Creates a new macro. When using this method to create a macro, the macro must be scripted manually.
	Rename	Renames the selected macro script.
	Delete	Deletes the selected macro.
	Select	Selects a new macro to add to the current macro library or document.
	Obfuscate	Encrypts the selected macro so that it cannot be edited. You are prompted to save the encrypted macro with a new name.

Macro Commands

An alternative way to access a macro is to add the macro to a toolbar in the CATIA interface, or specify a keyboard entry or sequence for the macro. To perform either of these tasks, open the Customize dialog box by selecting **Tools>Customize**. Select the *Commands* tab. In the Categories list, select **Macros** as shown in Figure 15–3.

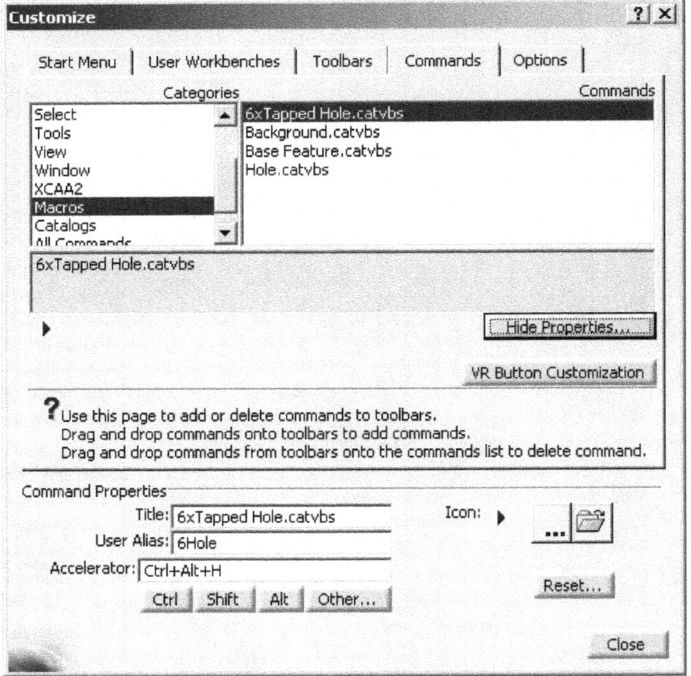

Figure 15–3

Executing a Macro from a Toolbar

Add a macro to a toolbar by selecting the macro in the *Commands* field and dragging it onto the required toolbar. [icon] is the default icon for a macro. This icon can be changed by clicking [...] in the Customize dialog box.

Executing a Macro Using the Keyboard

You can use accelerators and user aliases to execute a macro using the keyboard. You can create accelerators and user aliases in the *Command Properties* area in the Customize dialog box, as shown in Figure 15–4.

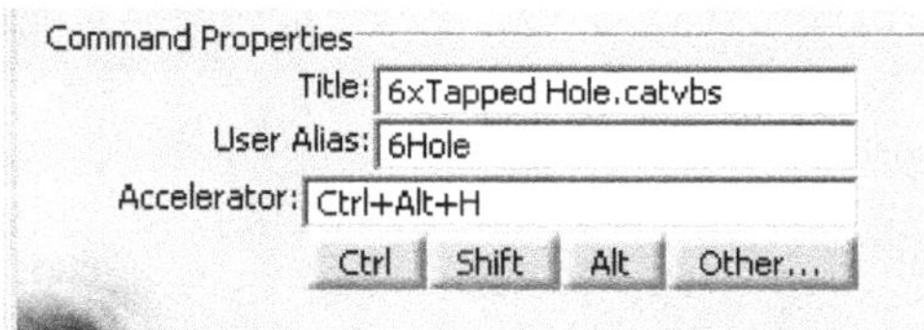

Figure 15–4

A user alias can be used to execute a mapkey by entering it into the command line. The alias must be preceded by **c:** as shown in Figure 15–5.

Figure 15–5

Adding the macro to the Standard toolbar makes it available in all workbenches.

An accelerator can only be specified for a macro if it has been added to a toolbar. The accelerator is a keyboard shortcut used to execute the macro. Add the key sequence using the buttons below the *Accelerator* field. The key sequence specified must be unique and not used by any other command. You must press the keys simultaneously when executing an accelerator.

Macro Libraries

By default, a new macro is stored with the current model. To make macros global to your installation of CATIA, you must create a macro library. The library indicates a location on the system or network in which the macro Visual Basic scripts are stored.

How To: Create a New Macro Library

1. Select **Tools>Macro>Macros**.
2. In the Macros dialog box, click **Macro libraries**.
3. In the Macro libraries dialog box, in the Library type drop-down list, select **Directories**, as shown in Figure 15–6.

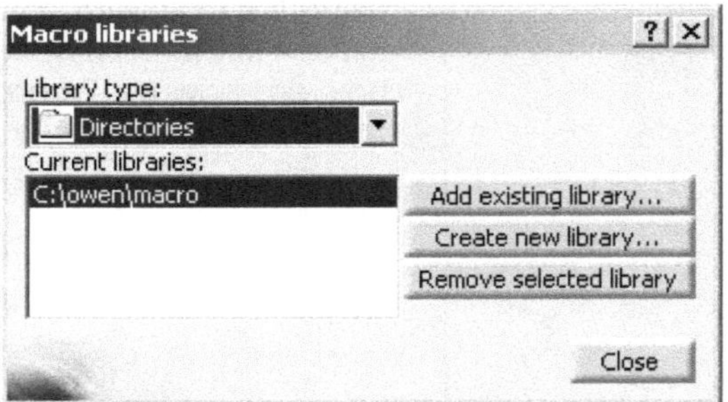

Figure 15–6

4. Click **Create new library** and browse to the required directory.

15.2 Visual Basic (VB) and VBA

Visual Basic is a programming language used for rapid application development. It was designed to be easy enough to develop so that non-programmers could use it. Many applications have a Visual Basic Editor that enables users to automate repetitive tasks.

VBA (Visual Basic for Applications) is a subset of Visual Basic. VBA is included in many applications, such as CATIA, Word, and Excel. It provides a programming environment in which you can create, edit, and run your own programs.

VBScript (Visual Basic Script) is a subset of VBA. It can call and use CATIA Objects. While the program is running, it calls the required objects, the functions of the objects, and the properties of the objects.

How Does it Work?

All programs are built in two sections: the interface and the code, as shown in Figure 15–7. To ease the use of the program, interfaces are provided between the user and the program. In this way, you do not need to enter most of the commands to use the program. Instead, you activate the commands using a keyboard and mouse, or by entering the required input.

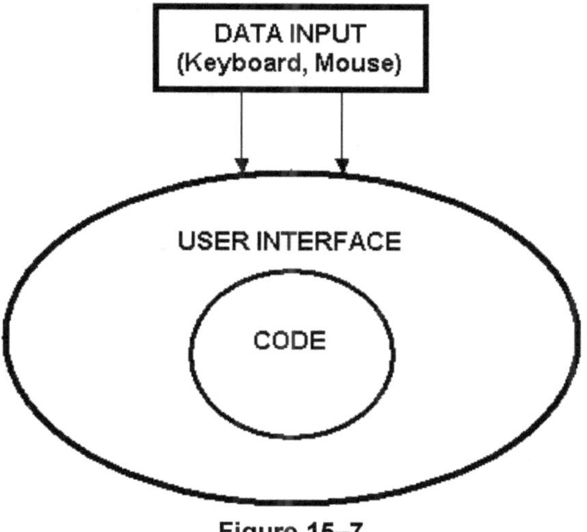

Figure 15–7

You do not see the code while using the program. The code is running in the background, and can interact with other applications as shown in Figure 15–8.

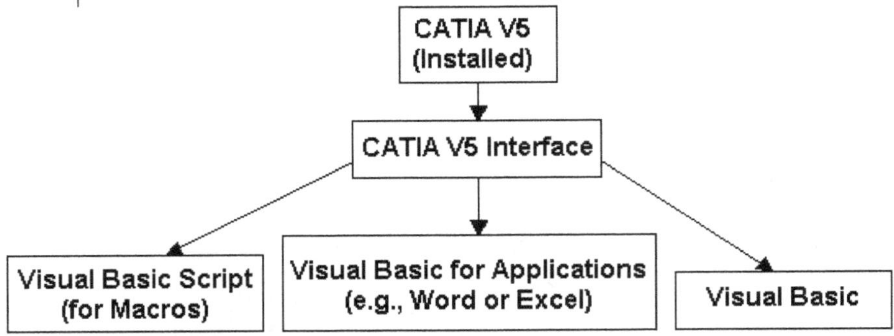

Figure 15–8

Object-Oriented Programming

Object-oriented programming uses objects. An object has its own properties and functions. An object's properties include color or name, and its function determines what it can do. Objects can have more than one function. Objects in CATIA include line, point, sketch, and pad.

All of the CATIA objects come from a single base object called **CATIA**. The CATIA object can be categorized in 2 main collections: **Documents** and **Windows**.

Documents

The **Documents** collection stores the data that is used in the program. The document types for CATIA can be:

- CATPart
- CATProduct
- CATDrawing
- CATProcess

The CATIA Object Model for Part Documents taken from the Dassault help documentation is shown in Figure 15–9.

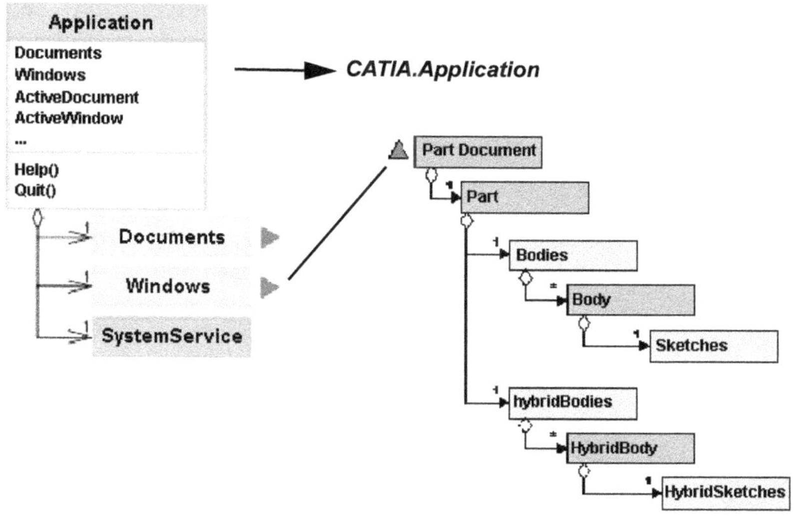

Figure 15–9

Each of these documents is associated with a number of properties and functions. The functions and properties vary for each document type. The object structure for a Part document is shown in Figure 15–10.

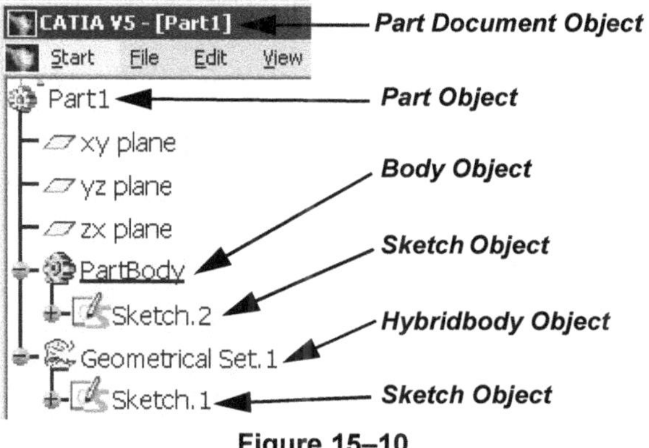

Figure 15–10

Windows

The Windows collection contains information about how the data is viewed.

Developing New Code

Instead of writing all of the code from scratch, you can use other methods to develop code. One way is to take an existing program and begin building from its code, adding and modifying for the required functionality. Another method is to record a macro and build from the code that the macro has generated. Disadvantages of these methods include:

- Does not work for Drafting, Manufacturing, and FEA Analysis.
- Recorded macros can create unnecessary extra code.

Before recording a macro, make sure a macro library is already created. These can be:

- In a CATPart file.
- In a directory.
- In a CATVBA Project.

Recording macros is a fast way to start your program. It enables you to have a better understanding of how the structure is working. While recording macros, use the following tips:

- Check the CATSettings when recording.
- Complete the feature before stopping recording.
- Investigate each macro after it is recorded.
- Record only the required actions.
- Do not use **Undo** when recording a macro.
- Do not switch between workbenches while recording a macro.

VBA Editor

The VBA Editor is the environment in which you can see and build your own programs. To open the VBA Editor, select **Tools>Macro>Visual Basic Editor**.

The Microsoft Visual Basic window opens as shown in Figure 15–11.

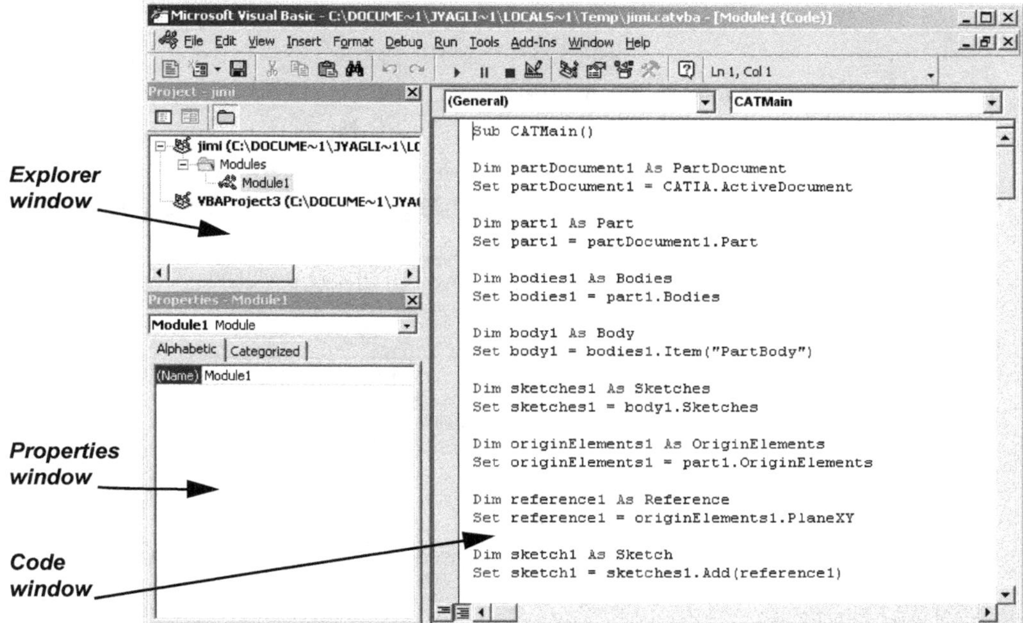

Figure 15–11

There are three main windows that are commonly used during program compilation. The windows are described as follows:

Windows	Description
Explorer window	Displays all of the stored projects.
Properties window	Displays the properties of an active object.
Code window	The window in which you write the code.

Object Browser

Object Browser is a search tool that indicates where the object is located and how it should be used. To open the Object Browser window, select **View>>Object Browser**, or click (Object Browser) in the Standard toolbar. Figure 15–12 shows a keyword search in the Object Browser for **pad**. In the *Member* area, find the function that makes the most sense (e.g., **AddNewPad**).

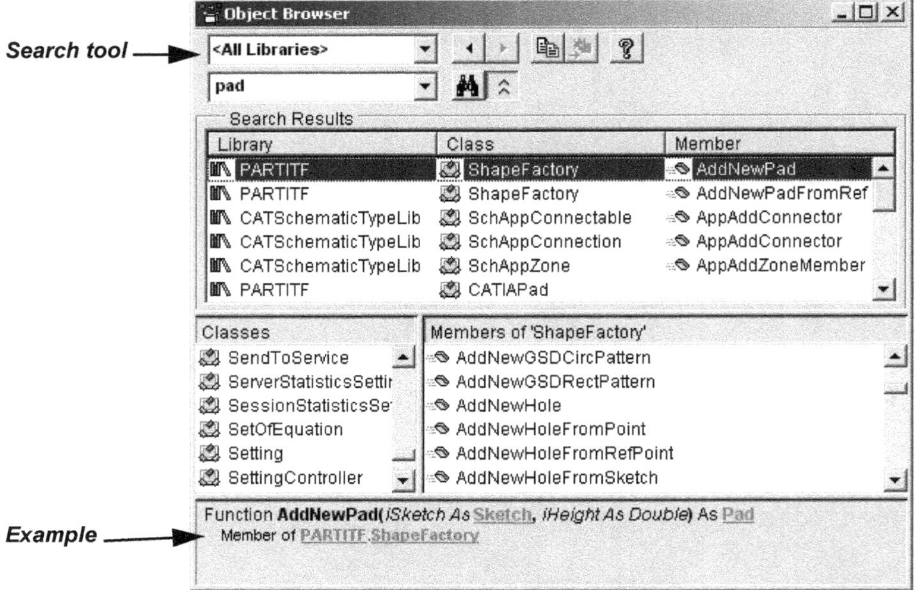

Figure 15–12

In Figure 15–12, the structure for creating a Pad feature is as follows:

To create a Pad feature, a ShapeFactory object is required. To create a ShapeFactory object, a Part object is required. To create a Part object, a Partdocument object is required. To create a Partdocument object, a CATIA object is required.

The *Class* area indicates which function belongs to which object. The bottom of the window describes how to use the function. This part is the Syntax portion of the object browser. In Figure 15–12, this part indicates that, when calling the **AddNewPad** function, you have to provide two parameters: one sketch object and one number (double precision value).

Underlined words (as shown in Figure 15–13) are the keywords that you can select to display more information about that object.

```
Function AddNewPad(iSketch As Sketch, iHeight As Double) As Pad
  Member of PARTITF.ShapeFactory
```

Figure 15–13

Code Window

The code window is the area in which you write the program. Some words can display in three colors: green, blue, and red. The colors are described as follows:

Color	Description
Green	Indicates that the line is only for comment. The comments begin with an apostrophe.
Blue	Indicates reserved words.
Red	Indicates that there is an error.

When compiling is finished, you need to test your program. To debug the program, click (Run Sub/UserForm) or press <F5>. If there is a problem with the code, an error box opens as shown in Figure 15–14.

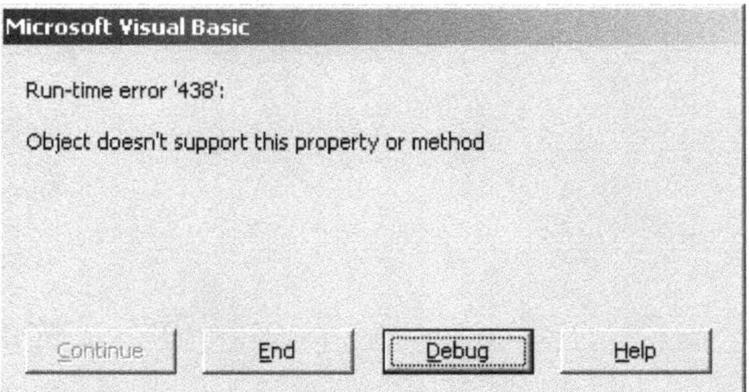

Microsoft Visual Basic
Run-time error '438':
Object doesn't support this property or method
Continue
End
Debug
Help

Figure 15–14

It is suggested that you run the program several times during the compilation. This makes it easier to identify and solve the problems.

Variables

Variables are the input data that is used by the program. Different variable types hold different kinds of data, such as numbers, text, etc. Some of the common variable types are:

- Integer (stores whole numbers)
- Double (stores decimal numbers)
- String (stores text)
- Boolean (its value can be either **True** or **False**)
- Date

Every variable must be named and the data type for the variable also must be specified. To declare a variable, use the following statement:

Dim *VariableName* as **VariableType**

Every program starts with **Sub (Subroutine)** commands, and ends with **End Sub** commands. You write the program between these lines.

Sub

Type the code here....

.....

End Sub

A simple example of code is shown in Figure 15–15.

```
Sub

Dim Total as Integer

Total = 5 + 5

MsgBox (Total)

End Sub
```

Figure 15–15

The second line declares the variable name (**Total**) and the type (**Integer**). The third line adds 5 to 5 and stores the result in the variable (**Total**).

The fourth line displays the result which is stored in the **Total** variable.

Practice 15a

Selection Automation

Practice Objectives

- Record and run a macro.
- Create a selection set.
- Search the model for features.

In this practice, you will use a variety of tools to automate menu and feature selections in CATIA.

Task 1 - Open the part.

1. Open **B12255Bushing.CATPart**. The model displays as shown in Figure 15–16.

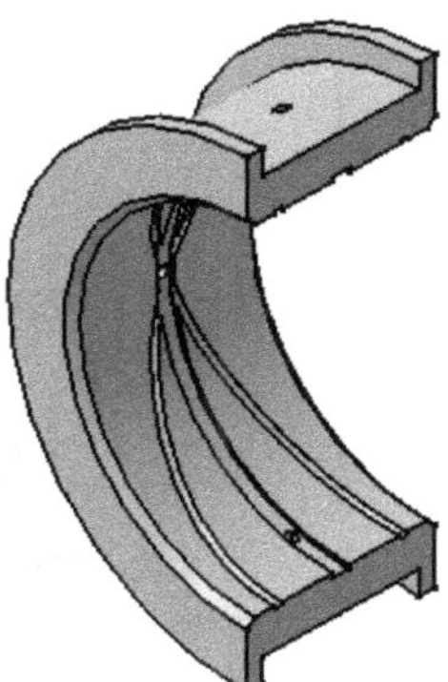

Figure 15–16

Task 2 - Search for features in the model.

In this task, you will perform a search for features by name.

1. Select **Edit>Search**. The Search dialog box opens.
2. In the *Name* field, enter ***plane*** and click (Search). The system highlights all of the plane features in the specification tree.
3. Before you can operate on the located features, you must select them. Click **Select**.

4. In the specification tree, right-click on the zx plane and show the selected features. All planes in the model display, as shown in Figure 15–17.

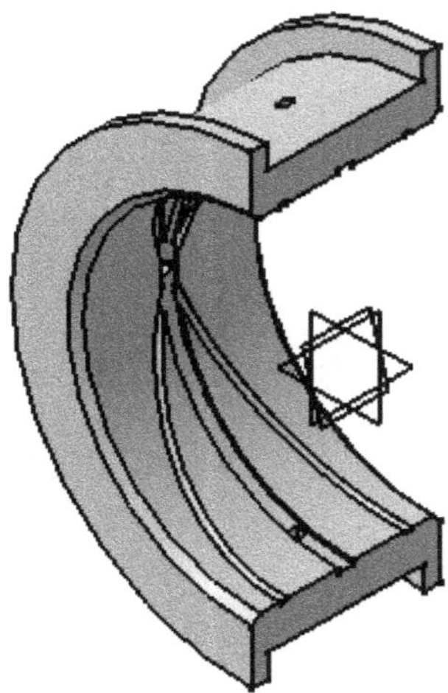

Figure 15–17

5. Click **Select** and hide the plane features.

Task 3 - Perform an advanced search.

In this task, you will perform advanced searches for multiple feature types. The search is saved as a favorite to be reused later.

1. In the Search dialog box, select the *Advanced* tab.
2. In the Workbench drop-down list, select **Part Design**.
3. In the Type drop-down list, select **Plane** and click **Or**. The query is added to the *Composed query* field, as shown in Figure 15–18.

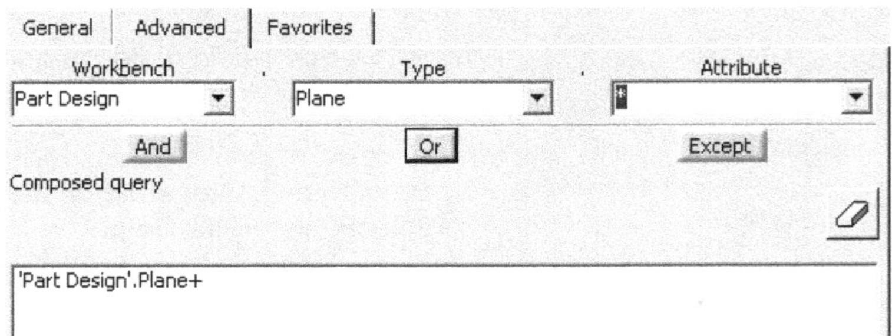

Figure 15–18

4. In the Type drop-down list, select **Point** and click **Or**.
5. Similarly, add queries for **Line** and **Curve** types. The Search dialog box opens as shown in Figure 15–19.

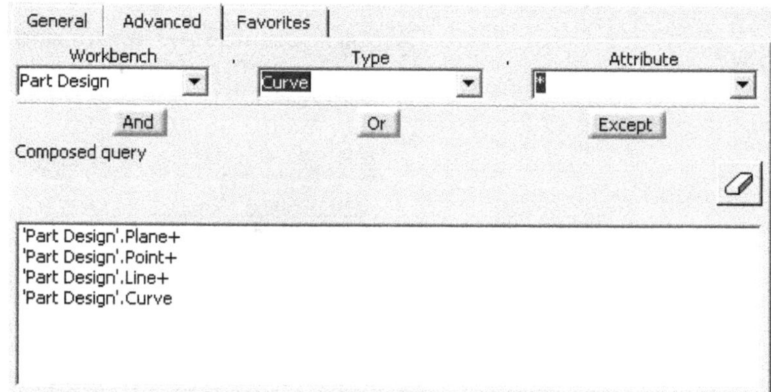

Figure 15–19

6. Click (Search). All of the reference elements in the model are highlighted.
7. Click (Add to favorites) and name the query as **RefElements**.
8. Close the Search dialog box.

Task 4 - Create a macro library directory.

In this task, you will define a directory in which the macros will be stored.

1. Select **Tools>Macro>Start Recording**. The Record macro dialog box opens as shown in Figure 15–20.

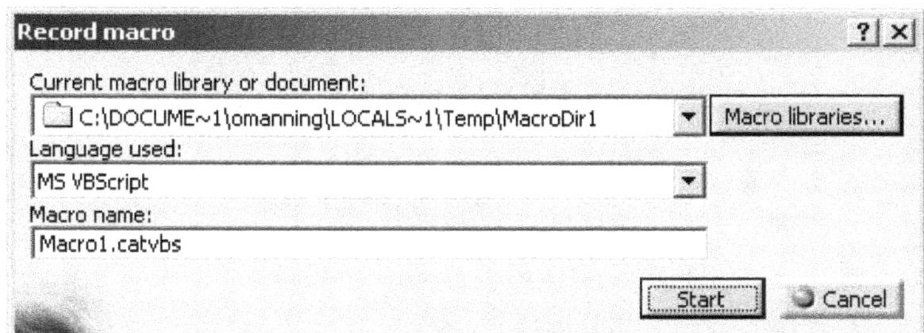

Figure 15–20

2. To create a new location to store macros, click **Macro libraries**.

3. In the Macro libraries dialog box, expand the Library type drop-down list, and select **Directories**.

4. Click **Create new library** and enter the path **C:\CATIA Advanced Part Designpractice\macros**, as shown in Figure 15–21.

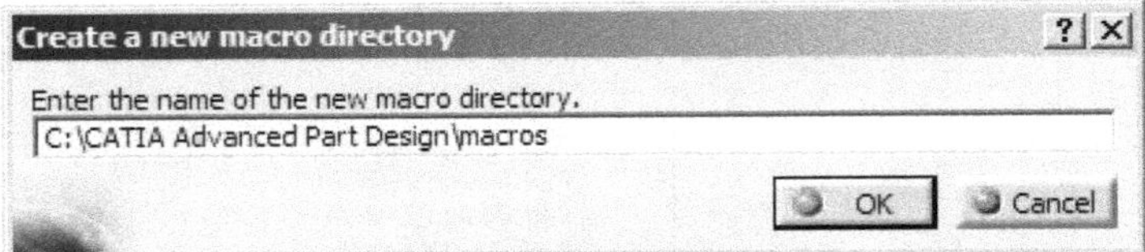

Figure 15–21

5. Click **OK** and **Close**. Keep the Record macro dialog box open.

Task 5 - Record a macro.

In this task, you will create a macro that will search for all of the reference elements in the model using the favorite search that you just created.

1. In the Record macro dialog box, configure the macro with the following options:

   - *Language Used:* Accept the default option
   - *Macro name:* **SelectRef.catvbs**

2. Click **Start**. The Record macro dialog box closes and (Stop macro recording) displays, which can be used to end the macro recording session. All of the menu selections that you make will be recorded in the macro.

3. Select **Edit>Search**.

4. Select the *Favorites* tab.

5. Highlight **RefElements** and click .

6. Click (Stop macro recording) to end macro recording. The macro is automatically saved to **C:\Advanced Part Design practice Files\macros\SelectRef.catvbs**.

7. Close the Search dialog box.

Task 6 - Add the macro to a toolbar.

In this task, you will create a toolbar button to run the macro you just created.

1. Select **Tools>Customize**. The Customize dialog box opens.

2. Select the *Commands* tab.

3. In the *Categories* column, select the **Macros** entry. The macro you just created displays in the *Commands* field, as shown in Figure 15–22.

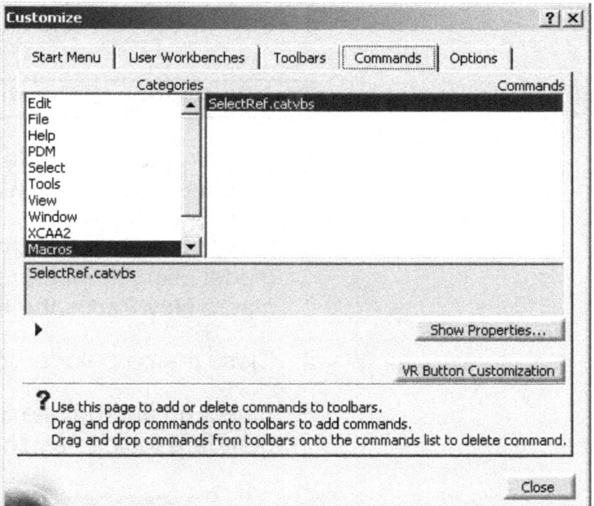

Figure 15–22

4. With **SelectRef.catvbs** selected, click **Show Properties**.

5. Click to change the icon for the macro.

You might need to advance a few pages of icons before finding the one shown. If you cannot find it, use any icon.

6. Click [icon] as the new icon and close the Icons Browser.
7. In the *Commands* field, select **SelectRef.catvbs** and drag it onto the Sketch toolbar, as shown in Figure 15–23.

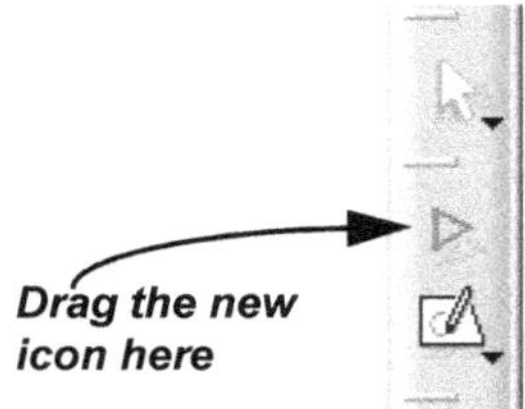

Figure 15–23

8. Close the Customize dialog box.
9. Test the macro to ensure that it selects the required elements. This macro can now be used as a selection tool to show and hide all reference elements in your models.
10. Save the model and close the window.

Task 7 - (Optional) Create an additional macro.

In this task, you will create a new macro and toolbar button that will be used to create a new part.

1. Create a new macro that will be used to create a new part model using the menu sequence **File>New>Part**. Name the macro **NewPart.catvbs**.
2. Close the part model created while recording the macro.
3. Select an appropriate icon for the macro and add it to the Standard toolbar, as shown in Figure 15–24.

Figure 15–24

4. Test the macro to ensure that it functions correctly.

Practice 15b

Editing a Macro

Practice Objectives

- Record a macro.
- Edit a macro.

In this practice, you will record a macro that will create a Pad feature. You will then modify the macro to add input boxes. You can control the shape of the Pad feature by entering values in the input boxes.

Task 1 - Create a new part.

1. Create a new part file.

Task 2 - Create a new VB project.

In this task, you will create a new VB project. When you save the macro in a project, you can open it in the VB Editor.

1. Select **Tools>Macro>Macros**.
2. To create a new location to store macros, click **Macro libraries**.
3. In the Library Type drop-down list, select **VBA projects** as shown in Figure 15–25.

Figure 15–25

4. Click **Create new library** and enter the path **C:\CATIA Advanced Part Designpractice\macros\Macro1.catvba**, as shown in Figure 15–26.

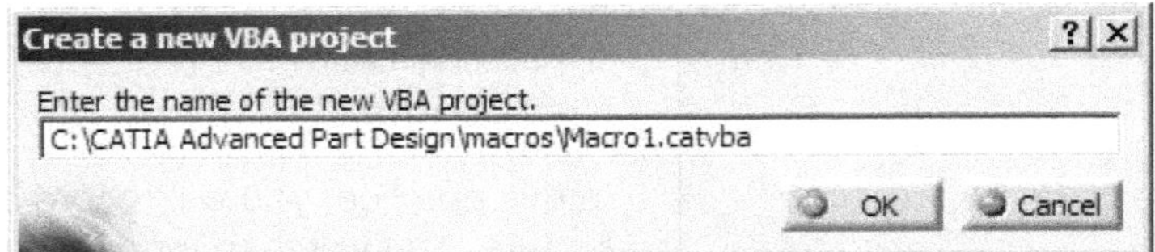

Figure 15–26

5. Click **OK**.

6. Click **Close** twice.

Task 3 - Record a macro.

In this task, you will record a Pad creation.

7. Select **Tools>Macro>Start Recording**. The Record macro dialog box opens as shown in Figure 15–27.

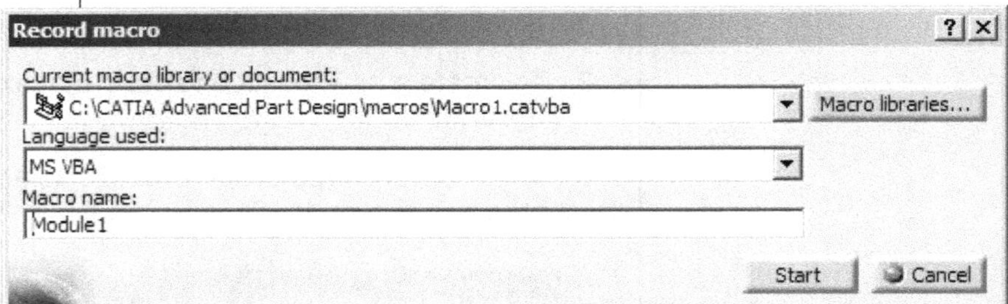

Figure 15–27

8. Click **Start**. The macro recording starts. Do not make any unnecessary selections during the creation of the macro.

9. Create a sketch on the xy plane and draw a rectangular profile with two dimensional constraints, as shown in Figure 15–28. The dimensional values do not need to match the figure. Do not modify the values.

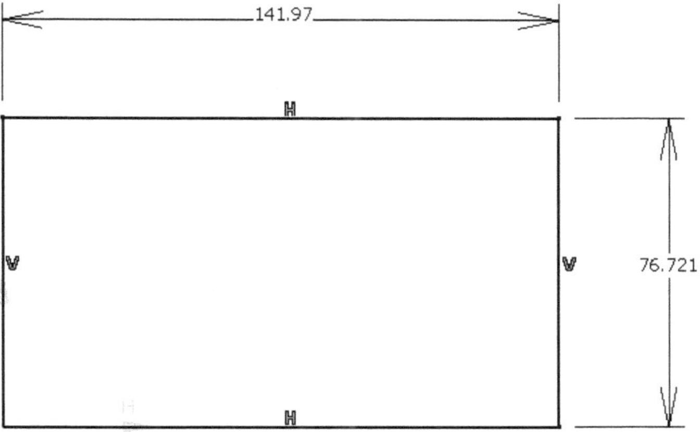

Figure 15–28

10. Exit from the Sketcher workbench.

11. Create a Pad feature that has a **20mm** height with the rectangular profile, as shown in Figure 15–29.

Figure 15–29

12. To end macro recording, click . The macro is automatically saved to **C:\CATIA Advanced Part Designpractice\macros\Macro1.catvbs**.

Task 4 - Edit a macro.

In this task, you will modify a previously created macro. If the recorded macro is run as is, it will create the same Pad. To create a Pad with different dimensions, you will modify the macro accordingly.

1. Select **Tools>Macro>Macros**. The Macros dialog box opens as shown in Figure 15–30.

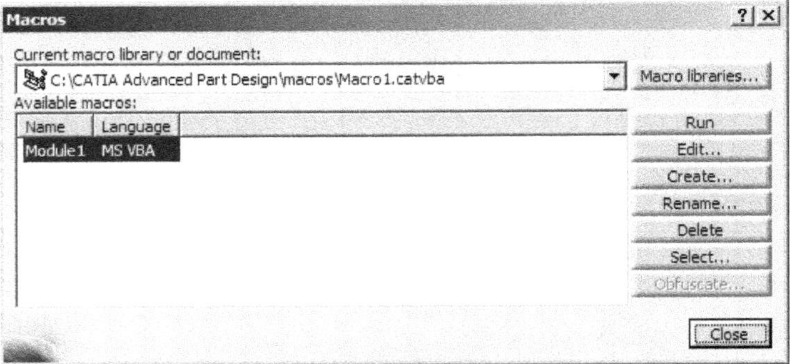

Figure 15–30

2. Click **Edit**. The Visual Basic Editor opens as shown in Figure 15–31.

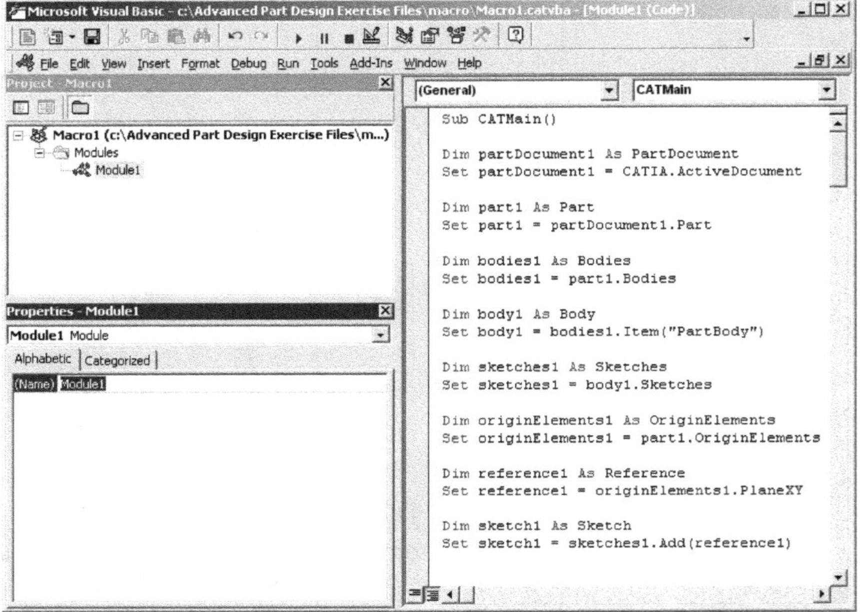

Figure 15–31

3. Scroll-down to the end of the code in the Code window and find the lines shown in Figure 15–32.

```
length1.Value = 76.721466          1

Dim reference11 As Reference
Set reference11 = part1.CreateReferenceFromObject(line2D5)

Dim constraint6 As Constraint
Set constraint6 = constraints1.AddMonoEltCst(catCstTypeLength, reference11)

constraint6.Mode = catCstModeDrivingDimension

Dim length2 As Length
Set length2 = constraint6.Dimension

length2.Value = 141.970413         2

sketch1.CloseEdition

part1.InWorkObject = body1

part1.Update

part1.InWorkObject = body1

Dim shapeFactory1 As ShapeFactory
Set shapeFactory1 = part1.ShapeFactory

Dim pad1 As Pad
Set pad1 = shapeFactory1.AddNewPad(sketch1, 20#)     3

part1.Update

End Sub
```

Figure 15–32

These are the lines that control the length, width, and height of the Pad.

Design Considerations

Use of the **InputBox()** command results in a dialog box that prompts the user for input data. While the macro is running, CATIA will create the rectangular shape and then prompt for the values for the profile. The creation order of the dimensions specifies whether line 1 drives the width or length of the Pad.

4. Modify the first line as shown in Figure 15–33.

```
length1.Value = InputBox("Enter the Width")
```

Figure 15–33

5. Modify the second line as shown in Figure 15–34.

```
length2.Value = InputBox("Enter the Length")
```

Figure 15–34

6. Add the two lines shown in Figure 15–35 above the third line.

Design Considerations

The Pad feature is created using the **sketch1** and **20#** values. To control the height of the Pad, you must declare a new variable using the double type. The double variable type can store decimal numbers. The height variable is equal to the entered value in the input box. If you replace the **20** value with the height variable, you can control the height of the Pad by entering a value during the creation of the Pad feature.

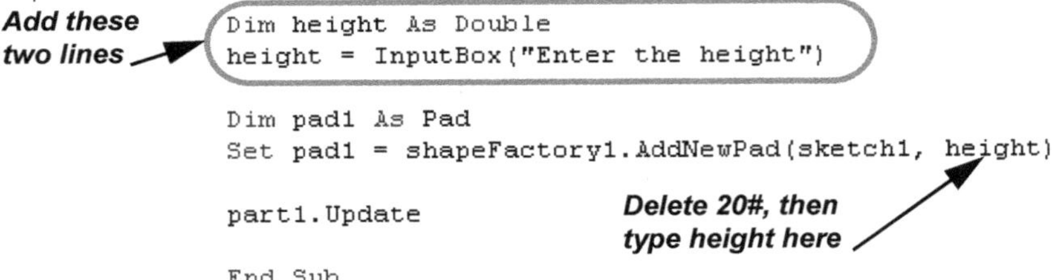
Add these two lines
Dim height As Double
height = InputBox("Enter the height")
Dim pad1 As Pad
Set pad1 = shapeFactory1.AddNewPad(sketch1, height)
part1.Update
Delete 20#, then type height here
End Sub

Figure 15–35

Task 5 - Run the macro.

In this task, you will run the macro that you just modified.

1. Switch to the CATIA window and close the part file.
2. Create a new part file.
3. Select **Tools>Macro>Macros** and run the macro. The CATIA V5 dialog box opens as shown in Figure 15–36.

CATIA V5
Enter the Width
OK
Cancel

Figure 15–36

4. Enter **50** in the dialog box. The CATIA V5 dialog box opens as shown in Figure 15–37.

Figure 15–37

5. Enter **100** in the dialog box. The CATIA V5 dialog box opens as shown in Figure 15–38.

Figure 15–38

6. Enter **150** in the dialog box. The model displays as shown in Figure 15–39.

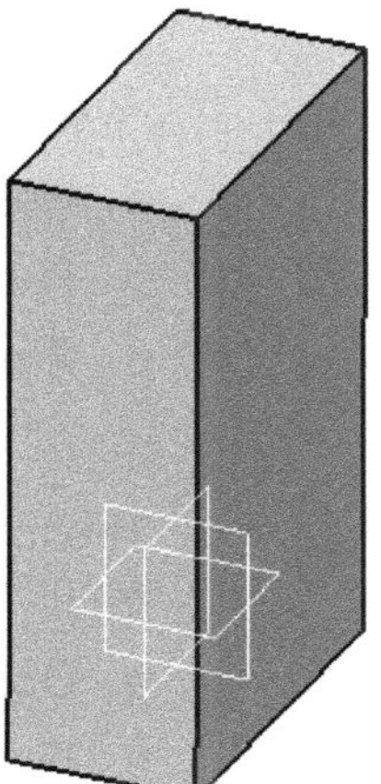

Figure 15–39

7. Save and close the file.

Chapter Review Questions

1. You can use Macros to record a series of actions in CATIA.
    a. True
    b. False
2. Macros are recorded using _____
    a. Macro script.
    b. Visual Basic script.
    c. Java Script.
    d. None of the above.
3. By default, a new macro is created ______
    a. Local to the current model.
    b. In a macro library.
    c. In a VB Script library.
    d. In the PLM system.
4. You can use keyboard accelerators to define keyboard shortcuts to run your macros.
    a. True
    b. False
5. A running VBScript calls:
    a. Required objects.
    b. Functions of the objects.
    c. Properties of the objects.
    d. All of the above.
6. The three main parts of the Microsoft Visual Basic editor window are:
    a. Object Browser, Parameters, and Script windows.
    b. File, Attributes, and Program windows.
    c. Explorer, Properties, and Code window.
    d. None of the above.

7. Words displayed in green in the code window area indicate:
    a. Reserved words.
    b. Errors.
    c. Warnings
    d. Comments
8. Variables can take the form of:
    a. Double
    b. String
    c. Boolean
    d. All of the above.

Projects

In this chapter, you will create three different projects with minimal instructions.

Practice 16a Bucket

Practice Objective

- Create a model using a design table.

In this practice, you will create a bucket for an hydraulic excavator cover. You will create a design table to create different configurations of the bucket, without instructions.

The completed model displays as shown in Figure 16–1.

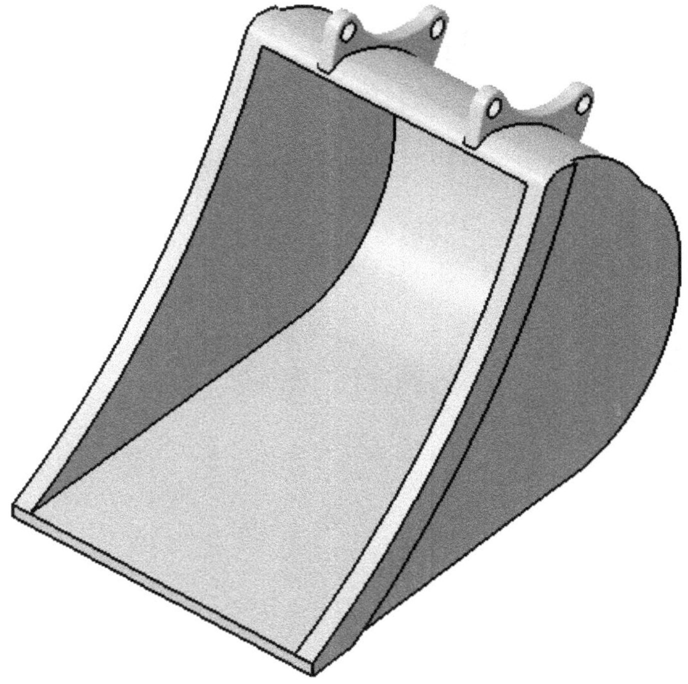

Figure 16–1

Task 1 - Create a new part.

1. Create a new part file.
2. Create the model using Figure 16–2, Figure 16–3, Figure 16–4, and Figure 16–5.

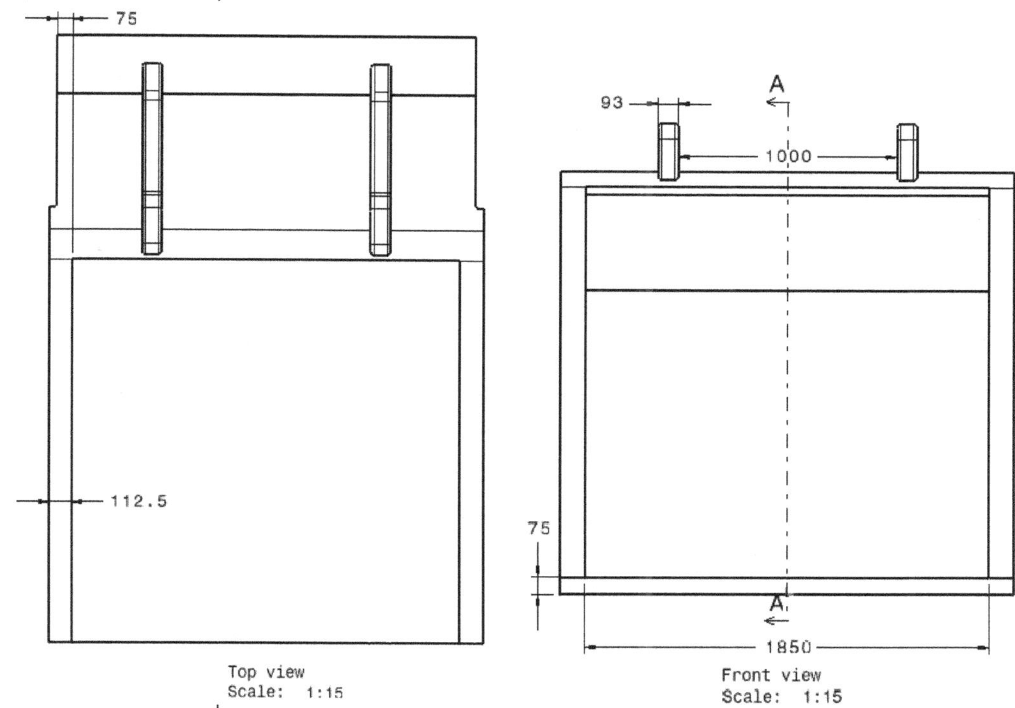

Figure 16–2

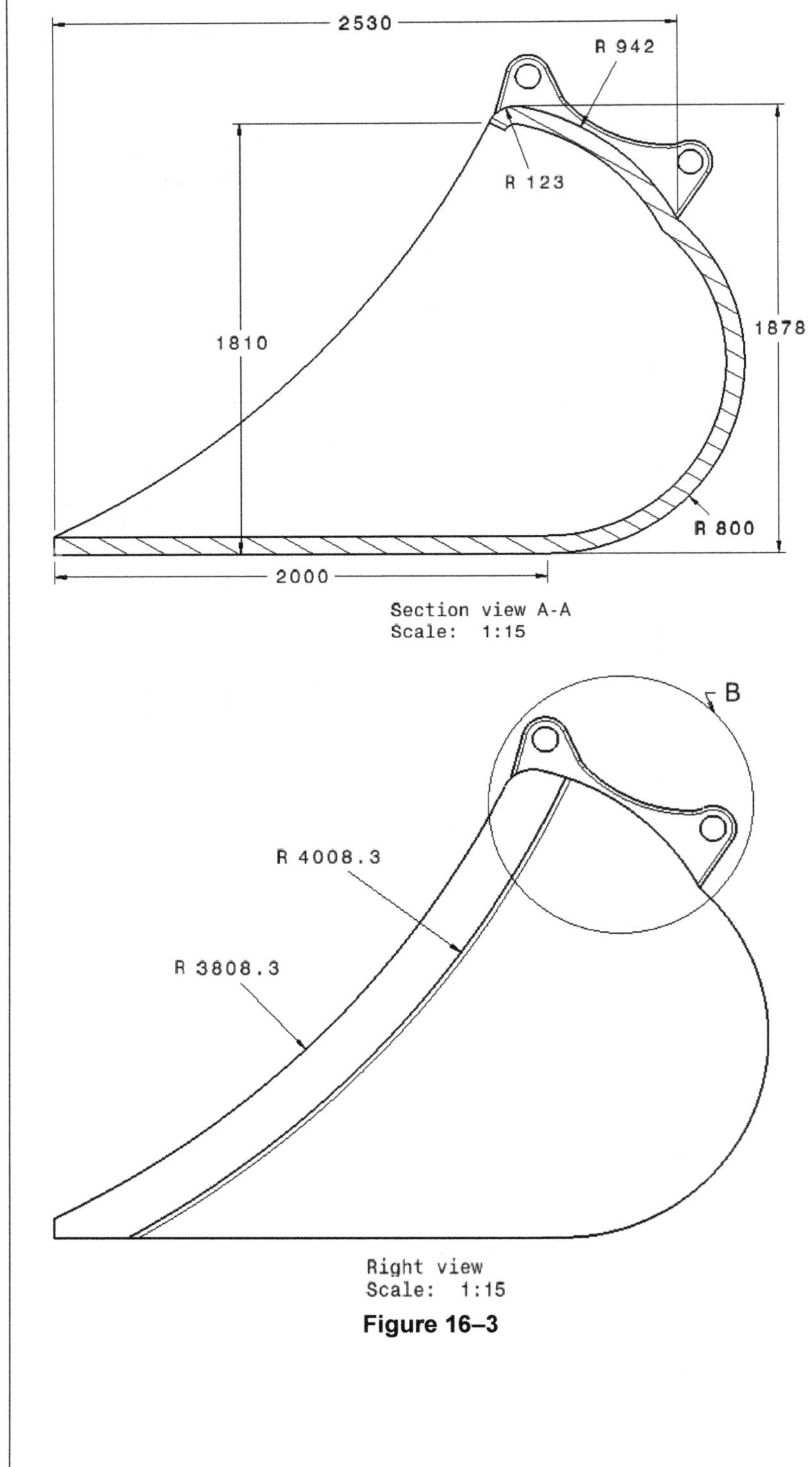
2530
R 942
R 123
1810
1878
R 800
2000
Section view A-A
Scale: 1:15
B
R 4008.3
R 3808.3
Right view
Scale: 1:15

Figure 16–3

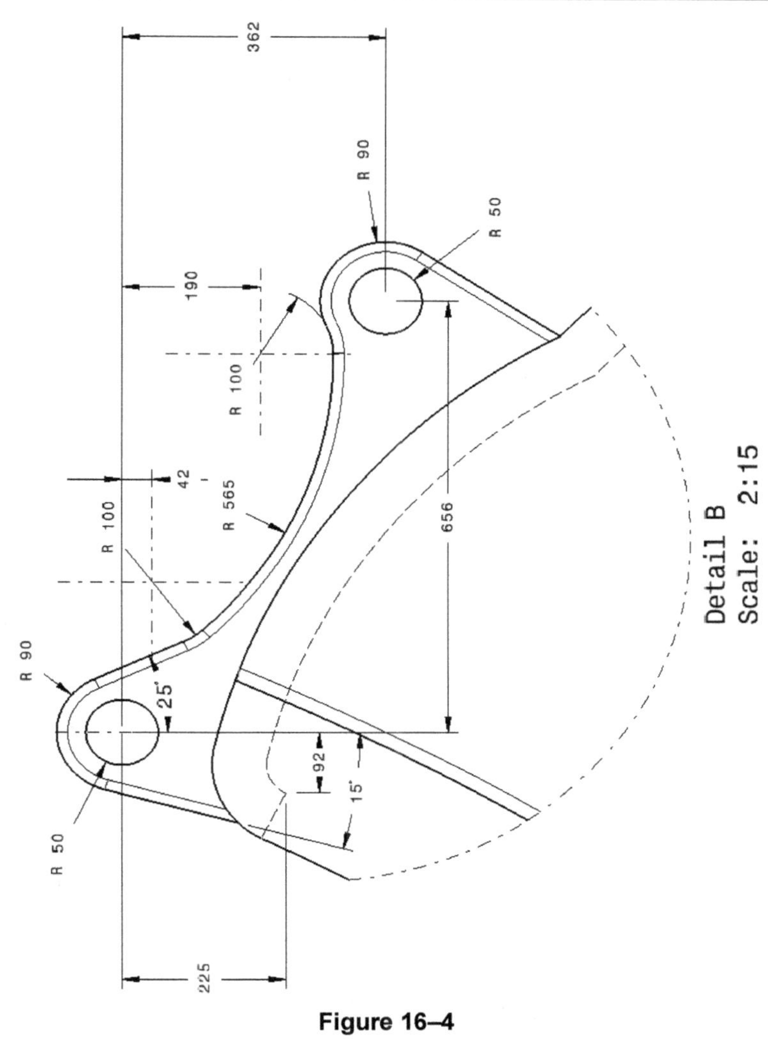
362
R 90
R 50
190
R 100
42
R 565
656
R 100
R 90
25°
92
15°
R 50
225
Detail B
Scale: 2:15

Figure 16–4

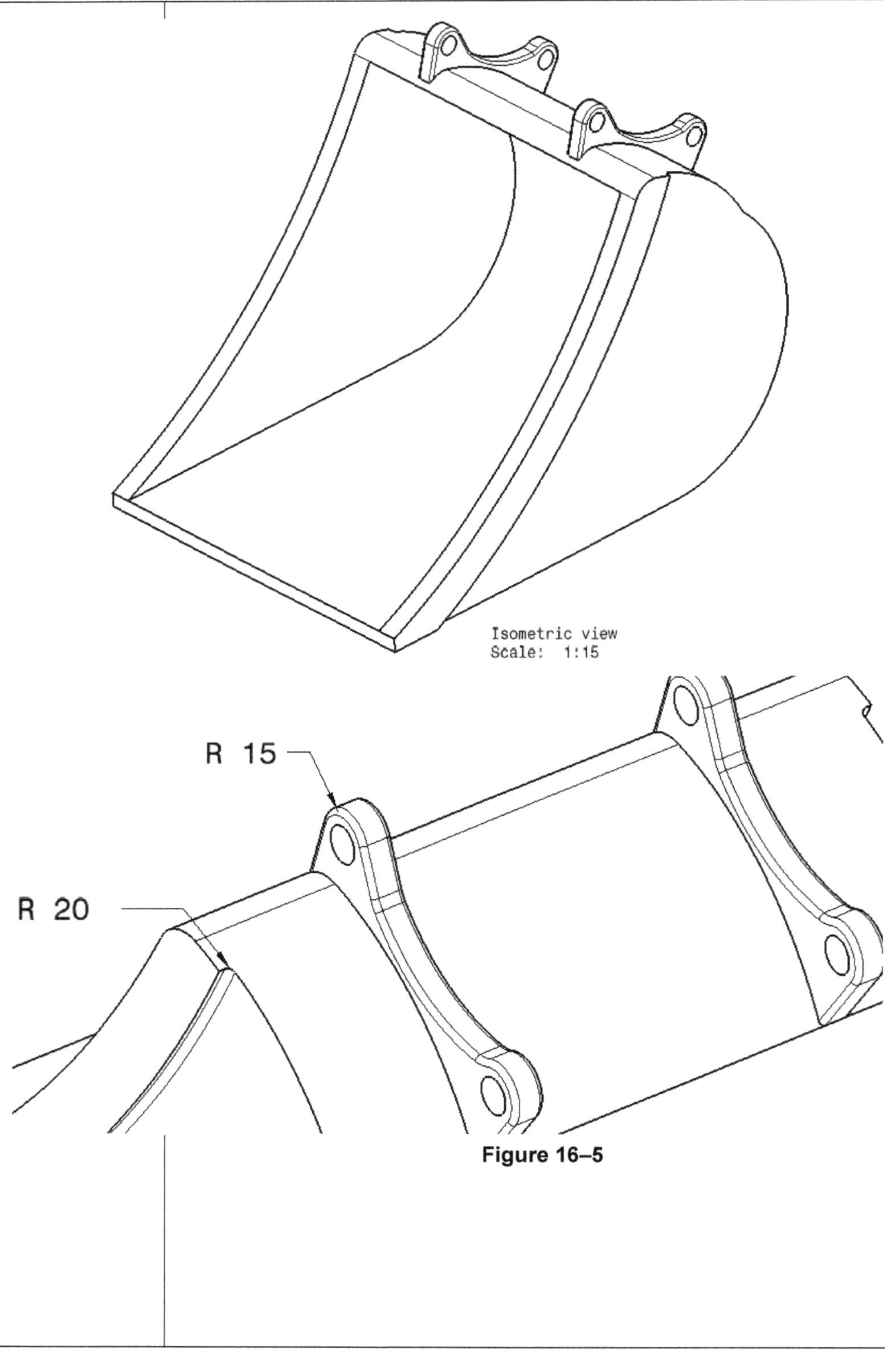

Figure 16–5

Task 2 - Create the design table.

1. Create the design table, as shown in Figure 16–6.

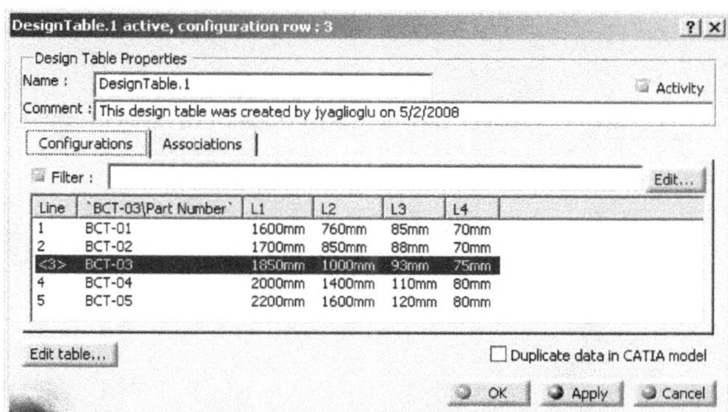

Line	`BCT-03\Part Number`	L1	L2	L3	L4
1	BCT-01	1600mm	760mm	85mm	70mm
2	BCT-02	1700mm	850mm	88mm	70mm
<3>	BCT-03	1850mm	1000mm	93mm	75mm
4	BCT-04	2000mm	1400mm	110mm	80mm
5	BCT-05	2200mm	1600mm	120mm	80mm

Figure 16–6

The parameters are shown in Figure 16–7.

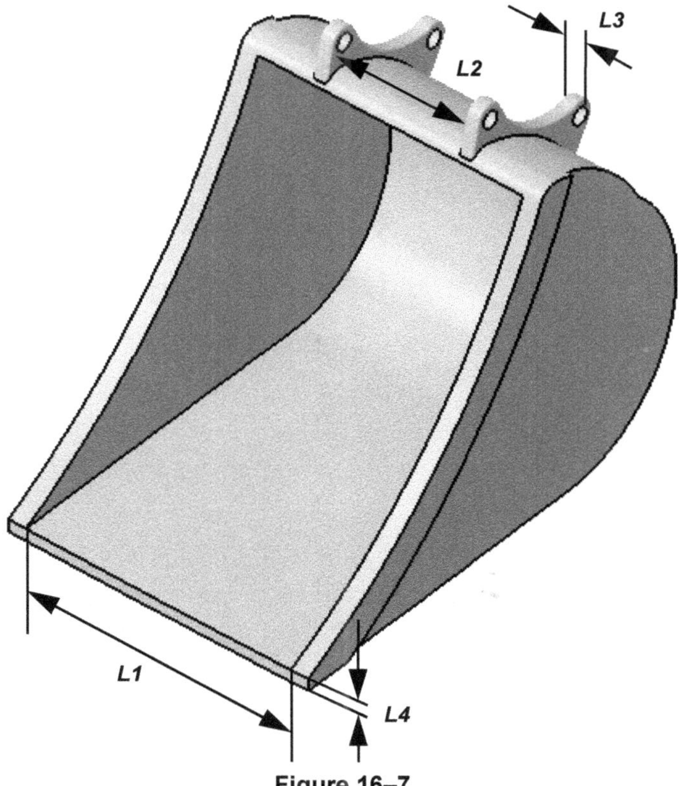

Figure 16–7

Practice 16b Housing Cover

Practice Objective

- Create a model with limited instruction.

In this practice, you will create a housing cover with minimal instructions. The completed model displays as shown in Figure 16–8.

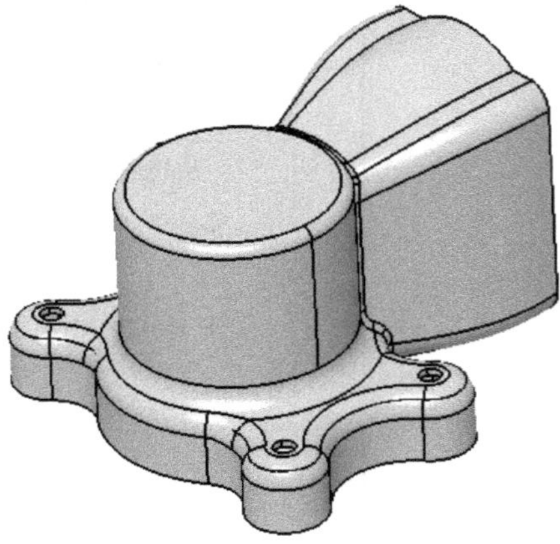

Figure 16–8

Task 1 - Create a new part.

1. Create a new part file.
2. Create a circular profile on the xy plane, as shown in Figure 16–9.

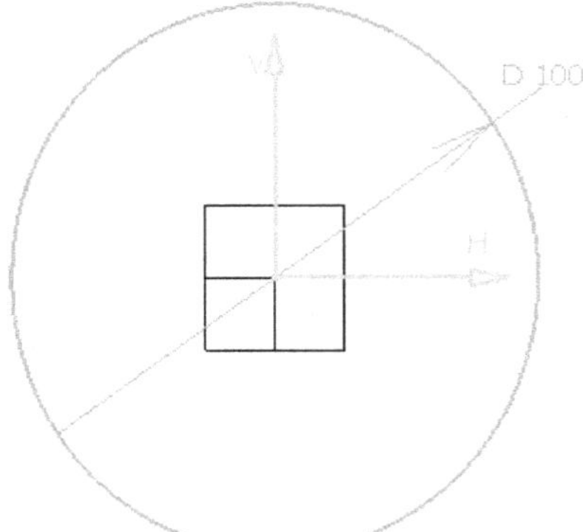

Figure 16–9

3. Create a Pad with the profile that you just created, as shown in Figure 16–10.

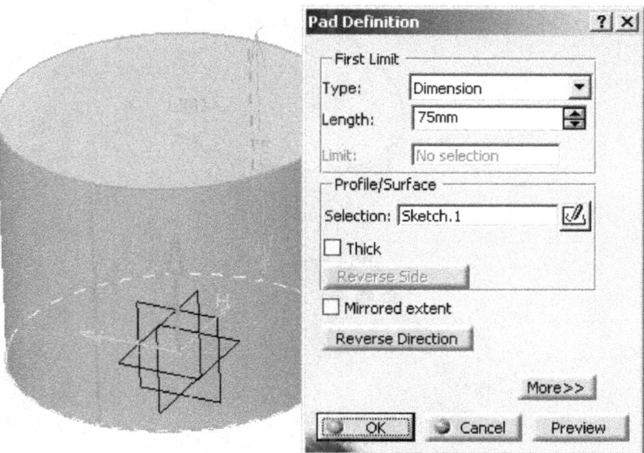

Figure 16–10

4. On the xy plane, create the sketch shown in Figure 16–11.

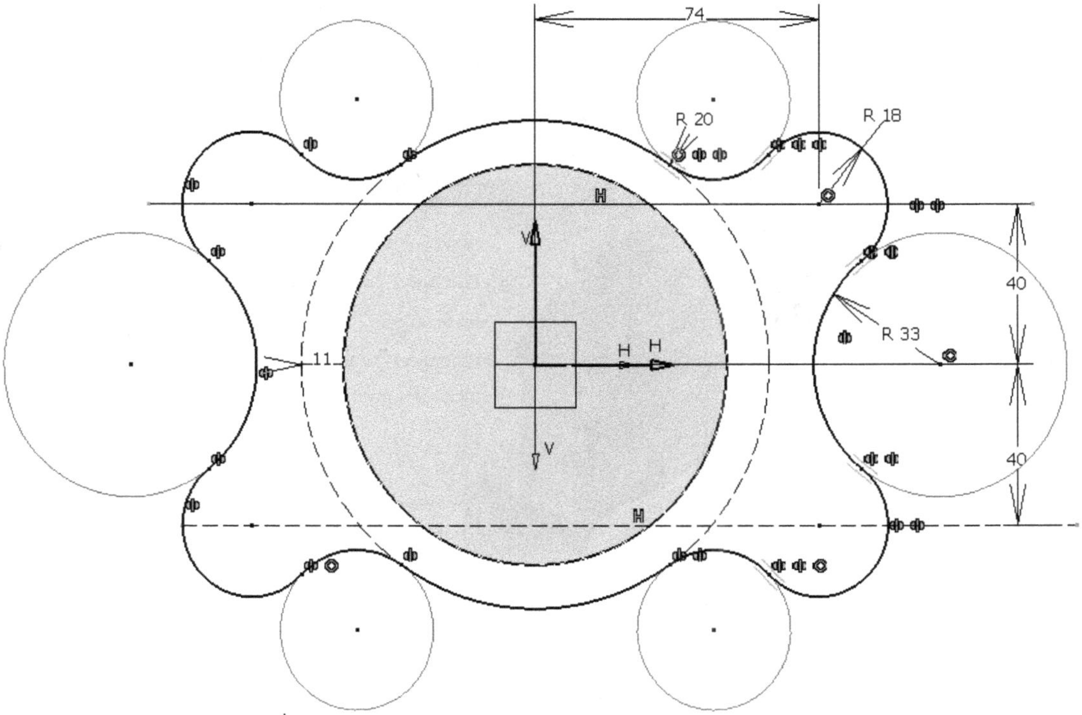

Figure 16–11

5. Create a Pad, as shown in Figure 16–12.

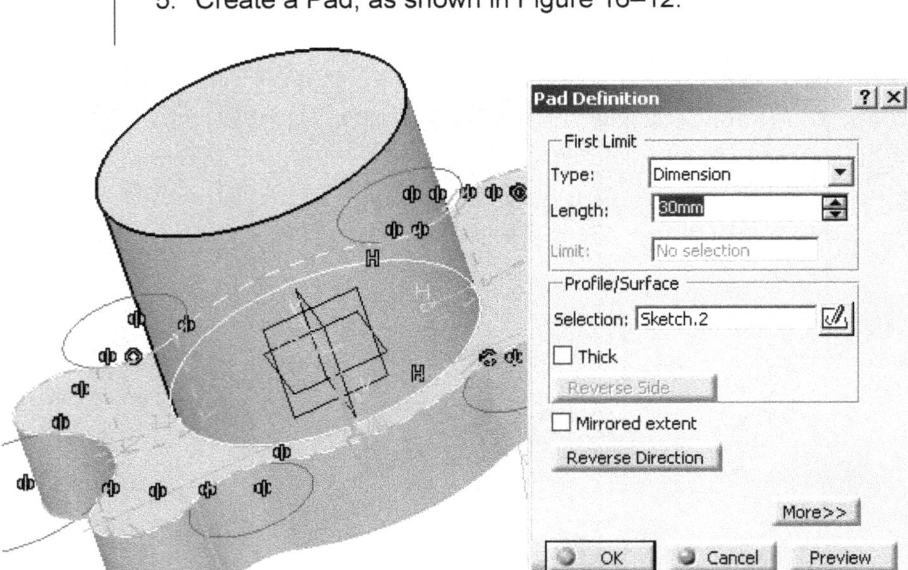

Figure 16–12

6. Create a Shell, as shown in Figure 16–13.

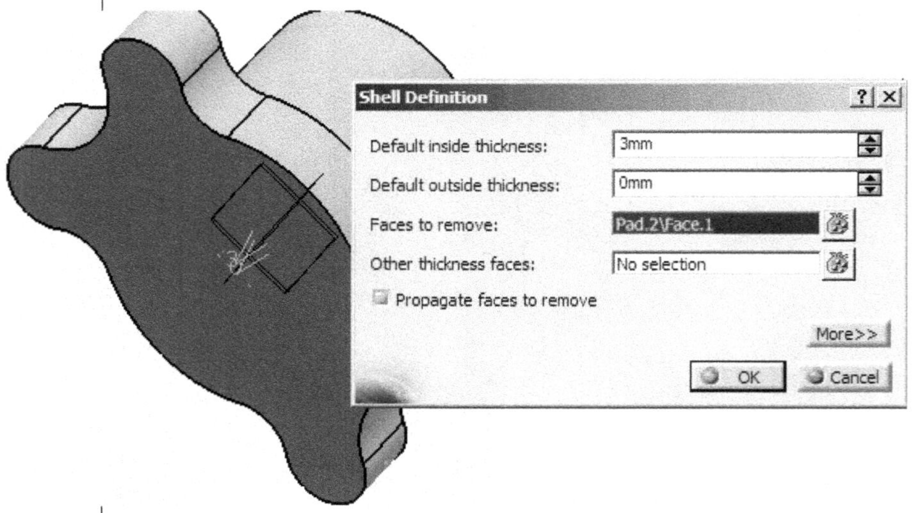

Figure 16–13

7. Create four Holes with a diameter of 10mm, as shown in Figure 16–14.

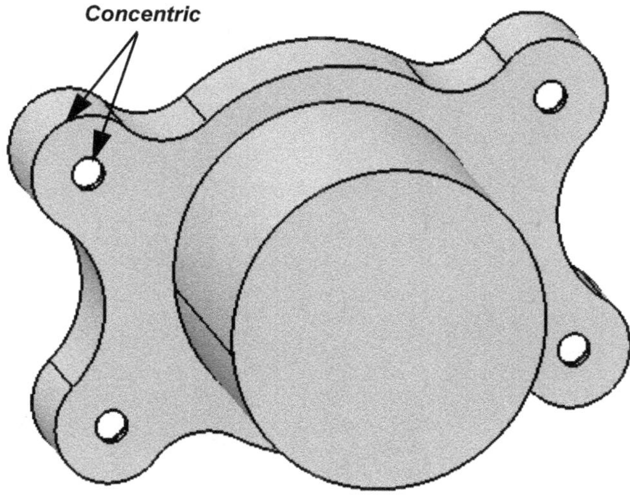

Figure 16–14

8. Create three reference planes, as shown in Figure 16–15.

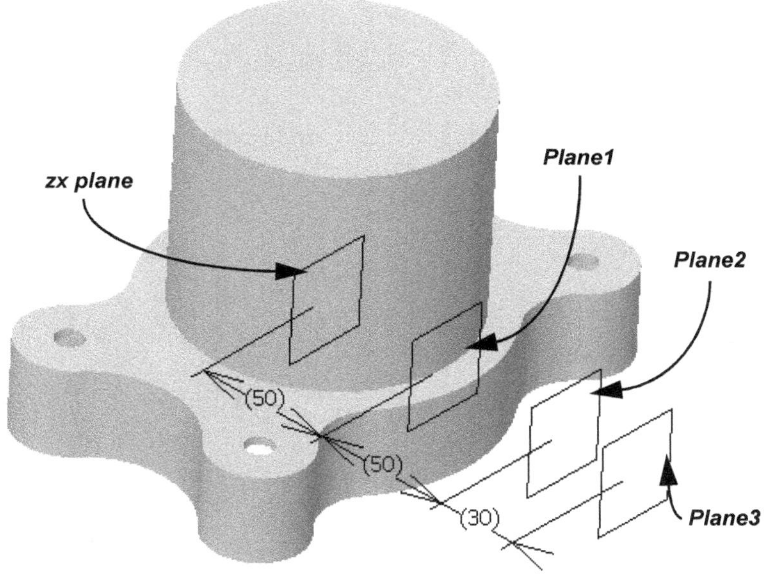

Figure 16–15

9. Insert a new body, and activate the body. It will be used to create a Multi-section solid feature.

10. On zx plane, create the profile shown in Figure 16–16.

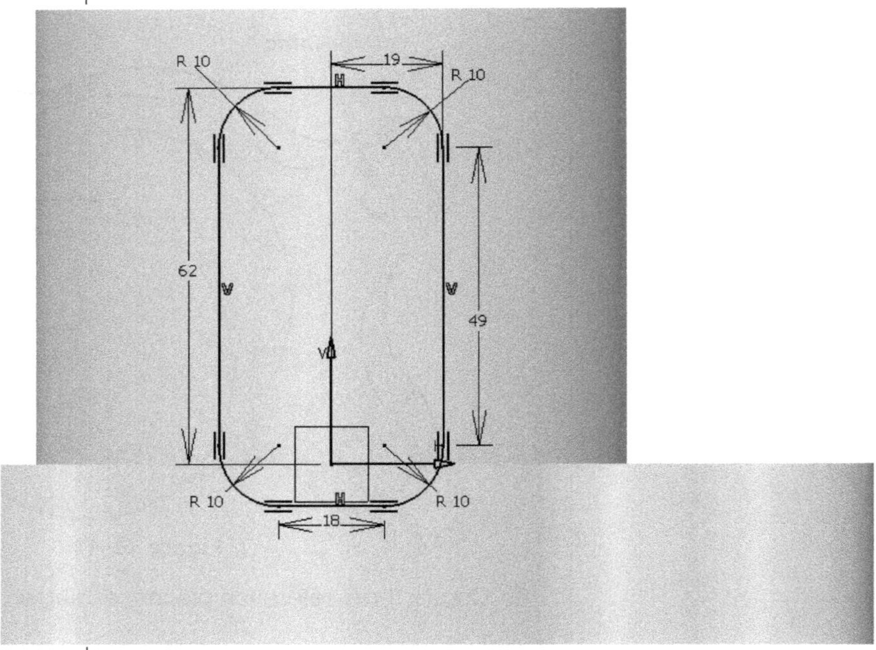

Figure 16–16

11. On Plane1, create the profile shown in Figure 16–17.

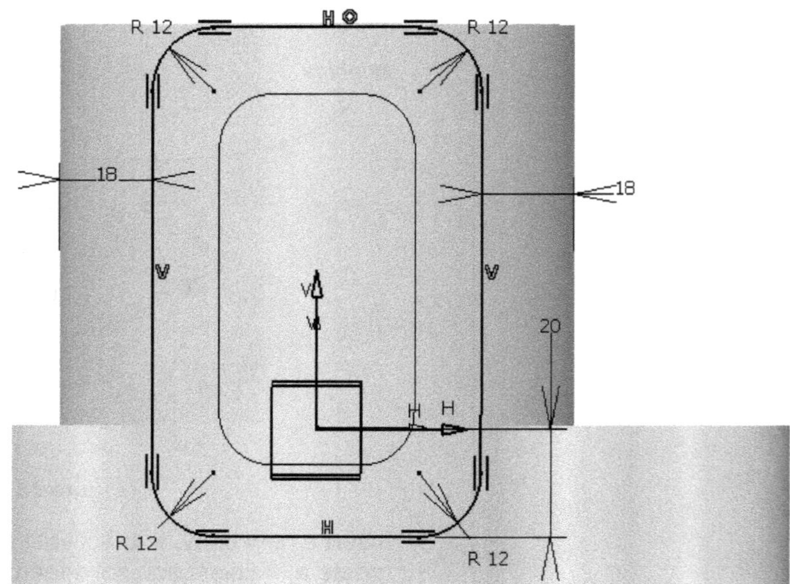

Figure 16–17

12. On Plane2, create the profile shown in Figure 16–18.

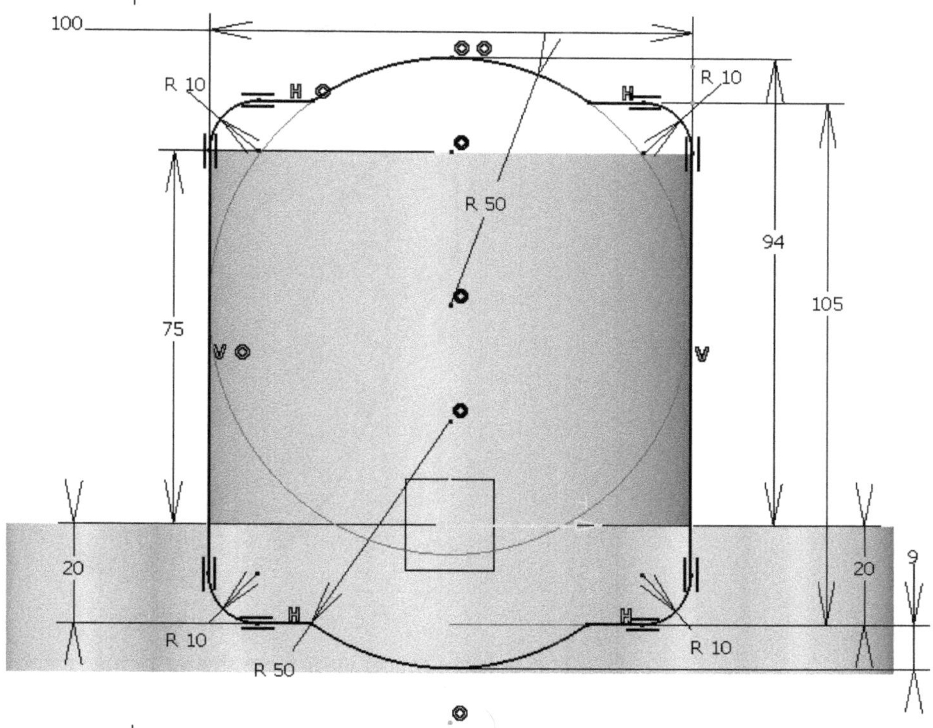

Figure 16–18

13. Copy and paste the last profile you created onto Plane3. The profiles display, as shown in Figure 16–19.

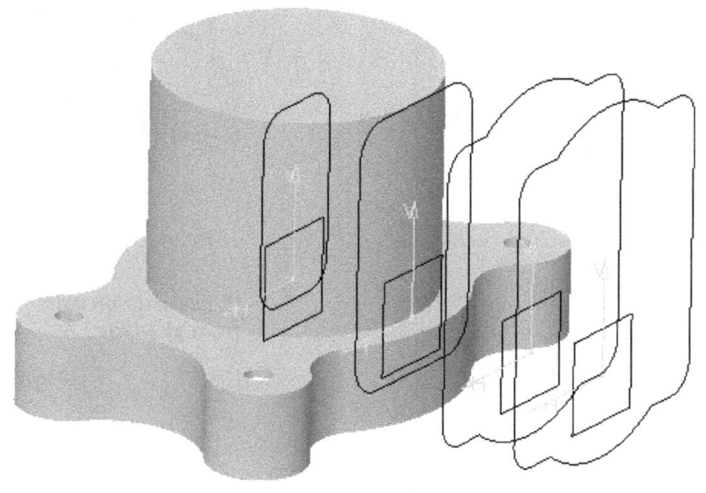

Figure 16–19

14. Create a multi-section solid, as shown in Figure 16–20.

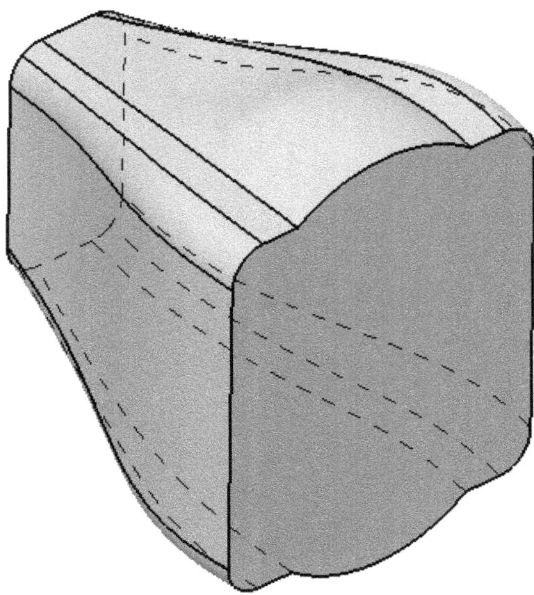

Figure 16–20

The cross-section view from the yz plane is shown in Figure 16–21.

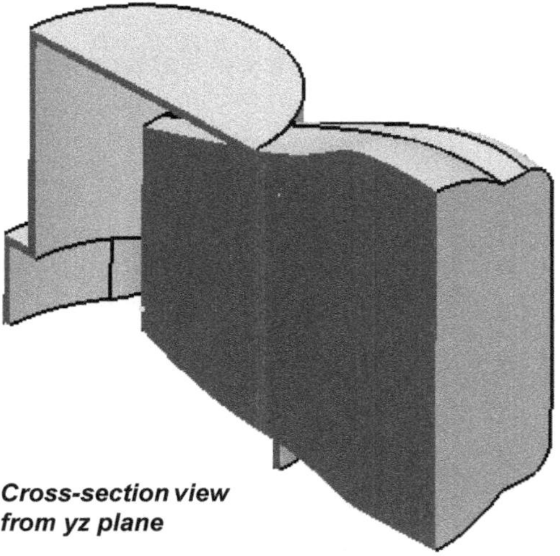

Figure 16–21

15. Insert a new body and activate the body, as shown in Figure 16–22. It will be used to create a removed Multi-section Solid feature.

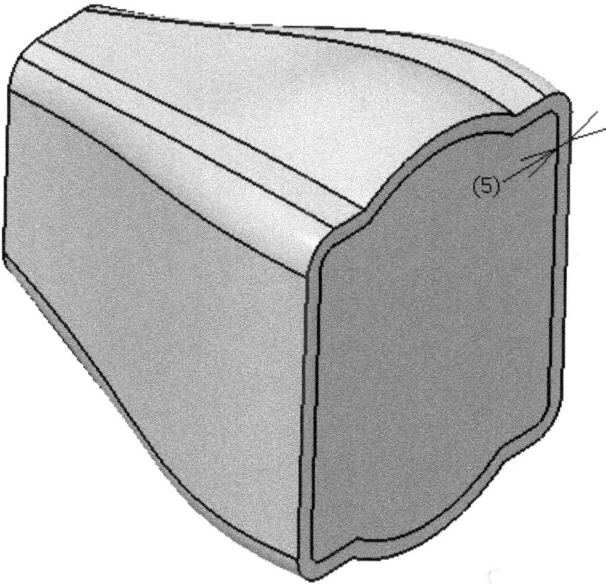

Figure 16–22

16. Use the correct Boolean operations to get the results shown in Figure 16–23, Figure 16–24, Figure 16–25, and Figure 16–26.

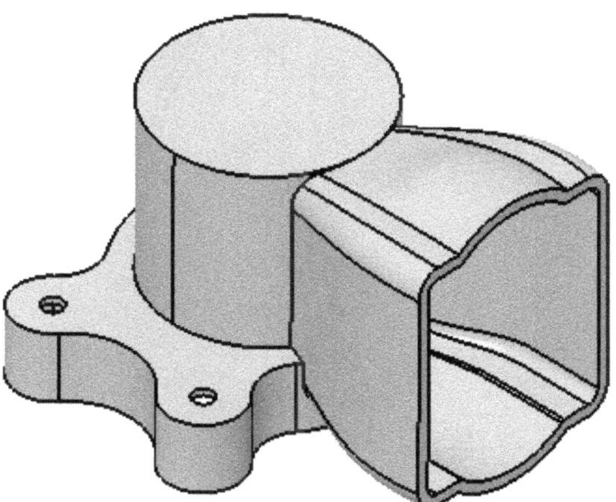

Figure 16–23

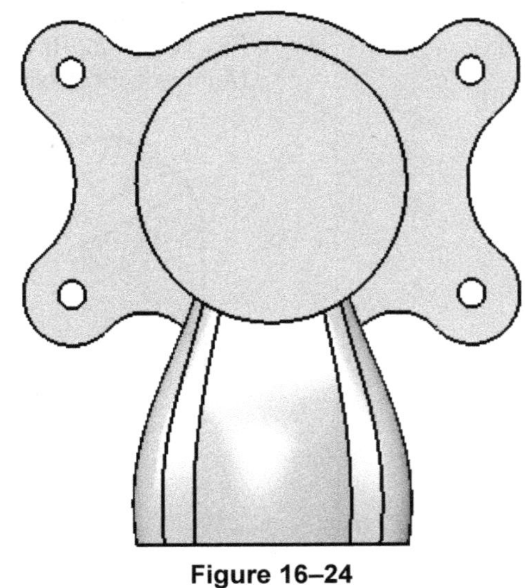

Figure 16–24

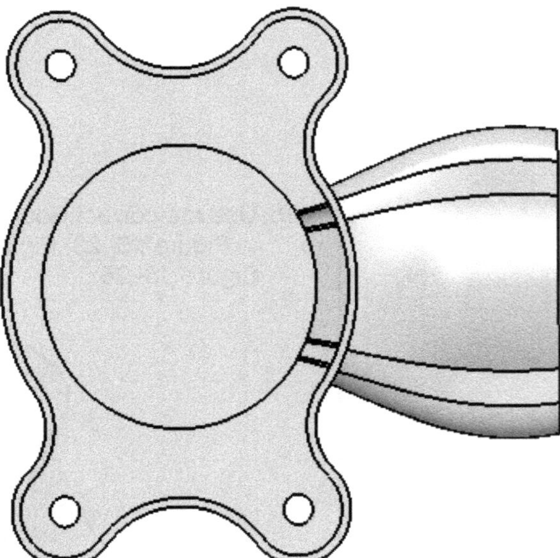

Figure 16–25

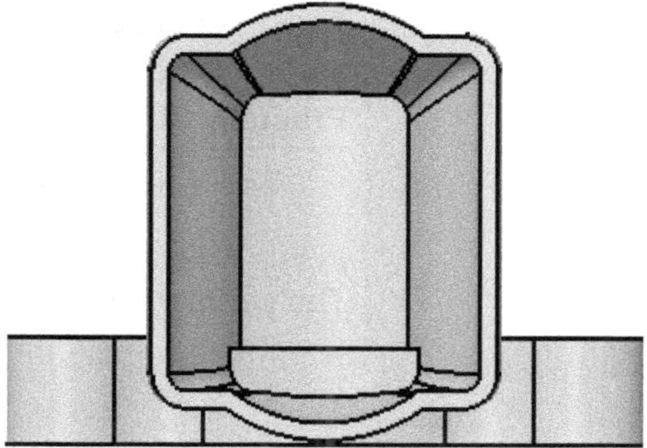

Figure 16–26

17. Create the Fillets, as shown in Figure 16–27.

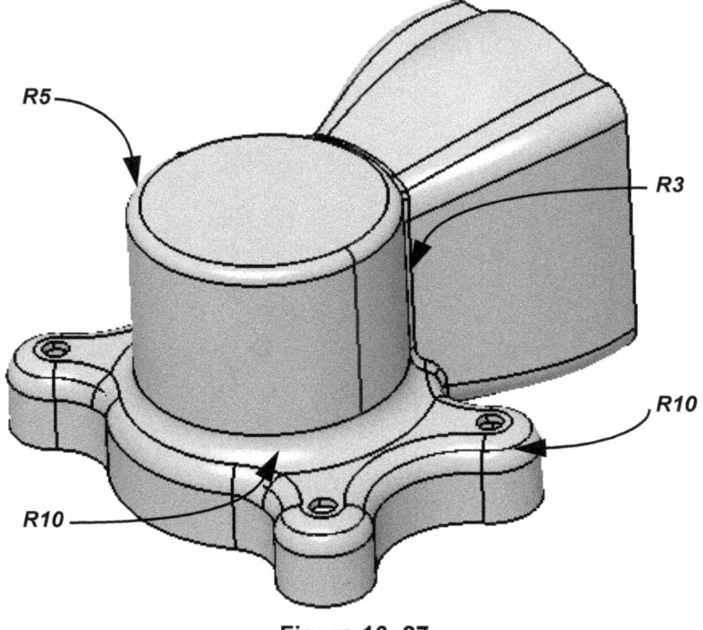

Figure 16–27

18. Save and close the file.

Practice 16c Landing Gear

Practice Objective

- Create a model with limited instruction.

In this practice, you will create a landing gear with given figures. The completed model displays as shown in Figure 16–28.

Figure 16–28

Task 1 - Create a new part.

In this task, you will create the model using the following drawings.

1. Create a new part file.
2. Create the model using Figure 16–29, Figure 16–30, Figure 16–31, Figure 16–32, and Figure 16–33.

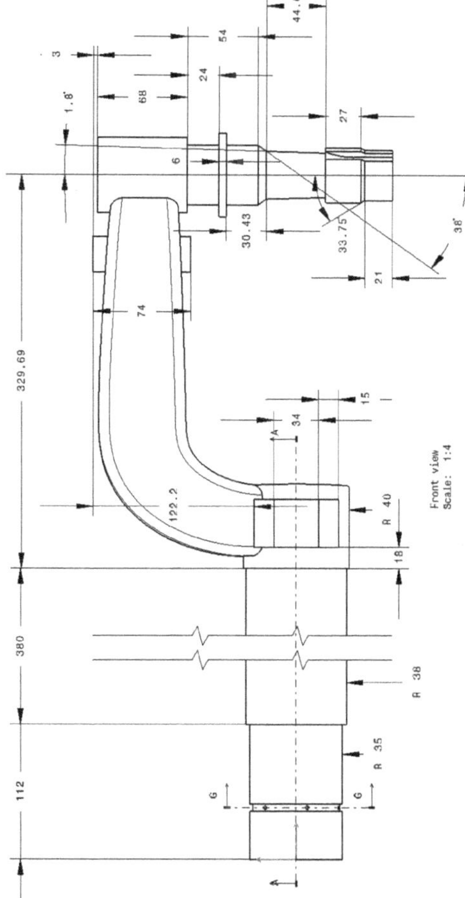

Figure 16–29

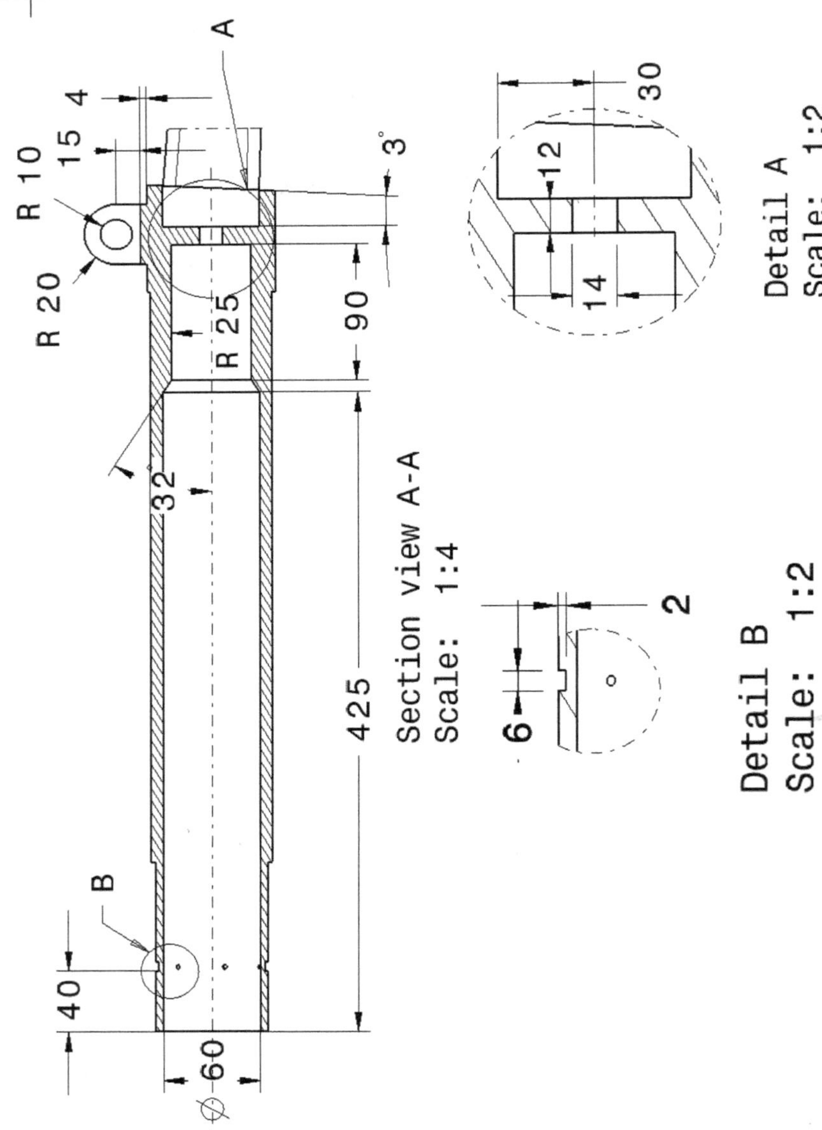
A
4
15
R 10
R 20
3°
R 25
90
32
425
Section view A-A
Scale: 1:4
B
40
⌀60
30
12
14
Detail A
Scale: 1:2
2
6
Detail B
Scale: 1:2

Figure 16–30

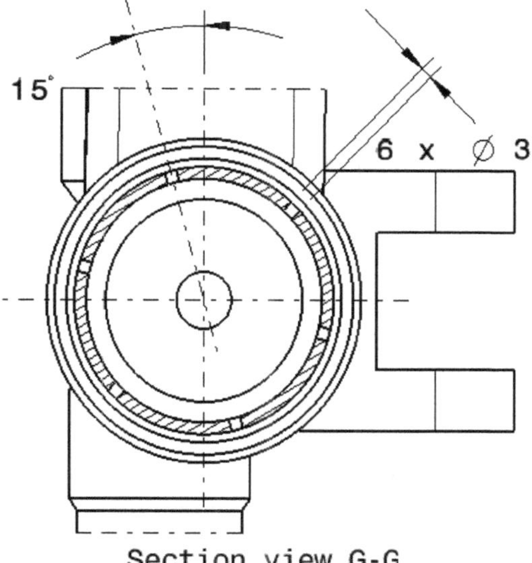

Figure 16–31

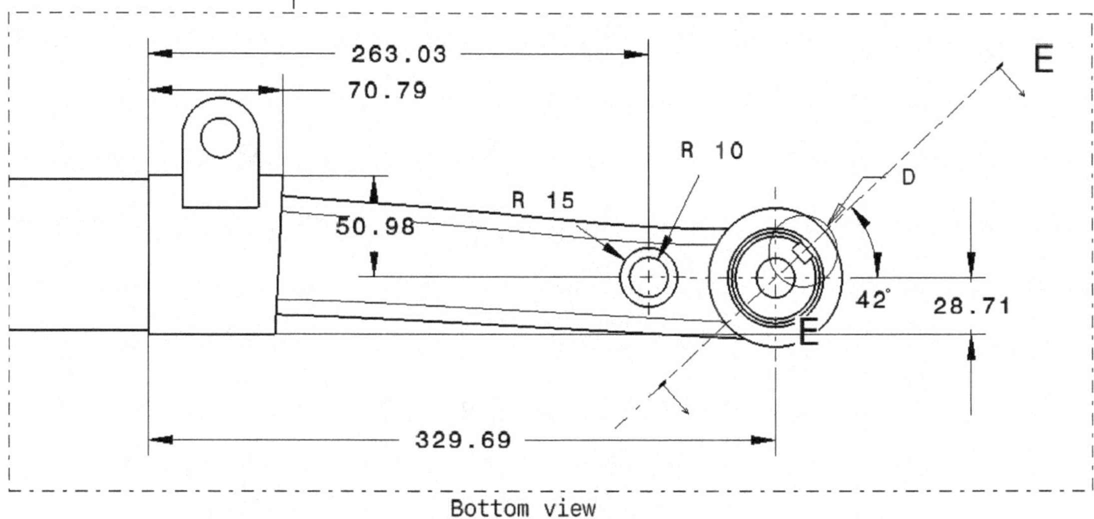

Figure 16–32

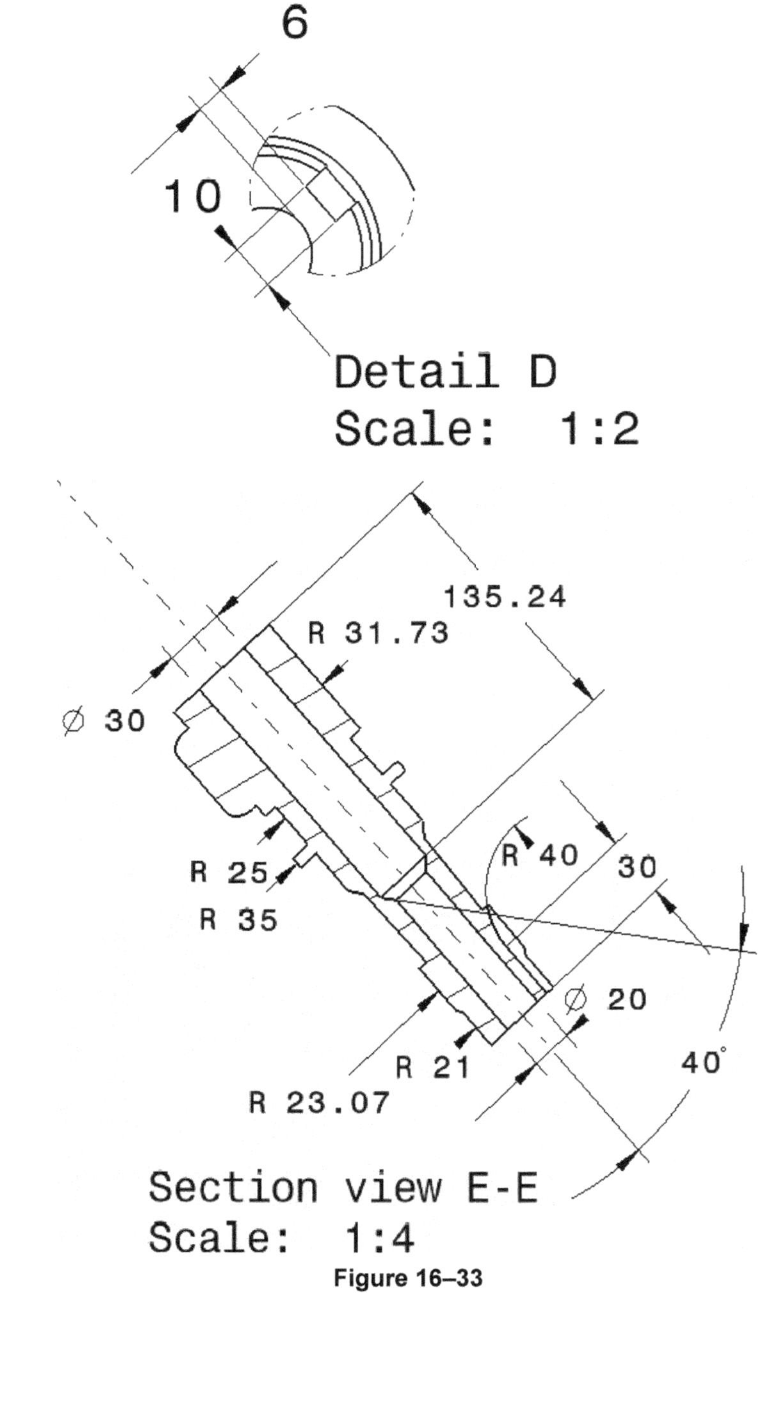
6
10
Detail D
Scale: 1:2
135.24
R 31.73
∅ 30
R 40
30
R 25
R 35
∅ 20
R 21
R 23.07
40°
Section view E-E
Scale: 1:4

Figure 16–33

Design Considerations

The information required to build the Multi-section Solid is shown in Figure 16–34, Figure 16–35, Figure 16–36, Figure 16–37, Figure 16–38, and Figure 16–39.

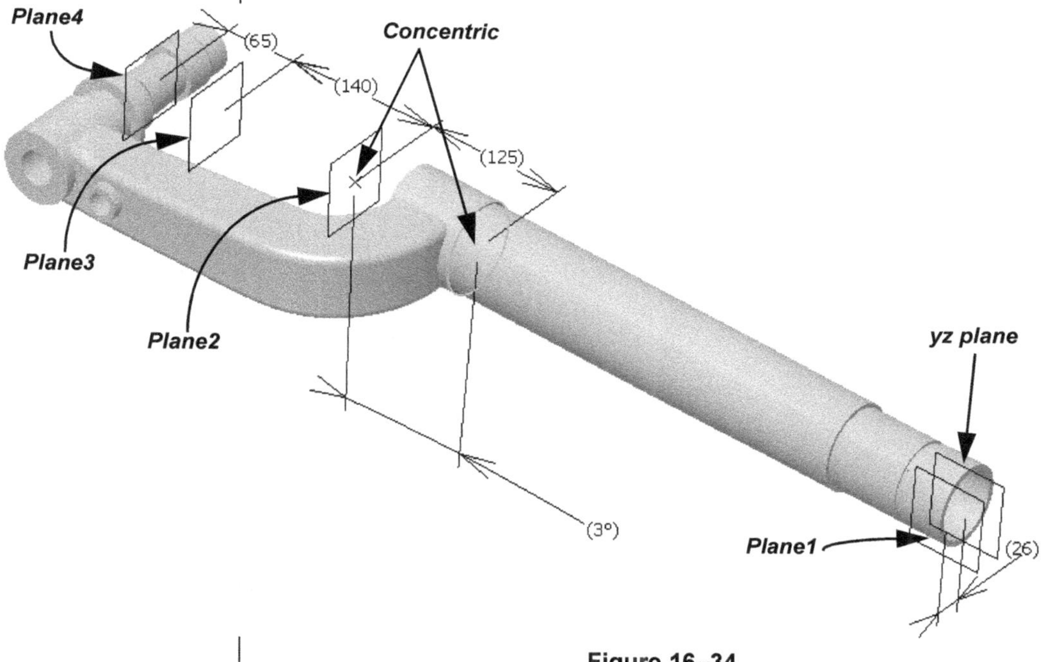

Figure 16–34

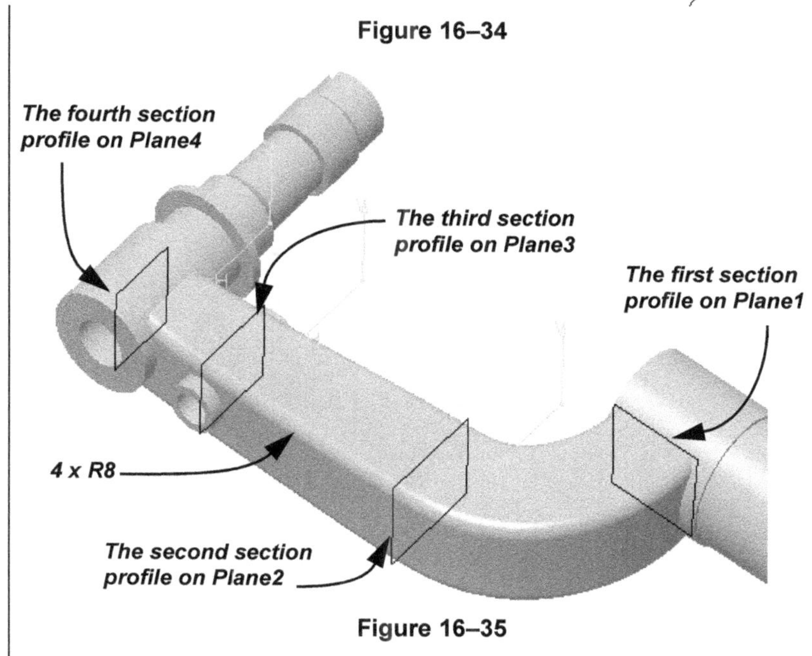

Figure 16–35

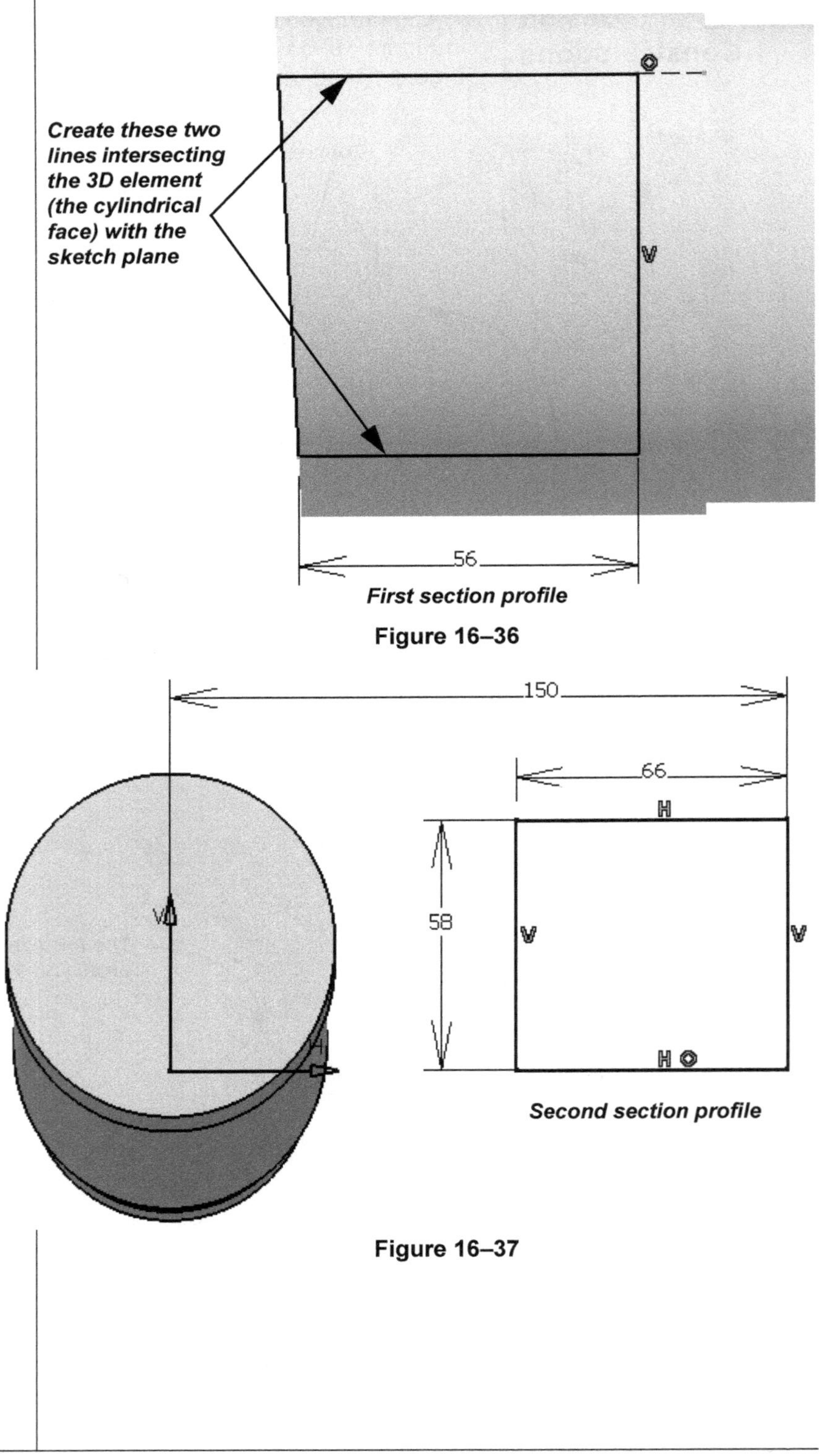
Create these two lines intersecting the 3D element (the cylindrical face) with the sketch plane
V
56
150
66
H
58
V
V
H

First section profile

Figure 16–36

Second section profile

Figure 16–37

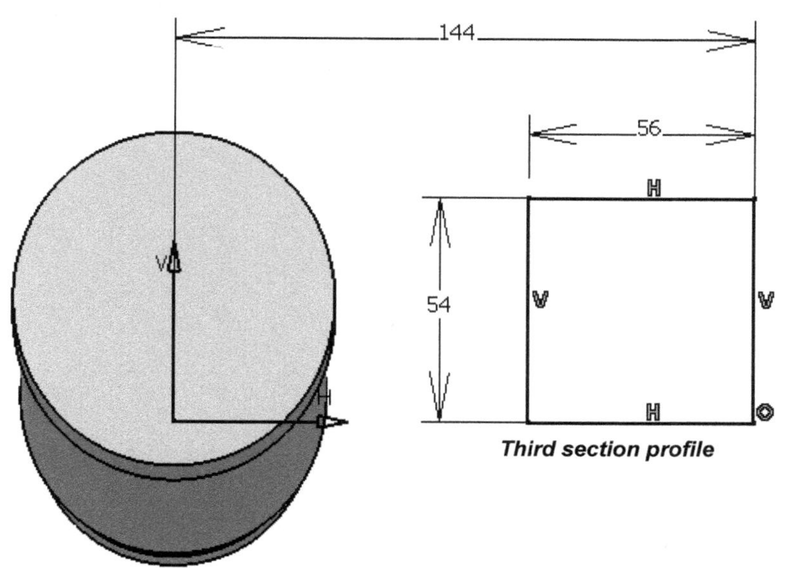

Figure 16–38

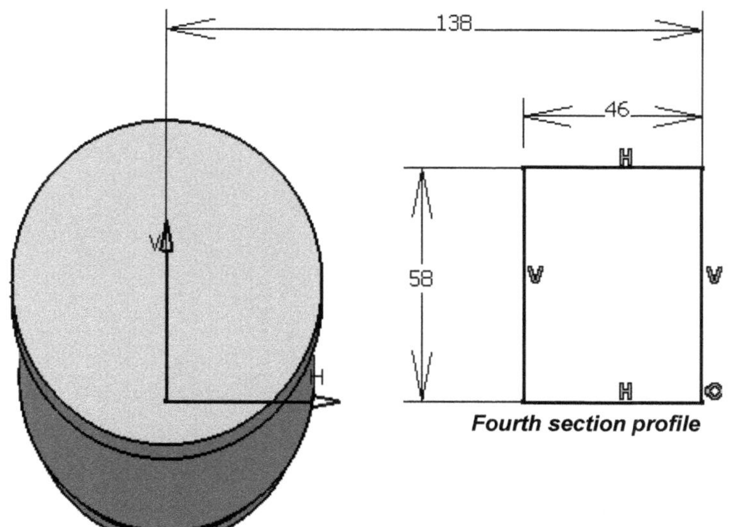

Figure 16–39

Feature Recognition

When a model is imported into CATIA using formats, such as IGES or STEP, the resulting geometry is represented by a single, isolated feature. You can use the Feature Recognition tool to have CATIA reconstruct the geometry using native CATIA V5 features. This enables a new level of manipulation for imported data.

Learning Objectives in this Chapter

- Understand Manual Feature Recognition.
- Use Automatic Feature Recognition to recognize multiple features.

A.1 Feature Recognition

Practice Objective

- Understand Manual Feature Recognition.

*A solid created using the **AsResultWithLink** option must be isolated before feature recognition can be used.*

If you paste a body using the **AsResult** option, only a solid.* is reported in the specification tree, even if the copied body consists of more than one feature. You can use Feature Recognition to manually recognize the features of the pasted solid. You can make modifications to the manually recognized feature.

Manual Feature Recognition

To use Manual Feature Recognition, click (Manual Feature Recognition) to open the Feature Recognition dialog box, as shown in Figure A–1.

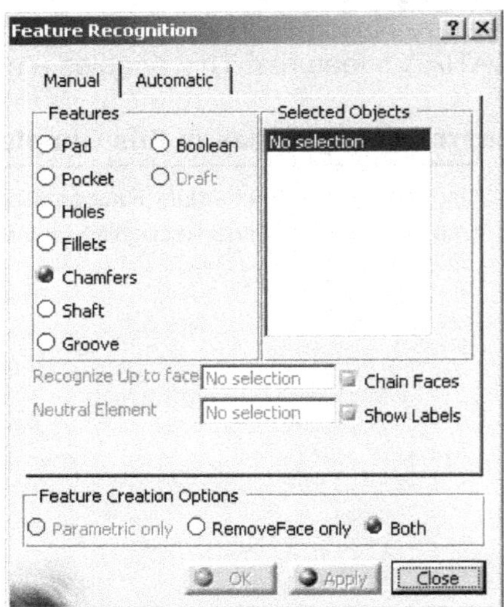

Figure A–1

You can manually recognize the following features:

- Pads
- Pockets
- Holes
- Fillets
- Draft
- Chamfers
- Shafts
- Grooves
- Boolean

To recognize a feature, select the type of element you want to recognize in the Feature Recognition dialog box.

Select a surface that defines the feature and click **Apply**, as shown in Figure A–2.

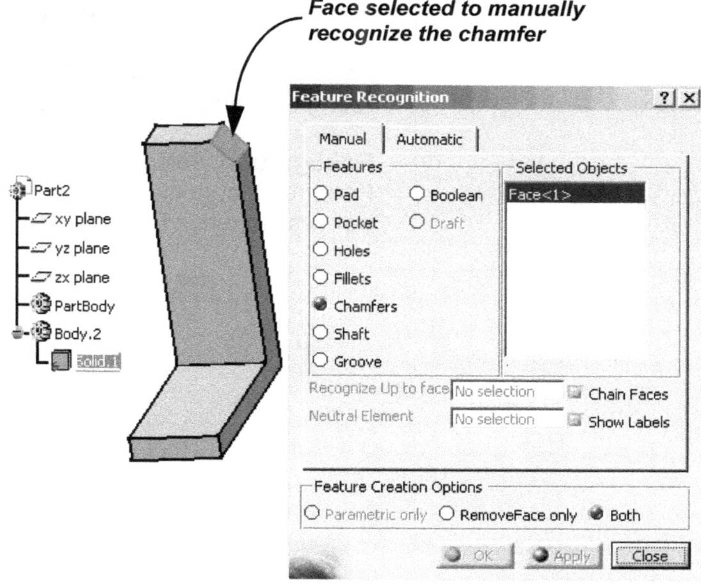

Figure A–2

The feature is removed from the display. CATIA places it below the object you are working with in the specification tree, as shown in Figure A–3. To display the element again, make the body the active object.

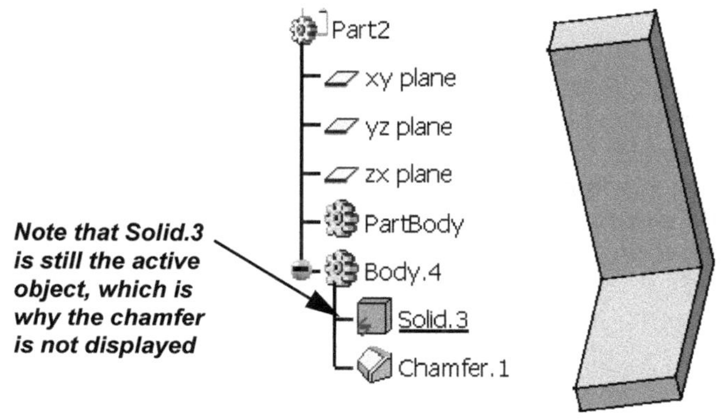

Figure A–3

A.2 Automatic Feature Recognition

Practice Objective

- Use **Automatic Feature Recognition** to recognize multiple features.

The **Automatic Feature Recognition** tool enables you to recognize multiple features at a time. To use **Automatic Feature Recognition**, select the *Automatic* tab or click (Automatic Feature Recognition) to open the Feature Recognition dialog box, as shown in Figure A–4.

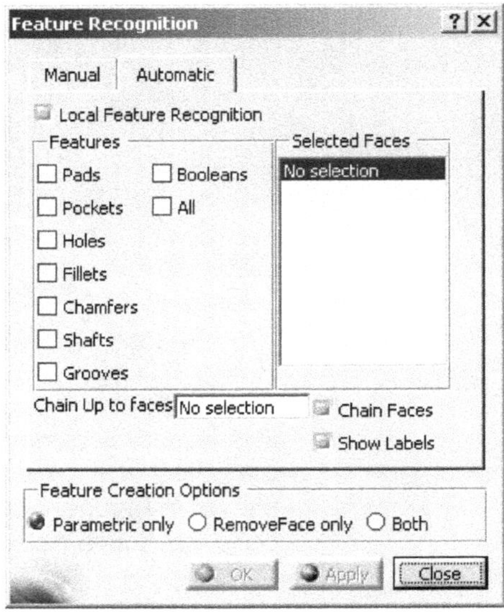

Figure A–4

Only Holes, Fillets, and Chamfers can be automatically recognized when the ***Local Feature Recognition*** *option is cleared.*

You can automatically recognize the following features:.

- Pads
- Pockets
- Holes
- Fillets
- Chamfers
- Shafts
- Grooves
- Booleans
- All

Select the types of elements that you want to recognize and click **Apply**. CATIA automatically scans the model for the selected features.

The recognized features are removed from the display. CATIA places them below the object you are working with in the specification tree, as shown in Figure A–5. To display the recognized features, define the Body as the work object.

Note that Solid.1 is still the active object. This is why the features below it in the specification tree are not displayed.

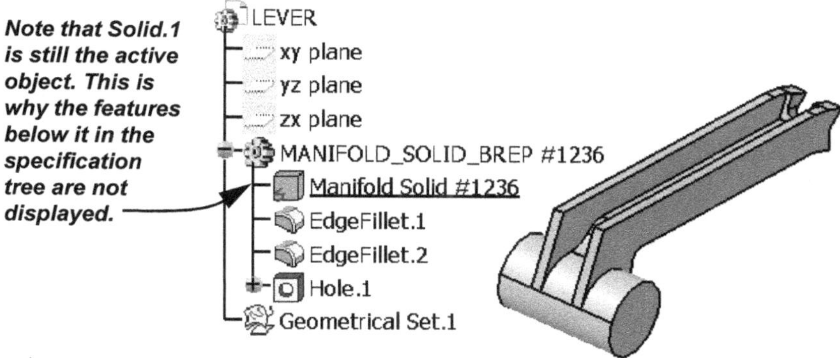

Figure A–5

Local Feature Recognition

You can use the **Local Feature Recognition** option to recognize features in a specific area in the model. Like the **Manual Recognition** tool, this option enables you to control which surfaces of the model are to be scanned and enables you to recognize multiple types of features at once. To recognize features, select **Local Feature Recognition**, and select the type of element you want to recognize in the Feature Recognition dialog box.

Select the surfaces that define the features and click **Apply**, as shown in Figure A–6.

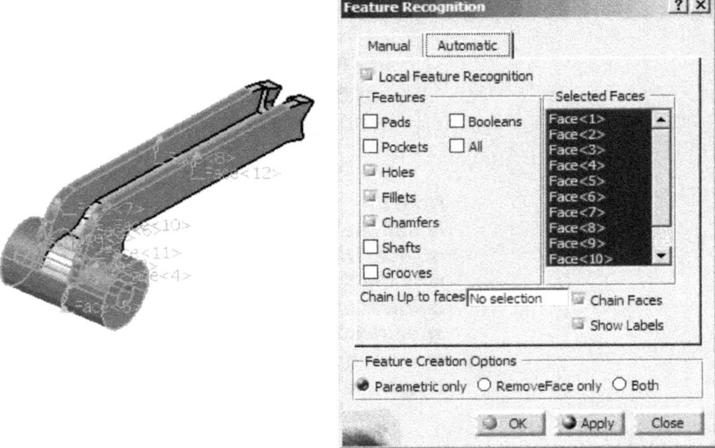

Figure A–6

Practice A1

Feature Recognition

Practice Objective

- Use the **Manual Feature Recognition** tool.

In this practice, you will practice manually recognizing features from an imported step file. The geometry shown in Figure A–7 has been created for you.

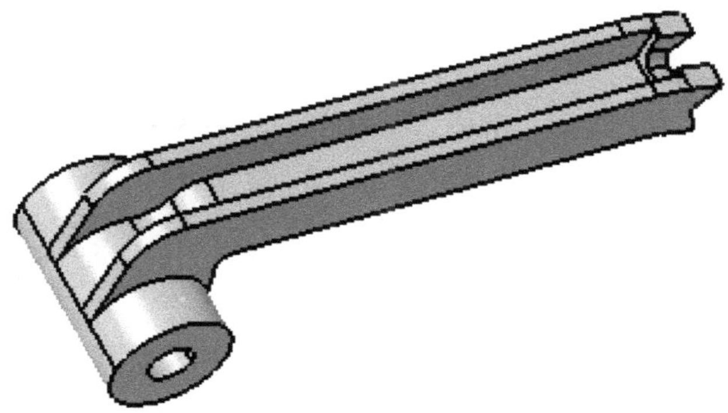

Figure A–7

Task 1 - Open the part.

1. Open **lever.stp**.
2. Pan, zoom, and rotate the model to see what the part looks like, and the features it includes.

   Note that the part body only contains a solid boundary representation of the original part, and no features.

Task 2 - Manually recognize the fillets.

1. Define the **MANIFOLD_SOLID_BREP #1236** solid as the Work Object.

2. Click (Manual Feature Recognition). The Feature Recognition dialog box opens. Ensure that the *Manual* tab is selected, as shown in Figure A–8.

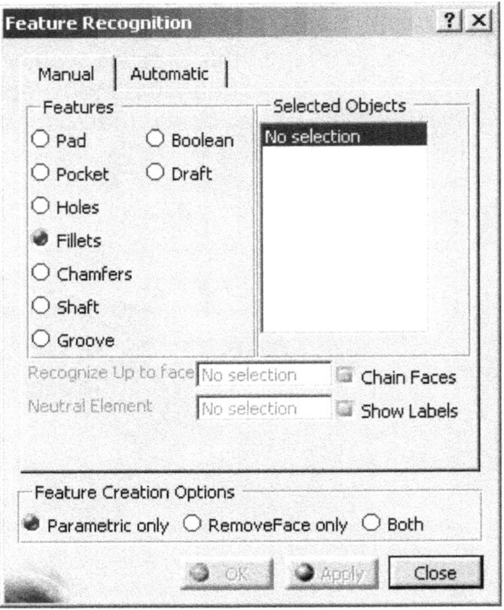

Figure A–8

3. Select the rounded edges shown in Figure A–9.

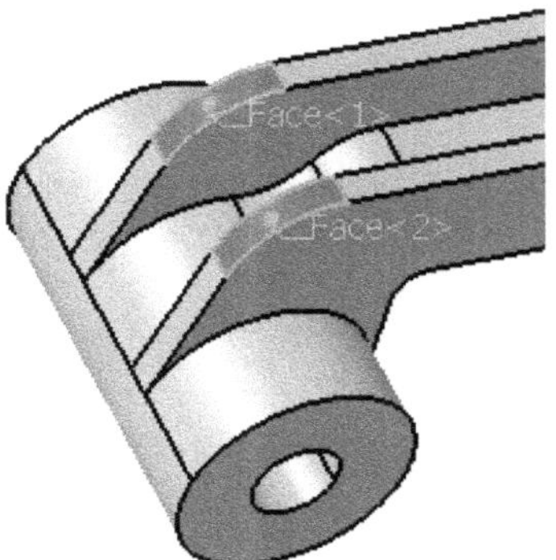

Figure A–9

4. Click **OK**.

Design Considerations

When a feature is recognized from an imported solid, CATIA removes the geometry from the solid and adds the new feature to the specification tree. Note that two Edge Fillets now display in the specification tree. These Fillets are not displayed on the model because the imported solid is still the active object, as shown in Figure A–10.

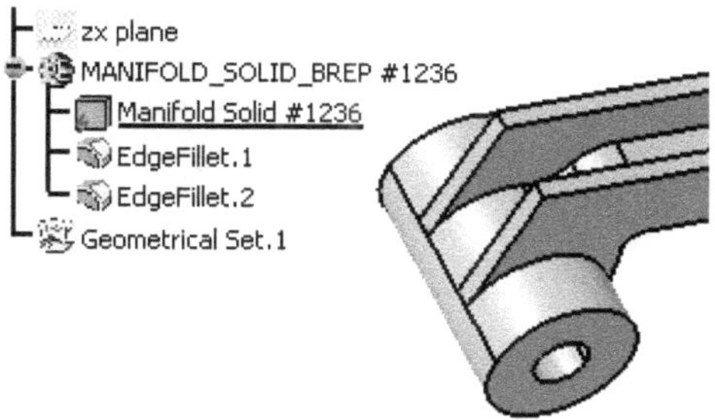

Figure A–10

5. Click (Manual Feature Recognition).
6. Select the two rounded edges shown in Figure A–11.

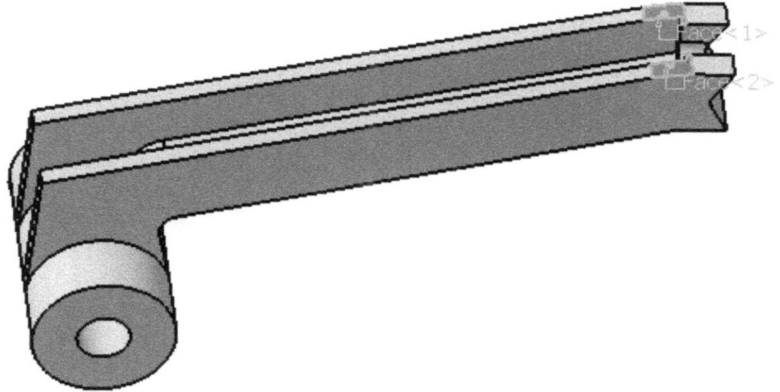

Figure A–11

7. Click **OK**. Two more Edge Fillets display in the specification tree, and the rounded edges are no longer visible.

8. Use the **Manual Feature Recognition** tool for the two rounded edges shown in Figure A–12.

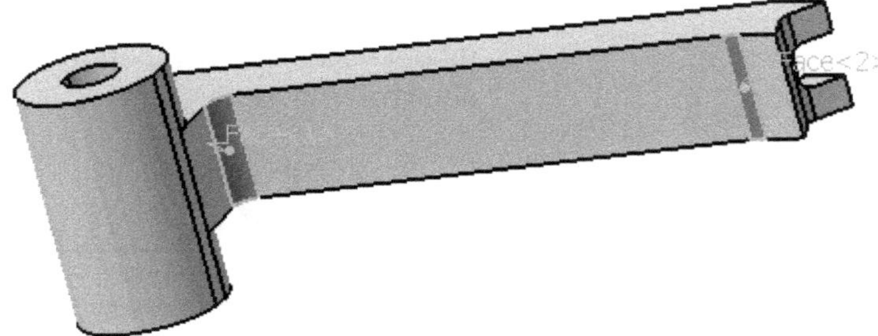

Figure A–12

The tree and model are updated, as shown in Figure A–13.

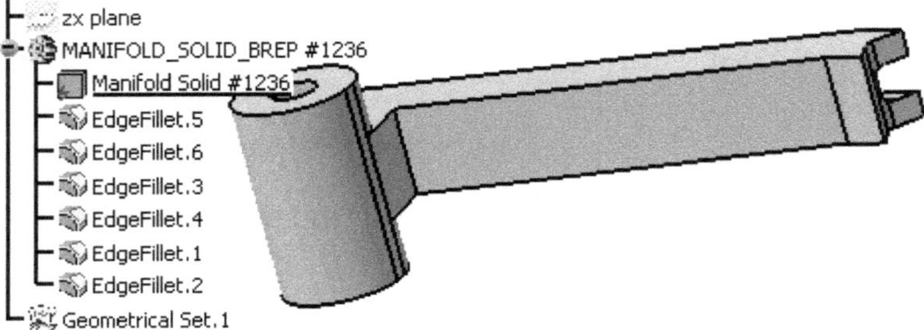

Figure A–13

9. Manually recognize the last set of rounded edges, as shown in Figure A–14.

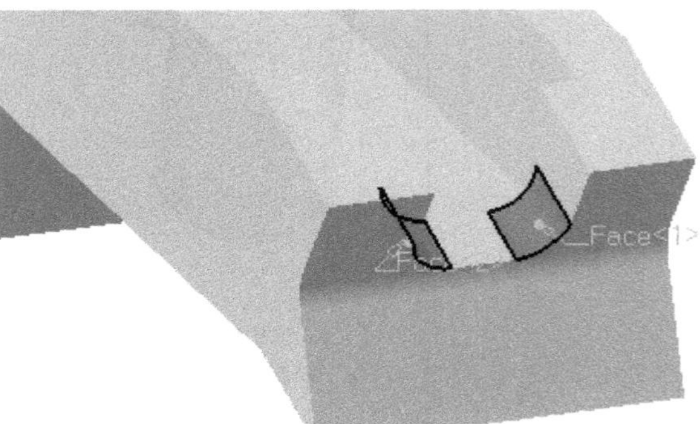

Figure A–14

The tree and model are updated, as shown in Figure A–15.

Figure A–15

Task 3 - Manually recognize the hole.

1. Click (Manual Feature Recognition).
2. Select **Holes**.
3. Select the curved surface shown in Figure A–16.

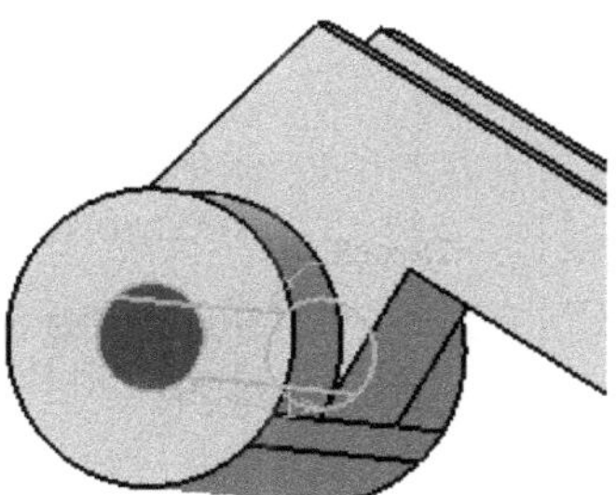

Figure A–16

4. Click **OK**. A Hole feature is added to the specification tree and removed from the display, as shown in Figure A–17.

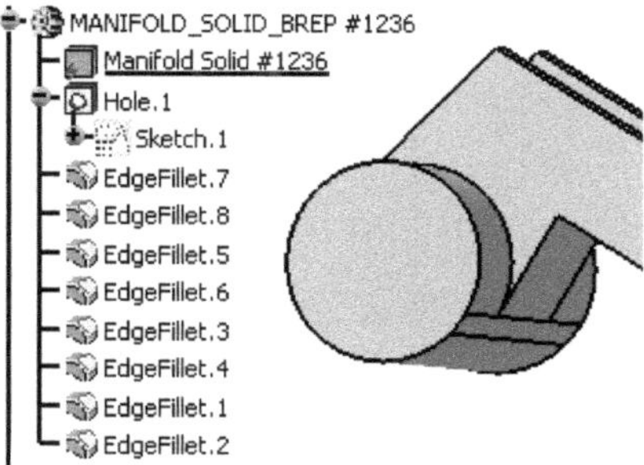

Figure A–17

Task 4 - Manually recognize the pockets.

1. Click (Manual Feature Recognition).
2. Select **Pocket**.
3. Select the surface shown in Figure A–18.

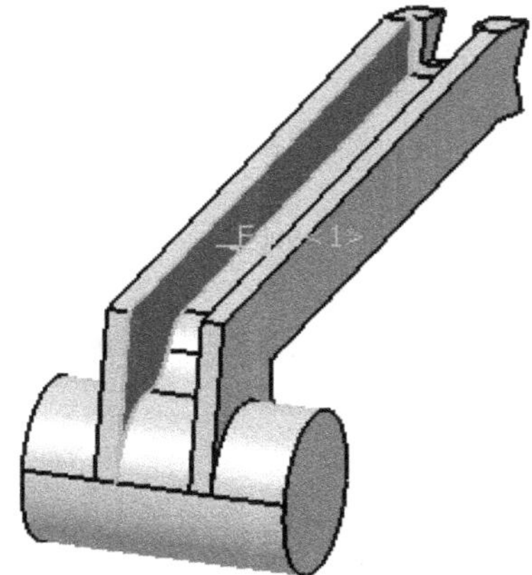

Figure A–18

4. In the Feature Recognition dialog box, activate the *Recognize Up to face* field.
5. Select the face opposite to the initial surface selected, as shown in Figure A–19.

Figure A–19

6. Click **OK** to complete the feature. The Pocket feature displays in the specification tree, as shown in Figure A–20.

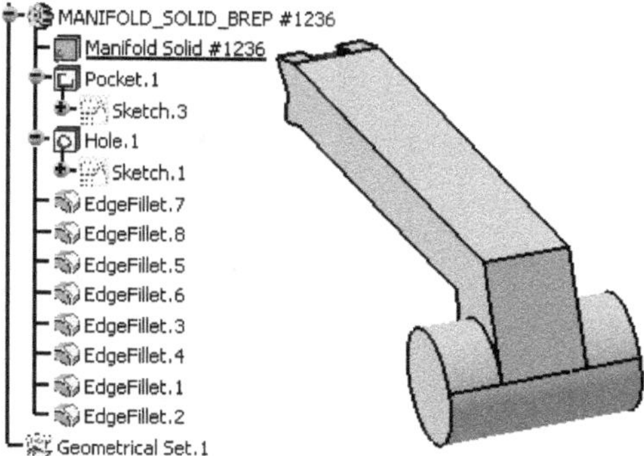

Figure A–20

7. Click (Manual Feature Recognition) and select **Pocket**.

8. Select the face shown in Figure A–21.

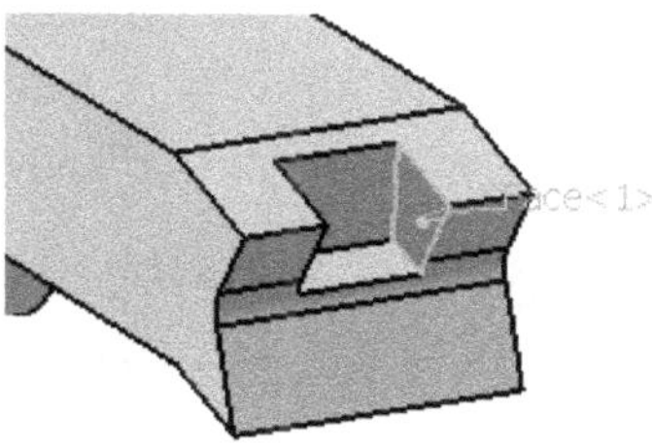

Figure A–21

9. In the Feature Recognition dialog box, activate the *Recognize Up to face* field.

10. Select the face opposite to the initial surface selected, as shown in Figure A–22.

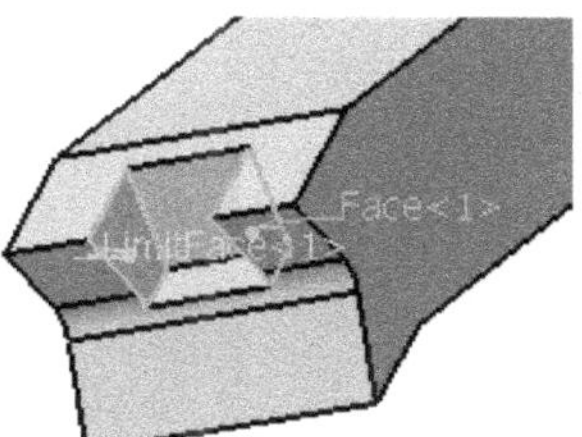

Figure A–22

11. Finish creating the feature. The model updates as shown in Figure A–23.

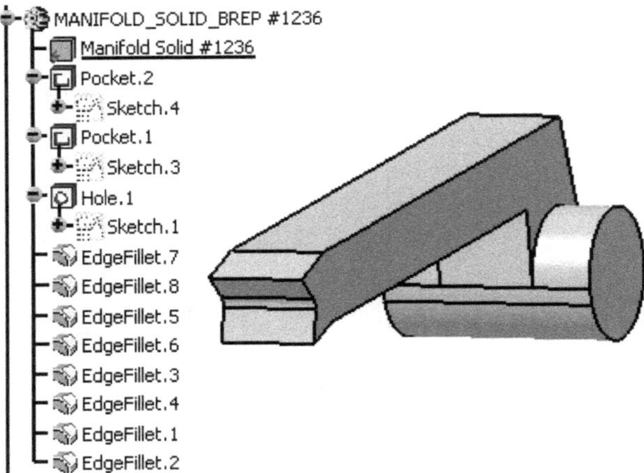

Figure A–23

Task 5 - Manually recognize the Pads.

1. Click (Manual Feature Recognition).
2. Select **Pad**.
3. Select the face shown in Figure A–24.

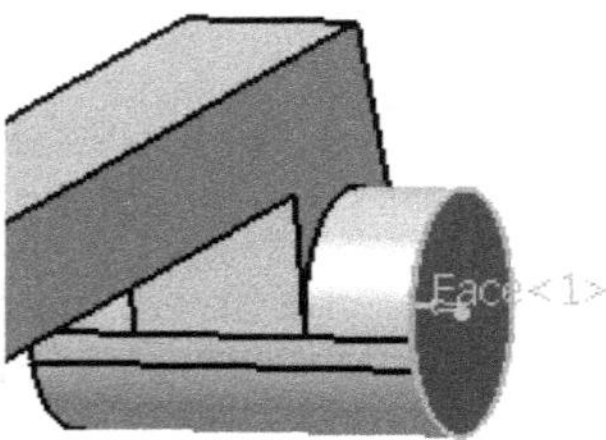

Figure A–24

4. In the Feature Recognition dialog box, activate the *Recognize Up to face* field.

5. Select the face opposite to the initial surface selected, as shown in Figure A–25.

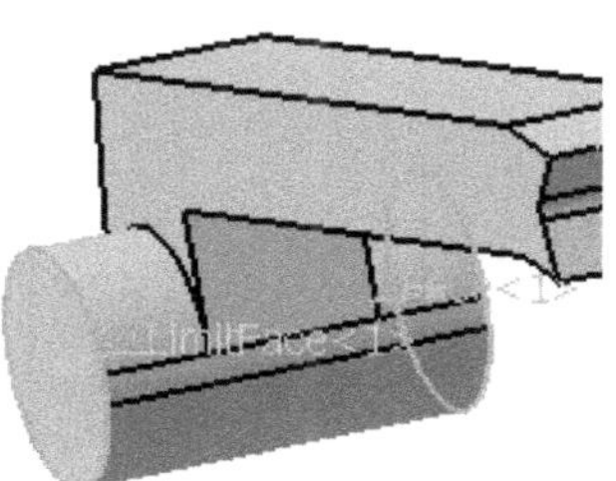

Figure A–25

The result displays as shown in Figure A–26.

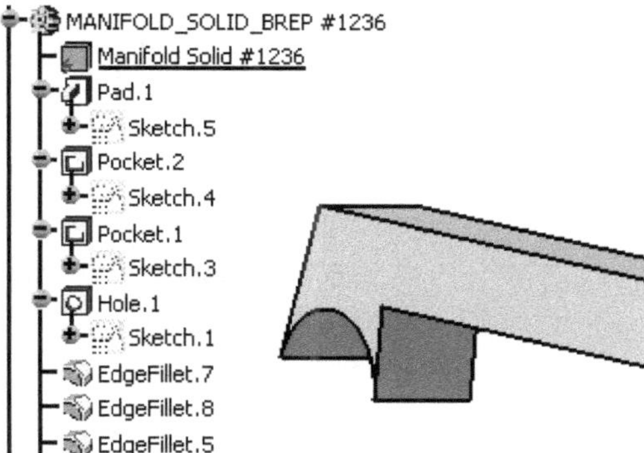

Figure A–26

6. Repeat Steps 1 to 5 by selecting the face shown in Figure A–27, and then selecting the face opposite to it as the *Recognize up to face* reference.

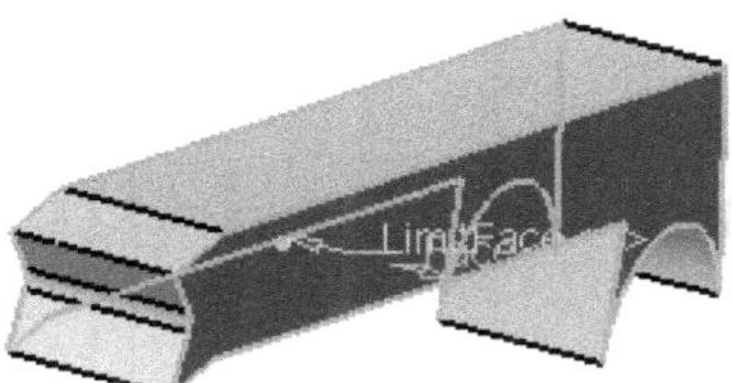

Figure A–27

7. The end result is shown in Figure A–28. Note that the imported solid no longer exists in the specification tree. All of the geometry has been recognized and converted to unique features.

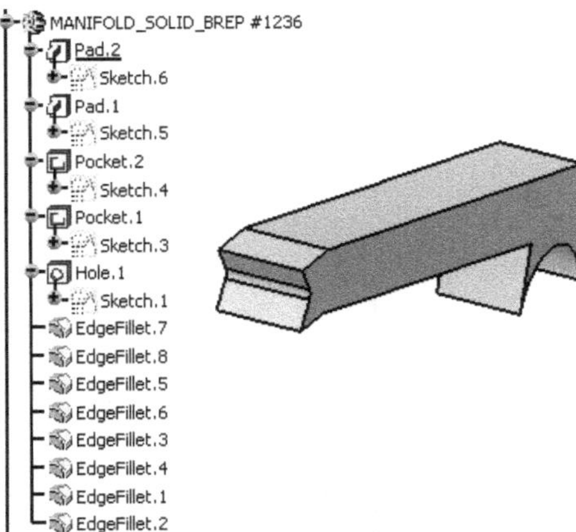

Figure A–28

8. To display the entire model with all of its features, switch the work object to the last Edge Fillet in the tree. The model displays as shown in Figure A–29.

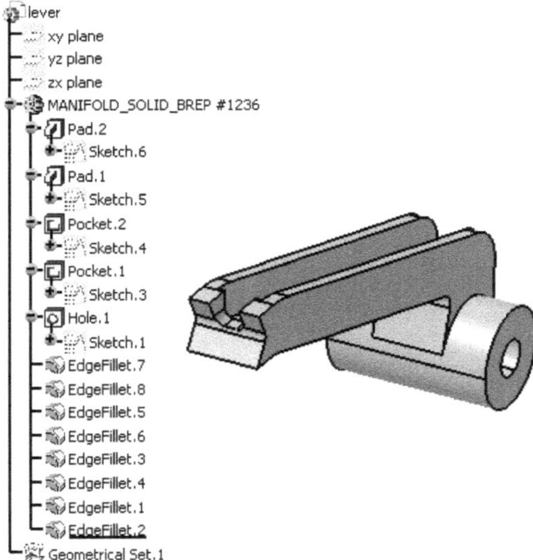

Figure A–29

9. Save and close the part.

Additional Practices

This appendix contains additional practices that can be done if time permits.

Practice B1

Re-using Existing Designs

Practice Objectives

- Copy and Paste AsResult.
- Investigate Links.

In this practice, you will reuse the existing design of **2ndStage.CATPart** shown on the left in Figure B–1 to create a new design, as shown on the right.

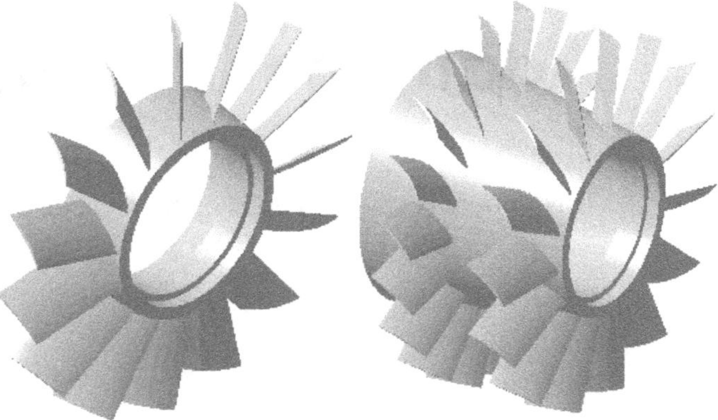

Figure B–1

Task 1 - Open the part.

1. Open the part named **2ndStage.CATPart** from the *Turbine* directory. The body displays as shown in Figure B–2.

Figure B–2

2. Set the units to millimeters.

Task 2 - Save the body with a different name.

1. Select **File>Save As**. For the new name, enter **2nd3rdStage**.

Task 3 - Copy and paste a part from a different body.

1. Open **2ndStage.CATPart**.
2. In the specification tree, right-click on the 2ndStage body and select **Copy**, as shown in Figure B–3.

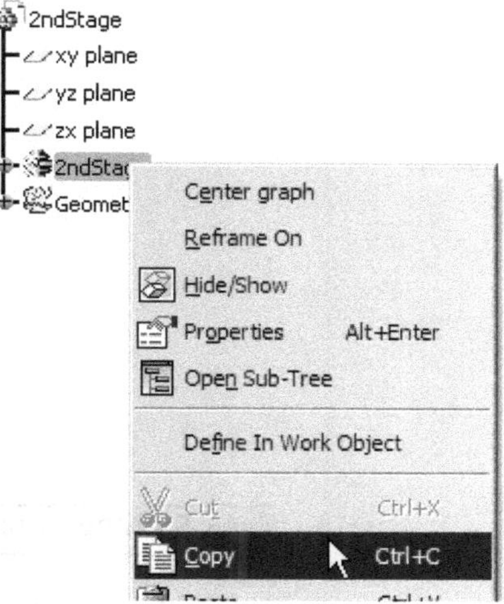

Figure B–3

3. Activate the **2nd3rdStage.CATPart** window.
4. In the specification tree, right-click on the part number 2ndStage and select **Paste Special**. The Paste Special dialog box opens as shown in Figure B–4.

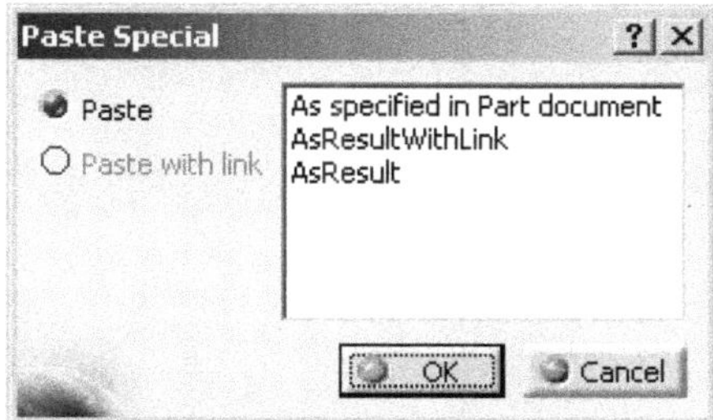

Figure B–4

5. Select **AsResultWithLink** and click **OK**. A new body named **2ndStage** has been added to the element list in the specification tree.

Task 4 - Rename elements in the specification tree.

1. Change the part number from **2ndStage** to **2nd3rdStage**.
2. Change the name of the first **2ndStage** body to **3rdStage**. The specification tree displays as shown in Figure B–5. Note the **Solid.1** element and its associated icon and status symbol.

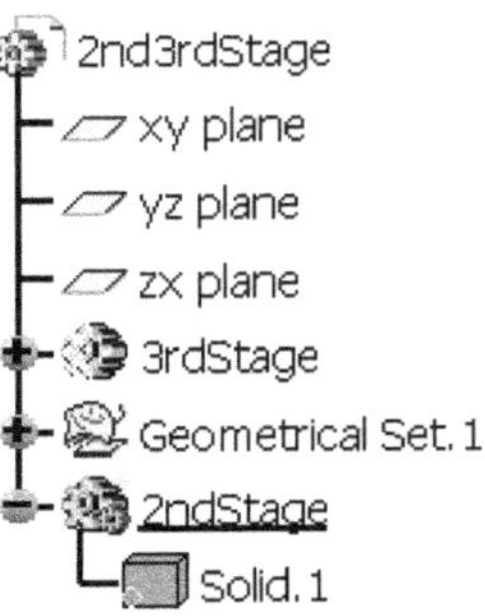

Figure B–5

Task 5 - Move the 2ndStage body.

1. Drag the compass onto the body so that the axis of the compass is oriented, as shown in Figure B–6.

Figure B–6

2. In the specification tree, select **2ndStage** and drag the axis of the compass to the location shown in Figure B–7.

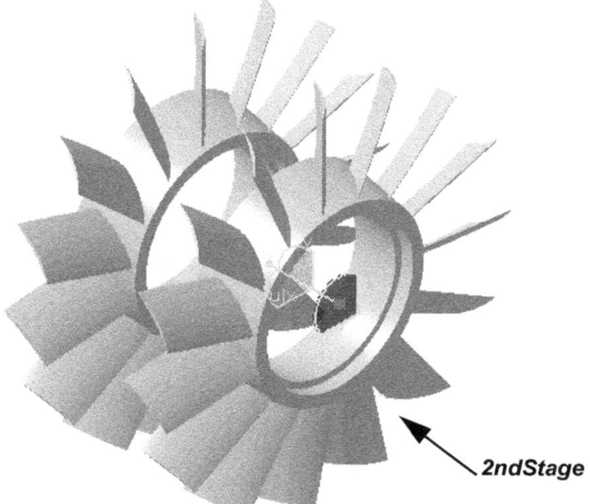

Figure B–7

Task 6 - Explore external links.

1. In the specification tree, select **2ndStage** and select **Edit> Links**. The Links of element 2ndStage dialog box opens as shown in Figure B–8.

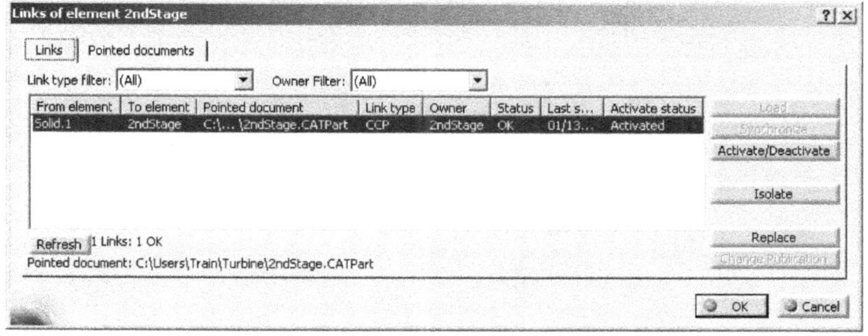

Figure B–8

Note that the path in the *Pointed document* column for **Solid.1** points to **2ndStage.CATPart** and that the status of the element is **OK**.

2. Click **OK**.

Task 7 - Modify the 3rdstage body.

1. Edit **Sketch.1**, which is located under **Shaft.1** of **3rdStage**. The sketch and specification tree display as shown in Figure B–9.

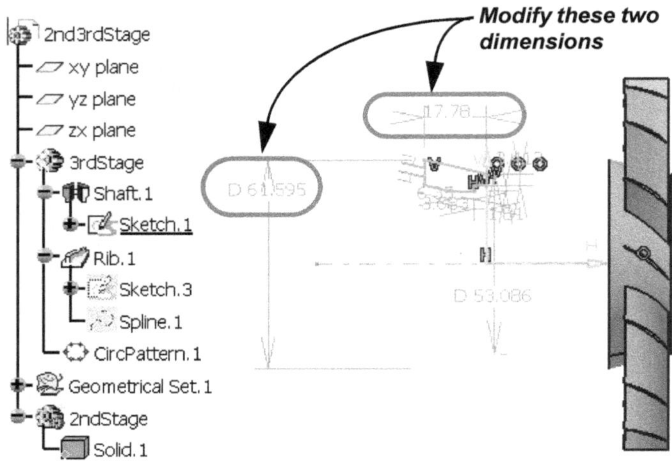

Figure B–9

2. Change the *17.78* value to **29.5**.

3. Change the *61.595* value to **71.2**.

4. Erase the four dimensions shown in Figure B–10.

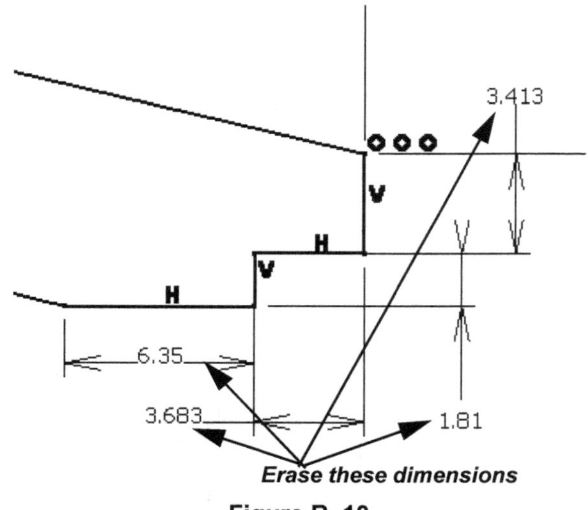

Figure B–10

5. Erase the two sketched lines shown in Figure B–11.

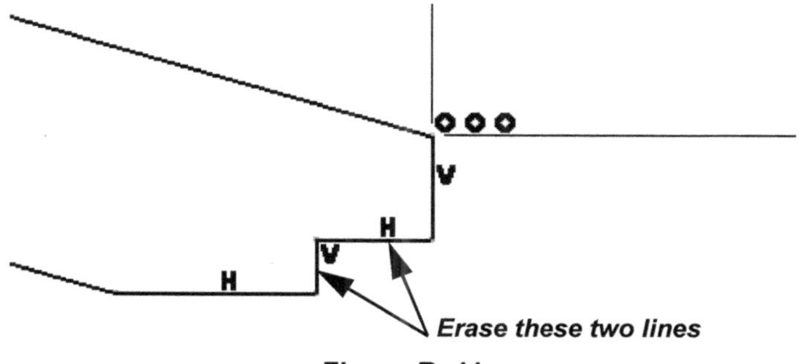

Figure B–11

6. Trim the remaining two lines together and dimension as shown in Figure B–12. Ensure that the sketch is fully constrained (green).

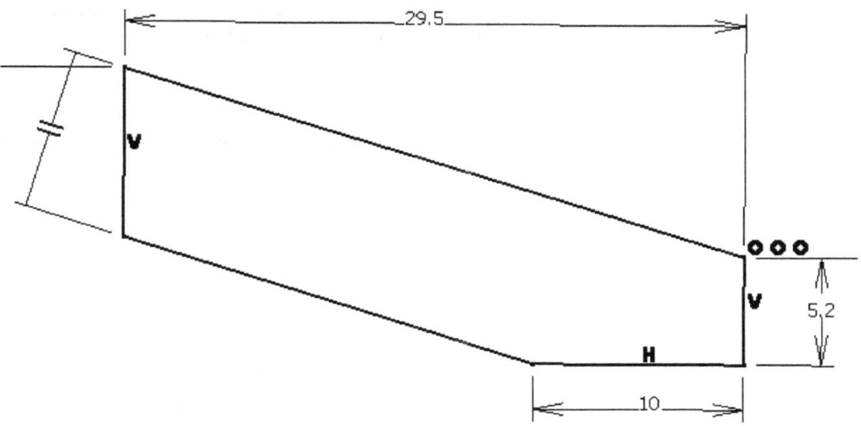

Figure B–12

7. Exit the Sketcher workbench. The **3rdStage** body displays as shown in Figure B–13.

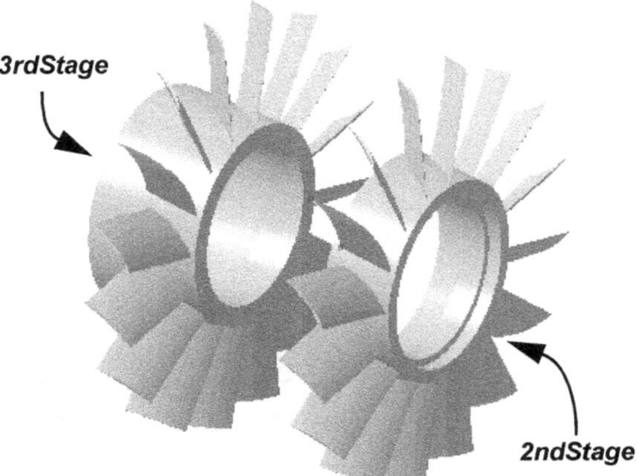

Figure B–13

Task 8 - Modify the pointed document.

1. Activate the **2ndStage** part window.
2. Modify the *17.78* value of **Shaft.1** to **28.5**, as shown in Figure B–14.

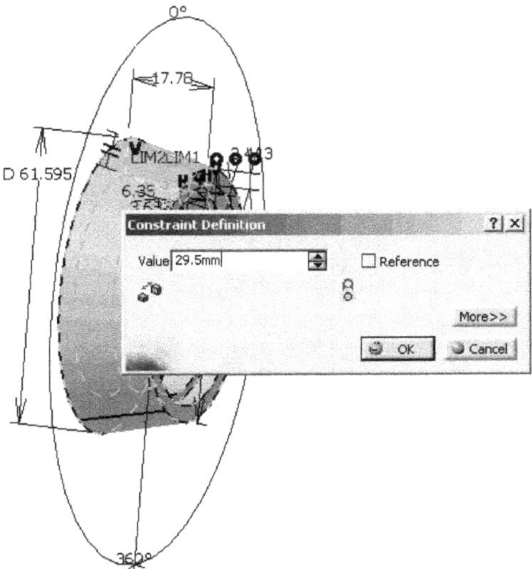

Figure B–14

The body displays as shown in Figure B–15.

Figure B–15

3. Activate the **2nd3rdStage** part window. Note that the system recognizes that changes have been made to a linked document. In the specification tree, expand **2ndStage** and note the status symbol of the **Solid.1** element, as shown in Figure B–16.

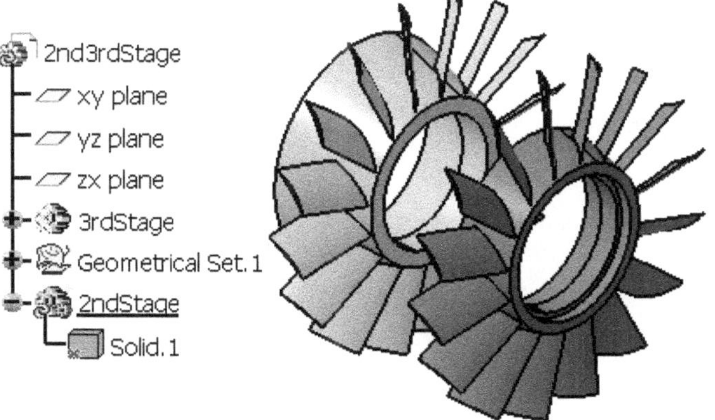

Figure B–16

4. Click to update the geometry. The updated body displays as shown in Figure B–17. Note the status symbol of the Solid.1 element.

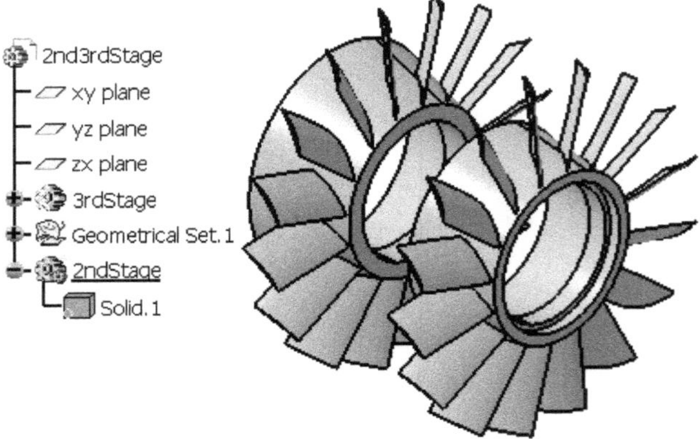

Figure B–17

Task 9 - Create a measurement of the large diameter of 3rdStage.

1. Click (Measure Item) to create a measure element.

2. Click **Customize** and ensure that only the **Diameter** option is selected under the *Arc* column, as shown in Figure B–18.

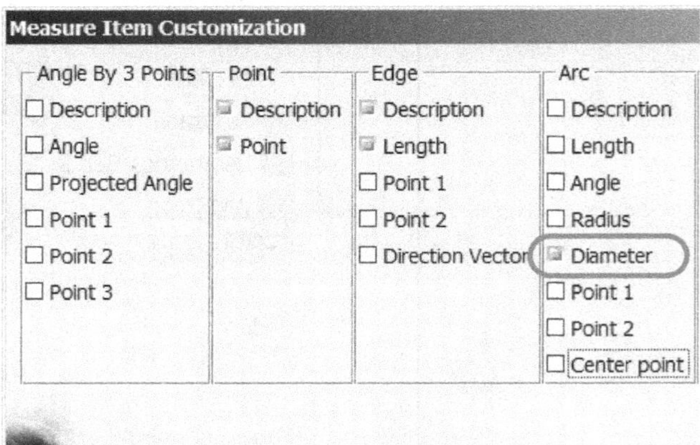

Figure B–18

3. Click **OK** and measure the edge of the **2ndStage**, as shown in Figure B–19.

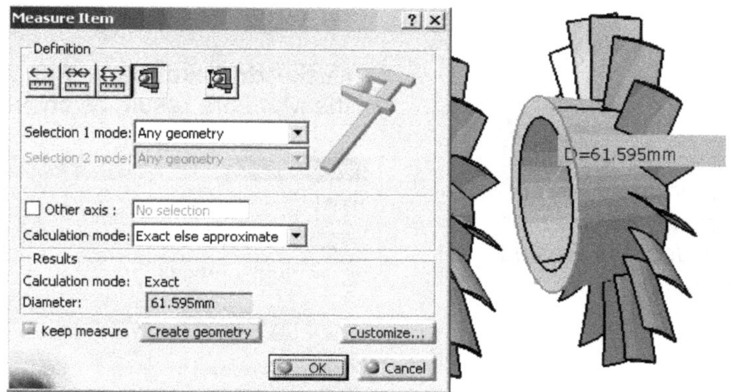

Figure B–19

4. Ensure that the **Keep Measure** option is selected and click **OK** to close the Measure Item dialog box.

Task 10 - Create a formula.

1. Click f(x) (Formula) and select the **3rdStage** geometry, as shown in Figure B–20.

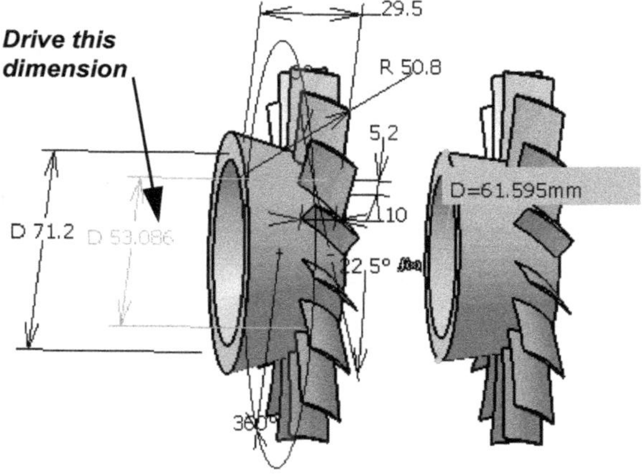

Figure B–20

2. Select the **53.086** dimension so that the parameter is highlighted in the Formulas dialog box. This will be a diameter parameter (named radius by CATIA) with a value of **26.543**.

3. Click **Add Formula** and equate the 53.086 dimension by half the Measure result, as shown in Figure B–21.

To display the radius measurement, select the body. Ensure that you select the Radius parameter.

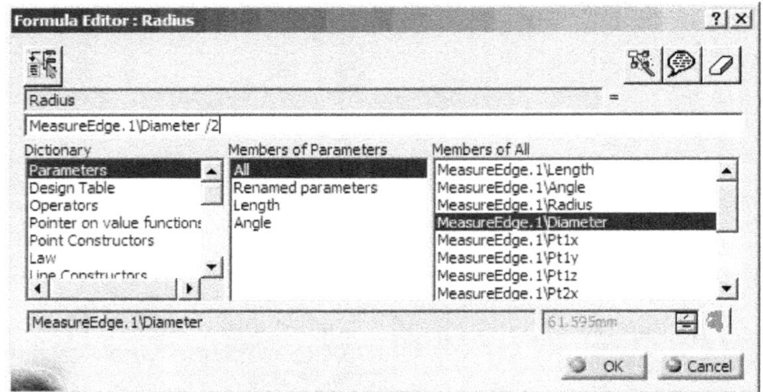

Figure B–21

4. Click **OK** to complete the formula. The body is updated, as shown in Figure B–22.

Figure B–22

Task 11 - Create a 3D constraint.

1. In the Constraints toolbar, click (Constraints).
2. Create the constraint shown in Figure B–23.

Note that the value might differ from that shown in Figure B–23.

Figure B–23

3. Set the constraint value to **0mm** with a formula, as shown in Figure B–24.

Include units with the entered value.

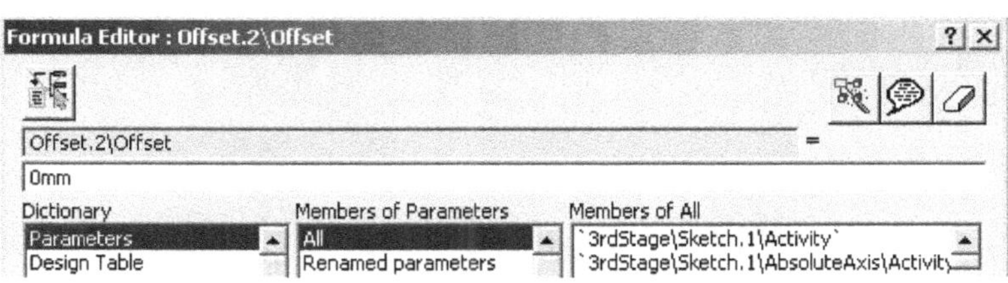

Figure B–24

4. To display the 3D constraint in the specification tree, select **Tools>Options>Infrastructure>Part Infrastructure**. In the dialog box, select the *Display* tab and select **Constraints**. The specification tree displays as shown in Figure B–25.

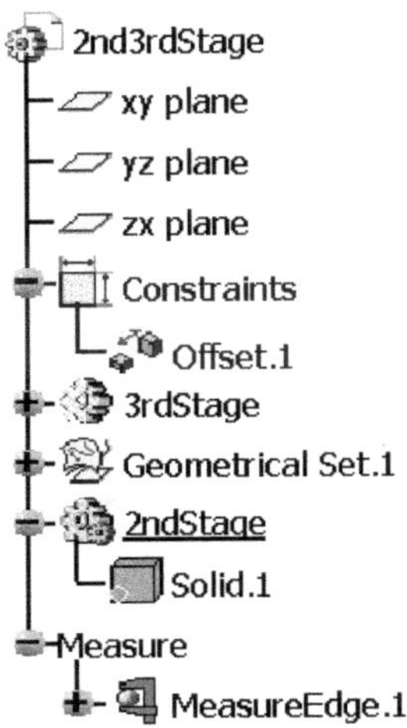

Figure B–25

5. Hide the constraint. The body displays as shown in Figure B–26.

The part now consists of two part bodies. These bodies can be combined into one body using a boolean ***Assemble*** *operation.*

Figure B–26

6. Save the model and close the window.

Practice B2

Managing Links

Practice Objectives

- Load a Document.
- Synchronize a Pointed Document.
- Break the Link.

In this practice, you will modify a linked document using the option in the Links dialog box. The completed body displays as shown in Figure B–27.

Figure B–27

Task 1 - Modify the pointed document.

1. Ensure that the **2ndStage** part is open from the previous practice.

   If you did not complete the last practice, open **2ndStage.CATPart** from the *Completed* directory instead. Note that the images in this practice use the models from the completed folder.

2. Redefine **CircPattern.1** of the **2ndStage** part and modify the number of pattern instances to **3**. The body displays as shown in Figure B–28.

Figure B–28

3. Save the part and close the file.

4. Open **2nd3rdStage.CATPart**. The body displays as shown in Figure B–29. Note the status symbol of the **Solid.1** element.

   If you did not complete the last practice, open **2nd3rdStage.CATPart** from the *Completed* directory instead. Note that the images in this practice use the models from the completed folder.

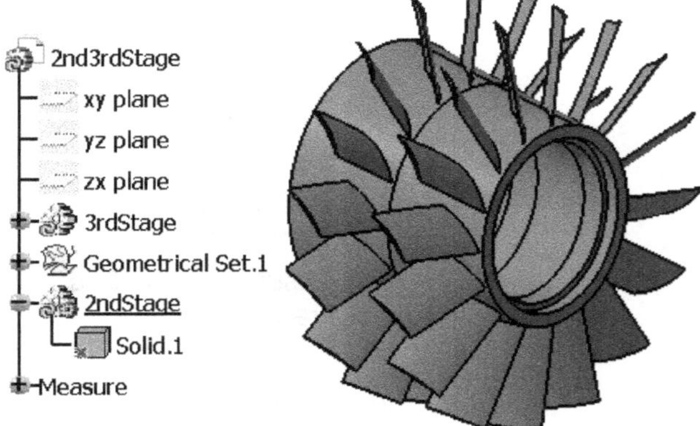

Figure B–29

Task 2 - Load pointed documents.

1. Select **Edit>Links**.

2. Select the *Pointed documents* tab and note that the Status is **Document not loaded**, as shown in Figure B–30.

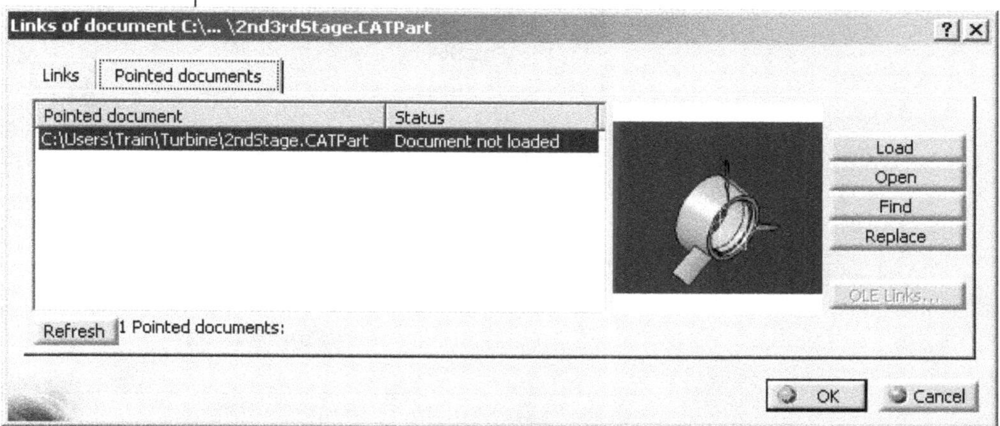

Figure B–30

3. Click **Load**. The system loads all of the pointed document information into session and recognizes that changes have been made. Note that the pointed document is not opened; it is only loaded. The **Load** functionality only loads body information but does not actually open the file.

4. The status symbol of the **Solid.1** element indicates that the element needs to be updated, as shown in Figure B–31.

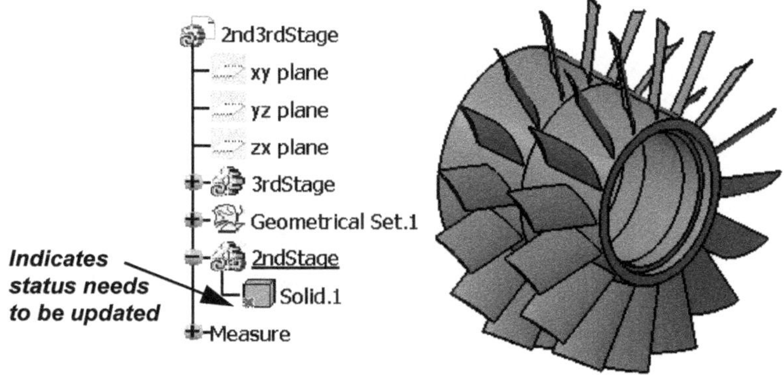

Figure B–31

5. Click [icon] to update the body. The body is updated to reflect the changes made to the pointed document, as shown in Figure B–32.

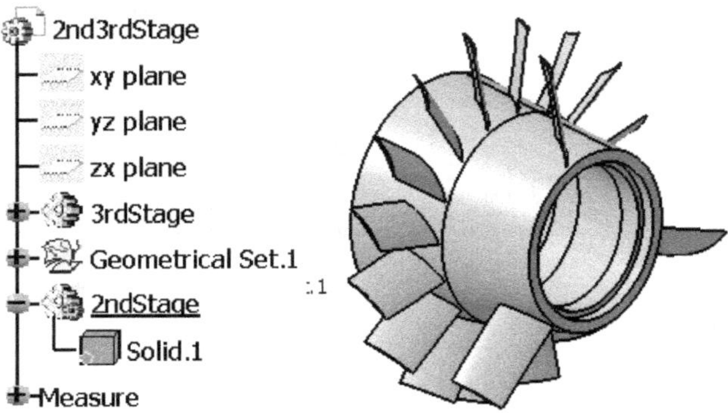

Figure B–32

Task 3 - Synchronize documents.

1. Select **Window** and note that **2nd3rdStage.CATPart** is the only file in session.
2. Select **Edit>Links** and select the *Pointed documents* tab.
3. Click **Open**. The **2ndStage** body displays.
4. Modify the circular pattern to **20** instances.
5. Activate the **2nd3rdStage** window. The model displays as shown in Figure B–33.

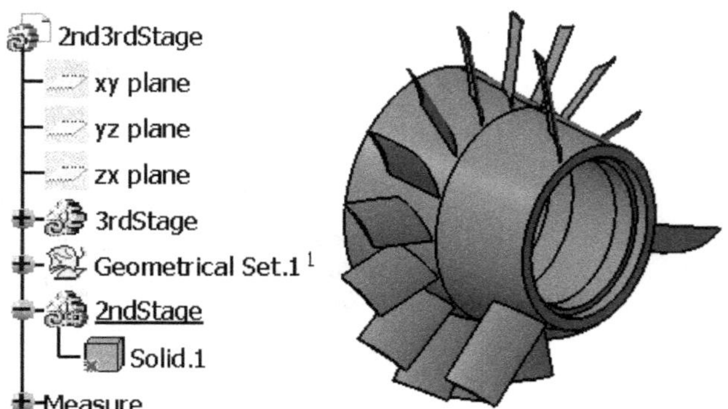

Figure B–33

6. Select **Edit>Links** and note the **Not synchronized** status in the *Status* column, as shown in Figure B–34.

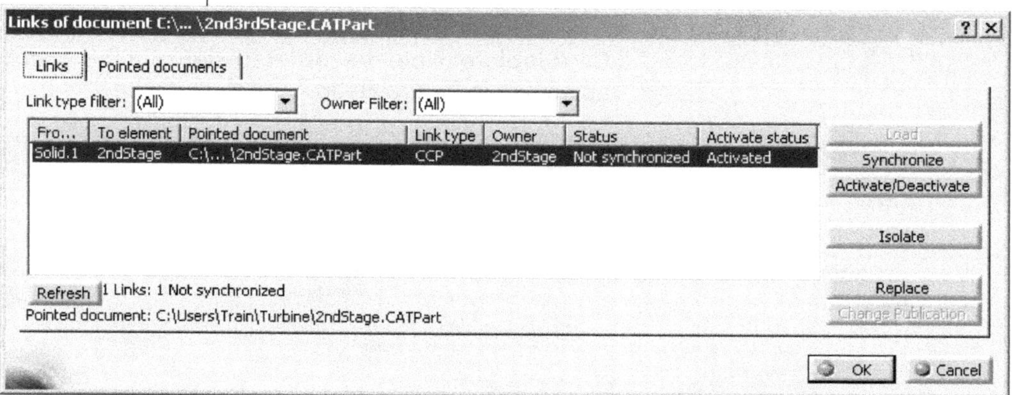

Figure B–34

7. Click **Synchronize**.

8. Click **OK** and click to update the body. The body displays as shown in Figure B–35.

Figure B–35

Task 4 - Break the external link.

1. Select **Edit>Links**.
2. Click **Isolate**. Note the **Isolated** status in the *Status* column, as shown in Figure B–36.

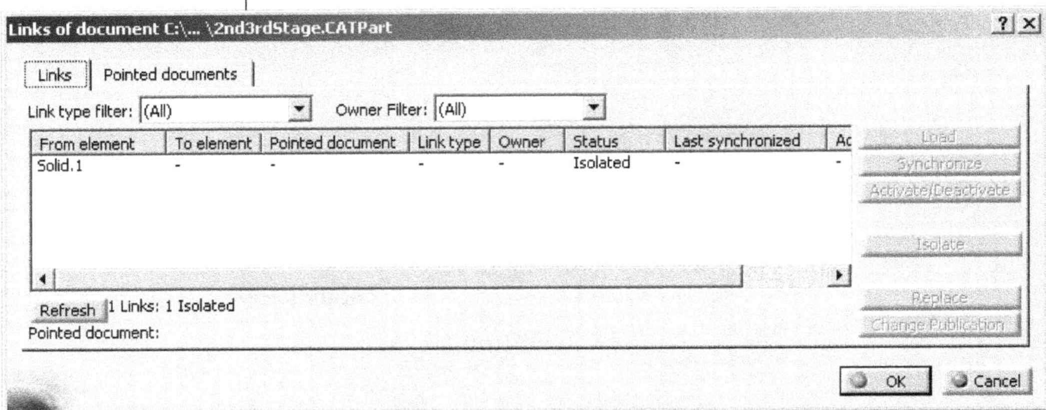

Figure B–36

3. Click **OK**. Note the status symbol of the **Solid.1** element, as shown in Figure B–37.

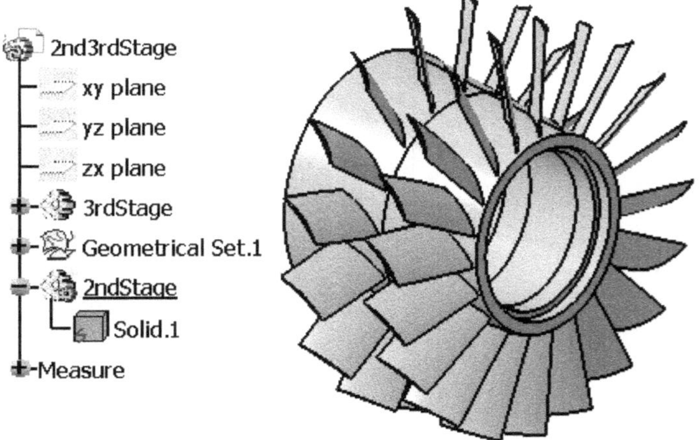

Figure B–37

4. Select **Edit>Links**. The Links message box opens as shown in Figure B–38, indicating that the document does not have external links.

Links
Document 2nd3rdStage.CATPart has no external links.
OK

Figure B–38

5. Save the part.

6. Activate the **2ndStage** window and modify the circular pattern to **16** instances.

7. Save the part and close the file.

8. Modify **CircPattern.1** of **2nd3rdStage** to **22** instances. The body displays as shown in Figure B–39.

Figure B–39

9. Save the model and close the file.

Advanced Practice Solutions

This appendix provides solutions to all of the advanced practices.

C.1 Step by Step Solution for Practice 1b

Practice Objective

- Capture design intent in Sketcher.

Task 1 - Create a new part.

1. Create a part file. Save it as **Pipe1.CATPart**. The best selection for a Base feature is a Rib, using the **Thick Profile** option.

Task 2 - Sketch a center curve.

1. Create the following sketch on the yz plane, as shown in Figure C–1.

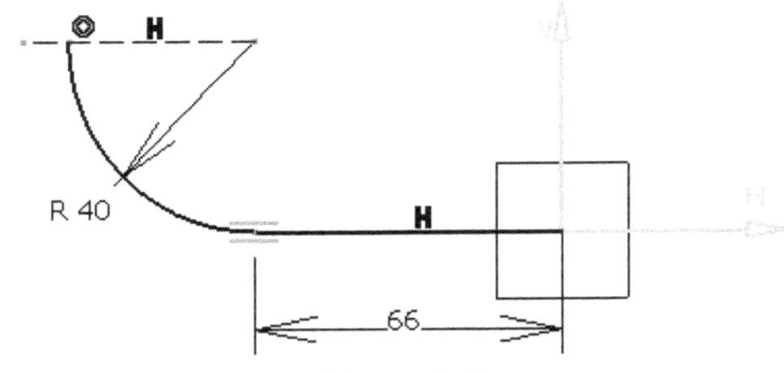

Figure C–1

Task 3 - Sketch a profile.

1. Create the following sketch on the zx plane, as shown in Figure C–2.

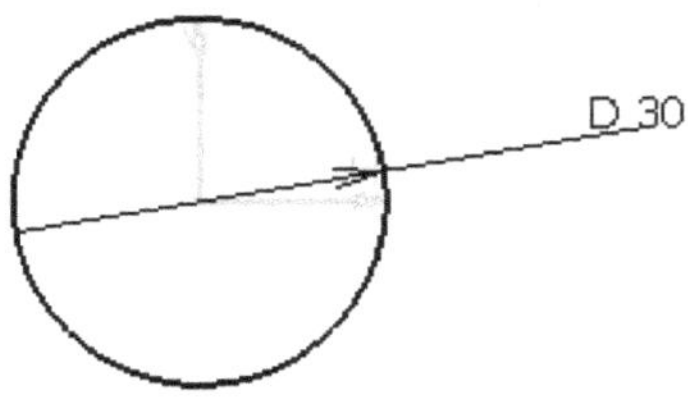

Figure C–2

Task 4 - Create a Rib feature.

1. Create a Rib feature, as shown in Figure C–3.

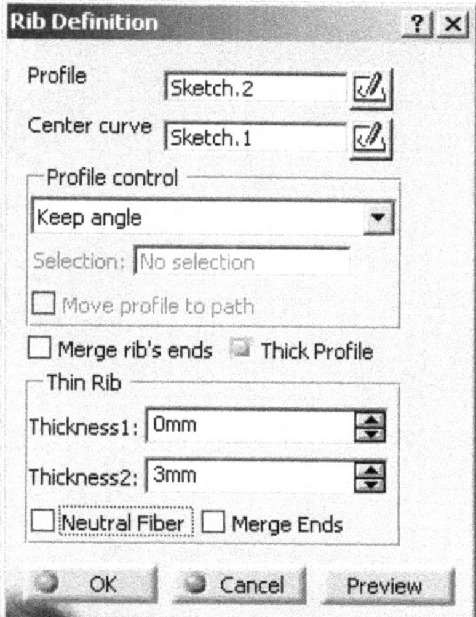

Figure C–3

Task 5 - Create a Pad for the holed flange.

1. Create the sketch shown in Figure C–4.

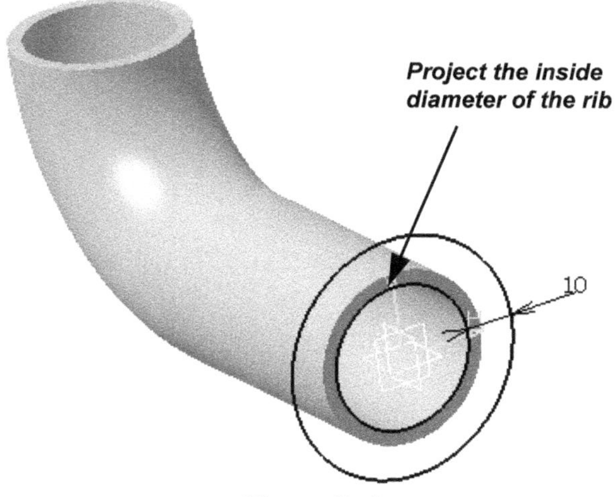

Figure C–4

2. Create a Pad feature, as shown in Figure C–5.

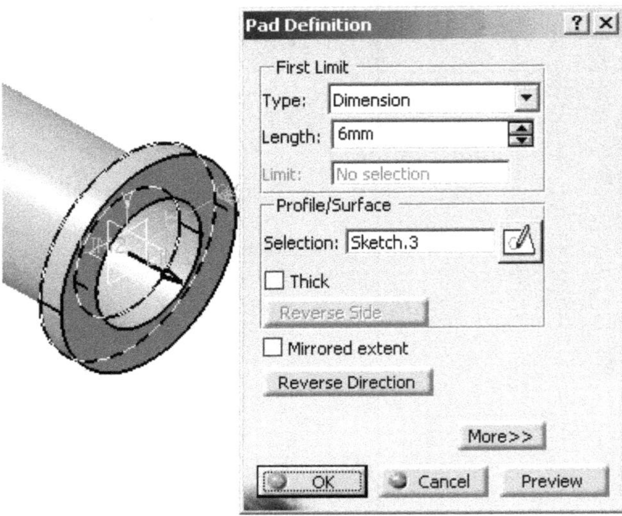

Figure C–5

Task 6 - Create a Pad for the grooved flange.

1. Create the sketch shown in Figure C–6.

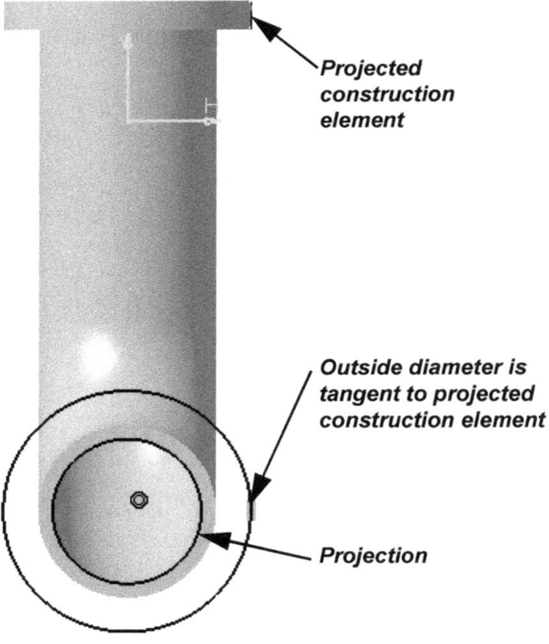

Figure C–6

2. Create the Pad shown in Figure C–7.

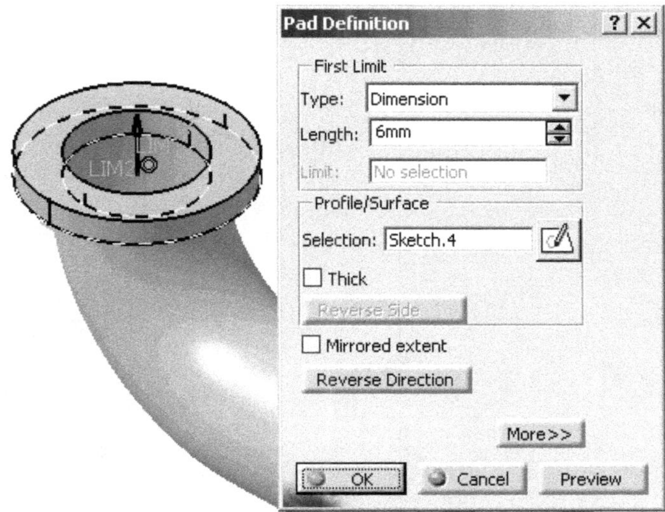

Figure C–7

Task 7 - Create a Pad for the pipe segment.

1. Create the sketch shown in Figure C–8.

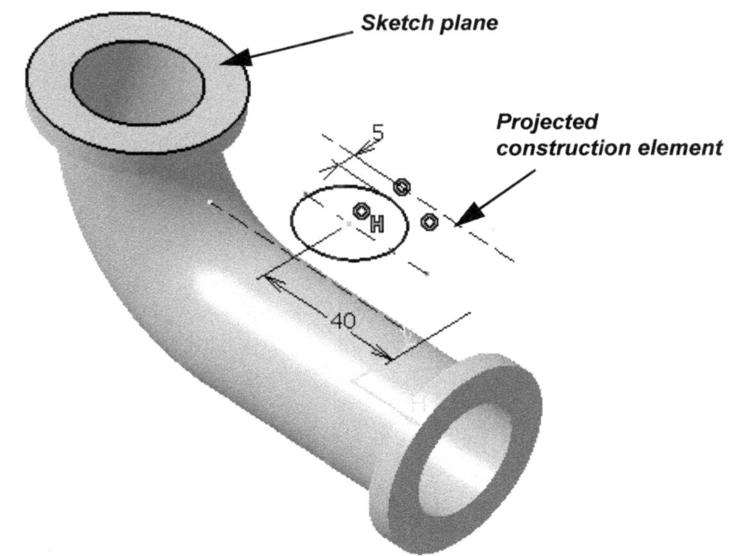

Figure C–8

2. Create the Pad feature shown in Figure C–9.

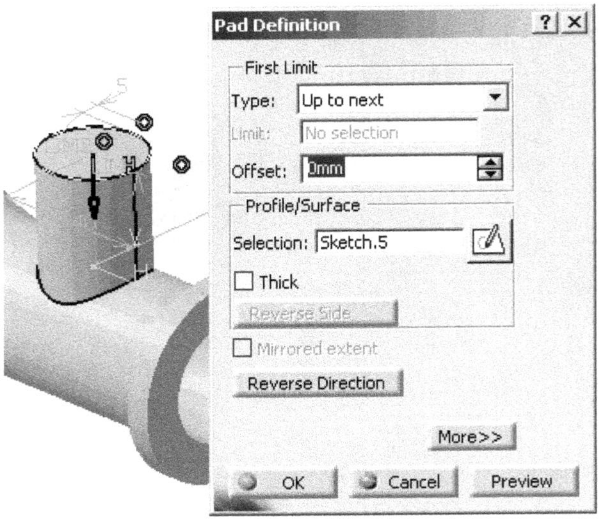

Figure C–9

Task 8 - Create a Pocket feature.

1. Create the sketch shown in Figure C–10.

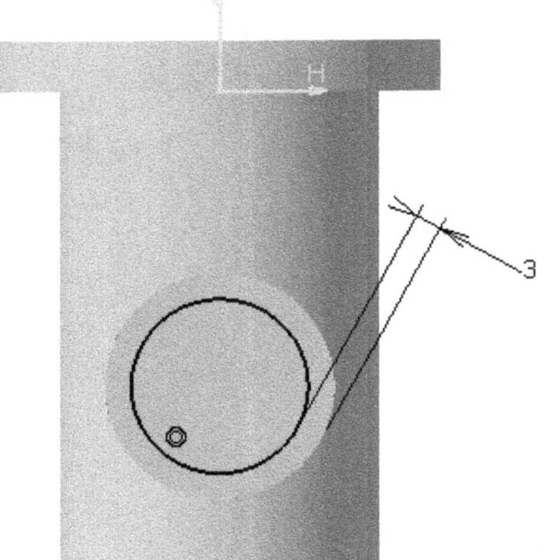

Figure C–10

2. Create the Pocket feature, as shown in Figure C–11.

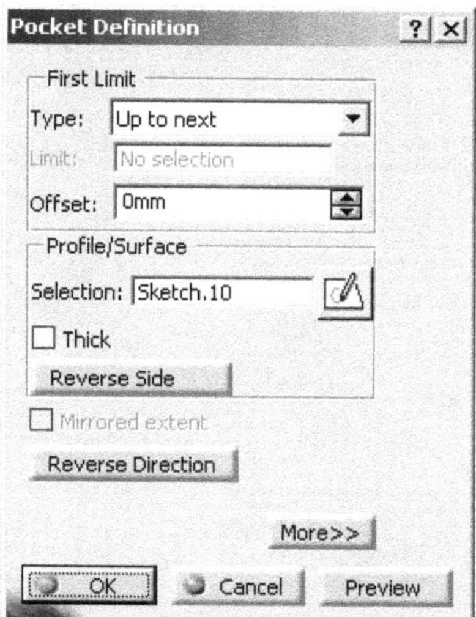

Figure C–11

Task 9 - Create a Groove feature.

1. Create the appropriate sketch and Groove feature shown in Figure C–12.

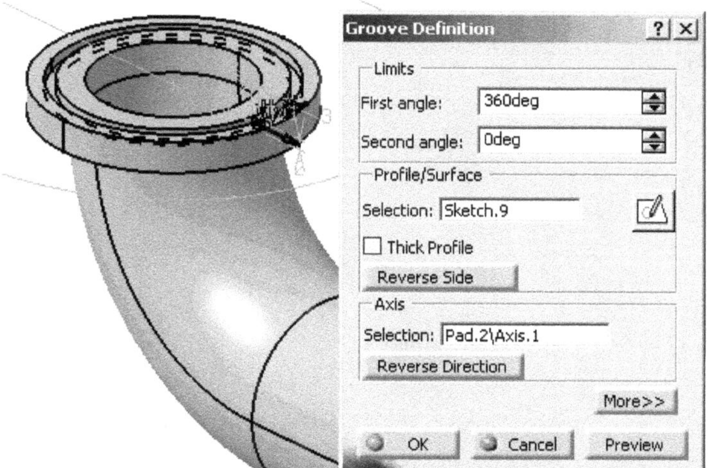

Figure C–12

Task 10 - Create a Hole feature.

1. Create the Hole feature shown in Figure C–13. The positioning sketch is shown in Figure C–14.

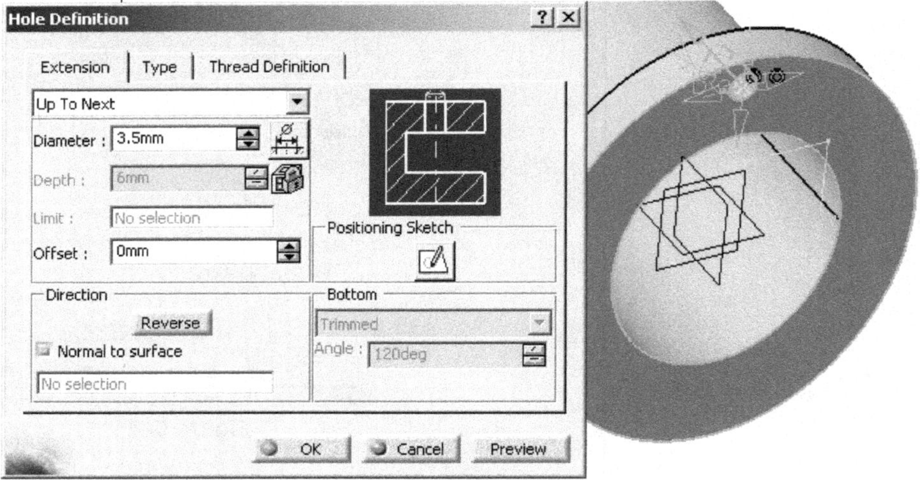

Figure C–13

2. Use the positioning sketch shown in Figure C–14 for the Hole feature.

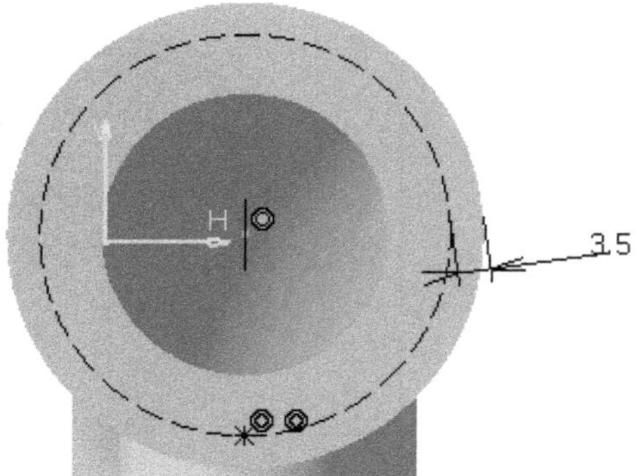

Figure C–14

3. Create a pattern of the Hole feature, as shown in Figure C–15.

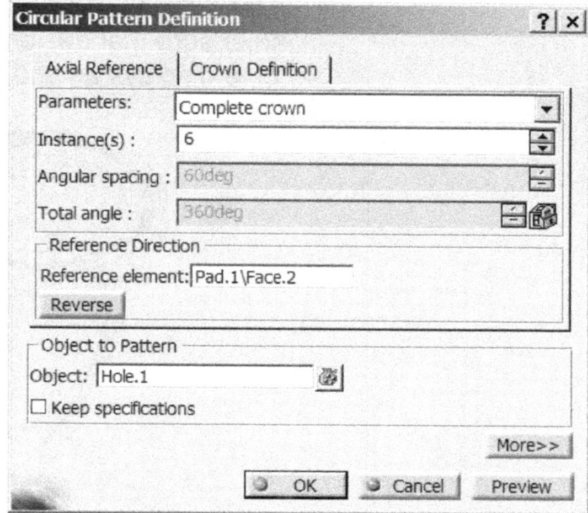

Figure C–15

Task 11 - Create dress-up features.

1. Create the appropriate chamfer.
2. Fillet the model using a single Fillet feature.

Task 12 - Make changes to the inside pipe diameter.

The completed model displays as shown in Figure C–16.

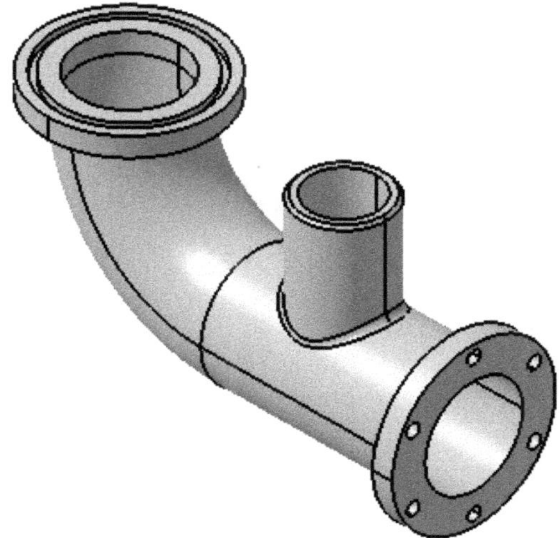

Figure C–16

1. Make dimensional changes to the inside diameter of the pipe to ensure that design requirements have been captured. The pipe displays as shown in Figure C–17.

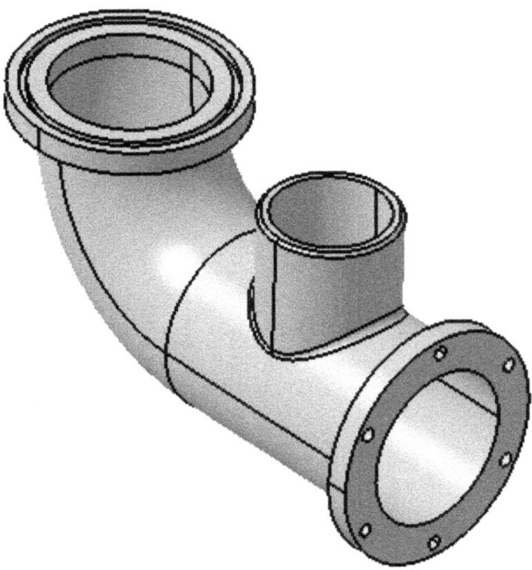

Figure C–17

2. Save the model and close the file.

www.ingramcontent.com/pod-product-compliance
Lightning Source LLC
Chambersburg PA
CBHW080339220326
41598CB00030B/4552
* 9 7 8 1 9 4 6 5 7 1 9 9 1 *